NATURAL SCIENCES IN AMERICA

HISTORY

OF

NORTH AMERICAN BIRDS

S[pencer] F[ullerton] Baird
T[homas] M. Brewer
R[obert] Ridgway

Volume II

ARNO PRESS
A New York Times Company
New York, N. Y. • 1974

Reprint Edition 1974 by Arno Press Inc.

Reprinted from copies in The American
  Museum of Natural History Library

.NATURAL SCIENCES IN AMERICA
ISBN for complete set: 0-405-05700-8
See last pages of this volume for titles.

Manufactured in the United States of America

Publisher's Note: The illustrations in this book
have been reproduced in black and white. The
pages have been reduced by 5%.

———————◆———————

Library of Congress Cataloging in Publication Data

Baird, Spencer Fullerton, 1823-1887.
    A history of North American birds: land birds.

    (Natural sciences in America)
    Reprint of the 1874 ed. published by Little, Brown,
Boston.
    1. Birds--North America. I. Brewer, Thomas Mayo,
1814-1880, joint author. II. Ridgway, Robert, 1850-
1929, joint author. III. Title. IV. Series.
QL681.B16 1974   598.2'97   73-17798
ISBN 0-405-05711-3

NORTH AMERICAN BIRDS.

LAND BIRDS.

VOL. II.

A

HISTORY

OF

NORTH AMERICAN BIRDS

BY

S. F. BAIRD, T. M. BREWER, AND R. RIDGWAY

LAND BIRDS

ILLUSTRATED BY 64 COLORED PLATES AND 593 WOODCUTS.

VOLUME II.

BOSTON
LITTLE, BROWN, AND COMPANY
1874

CONTENTS.

NORTH AMERICAN BIRDS.

FAMILY **FRINGILLIDÆ.** — THE FINCHES. (*Continued.*)

GENUS **SPIZELLA**, BONAP.

Spizella, BONAP. Geog. and Comp. List, 1838. (Type, *Fringilla canadensis*, LATH.)
Spinites, CABANIS, Mus. Hein. 1851, 133. (Type, *Fringilla socialis*, WILS.)

GEN. CHAR. Bill conical, the outlines slightly curved; the lower mandible decidedly larger than the upper; the commissure gently sinuated; the roof of the mouth not knobbed. Feet slender; tarsus rather longer than the middle toe; the hinder toe a little longer than the outer lateral, which slightly exceeds the inner; the outer claw reaching the base of the middle one, and half as long as its toe. Claws moderately curved. Tertiaries and secondaries nearly equal; wing somewhat pointed, reaching not quite to the middle of the tail. First quill a little shorter than the second and equal to the fifth; third longest. Tail rather long, moderately forked, and divaricated at the tip; the feathers rather narrow. Back streaked; rump and beneath immaculate. Young streaked beneath.

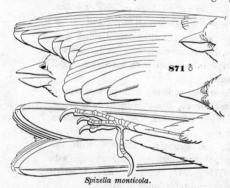

871 ♂

Spizella monticola.

This genus differs from *Zonotrichia* principally in the smaller size and longer and forked, instead of rounded tail.

Birds of the year of this genus are very difficult to distinguish, even by size, except in *monticola*. The more immature birds are also very closely related. In these the entire absence of streaks on a plumbeous head point to *atrigularis*; the same character in a reddish cap, and a reddish upper mandible to *pusilla*; a dusky loral spot with dark streaks and generally a rufous shade on top of head, to *socialis*. *S. breweri*, with a streaked head, lacks the dusky lore and chestnut shade of feathers. *S. pallida* generally has a median light stripe in the cap, and a dusky mandibular line.

COMMON CHARACTERS. Interscapular region with black streaks. Rump and lower parts without streaks (except in young). Wing with two narrow light bands (indistinct in *atrigularis*).

A. Crown different from the sides of the head, a plain light superciliary stripe. Young with crown and breast streaked.

   a. Crown rufous and plain in adult; in young, grayish and with streaks.

  I. *Streak behind eye, and tinge on side of breast, rufous. Egg pale blue, or bluish-white, blotched with pale brown, or sprinkled with reddish.*

    1. **S. monticola.** Crown bright rufous, undivided medially; a dusky spot on lore; wing-bands sharply defined, pure white. A black spot on breast; jugulum tinged with ashy. Bill black above, yellow below. Length, 6.25; wing, 3.00. *Hab.* Whole of North America; north of the United States only, in summer.

    2. **S. pusilla.** Crown dull rufous, indistinctly divided medially; lores entirely whitish; wing-bands not sharply defined, pale brown. No black spot on breast; jugulum tinged with buff. Bill entirely light brownish-red.

      Wing, 2.70; tail, 2.80; bill, from forehead, .37. *Hab.* Eastern Province United States . . . . . var. *pusilla.*

      "Similar, but colors clearer, and bill more robust." *Hab.* Peten, Guatemala . . . . . . var. *pinetorum.*[1]

  II. *Streak behind the eye blackish. No rufous tinge on side of breast. Egg deep blue, with black dots and streaks round larger end.*

    3. **S. socialis.** Crown bright rufous, not distinctly divided, generally plain. Forehead black, divided medially with white. Streak of black on lore and behind eye. Rump pure bluish-ash. Bill blackish, lower mandible paler.

      Auriculars deep ash, in strong contrast with pure white of the superciliary stripe and throat; breast without ashy tinge. Dorsal streaks broad. Wing, 2.80; tail, 2.30. *Hab.* Eastern Province of United States . . . . . var. *socialis.*

      Auriculars lighter ash, less strongly contrasted with the white above and below; breast strongly tinged with ash. Dorsal streaks narrow. Wing, 3.00; tail, 2.90. *Hab.* Western Province of United States, and table-lands of Mexico.

                            var. *arizonæ.*

  b. Crown light grayish-brown, with distinct black streaks; young differing in streaked. Egg deep blue, with black streaks and dots (precisely as in *socialis*).

    4. **S. pallida.**

      Crown divided medially by a distinct pale stripe; whitish superciliary stripe, and blackish post-ocular streak sharply defined. A dusky sub-maxillary streak. Nape ashy in contrast with the crown and back. Wing, 2.50; tail, 2.40. *Hab.* Plains of United States, from the Saskatchewan southward.

                            var. *pallida.*

      Crown without a distinct median stripe. Markings on side of head not sharply defined. No dusky sub-maxillary stripe, and nape scarcely different from crown and back. Wing, 2.50; tail, 2.60. *Hab.* Middle and western Provinces   var. *breweri.*

B. Crown not different from the sides of head; no light superciliary stripe.

---

[1] *Spizella pinetorum,* SALVIN, Pr. Z. S. 1863, p. 189. ("Similis *S. pusillæ,* ex Amer. Sept. et Mexico, sed coloribus clarioribus et rostro robustiore differt.")

5. **S. atrigularis.** Head and neck all round, and rump, uniform dark ash, gradually fading into white on the abdomen; wing-bands indistinct; bill light brownish-red. *Ad.* Lores, chin, and upper part of throat black. *Juv.* without black about the head. (Eggs unknown.) *Hab.* Adjacent portions of Mexico and southern Middle Province of United States (Fort Whipple, Arizona, Coues; Cape St. Lucas, Xantus).

Spizella monticola, BAIRD.

TREE SPARROW.

Fringilla monticola, GM. Syst. Nat. I, 1788, 912. *Zonotrichia monticola,* GRAY, Genera. *Spinites monticolus,* CABANIS, Mus. Hein. 1851, 134. *Spizella monticola,* BAIRD, Birds N. Am. 1858, 472. — COUES, P. A. N. S. 1861, 224 (Labrador). — COOPER & SUCKLEY, 203 (Washington Ter.). — DALL & BANNISTER, Tr. Ch. Ac. I, 1869, 285. — COOPER, Orn. Cal. I, 206. — SAMUELS, 317. *Passer canadensis,* BRISSON, Orn. III, 1760, 102. *Fringilla canadensis,* LATH. Index, I, 1790, 434. — AUD. Orn. Biog. II, 1834, 511; V, 504, pl. clxxxviii. — MAX. Cab. Jour. VI, 1858, 280. *Emberiza canadensis,* SW. F. B. Am. II, 1831, 252. — AUD. Syn. 1839. — IB. Birds Am. III, 1841, 83, pl. clxvi. *Spizella canadensis,* BON. List, 1838. — IB. Conspectus, 1850, 480. *Fringilla arborea,* WILS. Am. Orn. II, 1810, 12, pl. xii, f. 3. *Moineau du Canada,* BUFFON, Pl. Enl. 223, f. 2. *"Mountain Finch,"* LATH. Syn. II, I, 265.

Spizella monticola.

SP. CHAR. Middle of back with the feathers dark brown centrally, then rufous, and edged with pale fulvous (sometimes with whitish). Hood and upper part of nape continuous chestnut; a line of the same from behind the eye, as well as a short maxillary stripe. Sides of head and neck ashy. A broad light superciliary band. Beneath whitish, tinged with fulvous; the throat with ashy; a small circular blotch of brownish in the middle of the upper part of the breast; the sides chestnut. Edges of tail-feathers, primary quills, and two bands across the tips of the secondaries, white. Tertiaries nearly black; edged externally with rufous, turning to white near the tips. Lower jaw yellow; upper black. Young bird streaked on throat and breast, as well as on crown. Length, 6.25 inches; wing, 3.00.

HAB. Eastern North America to the Missouri, north to Arctic Ocean; also on Pole Creek and Little Colorado River, New Mexico; Western Nevada.

This species varies in the amount of whitish edging to the quills and tail.

HABITS. Essentially a northern bird, the Tree Sparrow breeds in high Arctic regions, only appearing in winter within the United States. It is then common as far south as Pennsylvania. A few winter in South Carolina.

It arrives on the Saskatchewan in the latter part of April, where it only makes a short halt, proceeding farther north to breed. Bischoff obtained a specimen at Sitka. Mr. Kennicott found its nest and eggs on the Yukon, and Mr. Dall obtained it at Nulato, and more sparingly below that point. Mr. MacFarlane met with it breeding in large numbers at Fort Anderson. The nests were in various situations, the larger proportion on the ground, a few in bushes near the ground, and only one is mentioned as having been several feet above it. One was in the cleft of a low willow on the edge of a small lake; another, in a bush, was nearly four feet from the ground; and a third was in a clump of willows and fourteen inches above the ground. Nearly all the other nests mentioned were built directly upon the ground.

The nests were constructed of dry bark and grasses, loosely put together, and very warmly lined with feathers. On the ground they were usually concealed in a tuft of grass. In all instances the female alone was found on the nests, the male being very rarely seen in their vicinity. The usual number of eggs in a nest was four or five, occasionally six, and even seven.

Dr. Suckley obtained a single specimen at Fort Dalles, and Dr. Cooper saw a flock in September, 1863, and again in 1864 at the mouth of the Columbia. Lieutenant Bryan met with them among the Rocky Mountains in latitude 39°, in August. Mr. Ridgway found them very common during the winter in the interior.

Dr. Coues found this Sparrow common in all the wooded districts of Labrador. It was very tame and unsuspicious, showing no fear even when closely approached. I have never met with any, in summer, in any part of New Brunswick or Nova Scotia.

This Sparrow is occasionally abundant in Massachusetts early in October, but rarely appears in full numbers until November. Some remain in the gardens in and about Boston during the winter, and during November the marshes of Fresh Pond are filled with them, when their wailing autumnal chant is in marked contrast with the sweet and sprightly song with which they enliven the spring, just before they are about to depart for their summer homes. They remain until the latter part of April, and Mr. Allen has observed them at Springfield till about the first of May.

In regard to their song, Mr. William Brewster informs me that they usually commence singing about the 25th of March. Their song is a loud, clear, and powerful chant, starting with two high notes, then falling rapidly, and ending with a low, sweet warble. He has heard a few singing with their full vigor in November and December, but this is rare.

Dr. Coues found them not common in South Carolina, but Dr. Kennerly states that they were quite abundant in December on the Little Colorado, in New Mexico, feeding on the fruit of the wild grape and upon seeds.

During the love-season the Tree Sparrow is quite a fine musician, its song resembling that of the Canary, but finer, sweeter, and not so loud. In their migrations, Mr. Audubon states, a flock of twenty or more will perch upon the same tree, and join in a delightful chorus. Their flight is elevated and graceful, and in waving undulations. On opening the stomachs of those he shot at the Magdeleine Islands, Mr. Audubon found them containing minute shell-fish, coleopterous insects, hard seeds, berries, and grains of sand.

Nests obtained near Fort Anderson confirm the descriptions given by Mr. Hutchins, as observed in the settlement at Hudson's Bay. The eggs, which are much larger than those of the other species of *Spizella*, measure .85 by .65 of an inch. Their ground-color is a light green, over which the eggs are very generally freckled with minute markings of a foxy brown. These markings are distributed with great regularity, but so sparsely as to leave the ground distinctly visible.

Spizella pusilla, BONAP.

FIELD SPARROW.

Fringilla pusilla, WILSON, Am. Orn. II, 1810, 121, pl. xvi, f. 2. — LICHT. Verzeich. Doubl. 1823, No. 252. — AUD. Orn. Biog. II, 1834, 299, pl. cxxxix. *Spizella pusilla*, BONAP. List, 1838. — IB. Conspectus, 1850, 480. — BAIRD, Birds N. Am. 1858, 473. — SAMUELS, 319. *Emberiza pusilla*, AUD. Syn. 1839, 104. — IB. Birds Am. III, 1841, 77, pl. clxiv. *Spinites pusillus*, CAB. Mus. Hein. 1851, 133. *Fringilla juncorum*, NUTT. Man. I, 1832, 499 (2d ed.,) 1840, 577 (supposed by him to be *Motacilla juncorum*, GMELIN, I, 952 ; *Sylvia juncorum*, LATHAM, Ind. II, 511 ; *Little Brown Sparrow*, CATESBY, Car. I, 35).

SP. CHAR. Bill red. Crown continuous rufous-red, with a faint indication of an ashy central stripe, and ashy nuchal collar. Back somewhat similar, with shaft-streaks of blackish. Sides of head and neck (including a superciliary stripe) ashy. Ear-coverts rufous. Beneath white, tinged with yellowish anteriorly. Tail-feathers and quills faintly edged with white. Two whitish bands across the wing-coverts. Autumnal specimens more rufous. Length about 5.75 ; wing, 2.34.

HAB. Eastern North America to the Missouri River ; San Antonio, Texas in winter (DRESSER, Ibis, 1865, 489).

This species is about the size of *S. socialis*, but is more rufous above ; lacks the black forehead and eye stripe ; has chestnut ears, instead of ash ; has the bill red, instead of black ; lacks the clear ash of the rump ; has a longer tail, etc. It is more like *monticola*, but is much smaller ; lacks the spot on the breast, and the predominance of white on the wings, etc. The young have the breast and sides streaked, and the crown slightly so.

HABITS. The common Field Sparrow occupies a well-defined and somewhat compact area, being resident within the United States, and in its migrations not removing far from its summer abode. In the summer it breeds from Virginia to Maine, as far as the central and western portions. It is not found near Calais, but occurs and breeds near Norway, Oxford County. In the interior it is found still farther north, in Canada, Iowa, and Wisconsin, to the Red River settlements, where it was found breeding by Donald Gunn. At Hamilton, Ontario, Mr. McIlwraith states it to be a rather rare summer resident. It breeds in Southern Wisconsin and in Iowa, but is not abundant. It does not appear to have been found west of the Missouri Valley.

This Sparrow arrives in Massachusetts early in April, and is found almost exclusively in open pastures, old fields, and in clearings remote from villages. It is a shy, retiring bird, and seems to avoid the near presence of man. Wilson states that it has no song, nothing but a kind of chirruping, not much superior to the chirping of a cricket. But this is quite a mistake, as it is in reality a very varied and fine singer. Its notes are not very powerful, and cannot be heard any distance, but they are very pleasing, although little known or appreciated. It continues in full song until into July, when the second brood is about hatching, when its notes relax, but do not cease until just before its departure in September or early October.

Mr. D. D. Hughes, of Grand Rapids, Mich., in an interesting paper on the habits of this species, speaks of its beautiful tinkling song as one of its most marked features. To his ear it resembles the ringing of a tiny bell more nearly than anything else. In the early morning and at evening the fields ring with their plaintive and tender peals. It sings at all hours of the day, during the nesting-season, even in the noonday heat of summer, when most other birds are silent.

In Virginia these birds may be found throughout the year, though probably not the same birds in the same localities, some retiring farther south and others coming to take their places from the north. In winter they are found in the greatest abundance in South Carolina and Georgia, occurring in large loose flocks, found chiefly along the roadsides and in old fields and pastures in the rural districts.

The Field Sparrow nests both on the ground and in low bushes, or among tangled clusters of vines. I have found their nests in all these situations, and have no doubt the nature of the surface may have something to do with the position. In high dry pastures, in sheltered situations, I have always found their nests on the ground. In the wet meadows and fields subject to a rise of water, as about the Potomac, near Washington, where these birds are very abundant, they almost invariably nest in bushes at a height of two or three feet.

Mr. Audubon says that during the winter these birds are quite common throughout Louisiana, and the country about the Mississippi, as far as Kentucky. They begin to depart from the South early in March, and move slowly northward as the season advances. He states that they begin to nest in May, and raise three broods in a season. This is not the case in New England, where they do not often have more than a single brood.

Their nests are constructed in a manner very similar to those of the Chipping Sparrow, loosely made of a few stems of vegetables, grasses, and sedges, and lined with hair or fine rootlets. Those placed on the ground are larger and more bulky, and those wrought into the twigs of a bush are made with more care and neatness of interweaving. The eggs are usually five in number, of an oblong-oval shape. The ground is a whitish clay-color, marked more or less fully with blotches of a ferruginous-brown. In some these markings are few, and arranged only about the larger end. In others they are generally diffused, and impart a deep ferruginous color to the whole egg, and disguise or conceal the ground. They vary also in size, — in length from .70 to .63 of an inch, and in breadth from .52 to .50. Their usual size is .70 by .52.

Two nests of this bird taken in Lynn, Mass., by Mr. George O. Welch, are characteristic of their usual style in architecture. One of these has a diameter of four and a height of two and a half inches. Its base, as well as the great mass of its periphery, is made of a very loose intertwining of minute stems of vegetables and dry grasses. The ends of these project from the exterior of the nest at the upper rim, and present a very peculiar appearance, as of an enclosure of palisades. The interior is lined with horsehair. The other is made of similar materials, of a less rigid character and closer texture. Its rim presents the same peculiarities of projecting ends, arranged like a fence above the nest itself. Its dimensions also are about the same. It is, however, much more compactly constructed, with thicker walls and a less open network of dry grasses, and stiff wiry stems of dried plants intermixed with a few pine leaves. The whole is very carefully and warmly lined with horsehair and the softer fur of small quadrupeds. These nests contained, one three, and the other four eggs.

Spizella socialis, BONAP.

CHIPPING SPARROW; CHIPPY.

Fringilla socialis, WILSON, Am. Orn. II, 1810, 127, pl. xvi, f. 5. — AUD. Orn. Biog. II, 1834, 21 ; V, 517, pl. civ. *Spizella socialis,* BON. List, 1838. — IB. Conspectus, 1850, 480. — BAIRD, Birds N. Am. 1858, 473. — COOPER & SUCKLEY, 203. — SAMUELS, 320. *Emberiza socialis,* AUD. Syn. 1839. — IB. Birds Am. III, 1841, 80, pl. clxv. *Spinites socialis,* CABANIS, Mus. Hein. 1851, 133.

SP. CHAR. Rump, back of neck, and sides of neck and head, ashy. Interscapular region with black streaks, margined with pale rufous. Crown continuous and uniform chestnut. Forehead black, separated in the middle by white. A white streak over the eye to nape, and a black one from the base of the bill through and behind the eye. Lores dusky. Under parts unspotted whitish, tinged with ashy on the sides and across the upper breast. Tail-feathers and primaries edged with paler, not white. Two narrow white bands across the wing-coverts. Bill black. Length, 5.75; wing, nearly 3.00; tail, 2.50 (or less).

Young. Immature birds and frequently the adult females with the cap streaked with blackish lines, the chestnut nearly or sometimes quite wanting. Birds of the year streaked beneath and on rump.

The color of bill varies; sometimes entirely black throughout, sometimes very light (but never reddish as in *S. pusilla*), with all intermediate stages. There is usually, however, a dusky tinge in the upper bill, wanting in *pusilla*, and the lores are almost always more or less dusky in all stages of plumage.

HAB. Eastern Province of North America; north to Great Slave Lake, and south to Orizaba, Eastern Mexico, where it is resident. Oaxaca (perhaps var. *arizonæ*), Jan. (SCL. 858, 304); Xalapa (SCL. 1859, 365); Cordova (SCL. 1856, 305); Cuba (LAWR. 1860, VII., 1269).

HABITS. The common Chipping Sparrow, so familiar to all in the eastern portion of the United States, is not only one of the most abundant, but one of the most widely distributed of our North American birds. It is found from the Atlantic to the Pacific in its two races, and breeds from Georgia to the Arctic Circle. At different seasons of the year it is found in all portions of North America to Mexico. Along the Atlantic coast it nests at least as far north as New Brunswick and Nova Scotia; in the extreme northern portion of the latter Province I found it one of the most abundant birds.

The late Mr. Robert Kennicott met with them in considerable numbers at Fort Resolution, on Great Slave Lake, and there he obtained quite a number of their nests, all of which were in trees or bushes, from two to three feet above the ground. These were all met with between the 1st and the 26th of June. Mr. B. R. Ross also met with these birds in considerable numbers at Fort Simpson and at Fort Rae.

On the Pacific coast the Chipping Sparrow is stated by Dr. Cooper to be quite as abundant in the northern parts of California, and in Oregon and Washington Territory, as on the Atlantic coast. He found them wintering in the Colorado Valley in large numbers, but met with none about San Diego. They spend their summers in the northern part of California, building their nests, as with us, in the shrubbery of the gardens, and coming familiarly about the doorsteps to pick up crumbs. In autumn they collect in large flocks, and frequent the open fields and pastures. Dr. Cooper found them in flocks on Catalina Island in June, but could discover no nests. They were all old birds, and the conclusion was that they had delayed their more northern migrations.

Dr. Suckley found this species extremely abundant in the open districts on the Columbia River, as well as upon the gravelly prairies of the Puget Sound district. It is not named as having been met with by Mr. Dall or any of the Russian Telegraph party in Alaska.

It was found in abundance during the summer by Mr. Ridgway in all the wooded portions of the country of the Great Basin. He did not meet with any among the cottonwoods of the river-valleys, its favorite haunts appearing to be the cedars and the nut-pines of the mountains. In July and August, in such localities, on the East Humboldt Mountains, it was not only the most numerous species, but also very abundant, nesting in the trees. About the middle of August they congregated in large numbers, preparing for their departure.

At Sacramento it was also very abundant among the groves of small oaks. He could not observe the slightest difference in habits or notes between the eastern and the western specimens of this form. He found them breeding at Salt Lake City, June 19, the nest being in a scrub-oak, six feet from the ground.

In Arizona, Dr. Coues found the Chippy a very abundant summer resident, arriving the third week of March and remaining until the latter part of November. A few may spend the winter there. As described, it seems more gregarious than it is with us, arriving in the spring, and remaining for a month or more in large flocks of fifty or upwards. In New England they always come in pairs, and only assemble in flocks just on the eve of their departure. Mr. Dresser met with these Sparrows, and obtained specimens of them, near San Antonio, on the 10th of April. Dr. Heermann, in his Report upon the birds observed in Lieutenant Williamson's route between the 32d and 35th parallels, speaks of finding this species abundant.

Dr. Gerhardt found this Sparrow not uncommon in the northern portions of Georgia, where it is resident throughout the year, and where a few remain in the summer to breed. Dr. Coues also states that a limited number summer in the vicinity of Columbia, S. C., but that their number is insignificant compared with those wintering there between October and April. They collect in large flocks on their arrival, and remain in companies of hundreds or more.

Mr. Sumichrast states that it is a resident bird in the temperate region of Vera Cruz, Mexico, where it remains throughout the year, and breeds as freely and commonly as it does within the United States.

Although found throughout the country in greater or less numbers, they are noticeably not common in the more recent settlements of the West, as on the unsettled prairies of Illinois and Iowa. Mr. Allen found them quite rare in both States, excepting only about the older settlements. As early as the first week in April, 1868, I noticed these birds very common and familiar in the streets of St. Louis, especially so in the business part of that city, along the wharves and near the grain-stores, seeking their food on the ground with a confidence and fearlessness quite unusual to it in such situations.

The tameness and sociability of this bird surpass that of any of the birds I have ever met with in New England, and are only equalled by similar traits manifested by the Snowbird (*J. hyemalis*) in Pictou. Those that live about our dwellings in rural situations, and have been treated kindly, visit our doorsteps, and even enter the houses, with the greatest familiarity and trust. They will learn to distinguish their friends, alight at their feet, call for their accustomed food, and pick it up when thrown to them, without the slightest signs of fear. One pair which, summer after summer, had built their nest in a fir-tree near my door, became so accustomed to be fed that they would clamor for their food if they were any morning forgotten. One of these birds, the female, from coming down to the ground to be fed with crumbs, soon learned to take them on the flat branch of the fir near her nest, and at last to feed from my hand, and afterwards from that of other members of the family. Her mate, all the while, was comparatively shy and distrustful, and could not be induced to receive his food from us or to eat in our presence.

This Sparrow is also quite social, keeping on good terms and delighting to associate with other species. Since the introduction of the European House Sparrow into Boston, I have repeatedly noticed it associating with them in the most friendly relations, feeding with them, flying up with them when disturbed, and imitating all their movements.

The Chipping Sparrow has very slight claims to be regarded as one of our song-birds. Its note of complaint or uneasiness is a simple *chip*, and its song, at its best, is but a monotonous repetition of a single note, sounding like the rapid striking together of two small pebbles. In the bright days of June this unpretending ditty is kept up incessantly, hours at a time, with only rare intermissions.

The nest of this bird is always in trees or bushes. I have in no instance known of its being built on the ground. Even at the Arctic regions, where so many of our tree-builders vary from this custom to nest on the ground, no exceptional cases are reported in regard to it, all its nests being upon trees or in bushes. These are somewhat rudely built, often so loosely that they may readily be seen through. Externally they are made of coarse stems of grasses and vegetable branches, and lined with the hair of the larger animals.

These birds are devoted parents, and express great solicitude whenever their nests are approached or meddled with. They feed their young almost exclusively with the larvæ of insects, especially with young caterpillars. When in neighborhoods infested with the destructive canker-worm, they will feed their young with this pest in incredible numbers, and seek them from a considerable distance. Living in a district exempt from this scourge, yet but shortly removed from them, in the summer of 1869, I noticed one of these Sparrows with its mouth filled with something which inconvenienced it to carry. It alighted on the gravel walk to adjust its load, and passed on to its nest, leaving two canker-worms behind it, which, if not thus detected, would have introduced this nuisance into an orchard that had previously escaped, showing that though friends to those afflicted they are dangerous to their neighbors. This Sparrow is also the frequent nurse of the Cow Blackbird, rearing its young to the destruction of its own, and tending them with exemplary fidelity.

Their eggs, five in number, are of an oblong-oval shape, and vary greatly in size. They are of a bluish-green color, and are sparingly spotted about the larger end with markings of umber, purple, and dark blackish-brown, intermingled with lighter shadings of faint purple. The largest specimen

I have ever noticed of this egg, found in the Capitol Grounds, Washington, measures .80 by .58 of an inch ; and the smallest, from Varrell's Station, Ga., measures .60 by .50. Their average measurement is about .70 by .54. They are all much pointed at the smaller end.

Spizella socialis, var. arizonæ, Coues.

WESTERN CHIPPING SPARROW.

Spizella socialis, var. *arizonæ*, Coues, P. A. N. S. 1866. — Cooper, Orn. Cal. I, 207.

Sp. Char. Similar to *socialis*, but tail and wing longer, the bill narrower, and colors paler and grayer. Rufous of the crown lighter and less purplish, generally (always in specimens from southern Rocky Mountains) with fine black streaks on the posterior part. Ash of the cheeks paler, throwing the white of the superciliary stripe and throat into less contrast. Black streaks of the back narrower, and without the rufous along their edges, merely streaking a plain light brownish-gray ground-color. A strong ashy shade over the breast, not seen in *socialis ;* wing-bands more purely white. Wing, 3.00; tail, 2.80; bill, .36 from forehead, by .18 deep. (40,813 ♂, April 24, Fort Whipple, Ariz., Dr. Coues.)

Hab. Western United States from Rocky Mountains to the Pacific; south in winter into Middle and Western Mexico.

All the specimens of a large series from Fort Whipple, Arizona, as well as most others from west of the Rocky Mountains to the Pacific coast, agree in the characters given above, as distinguished from eastern specimens of *socialis*. The variations with age and season are simple parallels of those in *socialis*.

HABITS. The references in the preceding article to the Chipping Sparrow as occurring in the Middle and Western Provinces of the United States, are to be understood as applying to the present race.

Spizella pallida, Bonap.

CLAY-COLORED SPARROW.

Emberiza pallida, Sw. F. Bor.-Am. II, 1831, 251 (not of Audubon). *Spizella pallida*, Bonap. List, 1838. — Baird, Birds N. Am. 1858, 474. *Spinites pallidus*, Cabanis, Mus. Hein. 1851, 133. *Emberiza shattucki*, Aud. Birds Am. VII, 1843, 347, pl. ccccxciii. *Spizella shattucki*, Bonap. Conspectus, 1850, 480.

Sp. Char. Smaller than *S. socialis*. Back and sides of hind neck ashy. Prevailing color above pale brownish-yellow, with a tinge of grayish. The feathers of back and crown streaked conspicuously with blackish. Crown with a median pale ashy and a lateral or superciliary ashy-white stripe. Beneath whitish, tinged with brown on the breast and sides, and an indistinct narrow brown streak on the edge of the chin, cutting off a light stripe above it. Ear-coverts brownish-yellow, margined above and below by dark brown, making three dark stripes on the face. Bill reddish, dusky towards tip. Legs yellow. Length, 4.75 ; wing, 2.55.

HAB. Upper Missouri River and high central plains to the Saskatchewan country. Cape St. Lucas, Oaxaca, March (SCL. 1859, 379); Fort Mohave (COOPER, P. A. N. S. Cal. 1861, 122); San Antonio, Texas, spring (DRESSER, Ibis, 1865, 489; common).

The ashy collar is quite conspicuous, and streaked above with brown. The rump is immaculate. The streaks on the feathers of the crown almost form continuous lines, about six in number. The brown line above the ear-coverts is a post-ocular one. That on the side of the chin forms the lower border of a white maxillary stripe which widens and curves around behind the ear-coverts, fading into the ashy of the neck. The wing-feathers are all margined with paler, and there is an indication of two light bands across the ends of the coverts.

The young of this species is thickly streaked beneath over the throat, breast, and belly, with brown, giving to it an entirely different appearance from the adult. The streaks in the upper parts, too, are darker and more conspicuous. The margins of the feathers are rather more rusty.

This species is readily distinguishable from the other American *Spizellas*, except *S. breweri* (which see), in the dark streaks and median ashy stripe on the crown, the paler tints, the dark line on the side of the chin, etc.

HABITS. The Clay-colored Bunting was first discovered by Richardson, and described by Swainson, in the Fauna Bor.-Amer. The only statement made in regard to it is that it visited the Saskatchewan in considerable numbers, frequented the farm-yard at Carlton House, and was in all respects as familiar and confiding as the common House Sparrow of Europe.

The bird given by Mr. Audubon as the *pallida* has been made by Mr. Cassin a different species, *S. breweri*, and the species the former gives in his seventh volume of the Birds of America as *Emberiza shattucki* is really this species. It was found by Mr. Audubon's party to the Yellowstone quite abundant throughout the country bordering upon the Upper Missouri. It seemed to be particularly partial to the small valleys found, here and there, along the numerous ravines running from the interior and between the hills. Its usual demeanor is said to greatly resemble that of the common Chipping Sparrow, and, like that bird, it has a very monotonous ditty, which it seems to delight to repeat constantly, while its mate is more usefully employed in the duties of incubation. When it was approached, it would dive and conceal itself amid the low bushes around, or would seek one of the large clusters of wild roses so abundant in that section. The nest of this species is mentioned as having been usually placed on a small horizontal branch seven or eight feet from the ground, and occasionally in the broken and hollow branches of trees. These nests are also stated to have been formed of slender grasses, but in so slight a manner as, with their circular lining of horse or cattle hair, to resemble as much as possible the nest of the common *socialis*. The eggs were five in number, and are described as being blue with reddish-brown spots. These birds were also met with at the Great Slave Lake region by Mr. Kennicott, in the same neighborhood by B. R.

Ross and J. Lockhart, and in the Red River settlements by Mr. C. A. Hubbard and Mr. Donald Gunn.

Captain Blakiston noted the arrival of this bird at Fort Carlton on the 21st of May. He speaks of its note as very peculiar, resembling, though sharper than, the buzzing made by a fly in a paper box, or a faint imitation of the sound of a watchman's rattle. This song it utters perched on some young tree or bush, sometimes only once, at others three or four times in quick succession.

Their nests appear to have been in all instances placed in trees or in shrubs, generally in small spruces, two or three feet from the ground. In one instance it was in a clump of small bushes not more than six inches from the ground, and only a few rods from the buildings of Fort Resolution.

Both this species and the *S. breweri* were found by Lieutenant Couch at Tamaulipas in March, 1855. It does not appear to have been met with by any other of the exploring expeditions, but in 1864, for the first time, as Dr. Heermann states, to his knowledge, these birds were found quite plentiful near San Antonio, Texas, by Mr. Dresser. This was in April, in the fields near that town. They were associating with the *Melospiza lincolni* and other Sparrows. They remained about San Antonio until the middle of May, after which none were observed.

The eggs of this species are of a light blue, with a slight tinge of greenish, and are marked around the larger end with spots and blotches of a purplish-brown, rather finer, perhaps, than in the egg of *S. socialis*, though very similar to it. They average .70 of an inch in length, and vary in breadth from .50 to .52 of an inch.

Spizella pallida, var. breweri, CASSIN.

BREWER'S SPARROW.

Emberiza pallida, AUD. Orn. Biog. V, 1839, 66, pl. cccxcviii, f. 2. — IB. Synopsis, 1839. — IB. Birds Am. III, 1841, 71, pl. clxi (not of SWAINSON, 1831). *Spizella breweri*, CASSIN, Pr. A. N. Sc. VIII, Feb. 1856, 40. — BAIRD, Birds N. Am. 1858, 475. — COOPER, Orn. Cal. I, 209.

SP. CHAR. Similar to *S. pallida;* the markings including the nuchal collar more obsolete; no distinct median and superciliary light stripes. The crown streaked with black. Some of the feathers on the sides with brown shafts. Length, 5 inches; wing, 2.50. Young streaked beneath, as in *pallida*.

HAB. Rocky Mountains of United States to the Pacific coast.

This race is very similar to the *S. pallida*, and requires close and critical comparison to separate it. The streaks on the back are narrower, and the central ashy and lateral whitish stripes of the crown are scarcely, if at all, appreciable. The clear unstreaked ash of the back of the neck, too, is mostly wanting. The feathers along the sides of the body, near the tibia, and occasionally elsewhere on the sides, have brownish shafts, not found in the other. The differences are perhaps those of race, rather than of species, though they are very appreciable.

HABITS. This species bears a very close resemblance to the *S. pallida* in its external appearance, but there are certain constant differences which, with the peculiarities of their distinctive distributions and habits, seem to establish their specific separation. The present bird is found from the Pacific coast to the Rocky Mountains, and from the northern portion of California to the Rio Grande and Mexico. Dr. Kennerly found it in February, 1854, throughout New Mexico, from the Rio Grande to the Great Colorado, along the different streams, where it was feeding upon the seeds of several kinds of weeds.

Dr. Heermann, while accompanying the surveying party of Lieutenant Williamson, between the 32d and 35th parallels, found these Sparrows throughout his entire route, both in California and in Texas. On the passage from the Pimos villages to Tucson he observed large flocks gleaning their food among the bushes as they were moving southward. In the Tejon valley, during the fall season, he was constantly meeting them associated with large flocks of other species of Sparrows, congregated around the cultivated fields of the Indians, where they find a bountiful supply of seeds. For this purpose they pass the greater part of the time upon the ground.

Dr. Woodhouse also met with this Sparrow throughout New Mexico, wherever food and water were to be found in sufficient quantity to sustain life.

In Arizona, near Fort Whipple, Dr. Coues states that this bird is a rare summer resident. He characterizes it as a shy, retiring species, keeping mostly in thick brush near the ground.

Mr. Ridgway states that he found this interesting little Sparrow, while abundant in all fertile portions, almost exclusively an inhabitant of open situations, such as fields or bushy plains, among the artemesia especially, where it is most numerous. It frequents alike the valleys and the mountains. At Sacramento it was the most abundant Sparrow, frequenting the old fields. In this respect it very much resembles the eastern *Spizella pusilla,* from which, however, it is in many respects very different.

The song of Brewer's Sparrow, he adds, for sprightliness and vivacity is not excelled by any other of the North American Fringillidæ, being inferior only to that of the *Chondestes grammaca* in power and richness, and even excelling it in variety and compass. Its song, while possessing all the plaintiveness of tone so characteristic of the eastern Field Sparrow, unites to this quality a vivacity and variety fully equalling that of the finest Canary. This species is not resident, but arrives about the 9th of April. He found its nest and eggs in the Truckee Reservation, early in June. The nests were in sage-bushes about three feet from the ground.

Dr. Cooper found small flocks of this species at Fort Mohave, after March

20, frequenting grassy spots among the low bushes, and a month later they were singing, he adds, much like a Canary, but more faintly. They are presumed to remain in the valley all summer.

The eggs, four in number, are of a light bluish-green color, oblong in shape, more rounded at the smaller end than the eggs of the *socialis*, and the ground is more of a green than in those of *S. pallida*. They are marked and blotched in scattered markings of a golden-brown color. These blotches are larger and more conspicuous than in the eggs of the other species. They measure .70 by .51 of an inch.

Spizella atrigularis, BAIRD.

BLACK-CHINNED SPARROW.

Spinites atrigularis, CABANIS, Mus. Hein. 1851, 133. *Spizella atrigularis*, BAIRD, Birds N. Am. 1858, 476, pl. lv, f. 1. — IB. Mex. Bound. II, Birds, p. 16, pl. xvii, f. 1. — COOPER, Orn. Cal. I, 210. *Struthus atrimentalis*, COUCH, Pr. A. N. Sc. Phil. VII, April, 1854, 67.

SP. CHAR. Tail elongated, deeply forked and divaricated. General color bluish-ash, paler beneath, and turning to white on the middle of the belly. Interscapular region yellowish-rusty, streaked with black. Forehead, loral region, and side of head as far as eyes, chin, and upper part of throat black. Quills and tail-feathers very dark brown, edged with ashy. Edges of coverts like the back. No white bands on the wings. Bill red, feet dusky. Immature birds, and perhaps adult female, without any black on head. Length, 5.50; wing, 2.50; tail, 3.00.

HAB. Mexico, just south of the Rio Grande; Fort Whipple, Ariz. (COUES); Cape St. Lucas.

This species is about the size of *S. pusilla* and *S. socialis*, resembling the former most in its still longer tail. This is more deeply forked and divaricated, with broader feathers than in either. The wing is much rounded; the fourth quill longest; the first almost the shortest of the primaries.

HABITS. This species is a Mexican bird, found only within the limits of the United States along the borders. But little is known as to its history. It is supposed to be neither very abundant nor to have an extended area of distribution. It was met with by Dr. Coues in the neighborhood of Fort Whipple, Arizona, where it arrives in April and leaves again in October, collecting, before its departure, in small flocks. In the spring he states that it has a very sweet and melodious song, far surpassing in power and melody the notes of any other of this genus that he has ever heard.

Dr. Coues furnishes me with the following additional information in regard to this species: " This is not a common bird at Fort Whipple, and was only observed from April to October. It unquestionably breeds in that vicinity, as I shot very young birds, in August, wanting the distinctive head-markings of the adult. A pair noticed in early April were seemingly about breeding, as the male was in full song, and showed, on dissection, highly developed sexual organs. The song is very agreeable, not in the least recalling the monotonous ditty of the Chip Bird, or the rather weak performances of some other species of the genus. In the latter part of summer and early autumn the birds were generally seen in small troops, perhaps families, in weedy places, associating with the western variety of *Spizella socialis*, as well as with Goldfinches."

Lieutenant Couch met with individuals of this species at Agua Nueva, in Coahuila, Mexico, in May, 1853. They were found in small flocks among the mountains. Their nest and eggs are unknown.

Genus **MELOSPIZA**, Baird.

Melospiza, Baird, Birds N. Am. 1868, 478.　(Type, *Fringilla melodia*, Wils.)

Gen. Char. Body stout. Bill conical, very obsoletely notched, or smooth; somewhat compressed. Lower mandible not so deep as the upper. Commissure nearly straight. Gonys a little curved. Feet stout, not stretching beyond the tail; tarsus a little longer than the middle toe; outer toe a little longer than the inner; its claw not quite reaching to the base of the middle one. Hind toe appreciably longer than the middle one. Wings quite short and rounded, scarcely reaching beyond the base of the tail; the tertials considerably longer than the secondaries; the quills considerably graduated; the fourth longest; the first not longer than the tertials, and almost the

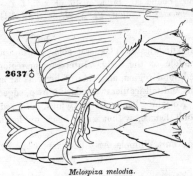

Melospiza melodia.

2637 ♂

shortest of the primaries. Tail moderately long, rather longer from coccyx than the wings, and considerably graduated; the feathers oval at the tips, and not stiffened. Crown and back similar in color, and streaked; beneath thickly streaked, except in *M. palustris*. Tail immaculate. Usually nest on ground; nests strongly woven of grasses and fibrous stems; eggs marked with rusty-brown and purple on a ground of a clay color.

This genus differs from *Zonotrichia* in the shorter, more graduated tail, rather longer hind toe, much more rounded wing, which is shorter; the tertiaries longer; the first quill almost the shortest, and not longer than the tertials. The under parts are spotted; the crown streaked, and like the back.

There are few species of American birds that have caused more perplexity to the ornithologist than the group of which *Melospiza melodia* is the type. Spread

Melospiza melodia.

over the whole of North America, and familiar to every one, we find each region to possess a special form (to which a specific name has been given), and yet these passing into each other by such insensible gradations as to render it quite impossible to define them as species. Between *M. melodia* of the Atlantic States and *M. insignis* of Kodiak the difference seems wide; but the connecting links in the intermediate regions bridge this over so completely that, with a series of hundreds of specimens before us, we abandon the attempt at specific separation, and unite into one no less than eight species previously recognized.

Taking, then, the common Song Sparrow of the Eastern Atlantic States (*M. melodia*) as the starting-point, and proceeding westward, we find quite a decided difference (in a variety *fallax*) when we reach the Middle Province, or that of the Rocky Mountains. The general tints are paler, grayer, and less rusty; the superciliary stripe anteriorly more ashy; the bill, and especially the legs, more dusky, the latter not at all to be called yellow. The bill is perhaps smaller and, though sometimes equal to the average of eastern specimens, more slender in proportion. In some specimens (typical *fallax*) the streaks are uniform rufous without darker centres, — a feature I have not noticed in eastern *melodia*. Another stage (*heermanni*) is seen when we reach the Pacific coast of California, in a darker brown color (but not rufous). Here the bill is rather larger than in var. *fallax*, and the legs colored more like typical *melodia*. In fact, the bird is like *melodia*, but darker. The stripes on the back continue well defined and distinct. *M. samuelis* (= *gouldi*) may stand as a smaller race of this variety.

Proceeding northward along the Pacific coast, another form (var. *guttata*), peculiar to the coast of California, is met with towards and beyond the mouth of the Columbia (coming into Southern California in winter). This is darker in color, more rufous; the stripes quite indistinct above, in fact, more or less obsolete, and none, either above or below, with darker or blackish centres. The sides, crissum, and tibia are washed with ochraceous-brown, the latter perhaps darkest. The bill is proportionally longer and more slender. This race becomes still darker northward, until at Sitka (var. *rufina*) it shows no rufous tints, but a dusky olive-brown instead, including the streaks of the under parts. The markings of the head and back are appreciable, though not distinct. The size has become considerably larger than in eastern *melodia*, the average length of wing being 3.00, instead of 2.60.

The last extreme of difference from typical *melodia* of the east is seen in the variety *insignis* from Kodiak. Here the size is very large: length, 7.00; extent, 10.75; wing, 3.20. The bill is very long (.73 from forehead), the color still darker brown and more uniform above; the median light stripe of vertex scarcely appreciable in some specimens; the superciliary scarcely showing, except as a whitish spot anteriorly. The bill and feet have become almost black.

The following synopsis may serve as a means by which to distinguish the several races of this species, as also the two remaining positive species of the genus : —

Species and Varieties.

A. Lower parts streaked.

1. **M. melodia.** White of the lower parts uninterrupted from the chin to the crissum ; the streaks of the jugulum, etc., broad and cuneate.

a. Streaks, above and below, sharply defined, and distinctly black medially (except sometimes in winter plumage).

Ground-color above reddish-gray, the interscapulars with the whitish and black streaks about equal, and sharply contrasted. Rump with reddish streaks. Wing, 2.70; tail, 2.90; bill .36 from nostril, and .30 deep. *Hab.* Eastern Province of United States, to the Plains on the west, and the Rio Grande on the south   var. *melodia.*[1]

Ground-color above ashy-gray, the interscapulars with the black streaks much broader than their rufous border, and the whitish edges not in strong contrast. Rump without streaks. Wing, 2.80; tail, 3.15; bill, .33 and .22. *Hab.* Middle Province of United States   .   .   .   .   var. *fallax.*[2]

Ground-color above nearly pure gray, the interscapulars with the black streaks much broader than the rufous, and the edges of the feathers not appreciably paler. Rump without streaks. Wing, 2.80; tail, 2.85; bill, .32 by .27. *Hab.* California, except along the coast; Sierra Nevada   .   .   .   .   var. *heermanni.*[3]

Ground-color above grayish-olive, the interscapulars with the black streaks much broader than their rufous border; edges of the feathers scarcely appreciably paler. Rump and tail-coverts, above and below, with distinct broad streaks of black. Wing, 2.40; tail, 2.50; bill, .37 and .24. *Hab.* Coast region of California var. *samuelis.*[4]

Ground-color above olive-rufous, the edges of the interscapulars alone, ashy ; dorsal black streaks very broad, without rufous border. Rump streaked with black. Wing, 2.60; tail, 2.85; bill, .34 and .25. *Hab.* Puebla, Mexico   .   .   .   var. *mexicana.*[5]

[1] *Winter plumage.* Rusty prevailing above, but hoary whitish edges to feathers still in strong contrast ; streaks beneath with a rufous suffusion externally, but still with the black in excess.

[2] *Winter plumage.* Gray above more olivaceous, the black streaks more subdued by a rufous suffusion ; streaks beneath with the rufous predominating, sometimes without any black.

[3] *Winter plumage.* Above rusty-olive, with little or no ashy, the black streaks broad and distinct. Streaks beneath with the black and rusty in about equal amount.

[4] In summer the streaks beneath are entirely intense black ; in winter they have a slight rufous external suffusion.

[5] *Melospiza melodia,* var. *mexicana,* Ridgway. Mexican Song Sparrow. *? ? Melospiza pectoralis,* von Müller.

Sp. Char. (Type, 60,046, Puebla, Mexico, A. Boucard.) Similar to *M. melodia,* but ground-color above olive-brown ; inner webs of interscapulars pale ashy, but not in strong contrast. Crown and wings rusty-brown, the former with broad black streaks, and divided by a just appreciable paler line ; back with broad black streaks without any rufous suffusion. Superciliary stripe pure light ash, becoming white anterior to the eye ; two broad, dark-brown stripes on side of head, — one from the eye back along upper edge of auriculars, the other back from the rictus, along their lower border. Lower parts pure white, the flanks and crissum distinctly ochraceous ; markings beneath broad and heavy, entirely pure deep black ; those on the jugulum deltoid, on the sides linear. Wing, 2.60 ; tail, 2.85 ; bill, .37 and .24 ; tarsus, .85 ;

b. Streaks, above and below, not sharply defined, and without black medially.

Above rufescent-olive, the darker shades castaneous ; streaks beneath castaneous-rufous. Wing, 2.60 ; tail, 2.50 ; bill, .35 and .23. *Hab.* Pacific Province from British Columbia, southward . var. *guttata.*

Above sepia-plumbeous, the darker shades fuliginous-sepia ; streaks beneath fuliginous-sepia. Wing, 3.00 ; tail, 3.00 ; bill, .41 and .25. *Hab.* Pacific Province from British Columbia northward. var. *rufina.*

Above plumbeous, the darker markings dull reddish-sepia in winter, clove-brown in summer ; streaks beneath castaneous-rufous in winter, dull sepia in summer. Wing, 3.40 ; tail, 3.60 ; bill, .50 and .30. *Hab.* Pacific coast of Alaska (Kodiak, etc.) . var. *insignis.*

2. **M. lincolni.** White of the lower parts interrutped by a broad pectoral band of buff ; streaks on the jugulum, etc., narrow linear. A vertex and superciliary stripe of ashy ; a maxillary one of buff. Wing, 2.60 ; tail, 2.40 ; bill, .30 and .25. *Hab.* Whole of North America ; south, in winter, to Panama.

B. Lower parts without streaks (except in young.)

3. **M. palustris.** Jugulum and nape tinged with ashy ; outer surface of wings bright castaneous, in strong contrast with the olivaceous of the back ; dorsal streaks broad, black, without rufous externally ; a superciliary and maxillary stripe of ashy. ♂. Crown uniform chestnut, forehead black. ♀. Crown similar, but divided by an indistinct ashy stripe, and more or less streaked with black (autumnal or winter ♂ similar). *Juv.* Head, back, and jugulum streaked with black on a yellowish-white ground ; black prevailing on the crown. *Hab.* Eastern Province of North America.

Melospiza melodia, BAIRD.

SONG SPARROW.

Fringilla melodia, WILSON, Am. Orn. II, 1810, 125, pl. xvi, f. 4. — LICHT. Verz. 1823, No. 249. — AUD. Orn. Biog. I, 1832, 126 ; V, 507, pl. 25. — IB. Syn. 1839, 120. — IB. Birds Am. III, 1841, 147, pl. clxxxix. — MAX. Cab. J. VI, 1858, 275. *Zonotrichia melodia,* BON. List, 1838. — IB. Conspectus, 1850, 478. *?? Fringilla fasciata,* GMELIN, Syst. Nat. I, 1788, 922. — NUTTALL, Man. I, (2d ed.,) 1840, 562. *?? Fringilla hyemalis,* GMELIN, Syst. Nat. I, 1788, 922. *Melospiza melodia,* BAIRD, Birds N. Am. 1858, 477. — SAMUELS, 321.

SP. CHAR. General tint of upper parts rufous and distinctly streaked with rufous-brown, dark-brown, and ashy-gray. The crown is rufous, with a superciliary and median stripe of dull gray, the former lighter ; nearly white anteriorly, where it sometimes has a faint shade of yellow, principally in autumn ; each feather of the crown with a narrow streak of black forming about six narrow lines. Interscapulars black in the centre, then rufous, then pale grayish on the margin, these three colors on each feather very sharply contrasted. Rump grayer than upper tail-coverts, both with obsolete dark streaks. There is

middle toe without claw, .68. This may possibly be the *M. pectoralis* of von Müller. The description cited above, however, does not agree with the specimen under consideration. The pectoral spots are expressly stated to be brown, not even a black shaft-streak being mentioned, whereas the pure black spots of the specimen before us render it peculiar in this respect, being, in fact, its chief characteristic.

a whitish maxillary stripe, bordered above and below by one of dark rufous-brown, and with another from behind the eye. The under parts are white; the jugulum and sides of body streaked with clear dark-brown, sometimes with a rufous suffusion. On the middle of the breast these marks are rather aggregated so as to form a spot. No distinct white on tail or wings. Length of male, 6.50; wing, 2.58; tail, 3.00. Bill pale brown above; yellowish at base beneath. Legs yellowish.

HAB. Eastern United States to the high Central Plains.

Specimens vary somewhat in having the streaks across the breast more or less sparse, the spot more or less distinct. In autumn the colors are more blended, the light maxillary stripe tinged with yellowish, the edges of the dusky streaks strongly suffused with brownish-rufous.

The young bird has the upper parts paler, the streaks more distinct; the lines on the head scarcely appreciable. The under parts are yellowish; the streaks narrower and more sharply defined dark brown.

As already stated, this species varies more or less from the above description in different parts of North America, its typical races having received specific names, which it is necessary to retain for them as varieties.

HABITS. The common Song Sparrow of eastern North America has an extended range of distribution, and is resident throughout the year in a large part of the area in which it breeds. It nests from about South Carolina north to the British Provinces of Nova Scotia and New Brunswick at the east, and to a not well-defined limit in British America. The most northern points to which it has been traced are the plains of the Saskatchewan and the southern shore of Lake Winnepeg, in which latter place Mr. Kennicott found it breeding. It is said by Dr. Coues to breed in South Carolina, and by Mr. Audubon in Louisiana, but I have never seen any of their eggs from any point south of Washington. In winter it is found from Massachusetts, where only a few are observed, to Florida. It is most abundant at this period in North and South Carolina. It is not mentioned in Dr. Gerhardt's list as being found in Northern Georgia at any season of the year. Mr. Ridgway informs me that it does not breed in Southern Illinois. Its song is not popularly known there, though he has occasionally heard it just before these Sparrows were leaving for the north. This species winters there in company with the *Z. albicollis* and *Z. leucophrys*, associating with the former, and inhabiting brush-heaps in the clearings.

To Massachusetts, where specimens have been taken in every month of the year, and where they have been heard to sing in January, they return in large numbers usually early in March, sometimes even in February. It is probable that these are but migrants, passing farther north, and that our summer visitants do not appear among us until the middle of April, or just as they are about to breed. They reach Maine from the 15th to the 25th, and breed there the middle of May. In Massachusetts they do not have eggs until the first week in May, except in very remarkable seasons, usually not until after the Bluebird has already hatched out her first brood, and a week later than the Robin.

The tide of returning emigration begins to set southward early in October. Collecting in small loose flocks, probably all of each group members of the same family, they slowly move towards the south. As one set passes on, another succeeds, until the latter part of November, when we no longer meet with flocks, but solitary individuals or groups of two or three. These are usually a larger and stouter race, and almost suggest a different species. They are often in song even into December. They apparently do not go far, and are the first to return. In early March they are in full song, and their notes seem louder, clearer, and more vibratory than those that come to us and remain to breed.

The Song Sparrow, as its name implies, is one of our most noted and conspicuous singers. It is at once our earliest and our latest, as also our most constant musician. Its song is somewhat brief, but is repeated at short intervals, almost throughout the days of spring and early summer. It somewhat resembles the opening notes of the Canary, and though less resonant and powerful, much surpasses them in sweetness and expression. Plain and homely as this bird is in its outward garb, its sweet song and its gentle confiding manners render it a welcome visitor to every garden, and around every rural home wherein such attractions can be appreciated. Whenever these birds are kindly treated they readily make friends, and are attracted to our doorsteps for the welcome crumbs that are thrown to them; and they will return, year after year, to the same locality, whenever thus encouraged.

The song of this Sparrow varies in different individuals, and often changes, in the same bird, in different parts of the year. It is even stated by an observing naturalist — Mr. Charles S. Paine, of Randolph, Vt. — that he has known the same bird to sing, in succession, nine entirely different sets of notes, usually uttering them one after the other, in the same order. This was noticed not merely once or during one season, but through three successive summers. The same bird returned each season to his grounds, and came each time provided with the same variety of airs.

Mr. Nuttall, who dwells with much force upon the beauty and earnestness of expression of the song of this species, has also noticed and remarked upon the power of individuals to vary their song, from time to time, with very agreeable effect, but no one has recorded so remarkable an instance as that thus carefully noted by Mr. Paine.

These birds are found in almost any cultivated locality where the grounds are sufficiently open. They prefer the edges of open fields, and those of meadows and low grounds, but are rarely found in woods or in thick bushes, except near their outer edges. They nest naturally on the ground, and in such situations a large majority build their nests. These are usually the younger birds. A portion, almost always birds of several summers, probably taught by sad experiences of the insecurity of the ground, build in bushes. A pair which had a nest in an adjoining field had been robbed, by a cat, of their young when just about to fly. After much lamentation, and an interval of a week, I found this same pair, which I easily recognized, building their nest among some vines near my house, some eight feet from the ground. They had abandoned my neighbor's grounds and taken refuge close to my house. This situation they resorted to afterwards for several successive summers, each season building two nests, never using the same nest a second time, although each time it was left as clean and in as good condition as when first made. Indeed, this species is remarkable for its cleanliness, both in its own person and in its care of nestlings and nests.

They feed their young chiefly with insects, especially small caterpillars ; the destructive canker-worm is one of their favorite articles of food, also the larvæ of insects and the smaller moths. When crumbs of bread are given them, they are eagerly gathered and taken to their nests.

In the Middle States they are said to have three broods in a season. This may also be so in New England, but I have never known one pair to have more than two broods in the same summer, even when both had been successfully reared. Nests found after July have always been in cases where some accident had befallen the preceding brood.

The nest of the Song Sparrow, whether built on ground, bush, or tree, is always well and thoroughly made. Externally and at the base it consists of stout stems of grasses, fibrous twigs of plants, and small sticks and rootlets. These are strongly wrought together. Within is made a neat, well-woven basket of fine long stems of grasses, rarely anything else. On the ground they are usually concealed beneath a tuft of grass ; sometimes they make a covered passage-way of several inches, leading to their nest. When built in a tree or shrub, the top is often sheltered by the branches or by dry leaves, forming a covering to the structure.

The eggs of the Song Sparrow are five in number, and have an average measurement of .82 by .60 of an inch. They have a ground of a clay-color or dirty white, and are spotted equally over the entire egg with blotches of a rusty-brown, intermingled with lighter shades of purple. In some these markings are so numerous and confluent as to entirely conceal the ground-color ; in others they are irregularly diffused over different parts, leaving patches unmarked. Occasionally the eggs are unspotted, and are then not unlike those of *Leucosticte griseinucha.*

Melospiza melodia var. fallax, BAIRD.

WESTERN SONG SPARROW.

Zonotrichia fallax, BAIRD, Pr. A. N. Sc. Ph. VII, June, 1854, 119 (Pueblo Creek, New Mexico). *? Zonotrichia fasciata*, (GM.) GAMBEL, J. A. N. Sc. Ph. 2d Series, I, 1847, 49. *Melospiza fallax*, BAIRD, Birds N. Am. 1858, 481, pl. xxvii, f. 2. — KENNERLY, P. R. R. X, *b*. pl. xxvii, f. 2. — COOPER, Orn. Cal. I, 215.

SP. CHAR. Similar to var. *melodia*, but with the bill on the whole rather smaller, more slender, and darker. Legs quite dusky, not yellow. Entire plumage of a more grayish cast, including the whole superciliary stripe. The streaks on throat and jugulum in spring are almost black, as in *melodia;* in autumn more rufous; in all cases quite as sharply defined as in *melodia.* The bill is nearly black in spring.

HAB. Middle Province of United States, to the Sierra Nevada.

This race, intermediate between *melodia* and *heermanni* in habitat, is, however, hardly so in characters. The bill is more slender than in either, being much like that of *guttata,* and the tail is longer in proportion to the wing. In colors it is paler than either, the ground-cast above being nearly clear grayish: the streaks, both on the back and jugulum, are more sparse, as well as narrower; very frequently, in the winter plumage, those beneath lack the central black, being wholly rufous; such is the case with the type. In summer, however, they are frequently entirely black, the external rufous having entirely disappeared. As in *heermanni,* the rump is immaculate. The young bird differs as does the adult, though the resemblance to those of *melodia* and *heermanni* is more close than in the adult. The very narrow bill and long tail are the most characteristic features of form.

HABITS. In habits and song, Dr. Cooper can find no appreciable differences between this variety and its nearest allies. He states that its nest, which he found in a willow thicket, was composed of bark and fine twigs and grass, and lined with hair. Its eggs he describes as bluish-white, blotched and streaked with reddish-brown, and as measuring .74 by .55 of an inch.

Dr. Coues found this species a common and permanent resident in Arizona, and he pronounces its habits, manners, and voice precisely like those of *M. melodia.* This species, he states, occurs throughout New Mexico, Arizona, and a part of Southern California, and is particularly abundant in the valley of the Colorado.

Dr. Kennerly observed this species only along Pueblo Creek, in the month of January. It did not confine itself to the open valley, but was often seen among the thick bushes that margined the creek, far up into the Aztec Mountains, where the snow covered the ground. In its habits it resembled the *Poospiza belli,* being very restless and rapid in its motions, accompanying them with a short chirp, feeding upon the seeds of the weeds that remained uncovered by the snow. Its flight was also rapid and near the earth. The bird being very shy, Dr. Kennerly found it difficult to procure many specimens.

According to Mr. Ridgway, the Western Song Sparrow is one of the most abundant of the resident species inhabiting the fertile portions of the Great Basin. It principally occupies the willows along the streams, but is also found in *tulé* sloughs of the river valleys. From a long acquaintance with the Western Song Sparrows, Mr. Ridgway is fully convinced of the propriety of recognizing this as a distinct variety from the eastern *M. melodia.* In all respects, as to habits, especially in its familiarity, it replaces at the West the well-known Song Sparrow of the East. When first heard, the peculiar measure and delivery of its song at once attracts attention. The precision of style and method of utterance are quite distinct and constant peculiarities. The song, though as pleasing, is not so loud as that of the eastern Song Sparrow, while the measure is very different. He noted the syllables of its song, and found them quite uniform. He expresses the song thus: *Cha-cha-cha-cha-cha—wit'—tur'-r-r-r-r-r—tut.* The first six syllables as to accent are exactly alike, but with a considerable interval or pause between the first and second notes. The second to the fifth follow in rapid succession, each being uttered with deliberation and distinctness. Then comes a pause between the last "cha" and the "wit," which is pronounced in a fine metallic tone with a rising inflection, then another pause, and a liquid trill with a falling inflection, the whole terminating abruptly with a very peculiar "tut," in an entirely different key from the other notes.

The nests and eggs were found in the Wahsatch Mountains, June 23. The nests were generally among bushes, in willow thickets, along the streams, about a foot from the ground. One of these nests found in a clump of willows, about two feet from the ground and near a stream, is a compact, firmly built nest, in the shape of an inverted dome. It is two and a half inches in height, and about the same in diameter. Externally it is composed of a coarse framework of strips of willow bark firmly bound around. Within is a compactly woven inner nest, composed of straws, mingled and interwoven with horse-hairs. The cavity has a depth and diameter of two inches. The eggs, four in number, measure .85 by .63 of an inch. Their form is a rounded oval, distinctly pointed at one end. They have a greenish-white ground, marked and blotched with splashes of purplish and reddish brown.

Melospiza melodia, var. heermanni, BAIRD.

HEERMANN'S SONG SPARROW.

Melospiza heermanni, BAIRD, Birds N. Am, 1858, 478, pl. 70, f. 1. — COOPER, Orn. Cal. I, 212.

SP. CHAR. Somewhat like *melodia*, but darker. The streaks on the back and under parts blacker, broader, more distinct, and scarcely margined with reddish, except in winter plumage. The median stripe on vertex indistinct. General shade of coloration olivaceous-gray rather than rusty. Length, 6.40; wing, 2.56; tail, 3. Bill and legs in size and color most like *melodia*.

HAB. Southern California; eastern slope of Sierra Nevada (Carson City), and West Humboldt Mountains, Nev.; RIDGWAY.

Of the various races of *M. melodia*, this one approaches nearest the typical style of the Atlantic region; agreeing with it in thicker bill and shorter tail, as compared with the var. *fallax*, which occurs between them. It differs from the var. *melodia*, however, in a more grayish cast to the ground-color of the upper plumage, being olivaceous-gray, rather than reddish; the black dorsal streaks are very much broader than the rusty ones, instead of about equal to them in width, and the edges to the interscapular feathers are not appreciably paler than the prevailing shade, instead of being hoary whitish, in strong contrast. In spring the " bridle " on the side of the throat and the spots on the jugulum have the black of their central portion in excess of their external rufous suffusion ; but in autumn the rusty rather predominates ; at this season, too, the rusty tints above overspread the whole surface, but the black streaks are left sharply defined. At all seasons, the spots on the jugulum are broader and rather more numerous than in *melodia*. The young can scarcely be distinguished from those of *melodia*, but they have the dark streaks on the crown and upper tail-coverts considerably broader.

HABITS. The California Song Sparrow has been named in honor of the late Dr. Heermann, who first obtained specimens of this bird in the Tejon Valley, and mistook them for the *Zonotrichia guttata* of Gambel (*M. rufina*), from which they were appreciably different. Whether a distinct species or only a local race, this bird takes the place and is the almost precise counterpart, in most essential respects, of the Song Sparrow of the East. The exact limits of its distribution, both in the migratory season and in that of reproduction, have hardly yet been ascertained. It has been found in California as far north as San Francisco, and to the south and southeast to San Diego and the Mohave River.

The California Song Sparrow is the characteristic *Melospiza* in all that portion of the State south of San Francisco. It is found, Dr. Cooper states, in every locality where there are thickets of low bushes and tall weeds, especially in the vicinity of water, and wherever unmolested it comes about the gardens and houses with all the familiarity of the common *melodia*. The ground, under the shade of plants or bushes, is their usual place of resort. There they diligently search for their food throughout the day, and rarely fly more than a few yards from the place, and remain about their chosen locality from one year's end to another, being everywhere a resident species. In the spring they are said to perch occasionally on some low bush or tree, and sing a lively and pleasant melody for an hour at a time. Each song, Dr. Cooper remarks, is a complete little stanza of a dozen notes, and is frequently varied or changed entirely for another of similar style, but quite distinct. Although no two birds of this species sing just alike, there is never any difficulty in distinguishing their songs when once heard. There is, he thinks, a similarity of tone and style in the songs of all the species of true *Melospiza*, which has led other observers to consider them as of only one species, when taken in connection with their other similarities in colors and habits.

Dr. Cooper found a nest, presumed to belong to this bird, at Santa Cruz, in June. It was built in a dense blackberry-bush, about three feet from the ground, constructed with a thick periphery and base of dry grasses and thin strips of bark, and lined with finer grasses. The eggs were of a smoky white, densely speckled with a dull brown. Although this bird was abundant around Santa Cruz, he was only able, after much searching, to find two of their nests. One was in a willow, close against the tree, and three feet from the ground, containing, on the 11th of May, four eggs partially hatched. This was built of coarse dry stems and leaves, lined with finer grasses and horse-hair. It was five inches in external diameter, and four high. The cavity was two and a half inches deep and two in diameter. These eggs had a ground of greenish-white, and were blotched and spotted with a purplish-brown, chiefly at the larger end. They were .82 by .62 of an inch in measurement. The ground-color was paler and the spots were darker than in eggs of *Z. gambeli*, the whole coloring much darker than in those of *M. fallax*. This nest was apparently an old one used for a second brood.

Another nest found as late as July 10, and doubtless a second brood, was in a thicket, six feet from the ground, and also contained four eggs. Dr. Cooper states that he has seen the newly fledged young by the 7th of May.

Dr. Heermann, in his account of this bird, which he supposed to be the *guttata* of Dr. Gambel, states that he found it abundant throughout the whole country over which he passed, and more especially so in the bushes bordering the streams, ponds, and marshes. Its notes, sweet, and few in number, resembled those of the common Song Sparrow. Its nests, usually built in thick tufts of bushes, were composed externally of grasses and lined with hair, and contained each four eggs, with a pale bluish-ash ground, thickly covered with dashes of burnt umber. Eggs of this species, from near Monterey, collected by Dr. Canfield, vary in measurement from .85 by .65 of an inch to .88 by .70, — larger than any eggs of *Melospiza melodia* that I have seen. Their ground-color is a light green. The blotches are large, distinct, and more or less confluent, and of a blended reddish and purplish brown. They are in some diffused over the entire egg, in others disposed around the larger end.

Melospiza melodia, var. samuelis, BAIRD.

SAMUELS'S SONG SPARROW.

Ammodromus samuelis, BAIRD, Pr. Boston Soc. N. H. VI, June, 1858, 381. — IB. Birds N. Am. 1858, 455, pl. lxxi, f. 1. — COOPER, Orn. Cal. I, 191. *Melospiza gouldi*, BAIRD, Birds N. Am. 1858, 479.

SP. CHAR. Somewhat like *Melospiza melodia*, but considerably smaller and darker. Bill slender and acute, the depth not more than half the culmen. Above streaked on the head, back, and rump with dark brown, the borders of the feathers paler, but without any rufous. Beneath pure white; the breast, with sides of throat and body, spotted and streaked with black, apparently farther back than on other species. Wings above nearly uniform dark brownish-rufous. Under tail-coverts yellowish-brown, conspicuously blotched with blackish. An ashy superciliary stripe, becoming nearly white to the bill, and a whitish maxillary one below which is a broad blackish stripe along the sides of neck; the crown with faint grayish median line. Length, 5 inches; wing, 2.20; tail, 2.35. Bill dusky; legs rather pale. Bill, .35 from nostril by .24 deep; tarsus, .71; middle toe without claw, .58. (5,553 ♂, Petaluma, Cal.)

HAB Coast region of California, near San Francisco.

The above description is of a specimen in worn summer plumage, when the markings have not the sharp definition seen in the autumnal plumage. The autumnal plumage is as follows: Ground-color above grayish-olive, outer surface of wings, with the crown, more rufous; crown with narrow, and dorsal region with broad, stripes of black, the latter with scarcely a perceptible rufous suffusion; crown with a distinct median stripe of ashy. Streaks on jugulum, etc., broader than in the type, and with a slight rufous suffusion. Wing, 2.20; tail, 2.35; bill from nostril .31, its depth .22; tarsus .74; middle toe without claw, .60.

The type of *Melospiza gouldi* resembles the last, and differs only in having a more distinct rufous suffusion to the black markings; the measurements are as follows : Wing, 2.20; tail, 2.35; bill, .33 by .23; tarsus, .73; middle toe without claw, .59.

This is probably a dwarfed race of the common species, the very small size being its chief distinctive character. The colors are most nearly like those of *heermanni*, but are considerably darker, caused by an expansion of the black and contraction of the rufous markings. The pattern of coloration is precisely the same as in the other races. The present bird appears to be peculiar to the coast region of California, the only specimens in the collection being from the neighborhood of San Francisco.

HABITS. Of the history, distribution, and general habits of this species, nothing is known. It was found at Petaluma, Cal., by Emanuel Samuels, and described in the Proceedings of the Boston Society of Natural History in 1858. The following description of the nest and eggs of this bird, in the Smithsonian collection, has been kindly furnished me by Mr. Ridgway.

Nests elaborate and symmetrical, cup-shaped, composed of thin grass-stems, but externally chiefly of grass-blades and strips of thin inner bark. Diameter about 3.50 inches; internal diameter 2.00, and internal depth 1.50; external, 2.00. Egg measures .78 by .62 ; regularly ovate in shape ; ground-color, greenish-white; this is thickly sprinkled with purplish and livid ashy-brown, the specks larger, and somewhat coalescent, around the larger circumference. (3553, San Francisco, Cal., J. Hepburn.)

Melospiza melodia, var. guttata, BAIRD.

OREGON SONG SPARROW.

Fringilla cinerea, (GM.) AUD. Orn. Biog. V, 1839, 22, pl. cccxc. — IB. Syn. 1839, 119. — IB. Birds Am. III, 1841, 145, pl. clxxxvii. *Passerella cinerea*, BP. List, 1839. — IB. Conspectus, 1850, 477. *Fringilla (Passerella) guttata*, NUTTALL, Man. I, (2d ed.,) 1840, 581. *Zonotrichia guttata*, GAMBEL, J. A. N. Sc. I, Dec. 1847, 50. *Melospiza rufina*, BAIRD, Birds N. Am. 1858, 480. — COOPER & SUCKLEY, 204. — DALL & BANNISTER, Tr. Ch. Ac. I, 1859, 285. — COOPER, Orn. Cal. I, 214.

SP. CHAR. Bill slender. Similar in general appearance to *M. melodia*, but darker and much more rufous, and without any blackish-brown streaks, or grayish edges of the feathers ; generally the colors more blended. General appearance above light rufous-brown, the interscapular region streaked very obsoletely with dark brownish-rufous, the feathers of the crown similar, with still darker obsolete central streaks. A superciliary and very indistinct median crown-stripe ashy. Under parts dull white, the breast and sides of throat and body broadly streaked with dark brownish-rufous; darker in the centre. A light maxillary stripe. Sides of the body and anal region tinged strongly with the colors of the rump. Under coverts brown. Length, 6.75; wing, 2.70; tail, 3.00. Legs rather darker than in *melodia*. Bill from nostril, .37; from forehead, .60.

HAB. Pacific coast of the United States to British Columbia.

A young bird from Napa Valley, Cal. (12,912, Colonel A. J. Grayson), probably referrible to this race, differs from the corresponding stage of *heermanni, fallax,* and *melodia* in the following respects : the ground-color above is much darker, being dull dingy-brown, and the dusky streaks broader ; the white beneath has a strong yellowish tinge, and the pectoral streaks are very broad.

HABITS. Dr. Cooper characterizes this species as the most northern and mountain-frequenting representative of the Song Sparrows, being a resident of the higher Sierra Nevada and on the borders of the evergreen forests towards the Columbia, and thence northward, where it is the only species of this genus, and where it is common down to the level of the sea. Specimens have been obtained at Marysville in the spring, by Mr. Gruber.

Dr. Cooper says that he has also met with this bird, and found it possessing habits and songs entirely similar to those of the eastern *M. melodia,* and resembling also those of the more southern *M. heermanni.* He was never able to meet with one of their nests, as, like other forest birds, they are more artful in concealing their treasures than birds that have become accustomed to the society and protection of man, and who, no longer wild, select gardens as the safest places in which to build. In the mild winters usual about the mouth of the Columbia, these birds do not evince any disposition to emigrate, but come familiarly around the houses for their food, when the snow has buried their usual supply.

Dr. Suckley remarks that this Finch is quite a common bird in the vicinity of Puget Sound, and that it is there resident throughout the year. He has found them in very different situations ; some in thickets at the edges of prairies, others in stranded drift-logs on open salt marshes, as well as in swamps, and in the dense forests of the Douglass firs, peculiar to the northwest coast. Its voice, he adds, is, during the breeding-season, singularly sweet and melodious, surpassing that of the Meadow Lark in melody and tone, but unequal to it in force.

This species is stated to be a constant resident in the district wherein it is found, never ranging far from the thicket which contains its nest, or the house in the neighborhood of which it finds food and protection. Almost every winter morning, as well as during the summer, as Dr. Cooper states, its cheerful song may be heard from the garden or the fence, as if to repay those whose presence has protected it from its rapacious enemies. When unmolested, it becomes very familiar, and the old birds bring their young to the door to feed, as soon as they can leave their nest. Their song is said to so closely resemble that of the eastern bird, in melody and variety, that it is impossible either to tell which is the superior or to point out the differences. In wild districts it is always to be found near the sides of brooks, in thickets, from which it jealously drives off other birds, whether of its own or other species, as if it considered itself the proprietor. Its nest is built on the ground or in a low bush. Dr. Cooper has seen newly fledged young as early as May 6, at Olympia, though the rainy season was then hardly over.

Mr. Nuttall pronounces its song as sweeter and more varied in tone than that of the Song Sparrow. He heard their cheerful notes throughout the summer, and every fine day in winter until the month of November, particularly in the morning, their song was still continued. Their nests and eggs were not distinguishable from those of *F. melodia.* The nests were composed of dry grasses, lined with finer materials of the same, and occasionally with deer's hair. He states that they keep much in low ground and alluvial situations, amidst rank weeds, willows, and brambles, where they are frequently to be seen hopping about and searching after insects, in the manner of the Swamp Sparrow, which they so much resemble in their plumage. They are usually very solicitous for the safety of their young or for their nests and eggs, keeping up an incessant chirp. They raise several broods in a season, and are, like the Song Sparrow, also engaged nearly the whole of the summer in the cares of rearing their young.

Mr. Townsend met with this species through several hundred miles of the Platte country in great numbers, as well as on the banks of the Columbia, generally frequenting the low bushes of wormwood (*Artemisia*). It appeared also to be a very pugnacious species. Two of the males were often observed fighting in the air, the beaten party going off crestfallen, and the conqueror repairing to the nearest bush to celebrate his triumph by his lively and triumphant strains. He again met with these birds, though not in abundance, in June, 1825, at the mouth of the Lewis River, on the waters of the Columbia.

This Sparrow was also found very numerous at Sitka, by Mr. Bischoff, but no mention is made of its habits.

Melospiza melodia, var. rufina, BAIRD.

RUSTY SONG SPARROW.

Emberiza rufina, " BRANDT, Desc. Av. Rossic. 1836, tab. ii, 5 (Sitka)," BONAPARTE. *Passerella rufina,* BONAP. Consp. 1850, 477. (This may refer to *Passerella townsendi,* but is more probably the present bird.) *Melospiza cinerea,* FINSCH, Abh. Nat. III, 1872, 41 (Sitka). (Not *Fringilla c.* GMEL.) *M. guttata,* FINSCH, Abh. Nat. III, 1872, 41 (Sitka). (Not *Fringilla g.* NUTT.)

SP. CHAR. Resembling *M. guttata* in the undefined markings, slender bill, etc., but olivaceous-brownish instead of rufous above, the darker markings sepia-brown instead of castaneous. The white beneath much tinged with ashy; jugulum-spots blended, and of a sepia-brown tint. Wing, 3.00; tail, 3.00; bill .41 from nostril, and .25 deep at base.

HAB. Northwest coast. from British Columbia northward. (Sitka.)

The above characters are those of a large series of specimens from Sitka, and a few points along the coast to the southward and northward, and represent the average features of a race which is intermediate between *guttata* and *insignis*, in appearance as well as in habitat. Tracing this variety toward the Columbia River, it gradually passes into the former, and northward into the latter.

We have no distinctive information relative to the habits of this race.

Melospiza melodia, var. insignis, BAIRD.

KODIAK SONG SPARROW.

? *Fringilla cinerea*, GMELIN, I, 1788, 922 (based on Cinereous Finch, LATH. II, 274). — PENN. Arc. Zoöl. II, 68 (Unalaschka). *Emberiza cinerea*, BONAP. Consp. 1850, 478. *Melospiza insignis*, BAIRD, Trans. Chicago Acad. I, ii, 1869, p. 319, pl. xxix, fig. 2. — DALL & BANNISTER, do. p. 285. — FINSCH, Abh. Nat. III, 1872, 44 (Kodiak).

SP. CHAR. *Summer plumage* (52,477 ♂, Kodiak, May 24, 1868). Above brownish-plumbeous, outer surface of wings somewhat more brown, the greater coverts slightly rufescent. Interscapulars with medial broad but obsolete streaks of sepia-brown; crown and upper tail-coverts with more sharply defined and narrower dusky shaft-streaks. Crown without medial light line. Beneath grayish-white, much obscured by brownish-plumbeous laterally. A whitish supraloral space, but no appreciable superciliary stripe; a whitish maxillary stripe; beneath it an irregular one of dusky sepia; irregular streaks of dark grizzly-sepia on breast and along sides, blended into a broad crescent across the jugulum. Wing, 3.30; tail, 3.50; bill, .48 from nostril, .28 deep at base, and .21 in the middle, the middle of the culmen being much depressed, its extremity rather abruptly decurved.

Autumnal plumage (60,162, Kodiak, received from Dr. J. F. Brandt). Differs very remarkably in appearance from the preceding. The pattern of coloration is everywhere plainly plotted, there being a distinct vertical and sharply defined superciliary stripe. Ground-color above ashy, somewhat overlaid by rusty, except on the sides of the neck. Whole crown, outer surface of wings, and dorsal streaks, rusty rufous; black streaks on crown and upper tail-coverts obsolete. Beneath pure white medially, the markings rusty rufous. Wing, 3.30; tail, 3.60; bill, .47 and .30.

HAB. Kodiak and Unalaschka.

This race represents the extreme extent of variation in the species, and it would be difficult for a species to proceed farther from the normal standard; indeed, the present bird is so different even in form, especially of bill, from *melodia*, that, were it not for the perfect series connecting them, few naturalists would hesitate to place them in different genera.

HABITS. No information has so far been published in reference to the nesting of this Sparrow, or of any peculiar habits.

Melospiza lincolni, Baird.

LINCOLN'S FINCH.

Fringilla lincolni, Aud. Orn. Biog. II, 1834, 539, pl. cxciii. — Nutt. Man. I, (2d ed.,) 1840, 569. *Linaria lincolni*, Rich. List. 1837. *Passerculus lincolni*, Bonap. List, 1838. *Peucæa lincolni*, Aud. Synopsis, 1839, 113. — Ib. Birds Am. III, 1841, 116, pl. clxxvii. — Bonap. Consp. 1850, 481. — Ib. Comptes Rendus, XXVII, 1854, 920. *Melospiza lincolni*, Baird, Birds N. Am. 1858, 482. — Dall & Bannister, Tr. Ch. Ac. I, 1869, 285 (Alaska). — Cooper, Orn. Cal. I, 216. *Passerculus zonarius*, (Bp.) Sclater, Pr. Zoöl. Soc. 1856, 305.

Sp. Char. General aspect above that of *M. melodia*, but paler and less reddish. Crown dull chestnut, with a median and lateral or superciliary ash-colored stripe; each feather above streaked centrally with black. Back with narrow streaks of black. Beneath white, with a maxillary stripe curving round behind the ear-coverts; a well-defined band across the breast, extending down the sides, and the under tail-coverts, of brownish-yellow. The maxillary stripe margined above and below with lines of black spots and a dusky line behind eye. The throat, upper part of breast, and sides of the body, with streaks of black, smallest in the middle of the former. The pectoral bands are sometimes paler. Bill above dusky; base of lower jaw and legs yellowish. Length, 5.60; wing, 2.60.

Hab. United States from Atlantic to Pacific, north to the Yukon River and the Mackenzie, and south through Mexico to Panama. Oaxaca (Scl. 1858, 303); Xalapa (Scl. 1859, 365); Guatemala (Scl. Ibis, I, 18); Vera Cruz, winter (Sum. M. B. S. I, 552).

There is little or no difference in specimens of this bird from the whole of its range, except that one from near Aspinwall is considerably smaller than usual, the streaks on the back narrower, and the color above more reddish. A young bird from Fort Simpson, on the Mackenzie, is much like the adult.

Habits. Lincoln's Finch was first met with by Mr. Audubon in Labrador, and named in honor of one of his companions, Mr. Thomas Lincoln, now residing at Dennysville, Maine, by whom the first specimen was procured. His attention was attracted to it by the sweet notes of its song, which, he states, surpass in vigor those of any of our American Sparrows with which he was acquainted. He describes this song as a compound of the notes of a Canary and a Woodlark of Europe. The bird was unusually wild, and was procured with great difficulty. Other specimens, afterwards obtained, did not exhibit the same degree of wildness, and they became more common as the party proceeded farther north. He did not meet with its nest.

He describes the habits of this species as resembling, in some respects, those of the Song Sparrow. It mounts, like that bird, on the topmost twig of some tall shrub to chant for whole hours at a time, or dives into the thickets and hops from branch to branch until it reaches the ground in search of those insects or berries on which it feeds. It moves swiftly away when it discovers an enemy, and, if forced to take to flight, flies low and rapidly to a considerable distance, jerking its tail as it proceeds, and throwing itself into the thickest bush it meets. Mr. Audubon found it mostly near streams, and always in the small valleys guarded from the prevalent cold winds of that country.

He also describes this species as eminently petulant and pugnacious. Two males would often pursue each other until the weaker was forced to abandon the valley, and seek refuge elsewhere. He seldom saw more than two or three pairs in a tract of several miles in extent. By the 4th of July the young had left their nests and were following their parents. As from that time the old birds ceased to sing, he inferred that they raised but one brood in a season. Before he left Labrador these birds had all disappeared.

Although first discovered on the coast of Labrador, subsequent explorations have shown this bird to be far more common at the West than it is at the East, where indeed it is exceedingly rare. Not a specimen, that I am aware of, has ever been found in Maine, although it probably does occasionally occur there; and only a very few isolated individuals had been taken in Massachusetts before the spring of 1872, when they were noticed by Mr. Brewster and Mr. Henshaw in considerable numbers. These birds, seven or eight in number, were shot, with two exceptions, in May, between the 14th and the 25th. Three were taken in Springfield by Mr. Allen, one in Newburyport by Mr. Hoxie, two in Hudson by Mr. Jillson, and two in Cambridge by Mr. Brewster. The latter were obtained, one in September and the other in October. In May, 1872, Mr. Brewster obtained six others. Mr. Allen had met with this Finch in Wayne County, N. Y., in May, where it was not uncommon, and in Northern Illinois, where it was quite numerous. A few have been taken near New York City, and in the neighborhood of Philadelphia, where they are regarded as very rare. Professor Baird, however, frequently met with them at Carlisle, Penn.

Farther west, from the Mississippi Valley to the Pacific, they are much more common. Mr. Ridgway states that they occasionally winter in Southern Illinois, where they frequent retired thickets near open fields. They have been found breeding near Racine, Wis., by Dr. Hoy, and have been met with also in Nebraska in considerable numbers; and, during the breeding-season, Mr. Audubon met with them on the Upper Missouri.

From March to May Mr. Dresser found these birds very abundant in the fields near the San Antonio River, and in some swampy grounds. They seemed to prefer that sort of locality, and the banks of the river, keeping among the flags and rushes. Their stomachs were found to contain small seeds. Mr. Lincecum also met with a few in Washington County of the same State.

It was not met with in Arizona by Dr. Coues, but Dr. Kennerly found it in the month of February from the Big Sandy to the Great Colorado River. It confined itself to the thick bushes along the streams, and when seen was generally busily hopping from twig to twig in search of food. When started up, its flight was very rapid and near the earth.

Dr. Heermann obtained this species, not unfrequently, both in Northern California and in the Tejon Valley. On all occasions he found it in company with flocks of Sparrows, composed of several species.

Lieutenant Couch took this species at Tamaulipas, Mexico, and at Browns-ville, Southwestern Texas, in March. It has also been seen in May, at the Forks of the Saskatchewan, by Captain Blakiston.

Lincoln's Finch was met with by Mr. Ridgway in abundance only during its spring and fall migrations. Towards the last of April it was quite common in wet brushy places in the vicinity of Carson City. It was next observed in October among the willows bordering Deep Creek, in Northern Utah. In the weedy pastures in Parley's Park it was a common species, frequenting the resorts of the *Z. leucophrys*. A nest, with young, was dis-covered near the camp. It was embedded in the ground, beneath a bush. Its song he did not hear, only a single *chuck*, almost as loud as that of the *Passerella schistacea*.

Dr. Cooper reports this species as near San Diego about March 25. Large flocks were then passing northward. During the day they kept among the grass, and were rather shy and silent. They seemed to have a good deal of the habits of the *Passerculus*, and to differ much in their gregariousness, their migratory habits, and their general form, from the other *Melospizæ*. Dr. Cooper did not meet with any of these birds in the Colorado Valley, nor has he seen or heard of any having been found in California during the summer. The *M. lincolni* has been found breeding up to high Arctic latitudes. It was met with by Mr. Kennicott at Fort Simpson and at Fort Resolution. At the latter place its nests were found between the 2d and the 14th of June. They were also obtained in May, June, and July, at Fort Simpson, by Mr. B. R. Ross, and at Yukon River, Fort Rae, Nulato, and other localities in the extreme northern regions, by Messrs. Reid, Lockhart, Clarke, Kirkby, and Dall. On Mt. Lincoln, Colorado, above eight thousand feet, Mr. Allen found this Sparrow very numerous.

This Finch was found by Salvin about the reeds on the margin of Lake Dueñas, Guatemala, in February, but was not common. It is common, in the winter months, near Oaxaca, Mexico, where it was taken by Mr. Boucard.

Mr. Kennicott saw its nest June 14. This was on the ground, built in a bunch of grass in rather an open and dry place, and containing five eggs. The female permitted him to approach very close to her, until he finally caught her on the nest with his beating-net. Another nest was placed in a bunch of grass growing in the water of a small grassy pond. The nest contained four eggs and one young bird.

The nest and eggs of this species had been previously discovered by Dr. Hoy, near Racine. This is, I believe, the first instance in which it was iden-tified by a naturalist, as also the most southern point at which it has ever been found. These eggs measure .74 by .60 of an inch. They have a pale greenish-white ground, and are thickly marked with dots and small blotches of a ferruginous-brown, often so numerous and confluent as to disguise and partially conceal the ground.

Melospiza palustris, BAIRD.

SWAMP SPARROW.

Fringilla palustris, WILSON, Am. Orn. III, 1811, 49, pl. xxii, f. 1. — AUD. Orn. Biog. I, 1831, 331 ; V, 508, pl. lxiv. *Fringilla (Spiza) palustris*, BONAP. Obs. Wilson, 1825, No. 105. *Passerculus palustris*, BONAP. List, 1838. — IB. Conspectus, 1850, 481. *Ammodromus palustris*, AUD. Syn. 1839. — IB. Birds Am. III, 1841, 110, pl. clxxv. *Melospiza palustris*, BAIRD, Birds N. Am. 1858, 483. — SAMUELS, 323. *? Fringilla georgiana*, LATH. Index Orn. I, 1790, 460 (perhaps *Peucæa æstivalis*). — LICHT. Verz. 1823, No. 251. *Fringilla (Ammodromus) georgiana*, NUTT. Man. I, (2d ed.,) 1840, 588.

SP. CHAR. Middle of the crown uniform chestnut; forehead black; superciliary streak, sides of head and back, and sides of neck, ash. A brown stripe behind the eye. Back with broad streaks of black, which are edged with rusty yellow. Beneath whitish, tinged with ashy anteriorly, especially across the breast, and washed with yellowish-brown on the sides. A few obsolete streaks across the breast, which become distinct on its sides. Wings and tail strongly tinged with rufous ; the tertials black, the rufous edgings changing abruptly to white towards the end. Length, 5.75 ; wing, 2.40.

Female with the crown scarcely reddish streaked with black, and divided by a light line. Young conspicuously streaked beneath the head, above nearly uniform blackish.

HAB. Eastern North America from the Atlantic to the Missouri ; north to Fort Simpson.

In autumn the male of this species has the feathers of the crown each with a black streak ; and the centre of the crown with an indistinct light stripe, materially changing its appearance.

The forehead is usually more or less streaked with black.

In the uncertainty whether the *Fringilla georgiana* of Latham be not rather the *Peucæa æstivalis* than the Swamp Sparrow, I think it best to retain Wilson's name. It certainly applies as well to the latter, which has the black sub-maxillary streak, and the chin and throat more mouse-colored than in *palustris*.

HABITS. Owing to the residence of this species in localities not favoring frequent visits or careful explorations, and still more to its shy and retiring habits, our writers have not been generally well informed as to the history and general manners of this peculiar and interesting Sparrow. Its irregular distribution, its abundance only in certain and unusually restricted localities, its entire absence from all the surrounding neighborhood, and its secretiveness wherever found, have all combined to throw doubt and obscurity over its movements. Unless purposely looked for and perseveringly hunted up, the Swamp Sparrow might exist in large numbers in one's immediate neighborhood and yet entirely escape notice. Even now its whole story is but imperfectly known, and more careful investigation into its distribution and general habits will doubtless clear up several obscure points in regard to its movements.

From what is now known, we gather that it occurs throughout the eastern portions of North America, from the Southern States, in which it passes the wintry months, to high northern latitudes, where some find their way in the breeding-season, extending as far to the west at least as the Missouri River region.

Three specimens were obtained at Fort Simpson, by Mr. Kennicott, in September, which indicates their probable summer presence in latitude 55°, and their near approach to the Pacific coast at the extreme northwestern portion of their distribution. Audubon also met with them in Newfoundland and in Labrador. They are known to breed as far to the south as Pennsylvania. They have been taken in the eastern portion of Nebraska, and breed in considerable numbers in Southern Wisconsin. Further investigations in regard to its distribution will probably show it to be a much more widely distributed as well as a more abundant bird than has been generally supposed.

Mr. Ridgway writes me that this bird winters in Southern Illinois, and remains there very late in the spring, but he thinks that none remain to breed.

Wilson states that it arrives in Pennsylvania early in April, where it frequents low grounds and river-courses, rears two and sometimes three broods in a season, and returns to the South as the cold weather commences. During the winter, he met with them in large numbers in the immense cypress swamps and extensive grassy flats of the Southern States, along the numerous rivers and rice plantations. These places abounded with their favorite seeds and other means of sustenance, and appeared to be their general places of resort at this season. From the river Trent, in North Carolina, to the Savannah River, and even farther south, Wilson found this species very numerous. They were not found in flocks, but skulked among the reeds and grass, were shy and timorous, and seemed more attached to the water than any others of this family. In April large numbers pass through Pennsylvania northward. Only a few remain behind, and these frequent the swamps and the reedy borders of creeks and rivers. He found their nests built in the ground, in tussocks of rank grass, surrounded by water, with four eggs of a dirty-white ground, spotted with rufous. He has found them feeding their young as late as the 15th of August. Their food seemed to be principally grass-seeds, wild oats, and insects. He supposed them to have no song, and that their only note was a single *cheep* uttered in a somewhat hoarse tone. They flirt their tails as they fly, seldom or never take to trees, but run and skulk from one low bush to another.

Except in regard to their song, Wilson's account of their habits, so far as it goes, is quite accurate, although this bird really does have quite a respectable song, and one that improves as the season advances. At first it is only a succession or repetition of a few monotonous trilling notes, which might easily be mistaken for the song of the Field Sparrow, or even confounded with the feebler chant of the *socialis*, although not so varied as the former, and is much more sprightly and pleasing than the other. Still later its music improves, and more effort is made. Like the Song Sparrow, it mounts some low twig, expands its tail-feathers, and gives forth a very sprightly trill that echoes through the swampy thicket with an effect which, once noticed and identified with the performer, is not likely to be ever mistaken. Nuttall calls this song loud, sweet, and plaintive. It is to my ear more sprightly than pathetic, and has a peculiarly ventriloquistic effect, as if the performer were at a much greater distance than he really is.

Their food, when they first arrive, and that which they feed to their young, consists very largely of insects, principally coleopterous ones, with such few seeds as they can glean. After the breeding-season, when their young can take care of themselves, they eat almost exclusively the ripened seeds of the coarse water grasses and sedges. They are very devoted to their young, and often display great solicitude for their safety, even when able to take care of themselves, and often expose themselves to dangers they carefully avoid at other times, and are thus more easily procured. At all other times they are difficult to shoot, running, as they do, through the grass and tangled thickets, and rarely rising on the wing. They dive from thicket to thicket with great rapidity, and even when wounded have a wonderful power of running and hiding themselves.

Mr. Audubon met with them, during autumn and winter, among the flat sand-bars of the Mississippi, which are overgrown with rank grasses. Though not in flocks, their numbers were immense. They fed on grass-seeds and insects, often wading for the latter in shallow water in the manner of the *Tringidæ*, and when wounded and forced into the water swimming off to the nearest shelter. He also met with these birds abundantly dispersed in the swamps of Cuyaga Lake, as well as among those along the Illinois River in the summer, and in the winter up the Arkansas River.

Mr. Townsend observed these birds on the head-waters of the Upper Missouri, but did not meet with them beyond.

In Maine, Mr. Boardman gives it as a regular summer visitant at Calais, arriving there as early as March, becoming common in May, and breeding in that locality. Professor Verrill found it in Western Maine, a summer visitant and breeding, but did not regard it as common. From my own experience, in the neighborhood of Boston, I should have said the same as to its infrequency in Eastern Massachusetts, yet in certain localities it is a very abundant summer resident. Mr. William Brewster has found it breeding in large numbers in the marshes of Fresh Pond, where it arrives sometimes as early as the latter part of March, and where it remains until November. In the western part of the State it is more common as a migratory bird, and has not been found, in any numbers, stopping to breed. Mr. Allen never met with any later than May 25. They were observed to be in company with the Water Thrush, and to be in every way as aquatic in their habits. In the autumn he again met with it from the last of September through October, always in bushy marshes or wet places. Mr. McIlwraith states that in the vicinity of Hamilton, Ontario, it is a common summer resident, breeding there in marshy situations. At Lake Koskonong, in Wisconsin, Mr. Kumlien has also met with these birds abundantly in suitable localities, and found their nests and eggs quite plentiful.

Mr. Ridgway has recently found this Sparrow to be a very abundant winter resident in Southern Illinois, where it inhabits swampy thickets, and where it remains until May, but is not known to breed there.

They always nest on the ground, usually in a depression sheltered by a tuft of grass. The nest is woven of fine grass-stems, but is smaller than the nest of *M. melodia.*

The eggs of this species, usually five in number, have an average measurement of .78 by .60 of an inch. Their ground-color is usually a light green, occasionally of a light clay, marked and blotched with reddish and purplish brown spots, varying in size and number, occasionally forming a confluent ring around the larger end.

Genus **PEUCÆA**, Audubon.

Peucæa, Aud. Synopsis, 1839. (Type, *Fringilla æstivalis.*) Sclater & Salvin, 1868, 322 (Synopsis.)

Gen. Char. Bill moderate. Upper outline and commissure decidedly curved. Legs and feet with the claws small; the tarsus about equal to the middle toe; the lateral toes equal, their claws falling considerably short of the middle one; the hind toe reaching about to the middle of the latter. The outstretched feet reach rather beyond the middle of the tail. The wing is very short, reaching only to the base of the tail; the longest tertials do not exceed the secondaries, while both are not much short of the primaries; the outer three or four quills are graduated. The tail is considerably longer than the wings; it is much

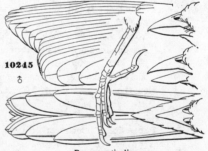

10245

♂

Peucæa æstivalis.

graduated laterally; the feathers, though long, are peculiarly narrow, linear, and elliptically rounded at the ends.

Color beneath plain whitish or brownish, with a more or less distinct dusky line each side of the chin. Above with broad obsolete brown streaks or blotches. Crown uniform, or the feathers edged with lighter.

Species and Varieties.

Common Characters. A light superciliary stripe, with a brownish one below it from the eye along upper edge of ear-coverts (not one along lower edge of ear-coverts, as in *Melospiza*). A narrow blackish "bridle" along side of throat (sometimes indistinct). Crown without a distinct median stripe, and lower parts without markings. Ground-color above ashy, sometimes of a brownish cast; dorsal region and nape with brown blotches, with or without dark centres. Crown blackish-brown streaked with ashy or plain rufous. Beneath plain brownish-white, lightest on the abdomen, darker across jugulum and along sides.

A. Crown plain rufous; interscapulars without distinct black centres, and tertials without whitish border. Blackish "bridle" conspicuous. Bend of wing edged with white.

1. **P. ruficeps.**

Above olivaceous-ash, interscapulars with broad streaks of dull rufous, the shafts scarcely blackish. Crown bright rufous. Wing, 2.40; tail, 2.70; bill, .29 from forehead, .20 deep; tarsus, .70; middle toe without claw, .55. *Hab.* California (and Mexico in winter?) . . . . var. *ruficeps.*

Darker, above brownish-plumbeous, dorsal streaks scarcely rufous, and with distinctly black shaft-streaks; crown darker rufous. Wing, 2.40; tail, 2.60; bill, .34 and .25; tarsus, .77; middle toe, .57. *Hab.* Mexico (Orizaba; Oaxaca), in summer . var. *boucardi.*[1]

B. Crown streaked; interscapulars with distinct black centres; tertials sharply bordered terminally with paler. "Bridle" obsolete; bend of wing edged with yellowish.

2. **P. æstivalis.** Above uniformly marked with broad streaks or longitudinal blotches of deep rufous; black streaks confined to interscapulars and crown. Tail-feathers without darker shaft-stripe, and without indications of darker bars; the outer feathers without distinct white. Black marks on upper tail-coverts inconspicuous, longitudinal.

The bluish-ash, and chestnut-rufous streaks above sharply contrasted; black dorsal streaks broad. Wing, 2.45; tail, 2.65; bill, .30 and .30; tarsus, .73; middle toe, .60. *Hab.* Southern States from Florida and Georgia to Southern Illinois . . var. *æstivalis.*

The dull ash and light rufous streaks above not sharply defined; black dorsal streaks narrow. Wing, 2.65; tail, 3.00; bill, .32 and .25; tarsus, .80; middle toe, .63. *Hab.* Southern border of the Arizona region of Middle Province of United States . . var. *arizonæ.*

Markings badly defined as in the last, but the rufous streaks darker (in summer plumage almost entirely black), with more black on the crown. Wing, 2.55; tail, 2.65; bill, .32 and .25; tarsus, .80; middle toe, .60. *Hab.* Mexico (Orizaba; Mirador, Colima).

var. *botterii.*[2]

3. **P. cassini.** Above marked everywhere with broad short streaks of pale (not reddish) brown streaks, all black medially. Tail-feathers with

[1] *Zonotrichia boucardi,* SCLATER, P. Z. S. 1867, 1, pl. i, La Puebla, Mex. (scarcely definable as distinct from *ruficeps*).

[2] *Peucæa botterii,* SCLATER, Cat. Am. B. 1862, 116 (*Zonotrichia b.* P. Z. S. 1857, 214), Orizaba. *Coturniculus mexicana,* LAWR. Ann. N. Y. Lyc. VIII, 1867, 474 (Colima). This form can scarcely be defined separately from *æstivalis.* The type of *C. mexicanus,* LAWR., is undistinguishable from Orizaba specimens. A specimen in the worn summer plumage (44,752♀, Mirador, July) differs in having the streaks above almost wholly black, with scarcely any rufous edge; the crown is almost uniformly blackish. The feathers are very much worn, however, and the specimen is without doubt referrible to *botteri.*

The *Peucæa notosticta* of SCLATER (P. Z. S. 1868, 322) we have not seen; it appears to differ in some important respects from the forms diagnosed above, and may, possibly, be a good species. Its place in our system appears to be with section "A," but it differs from *ruficeps* and *boucardi* in the median stripe on the crown, and the black streaks in the rufous of the lateral portion, the blacker streaks of the dorsal region, and some other less important points of coloration. The size appears to be larger than in any of the forms given in our synopsis (wing, 2.70; tail, 3.00). *Hab.* States of Puebla and Mexico, Mex.

distinct blackish shaft-stripe, throwing off narrow, obsolete bars toward the edge of the feathers. Outer tail-feathers distinctly tipped (broadly) and edged with dull white. Black marks on upper tail-coverts very large, transverse. Beneath nearly uniform dull white, scarcely darker along sides and across breast; flanks with broad streaks of blackish-brown. Wing, 2.55; tail, 2.80; bill, .28 and .23; tarsus, .68; middle toe, .55. *Hab.* Rio Grande, region (San Antonio and Laredo), north to Kansas (ALLEN).

Peucæa æstivalis, CABANIS.

BACHMAN'S SPARROW.

Fringilla æstivalis, LICHT. Verz. Doubl. 1823, 25, No. 254. — BONAP. Conspectus, 1850, 481. *Peucæa æstivalis*, CABANIS, Mus. Hein. 1850, 132. — BAIRD, Birds N. Am. 1858, 484. *Fringilla bachmani*, AUD. Orn. Biog. II, 1834, 366, pl. clxv. *Ammodromus bachmani*, BON. List, 1838. *Peucæa bachmani*, AUD. Syn. 1839. — IB. Birds Am. III, 1841, 113, pl. clxxvi. — BON. Consp. 1850, 481 (type). *Fringilla æstiva*, NUTT. I, (2d ed.,) 1840, 568. "*Summer finch*, LATHAM, Synopsis, (2d ed.,) VI, 136." NUTTALL.

SP. CHAR. All the feathers of the upper parts rather dark brownish-red or chestnut. margined with bluish-ash, which almost forms a median stripe on the crown. Inter-scapular region and upper tail-coverts with the feathers becoming black in the centre. An indistinct ashy superciliary stripe. Under parts pale yellow-brownish, tinged with ashy on the sides, and with darker brownish across the upper part of the breast. A faint maxillary dusky line. Indistinct streaks of chestnut along the sides. Edge of wing yellow; lesser coverts tinged with greenish. Innermost secondaries abruptly margined with narrow whitish. Legs yellow. Bill above dusky, yellowish beneath. Outer tail-

Peucæa æstivalis.

feathers obsoletely marked with a long blotch of paler at end. Female considerably smaller. Young with rounded dusky specks on the jugulum, which is more ochraceous. Length, 6.25; wing, 2.30; tail, 2.78.

HAB. Georgia; Florida; South Illinois, breeding (RIDGWAY). (Perhaps whole of Southern States from Florida to South Illinois.)

Specimens from Southern Illinois (Wabash Co., July, 1871; coll. of R. Ridgway) are similar to Florida examples.

HABITS. Bachman's Finch has only been known, until very recently, as a species of a very restricted range, and confined within the limits of the States of South Carolina, Georgia, and Florida. Our principal, and for some time our only, knowledge of its habits was derived from the account furnished by Rev. Dr. Bachman to Mr. Audubon. That observing naturalist first met with it in the month of April, 1832, near Parker's Ferry, on the Edisto River, in South Carolina. Dr. Henry Bryant afterwards met with this species at Indian River, in Florida, where he obtained specimens of its nests and eggs. Dr. Alexander Gerhardt also found these Sparrows common at Varnell's Station, in the northern part of Georgia. Professor Joseph Leconte has taken it near Savannah, and Mr. W. L. Jones has also obtained several specimens in Liberty County, in the same State.

After meeting with this species on the Edisto, Dr. Bachman ascertained, upon searching for them in the vicinity of Charlestown, that they breed in small numbers on the pine barrens, about six miles north of that city. He was of the opinion that it is by no means so rare in that State as has been supposed, but that it is more often heard than seen. When he first heard it, the notes so closely resembled those of the Towhee Bunting that for a while he mistook them for those of that bird. Their greater softness and some slight variations at last induced him to suspect that the bird was something different, and led him to go in pursuit. After that it was quite a common thing for him to hear as many as five or six in the course of a morning's ride, but he found it almost impossible to get even a sight of the bird. This is owing, not so much to its being so wild, as to the habit it has of darting from the tall pine-trees, on which it usually sits to warble out its melodious notes, and concealing itself in the tall broom-grass that is almost invariably found in the places it frequents. As soon as it alights it runs off, in the manner of a mouse, and hides itself in the grass, and it is extremely difficult to get a sight of it afterwards.

It was supposed by Dr. Bachman — correctly, as it has been ascertained — to breed on the ground, where it is always to be found when it is not singing. He never met with its nest. In June, 1853, he observed two pairs of these birds, each having four young. They were pretty well fledged, and were following their parents along the low scrub-oaks of the pine lands.

Dr. Bachman regarded this bird as decidedly the finest songster of the Sparrow family with which he was acquainted. Its notes are described as very loud for the size of the bird, and capable of being heard at a considerable distance in the pine woods where it occurs, and where at that season it is the only singer.

He also states that, by the middle of November, they have all disappeared, probably migrating farther south. It is quite probable that they do not go beyond the limits of the United States, and that some remain in South Carolina during the whole of winter, as on the 6th of February, the coldest part of the year, Dr. Bachman found one of them in the long grass near Charleston.

Mr. Audubon says that on his return from Florida, in June, 1832, travelling through both the Carolinas, he observed many of these Finches on the sides of the roads cut through the pine woods of South Carolina. They filled the air with their melodies. He traced them as far as the boundary line of North Carolina, but saw none within the limits of that State. They were particularly abundant about the Great Santee River.

This Finch, hitherto assumed to be an exclusively southeastern species, has recently been detected by Mr. Ridgway in Southern Illinois, where it is a summer resident, and where it breeds, but is not abundant. It inhabits old fields, where, perched upon a fence-stake or an old dead tree, it is described as chanting a very delightful song. It was first taken on the 12th of July, 1871, on the road about half-way between Mount Carmel and Olney. The bird was then seen on a fence, and its unfamiliar appearance and fine song at once attracted his notice as he was riding by. As several were heard singing in the same neighborhood, it seemed common in that locality, and as a young bird was taken in its first plumage there is no doubt that it is a regular summer visitant of Southern Illinois, and breeds there. Mr. Ridgway speaks of its song as one of the finest he has ever heard, most resembling the sweet chant of the Field Sparrow, but is stronger, and varied by a clear, high, and very musical strain. He describes its song as resembling the syllables *théééééé-til-lūt, lūt-lūt*, the first being a very fine trill pitched in a very high musical key, the last syllable abrupt and metallic in tone.

The food of this species, Dr. Bachman states, consists of the seeds of grasses, and also of coleopterous insects, as well as of a variety of the small berries so abundant in that part of the country. He speaks of its flight as swift, direct, and somewhat protracted, and adds that it is often out of sight before it alights.

Dr. Coues did not meet with this Sparrow in South Carolina, but he was informed by Professor Leconte that it occurs about Columbia and elsewhere in the State, frequenting open pine woods and old dry fields.

Dr. Bryant met with its nest in Florida, April 20. It was similar, in construction, to that of the Savannah Sparrow, and contained five eggs. It was the only Sparrow found by him in the pine barrens near Enterprise, and was only seen occasionally, when it was a very difficult bird to shoot, as it runs round in the grass more like a mouse than a bird, and will not fly until almost trodden on, then moving only a few feet at a time.

The nests of this bird, found by Dr. Bryant in Florida and by Dr. Gerhardt in Northern Georgia, were all placed upon the ground and concealed in tufts of thick grass, and constructed entirely of coarse wiry grasses, with no other lining than this material. The eggs, four in number, are of a pure, almost brilliant white, of a rounded oval shape, and measure .74 by .60 of an inch.

Peucæa æstivalis var. arizonæ, RIDGWAY.

ARIZONA SPARROW.

Peucæa cassini, BAIRD, Birds N. Am. 1858, 486. (Los Nogales specimen.)

SP. CHAR. (6,327 ♂, Los Nogales, Northern Sonora, June, C. B. Kennerly.) Similar to *P. æstivalis*, but paler; wings and tail longer. Above light chestnut, all the feathers margined and tipped with bluish-gray, but the reddish prevailing. Interscapular and crown feathers with a narrow streak of black, those on crown indistinct. Beneath dull white, tinged with ashy-ochraceous across the breast and along the sides; crissum pale ochraceous. An obsolete light superciliary, and narrow dusky maxillary stripe. Bend of wing yellow; lesser coverts tinged with greenish-yellow. Length, 6 inches; wing, 2.65; tail, 3.00; bill, .32 from nostril, .25 deep at base; tarsus, .80; middle toe, .63.

HAB. Los Nogales, Sonora, and Southern Arizona.

This race has a considerable resemblance to *P. æstivalis*, but differs in some appreciable points. The brown of the upper parts is paler, and the ashy edging to the feathers appears rather less extensive. The dark brown blotches on the back are of greater extent, the black streaks on the back confined to a mere streak along the shaft. There is less of an olive tinge across the breast.

The proportions of the present race differ more from those of *æstivalis* than do the colors, the bill being more slender, and the wings and tail considerably longer.

The resemblance to *P. botterii* (= *æstivalis*, var. *botterii*) of Sclater, from Middle Mexico (Orizaba, Colima, etc.), is very close; the difference being greater in the proportions than in the colors, the latter having a shorter wing and tail, with thicker bill, as in var. *æstivalis*. In *botterii* there is rather a predominance of the black over the rufous in the streaks above.

HABITS. This, in its general habits, nesting, eggs, etc., probably resembles the variety *æstivalis*.

Peucæa cassini, BAIRD.

CASSIN'S SPARROW.

Zonotrichia cassini, WOODHOUSE, Pr. A. N. Sc. Ph. VI, April, 1852, 60 (San Antonio). *Passerculus cassini*, WOODHOUSE, Sitgreaves's Rep. Zuñi and Colorado, 1853, 85; Birds, pl. iv. *Peucæa cassini*, BAIRD, Birds N. Am. 1858, 485, pl. iv, f. 2. — HEERMANN, X, c, p. 12, pl. iv, f. 2. — COOPER, Orn. Cal. I, 219 (not from Cal.).

SP. CHAR. (6,329 ♂, Texas; compared with type of species.) Ground-color of upper parts grayish-ash; the middle portion of each feather dull brown, in the form of a blotch, and with a black shaft-streak, the latter becoming modified on scapulars, rump, and upper tail-coverts, into transverse spots, those on the upper tail-coverts being large and conspicuous, and in the form of crescentic spots, the terminal margin of the feathers being lighter ashy in sharp contrast. Middle tail-feathers clear ashy, with a sharply defined shaft-streak of blackish, throwing off obsolete, narrow, transverse bars toward the edge; rest of tail clear dusky-brown, the lateral feather with whole outer web, and margin of the inner, dull white, all, except the intermediate, with a large, abruptly defined, terminal space of dilute brown (decreasing in size from the outer), the margin whitish. Upper secondaries broadly and sharply margined along both edges with dull ashy-white, the enclosed portion being clear dusky brown, intensified where adjoining the whitish. A very obsolete superciliary stripe of ashy, becoming whitish over the lore; auriculars more dingy, but without distinct stripe along upper edge. An uninterrupted but indistinct "bridle" along sides of throat. Lower parts dull white, without any ochraceous, but with a very faint ashy tinge over the jugulum; flanks with broad, somewhat blended streaks of mixed brownish and dusky. Bend of wing edged with light yellow. Wing, 2.55 ; tail, 2.80 ; bill, .28 from nostril and .23 deep ; tarsus, .68 ; middle toe, .55.

Young. (45,277, Laredo, Texas, June 28.) Very similar, but with a few drop-shaped streaks of dark brown on the jugulum and along sides. The feathers above have a more appreciable terminal border of buff.

HAB. Rio Grande region of Southern Middle Province ; Kansas, breeding (ALLEN). San Antonio, Texas, summer (DRESSER, Ibis, 1865, 489 ; eggs) ; ? Orizaba, temp. reg. (SUM. M. B. S. I, 551).

In the Birds of North America, the specimen characterized on p. 637 of the present work as *æstivalis,* var. *arizonæ,* was referred to *P. cassini,* those specimens which are here retained as such being considered as in quite immature plumage. A more recent examination of additional material, however, has compelled us to change our view. In consequence of the similarity of the specimen in question to *æstivalis,* as noted in the article referred to above, the general acceptation of the name *cassini* has been that of a term designating a variety of the common species ; but we have as the result of the investigation in question found it necessary to retain under the head of "*cassini*" only the typical specimens from the Rio Grande region, and refer the supposed aberrant specimen to *æstivalis.* In this Los Nogales specimen we find existing such differences in proportions and colors as are sufficient to warrant our bestowing upon it a new name, and establishing it as the Middle Province race of *æstivalis,* in this way connecting the South Atlantic and Mexican races (var. *æstivalis* and var. *botterii*) by a more similar form than the *P. cassini,* which must be set apart as an independent form, — in all probability a good species. Several facts are favorable to this view. First, we have of the *P. cassini* specimens which are beyond question in perfect adult plumage, and others which are undoubtedly immature ; they differ from each other only in such respects as would be expected, and agree substantially in other characters, by which they are distinguished from the different styles of *æstivalis.* Secondly, the region to be filled by a peculiar race of *æstivalis* is represented by the var. *arizonæ,* which is undoubtedly referrible to that species ; thus we have in one province these two different forms, which therefore are probably distinct.

The present bird is hardly less distinct from the races of *æstivalis* than is *ruficeps ;* and we would be as willing to consider all the definable forms presented in the synopsis as varieties of a single species, as to refer the present bird to *æstivalis.*

HABITS. This Finch, in its general appearance, as well as in respect to habits, nesting, and eggs, is quite similar to Bachman's Finch. It was first met with by Dr. Woodhouse, in the expedition to the Zuñi River, when he found it in Western Texas. He shot it on the prairies near San Antonio, on the 25th of April, 1851, mistaking it for *Passerculus savanna,* which, in its habits, it seemed to him very much to resemble, but upon examination it was found to be totally distinct.

Dr. Heermann afterwards, being at Comanche Springs in Texas, had his attention attracted by the new note of a bird unfamiliar to him. It was found, after some observation, to proceed from this species. He describes it as rising with a tremulous motion of its wings some twenty feet or more, and then descending again, in the same manner, to within a few yards of the spot whence it started, and as accompanying its entire flight with a lengthened and pleasing song. The country in that neighborhood is very barren, covered with low stunted bushes, in which the bird takes refuge on being alarmed, gliding rapidly through the grass and shrubbery, and very adroitly and effectually evading its pursuer. He observed them during four or five days of the journey of his party, and after that saw no more of them. They seemed, at the time, to be migrating, though their continued and oft-repeated song also showed that they were not far from readiness for the duties of incubation.

The *Peucœa cassini* is said, by Mr. Sumichrast, to be a resident species in the valley of Orizaba, in the State of Vera Cruz, Mexico, and to be gen-erally·distributed throughout the temperate region of that district. It is very probable, however, that he has in view the Mexican race of *P. œstivalis* (var. *botterii*), and not the present species.

Mr. J. A. Allen, who considers this bird only a western form of *P. œstiva-lis*, mentions (Am. Naturalist, May, 1872) finding it quite frequently near the streams in Western Kansas, where its sweetly modulated song greets the ear with the first break of dawn, and is again heard at night till the last trace of twilight has disappeared. Mr. Allen also states, in a letter, that this bird was " tolerably common along the streams near Fort Hays, but very retiring, singing mostly after nightfall and before sunrise, during the morning twilight. When singing, it had the habit of rising into the air. I shot three one morning thus singing, when it was so dark I could not find the birds. The one I obtained does not differ appreciably from specimens from Mr. Cassin's collection, labelled by him *Peucœa cassini*, collected in Texas."

Mr. Ridgway regards this record of the manners of this bird, while sing-ing, as indicating a specific difference from *P. œstivalis*. The latter, in Southern Illinois, has never been heard by him to sing at night, or in the morning, nor even on the wing; but in broad midday, in the hottest days of June, July, and August, he often heard them singing vigorously and sweetly, as they perched upon a fence or a dead tree in a field, exactly after the man-ner of our common *Spizella pusilla*.

Among Dr. Heermann's notes, quoted by Mr. Dresser, is one containing the statement that he found this species not rare on the prairies near the Medina River, in Texas, where it breeds. Mr. Dresser also states that when at Howard's Ranche, early in May, he found this bird by no means uncom-mon. He confirms Dr. Heermann's account, that it is easily distinguished as it rises in the air, from a bush, with a peculiar fluttering motion of the wings, at the same time singing, and then suddenly dropping into the bushes again.

He adds that, in his absence, Dr. Heermann procured the eggs of this species on the Medina, and while he was himself travelling in July towards Loredo, he found a nest which he was fully confident belonged to this bird. It was placed in a low bush not above a foot from the ground, and in its construction resembled that of the *Poospiza bilineata.* The eggs were three in number, pure white, closely agreeing with those taken by Dr. Heermann, and larger and more elongated than those of the *bilineata.*

An egg of this species, taken in Texas by Dr. H. R. Storer, the identification of which, however, was incomplete, is more oblong than the eggs of *P. œstivalis,* and smaller, measuring .72 by .58 of an inch. It is pure white also.

Peucæa ruficeps, BAIRD.

RUFOUS-CROWNED SPARROW.

Ammodromus ruficeps, CASSIN, Pr. A. N. Sc. VI, Oct. 1852, 184 (California). — IB. Illust. I, v, 1854, 135, pl. xx. *Peucæa ruficeps,* BAIRD, Birds N. Am. 1858, 486. — COOPER, Orn. Cal. I, 1870, 218.

SP. CHAR. Above brownish-ashy. The crown and nape uniform brownish-chestnut, the interscapular region and neck with the feathers of this color, except around the margins. A superciliary ashy stripe, whiter at the base of the bill. Beneath pale yellowish-brown, or brownish-yellow, darker and more ashy across the breast and on the sides of body; middle of belly and chin lighter; the latter with a well-marked line of black on each side. Edge of wing white. Under tail-coverts more rufous. Legs yellow. Length, 5.50; wing, 2.35; tail, 2.85.

HAB. Coast of California, to Mexico; ? Oaxaca, March (SCL. 1859, 380); ? Vera Cruz, temperate region; resident (SUM. M. B. S. I, 552).

This plainly colored species has the bill rather slender; tail rather long, and considerably rounded; the outer feathers .40 of an inch shorter than the middle; the feathers soft, and rounded at the tip. The wing is short; the primaries not much longer than the tertials; the second, third, fourth, and fifth nearly equal; the first scarcely longer than the secondaries.

There is a blackish tinge on the forehead, separated by a short central line of white, as in *Spizella socialis.* The eyelids are whitish, and there is a short black line immediately over the upper lid. There is a faint chestnut streak back of the eye. The chestnut of the nape is somewhat interrupted by pale edgings. The blotches on the back melt almost insensibly into the colors of the margins of the feathers. The outer edges of the secondaries and tertials, and the outer surface of the tail, are yellowish-rusty.

This bird is similar in general appearance to the *P. œstivalis,* but has the head above more continuous chestnut; the black cheek-stripe more distinct, and the edge of wing whitish, not yellow, the bill more slender. A Mexican specimen has a stouter bill.

The *P. boucardi* of Sclater (= *ruficeps,* var. *boucardi;* see table, p. 634), from Mexico, is exceedingly similar, it being very difficult to present the differences in a diagnosis. This trouble is partly the result of the insufficient series at our command, for there are such different combinations of colors, according to the season, that it is almost impossible to select the average characters of two definable forms.

HABITS. This species was first described, in 1852, by Mr. Cassin, from a specimen obtained in California by Dr. Heermann. Very little is known as to its history, and it appears to have been generally overlooked by naturalists who have studied the ornithology of that State. The extent of its distribution or of its numbers remains unknown, — a circumstance due undoubtedly to the nature of the country which it frequents.

Dr. Heermann states that in the fall of 1851 he shot on the Cosumnes River a single specimen of this bird from among a large flock of Sparrows of various kinds. In the spring of the following year, among the mountains, near the Calaveras River, he found it quite abundant. It was then flying in pairs, engaged in picking grass-seed from the ground, and when started it never extended its flight beyond a few yards. Its notes, in their character, reminded him of the ditty of our common little Chipping Sparrow (*Spizella socialis*). He obtained several specimens. Its flight seemed feeble, and when raised from the ground, from which it would not start until almost trodden on, it would fly but a short distance, and almost immediately drop again into the grass.

Dr. Cooper has only met with this species on Catalina Island, in June, where a few kept about the low bushes, feeding on the ground. They were very difficult even to get a sight of. He heard them sing a few musical notes, that reminded him of those of the *Cyanospizæ*. They flew only a short distance, and in their habits reminded him of the *Melospizæ*. Their favorite places of resort he supposes to be pine woods, as in the eastern species.

The fact that this species has been found by Mr. Sumichrast to be a permanent resident throughout all the temperate regions of Vera Cruz is a very interesting one, and is suggestive of different manners and habits from those supposed to belong to it as a bird allied with the *Ammodrami*. They are abundant, and breed there, as in the United States, but nothing is given throwing any positive light upon their general habits.

GENUS **EMBERNAGRA**, LESSON.

Embernagra, LESSON, Traité d'Ornith. 1831 (AGASSIZ). (Type, *Saltator viridis*, VIEILLOT.)

GEN. CHAR. Bill conical, elongated, compressed; the upper outline considerably curved, the lower straight; the commissure slightly concave, and faintly notched at the end. Tarsi lengthened; considerably longer than the middle toe. Outer toe a little longer than the inner, not reaching quite to the base of the middle claw. Hind toe about as long as the middle without its claw. Wings very short, and much rounded; the tertials nearly equal to the primaries; the secondaries a little shorter; the outer four primaries much graduated, even the second shorter than any other quill. The tail is moderate, about as long as the wings, much graduated; the feathers rather narrow, linear, and elliptically rounded at the end; the outer webs more than usually broad in proportion to the inner, being more than one third as wide. The upper parts are olive-green, the under whitish.

The position of this genus is a matter of considerable uncertainty. On some accounts it would be better placed among the *Spizinæ*.

There are numerous tropical species of this genus; none of them are nearly allied, however, to the single North American species.

Embernagra rufivirgata, LAWRENCE.

TEXAS SPARROW.

Embernagra rufivirgata, LAWRENCE, Ann. N. Y. Lyc. V, May, 1851, 112, pl. v, f. 2 (Texas). — SCLATER, Pr. Zoöl. Soc. 1856, 306. — BAIRD, Birds N. Am. 1858, 487, pl. lv. f. 2. — IB. Mex. Bound. II, Birds, 16, pl. xvii, f. 2. *Zonotrichia plebeja*, LICHT. BON. Comptes Rend. 43, 1856, 413.

SP. CHAR. Above uniform olivaceous-green. one behind the eye, dull brownish-rufous, an ashy superciliary stripe whiter anteriorly. Under parts brownish-white, tinged with yellowish posteriorly, and with olivaceous on the sides; white in the middle of the belly. Edge of wing, under coverts, and axillaries bright yellow. Young with the head-stripes obsolete. Length, 5.50; wing, 2.60; tail, 2.70.

HAB. Valley of the Rio Grande, and probably of Gila, southward; Mazatlan, Mexico. Oaxaca, April (SCL. 1859. 380); Cordova; Vera Cruz, temperate and hot regions, breeding (SUM. M. B. S. I, 551); Yucatan (LAWR. IX, 201).

A stripe on each side of the head, and

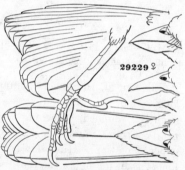

Embernagra rufivirgata, Lawr.

In this species the bill is rather long; the wings are very short, and much rounded; the tertials equal to the primaries; the secondaries rather shorter; the first quill is .65 of an inch shorter than the seventh, which is longest. The tail is short; the lateral feathers much graduated; the outer half an inch shorter than the middle.

All the Mexican specimens before us have the bill stouter than those from the Rio Grande of Texas, the stripes on the head apparently better defined. The back is darker olive; the flanks brighter olive-green, not olive-gray, the wings are apparently shorter. The series is not sufficiently perfect to show other differences, if any exist.

HABITS. In regard to the habits and distribution of this species we are entirely without any information, other than that it has been met with in the valley of the Rio Grande, and at various places in Mexico. Specimens were obtained at New Leon, Mexico, by Lieutenant Couch, and at Ringgold Bar-

racks, in Texas, by Mr. J. H. Clark. The season when these birds were met
with is not indicated by him.

Embernagra rufivirgata.

It is stated by Mr. Sumichrast
that this species is found throughout
both the temperate and the hot districts of the State of Vera Cruz,
Mexico. He also mentions that he
has found this bird in localities quite
remote from each other, and belonging both to the hot and to the temperate regions. In the latter it is
found to the height of at least four
thousand feet.

This species was met with by Mr.
Boucard, during the winter months,
at Plaza Vicente, in the hot lowlands of the State of Oaxaca, Mexico.

Subfamily PASSERELLINÆ.

CHAR. Toes and claws very stout; the lateral claws reaching beyond the middle of the
middle one; all very slightly curved.

Bill conical, the outlines straight; both mandibles equal; wings long,

longer than the even tail or
slightly rounded, reaching
nearly to the middle of its
exposed portion. Hind claw
longer than its digit; the toe
nearly as long as the middle
toe; tarsus longer than the
middle toe. Brown above,
either uniformly so or faintly
streaked; triangular spots below.

This section embraces a

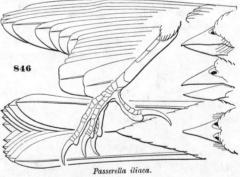

846

Passerella iliaca.

single North American genus, chiefly characterized by the remarkable elongation of the lateral claws, as well as by the peculiar shape and large size
of all the claws; the lateral, especially, are so much lengthened as to extend
nearly as far as the middle. The only approach to this, as far as I recollect,
among United States *Conirostres*, is in *Pipilo megalonyx*, and *Xanthocephalus
icterocephalus.*

Genus PASSERELLA, Swainson.

Passerella, Swainson, Class. Birds, II, 1837, 288.   (Type, *Fringilla iliaca*, Merrem.)

Gen. Char. Body stout. Bill conical, not notched, the outlines straight; the two jaws of equal depth; roof of upper mandible deeply excavated, and vaulted; not knobbed. Tarsus scarcely longer than the middle toe; outer toe little longer than the inner, its claw reaching to the middle of the central one. Hind toe about equal to the inner lateral; the claws all long, and moderately curved only; the posterior rather longer than the middle, and equal to its toe. Wings long, pointed, reaching to the middle of the tail; the tertials scarcely longer than secondaries; second and third quills longest; first equal to the fifth. Tail very nearly even, scarcely longer than the wing. Inner claw contained scarcely one and a half times in its toe proper.

Color. Rufous or slaty; obsoletely streaked or uniform above; thickly spotted with triangular blotches beneath.

Species and Varieties.

Common Characters. Ground-color above, slaty-ash, or sepia; wings, upper tail-coverts, and tail more rufescent. Beneath, pure white, with numerous triangular spots over breast and throat, streaks along sides, and a triangular blotch on side of throat, of the same color as the wings. The pectoral spots aggregated on the middle of the breast.

A. Hind claw not longer than its digit. Back with broad streaks of dark rufous.

1. **P. iliaca.** Ground-color above ash (more or less overlaid in winter with a rufous wash); wings, dorsal spots, upper tail-coverts, tail, auriculars, and markings of lower parts, bright reddish-rufous. Wing, 3.50; tail, 2.90; tarsus, .87; middle toe, without claw, .67; hind claw, .35. *Hab.* Eastern Province of North America.

B. Hind claw much longer than its digit. Back without streaks.

2. **P. townsendi.**

Head and neck above with back, scapulars, and rump, rich sepia-brown, almost uniform with wings and tail. Belly thickly spotted; tibiæ deep brown; supraloral space not whitish. Wing, 3.05; tail, 2.85; tarsus, .80; middle toe, .62; hind claw, .43. *Hab.* Pacific Province of North America, from Kodiak south to Fort Tejon, Cal. (in winter) . . . . var. *townsendi.*

Head and neck above, with back, scapulars, and rump, slaty-ash, in strong contrast with the rufescent-brown of wings and tail. Belly with only minute specks, or immaculate; tibiæ grayish; supraloral space distinctly white. Spots beneath clove-brown.

Bill, .34 from nostril, by .25 deep at base; wing, 3.30; tail, 3.50; tarsus, .85; middle toe, .60; hind claw, .45. *Hab.* Middle Province of United States . . . var. *schistacea.*

Bill, .35 from nostril and .47 deep; wing, 3.30; tail, 3.50; tarsus, .83; middle toe, .63; hind claw, .50. *Hab.* Sierra Nevada, from Fort Tejon, north to Carson City, Nev.

var. *megarhynchus.*

No great violence would be done by considering all the above forms as races of one species, the characters separating *iliaca* from the rest being of no great importance. However, in the large series examined, there is no specimen of *iliaca* at all aberrant, and none approach in the slightest degree to any of the other forms. There can be no doubt whatever of the specific identity of the three forms presented under section " B," as is plainly shown by specimens of intermediate characters. These western forms are parallels of the western race of *Melospiza ; schistacea* representing *M. fallax, megarhynchus* the *M. heermanni,* and *townsendi* the *M. guttata* or *rufina.*

Passerella iliaca, SWAINSON.

FOX-COLORED SPARROW.

Fringilla iliaca, MERREM. "Beitr. zur besond. Gesch. der Vögel, II, 1786 – 87, 40, pl. x." — GM. Syst. Nat. I, 1788, 923. — AUD. Orn. Biog. II, 1834, 58 ; V, 512, pl. cviii. — IB. Syn. 1839. — IB. Birds Am. III, 1841, 139, pl. clxxxvi. *Passerella iliaca,* Sw. Birds, II, 1837, 288. — BON. List. 1838. — IB. Conspectus, 1850, 477. — BAIRD, Birds N. Am. 1858, 488. — DALL & BANNISTER, Tr. Ch. Ac. I, 1869, 285. — SAMUELS, 325. *Fringilla rufa,* WILSON, Am. Orn. III, 1811, 53, pl. xxiv, f. 4. — LICHT. Verz. 1823, No. 248. *Fringilla ferruginea,* WILSON, Catalogue, VI, 1812. — Hall's ed. WILSON, II, 255. "*Emberiza pratensis,* VIEILL.," GRAY.

Passerella townsendi.

SP. CHAR. General aspect of upper parts foxy-red, the ground-color and the sides of neck being ashy ; the interscapular feathers each with a large blotch of fox-red ; this color glossing the top of head and nape ; sometimes faintly, sometimes more distinctly ; the rump unmarked ; the upper coverts and surface of the tail continuous fox-red. Two narrow white bands on the wing. Beneath, with under tail-coverts and axillars, clear white, the sides of head and of throat, the jugulum, breast, and sides of body, conspicuously and sharply blotched with fox-red ; more triangular across breast, more linear and darker on sides. Sometimes the entire head above is continuously reddish. First quill rather less than fifth. Hind toe about equal to its claw. Length, 7.50 ; wing, 3.50 ; tail, 2.90 ; tarsus, .87 ; middle toe, without claw, .67 ; hind claw, .35.

HAB. Eastern North America to the Mississippi, to the north along valley of the Mackenzie, almost or quite to the Arctic coast, and down the valley of the Yukon to the Pacific. Breeds throughout the interior of British America.

In summer, the ash is more predominant above ; in winter, it is overlaid more or less by a wash of rufous, as described above.

The young plumage we have not seen. The *P. obscura,* Verrill,[1] may be referrible to it.

---

[1] *Passerella obscura,* VERRILL, Pr. Bost. N. H. Soc. IX, Dec. 1862, 143 (Anticosti). (Type in Museum Comp. Zoöl., Cambridge.)

"Size somewhat smaller than that of *P. iliaca.* Legs and wings a little shorter in proportion. Claws less elongated. Bill somewhat shorter, thicker, and less acute. Color above rufous-brown,

HABITS. The Fox-colored Sparrow, in its seasons of migrations, is a very common bird throughout the United States east of the Mississippi River. It has not been ascertained to breed in any part of the United States, though it may do so in Northeastern Maine. Mr. Boardman has not met with it near Calais, nor did I see nor could I hear of it in any part of Nova Scotia or New Brunswick that I visited. In passing north, these birds begin their northern movements in the middle of March, and from that time to the last of April they are gradually approaching their summer quarters. Their first appearance near Boston is about the 15th of March, and they linger in that vicinity, or successive parties appear, until about the 20th of April. The last comers are usually in song. On their return, the middle or last of October, they pass rapidly, and usually make no stay. In Southwestern Texas these birds were not observed by Mr. Dresser, nor in Arizona by Dr. Coues, but in the Indian Territory Dr. Woodhouse found them very abundant on the approach of winter. Dr. Coues speaks of them as common in South Carolina from November to April, but less numerous than most of the Sparrows.

In the vicinity of Washington this bird is found from October to April. I have met with small groups of them through all the winter months among the fallen leaves in retired corners of the Capitol grounds, where they were busily engaged, in the manner of a *Pipilo*, in scratching in the earth for their food. At those periods when the ground was open, their habits were eminently similar to those of the gallinaceous birds. In March and April they were in company with the White-throated Sparrows, but passed north at least a month earlier.

becoming bright rufous on the rump and exposed portion of the tail, but a shade darker than in *P. iliaca;* head uniform brown, with a slight tinge of ash ; feathers of the back centred with a streak of darker brown. Wings nearly the same color as the back, with no white bands ; outer webs of the quills rufous, inner webs dark brown ; secondary coverts rufous, with dark brown centres ; primary coverts uniform brown. Beneath dull white, with the throat and breast thickly covered with elongated triangular spots and streaks of dark reddish-brown ; sides streaked with rufous-brown ; middle of abdomen with a few small triangular spots of dark brown ; under tail-coverts brownish-white, with a few small spots of bright rufous ; tibiæ dark brown. The auriculars are tinged with reddish-brown. Bristles at the base of the bill are numerous, extending over the nostrils. Tail rather long, broad, and nearly even. Third quill longest ; second and fourth equal, and but slightly shorter ; first intermediate between the fifth and sixth, and one fourth of an inch shorter than the third.

"Length, 6.75 ; extent of wings, 10.75 ; wing, 3.35 ; tarsus, 1 inch.

"This species differs greatly in color from *P. iliaca.* It is darker in all parts ; the feathers of the back are rufous-brown, centred with darker, instead of ash centred with brownish-red ; the two white bands on the wing are wanting ; the breast and throat are thickly streaked with elongated spots of dark reddish-brown, while in *P. iliaca* the spots are less numerous, shorter and broader, and bright rufous, and the central part of the throat is nearly free from spots ; the under tail-coverts are brownish-white, with rufous spots, instead of nearly pure white."

There are some features in this bird, as described by Mr. Verrill, which seem to characterize it as different from *P. iliaca*, although it is barely possible that it is this bird in immature dress. The streaked back at once separates it from all our species excepting *iliaca.* Nothing is said of its habits. One specimen was killed in Anticosti, July 1 ; the other, August 8. The true *iliaca* was found on the island, which fact renders it still more probable that this is its young.

During their stay in the United States these birds keep in small distinctive flocks, never mingling, though often in the same places, with other species. They are found in the edges of thickets and in moist woods. They are usually silent, and only occasionally utter a call-note, low and soft. In the spring the male becomes quite musical, and is one of our sweetest and most remarkable singers. His voice is loud, clear, and melodious; his notes full, rich, and varied; and his song is unequalled by any of this family that I have ever heard. They soon become reconciled to confinement and quite tame, and sing a good part of the year if care is taken in regard to their food. If allowed to eat to excess, they become very fat and heavy, and lose their song.

Dr. Coues did not meet with these birds in Labrador, but Mr. Audubon found them there and in Newfoundland in large numbers; and, according to the observations of Sir John Richardson, they breed in the wooded districts of the fur countries, up to the 68th parallel of latitude.

These birds were also found abundantly at Fort Simpson and Great Slave Lake by Mr. Robert Kennicott and Mr. B. R. Ross; at Fort Anderson, Anderson River, Swan River, and in various journeys, by Mr. R. MacFarlane; at Fort Resolution, Fort Good Hope, La Pierre House, and Fort Yukon, by Mr. Lockhart; at Peel's River, by Mr. J. Flett; at St. Michael's, by Mr. H. M. Bannister; and at Nulato, by Mr. W. H. Dall. They were observed at Fort Simpson as early as May 17, and by Mr. Kennicott as late as September 17. Mr. Dall states that at Nulato he found this Sparrow in abundance. It arrived there from the 10th to the 15th of May. It breeds there, and its eggs were obtained on the Yukon River. In the month of August in 1867 and of July in 1868 it was abundant at the mouth of the Yukon and at St. Michael's. One was also shot at Unalaklik. The birds seemed to prefer thickets to the more open country. Mr. Bannister did not find it abundant. He shot only one specimen during the season, in an alder thicket near the fort; and Mr. Pease, who was familiar with the species, only saw a single individual.

According to the reports of both Mr. MacFarlane and Mr. Kennicott, the nest of this species was found both on the ground and in trees. In one instance it was in a tree about eight feet from the ground, and in its structure was said to be similar to the nests of *Turdus aliciæ*. They were nearly all found after the middle of June, a few as early as the 7th. One was found on the ground at the foot of a tuft of dwarf willows, which helped to conceal it from view. This was composed of coarse hay, lined with some of a finer quality, a few deer-hairs, and a small quantity of fresh and growing moss, intermingled together. In speaking of this nest Mr. MacFarlane states that all the nests of this Sparrow he had previously met with had been built in the midst of branches of pine or spruce trees, and had been similar to those of the *T. aliciæ*, which, in this instance, it did not resemble. He adds that this species, though not numerous, extended quite to the borders of the wooded country, to the north and northwest of

Fort Anderson. Afterwards he observed several other nests on the ground, all of which were similar to the last, and it is by no means impossible that in certain instances these birds may have occupied old nests of the *T. aliciæ*, and used them for purposes of incubation. Richardson states that its nests are constructed in a low bush, and are made of dry grass, hair, and feathers. He states that the eggs are five in number, of a pale mountain-green tint, and marbled with irregular spots of brown.

Mr. Audubon, who found several of the nests of this bird in Labrador, near the coast, describes them as large for the size of the bird, and as usually placed on the ground among moss or tall grass near the stem of a creeping fir, the branches of which usually conceal it from view. Its exterior is loosely formed of dry grasses and moss, with a carefully disposed inner layer of fine grasses, circularly arranged. The lining consists of very delicate fibrous roots, with feathers of different kinds of water-fowl. In one instance he noted the down of the eider-duck. He found their eggs from the middle of June to the 5th of July. When their nest was approached, the female affected lameness, and employed all the usual arts to decoy the intruder away. They raised but one brood in a season, and about the first of September left Labrador for the south in small flocks, made up of members of one family.

Their eggs measure from .92 to an inch in length, and .70 in breadth. They are oblong in shape. Their ground-color is a light bluish-white, thickly spotted with a rusty-brown, often so fully as to conceal the ground.

Passerella townsendi, Nuttall.

TOWNSEND'S SPARROW.

? *Emberiza unalaschkensis*, GMEL. II, 1788, 875 (based on *Aonalaschka Bunting*, LATH. II, 202, 48 ; *Unalaschka B.*, PENNANT, 52). *Passerella u.* FINSCH, Abh. Nat. III, 1872, 53 (Alaska). *Fringilla townsendi*, AUD. Orn. Biog. V, 1839, 236, pl. ccccxxiv, f. 7. — IB. Syn. 1839. — IB. Birds Am. III, 1841, 43, pl. clxxxvii. *Fringilla (Passerella) townsendi*, NUTT. Man. I, (2d ed.,) 1840, 533. *Passerella townsendi*, BON. Conspectus, 1850, 477. — BAIRD, Birds N. Am. 1858, 489. — COOPER & SUCKLEY, 204. — DALL & BANNISTER, Tr. Ch. Ac. I, 1869, 285. *Fringilla meruloides*, VIG. Zoöl. Blossom (Monterey, Cal.), 1839, 19. ? *Emberiza (Zonotrichia) rufina*, KITTLITZ, Denkw. 1858, 200. (He compares it with *P. iliaca*, but says it is darker. Sitka.)

SP. CHAR. Above very dark olive-brown, with a tinge of rufous, the color continuous and uniform throughout, without any trace of blotches or spots; the upper tail-coverts and outer edges of the wing and tail feathers rather lighter and brighter. The under parts white, but thickly covered with approximating triangular blotches colored like the back, sparsest on the middle of the body and on the throat; the spots on the belly smaller. Side almost continuously like the back; tibiæ and under tail-coverts similar, the latter edged with paler. Axillars brown; paler on edges. Claws all very large and long; the hinder claw longer than its toe. First and sixth quills about equal. Length, about 7 inches; wing, about 3.00.

HAB. Pacific coast of United States, as far south as Sacramento, and Fort Tejon? north to Kodiak (and Unalaschka?).

This species differs a good deal in form from *P. iliaca*. The claws are

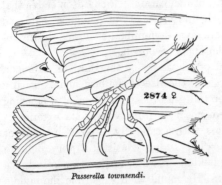

Passerella townsendi.

2874 ♀

much larger and stouter, the wing a good deal shorter and more rounded. The differences in color are very appreciable, the tints being dark sepia-brown instead of red, and perfectly uniform above, not spotted ; the under parts much more thickly spotted.

Specimens from Alaska show a tendency to longer and perhaps more slender bills. Some are rather more rufous-brown than the type ; others have a faint tinge of ashy anteriorly, although scarcely appreciable. This is especially noticeable in some skins from Fort Tejon, they being almost exactly intermediate between *townsendi* and *schistacea*, or *megarhynchus*.

Young birds are not materially different from the adult, except in having the white of under parts replaced by pale rusty ; the back is rather duller in color, but without spots or stripes of any kind.

No. 46,620 from British Columbia has the bill much stouter than in the average.

It is by no means certain, however probable, that this bird is the *E. una-laschkensis* of Gmelin, an important objection being its absence so far in collections received by the Smithsonian Institution from that island. We therefore leave the question open for the present.

HABITS. The history of this western analogue of the Fox-colored Sparrow is still quite imperfectly known. It was first obtained in Oregon by Mr. Townsend, on the 15th of February. He describes it as a very active and a very shy bird, keeping constantly among the low bushes of worm-wood, and on the ground in their vicinity. It was partially gregarious, six or eight being usually seen together. Its call-note was a short, sharp, quick chirp, and it also had occasionally a low weak warble.

Dr. Gambel, referring probably to its occurrence in winter in California, speaks of this bird as an abundant resident in that State, which is not correct, it being only a winter visitant, and not abundant south of San Francisco. He describes its habits as very different from those of any other Sparrow, and more like those of a Thrush. It is said to keep in retired bushy places, or in underwood, and was scarcely ever seen except on the ground, and then would scarcely ever be discovered but for the noise it made in scratching among the leaves. It was silent and unsuspicious, and he rarely heard it utter even its occasional chirp.

Dr. Cooper states that he found this Sparrow only a winter resident in Washington Territory, where, in company with other Sparrows, it kept constantly on the ground, frequenting the thickets and scratching among the fallen leaves for its food. It was most common in the interior, but in very cold weather sought the coast, in company with the Snowbird and other species. He observed a few lingering about the Straits of Fuca until April. After that he saw no more of them until their return southward in October. During their winter residence Dr. Cooper never heard them sing. Dr. Suckley found them rather abundant near Fort Steilacoom, though not so common as the *Melospiza rufina*, which they greatly resembled in habits and in general appearance.

Dr. Heermann describes them as abundant and migratory in California, visiting that State only in winter. He speaks of them as of a solitary and quiet nature, resorting to the thickets and underwood for its food, turning over the leaves and scratching up the ground in the manner of the Brown Thrush, occasionally hopping backwards as if to ascertain the results of its labors.

Dr. Cooper, in his Report on the Birds of California, reaffirms that this bird is only a winter visitant to the lower country near the Columbia, but also conjectures that it spends the summer in the Cascade Mountains, between April and October. Specimens have been obtained near San Francisco in winter. It seemed to him to be both a shy and a silent bird, frequenting only woods or thick bushes, and while there constantly scratching among the fallen leaves, and feeding both on seeds and insects. He has seen either this bird or the *P. megarhynchus* as far south as San Diego in winter. He has also noticed its arrival near San Francisco as early as October 20.

On the Spokan Plains, in British Columbia, Mr. J. K. Lord first met with this species. They were there not uncommon in dark swampy places east of the Cascades. These birds he found remarkable for their singular habit of scratching dead leaves or decayed material of any sort with their feet, exactly as do barn-door fowls, — sending the dirt right, left, and behind. It picks up seeds, insects, larvæ, or anything eatable that it thus digs out, and then proceeds to scratch for more. The long and unusually strong claws with which this bird is provided seem particularly well adapted for these habits, so unusual in a Sparrow. At almost any time, by waiting a few moments, one may be pretty sure to hear the scratching of several of these birds from under the tangle of fallen timber.

Several specimens were obtained in Sitka by Bischoff and others, but without any record of their habits.

Passerella townsendi, var. schistacea, BAIRD.

Passerella schistacea, BAIRD, Birds N. Am. 1858, 490, pl. lxix, f. 3.

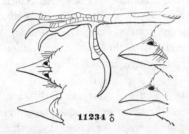

SP. CHAR. Bill slender, the length being .34 from nostril, the depth .25; the upper mandible much swollen at the base; the under yellow. Above and on the sides uniform slate-gray; the upper surface of wings, tail-feathers, and upper coverts dark brownish-rufous; ear-coverts streaked with white. Beneath pure white, with broad triangular arrow-shaped and well-defined spots of slate-gray like the back everywhere, except along the middle of the belly; not numerous on the throat. A hoary spot at the base of the bill above the loral region; axillars nearly white. Length, 6.80; wing, 3.30; tail, 3.50.

11234 ♂

HAB. Head-waters of Platte and middle region of United States to Fort Tejon and to Fort Crook, California.

This species is readily distinguished from *P. iliaca* by the slaty back and spots on the breast, the absence of streaks above, and the longer claws. From *townsendi* it differs in having the head, back, sides, and spots beneath slate-colored, instead of dark reddish-brown. The spotting beneath is much more sparse, the spots smaller, more triangular, and confined to the terminal portion of the feathers, instead of frequently involving the entire outer edge. The axillars are paler. The wings and tail are the same in both species.

The young bird is quite similar; but the spots beneath are badly defined, more numerous, and longitudinal rather than triangular.

There can be little doubt, however, that this bird is a geographical race of *P. townsendi.*

HABITS. For all that we know in regard to the habits and general distribution of this species, we are indebted to the observations of Mr. Ridgway, who met with it while accompanying Mr. Clarence King's geological survey. It was first obtained in July, 1856, by Lieutenant F. T. Bryan, on the Platte River, and others were afterwards collected at Fort Tejon by Mr. Xantus.

Mr. Ridgway found the Slate-colored Sparrow at Carson City, during its spring migrations northward, in the early part of March. At this time it was seen only among the willows along the Carson River, and was by no means common. It had the habit of scratching among the dead leaves, on the ground in the thickets, precisely after the manner of the eastern *P. iliaca.* In the following September he again found it among the thickets in the Upper Humboldt Valley. In Parley's Park, among the Wahsatch Mountains, he found it a very plentiful species in June, nesting among the willows and other shrubbery along the streams. There it was always found in company with the *M. fallax,* which in song it greatly resembles, though its other notes are quite distinct, the ordinary one being a sharp *chuck.* The nest of the two species, he adds, were also so much alike in manner of construction and situation, and the eggs so similar, that it required a careful observation to identify a nest when one was found.

The eggs from one nest of the *Passerella schistacea* measure .90 by .70 of an inch, have a ground of a light mountain-green, and are profusely spotted with blotches of a rufous-brown, generally diffused over the entire egg.

Another nest of this species, obtained in Parley's Park, in the Wahsatch Mountains, by Mr. Ridgway, June 23, 1869, was built in a clump of willows, about two feet from the ground. The nest is two inches in height, two and a half in diameter, cavity one and a half deep, with a diameter of two. It is composed externally of coarse decayed water-grass, is lined with fine hair and finer material like the outside. The eggs, four in number, are .80 by .67 of an inch, of a very rounded oval shape, the ground-color of a pale green, blotched and marked chiefly at the larger end with brown spots of a wine-colored hue.

Passerella townsendi, var. megarhynchus, BAIRD.

THICK-BILLED SPARROW.

Passerella schistacea, BAIRD, Birds N. Am. 1858, p. 490 (in part ; Ft. Tejon specimens). *Passerella megarhynchus*, BAIRD, Birds N. Am. 1858, p. 925 (Appendix). — COOPER, Orn. Cal. I, 222. *Passerella schistacea*, var. *megarhynchus*, RIDGWAY, Rept. Geol. Expl. 40th Par.

SP. CHAR. Similar to var. *schistacea* in colors, size, and general proportions ; but bill enormously thick, its depth being very much greater than the distance from nostril to tip, instead of much less ; color of lower mandible rosy milk-white, instead of maize-yellow. Bill, .35 from nostril, .47 deep ; wing, 3.30 ; tail, 3.50 ; tarsus, .83 ; middle toe without claw, .63 ; hind claw, 50.

HAB. Sierra Nevada, from Fort Tejon north to 40° latitude (Carson City, Nevada, breeding, RIDGWAY).

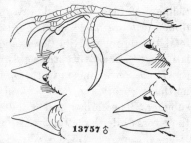

13757 ♂

This very remarkable variety of *P. townsendi* is quite local in its distribution, having been observed only in the Sierra Nevada region, as above indicated. The first specimens were brought from Fort Tejon by Mr. J. Xantus, but at what season they were found there is not indicated on the labels. Recently, specimens were procured by Mr. Ridgway at Carson City, Nev., in April, they having arrived there about the 20th of April, frequenting the ravines of the Sierra near the snow. At the same place the var. *schistacea* was found earlier in the spring, but among the willows along the streams in the valleys, and not met with in the mountains ; and all the individuals had passed northward before those of *megarhynchus* arrived.

In this restricted distribution the present bird is a companion of the *Melospiza melodia*, var. *heermanni*, and the characteristics of form are the same in both as compared with their Middle Province and Northern representatives ; while they both differ from the latter (*townsendi* of *Passerella*, and *rufina* of *Melospiza*) in purer, lighter, and less brown colors.

HABITS. Dr. Cooper met with several individuals of this bird towards the summits of the Sierra Nevada, in September, 1863, but was unable to preserve any of them. So far as he was able to observe them, they had no song, and their habits were generally similar to those of the *P. townsendi*.

The Thick-billed Sparrow was found by Mr. Ridgway as a very common bird among the alder swamps in the ravines of the eastern slope of the Sierra Nevada during the summer. Near Carson City, April 25, in a swampy thicket near the streams in the level slopes, he heard, for the first time, its beautiful song, and killed a specimen in the midst of its utterance of what, he adds, was one of the most exquisitely rich utterances he ever heard. This song, he states, resembles, in richness and volume, that of the Louisiana Water Thrush (*Seiurus ludovicianus*), qualities in which that bird is hardly equalled by any other North American bird. They were singing in all parts of that swampy thicket, and up the ravines as far as the snow. From the nature of the place and the character of their song, they were at first supposed to be the Water Thrush, until specimens of these exquisite songsters were secured. He regards this bird as second to none of our singers belonging to this family. and though in variety, sprightliness, and continuity, and also in passionate emotional character, its song is not equal to that of the *Chondestes grammaca*, yet it is far superior in power and richness of tone. Mr. Ridgway regards this bird as easily distinguishable from the *P. schistacea*, of which, however, it is only a variety. There is a total discrepancy in its notes, and while neither species is resident in the latitude of Carson City, through which both kinds pass in their migrations, the *P. schistacea* lingers in the spring only a short time, soon passing to the northward, while the *P. megarhynchus* arrives later and remains through the summer. The former makes its temporary abode among the willows along the river, while the latter breeds in the shrubbery of the mountain ravines.

SUBFAMILY **SPIZINÆ**.

CHAR. Bill variable, always large, much arched, and with the culmen considerably curved ; sometimes of enormous size, and with a greater development backward of the lower jaw, which is always appreciably, sometimes considerably, broader behind than the upper jaw at its base ; nostrils exposed. Tail rather variable. Bill generally black, light blue, or red. Wings shorter than in the first group. Gape almost always much more strongly bristled. Few of the species sparrow-like or plain in their appearance ; usually blue, red, or black and white ; except in one or two instances the sexes very different in color.

The preceding diagnosis is intended to embrace the brightly colored passerine birds of North America, different in general appearance from the common Sparrows. It is difficult to draw the line with perfect strictness, so as to separate the species from those of the preceding group, but the bill is always more curved, as well as larger, and the colors are brighter. They resemble quite closely, at a superficial glance, the *Coccothraustinæ*, but may be readily distinguished by absence of the projecting tufts surrounding the base of the upper mandible, shorter, more rounded wings, and longer tarsi.

The genera may be most conveniently arranged as follows: —

A. Wings decidedly longer than the tail. Eggs plain blue or white, unspotted.
   a. Feet very stout, reaching nearly to the end of the tail. Species terrestrial.

      Calamospiza. Bill moderate, the commissure with a deep angle posteriorly and prominent lobe behind it; anteriorly nearly straight; commissure of lower mandible with a prominent angle. Outer toe longer than the inner, both nearly as long as the posterior. Outer four primaries about equal, and abruptly longer than the rest. Tertials nearly equal to primaries. Tail-feathers broad at tips. Color: black with white spot on wing in ♂, brownish streaks in ♀. Nest on or near ground; eggs plain pale blue.

      Euspiza. Bill weaker, the commissure with a more shallow angle, and much less prominent sinuation behind it; anteriorly distinctly sinuated. Outer toe shorter than inner, both much shorter than the posterior one. First primary longest, the rest successively shorter. Tertials but little longer than secondaries. Tail-feathers attenuated at tips. Color: back brown streaked with black; throat white; jugulum yellow or ashy; with or without black spot on fore neck. A yellow or white superciliary stripe. Nest on or near ground; eggs plain pale blue.

   b. Feet weaker, scarcely reaching beyond lower tail-coverts; species arboreal.

      a. Size large (wing more than 3.50 inches).

      Hedymeles. Upper mandible much swollen laterally. Colors: no blue; upper parts conspicuously different from the lower. Wings and tail with white patches; axillars and lining of wing yellow or red. Female streaked. Nest in a tree or bush; eggs greenish, thickly spotted.

      Guiraca. Upper mandible flat laterally. Colors: ♂ deep blue, with two rufous bands on wings; no white patches on wings or tail; axillars and lining of wing blue; ♀ olive-brown without streaks. Nest in a bush; eggs plain bluish-white.

      b. Size very small (wing less than 3.00 inches).

      Cyanospiza. Similar in form to *Guiraca*, but culmen more curved, mandible more shallow, the angle and sinuations of the commissure less conspicuous. Color: ♂ more or less blue, without any bands on wing (except in *C. amœna* in which they are white); ♀ olive-brown. Nest in a bush; eggs plain bluish-white (except in *C. ciris*, in which they have reddish spots).

B. Wing and tail about equal. The smallest of American *Conirostres*. Nest in bushes. Eggs white, spotted.

Spermophila. Bill very short and broad, scarcely longer than high, not compressed; culmen greatly curved. Color: chiefly black and white, or brown and gray.

Phonipara. Bill more triangular, decidedly longer than deep, much compressed; culmen only slightly curved, or perfectly straight. Colors: dull olive-green and blackish, with or without yellow about the head.

C. Wing much shorter than the tail.

a Head crested. Prevailing color red. Bill red or whitish.

Pyrrhuloxia. Bill pyrrhuline, very short, and with the culmen greatly convex; shorter than high. Hind claw less than its digit; not much larger than the middle anterior one. Tarsus equal to the middle toe. Nest in bush or low tree; eggs white, spotted with lilac and olive.

Cardinalis. Bill coccothraustine, very large; culmen very slightly convex. Wings more rounded. Feet as in the last, except that the tarsus is longer than the middle toe. Nest in bush or low tree; eggs white, spotted with lilac and olive.

b. Head not crested. Colors black, brown, or olive, without red. Bill dusky, or bluish.

Pipilo. Bill moderate; culmen and commissure curved. Hind claw very large and strong; longer than its digit. Tarsus less than the middle toe. Nest on ground or in low bush; eggs white sprinkled with red, or pale blue with black dots and lines round larger end.

Genus **CALAMOSPIZA**, Bonap.

Calamospiza, Bonap. List, 1838. (Type, *Fringilla bicolor*, Towns.)
Corydalina, Audubon, Synopsis, 1839. (Same type.)

Gen. Char. Bill rather large, much swollen at the base; the culmen broad, gently but

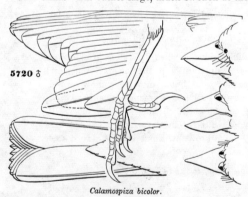

5720 ♂

Calamospiza bicolor.

decidedly curved; the gonys nearly straight; the commissure much angulated near the base, then slightly sinuated; lower mandible nearly as deep as the upper, the margins much inflected, and shutting under the upper mandible. Nostrils small, strictly basal. Rictus quite stiffly bristly. Legs large and stout. Tarsi a little longer than the middle toe; outer toe rather longer than the inner, and reaching to the concealed base of the middle claw; hind toe reaching to the base of the middle claw; hind claw about as long as its toe. Claws all strong, compressed, and considerably curved. Wings long and pointed; the first four nearly equal, and abruptly longest; the tertials much elongated, as long as the primaries. Tail a little shorter than the wings, slightly graduated; the feathers rather narrow and obliquely oval, rounded at the end.

Color. Male, black, with white on the wings. *Female*, brown above, beneath white, with streaks.

This genus is well characterized by the large swollen bill, with its curved culmen ; the large strong feet and claws ; the long wings, a little longer than the tail, and with the ter- tials as long as the primaries ; the first four quills about equal, and abruptly longest ; the tail short and graduated.

The only group of North American *Spizellinæ*, with the tertials equal to the primaries in the closed wing, is *Passerculus.* This, however, has a differently formed bill, weaker feet, the

Calamospiza bicolor.

inner primaries longer and more regularly graduated, the tail-feathers more acute and shorter, and the plumage streaked brownish and white instead of black.

Calamospiza bicolor, BONAP.

LARK BUNTING ; WHITE-WINGED BLACKBIRD.

Fringilla bicolor, TOWNSEND, J. A. N. Sc. Ph. VII, 1837, 189. — IB. Narrative, 1839, 346. — AUD. Orn. Biog. V, 1839, 19, pl. cccxc. *Calamospiza bicolor,* BONAP. List, 1838. — IB. Conspectus, 1850, 475. — BAIRD, Birds N. Am. 1858, 492. — HEERM. X, c, 15. *Corydalina bicolor,* AUD. Synopsis, 1839, 130. — IB. Birds Am. III, 1841, 195, pl. cci. — MAX. Cab. J. VI, 1858, 347. — COOPER, Orn. Cal. I, 225. *Dolichonyx bicolor,* NUTTALL, Manual, I, (2d ed.,) 1840, 203.

SP. CHAR. *Male* entirely black ; a broad band on the wing (covering the whole of the greater coverts), with the outer edges of the quills and tail-feathers, white. Length, about 6.50 ; wing, 3.50 ; tail, 3.20 ; tarsus, 1.00 ; bill above, .60.

Female pale brown, streaked with darker above ; beneath white, spotted and streaked rather sparsely with black on the breast and sides. Throat nearly immaculate. A maxillary stripe of black, bordered above by white. Region around the eye, a faint stripe above it, and an obscure crescent back of the ear-coverts, whitish. A broad fulvous white band across the ends of the greater wing-coverts ; edge of wing white. Tail-feathers with a white spot at the end of the inner web.

Young. Similar to the female ; a faint buff tinge prevalent beneath, where the streaks are narrower ; dark streaks above broader, the feathers bordered with buffy-white.

HAB. High Central Plains to the Rocky Mountains ; southwesterly to Valley of Mimbres and Sonora ; San Antonio, Texas, winter (DRESSER, Ibis, 1865, 490). Fort Whipple, Arizona (COUES, P. A. N. S. 1866, 84). Parley's Park, Utah (RIDGWAY).

HABITS. This peculiar species, known by some writers as the Lark Bunt- ing, and by others as the White-winged Blackbird, was first described by Townsend in 1837. He met with it when, in company with Mr. Nuttall, he made his western tour across the continent, on the 24th of May, soon after crossing the north branch of the Platte River. The latter writer regarded it as closely allied to the Bobolink, and described it as a *Dolichonyx*. He describes the birds as gregarious, consorting with the Cowbirds, and, at the time he met with them, uttering most delightful songs.   Towards evening they sometimes saw these birds in all directions around them, on the hilly grounds, rising at intervals to some height, hovering and flapping their wings, and, at the same time, giving forth a song which Mr. Nuttall describes as being something like *weet-weet-wt-wt-wt*, notes that were between the hurried warble of the Bobolink and the melody of a Skylark.   It is, he says, one of the sweetest songsters of the prairies, is tame and unsuspicious, and the whole employment of the little band seemed to be an ardent emulation of song.

It feeds on the ground, and, as stated by Mr. Townsend, may be seen in flocks of from sixty to a hundred together.   It was, so far as their observations went, found inhabiting exclusively the wide grassy plains of the Platte. They did not see it to the west of the Black Hills, or the first range of the Rocky Mountains.

To Mr. Nuttall's account Mr. Townsend adds that this bird is strictly gregarious, that it feeds on the ground, around which it runs in the manner of the Grass Finch, to which, in its habits, it seems to be somewhat allied.   Mr. Townsend adds that, as their caravan moved along, large flocks of these birds, sometimes to the number of sixty or a hundred individuals, were started from the ground, and the piebald appearance of the males and females promiscuously intermingled presented a very striking and by no means unpleasing effect.   While the flock was engaged in feeding, some of the males were observed to rise suddenly to considerable height in the air, and, poising themselves over their companions with their wings in constant and rapid motion, continued nearly stationary.   In this situation they poured forth a number of very lively and sweetly modulated notes, and, at the expiration of about a minute, descended to the ground and moved about as before. Mr. Townsend also states that he met with none of these birds west of the Black Hills.

Mr. Ridgway also mentions that though he found these birds very abundant on the plains east of the Black Hills, he met with only a single specimen to the westward of that range.   This was at Parley's Park, among the Wahsatch Mountains.

Dr. Gambel, in his paper on the Birds of California, states that he met with small flocks of this handsome species in the bushy plains, and along the margins of streams, during the winter months.   And Dr. Heermann states that he also found this species numerous in California, New Mexico, and Texas.   Arriving in the last-named State in May, he found this species there already mated, and about to commence the duties of incubation.

Mr. Dresser found these birds common near San Antonio during the winter.   In December he noticed several flocks near Eagle Pass. . They frequented the roads, seeking the horse-dung.   They were quite shy, and when disturbed the whole flock would go off together, uttering a low and melodious whistle. In May and June several were still about near Howard's Rancho, and on his return from Houston, in June, he succeeded in shooting one in its full summer plumage, when its specific name is peculiarly appropriate. He does not, however, think that, as a general thing, any of them remain about San Antonio to breed.

They breed in great numbers on the plains of Wyoming Territory, and probably also in Colorado, Montana, and Dakota. The Smithsonian collection embraces specimens obtained in July from the Yellowstone, from Platte River, Pole Creek, the Black Hills, and Bridger's Pass, indicating that they breed in these localities; also specimens from Texas, New Mexico, Sonora, and Espia, in Mexico, but none from California.

Dr. Kennerly, who met with these birds both in Sonora and at Espia, on the Mexican Boundary Survey, states that he observed them in the valley of the river early in the morning, in very large flocks. During the greater part of the day they feed on the hills among the bushes. When on the wing they keep very close together, so that a single discharge of shot would sometimes bring down twenty or thirty. Mr. J. H. Clark, on the same survey, also states that he sometimes found them occurring in flocks of hundreds. The greatest numbers were seen near Presidio del Norte. Great varieties of plumage were observed in the same flock. The food seemed to be seeds almost exclusively. They were very simultaneous in all their movements. Stragglers were never observed remaining behind after the flock had started. They are, he states, the most absolutely gregarious birds he has ever met with.

Dr. Coues, who regarded this bird as one highly characteristic of the prairie fauna, writes me that he met with it in great numbers in Kansas, soon after leaving Fort Riley, and saw it every day until he reached the Raton Mountains in New Mexico. "For two or three days, in fact, from Fort Larned to the mountains," he writes, "I scarcely saw anything else. This was the first week in June, and most of the birds seemed to be paired and nesting, though occasionally a dozen or more were seen together, flocking like the Blackbirds that they strongly recall. They were in full song, and proved delightful vocalists. Sometimes they warble from some spray or low bush offering a stand a little above the level flower-beds of the prairie, but oftener they mount straight up, hovering high in the air on tremulous wings, pouring forth their melodious strains until, seemingly exhausted, they sink back to the ground. At such times it is interesting to watch two rival males, each straining every nerve to mount higher than the other, and sing more acceptably to its mate hidden in the verdure below. This habit of rising on the wing to sing, so famed in the case of the Skylark, seems not confined to particular species, but to be a forced practice of a number of different birds residing in open level regions, that do not afford the elevated perches usually chosen by woodland songsters for their performances. The ordinary flight of this species is altogether of a different character, being a low gliding motion, overtopping the weeds and bushes. That the birds were nesting at this time is rendered still more probable by the fact that the males noticed as we passed along were out of all proportion, in numbers, to the females seen. They were very heedless of approach, and any number could have been readily destroyed. I never saw any at Fort Whipple, or elsewhere in Arizona, though Dr. Heermann says that they are abundant in the southern portions of the Territory, and specimens are recorded from Lower California."

Mr. Allen found the Lark Bunting one of the few birds that seemed strictly confined to the arid plains near Fort Hays, in Kansas. He met with it in great abundance, but only on the high ridges and dry plateaus, where they seemed to live in colonies. He describes them as very wary, and very tenacious of life, often flying long distances, even after having been mortally wounded. They seemed to delight to fly in strong winds, when most other birds kept in shelter. They sing while on the wing, hovering in the wind and shaking the tail and legs after the well-known manner of the Yellow-breasted Chat. Its song seemed to him to strongly resemble that of the Chat, with which, at such times, its whole demeanor strikingly accorded.

Dr. Heermann, in his Report on the birds collected in the survey on the 32d parallel, states that he first observed these birds on approaching the Pimos villages. They were associated with large flocks of Sparrows, gleaning grain and grass-seed upon the ground. When started up they flew but a short distance before they resumed their occupation. After crossing the San Pedro he again found them in large flocks. At Fort Fillmore, in Mesilla Valley, it was also quite common and associated with the Cowbird and Blackbird, searching for grain among the stable offals. He again met with them in Texas, in the month of April, most of them still retaining their winter coat. He describes the tremulous fluttering motion of the wings with which the male accompanies its song while on the wing as very much after the manner of the Bobolink, and he speaks of their song as a disconnected but not an unmusical chant. He found their nests on the ground, made of fine grasses, lined with hair, and in one instance he found the eggs spotted with faint red dashes.

At Gilmer, in Wyoming Territory, their nests were found by Mr. Durkee built on the ground, and composed of dry grasses very loosely arranged. The eggs, four or five in number, are of a uniform and beautiful light shade of blue, similar to those of the *Euspiza americana*. They measure .90 by .70 of an inch, are of a rounded-oval shape, and, so far as I have observed, are entirely unspotted, although eggs with a few reddish blotches are said to have been met with.

Genus **EUSPIZA**, Bonap.

Euspiza, Bonap. List, 1838. (Type, *Emberiza americana*, Gmelin.)
Euspina, Cabanis, Mus. Hein. 1851, 133. (Same type.)

Gen. Char. Bill large and strong, swollen, and without any ridges; the lower mandible nearly as high as the upper; as broad at the base as the length of the gonys, and considerably broader than the upper mandible; the edges much inflexed, and shutting much within the upper mandible; the commissure considerably angulated at the base, then decidedly sinuated. The tarsus barely equal to the middle toe; the lateral toes nearly equal, not reaching to the base of the middle claw; the hind toe about equal to the middle one without its claw. The wings long and acute, reaching nearly to the middle of the tail; the

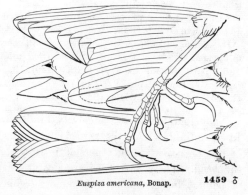

Euspiza americana, Bonap.   **1459** ♂

tertials decidedly longer than the secondaries, but much shorter than the primaries; first quill longest, the others regularly graduated. Tail considerably shorter than the wings, though moderately long; nearly even, although slightly emarginate; the outer feathers scarcely shorter. Middle of back only striped; beneath without streaks.

This genus comes nearer to *Calamospiza*, but has shorter tertials, more slender bill, weaker and more curved claws, etc.

Species.

E. americana. Top and sides of head light slate; forehead tinged with greenish-yellow. A superciliary stripe, a maxillary spot, sides of breast, and middle line of breast and belly, yellow. Chin white, throat black, shoulders chestnut. Female with the black of the throat replaced by a crescent of spots. *Hab.* Eastern Province of United States; south to New Grenada.

E. townsendi. Body throughout (including the jugulum), dark ash, tinged with brownish on the back and wings. Superciliary and maxillary stripe, chin, throat, and middle of belly, white. A maxillary line and a pectoral crescent of black spots. No chestnut shoulders. *Hab.* Chester Co., Pennsylvania.

Euspiza americana, Bonap.

BLACK-THROATED BUNTING.

Emberiza americana, Gmelin, Syst. Nat. I, 1788, 872. — Wilson, Am. Orn. III, 1811, 86, pl. iii, f. 2. — Aud. Orn. Biog. IV, 1838, 579, pl. ccclxxxiv. — Ib. Syn. 1839, 101. — Ib. Birds Am. III, 1841, 58, pl. clvi. — Max. Cab. J. VI, 1858, 341. *Fringilla (Spiza) americana*, Bonap. Obs. Wils. 1825, No. 85. *Euspiza americana*, Bonap. List, 1838 (type). — Ib. Conspectus, 1850, 469. — Baird, Birds N. Am. 1858, 494. — Samuels, 327. *Euspina americana*, Cabanis, Mus. Hein. 1851, 133 (type). *Fringilla flavicollis*, Gmelin, Syst. Nat. I, 926. "*Emberiza mexicana*, Latham," Syn. I, 1790, 412 (Gray). *Passerina nigricollis*, Vieillot. *Yellow-throated Finch*, Pennant, Arc. Zoöl. II, 374.

Sp. Char. *Male.* Sides of the head and sides and back of the neck ash ; crown tinged with yellowish-green and faintly streaked with dusky. A superciliary and short maxillary line, middle of the breast, axillaries, and edge of the wing yellow. Chin, loral region, patch on side of throat, belly, and under tail-coverts white. A black patch on the throat diminishing to the breast, and ending in a spot on the upper part of the belly. Wing-coverts chestnut. Interscapular region streaked with black ; rest of back immaculate. Length, about 6.70 ; wing, 3.50.

Female with the markings less distinctly indicated ; the black of the breast replaced by a black maxillary line and a streaked collar in the yellow of the upper part of the breast.

Hab. United States from the Atlantic to the border of the high Central Plains, south to Panama and New Granada. Xalapa (Scl. 1857, 205) ; Guatemala (Scl. Ibis, I, 18) ; Turbo, N. G. (Cassin, P. A. N. S. 1860, 140) ; Panama (Lawr. VII, 1861, 298) ; Nicaragua, Graytown (Lawr. VIII, 181) ; Veragua (Salv. 1867, 142) ; Costa Rica (Lawr. IX, 103) ; Vera Cruz, winter (Sum. M. B. S. I, 552).

Among adult males, scarcely two individuals exactly alike can be found. In some the black of the throat is continued in blotches down the middle of the breast, while in others it is restricted to a spot immediately under the head. These variations are not at all dependent upon any difference of habitat, for specimens from remote regions from each other may be found as nearly alike as any from the same locality. Some specimens from Central America are more deeply colored than North American ones, owing, no doubt, to the freshness of the plumage.

Habits. The history of the Black-throated Bunting has, until very recently, been much obscured by incorrect observations and wrong descriptions. Evidently this bird has been more or less confounded with one or two other species entirely different from it. Thus Wilson, Audubon, and Nuttall, in speaking of its nest and eggs, give descriptions applicable to *Coturniculus passerinus* or to *C. henslowi*, but which are wholly wrong as applied to those of this bird. Nuttall, whose observations of North American birds were largely made in Massachusetts, speaks of this bird being quite common in that State, where it is certainly very rare, and describes, as its song, notes that have no resemblance to those of this Bunt-

Euspiza americana.

ing, but which are a very exact description of the musical performances of the Yellow-winged Sparrow.

It is found in the eastern portion of North America, from the base of the Black Hills to the Atlantic States, and from Massachusetts to South Carolina. I am not aware that on the Atlantic it has ever been traced farther south than that State, but farther west it is found as far at least as Southwestern Texas. During winter it is found in Central America, and in Colombia, South America.

In Massachusetts it is extremely rare. Mr. Hopkins found it breeding in Williamstown, and sent me its eggs. I have also met with its nest and eggs, in a low meadow near the sea, in Hingham. In both of these instances the nest was on the ground. A specimen was shot in Newton by Mr. John Thaxter, June 26, 1857, that had all the appearance of being then in the process of incubation. Throughout Pennsylvania, and in the vicinity of Washington, these birds are quite common.

Wilson states that they are very common in the vicinity of Philadelphia, where they make their appearance in the middle of May, and where they seem to prefer level fields covered with rye-grass, clover, or timothy. They are described as more conspicuous for the quantity than for the quality of their song. This consists of three notes, sounding like *chip-chip-chē-chē-chē*. Of this unmusical ditty they are by no means parsimonious, and for nearly three months after their first arrival, every level field of grain or grass resounds with their quaint serenade. In their shape and manners, Wilson states, they bear a close resemblance to the *Emberiza citrinella* of Europe. They become silent by September, and in the course of that month depart for the southwest. It is a rare bird in South Carolina, but is very abundant in Texas, where it is also resident, and undoubtedly breeds. Audubon states that he was surprised to see how numerous they were in every open piece of ground throughout that State, especially those covered with tufts of grass. They are, he states, not so common in Ohio, and quite rare in Kentucky. They are especially abundant in the open lands of Indiana, Illinois, Wisconsin, Iowa, Missouri, Kansas, and Nebraska; and they have been found breeding as far to the west as Wyoming Territory, near to the base of the eastern range of the Rocky Mountains. Mr. Allen found this species one of the most abundant birds of Western Iowa, characterizing it as eminently a prairie species, and one of the few inhabitants of the wide open stretches.

Mr. Dresser found, early in May, numbers of these birds in the mesquite thickets near the San Antonio and Medina Rivers, and, as he found them equally numerous there in July, he naturally infers that they breed in that neighborhood. Dr. Heermann obtained some eggs which he had no doubt belonged to this species, though he was unable to secure the parent.

It has also been found in Western Texas and in the Indian Territory by Mr. J. H. Clark, in Texas by Dr. Lincecum, at the Kiowa agency by Dr. Palmer, and on the Yellowstone by Dr. Hayden.

This bird is not gregarious, always moving in pairs, and although, as they are preparing for their migrations, they congregate in particular localities, they always keep somewhat apart in family groups, and do not mingle promiscuously as do many others of this family. They are, at all times, unsuspicious and easily approached, and when fired at will often return to the same field from which they were startled. They are very partial to certain localities, and are rarely to be met with in sandy regions.

Mr. Audubon states that the notes of this species very closely resemble those of the *Emberiza miliaria* of Europe. Its unmusical notes are almost continuously repeated from sunrise to sunset. When the female is startled from her nest she creeps quietly away through the grass, and then hides herself, making no complaint, and not showing herself even if her treasures are taken from her. Their nests are constructed of coarse grasses and stems, lined with finer and similar materials. They are, in certain localities, placed on the ground, but more frequently, in many parts of the country, they are built in positions above the ground. This is almost invariably the case where they nest among the tall coarse grasses of the prairies. My attention was first called to this peculiarity by Dr. J. W. Velie, then of Rock Island, Ill. He informed me that in no instance had he found the nest of this species on the ground, but always raised a few inches above it. It was usually constructed of the tops of the red-top grasses, worked in among a bunch of thick grass, so as to make the nest quite firm. The meadows in which Dr. Velie found these nests were quite dry, so that there was no necessity for their thus building clear from the ground in order to escape being wet. I was afterwards informed by the late Mr. Robert Kennicott that his experience in regard to the nests of these birds had been invariably the same. Dr. P. R. Hoy, of Racine, is confident that these birds in Wisconsin never nest on the ground, or else very rarely, as he has never noticed their doing so. He writes that during one season he visited and made notes of nineteen different nests. Ten of these were built in gooseberry-bushes, four on thorn-bushes, three among blackberry-brambles, one on a raspberry-bush, and one on a wild rose. None were within a foot of the ground, and some were six feet from it. They have two broods in a season.

On the other hand, Mr. Ridgway informs me that in Southern Illinois the nest of this species is always placed on the ground, usually in a meadow, and that he has never found its nest placed anywhere else than on the ground, in a tuft of grass or clover. Professor Baird has had a similar experience in Pennsylvania. Mr. B. F. Goss found them nesting both in bushes and on the ground at Neosho Falls, Kansas.

The eggs of this species are of a uniform light blue color, similar in shade to the eggs of the common Bluebird, as also to those of the *Calamospiza bicolor*. They vary considerably in size, the smallest measuring .80 of an inch in length by .60 in breadth, while the larger and more common size is .90 by .70 of an inch.

Euspiza townsendi, BONAP.

TOWNSEND'S BUNTING.

Emberiza townsendi, AUD. Orn. Biog. II, 1834, 183 ; V, 90, pl. cccc. — IB. Syn. 1839. — IB. Birds Am. III, 1841, 62, pl. clvii. — NUTTALL, Man. I, (2d ed.,) 1840, 528. *Euspiza townsendi*, BON. List, 1838. — BAIRD, Birds N. Am. 1858, 495.

SP. CHAR. *Male.* Upper parts, head and neck all round, sides of body and forepart of breast, slate-blue ; the back and upper surface of wings tinged with yellowish-brown ; the interscapular region streaked with black. A superciliary and maxillary line, chin and throat, and central line of under parts from the breast to crissum, white; the edge of the wing, and a gloss on the breast and middle of belly, yellow. A black spotted line from the lower corner of the lower mandible down the side of the throat, connecting with a crescent of streaks in the upper edge of the slate portion of the breast. Length, 5.75; wing, 2.86; tail, 2.56.

HAB. Chester County, Penn. But one specimen known (in the Mus. Smith.).

It is still a question whether this is a distinct species, or only a variety of *E. americana.* There is, however, little ground for the last supposition, although its rarity is a mystery.

The original type specimen of this species, collected by Dr. J. K. Townsend, still continues to be the only one known, and has been presented by its owner, Dr. E. Michener, to the Smithsonian Institution.

HABITS. Only a single specimen of this apparently well-marked species has been observed, and nothing is known as to its history. The bird was shot by Mr. J. K. Townsend, in an old field grown up with cedar-bushes, near New Garden, Chester Co., Penn., May 11, 1833.

GENUS **HEDYMELES**, CABANIS.

? Goniaphea, BOWD. "Excurs. in Madeira, 1825," Agassiz. (Type, *Loxia ludoviciana,* according to Gray.)

Habia, REICHENB. Av. Syst. Nat. 1850, pl. xxviii. (Type, *L. ludoviciana;* not *Habia* of LESSON, 1831).

Hedymeles, CABANIS, Mus. Hein. 1851, 153. (Same type.)

GEN. CHAR. Bill very large, much swollen; lower mandible scarcely deeper than the upper; feet almost coccothraustine, tarsi and toes very short, the claws strong and much curved, though blunt. First four primaries longest, and nearly equal, abruptly longer than the fifth. Tail broad, perfectly square. *Colors:* Black, white, and red, or black, cinnamon, yellow, and white, on the male; the females brownish, streaked, with the axillars and lining of the wing yellow.

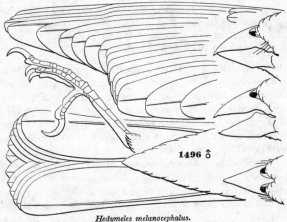

1496 ♂

Hedymeles melanocephalus.

There seems to be abundant reason for separating this genus from *Guiraca ;* the latter is, in reality, much more nearly related to *Cyanospiza,* it being impossible to define the dividing line between them.

Species and Varieties.

COMMON CHARACTERS.   ♂. Head and upper parts (except rump) deep black. Two broad bands across coverts, a large patch on base of primaries, and terminal half of inner webs of tail-feathers, pure white. Breast carmine or cinnamon; axillars and lining of wing carmine or gamboge. ♀. Black replaced by ochraceous-brown; other parts more streaked.

H. ludovicianus. Rump and lower parts white; lining of wing, and patch on breast, rosy carmine. No nuchal collar. *Female.* Lining of wing saffron-yellow; breast with numerous streaks. *Hab.* Eastern Province of North America, south, in winter, to Ecuador.

H. melanocephalus. Rump and lower parts cinnamon-rufous; lining of wing and middle of abdomen gamboge-yellow. A nuchal collar of rufous. *Female.* Lining of wing lemon-yellow; breast without streaks; abdomen tinged with lemon-yellow.

Crown continuous black. No post-ocular rufous stripe. *Hab.* Mountains of Mexico, and Central Rocky Mountains of United States.

var. *melanocephalus*.

Crown divided by a longitudinal rufous stripe; a distinct post-ocular stripe of the same. *Hab.* Western Province of United States, south, in winter, to Colima   .   .   .   .   var. *capitalis*.

Hedymeles ludovicianus, SWAINSON.

ROSE-BREASTED GROSBEAK.

Loxia ludoviciana, LINN. Syst. Nat. I, 1766, 306. — WILSON, Am. Orn. II, 1810, 135, pl. xvii, f. 2. *Guiraca ludoviciana,* SWAINSON, Phil. Mag. I, 1827, 438. — BONAP. List, 1838. — IB. Consp. 1850, 501. — BAIRD, Birds N. Am. 1858, 497. — SAMUELS, 328. *Fringilla ludoviciana,* AUD. Orn. Biog. II, 1834, 166; V, 513, pl. cxxvii. *Pyrrhula ludoviciana,* SAB. Zoöl. App. Franklin's Narr. *Coccothraustes ludoviciana,* RICH. List, Pr. Br. Ass. 1837. *Coccoborus ludovicianus,* AUD. Syn. 1839, 133. — IB. Birds Am. III, 1841, 209, pl. 205. — MAX. Cab. J. VI, 1858, 267. "*Goniaphea ludoviciana,* BOWDICH." *Hedymeles ludoviciana,* CABANIS, Mus. Hein. 1851, 153. *Fringilla punicea,* GMELIN, Syst. Nat. I, 1788, 921 (male). *Loxia obscura,* GMELIN, I, 1788, 862. *Loxia rosea,* WILSON, Am. Orn. pl. xvii, f. 2. *Coccothraustes rubricollis,* VIEILLOT, Galerie des Ois. I, 1824, 67, pl. lviii.

SP. CHAR. Upper parts generally, with head and neck all round, glossy black. A broad crescent across the upper part of the breast, extending narrowly down to the belly, axillaries, and under wing-coverts, carmine. Rest of under parts, rump and upper tail-coverts, middle wing-coverts, spots on the tertiaries and inner great wing-coverts, basal half of primaries and secondaries, and a large patch on the ends of the inner webs of the outer three tail-feathers, pure white. Length, 8.50 inches; wing, 4.15.

Female without the white of quills, tail, and rump, and without any black or red. Above yellowish-brown streaked with darker; head with a central stripe above, and a superciliary on each side, white. Beneath dirty white, streaked with brown on the breast and sides. Under wing-coverts and axillars saffron-yellow.

In the male the black feathers of the back and sides of the neck have a subterminal white bar. There are a few black spots on the sides of the breast just below the red.

The young male of the year is like the female, except in having the axillaries, under wing-coverts, and a trace of a patch on the breast, light rose-red.

The depth of the carmine tint on the under parts varies a good deal in different specimens, but it is always of the same rosy hue.

HAB. Eastern United States to the Missouri plains; south to Ecuador. Honduras (MOORE, P. Z. S. 1859, 58); Xalapa (SCL. 1859, 365); Bogota (SCL. 1855, 154); Cordova (SCL. 1856, 301); Guatemala (SCL. Ibis, I, 17); Cuba (CAB. J. VI, 9); Ecuador (SCL. 1860, 298); Costa Rica (CAB. J. 61, 71); (LAWR. IX, 102); Panama (LAWR. VII, 1861, 297); Vera Cruz, winter (SUM. M. B. S. I, 552); Yucatan (LAWR. Ann. IX, 210).

HABITS. The Rose-breasted Grosbeak, during the summer months, appears to have a widely extended area of distri-
bution, though nowhere a very abundant species, and one of somewhat irregular occurrence. It is found as far to the east as Nova Scotia, to the north as Selkirk Settlement and the valley of the Sas-katchewan, and to the west as Nebraska. It winters in great numbers in Guate-mala. In the last-named country, while abundant in the Vera Paz, it was not found at Dueñas, but was a common cage-bird in the city of Guatemala. It

Hedymeles melanocephalus.

was also found common at Herradura, in Colombia, South America, by Mr. C. W. Wyatt.

This bird was noticed on a single occasion near San Antonio by Mr. Dresser, but was not observed by Dr. Woodhouse in Texas, or in the Indian Territory. Sumichrast did not meet with it in Vera Cruz. At St. Stephens, N. B., Mr. Boardman found this species a regular summer visitant, but rare, nor did Mr. Verrill find it common in the western part of Maine. In Mas-sachusetts this bird becomes more common, but is nowhere very abun-dant. It has been met with in various places in the eastern part of the State, but rarely, and only in restricted localities. In the western part of the State it is more numerous, as well as throughout the whole of the Connecti-cut Valley. At Springfield, Mr. Allen notes it as a summer visitant, breed-ing in the open woods, but not abundant. He is of the opinion that during the past twenty-five years this bird has increased in numbers in all parts of the State. Mr. Allen found this bird quite common in Southern Indiana, in Northern Illinois, and in Western Iowa, where he found it fre-quent in the groves along the streams. Dr. Coues mentions it as rare and only migratory in South Carolina. Mr. McIlwraith gives it as a summer resident in the vicinity of Hamilton, Canada, where it is very generally dis-tributed throughout the open woods, arriving there the second week in May. It is also found throughout Vermont, in favorable situations in open woods, on the borders of streams. It is not uncommon in the vicinity of Randolph, where it regularly breeds.

Wilson, who enjoyed but few opportunities of studying the habits of this species, states that it eagerly feeds on the ripe fruit of the sour gum-tree. He was also aware of its fine song, its value as a caged bird, and that it frequently sings during the night.

Sir John Richardson met with a single specimen of this bird near the Saskatchewan during his first expedition with Sir John Franklin, but did not afterwards meet with it. He states that it frequents the deep recesses of the forests, and there sings a clear, mellow, and harmonious song.

Nuttall appears to have seen little or nothing of this bird, except in confinement. He describes it as thriving very well in a cage, and as a melodious and indefatigable warbler, frequently passing the greater part of the night in singing, with great variety of tones. It is said, while thus earnestly engaged, to mount on tiptoe, as if seemingly in an ecstasy of enthusiasm and delight at the unrivalled harmony of its own voice. These notes, he adds, are wholly warbled, now loud and clear, now with a querulous and now with a sprightly air, and finally lower and more pathetic. In Mr. Nuttall's opinion it has no superior in song, except the Mocking-Bird.

Mr. Say met with these birds in the spring, on the banks of the Missouri, and afterwards, on the 5th of August, at Pembina in the 49th degree of latitude.

This bird arrives in Eastern Massachusetts about the 15th of May, and leaves in September. It nests during the first week in June.

Mr. Audubon states that he has frequently observed this species, early in the month of March, in the lower parts of Louisiana, making its way eastward, and has noticed the same circumstance both at Henderson, Ky., and at Cincinnati, O. At this period it passes at a considerable height in the air. He never saw it in the maritime parts of Georgia or Carolina, but they have been procured in the mountainous parts of those States. On the banks of the Schuylkill, early in May, he has observed this bird feeding on the tender buds of the trees. When in Texas, in 1837, Mr. Audubon also found it very abundant in April.

Dr. Bachman, quoted by Audubon, states that, having slightly wounded a beautiful male of this species, he kept it three years in confinement. It very soon became quite tame, fed, in an open room, on moistened bread. It was at once reconciled to live in a cage, and fed readily on various kinds of food, but preferred Indian meal and hemp-seed. It was also very fond of insects, and ate grasshoppers and crickets with peculiar relish. It watched the flies with great apparent interest, and often snatched at and secured the wasps that ventured within its cage. During bright moonshiny nights it sang sweetly, but not loudly, remaining in the same position on its perch. When it sang in the daytime it was in the habit of vibrating its wings, in the manner of the Mocking-Bird. It was a lively and a gentle companion for three years, but suffered from cold in severe wintry weather, and finally died from this cause. It would frequently escape from its cage, and never exhibited the least desire to leave him, but always returned to the house at night. It sang about eight weeks, and the rest of the year had only a faint *chuck*.

This Grosbeak builds in low trees on the edge of woods, frequently in small groves on the banks of streams. Their nests are coarsely built, with a base composed of waste stubble, fragments of leaves, and stems of plants. These are intermingled with and strengthened by twigs and coarser stems. They have a diameter of eight inches, and a height of three and a half. The upper portion of the nest is usually composed of dry *usnea* mosses, mingled with a few twigs, and lined with finer twigs. Its cavity is three inches in diameter and one in depth, being quite shallow for so large a nest.

The eggs bear some resemblance to those of the *Pyrangæ*, but are usually much larger, though they vary greatly in size. Their ground-color is usually a light but well-marked shade of verdigris-green, varying occasionally to a greenish-white, and are marked, more or less, over their entire surface, with blotches of reddish-brown. They vary in length from 1.05 to .90 of an inch, and from .78 to .60.

During incubation, and in the presence of its mate, this Grosbeak is a persistent and enthusiastic singer, and, at times, carries his love of song so far as to betray his nest. This is more especially so when he relieves his mate, takes her place on the nest, and then, apparently oblivious of the danger of lifting up his voice in song when upon so responsible a duty, attracts, by his melody, the oölogist to his treasures.

Dr. Hoy, of Racine, supplies some interesting information in regard to the habits and nesting of this species. On the 15th of June, within six miles of that city, he found seven nests, all within a space of not over five acres, and he was assured that each year they resort to the same locality and nest thus socially. Six of these nests were in thorn-trees, all were within six to ten feet from the ground, and all were in the central portion of the top. Three of the four parent birds sitting on the nests were males, and this he was told was usually the case. When a nest was disturbed, all the neighboring Grosbeaks gathered around and appeared equally interested. Both nest and eggs so closely resemble those of the Tanagers that it is difficult to distinguish them. Their position is, however, usually different, the Grosbeaks generally nesting in the central portion of a small tree, the Tanagers' being placed on a horizontal limb.

Hedymeles melanocephalus, SWAINSON.

BLACK-HEADED GROSBEAK.

Guiraca melanocephala, Sw. Syn. Mex. Birds Philos. Mag. I, 1827, 438. — BON. List, 1838. — IB. Consp. 1850, 502. — BAIRD, Birds N. Am. 1858, 498. — COOPER & SUCKLEY, 206. *Coccothraustes melanocephala*, RICH. List, Pr. Brit. Ass. for 1836, 1837. *Fringilla melanocephala*, AUD. Orn. Biog. IV, 1838, 519, pl. ccclxxiii. *Coccoborus melanocephalus*, AUD. Synopsis, 1839, 133. — IB. Birds Am. III, 1841, 214, pl. 206. — HEERM. X, S, 51 (nest). — COOPER, Orn. Cal. I, 228. *Goniaphea melanocephala*, SCLATER ? *Hedymeles melanocephala*, CABANIS, Mus. Hein. 1851, 153. *Fringilla xanthomaschalis*, WAGLER, Isis, 1831, 525. *Pitylus guttatus*, LESSON, Rev. Zoöl. II, 1839, 102. ? *Guiraca tricolor*, LESSON, Rev. Zoöl. II, 1839, 102.

Sp. Char. *Male.* Head above and on the sides, with chin, back, wings, and tail, black.
A well-marked collar on the hind neck all round (and in var. *capitalis* a more or less distinct median stripe on crown, and one behind the eye), edges of interscapular feathers,
rump, and under parts generally pale brownish-orange, almost light cinnamon. Middle
of belly, axillaries, and under wing-coverts, yellow. Belly just anterior to the anus,
under tail-coverts, a large blotch at the end of the inner webs of first and second tail-
feathers, a band across the middle and greater wing-coverts, some spots on the ends of
the tertiaries, the basal portions of all the quills, and the outer three primaries near the
tips, white. Length nearly 8 inches; wing, 4.25; tail, 3.50.

Female has the chin, sides of throat, and superciliary stripe white; the black markings
replaced by olivaceous-brown; the cinnamon markings paler, and almost white; the
white of wings more restricted; that of tail wanting. Usually there are few or no
streaks beneath as in *ludovicianus* (faint ones on flanks); in young males, however, they
are more appreciable. The lemon or gamboge yellow axillars and under coverts in all
ages and stages separate this species from *H. ludovicianus*, the female and young of which
have those regions of a saffron or fulvous yellow.

Hab. High Central Plains from Yellowstone to the Pacific. Table-lands of Mexico.
Xalapa (Scl. 1859, 365); Orizaba (Scl. 1857, 213); Vera Cruz, Alpine and plateau,
breeding (Sum. M. B. S. I, 551).

This bird, in its range of habitat, appears to be represented by two varieties, which, however, run into each other, so that it is often difficult to determine to which variety specimens from intermediate regions should be
referred.

Taking the series from Eastern Mexico (Orizaba and Mirador) and northward along the Rocky Mountains of the United States, we find the black of
the head continuous, sharply defined by a gently curved outline behind, and
without a trace of either the vertex or post-ocular stripes. This is the true
melanocephalus, as restricted, and may be regarded as the Rocky Mountain
form. The most western specimen is 11,241, from Fort Bridger; the most
northern (19,355), from Stinking River, Northern Wyoming. All specimens
from the Pacific coast eastward to the western base of the Rocky Mountains,
including Cape St. Lucas and Western Mexico south to Colima, differ from
the Rocky Mountain series in having the posterior outline of the black hood
ragged, and irregularly indented by the rufous of the nape, which always
extends in a quite broad stripe toward the eye, along the side of the occiput,
and quite frequently forms a conspicuous median vertex stripe, though the
latter feature is sometimes not distinct. These differences are observable
only in the males, and, although apparently slight, are yet sufficiently constant to justify distinguishing them as races. The Rocky Mountain form
being the true *melanocephalus*, the name *capitalis* is proposed for the western
one.

Habits. This bird occurs from the high Central Plains to the Pacific,
and from the northern portions of Washington Territory to the table-lands
of Mexico. Mr. Ridgway found this species abundant, during the summer
months, in all the fertile wooded districts along the entire route of the
survey. At Sacramento it was common in the willow copses, and was ob-

served in the greatest numbers, in May, in the rich valley of the Truckee, in
company with Bullock's Oriole, the Louisiana Tanager, and other species,
feeding upon the buds of the "grease-wood." It principally inhabits the
willows along the rivers, and the shrubbery skirting the streams of the
mountain cañons.   In its manners and notes Mr. Ridgway regards this
bird as an exact counterpart of the eastern species, the *Hedymeles ludovicianus*, its song being by no means superior.   The peculiar and very odd *click*
of the *ludovicianus* is said to be equally characteristic of this bird.   Mr.
Ridgway met with its nests in willows, about ten feet from the ground.   He
had evidence that the male bird assists the female in the duties of incubation.

This bird, though a common summer resident in the Great Salt Lake Valley, had all migrated, according to Mr. Allen, by the 1st of September.   It
is well known there as the Peabird, from its fondness for green peas, of
which it is very destructive.

According to Dr. Cooper, this Grosbeak arrives in California, near San
Diego, about April 12.   It is numerous during the summer throughout the
mountains both of the coast and of the Sierra Nevada, and extends its migrations at least as far as Puget Sound.   It is often kept in confinement
on account of its loud, sweet song.   In the Coast Mountains, in May, its
music is said to be delightful, the males vying with each other from the tops
of the trees, and making the hills fairly ring with their melody.

Dr. Cooper found a nest of this bird, May 12, at the eastern base of the
Coast Range.   It was built in a low horizontal branch of an alder, and consisted of a few sticks and weeds, very loosely put together, with a lining of
grass and roots.   The eggs, three in number, he describes as of a pale bluish-
white ground, thickly spotted with brown, more densely near the larger end.
Their size he gives as .95 by .70 of an inch.

Dr. Cooper also states that they frequent the ground in search of food, but
also live much on trees, feeding on their buds.   They are not gregarious,
assembling only in family groups in the fall.   They do not fly high, nor do
they make any noise in flying.

He has observed these birds at Santa Cruz April 12, or as early as he saw
them at San Diego, three hundred and fifty miles farther south, and has
found a young bird fledged as early as May 23.

Dr. Coues speaks of this bird as an abundant summer resident of Arizona,
where it arrives by the first of May, and remains until the latter part of
September.   He speaks of it as frequenting the thick brush of the ravines
and the cottonwood and willow copses of the river-bottoms.   Its call-note
resembles that of *Lophortyx gambeli*.   Its song, he says, is superb, — a
powerful, but melodious succession of clear, rich, rolling notes, reminding
one somewhat of the *Icterus baltimore*.

Dr. Suckley speaks of this bird being sparingly found in the vicinity of
Fort Steilacoom, Puget Sound, where he obtained two specimens.

Dr. Heermann speaks of the song of this bird as clear and musical, and as very closely resembling that of our *Turdus migratorius*. He describes its nests as formed with very little care, of twigs loosely thrown together, and lined with roots, placed in the branches of bushes. The eggs, four in number, he describes as of a greenish-blue ground, marked with irregular spots of umber-brown, varying in intensity of shade.

The song of the western species is described by Mr. Nuttall as fully equal, if not superior, to that of the Rose-breasted. He met with it on the central table-lands of the Rocky Mountains, along the upper branches of the Colorado River, where he found it frequenting the thick groves of the streams, and where, throughout its dense forests, the powerful song and the inimitable voice of this "most delightful Finch" cheered that naturalist amidst the wildest desolation of that "forest primeval," where this superb vocalist made the woods echo and re-echo to its untiring song. These notes, greatly resembling those of its eastern relative, may be heard from early dawn almost even to the close of the following night. These are described as loud, varied, high-toned, and melodious, rising and falling with the sweetest cadence, fascinating the listener most powerfully with sensations of a pleasing sadness, its closing note seeming like a shrill cry of appealing distress, and then sinking faintly on the ear. It is described as very shy and retiring in its habits, and can be but very rarely observed closely while thus engaged in song. On these occasions the bird is said to sit up conspicuously on a lofty bough, near the summit of the tree, his throat swelling with the excitement, and seeming to take a great delight in the sound of his own music.

Mr. Sumichrast found this bird on the Plateau of Mexico, and also in the alpine regions of Vera Cruz. It was found to the height of 8,300 feet, and never lower than 4,000.

The eggs of this species are of an oblong-oval shape, one end but slightly more rounded than the other, and measure 1.10 of an inch in length by .65 in breadth. They have a bluish-green ground, blotched and splashed with markings of a rusty-brown, for the most part more numerous about the larger end.

Genus GUIRACA, Swainson.

Guiraca, Swainson, Zoöl. Jour. III, Nov. 1827, 350. (Type, *Loxia cærulea*, L.)
Coccoborus, Swainson, Class. Birds, II, 1837, 277. (Same type.)

Gen. Char. Bill very large, nearly as high as long; the culmen slightly curved, with a rather sharp ridge; the commissure conspicuously angulated just below the nostril, the posterior leg of the angle nearly as long as the anterior, both nearly straight. Lower jaw deeper than the upper, and extending much behind the forehead; the width greater than the length of the gonys, considerably wider than the upper jaw. A prominent knob in the roof of the mouth. Tarsi shorter than the middle toe; the outer toe a little longer, reaching not quite to the base of the middle claw; hind toe rather longer than to this base. Wings long, reaching the middle of the tail; the secondaries and tertials nearly equal; the second quill longest; the first less than the fourth. Tail very nearly even, shorter than the wings.

The single North American species of this genus has no near relative in tropical America ; indeed, no other species at present known can be said to be strictly congeneric.

In all essential details of external structure, and in every respect as to habits and nidification, the type of the genus (*G. cærulea*) is

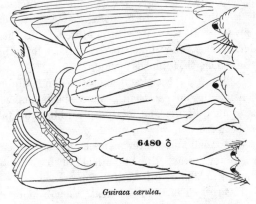

6480 ♂

Guiraca cærulea.

much more like the species of *Cyanospiza* than those of *Hedymeles*, with which latter it has usually been included.

Guiraca cærulea, SWAINSON.

BLUE GROSBEAK.

Loxia cærulea, LINN. Syst. Nat. I, 1766, 306. — WILSON, Am. Orn. III, 1811, 78, pl. xxiv, f. 6. — ? WAGLER, Isis, 1831, 525. *Guiraca cærulea*, SWAINSON, Birds Mex. in Phil. Mag. I, 1827, 438. — BAIRD, Birds N. Am. 1858, 499. — COOPER, Orn. Cal. I, 230. *Fringilla cærulea*, AUD. Orn. Biog. II, 1834, 140 ; V, 508, pl. cxxii. *Coccoborus cæruleus*, Sw. Birds II, 1837, 277. — AUD. Syn. 1839. — IB. Birds Am. III, 1841, 204, pl. cciv. — CABANIS, Mus. Hein. 1851, 152. — FINSCH, Abh. Nat. Brem. 1870, 339 (Mazatlan). *Cyanoloxia cærulea*, BP. Conspectus, 1850, 502. *Goniaphœa cærulea*, BP. *Blue Grosbeak*, PENNANT, Arc. Zoöl. II, 1785, 351.

SP. CHAR. Brilliant blue; darker across the middle of the back. Space around base of the bill and lores, with tail-feathers, black. Two bands on the wing across the tips of the middle and secondary coverts, with outer edges of tertiaries, reddish-brown, or perhaps chestnut. Feathers on the posterior portion of the under surface tipped narrowly with grayish-white. Length, 7.25 ; wing, 3.50 ; tail, 2.80.

Guiraca cærulea.

Female yellowish-brown above, brownish-yellow beneath ; darkest across the breast. Wing-coverts and tertials broadly edged with brownish-yellow. Sometimes a faint trace of blue on the tail. The young resembles the female.

HAB. More southern United States from Atlantic to Pacific, south to Costa Rica. Xalapa (SCL. 1859, 365) ; Oaxaca (SCL. 1859, 378) ; Cordova (SCL. 1856, 301) ; Cuba (CAB. J. IV, 9) ; Vera Paz (SALVIN, Ibis, III, 352) ; Costa Rica (LAWR. IX, 102) ; Vera Cruz, winter (SUM. M. B. S. I, 552) ; Yucatan (LAWR. IX, 200).

The species described as *Cyanospiza parellina* in the Birds of North America, but which so far has not been actually detected north of Mexico, is a miniature *Guiraca*, more related, however, to the *G. concreta* than to *cœrulea*. It is easily distinguished from the latter by more lobed bill, darker back and under parts, absence of rufous wing-bands, and inferior size. Length, 5 inches; wing, 2.50.

Males from the Pacific coast region (California, Colima, etc.) have tails considerably longer than eastern specimens, while those from California are of a much lighter and less purplish blue, the difference being much the same as between *Sialia sialis* and *S. azurea*.

Autumnal and winter males have the feathers generally, especially on the back and breast, tipped with light brown, obscuring somewhat the blue, though producing a beautiful appearance.

HABITS. The Blue Grosbeak, though more a bird of the Southern States, is also one both of an extended and of an irregular distribution. It was even met with one year in the vicinity of Calais, Me., although none have been known to occur in any part of the country between that point and New York City. It is found from the Atlantic to the Pacific coast.

The extent to which it is distributed throughout California is inferred, rather than known. Dr. Cooper noticed one at Fort Mohave, May 6, and afterwards saw many more frequenting the trees and bushes along the river, and singing a lively song, which he compares with that of the *Carpodacus frontalis*. He also saw them at Los Angeles and at Santa Barbara, and states that they were found at Pit River, in the extreme northeastern part of the State, by Dr. Newberry. They were observed to frequent the banks of streams crossing the great interior plains and deserts, where there was little vegetation except a few bushes.

The Blue Grosbeak was only met with by Mr. Ridgway and his party at Sacramento. It does not occur — or, if so, it was not seen — in the interior so far to the north as the route of Mr. King's survey. At Sacramento it was found frequenting the same localities as the *Cyanospiza amœna*, and appeared to be characteristic of the cottonwood copses. Their nests were found between the 18th and the 29th of June, and were all in similar situations. These were built in small cottonwood-trees, on the edge of the copse, and were all about six feet from the ground.

Mr. John Burroughs, in one of his charming popular essays [1] on the general habits of our birds, refers to their occasional preference, in sites for their nests, of the borders of frequented roadsides, and mentions finding a nest of the Blue Grosbeak among the trees that line one of the main streets and fashionable drives leading out of Washington City, less than half a mile from the boundary. There, he states, this bird, which, according to Audubon's observations, is shy and recluse, affecting remote marshes and the borders of large ponds of stagnant water, had placed its nest in the lowest twig

[1] Atlantic Monthly, XXIII, p. 707.

of the lowest branch of a large sycamore immediately over a great thorough-fare, and so near the ground that a person standing in a cart or sitting on a horse could have reached it with his hand. The nest was composed mainly of fragments of newspaper and stalks of grass, and though so low, was re-markably well concealed by one of the peculiar clusters of twigs and leaves which characterize this tree. The nest contained young when he discovered it, and though the parent birds were much annoyed by his loitering about beneath the tree, they paid but little attention to the stream of vehicles that was constantly passing. It was a source of wonder to him when the birds could have built it, as they are so much shyer when building than at other times. They must have worked mostly in the early morning, when they could have the place all to themselves. The same observer also noticed another pair of Blue Grosbeaks that had built their nest in a graveyard within the city limits. This was placed in a low bush, and the male con-tinued to sing at intervals till the young were ready to fly. The song of this bird he describes as a rapid, intricate warble, like that of the Indigo Bird, though stronger and louder. Indeed, these two birds so much resemble each other in color, form, voice, manner, and general habits, that, were it not for the difference in size, — the Grosbeak being nearly as large again as the Indigo Bird, — he thinks it would be a hard matter to tell them apart. The females of both birds are clad in the same reddish-brown suits, as are also the young during the first season.

The nest of this species has also been found built in a tree within the grounds of the Smithsonian Institution, Washington.

The only time I ever met with this species was at Carlisle, Penn., in June, 1843. The previous month Professor Baird had found its nest in a low tree, in open ground, and we found these birds still frequenting the same grounds, where we found another nest containing three eggs. It was in a low thorn-tree on the edge of a wood, but standing out in open ground. The nest was about five feet from the ground.

The Smithsonian specimens are from Carlisle, Penn., obtained in April, May, and August; from Georgia, Texas, New Mexico, Nebraska, Mexico, etc. Mr. Lawrence enumerates this among the birds found near New York City. Mr. Dresser found it common near Matamoras in July and August. It was breeding there, though, owing to the lateness of the season, he was unable to procure any of its eggs. Dr. Coues speaks of it as generally distributed in Arizona, but nowhere very common. A single specimen was taken near Fort Whipple, August 10. Turnbull regarded it as a rare straggler to the southern counties of Pennsylvania and New Jersey, arriving there in the middle of May. Dr. Woodhouse found it common in the Indian Territory and Texas. Lieutenant Couch mentions seeing this bird first near Monterey, the male always preceding the female. He speaks of them as exceedingly tame. Mr. J. H. Clark states that this bird was not often seen, and, when observed, was generally solitary, preferring the dark ravines and the cañons on the mountain-sides. It is not mentioned by Sumichrast as a bird of Vera Cruz, but was found during the winter months at Oaxaca, Mexico, by Mr. Boucard.

Mr. O. Salvin states (Ibis, III. p. 352) that he found this species, though not of very common occurrence, pretty generally distributed, in winter, throughout Vera Paz. He met with it on the Plains of Salamà, and all the collections from the warmer districts to the northward of Coban contained specimens. It was found by Mr. George H. White near Mexico.

Wilson speaks of this bird as retired and solitary, and also as a scarce species, and as having but few notes, its most common one being a loud *chuck*. He was, however, aware that at times they have a few low sweet-toned notes. He mentions their being kept in Charleston in cages, but as seldom singing in confinement. He fed a caged bird of this species on Indian corn, which it easily broke with its powerful bill; also on hemp-seed, millet, and berries. He speaks of them as timid, watchful, silent, and active.

Mr. Audubon was, apparently, somewhat at fault in regard to the pecu-liarities of this species. His accounts of the eggs of the *Pyranga œstiva* are entirely inapplicable to that species, and, so far as I know, apply to no other bird than the Blue Grosbeak, to which they exactly correspond. He makes no mention and gives no description of the eggs of the latter. His statements as to the nest appear to be correct.

Dr. Bachman kept several of these birds in an aviary; two of these mated, took possession of the nest of a Cardinal Grosbeak, which they drove off, and laid two eggs that were unfortunately destroyed. In the aviary these birds were silent. Mr. Audubon kept one, in confinement, with him in Edin-burgh. It had been raised from the nest. This bird frequently sang in the night, and before dawn. It was extremely tame, coming out or going into its cage at pleasure, perching on the head-dress of Mrs. Audubon, or on the heads of other members of the family, alighting on the table and feeding on almost anything given to it. If a gold or silver coin was thrown upon the table he would go to it, take it up in his bill, and apparently toss it about with pleasure. After bathing he would go to the fire and perch on the fender to dry himself. He would attack other birds, if put into the cage with him. In feeding he sometimes held his food in his claws like a Hawk.

The eggs of this bird are of a uniform light-blue color, and most resemble those of the *Sialia arctica*, but are larger and of a lighter color. Their color is quite fugitive, and readily fades into a dull white upon even a slight ex-posure to light. They are of an oval shape, equally rounded at either end, and measure .98 of an inch in length by .65 in breadth.

Genus CYANOSPIZA, BAIRD.

Passerina, VIEILLOT, Analyse, 1816.   Not of LINNÆUS, used in Botany.
Spiza, BONAPARTE, Synopsis, 1828.   Not of 1825.
Cyanospiza, BAIRD.   (Type, *Tanagra cyanea*, L.)

GEN. CHAR. Bill deep at the base, compressed; the upper outline considerably curved; the commissure rather concave, with an obtuse, shallow lobe in the middle. Gonys slightly curved. Feet moderate; tarsus about equal to middle toe; the outer lateral toe barely longer than the inner, its claw falling short of the base of the middle; hind toe about equal to the middle without claw. Claws all much curved, acute. Wings long and pointed, reaching nearly to the middle of the tail; the second and third quills longest. Tail appreciably shorter than the wings; rather narrow, very nearly even.

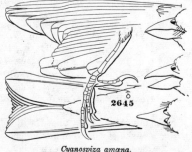

Cyanospiza amœna.

The species of this genus are all of very small size and of showy plumage, usually blue, red, or green, in well-defined areas. The females plain olivaceous or brownish; paler beneath.

Species.

A. Head all round uniform blue; eyelids not different, commissure distinctly sinuated.

　　a. Lower parts blue; no white bands on wing.

　　　1. C. cyanea. Entirely deep ultramarine-blue, more purplish on the head, somewhat greenish posteriorly. *Female* dull umber above, grayish-white beneath, the breast with obsolete darker streaks. *Hab.* Eastern Province of United States, south, in winter, to Panama.

　　b. Lower parts white, the breast rufous. One broad and distinct, and a narrower, more obsolete white band on the wing.

　　　2. C. amœna. Head and neck, all round, and rump, bright greenish-blue; back, wings, and tail more dusky; a narrow white collar between rufous of the breast and blue of the throat. *Female* grayish-brown above, the rump tinged with blue. Beneath dull whitish, the breast and jugulum more buffy. *Hab.* Western Province of United States.

B. Head party-colored; eyelids different from adjoining portions. Commissure hardly appreciably sinuated, or even concave.

　　a. Back and breast similar in color. Upper mandible much less deep than lower, the commissure concave.

　　　3. C. versicolor. Back and breast dark wine-purple, occiput and throat claret-red, forehead and rump purplish-blue. Eyelids purplish-red. *Female* fulvous-gray above, uniform pale fulvous below. *Hab.* Northern Mexico, and adjacent borders of United States; Cape St. Lucas.

　　b. Back and breast very different in color. Upper mandible scarcely less deep than the lower, the commissure straight, or slightly sinuated.

　　　4. C. ciris. Lower parts vermilion-red. Back green, crown blue; rump dull red; eyelids red. *Female* dull green above, light olivaceous-yellow below.   *Hab.* Gulf States of United States, and whole of Middle America.

5. **C. leclancheri.**[1]   Lower parts gamboge-yellow.   Back blue, crown green, rump blue; eyelids yellow.   *Female* not seen.   *Hab.* Southern Mexico.

Cyanospiza cyanea, BAIRD.

INDIGO BIRD.

Tanagra cyanea, LINN. Syst. Nat. I, 1766, 315.   *Emberiza cyanea*, GM. Syst. Nat. I, 1788, 876.   *Fringilla cyanea*, WILSON, I, 1810, 100, pl. vi, f. 5. — AUD. Orn. Biog. I, 1832, 377 ; V, 503, pl. lxxiv.   *Passerina cyanea*, VIEILL. Dict.   *Spiza cyanea*, BON. List, 1838. — IB. Consp. 1850, 474. — AUD. Syn. 1839, 109. — IB. Birds Am. III, 1841, 96, pl. clxx.   *Cyanospiza cyanea*, BAIRD, Birds N. Am. 1858, 505.— SAMUELS, 330.   *? Emberiza cyanella*, GM. I, 1788, 887.   *? Emberiza cœrulea*, GM. Syst. Nat. I, 1788, 876.   *Indigo Bunting,* and *Blue Bunting,* PENNANT and LATHAM.

SP. CHAR.   *Male.* Blue, tinged with ultramarine on the head, throat, and middle of breast; elsewhere with verdigris-green.   Lores and anterior angle of chin velvet-black. Wing-feathers brown, edged externally with dull bluish-brown.   *Female.* Brown above ; whitish, obscurely streaked or blotched with brownish-yellow, beneath ; tinged with blue on shoulders, edges of larger feathers, and on rump.   Immature males similar, variously blotched with blue.   Very young birds streaked beneath.   Length, about 5.75 inches ; wing, nearly 3.00.

HAB.   Eastern United States to the Missouri ; south to Guatemala.   Oaxaca (SCL. 1859, 379) ; Cordova (SCL. 1856, 304) ; Guatemala (SCL. Ibis, I, 17) ; Cuba (CAB. J. IV, 8) ; Costa Rica (CAB. JOUR. 1861, 4 ; LAWR. IX, 103) ; Vera Cruz, winter (SUM. M. B. S. I, 552).

In this species, which may be considered the type of the genus, the tail is slightly emarginate ; the second quill is longest, the first shorter than the fourth.

HABITS.   The common Indigo Bird of the Eastern States is found in nearly uniform and tolerable abundance in various parts of the United States, from the valley of the Missouri to the Atlantic, and from Florida to New Brunswick.   It is a summer visitant, but rare, in Eastern Maine, but is common in the western part of the State, where it arrives early in May, and where it breeds.   Mr. Allen speaks of it as not very common in the vicinity of Springfield, Mass., arriving there about the middle of May, and breeding in gardens, orchards, and the edges of woods, and making its nests in bushes. It leaves there about the middle of September.

In the eastern part of the State it is very unequally distributed.   In certain localities it has not been met with, but in other favorite places it seems to be quite common, and to be on the increase.   In the gardens of Brookline and Roxbury they are comparatively quite abundant.   Mr. Maynard gives May 10 as the earliest date of their coming.   He also states that in the autumn they are found in flocks, and frequent roadsides, high sandy fields,

---

[1] *Cyanospiza leclancheri.*   *Spiza leclancheri,* LAFR. Mag. Zoöl. 1841, pl. xxii. — LESS. R. Z. 1842, 74.

and rocky pastures, which I have never noticed. According to Dr. Coues, it is common and breeds as far south as Columbia, S. C., and, according to Mr. McIlwraith, it is a common summer resident in the neighborhood of Hamilton, Canada West. Specimens have been procured as far west as Fort Riley in Kansas. It passes the winter in Guatemala, where it is quite abundant, though a very large proportion of specimens received from there, in collections, are immature birds. It was not found in Vera Cruz by Mr. Sumichrast, nor is it given by Mr. Allen as found by him in Western Iowa, while it was common both in Northern Illinois and in Indiana. It was, however, found by Mr. Allen, in Kansas, in considerable numbers, near Leavenworth, in the spring of 1871. It was not met with by Mr. Dresser in Southwestern Texas, though Dr. Woodhouse found it quite common in the prairies of that State, where its pleasant song was heard in the timber on their edges, or in the thickets on the borders of the streams in the Indian Territory, where it was quite abundant. It was not observed on the Mexican Boundary Survey.

These birds were found, by Mr. Boucard, abundant throughout the State of Oaxaca, Mexico, having been taken both among the mountains near Totontepec, and among the hot lowlands near Plaza Vicente.

According to Wilson, this bird is not noticed in Pennsylvania much, if any, earlier than its first appearance in New England, and it leaves at about the same time. He observed it in great abundance both in South Carolina and Georgia.

In manners it is active and sprightly, and its song is vigorous and pleasant. It is considered a better singer than either the *ciris* or the *amœna*. It usually stations itself, in singing, on some high position, the top of a tree or of a chimney, where it chants its peculiar and charming song for quite a space of time. Its song consists of a repetition of short notes, at first loud and rapid, but gradually less frequent, and becoming less and less distinct. It sings with equal animation both in May and July, and its song may be occasionally heard even into August, and not less during the noonday heat of summer than in the cool of the morning. Nuttall describes its animated song as a lively strain, composed of a repetition of short notes. The most common of its vocal expressions sounds like *tshe-tshe-tshe*, repeated several times. While the female is engaged in the cares of incubation, or just as the brood has appeared, the song of the male is said to be much shortened. In the village of Cambridge, Nuttall observed one of this species regularly chanting its song from the point of a forked lightning-rod, on a very tall house.

The Indigo Bird usually builds its nest in the centre of a low thick bush. The first nest I ever met with was built in a thick sumach that had grown up at the bottom of a deep excavation, some fifteen feet below the surface, and but two feet above the base of the shrub. This same nest was occupied five successive summers. It was almost wholly built of matting that the birds had evidently taken from the ties of our grapevines. Each year the nest was repaired with the same material. Once only they had two broods in one season. The second brood was not hatched out until September, and the family was not ready to migrate until after nearly all its kindred had assembled and gone. This nest, though principally made of bare matting, was very neatly and thoroughly lined with hair. Other nests are made of coarse grasses and sedges, and all are usually lined in a similar manner.

Audubon and Wilson describe the eggs of this bird as blue, with purplish spots at the larger end. All that I have ever seen are white, with a slight tinge of greenish or blue, and unspotted. I have never been able to meet with a spotted egg of this bird, the identification of which was beyond suspicion. They are of a rounded-oval shape, one side is only a little more pointed than the other. They measure .75 of an inch in length by .58 in breadth. They resemble the eggs of *C. amœna*, but are smaller, and are not so deeply tinged with blue.

Cyanospiza amœna, BAIRD.

LAZULI FINCH.

Emberiza amœna, SAY, Long's Exped. II, 1823, 47. *Fringilla (Spiza) amœna*, BONAP. Am. Orn. I, 1825, 61, pl. vi, f. 5. *Fringilla amœna*, AUD. Orn. Biog. V, 1839, 64, 230, pls. cccxcviii and ccccxxiv. *Spiza amœna*, BONAP. List, 1838. — AUD. Syn. 1839, 109. — IB. Birds Am. III, 1841, 100, pl. clxxi. — MAX. Cab. Jour. VI, 1858, 283. — HEERM. X, s, 46. *Cyanospiza amœna*, BAIRD, Birds N. Am. 1858, 504. — COOPER & SUCKLEY, 205. — COOPER, Orn. Cal. I, 233.

SP. CHAR. *Male.* Upper parts generally, with the head and neck all round, greenish-blue; the interscapular region darker. Upper part of breast pale brownish-chestnut extending along the sides and separated from the blue of the throat by a faint white crescent; rest of under parts and axillars white. A white patch on the middle wing-coverts, and an obscurely indicated white band across the ends of the greater coverts. Loral region black. Length, about 5.50; wing, 3.90; tail, 2.60.

Female. Brown above, tinged with blue on rump and tail; whitish beneath, tinged with buff on the breast and throat; faint white bands on wings.

HAB. High Central Plains to the Pacific.

Cyanospiza amœna.

This species is about the size of *C. cyanea;* the bill exactly similar. The females of the two species are scarcely distinguishable, except by the faint traces of one or two white bands on the wings in *amœna*. Sometimes both the throat and the upper part of the breast are tinged with pale brownish-buff.

HABITS. The Lazuli Finch was first obtained by Mr. Say, who met with it in Long's expedition. It was observed, though rarely, along the banks of the Arkansas River during the summer months, as far as the base of the Rocky Mountains. It was said to frequent the bushy valleys, keeping much in the grass, after its food, and seldom alighting on either trees or shrubs.

Townsend, who found this rather a common bird on the Columbia, regarded it as shy and retiring in its habits, the female being very rarely seen. It possesses lively and pleasing powers of song, which it pours forth from the upper branches of low trees. Its nests were usually found placed in willows along the margins of streams, and were composed of small sticks, fine grasses, and buffalo-hair.

Mr. Nuttall found the nest of this bird fastened between the stem and two branches of a large fern. It was funnel-shaped, being six inches in height and three in breadth.

This bird possibly occurs quite rarely, as far east as the Mississippi, as I have what is said to be its egg taken from a nest near St. Louis. It only becomes abundant on the plains. Mr. Ridgway found it very generally distributed throughout his route, inhabiting all the bushy localities in the fertile districts. He regarded it as, in nearly every respect, the exact counterpart of the eastern *C. cyanea*. The notes of the two birds are so exactly the same that their song would be undistinguishable but for the fact that in the *amœna* it is appreciably weaker. He found their nests usually in the low limbs of trees, near their extremity, and only a few feet from the ground. Mr. J. A. Allen found this species common in Colorado, more so among the foot-hills than on the plains, but does not appear to have met with it in Kansas.

This species, Mr. Lord states, visits Vancouver Island and British Columbia early in the summer, arriving at the island in May, and rather later east of the Cascades. The song of the male is said to be feeble, and only now and then indulged in, as if to cheer his more sombre partner during incubation. The nest, he adds, is round and open at the top, composed of various materials worked together, lined with hair, and placed in a low bush, usually by the side of a stream.

The Lazuli Finch was met with in large numbers, and many of their nests procured, by Mr. Xantus, in the neighborhood of Ft. Tejon, California. Indeed, it is a very abundant species generally on the Pacific coast, and is found at least as far north as Puget Sound, during the summer. It arrives at San Diego, according to Dr. Cooper, about April 22, and remains there until October. A male bird, kept in a cage over winter, was found to retain its blue plumage. It is a favorite cage-bird in California, where it is absurdly known as the Indigo Bird. During the summer months, according to Dr. Cooper, there is hardly a grove in the more open portions of the State uninhabited by one or more pairs of this beautiful species. Although the female is very shy and difficult to obtain, except on the nest, the male is not timid, and frequently sings his lively notes from the top of some bush or tree, continuing musical in all weathers and throughout the summer. He describes its song as unvaried, as rather monotonous, and closely resembling that of *C. cyanea*.

Their nest, he adds, is usually built in a bush, not more than three or four feet from the ground, formed of fibrous roots, strips of bark, and grass, with a lining of vegetable down or hair, and securely bound to the surrounding branches. The eggs, five in number, he describes as white, faintly tinged with blue. At Santa Barbara he found them freshly laid May 6.

These birds are never gregarious, though the males come in considerable flocks in the spring, several days before the females. They travel at night, arriving at Santa Cruz about April 12. A nest found by Dr. Cooper, May 7, in a low bush close to a public road, was about three feet from the ground. It was véry strongly built, supported by a triple fork of the branch, and was composed of blades of grass firmly interwoven, and lined with horsehair and cobwebs. It measured three inches in height and three and three fourths in width. The cavity was two inches deep and one and three fourths wide.

In Arizona Dr. Coues found this bird a summer resident, but not abundant.

At Puget Sound this bird arrives about May 15. Dr. Suckley states that in Oregon it was observed returning from the south, in large flocks, in one instance of several hundred individuals.

The eggs of the Lazuli, when fresh, are of a light blue, which on the least exposure soon fades into a bluish-white. They are almost exactly oval in shape, and measure .75 by .60 of an inch. One end is somewhat more rounded, but the difference is slight.

Cyanospiza versicolor, BAIRD.

VARIED BUNTING.

Spiza versicolor, BON. Pr. Zoöl. Soc. 1837, 120. — IB. Conspectus Av. 1850, 475. — CAB. Mus. Hein. 1851, 148. *Carduelis luxuosus*, LESSON, Rev. Zoöl. 1839, 41. *Cyanospiza versicolor*, BAIRD, Birds N. Am. 1858, 503, pl. lvi, f. 2. — COOPER, Orn. Cal. I, 234.

SP. CHAR. Posterior half of hood, with throat, dark brownish-red; interscapular region similar, but darker. Forepart of hood, lesser wing-coverts, back of the neck, and rump, purplish-blue; the latter purest blue; the belly reddish-purple, in places tinged with blue, more obscure posteriorly. Feathers of wing and tail dark-brown, edged with dull bluish. Loral region and narrow frontal band black. Feathers on side of rump white at base. Length, 5.50; wing, 2.75; tail, 2.38.

Female. Yellowish-brown; paler beneath, and lightest behind. No white on wing. Tail with a bluish gloss.

HAB. Northern Mexico, and Cape St. Lucas. Xalapa (SCL. 1859, 365); Oaxaca (SCL. 1859, 379); Orizaba (SCL. 1857, 214); (SUM. M. B. S. I, 551; breeding); Guatemala (SCL. Ibis, I, 17).

The bill is stouter and more swollen to the end, and the mandible is much more curved than that of *C. cyanea*; and its perfectly concave commissure, without any shallow lobe in the middle, and the much more arched ridge, would almost separate the two generically. The wing is shorter and more rounded, the fourth quill longest, then the third, second, and fifth. The first is only a little longer than the seventh. The tail is decidedly rounded; rather more so than in *C. cyanea.*

The female is very similar to those of *C. amœna* and *cyanea.* The former has whitish bands on the wing; the latter differs in shape of bill, and has the first quill but little less than the second, or longest; not shorter than the sixth. In 34,033 ♂, Cape St. Lucas (June 26), the colors are much brighter than in any other of the collection. The whole occiput is bright scarlet, and the forehead nearly pure light blue, neither having scarcely a tinge of purple.

Autumnal and winter males have the bright tints very slightly obscured by grayish-brown tips to the feathers, especially on the back. The female in autumn is much more brown above and more rusty beneath than in spring.

HABITS. This beautiful species has only doubtful claims to a place in our fauna. It is a Mexican species, and may occasionally cross into our territory. It was met with at Boquillo, in the Mexican State of New Leon, by Lieutenant Couch. It was procured in Guatemala by Dr. Van Patten and by Salvin, and is given by Bonaparte as from Peru. It is also found at Cape St. Lucas, where it is not rare, and where it breeds.

This bird is also found at Orizaba, according to Sumichrast, but is quite rare in the State of Vera Cruz. Its common name is *Prusiano.* Its geographical distribution he was not able satisfactorily to ascertain.

Among the memoranda of Mr. Xantus made at Cape St. Lucas, we find the following in connection with this species: 517, nest and three eggs of *Cyanospiza versicolor ;* obtained May 5 on a myrtle hanging down from very high perpendicular bluffs, off the Trajoles, at Cape St. Lucas. 1535, nest and eggs of the same found on a vine ten feet high.

Specimens of this species were taken by Mr. Boucard at Oaxaca, Mexico, during the winter months.

Cyanospiza ciris, BAIRD.

NONPAREIL; PAINTED BUNTING.

Emberiza ciris, LINN. Kong. Sv. Vet. Akad. Hand. 1750, 278 ; tab. vii, f. 1. — IB. Syst. Nat. I, 1766, 313. — WILSON, Am. Orn. III, 1811, 68, pl. xxiv, f. 1, 2. *Passerina ciris,* VIEILLOT, Gal. Ois. I, 1824, 81, pl. lxvi. *Fringilla ciris,* AUD. Orn. Biog. I, 1832, 279 ; V, 517, pl. liii. *Spiza ciris,* BON. List, 1838. — IB. Conspectus, 1850, 476. — AUD. Syn. 1839, 108. — IB. Birds Am. III, 1841, 93, pl. clxix. *Cyanospiza ciris,* BAIRD, Birds N. Am. 1858, 503. — IB. Mex. Bound. II, Birds, 17, pl. xviii, f. 2. — HEERM. X, c, p. 14. *? Fringilla mariposa,* SCOPOLI, Annals Hist. Nat. I, 1769, 151. *Painted Finch,* CATESBY, PENNANT.

SP. CHAR. *Male.* Head and neck all round ultramarine-blue, excepting a narrow stripe from the chin to the breast, which, with the under parts generally, the eyelids, and the rump (which is tinged with purplish), are vermilion-red. Edges of chin, loral region, greater wing-coverts, inner tertiary, and interscapular region, green; the middle of the latter glossed with yellow. Tail-feathers, lesser wing-coverts, and outer webs of quills, purplish-blue. Length, about 5.50 inches; wing, 2.70.

Female. Clear dark green above; yellowish beneath. *Young,* like female.

HAB. South Atlantic and Gulf States to the Pecos River, Texas; south into Middle America to Panama; S. Illinois (RIDGWAY); Honduras (SCL. 1858, 358); Oaxaca (SCL. 1859, 379); Cordova (SCL. 1856, 304); Guatemala (SCL. Ibis, I, 17); Honduras (SCL. II, 10); Cuba (CAB. J. IV, 8); Veragua (SALV. 1867, 142); Costa Rica (LAWR. IX, 102); Vera Cruz, winter (SUM. M. B. S. I, 552); Yucatan (LAWR. IX, 200).

Tail very slightly emarginated and rounded; second, third, and fourth quills equal; first rather shorter than the fifth.

The female is readily distinguishable from that of *C. cyanea* by the green instead of dull brown of the back, and the yellow of the under parts.

Specimens of this species from all parts of its range appear to be quite identical.

HABITS. The Nonpareil or Painted Bunting of the Southern and Southeastern States has a somewhat restricted distribution, not being found any farther to the north on the Atlantic Coast than South Carolina and Georgia, and probably only in the more southern portions of those States. It has been traced as far to the west as Texas. It was also met with at Monterey, Mexico, by Lieutenant Couch, and in winter by Mr. Boucard, at Plaza Vicente, Oaxaca.

Mr. Dresser found it very common both at Matamoras and at San Antonio, breeding in both places. Dr. Coues did not meet with it in Columbia, S. C., and considers it as confined to the low country, and as rare even there. It breeds about the city of Charleston, S. C., from which neighborhood I have received its eggs in considerable numbers, from Dr. Bachman. It is also found in the lower counties of Georgia, and breeds in the vicinity of Savannah. It was not met with by Dr. Gerhardt in the northern portion of that State. Dr. Woodhouse found it quite abundant in all parts of Texas, where he tells us the sweet warblings of this beautiful and active little Finch added much to the pleasures of his trip across the prairies. Its favorite places of resort appeared to be small thickets, and when singing it selected the highest branches of a bush.

In the Report on the birds of the Mexican Boundary Survey, Lieutenant Couch met with this species among the low hedges in the suburbs of Pesqueria Grande. Mr. J. H. Clark observed that the individuals of this species diminished as they proceeded westward. The male was almost always seen alone, flying a long distance for so small a bird. Their nests, he adds, were built of very fine grass, in low bushes, and resting in the crotch of the twigs. Males were never seen about the nest, but the females were so gentle as to allow themselves to be taken off the nest, which was deliberately done on more than one occasion.

Dr. Kennerly reports having often listened to the melodious warblings of this beautiful Finch in the vicinity of San Antonio, Texas, where he found it very abundant among the thick mesquite-bushes, in the month of July. It was deservedly a great favorite there, both on account of the beauty of its plumage and its notes.

Wilson found this bird one of the most numerous summer birds of Lower Louisiana, where it was universally known among the French inhabitants as *Le Pape*. Its gay dress and its docility of manners procured it many admirers. Wilson also states that he met with these birds in the low countries of all the Southern States, in the vicinity of the sea and along the borders of the large rivers, particularly among the rice plantations. He states that a few were seen near the coast in North Carolina, but they were more numerous in South Carolina, and still more so in Georgia, especially the lower parts. At Natchez, on the Mississippi, they were comparatively scarce, but below Baton Rouge, on the levee, they appeared in great numbers. Around New Orleans they were warbling from almost every fence. Their notes very much resemble those of the Indigo Bird, but lack their energy, and are more feeble and concise.

Wilson met with these birds very generally in the houses of the French inhabitants of New Orleans. In the aviary of a wealthy French planter near Bayou Fourche, he found two pairs of these birds so far reconciled to their confinement as to have nests and hatch out their eggs. Wilson was of the opinion that with the pains given to the Canary these birds would breed with equal facility. Six of them, caught only a few days before his departure, were taken with him by sea. They soon became reconciled to their cage, and sang with great sprightliness. They were very fond of flies, and watched with great eagerness as the passengers caught them for their benefit, assembling in the front of the cage and stretching their heads through the wires to receive them.

These birds, he states, arrive in Louisiana from the South about the middle of April, and build early in May. They reach Savannah about the 20th of April. Their nests are usually fixed in orange hedges or in the lower branches of the trees. He often found them in common bramble and blackberry bushes. They are formed exteriorly of dry grass intermingled with the silk of caterpillars, with hair and fine rootlets. Some nests had eggs as late as the 25th of June, which were probably a second brood. The food of this bird consists of rice, insects, and various kinds of seeds. They also feed on the seeds of ripe figs.

A single specimen of this species was detected by Mr. Ridgway in Southern Illinois between Olney and Mount Carmel, on the 10th of June. It is therefore presumed to be a rare summer resident in that locality.

The Nonpareil is possessed of a very pugnacious disposition, and, according to Mr. Audubon, the bird-dealers of New Orleans take advantage of this peculiarity in a very ingenious manner to trap them. A male bird is stuffed and set up in an attitude of defence on the platform of a trap-cage. The first male bird of this species that notices it is sure to make an attack upon it, and is at once trapped. So pertinacious are they that even when thus imprisoned the captive repeats its attack upon its supposed rival. They feed almost immediately upon being caught, and usually thrive in confinement, Audubon mentioning one that had been caged for ten years.

This bird is very easily made to breed in confinement. Dr. Bachman has had a single pair thus raise three broods in a season.

The eggs of this species measure .80 by .65 of an inch, and do not at all resemble the eggs of the *cyanea* or *amœna*. They have a dull or pearly-white ground, and are very characteristically marked with blotches and dots of purplish and reddish brown.

Genus SPERMOPHILA, Swainson.

Spermophila, Swainson, Zoöl. Jour. III, Nov. 1827, 348. (Type, *Pyrrhula falcirostris*, Temm. Sufficiently distinct from *Spermophilus*, F. Cuv. 1822.)
Sporophila, Cabanis, Mus. Hein. 1851, 148. (Type, *Fringilla hypoleuca*, Licht.)

Gen. Char. Bill very short and very much curved, as in *Pyrrhula*, almost as deep as

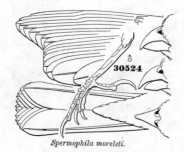

Spermophila moreleti.

long; the commissure concave, abruptly bent towards the end. Tarsus about equal to middle toe; inner toe rather the longer (?), reaching about to the base of the middle one; hind toe to the middle of this claw. Wings short, reaching over the posterior third of the exposed part of the tail; the tertiaries gradually longer than the secondaries, neither much shorter than the primaries, which are graduated, and but little different in length, the first shorter than the sixth, the second and fourth equal. The tail is about as long as the wings, rounded, all the feathers slightly graduated, rather sharply acuminate and decidedly mucronate. Smallest of American passerine birds.

The essential characters of this genus are the small, very convex bill, as high as long; the short broad wings, with the quills differing little in length, the outer ones graduated; the tail as long as the wings, widened towards the end, and slightly graduated, with the acuminate and mucronate tip to the feathers.

Many species of the genus occur in Middle and South America, although none not readily distinguishable from the single North American one.

Spermophila moreleti, Pucheran.

LITTLE SEED-EATER.

Spermophila moreleti, (Pucheran,) Bonap. Conspectus, 1850, 497. — Sclater, Pr. Zoöl. Soc. 1856, 302. — Baird, Birds N. Am. 1858, 506, pl. liv, f. 2, 3. — Ib. Mex. Bound. II, Birds, 17, pl. xvi, f. 2, 3. *Sporophila moreleti*, Cab. Mus. Hein. 1851, 150. — Ib. Journ. fur. Orn. IX, 1861, 4 (with synonomy). *Spermophila albigularis*, (Spix,) Lawrence, Ann. N. Y. Lyceum, V, Sept. 1851, 124 (Texas. Not of Spix).

Sp. Char. The top and sides of the head, back of the neck, a broad band across the upper part of the breast extending all round, the middle of the back, the wings and tail, with the posterior upper coverts, black. The chin, upper throat and neck all round, but interrupted behind, the rump, with the remaining under and lateral portions of the body, white; the latter tinged with brownish-yellow. Two bands on the wing, across the greater and middle coverts, with the concealed bases of all the quills, also white. Length, about 4 inches; wing, 2.05; tail, 1.90.

Female. Dull yellow; olivaceous above, brownish-yellow beneath. Wings and tail somewhat as in the male.

Hab. Rio Grande of Texas; south to Costa Rica. Xalapa (Scl. 1859, 365); Oaxaca (Scl. 1859, 378); Cordova (Scl. 1856, 302); Guatemala (Scl. Ibis, I, 17; Salv. Ibis, I, 468; nest); Costa Rica (Cab. J. 1861, 4); Vera Cruz, winter, alpine region, breeding (Sum. M. B. S. I, 551).

The specimen upon which the preceding description of the male has been based is the only one in full plumage we have seen, and was kindly lent by Mr. P. L. Sclater. It was collected in Honduras. Some of the feathers of the back have grayish tips. The specimen described by Mr. Lawrence as *S. albogularis*, though male, is, in most respects, like the female, except that the wings and tail are darker, the color of the upper part grayer, and the interscapular feathers blotched with black. The black of the head is strongly indicated, the feathers, however, all with gray margins. In this

Spermophila moreleti.

and another, a little further advanced, from San Diego, Mexico, (4096,) there is a very faint indication of the black pectoral band, and there is no trace of the whitish of the rump.

Habits. This pretty little tropical form of Sparrow can only rest a claim to be included in our fauna by its occasional presence on the Rio Grande in Texas. It is found throughout Mexico and Central America.

Mr. Sumichrast found it throughout the State of Vera Cruz, except only in the elevated or alpine regions. Its common name was *Frailecito*. It was abundant throughout the hot and the temperate regions as well as the plateau.

This species was first met with near the Lake of Peten, in Guatemala, by

M. Morelet, and was described from his specimens in the Paris Museum by Prince Bonaparte. Mr. Salvin found it a not uncommon species about Dueñas, where it is generally to be found amongst the tall weeds on the edge of the lake. It was also found at Belize. From a letter of Mr. Salvin, published in the Ibis of 1859 (p. 468), we quote the following in reference to the nest of this species, which is all the information we have in relation to this diminutive Sparrow: "A day or two ago I found two nests of *Spermophila moreleti*, and took one rotten dried-up egg from one with a young one in it. Nothing could be more different than this nest and that of *S. bicolor*, so well described by Mr. Newton. That of *S. moreleti*, instead of the loose domed structure of *S. bicolor*, with a large side-entrance, composed entirely of one material, is one of the neatest nests you ever saw, — a beautiful, open, transparent nest, composed of fine roots and fibres, and lined with horsehair. It is not placed resting on a branch, but is suspended like a Reed Warbler's (*Salicaria arundinacea*), by several small twigs. The eggs, too, differ materially." Mr. Salvin gives no description of these eggs.

This bird was found a resident during the winter months, and in May also, at Plaza Vicente, in the State of Oaxaca, Mexico. This is in the low or hot lands of that region.

Genus **PHONIPARA**, Bonap.

Phonipara, BONAPARTE, 1850. (Type, *Loxia canora*, GM.)

GEN. CHAR. Size very small. Wing considerably longer than the tail, but much rounded; third or fourth quill longest; first about equal to seventh. Tail very slightly rounded, the feathers broad. Bill very short and deep, but the depth through the base less than the culmen; culmen but slightly, or not appreciably, curved; bill much compressed. Feet stout; tarsi longer than the middle toe; outer toe longer than the inner, its claw just reaching the base of the middle claw; hind toe with the claw

Phonipara zena.

very large, and strongly curved. Among the least of American *Fringillidœ*.

The introduction of this genus into the North American fauna is the result of Mr. Maynard's indefatigable labors in the exploration of Florida. The species are principally West Indian, a single race alone belonging to the continental portion of Middle America.

Species and Varieties.

COMMON CHARACTERS. Sexes very different. Above olive-green, beneath blackish or whitish. ♂. Head and breast black, the former with or without yellow patches. ♀ with the yellow and black indicated only, or wanting. Length, about 4.00.

A. Head without any yellow.

1. **P. zena.** Culmen decidedly curved. Above dull grayish olive-green. ♂. Head and lower parts, especially anteriorly, dull black, mixed with whitish posteriorly. ♀. Head and beneath ashy. Wing, about 2.00; tail, 1.75. *Hab.* West Indies (Cuba, Hayti, Porto Rico, St. Bartholomew, Jamaica, etc.); also Key West, Florida (MAYNARD).

B. Head with yellow patches.

2. **P. pusilla.** Culmen perfectly straight. Above rather bright olive-green. ♂, a supraloral stripe, a patch on chin, and upper part of throat, with edge of wing, bright yellow; forehead, lores, and jugulum black. ♀ with the black and yellow only indicated, or wanting.

Whole crown, cheeks, breast, and upper part of abdomen black. *Hab.* Middle America, from Mirador to Panama, and southward.

var. *pusilla.*[1]

Only isolated spots, covering forehead, lore, and base of lower jaw, and patch on jugulum, black. *Hab.* West Indies. (Porto Rico, Hayti, Jamaica, Cuba, etc.) . . . . . var. *olivacea.*[2]

3. **P. canora.**[3] Culmen decidedly curved. Above bright olive-green; beneath pale ashy, whitish on anal region. A bright yellow broad crescent across the lower part of the throat, curving upward and forward, behind and over the auriculars, to above the eye. ♂. Lores, auriculars, and chin, and a band across the jugulum, black. ♀. Chin, etc., chestnut-brown; no black on jugulum. *Hab.* Cuba.

Phonipara zena, BRYANT.

THE BLACK-FACED FINCH.

Fringilla zena, LINN. Syst. Nat. I, (ed. 10,) 1758, 183 (based on *Passer bicolor bahamensis,* CATESBY, Carol. I, tab. 37, Bahamas). — BRYANT, Pr. Bost. Soc. N. H. X, 1865, 254. *Fringilla bicolor,* LINN. Syst. Nat. I, (ed. 12,) 1766, 324 (same original as *zena*). *Spermophila bicolor,* GOSSE (Jamaica). *Phonipara bicolor,* NEWTON (St. Croix). *? Tiaris omissa,* JARDINE, Ann. Nat. Hist. 1847, 332 (Tobago). *Phonipara omissa,* SCLATER. *Phonipara marchi,* BAIRD, Pr. A. N. Sc. Phila. Nov. 1863, 297 (Jamaica). *Fringilla zena,* var. *marchi,* BRYANT, Pr. Bost. Soc. 1867, 43. *Fringilla (Phonipara) zena,* var. *portoricensis,* BRYANT, Pr. Bost. Soc. X, 1865, 254 (Porto Rico).

SP. CHAR. *Male adult* (627, Bryant coll.; Inagua). Above dull olive-green, the head and lower parts black, the two colors blending insensibly into each other; feathers of the middle of the abdomen and crissum edged with whitish. Wing, 2.10; tail, 1.80, culmen, .35; tarsus, .63; middle toe, .50.

Female adult (983, Bryant coll.; Inagua). Above dull olive-green, beneath ashy, whitish on the abdomen and crissum; no black. Wing, 2.10.

Male juv. (981, Bryant coll.; Inagua). Like the adult female, but the head anteriorly, the chin, throat, and jugulum medially, black. Wing, 2.05.

HAB. West Indies (Bahamas; Jamaica, Porto Rico; St. Croix, Tobago?).

---

[1] *Tiaris pusilla,* SWAINSON, Phil. Mag. I, 1827, 438. *Phonipara pusilla,* SCLATER, P. Z. S. 1855, 159.

[2] *Emberiza olivacea,* GMELIN, Syst. Nat. I, 309. *Phonipara olivacea,* SCLATER, P. Z. S. 1855, 159.

[3] *Loxia canora,* GMELIN, Syst. Nat. I, 858. *Phonipara canora,* BONAP.

Quite a large series of this species from the various West Indian Islands show a considerable variation in the amount of black in male birds; nothing characteristic of the different islands, however, for, in specimens from each, individuals are to be found agreeing in every respect with the stages described above.

HABITS. The Black-faced Finch of Jamaica and other West India Islands claims a place in the fauna of the United States as an occasional visitant of Florida; of how common occurrence on that peninsula we cannot determine. It was taken there in the spring of 1871 by Mr. Maynard, and is possibly an accidental rather than a regular visitant. It is found in many of the West India Islands, though being resident in their several places of abode, they naturally exhibit certain characteristics as of distinct races. The eggs of the St. Croix bird differ considerably from those of the Jamaica one.

The Messrs. Newton, in their account of the birds of St. Croix, mention this bird as having a Bunting-like song, heard always very early in the morning. It is said to frequent the curing-houses, hopping on the uncovered sugar-hogsheads, and making a plentiful meal therefrom. It is very sociable, and feeds in small flocks, mostly on the ground among the guinea-grass. The crops of those dissected were usually found to contain small seeds. They build domed nests in low bushes, thickets of bamboo, or among creepers against the side of a house, seldom more than four feet from the ground, composed entirely of dry grass, the interior being lined with finer materials of the same. The opening is on one side, and is large for the size of the nest. They breed from the middle of May to the end of July. The eggs are white, spotted with red, especially at the larger end. The usual number of eggs is three, very rarely four. Their measurement is .65 by .50 of an inch.

In Jamaica Mr. March speaks of it as the most common of the Grass Finches, of which there are three other species, and as nesting at all seasons of the year in low trees and bushes. Near homesteads, in building their domed nests, they make use of shreds, scraps of cloth, bits of cotton, and other trash. Their eggs, he says, are three and sometimes even six in number; and he mentions their varying both as to dimensions and coloring, which may explain the difference between the eggs from St. Croix and Jamaica. Those from the latter place measure .72 by .50 of an inch, and the markings are more of a brown than a red color.

Mr. Hill adds that the Grass Finch very frequently selects a shrub on which the wasps have built, fixing the entrance close to their cells.

Mr. Gosse states that the only note of this species is a single harsh guttural squeak, difficult either to imitate or to describe.

Genus **PYRRHULOXIA**, Bonap.

Pyrrhuloxia, Bonaparte, Conspectus, 1850, 500. (Type, *Cardinalis sinuatus,* Bon.)

Gen. Char. The bill is very short and much curved, the culmen forming an arc of a circle of 60 degrees or more, and ending at a right angle with the straight gonys; the commissure abruptly much angulated anterior to the nostrils in its middle point; the

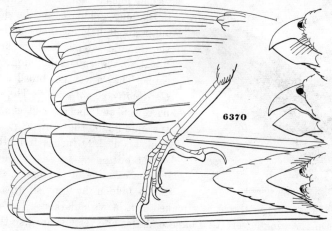

Pyrrhuloxia sinuata.

lower jaw very much wider than the upper, and wider than the gonys is long; anterior portion of commissure straight. Tarsus longer than middle toe; outer lateral toes longer, not reaching the base of the middle; wing considerably rounded, first quill longer than secondaries. Tail much longer than the wing, graduated; the feathers broad, truncate. Head crested.

Color. Gray, with red feathers and patches.

The essential character of this genus lies in the greatly curved, very short, and broad bill, something like that of *Pyrrhula.* In other respects like *Cardinalis,* but with less graduated wing, and longer and broader tail.

Pyrrhuloxia sinuata, Bonap.

TEXAS CARDINAL.

Cardinalis sinuatus, Bp. Pr. Zoöl. Soc. Lond. V, 1837, 111 (Mexico). — Lawrence, Ann. N. Y. Lyc. V, 1851, 116. — Cassin, Illust. I, vii, 1854, 204, pl. xxxiii. *Pyrrhuloxia sinuata,* Bon. Consp. 1850, 500. — Baird, Birds N. Am. 1858, 508. — Heerm. X, c. 16. — Cooper, Orn. Cal. I, 236.

Sp. Char. Head with an elongated, pointed crest, springing from the crown. Upper parts generally pale ashy-brown; hood, sides of neck, and under parts of body, rather paler. Long crest-feathers, bill all round including lores and encircling the eye, wing and tail, dark crimson. Chin and upper part of throat, breast, and median line of the belly, under tail-coverts, tibia, edge and inner coverts of the wings, bright carmine-red. Bill yellowish. Length, about 8.50; wing, 3.75; tail, 4.50.

Female similar, with the under part brownish-yellow; middle of belly and throat only tinged with red.

HAB. Valley of the Rio Grande of Texas and westward; Cape St. Lucas; Mazatlan, Mexico.

The wing is considerably rounded, the fourth and fifth quills longest; the first as long as the secondaries, the second longer than the seventh. The tail is long, graduated on the sides, the outer about half an inch shorter than the middle. The feathers are very broad to the end and obliquely truncate. They are rather broader than in *Cardinalis virginianus.* The crest is narrower and longer, and confined to the middle of the crown; it extends back about 1.80 inches from the base of the bill.

The carmine of the breast is somewhat hidden by grayish tips to the

Pyrrhuloxia sinuata.

feathers; that of the throat is streaked a little with darker. The exposed surfaces of the wing-coverts and of secondaries and tertials are like the back. The tail-feathers are tipped with brownish.

Specimens from Cape St. Lucas are very much smaller than any others, measuring only, wing, 3.30; tail, 3.80. The crest is dull carmine, instead of dark wine-purple; the red tinge on wing and tail much fainter, and the sides, as well as the gray tints everywhere, more brownish; there is none of that dark burnt-carmine tint to the red of lores and cheeks observable in all the Texas specimens. No. 49,758, Camp Grant, Arizona, is like the Cape St. Lucas birds in colors, except that the crest is dusky, but the proportions are those of the Rio Grande series.

HABITS. The Texan Cardinal was originally described as a bird of Mexico by Prince Charles Lucien Bonaparte in the Proceedings of the Zoölogical Society of London. It has since been ascertained to inhabit the southern central portions of our country, its range of extension northerly bringing it within the limits of the United States. In Texas, on the Rio Grande, it is resident throughout the year, or of but limited migration in the coldest weather. It was not observed by Dr. Coues in Arizona, but is said to occur in the southern portion of that Territory. It was found breeding at Cape St. Lucas by Mr. Xantus. It is not named by Sumichrast among the birds of Vera Cruz.

Its habits are said to be of the same general character with those of our common Cardinal.

The specimens from which this bird was first described were procured in the vicinity of the city of Mexico. The first obtained within the limits of the United States were observed by Captain McCown of the U. S. Army, at Ringgold Barracks, in Texas. Since then it has been procured by several of the naturalists accompanying the government expeditions. It was obtained in New Leon, Mexico, by Lieutenant Couch; in Texas, by Major Emory; in Texas and at El Paso, by Lieutenant Parke.

When first seen, in March, in the State of Tamaulipas, by Lieutenant Couch, it was in flocks, very shy and difficult of approach. It did not occur much in open fields, but seemed to prefer the vicinity of fences and bushes. It was often seen in company with the common Cardinal.

Dr. Kennerly found this bird quite abundant in the vicinity of El Paso, but did not observe it elsewhere. It kept generally in flocks of from three to six, frequenting the hedges and fruit-trees in the vicinity of houses. It became very restless when approached, flying from branch to branch and from tree to tree, uttering its peculiar note with great vehemence.

Dr. Heermann met with the first specimen of this bird in a dry cañon, a little to the east of the crossing of San Pedro River. It was perched on a bush, seemed wearied and lost, and was probably a wanderer. No more were seen until he reached El Paso. There he found it everywhere among the hedges and trees, and continued to meet with it occasionally on his road, until his party left civilization behind. It erects its crest as it moves actively about in search of food, and utters at intervals a clear, plaintive whistle, varied by a few detached notes.

Mr. Dresser considers this species rather a straggler from Mexico than as a Texan bird. Near Eagle Pass and Piedras Negras he found it abundant, but it became scarce as soon as he travelled a few miles into Texas. He saw none north or east of the Leona. He was told that quantities breed near Eagle Pass, and he saw not a few in cages that had been reared from the nest. He found it a shy bird, and difficult to shoot. When followed, it flies about uneasily, perching on the top of some high bush, and erecting its long crest, uttering a clear, plaintive whistle. Sometimes it would take to the thick brushwood and creep through the bushes so that it was impossible to get a shot at it. On the Lower Rio Grande it was of uncommon occurrence. He noticed a single pair near Matamoras in August, 1864.

Captain McCown, in his account of this species, published by Cassin, writes that, so far as seen on the Rio Grande, this handsome species appeared to have a strong partiality for damp and bushy woods. So far as he observed, it never ventured far from the river. He was under the impression that this bird remains in Texas all the year, having met with it so late in the fall and again so early in the spring, that, if not constantly resident, its migrations must be very limited. He describes it as a gay, sprightly bird, generally seen in company with others of the same species, frequently erecting its crest and calling to its mate or comrades. It is rather shy, and not easily approached. In its voice and general habits it appeared to him very similar to the common species.

The eggs of this species are of an oval shape, one end being only a little less rounded than the other. Their average measurement is one inch in length by .80 in breadth. Their ground-color is a dull chalky-white, over which are distributed well-defined blotches of a light umber-brown, and also a number of indistinct markings of purple. The spots are pretty uniform in these colors, but vary greatly in size and distribution. In some eggs they largely consist of fine dots, in others they are in bold blotches. In some the brown is more confluent and the effect that of a deeper shade.

Genus CARDINALIS, BONAP.

Cardinalis, BONAPARTE, Saggio di una distribuzione metod. dei Animagli Vertebrati, 1831 (Agassiz). (Type, *Loxia cardinalis*, LINN.)

GEN. CHAR. Bill enormously large; culmen very slightly curved, commissure sinuated; lower jaw broader than the length of the gonys, considerably wider than the upper jaw, about as deep as the latter. Tarsi longer than middle toe; outer toe rather the longer, reaching a little beyond the base of the middle one; hind toe not so long. Wings

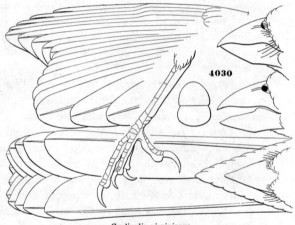

Cardinalis virginianus.

moderate, reaching over the basal third of the exposed part of the tail. Four outer quills graduated; the first equal to the secondaries. Tail long, decidedly longer than the wings, considerably graduated; feathers broad, truncated a little obliquely at the end, the corners rounded. Colors red. Head crested.

The essential characters of this genus are the crested head; very large and thick bill extending far back on the forehead, and only moderately curved above; tarsus longer than middle toe; much graduated wings, the first primary equal to the secondary quills; the long tail exceeding the wings, broad and much graduated at the end.

Of this genus, only two species are known, one of them being exclusively South American, the other belonging to North America, but in different regions modified into representative races. They may be defined as follows.

Species and Varieties.

COMMON CHARACTERS. *Male.* Bright vermilion-red, more dusky purplish on upper surface; feathers adjoining base of bill black for greater or less extent. *Female.* Above olivaceous, the wings, tail, and crest reddish; beneath olivaceous-whitish, slightly tinged on jugulum with red.

C. virginianus. Culmen nearly straight; commissure with a slight lobe; upper mandible as deep as the lower, perfectly smooth. Bill red. Black patch covering whole throat, its posterior outline convex. *Female.* Lining of wing deep vermilion. Olivaceous-gray above, the wings and tail strongly tinged with red; crest only dull red, without darker shaft-streaks. Beneath wholly light ochraceous. No black around bill.

A. Crest-feathers soft, blended. Rump not lighter red than back.

  a. Black of the lores passing broadly across forehead. Crest brownish-red. Bill moderate.

    Culmen, .75; gonys, .41; depth of bill, .54. Feathers of dorsal region broadly margined with grayish. Wing, 4.05; tail, 4.50; crest, 1.80. *Hab.* Eastern Province of United States, south of 40°. Bermudas . . . . var. *virginianus.*

  b. Black of the lores not meeting across forehead; crest pure vermilion. Bill robust.

    Culmen, .84; gonys, .47; depth of bill, .70. Feathers of dorsal region without grayish borders; red beneath more intense; wing, 3.60; tail, 4.20; crest, 2.00. *Hab.* Eastern Mexico (Mirador; Yucatan; "Honduras"). . . . . var. *coccineus.*[1]

    Culmen, .82; gonys, .47; depth of bill, .65. Feathers of dorsal region with distinct gray borders; red beneath lighter. Wing, 4.00; tail, 5.00; crest, 2.00. *Hab.* Cape St. Lucas, and Arizona; Tres Marias Islands. (Perhaps all of Western Mexico, north of the Rio Grande de Santiago.) . . . . . . var. *igneus.*

B. Crest-feathers stiff, compact. Rump decidedly lighter red than the back.

    Culmen, .75; gonys, .41; depth of bill, .57. Dorsal feathers without grayish margins; red as in the last. Wing, 3.40; tail, 3.80; crest, 2.00. *Hab.* Western Mexico; Colima. "Acapulco et Realejo." . . . . var. *carneus.*[2]

C. phœniceus.[3] Culmen much arched; commissure arched; upper mandible not as deep as lower, and with grooves forward from the nostril, parallel with the curve of the culmen. Bill whitish-brown. Black patch restricted to the chin, its posterior outline deeply concave.

---

[1] *Cardinalis virginianus,* var. *coccineus,* RIDGWAY.

[2] *Cardinalis virginianus,* var. *carneus.* ? *Cardinalis carneus,* LESS. R. Z. 1842, 209. — BONAP. Consp. I, 501.

According to the locality quoted ("Acapulco et Realejo") this name is the one to be applied to the variety diagnosed in the synopsis; it is difficult, however, to make anything out of the description, as it is evidently taken from a female or immature bird. If the locality quoted be correct, this form ranges along the Pacific Coast, probably from latitude 20° south, as far at least as Nicaragua. North of 20°, and on the Tres Marias Islands, it is replaced by var. *igneus,* and on the Atlantic coast, from Tampico south to Honduras, is represented by the var. *coccineus.*

In the very long, stiff crest-feathers, and light red rump, this variety of *C. virginianus* closely approximates to *C. phœniceus,* but in other respects is very distinct.

[3] *Cardinalis phœniceus,* (GOULD,) BONAP. P. Z. S. 1837, p. 111; Consp. I, 501. — SCLATER & SALVIN, Ex. Orn. Pt. VIII, 1868, pl. lxiii.

Crest-feathers stiff and compact. No black above, or on lores; crest pure vermilion; rump light vermilion, much lighter than the back, which is without gray edges to feathers. Culmen, .75; gonys, 39; height of bill, .67; wing, 3.50; tail, 3.90; crest, 2.20. *Female.* Lining of wing buff; above ashy-olivaceous, becoming pure ash on head and neck, except their under side. Crest-feathers vermilion with black shafts; no red tinge on wings, and only a slight tinge of it on tail. Forepart of cheeks and middle of throat white; rest of lower part deep ochraceous. Black around bill as in the male. *Hab.* Northern South America; Venezuela; New Granada.

Cardinalis virginianus, Bonap.

REDBIRD; CARDINAL GROSBEAK.

Coccothraustes virginiana, BRISSON, Orn. III, 1760, 253. *Loxia cardinalis,* LINN. Syst. I, 1766, 300. — WILSON, Am. Orn. II, 1810, 38, pl. vi, f. 1, 2. *Coccothraustes cardinalis,* VIEILL. Dict. *Fringilla (Coccothraustes) cardinalis,* BON. Obs. Wils. 1825, No. 79. *Fringilla cardinalis,* NUTT. Man. I, 1832, 519. — AUD. Orn. Biog. II, 1834, 336 ; V, 514, pl. clix. *Pitylus cardinalis,* AUD. Syn. 1839, 131. — IB. Birds Am. III, 1841, 198, pl. cciii. *Cardinalis virginianus,* BON. List, 1838. — IB. Consp. 1850, 501. — BAIRD, Birds N. Am. 1858, 509. — MAX. Cab. J. VI, 1858, 268. *Grosbec de Virginie,* BUFF. Pl. enl. 37.

SP. CHAR. A flattened crest of feathers on the crown. Bill red. Body generally bright vermilion-red, darker on the back, rump, and tail. The feathers of the back and rump bordered with brownish-gray. Narrow band around the base of the bill, extending to eyes, with chin and upper part of the throat black.

Cardinalis virginianus.

Female of a duller red, and this only on the wings, tail, and elongated feathers of the crown. Above light olive; tinged with yellowish on the head ; beneath brownish-yellow, darkest on the sides and across the breast. Black about the head only faintly indicated. Length, 8.50; wing, 4.00; tail, 4.50; culmen, .75; depth of bill, .58; breadth of upper mandible, .35. (28,286 ♂, Mount Carmel, Southern Illinois.)

HAB. More southern portions of United States to the Missouri. Probably along valley of Rio Grande to Rocky Mountains.

The bill of this species is very large, and shaped much as in *Hedymeles ludovicianus.* The central feathers of the crest of the crown are longer than the lateral; they spring from about the middle of the crown, and extend back about an inch and a half from the base of the bill. The wings are much rounded, the fourth longest, the second equal to the seventh, the first as long as the secondaries. The tail is long, truncate at the end, but graduated on the sides ; the feathers are broad to the end, truncated obliquely at the end.

Most North American specimens we have seen have the feathers of the back edged with ashy ; the more northern the less brightly colored, and larger. Mexican skins (var. *coccineus*) are deeper colored and without the olivaceous. In all specimens from eastern North America the frontal black is very distinct.

Specimens from the Eastern Province of United States, including Florida and the Bermudas, are all alike in possessing those features distinguishing the restricted var. *virginianus* from the races of Mexico, namely, the wide black frontal band, and distinct gray edges to dorsal feathers, with small bill. Specimens from Florida are scarcely smaller, and are not more deeply colored than some examples from Southern Illinois. Rio Grande skins, however, are slightly less in size, though identical in other respects.

HABITS. The Cardinal Grosbeak, the Redbird of the Southern States, is one of our few birds that present the double attraction of a brilliant and showy plumage with more than usual powers of song. In New England and the more northern States it is chiefly known by its reputation as a cage-bird, both its bright plumage and its sweet song giving it a high value. It is a very rare and only an accidental visitor of Massachusetts, though a pair was once known to spend the summer and to rear its brood in the Botanical Gardens of Harvard College in Cambridge. It is by no means a common bird even in Pennsylvania. In all the Southern States, from Virginia to Mexico, it is a well-known favorite, frequenting gardens and plantations, and even breeding within the limits of the larger towns and cities. A single specimen of this bird was obtained near Dueñas, Guatemala, by Mr. Salvin.

The song of this Grosbeak is diversified, pleasant, and mellow, delivered with energy and ease, and renewed incessantly until its frequent repetitions somewhat diminish its charms. Its peculiar whistle is not only loud and clear, resembling the finest notes of the flageolet, but is so sweet and so varied that by some writers it has been considered equal even to the notes of the far-famed Nightingale of Europe. It is, however, very far from being among our best singers ; yet, as it is known to remain in full song more than two thirds of the year, and while thus musical to be constant and liberal in the utterance of its sweet notes, it is entitled to a conspicuous place among our singing birds.

In its cage life the Cardinal soon becomes contented and tame, and will live many years in confinement. Wilson mentions one instance in which a Redbird was kept twenty-one years. They sing nearly throughout the year, or from January to October. In the extreme Southern States they are more or less resident, and some may be found all the year round. There is another remarkable peculiarity in this species, and one very rarely to be met with among birds, which is that the female Cardinal Grosbeak is an excellent singer, and her notes are very nearly as sweet and as good as those of her mate.

. This species has been traced as far to the west in its distribution as the base of the Rocky Mountains, and into Mexico at the southwest. In Mexico it is also replaced by a very closely allied variety, and at Cape St. Lucas by still another. It is given by Mr. Lawrence among the birds occurring near New York City. He has occasionally met with it in New Jersey and at Staten Island, and, in one instance, on New York Island, when his attention was attracted to it by the loudness of its song.

It is given by Mr. Dresser as common throughout the whole of Texas during the summer, and almost throughout the year, excepting only where the *P. sinuata* is found. At Matamoras it was very common, and may be seen caged in almost every Mexican hut. He found it breeding in great abundance about San Antonio in April and May.

Mr. Cassin states that the Cardinal Bird is also known by the name of Virginia Nightingale. He adds that it inhabits, for the greater part, low and damp woods in which there is a profuse undergrowth of bushes, and is particularly partial to the vicinity of watercourses. The male bird is rather shy and careful of exposing himself.

Wilson mentions that in the lower parts of the Southern States, in the neighborhood of settlements, he found them more numerous than elsewhere. Their clear and lively notes, even in the months of January and February, were, at that season, almost the only music. Along the roadsides and fences he found them hovering in small groups, associated with Snowbirds and various kinds of Sparrows. Even in Pennsylvania they frequent the borders of creeks and rivulets during the whole year, in sheltered hollows, covered with holly, laurel, and other evergreens. They are very fond of Indian corn, a grain that is their favorite food. They are also said to feed on various kinds of fruit.

The males of this species, during the breeding season, are described as very pugnacious, and when confined together in the same cage they fight violently. The male bird has even been known to destroy its mate. In Florida Mr. Audubon found these birds mated by the 8th of February. The nest is built in bushes, among briers, or in low trees, and in various situations, the middle of a field, near a fence, or in the interior of a thicket, and usually not far from running water. It has even been placed in the garden close to the planter's house. It is loosely built of dry leaves and twigs, with a large proportion of dry grasses and strips of the bark of grapevines. Within, it is finished and lined with finer stems of grasses wrought into a circular form. There are usually two, and in the more Southern States three, broods in a season.

Mr. Audubon adds that they are easily raised from the nest, and have been known to breed in confinement.

The eggs of this species are of an oblong-oval shape, with but little difference at either end. Their ground-color appears to be white, but is generally so thickly marked with spots of ashy-brown and faint lavender tints as to permit but little of its ground to be seen. The eggs vary greatly in size, ranging from 1.10 inches to .98 of an inch in length, and from .80 to .78 in breadth.

Cardinalis virginianus, var. igneus, BAIRD.

CAPE CARDINAL.

Cardinalis igneus, BAIRD, Pr. Ac. Sc. Phila. 1859, 305 (Cape St. Lucas). — ELLIOT, Illust. N. Am. Birds, I, xvi. — COOPER, Orn. Cal. I, 238. *Cardinalis virginianus*, FINSCH, Abh. Nat. Brem. 1870, 339.

SP. CHAR. Resembling *virginianus*, having, like it, the distinct grayish edges to feathers of the dorsal region. Red lighter, however, and the top of head, including crest, nearly pure vermilion, instead of brownish-red. Black of the lores not passing across the forehead, reaching only to the nostril. Wing, 4.00; tail, 5.00; culmen, .83; depth of bill, .66; breadth of upper mandible, .38. (No. 49,757 ♂. Camp Grant, 60 miles east of Tucson, Arizona).

Female distinguishable from that of *virginianus* only by more swollen bill, and more restricted dusky around base of bill. *Young:* bill deep black.

HAB. Cape St. Lucas; Camp Grant, Arizona; Tres Marias Islands (off coast of Mexico, latitude between 21° and 22° north). Probably Western Mexico, from Sonora south to latitude of about 20°.

In the features pointed out above, all specimens from Arizona and Tres Marias, and of an exceedingly large series collected at Cape St. Lucas, differ from those of other regions.

No specimens are in the collection from Western Mexico as far south as Colima, but birds from this region will, without doubt, be found referrible to the present race.

HABITS. There appears to be nothing in the habits of this form of Cardinal, as far as known, to distinguish it from the Virginia bird; the nest and eggs, too, being almost identical. The latter average about one inch in length, and .80 in breadth. Their ground-color is white, with a bluish tint. Their markings are larger, and more of a rusty than an ashy brown, and the purple spots are fewer and less marked than in *C. virginianus*.

The memoranda of Mr. John Xantus show that in one instance a nest of this bird, containing two eggs, was found in a mimosa bush four feet from the ground; another nest, with one egg, in a like situation; a third, containing three eggs, was about three feet from the ground; a fourth, with two eggs, was also found in a mimosa, but only a few inches above the ground.

Genus **PIPILO**, Vieillot.

Pipilo, Vieillot, Analyse, 1816 (Agassiz).   (Type, *Fringilla erythrophthalma*, Linn.)

Gen. Char.   Bill rather stout; the culmen gently curved, the gonys nearly straight; the commissure gently concave, with a decided notch near the end; the lower jaw not so

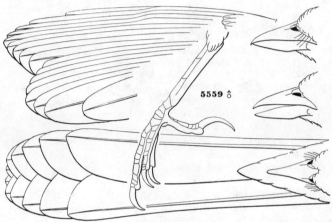

5559 ♂

Pipilo fuscus.

deep as the upper; not as wide as the gonys is long, but wider than the base of the upper mandible.   Feet large, the tarsus as long as or a little longer than the middle toe; the outer lateral toe a little the longer, and reaching a little beyond the base of the middle claw.   The hind claw about equal to its toe; the two together about equal to the outer toe.   Claws all stout, compressed, and moderately curved; in some western speci-

Pipilo erythrophthalmus.

mens the claws much larger.   Wings reaching about to the end of the upper tail-coverts; short and rounded, though the primaries are considerably longer than the nearly equal secondaries and tertials; the outer four quills are graduated, the first considerably shorter than the second, and about as long as the secondaries.   Tail considerably longer than the wings, moderately graduated externally; the feathers rather broad, most rounded off on the inner webs at the end.

The colors vary; the upper parts are generally uniform black or brown, sometimes olive; the under white or brown; no central streaks on the feathers.   The hood sometimes differently colored.

In the large number of species or races included in this genus by authors, there are certain differences of form, such as varying graduation of tail, length of claw, etc., but scarcely sufficient to warrant its further subdivision. In coloration, however, we find several different styles, which furnish a convenient method of arrangement into groups.

Few genera in birds exhibit such constancy in trifling variations of form and color, and as these are closely connected with geographical distribution, it seems reasonable to reduce many of the so-called species to a lower rank. In the following synopsis, we arrange the whole of North American and Mexican Pipilos into four sections, with their more positive species, and in the subsequent discussion of the sections separately we shall give what appear to be the varieties.

Species.

A. Sides and lower tail-coverts rufous, in sharp contrast with the clear white of the abdomen. Tail-feathers with whitish patch on end of inner webs.

 a. Head and neck black, sharply defined against the white of breast. Rump olive or blackish.

  Black or dusky olive above.

 1. **P. maculatus.** White spots on tips of both rows of wing-coverts, and on scapulars. No white patch on base of primaries. *Hab.* Mexico, and United States west of the Missouri. (Five races.)

 2. **P. erythropthalmus.** No white spots on wing-coverts, nor on scapulars. A white patch on base of primaries. *Hab.* Eastern Province of United States. (Two races.)

  Bright olive-green above.

 3. **P. macronyx.**[1] Scapulars and wing-coverts (both rows) with distinct greenish-white spots on tips of outer webs.

 4. **P. chlorosoma.**[2] Scapulars and wing-coverts without trace of white spots. *Hab.* Table-lands of Mexico. (Perhaps these are two races of one species, *macronyx*.)

[1] *Pipilo macronyx*, SWAINSON, Phil. Mag. I, 1827, 434. Real del Monte, Mex.—IB. Anim. in Men. 1838, 347.—BP. Consp. 487.—SCLATER & SALVIN, 1869, 361. *Pipilo virescens*, HARTLAUB, Cab. Jour. 1863, 228, Mex.

SP. CHAR. Prevailing color above olive-green ; the head and neck all round black, abruptly contrasted below with the white under parts ; above passing insensibly into the green of the back ; feathers of interscapular region obscurely dusky medially ; sides and crissum rufous. Scapulars and greater and middle coverts with outer webs pale greenish-yellow at ends ; these blotches faintly margined externally with olive-green. Edge of wing yellow ; outer primary edged with whitish, edges of other primaries and of secondaries uniform olive-green. Fifth quill longest, fourth and sixth scarcely shorter ; first shorter than ninth. Legs stout, claws much curved. Tail wanting in the single specimen before us (a male from the city of Mexico, belonging to Mr. G. N. Lawrence).

Dimensions (prepared specimen) : Wing, 3.70. Exposed portion of first primary, 2.30 ; of second, 2.73 ; of longest (measured from exposed base of first primary), 2.85. Bill : Length from forehead, .75 ; from nostril, .45. Legs : Tarsus, 1.14 ; middle claw, .38 ; hind toe and claw, .85 ; claw alone, .52.

In describing this species, Swainson mentions an accompanying specimen as similar, but without any white spots on wings, suggesting that it may be the female. A specimen in the plumage from Oaxaca is characterized as follows.

[2] *Pipilo chlorosoma*, BAIRD. 50,225 ♂, Oaxaca. Similar to *P. macronyx* in color, but without any trace of white markings on the wings. Outer tail-feathers with an obscurely defined greenish-white patch about an inch long, at the end of inner web ; similar, but successively smaller patches on the second and third feathers, all whiter on upper than lower surface. Fifth quill longest ; first shorter than ninth.

Dimensions (prepared specimen) : Total length, 8.20 ; wing, 3.75 ; tail, 4.80. Bill : Length *b.* Head and neck ashy, paler on jugulum, where the color fades gradually into the white of breast. Rump and upper tail-coverts bright rufous.

5. **P. supercilioss.**[1] An obsolete whitish superciliary stripe. Greater wing-coverts obsoletely whitish at tips; no other white markings on upper parts, and the tail-patches indistinct. *Hab.* Brazil. (Perhaps not genuine *Pipilo.*)

B. Sides ashy or tinged with ochraceous; lower tail-coverts ochraceous, not sharply contrasted with white on the abdomen, or else the abdomen concolor with the side. Head never black, and upper parts without light markings (except the wing in *fuscus* var. *albicollis*).

a. Wings and tail olive-green.

6. **P. chlorurus.** Whole pileum (except in young) deep rufous, sharply defined. Whole throat pure white, immaculate, and sharply defined against the surrounding deep ash; a maxillary and a short supraloral stripe of white. Anterior parts of body streaked in young. *Hab.* Western Province of United States.

b. Wings and tail grayish-brown.

7. **P. fuscus.** A whitish or ochraceous patch covering the throat contrasting with the adjacent portions, and bounded by dusky specks. Lores and chin like the throat. *Hab.* Mexico, and United States west of Rocky Mountains. (Five races.)

8. **P. aberti.** Throat concolor with the adjacent portions, and without distinct spots. Lores and chin blackish. *Hab.* Colorado region of Middle Province, United States. (Only one form known.)

SECTION I.

Head black.

Pipilo erythrophthalmus.

After a careful study of the very large collection of Black-headed Pipilos (leaving for the present the consideration of those with olive-green bodies) in the Smithsonian Museum, we have come finally to the conclusion that all the species described as having the scapulars and wing-coverts spotted with white — as *arcticus, oregonus,* and *megalonyx,* and even including the differently colored *P. maculatus* of Mexico — are probably only geographical races of one species, representing in the trans-Missouri region the *P. erythrophthalmus* of the eastern division of the continent. It is true that specimens may be selected of the four races capable of accurate definition, but the transition

from forehead, .73; from nostril, .43. Legs: Tarsus, 1.24; middle toe and claw, 1.10; claw alone, .36; hind toe and claw, .85; claw alone, .50. No. 60,050, Mexico, is similar, in all essential respects.

From the analogies of the black Pipilos, it is reasonable to consider these two birds as distinct species, or at least varieties, especially as the specimen before us of that with unspotted wings is marked male. The general appearance is otherwise much the same, the unspotted bird rather smaller, and without the dusky interscapular markings described in *macronyx.* Should No. 50,225 represent a distinct species, it may be called *P. chlorosoma,* and distinguished as above. (60,050, Mexico, Boucard.)

[1] *Pipilo lateralis* (Natt.). *Emberiza lateralis,* Natt. Mus. Vind. MSS. *Poospiza lat.* Burm. Th. Bras. III, Av. 2, p. 215. *Pipilo superciliosa,* Swains. An. Menag. 311, 95, fig. 59.

from one to the other is so gradual that a considerable percentage of the collection can scarcely be assigned satisfactorily ; and even if this were possible, the differences after all are only such as are caused by a slight change in the proportion of black, and the varying development of feet and wings.

Taking *maculatus* as it occurs in the central portion of its wide field of distribution, with wing-spots of average size, we find these spots slightly bordered, or at least often, with black, and the primaries edged externally with white only towards the end. The exterior web of lateral tail-feather is edged mostly with white ; the terminal white patches of outer feather about an inch long ; that of inner web usually separated from the outer by a black shaft-streak. In more northern specimens the legs are more dusky than usual. The tail is variable, but longer generally than in the other races. The claws are enormously large in many, but not in all specimens, varying considerably ; and the fourth primary is usually longest, the first equal to or shorter than the secondaries. This is the race described as *P. megalonyx*, and characterizes the Middle Province, between the Sierra Nevada of California and the eastern Rocky Mountains, or the great interior basin of the continent ; it occurs also near the head of the Rio Grande.

On the Pacific slope of California, as we proceed westward, we find a change in the species, the divergence increasing still more as we proceed northward, until in Oregon and Washington the extreme of range and alteration is seen in *P. oregonus*. Here the claws are much smaller, the white markings restricted in extent so as to form quite small spots bordered externally by black ; the spots on the inner webs of tail much smaller, and even bordered along the shaft with black, and the outer web of the lateral entirely black, or with only a faint white edging. The concealed white of the head and neck has disappeared also.

Proceeding eastward, on the other hand, from our starting-point, we find another race, in *P. arcticus*, occupying the western slope of the Missouri Valley and the basin of the Saskatchewan, in which, on the contrary, the white increases in quantity, and more and more to its eastern limit. The black borders of the wing-patches disappear, leaving them white externally ; and decided white edgings are seen for the first time at the bases of primaries, as well as near their ends, the two sometimes confluent. The terminal tail-patches are larger, the outer web of the exterior feather is entirely white except toward the very base, and we thus have the opposite extreme to *P. oregonus*. The wings are longer ; the third primary longest ; the first usually longer than the secondaries or the ninth quill.

Finally, proceeding southward along the table-lands of Mexico, and especially on their western slope, we find *P. maculatus* (the first described of all) colored much like the females of the more northern races, except that the head and neck are black, in decided contrast to the more olivaceous back. The wing formula and pattern of markings are much like *megalonyx*, the claws more like *arcticus*. Even in specimens of *megalonyx*, from the southern portion of its area of distribution, we find a tendency to an ashy or brownish tinge on the rump, extending more or less along the back ; few, if any indeed, being uniformly black.

As, however, a general expression can be given to the variations referred to, and as they have an important geographical relationship, besides a general diagnosis, we give their characters and distribution in detail.

The general impression we derive from a study of the series is that the amount of white on the wing and elsewhere decreases from the Missouri River to the Pacific, exhibiting its minimum in Oregon and Washington, precisely as in the small black Woodpeckers ; that in the Great Basin the size of the claws and the length of tail increases considerably ; that the northern forms are entirely black, and the more southern brown or olivaceous, except on the head.

The following synopsis will be found to express the principal characteristics of the species and their varieties, premising that *P. arcticus* is more distinctly definable than any of the others. We add the character of the green-bodied Mexican species to complete the series.

Synopsis of Varieties.

I. *P. erythrophthalmus.*

1. Wing, 3.65 ; tail, 4.20. Outer tail-feather with terminal half of inner web white. Iris bright red, sometimes paler. *Hab.* Eastern Province United States. (Florida in winter.) . . . . . var. *erythropthalmus.*
2. Wing, 2.90 ; tail, 3.75. Outer tail-feather with only terminal fourth of inner web white. Iris white. *Hab.* Florida (resident) . . var. *alleni.*

II. *P. maculatus.*

A. Interscapulars with white streaks.
 a. Outer webs of primaries not edged with white at the base.
1. Above olive-brown, the head and neck, only, continuous black ; back streaked with black. White spots on wing-coverts not bordered externally with black. Wing, 3.25 ; tail, 4.00 ; hind claw, .44. *Hab.* Table-lands of Mexico . . . . var. *maculatus.*[1]
2. Above black, tinged with olive on rump, and sometimes on the nape. White spots as in last. Inner web of lateral tail-feathers with terminal white spot more than one inch long ; outer web broadly edged with white. Wing, 3.45 ; tail, 4.10 ; hind claw, .55. *Female* less deep black than male, with a general slaty-olive cast. *Hab.* Middle Province of United States, from Fort Tejon, California, to Upper Rio Grande, and from Fort Crook to Fort Bridger . . . . var. *megalonyx.*
3. Above almost wholly black, with scarcely any olive tinge, and this only on rump. White spots restricted, and with a distinct black external border. White terminal spot on inner web of lateral tail-feather less than one inch long ; outer web almost wholly black. Wing, 3.40 ; tail, 3.90 ; hind claw, .39. *Female* deep umber-brown, instead of black. *Hab.* Pacific Province of United States, south to San Francisco ; West Humboldt Mountains. var. *oregonus.*

---

[1] *Pipilo maculatus*, SWAINSON, Philos. Mag., 1827.

b. Outer webs of primaries distinctly edged with white at base.

4. Above black, except on rump, which is tinged with olivaceous. White spots very large, without black border. Inner web of lateral tail-feather with terminal half white, the outer web almost wholly white. Wing, 3 50; tail, 3.90; hind claw, .39. *Female* umber-brown, replacing black. *Hab.* Plains between Rocky Mountains and the Missouri; Saskatchewan Basin.

var. *arcticus.*

B. Interscapulars without white streaks.

5. Above dusky olive; white spots on scapulars and wing-coverts small, and without black edge. Tail-patches very restricted (outer only .40 long). No white on primaries. Wing, 2.85; tail, 3.10. *Female* scarcely different. *Hab.* Socorro Island, off west coast of Mexico . . . var. *carmani.*[1]

Pipilo erythrophthalmus, VIEILLOT.

GROUND ROBIN; TOWHEE; CHEWINK.

Fringilla erythrophthalma, LINN. Syst. Nat. I, 1766, 318. — AUD. Orn. Biog. I, 1832, 151; V, 511, pl. xxix. *Emberiza erythrophthalma,* GM. Syst. Nat. I, 1788, 874. — WILSON, Am. Orn. VI, 1812, 90, pl. liii. *Pipilo erythrophthalmus,* VIEILL. Gal. Ois. I, 1824, 109, pl. lxxx. — BON. List, 1838. — IB. Conspectus, 1850, 487. — AUD. Syn. 1839, 124. — IB. Birds Am. III, 1841, 167, pl. cxcv. — BAIRD, Birds N. Am. 1858, 512. — SAMUELS, 333. *Pipilo ater,* VIEILL. Nouv. Dict. XXXIV, 1819, 292. *Towhee Bird,* CATESBY, Car. I, 34. *Towhee Bunting,* LATHAM, Syn. II, I, 1783, 199. — PENNANT, II, 1785, 359.

SP. CHAR. Upper parts generally, head and neck all round, and upper part of the breast, glossy black, abruptly defined against the pure white which extends to the anus, but is bounded on the sides and under the wings by light chestnut, which is sometimes streaked externally with black. Feathers of throat white in the middle. Under coverts 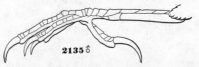 similar to sides, but paler. Edges of outer six primaries with white at the base and on the middle of the outer web; inner two tertiaries also edged externally with white. Tail-feathers black; outer web of the first, with the ends of the first to the third, white, decreasing from the exterior one. Outermost quill usually shorter than ninth, or even than secondaries; fourth quill longest, fifth scarcely shorter. Iris red; said to be sometimes paler, or even white, in winter. Length, 8.75; wing, 3.75; tail, 4.10. Bill black, legs flesh-color. *Female* with the black replaced by a rather rufous brown.

HAB. Eastern United States to the Missouri River; Florida (in winter).

The tail-feathers are only moderately graduated on the sides; the outer about .40 of an inch shorter than the middle. The outer tail-feather has the terminal half white, the outline transverse; the white of the second is about half as long as that of the first; of the third half that of the second. The chestnut of the sides reaches forward to the black of the neck, and is visible when the wings are closed.

[1] *Pipilo carmani,* BAIRD, MSS.; LAWRENCE, Ann. N. Y. Lyc. X, 7. (Specimens in collection made by Colonel A. J. Grayson.)

A young bird has the prevailing color reddish-olive above, spotted with lighter ; beneath brownish-white, streaked thickly with brown.

The description above given may be taken as representing the average of the species in the Northern and Middle States. Most specimens from the Mississippi Valley differ in having the two white patches on the primaries confluent ; but this feature is not sufficiently constant to make it worthy of

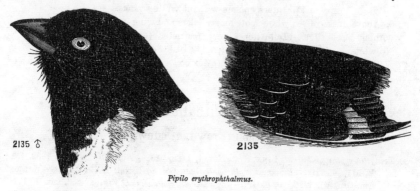

2135 ♂   2135

Pipilo erythrophthalmus.

more than passing notice, for occasionally western specimens have the white spaces separated, as in the majority of eastern examples, while among the latter there may, now and then, be found individuals scarcely distinguishable from the average of western ones.

In Florida, however, there is a local, resident race, quite different from these two northern styles, which are themselves not enough unlike to be considered separately. This Florida race differs in much smaller size, very restricted white on both wing and tail, and in having a yellowish-white instead of blood-red iris. Further remarks on this Florida race will be found under its proper heading (p. 708), as *P. erythrophthalmus*, var. *alleni*.

Specimens of *erythrophthalmus*, as restricted, from Louisiana, as is the case with most birds from the Lower Mississippi region, exhibit very intense colors compared with those from more northern portions, or even Atlantic coast specimens from the same latitude.

HABITS. The Ground Robin, Towhee, Chewink, Charee, or Joreet, as it is variously called, has an extended distribution throughout the eastern United States, from Florida and Georgia on the southeast to the Selkirk Settlements on the northwest, and as far to the west as the edge of the Great Plains, where it is replaced by other closely allied races. It breeds almost wherever found, certainly in Georgia, and, I have no doubt, sparingly in Florida.

This bird was not observed in Texas by Mr. Dresser. It has been found in Western Maine, where it is given by Mr. Verrill as a summer visitant, and where it breeds, but is not common. It arrives there the first of May. It is not given by Mr. Boardman as occurring in Eastern Maine. In Massachusetts it is a very abundant summer visitant, arriving about the last of April, and leaving about the middle of October. It nests there the last of

May, and begins to sit upon the eggs about the first of June. It is slightly gregarious just as it is preparing to leave, but at all other times is to be met with only in solitary pairs.

The Ground Robin is in many respects one of the most strongly characterized of our North American birds, exhibiting peculiarities in which all the members of this genus share to a very large degree. They frequent close and sheltered thickets, where they spend a large proportion of their time on the ground among the fallen leaves, scratching and searching for worms, larvæ, and insects. Though generally resident in retired localities, it is far from being a shy or timid bird. I have known it to show itself in a front yard, immediately under the windows of a dwelling and near the main street of the village, where for hours I witnessed its diligent labors in search of food. The spot was very shady, and unfrequented during the greater part of the day. It was not disturbed when the members of the family passed in or out.

The call-note of this bird is very peculiar, and is variously interpreted in different localities. It has always appeared to me that the Georgian *jo-rēēt* was at least as near to its real notes as *tow-hēē*. Its song consists of a few simple notes, which very few realize are those of this bird. In singing, the male is usually to be seen on the top of some low tree. These notes are uttered in a loud voice, and are not unmusical. Wilson says its song resembles that of the Yellow-Hammer of Europe, but is more varied and mellow. Nuttall speaks of its notes as simple, guttural, and monotonous, and of its voice as clear and sonorous. The song, which he speaks of as quaint and somewhat pensive, he describes as sounding like *t'sh'd-wĭtee-tĕ-tĕ-tĕ-tĕ-tĕ*.

Wilson says this bird is known in Pennsylvania as the "Swamp Robin." If so, this is a misnomer. In New England it has no predilection for low or moist ground, and I have never found it in such situations. Its favorite haunts are dry uplands, near the edges of woods, or high tracts covered with a low brushwood, selecting for nesting-places the outer skirts of a wood, especially one of a southern aspect. The nest is sunk in a depression in the ground, the upper edges being usually just level with the ground. It is largely composed of dry leaves and coarse stems as a base, within which is built a firmer nest of dry bents well arranged, usually with no other lining. It is generally partially concealed by leaves or a tuft of grass, and is not easily discovered unless the female is seen about it.

Dr. Coues says these Buntings are chiefly spring and autumnal visitants near Washington, only a few breeding. They are very abundant from April 25 to May 10, and from the first to the third week of October, and are partially gregarious. Their migrations are made by day, and are usually in small companies in the fall, but singly in the spring. Wilson found them in the middle districts of Virginia, and from thence south to Florida, during the months of January, February, and March. Their usual food is obtained among the dry leaves, though they also feed on hard seeds and gravel. They are not known to commit any depredations upon harvests. They may be easily accustomed to confinement, and in a few days will become quite tame. When slightly wounded and captured, they at first make a sturdy resistance, and bite quite severely. They are much attached to their young, and when approached evince great anxiety, the female thrusting herself forward to divert attention by her outcries and her simulated lameness.

The eggs of this species are of a rounded-oval shape, and have a dull-white ground, spotted with dots and blotches of a wine-colored brown. These usually are larger than in the other species, and are mostly congregated about the larger end, and measure .98 of an inch in length by .80 in breadth.

Pipilo erythrophthalmus, var. alleni, Coues.

WHITE-EYED CHEWINK; FLORIDA CHEWINK.

Pipilo alleni, Coues, American Naturalist, V, Aug. 1871, 366.

Sp. Char. Similar to *erythrophthalmus*, but differing in the following respects: White spaces on wings and tail much restricted, those on inner webs of lateral tail-feathers only .50 to .75 long. Size very much smaller, except the bill, which is absolutely larger. Iris white.

♂. (55,267, Dummits's Grove, Florida, March, 1869.) Length, 7.75; wing, 3.00; tail, 3.75; bill from nostril, .38; tarsus, .97.

♀. (55,271, same locality and date.) Wing, 3.00; tail, 3.50; bill from nostril, .37; tarsus, .91. White on primaries almost absent.

This interesting variety of *Pipilo erythrophthalmus* was found in Florida, in the spring of 1869, by Mr. C. J. Maynard, and probably represents the species as resident in that State. It is considerably smaller than the average (length, 7.75; extent, 10.00; wing, 3.00; tarsus, .95), and has very appreciably less white on the tail. The outer web of outer feather is only narrowly edged with white, instead of being entirely so to the shaft (except in one specimen), and the terminal white tip, confined to the inner web, is only from .50 to .75 of an inch long, instead of 1.25 to 1.75, or about the

2135, *Pipilo erythropthalmus.* 247, var. *alleni.*

amount on the second feather of northern specimens, as shown in the accompanying figures. There is apparently a greater tendency to dusky streaks and specks in the rufous of the side of the breast or in the adjacent white. Resident specimens from Georgia are intermediate in size and color between the northern and Florida races.

The bill of Mr. Maynard's specimen is about the size of that of more northern ones ; the iris is described by him as pale yellowish-white, much lighter than usual.

Pipilo maculatus,[1] var. megalonyx, Baird.

LONG-CLAWED TOWHEE BUNTING.

Pipilo megalonyx, Baird, Birds N. Am. 1858, 515, pl. lxxiii. — Heerm. X, *S*, 51 (nest). — Cooper, Orn. Cal. I, 242.

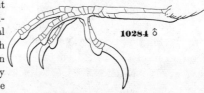

10284 ♂

Sp. Char. Similar to *P. arcticus* in amount of white on the wings and scapulars, though this frequently edged with black, but without basal white on outer web of primaries. Outer edge of outer web of external tail-feather white, sometimes confluent with that at tip of tail. Concealed white spots on feathers of side of neck. Claws enormously large, the hinder longer than its digit; the hind toe and claw reaching to the middle of the middle claw, which, with its toe, is as long as or longer than the tarsus. Inner lateral claw reaching nearly to the middle of middle claw. Length, 7.60; wing, 3.25; hind toe and claw, .90. *Female* with the deep black replaced by dusky slaty-olive.

Hab. Southern coast of California and across through valleys of Gila and Rio Grande; north through the Great Basin across from Fort Crook, California, to Fort Bridger, Wyoming.

This form constitutes so strongly marked a variety as to be worthy of particular description. The general appearance is that of *P. arcticus*, which it resembles in the amount of white spotting on the wings. This, however, does not usually involve the whole outer web at the end, but, as in *oregonus*, has a narrow border of black continued around the white terminally and sometimes externally. There is not quite so much of a terminal white blotch on the outer tail-feather, this being but little over an inch in length, and the outer web of the same feather is never entirely white, though always with an external white border, which sometimes is confluent with the

---

[1] *Pipilo maculatus*, Swainson. Sp. Char. *Male.* Similar to the female of *Pipilo arcticus*, but rather more olivaceous ; only the head and neck all round black ; shading above insensibly into the back. The white markings mostly edged narrowly externally with black, and clouded with rusty ; the nape-feathers faintly, the interscapular broadly, streaked centrally with blackish ; lower back and rump, with outer edges of quill and tail feathers, olivaceous-brown. A narrow shaft-streak in white at end of tail. Fourth quill longest ; fifth scarcely shorter ; first about equal to secondaries. Claws moderate ; perhaps larger than in *erythrophthalmus*. Length of skin, 7.80 ; wing, 3.15 ; tail, 4.20 ; tarsus, 1.10 ; middle toe and claw, .96 ; claw alone, .34 ; hind toe and claw, .81 ; claw alone, .45. *Hab.* Mexico (Oaxaca ; Real del Monte, Philos. Mag., 1827).

It is a serious question whether this comparatively little known Mexican species of *Pipilo* is not to be considered as identical with some or all of the species of the United States, with spotted wing-coverts, notwithstanding the difference in the color of the body. It appears, however, to be constant in the olivaceous character of the back, — no reference being made to Mexican specimens entirely black above, — and as such it may be considered a permanent geographical race.

terminal spot, but usually leaves a brown streak near the end never seen in *arcticus*, which also has the whole outer web white except at the base. From *oregonus* the species differs in the much greater amount of white on the wings and the less rounded character of the spots. *Oregonus*, too, has the whole outer web of external tail-feather black, and the terminal white spot of the inner web less than an inch in length. We have never seen in *oregonus* any concealed white spotting on the sides of the head.

The greatest difference between this race and the two others lies in the stout tarsi and enormously large claws, as described, both the lateral extending greatly beyond the base of the middle one, the hinder toe and claw nearly as long as the tarsus. The only North American passerine birds having any approach to this length of claw are those of the genus *Passerella*.

This great development of the claws is especially apparent in specimens from the Southern Sierra Nevada, the maximum being attained in the Fort Tejon examples; those from as far north as Carson City, Nev., however, are scarcely smaller. In most Rocky Mountain Pipilos, the claws are but little longer than in *arcticus*.

In this race the female is not noticeably different from the male, being of a merely less intense black, — not brown, — and conspicuously different as in *arcticus* and *oregonus;* there is, however, some variation among individuals in this respect, but none are ever so light as the average in the other races.

The young bird is dusky-brown above, with a slight rusty tinge, and obsolete streaks of blackish. White markings as in adult, but tinged with rusty. Throat and breast rusty-white, broadly streaked with dusky; sides only tinged with rufous.

HABITS. According to Mr. Ridgway's observations, the *P. megalonyx* replaces in the Rocky Mountain region and in the greater portion of the Great Basin the *P. arcticus* of the Plains, from their eastern slope eastward to the Missouri River, and the *P. oregonus* of the Northern Sierra Nevada and Pacific coast. It is most nearly related to the latter. He became familiar with the habits of this species near Salt Lake City, having already made like observations of the *oregonus* at Carson. A short acquaintance with the former, after a long familiarity with the latter, enabled him to note a decided difference in the notes of the two birds, yet in their external appearance they were hardly distinguishable, and he was at first surprised to find the same bird apparently uttering entirely different notes, the call-note of *P. megalonyx* being very similar to that of the common Catbird. The song of this species, he adds, has considerable resemblance in style to that of the eastern *P. erythrophthalmus*, and though lacking its musical character, is yet far superior to that of *P. oregonus*. This bird is also much less shy than the western one, and is, in fact, quite as unsuspicious as the eastern bird.

Nests, with eggs, were found on the ground, among the scrub-oaks of the hillsides, from about the 20th of May until the middle of June.

This species has been obtained on the southern coast of California, and through to the valleys of the Gila and the Rio Grande. In California it was obtained near San Francisco by Mr. Cutts and Mr. Hepburn ; at Santa Clara by Dr. Cooper ; at Monterey by Dr. Canfield ; in the Sacramento Valley by Dr. Heermann ; at San Diego by Dr. Hammond ; at Fort Tejon by Mr. Xantus ; at Saltillo, Mexico, by Lieutenant Couch ; in New Mexico by Captain Pope ; and at Fort Thorn by Dr. Henry.

Lieutenant Couch describes it as a shy, quiet bird, and as found in woody places.

Dr. Kennerly met with this bird at Pueblo Creek, New Mexico, January 22, 1854. It first attracted his attention early in the month of January, in the Aztec Mountains, along Pueblo Creek. There it was often met with, but generally singly. It inhabited the thickest bushes, and its motions were so constant and rapid, as it hopped from twig to twig, that they found it difficult to procure specimens. Its flight was rapid, and near the ground.

Dr. Cooper speaks of this species as a common and resident bird in all the lower districts of California, and to quite a considerable distance among the mountains. It was also found on the islands of Catalina and San Clemente, distant sixteen miles from the mainland. Though found in New Mexico, Dr. Cooper has met with none in the barren districts between the Coast Range and the Colorado, nor in the valley of the latter.

Their favorite residence is said to be in thickets and in oak groves, where they live mostly on the ground, scratching among the dead leaves in the concealment of the underbrush, and very rarely venturing far from such shelter. They never fly more than a few yards at a time, and only a few feet above the ground. In villages, where they are not molested, they soon become more familiar, take up their abodes in gardens, and build their nests in the vicinity of houses.

Dr. Cooper gives them credit for little musical power. Their song is said to be only a feeble monotonous trill, from the top of some low bush. When alarmed, they have a note something like the mew of a cat. On this account they are popularly known as Catbirds. He adds that the nest is made on the ground, under a thicket, and that it is constructed of dry leaves. stalks, and grass, mingled with fine roots. The eggs, four or five in number, are greenish-white, minutely speckled with reddish-brown, and measure one inch by .70.

Dr. Coues found this species a very abundant and resident species in Arizona. It was rather more numerous in the spring and in the fall than at other times. He found it shy and retiring, and inhabiting the thickest brush. Its call-note is said to be almost exactly like that of our eastern Catbird. He describes its song as a rather harsh and monotonous repetition of four or six syllables, something like that of the *Euspiza americana.* He found females with mature eggs in their ovaries as early as May 5.

A nest of this species, collected by Mr. Ridgway near Salt Lake City,

May 26, was built on the ground, among scrub-oak brush. It is a very slight structure, composed almost entirely of coarse dry stems of grass, with a few bits of coarse inner bark, and with a base made up wholly with the latter material, and having a diameter of about four inches.

The eggs of this nest, four in number, have an average measurement of .95 of an inch in length by .73 in breadth. Their ground-color is crystalline-white, covered very generally with spots and small blotches of purplish and wine-colored brown, somewhat aggregated at the larger end.

Pipilo maculatus, var. oregonus, BELL.

OREGON GROUND ROBIN.

Pipilo oregonus, BELL, Ann N. Y. Lyc. V, 1852, 6 (Oregon). — BONAP. Comptes Rendus, XXXVII, Dec. 1853, 922. — IB. Notes Orn. Delattre, 1854, 22 (same as prec.). — BAIRD, Birds N. Am. 1858, 513. — LORD, Pr. R. A. Inst. IV, 64, 120 (British Col.). — COOPER & SUCKLEY, 200. — COOPER, Orn. Cal. I, 241. *Fringilla arctica*, AUD. Orn. Biog. V, 1839, 49, pl. cccxciv. (not of SWAINSON). *Pipilo arctica*, AUD. Syn. 1839, 123. — IB. Birds Am. III, 1841, 164, pl. cxciv.

SP. CHAR. Upper surface generally, with the head and neck all round to the upper  part of the breast, deep black; the rest of lower parts pure white, except the sides of the body and under tail-coverts, which are light chestnut-brown; the latter rather paler. The outer webs of scapulars (usually edged narrowly with black) and of the superincumbent feathers of the back, with a rounded white spot at the end of the outer webs of the greater and middle coverts; the outer edges of the innermost tertials white; no white at the base of the primaries. Outer web of the first tail-feather black, occasionally white on the extreme edge; the outer three with a white tip to the inner web. Outer quill shorter than ninth, or scarcely equalling the secondaries; fourth quill longest; fifth scarcely shorter. Length, 8.25; wing, 4.40; tail, 4.00. *Female* with the black replaced by a more brownish tinge. Claws much as in *erythrophthalmus*.

HAB. Coasts of Oregon and Washington Territories, south to San Francisco, California. Melting eastward and south into *megalonyx*. West Humboldt Mountains and Northern Sierra Nevada.

Comparing this race with *arcticus*, we do not find much difference in the white of the scapular region, except that the white marks here, as elsewhere on the wing, are rounded, the extreme end of the outer web of the feather being black instead of running out acutely white to the very tip of the outer webs of the feathers. This gives rather less extension to the white. In fact, most of the white marks are edged externally with black, converting them into spots. There is no white whatever at the exposed base of the

outer web of the second to fifth primaries, and there is only a trace of white near the end, instead of having a conspicuous white edging from base to near the tip.

The outer web of the outer tail-feather, instead of being entirely white for the exposed portion, is only very slightly edged with white; usually entirely black. The white at the end of the feathers is much more restricted, and extends only over the three outer feathers; usually not reaching to the shaft. The relations to var. *megalonyx* have been given under the latter head.

HABITS. The Oregon Ground Robin, so far as known, has a restricted residence, the western portion of Oregon and Washington Territory during the summer, and in the more northern portions of California. Its occurrence in the latter State seems to have escaped the notice of Dr. Cooper, though he gives it conjecturally, having seen birds which he supposed to be of this species in the higher Sierra Nevada. In its habits and notes Dr. Cooper could observe no difference between this species and *P. megalonyx*, both having the complaining *mew*, from which they have obtained the name of Catbird on that coast.

Mr. J. K. Lord found a nest containing six eggs, which he supposed to belong to a bird of this species, at Fort Colville. It was built on the top of a stump, round which young shoots had grown like a fringe, completely hiding it from the sharpest eye. Mr. Hepburn met with it at Victoria.

Dr. Cooper, in his Report on the Birds of Washington Territory, states that the song of this species in spring, as it sits on a low bush enjoying the sunshine, is like the final trill of the Redwing, or the lisping faint notes of the Cowbird. It is a constant resident of the Territory, but only frequents the edge of the coast in winter. He also mentions finding it about thirty miles south of San Francisco in autumn. Dr. Suckley met with it west of the Cascade Mountains.

In very many respects, in the opinion of Mr. Ridgway, the Oregon Ground Robin very closely resembles the common and familiar eastern " Chewink." There is noticeable in this western representative a peculiar manner of flight, and a predilection for bushy places, closely corresponding with those of the eastern bird. It differs, in the most marked manner, however, in its extreme shyness, and in the total absence of the agreeable and striking notes of the Towhee. The notes of this bird are, he states, of the rudest description, and instead of being familiar and unsuspicious, it is one of the shyest and most difficult to approach of any of the western birds.

He found it quite plentiful about Sacramento, where it inhabits the thickets in company with the western Chat. After crossing the Sierra Nevada it was found more abundant still in the chaparrals of the sheltered ravines on the eastern base of those mountains, as well as in the shrubbery of the river valleys. During the winter it forsakes the former for the latter localities. Eastward this species was found as far as the West Humboldt Mountains, where typical examples were obtained.

At Carson City, early in March, his attention was attracted by the peculiar notes of this *Pipilo*; the bird was sitting on a high rock above the thick chaparral of the hillside, and sharply defined against the sky. It was readily distinguishable by the black of its head and breast, in sharp contrast with the pure white of its lower parts. Every few moments it would raise its head to utter, in a short trill, its rude song. When approached, it would jerk its expanded white-tipped tail, and disappear among the bushes. It was abundant in the chaparrals, on the hillsides, and among the thickets and buffalo-berry bushes along the rivers. The males were in full song, perching, as they sang, on a prominent rock or bush.

Mr. Nuttall met with a nest of this species on the 14th of June. It was built in the shelter of a low undershrub, in a depression scratched out for its reception. It was made of a rather copious lining of clean wiry grass, with some dead leaves beneath, as a foundation. The eggs were four, nearly hatched, very closely resembling those of the Towhee, thickly spotted over, but more so at the larger end, with very small round and very numerous reddish-chocolate spots. The pair showed great solicitude about their nest, the male, in particular, approaching boldly to scold and lament at the dangerous intrusion.

The Oregon Ground Robin Mr. Lord considered a quaint and restless bird. He found it very abundant from the coast to the summit of the Rocky Mountains, and also very common on Vancouver Island. It arrives the last of April and first of May, and frequents dark woods and thick tangled underbrush. He describes it as stealthy and shy, with a habit of hiding, but its cry usually betrays its place of concealment. This cry he states to be like the squall of the Catbird.

Mr. Townsend found it abundant on the Columbia, where, as he observed, it lived mostly on the ground, or on bushes near the ground, rarely ascending trees. Mr. Audubon gives the measurement of its egg as 1.12 inches in length and .87 in breadth.

The egg of this species is more rounded than are those of this genus generally, and there is but little difference between the two ends. The ground-color is white, with a greenish tinge, and is very generally and profusely spotted with fine markings of reddish and purplish-brown. They measure .95 by .80 of an inch.

Pipilo maculatus, var. arcticus, SWAINSON.

ARCTIC TOWHEE BUNTING.

Pyrgita (Pipilo) arctica, Sw. F. Bor.-Am. II, 1831, 260. *Pipilo arcticus,* NUTTALL, Man. I, 1832, 589. — IB., (2d ed.,) 1840, 610. — BELL, Ann. N. Y. Lyc. V, 1852, 7. — BAIRD, Birds N. Am. 1858, 514.

SP. CHAR. Upper parts generally, with head and neck all round to the upper part of the breast, black; the rump usually tinged with ashy. Middle of breast and of belly white; sides chestnut; under tail-coverts similar, but paler. Entire outer webs of scapulars and of dorsal feathers immediately above them, and of ends of primary and secondary coverts, to the shaft, with edges of outer webs of three innermost tertials, and of the second to the fifth primaries, conspicuously white. Whole outer web of the first and ends of the first to the fourth tail-feathers, white, the amount diminishing not very rapidly. Outermost quill longer than ninth, sometimes than eighth, nearly always exceeding the secondaries; third quill longest; fourth scarcely shorter. Length about 8 inches; wing, 4.40; tail, 4.10; hind toe and claw, .74. *Female* paler brown instead of black; the rufous, seen in *P. erythrophthalmus,* tinged with ashy.

HAB. High central plains of Upper Missouri, Yellowstone, and Platte; basin of Missouri River, especially west, including eastern slope of Rocky Mountains; San Antonio, Texas (DRESSER, Ibis, 1865, 492).

P. arcticus is similar in form to *P. erythrophthalmus,* which, however, is readily distinguished by the entire absence of white on the scapulars and wing-coverts. The amount of white on the tail decreases much less rapidly. The differences between it and *P. oregonus* will be found detailed under the head of the latter species.

One specimen (8,193) from Fort Leavenworth, with a few white spots only on the scapulars, may perhaps be considered a hybrid between *arcticus* and *erythrophthalmus.*

In some specimens the interscapulars are edged externally with white. The feathers of throat and sides of head show occasional concealed spots of white about the middle. As in *erythrophthalmus,* the bases of the primaries are white along the outer edge, showing under the primary coverts, sometimes, but perhaps not generally, confluent with the white towards the end of the same web.

The female is of a dull ashy-brown, difficult to describe, but with only a slight tinge of the rufous seen in *P. erythrophthalmus,* which is most distinct on top of head and back. There is an almost inappreciable ashy superciliary stripe.

The young bird resembles in general appearance that of *megalonyx,* but is lighter colored, and with the dusky streaks on the jugulum much narrower. The brown above is as light as in *erythrophthalmus,* but without the reddish cast seen in the latter, and not blackish, as in *megalonyx.*

HABITS. The Saskatchewan or Arctic Ground Finch was first met with by Sir John Richardson. It was observed by him only on the plains of the Saskatchewan, where he had no doubt of its breeding, as one specimen was killed late in July.   It was said to arrive in that region in the end of May, and to frequent shady and moist clumps of wood.   It was generally seen on the ground.   Its habits, so far as they were observed, correspond with those of the Towhee Bunting, which it closely resembles in external appearance.   It feeds on grubs, and is a solitary and retired, but not a distrustful bird.

Besides its occurrence in the Valley of the Saskatchewan, these birds have often been found on the high central plains of the Upper Missouri, on the Yellowstone and Platte Rivers.   Audubon met with it at Fort Union. Dr. Hayden obtained it on the Yellowstone, in August; at Fort Lookout, June 22 ; at Bijou Hills, from May 1 to the 15th ; at Bon Homme Island, May 9.   Dr. Cooper obtained it at Fort Laramie in September.   Mr. Allen found it in Colorado, where it was more abundant on the foothills than on the plains.   He also found this species an abundant inhabitant of the thickets in the valley of the Great Salt Lake, in its habits strongly resembling the common birds of the Eastern States.   Though its song is also somewhat similar, its call-note, he adds, is totally different, very nearly resembling that of the Catbird.

Dr. Woodhouse met with but few of these birds either in the Indian Territory or in New Mexico.   Mr. Dresser, in November, 1863, when hunting in the Bandera Hills, noticed several of these birds near the camp, and obtained several near San Antonio during the winter.   None of these birds appear to have been observed in the Arctic regions beyond the Saskatchewan Plains.

Mr. Nuttall met with this species on the western slopes of the Rocky Mountains, but as he apparently did not appreciate the difference between this form and the *oregonus*, we cannot determine with certainty to which his descriptions apply in all cases.   He found it, in manners and habits, the counterpart of our common eastern species, frequenting forests and scratching among the dead leaves among bushes and thickets.   He describes it as more shy than the common species.   If the nest be invaded, the male shows more boldness, and reiterates his complaints until the cause of his alarm is removed.   He speaks of its warble as quaint and monotonous, and very similar to the notes of the Towhee, — but the note of our bird, *towhee*, is never heard west of the mountains.   In its stead this bird is said to have a note like the mew of a cat.

The egg of the *arcticus* is oval in shape, and measures one inch in length by .70 in breadth.   It has a white ground, but is so generally and so thickly covered with fine dots of umber-brown, intermingled with paler markings of lavender and neutral tints, that the ground can hardly be distinguished.

SECTION II.

Head and body above brown ; throat with a light patch.

Pipilo fuscus, Swainson.

Synopsis of the Varieties.

Common Characters. Grayish-brown above, with a more or less appreciable rufous tinge on the crown. A patch covering the throat, ochraceous or white, contrasting with the surrounding portions, and encircled more or less completely, especially posteriorly, by dusky spots ; lores like the chin. Crissum deep ochraceous, the lower part of abdomen tinged more or less with the same.

A. No trace of white tips to middle wing-coverts. Throat ochraceous.

a. Crown only faintly tinged with rufous.

1. Abdomen pale grayish-brown ; throat and lores deep reddish-ochraceous ; the deep ochraceous confined posteriorly to lower tail-coverts. Wing, 3.90 ; tail, 5.00. *Hab.* California. var. *crissalis.*

2. Abdomen distinctly white centrally, but surrounded by grayish laterally and anteriorly ; throat and lores pale ochraceous ; deep ochraceous of crissum extending forward over lower part of abdomen. Wing, 3.80 ; tail, 4.00. *Hab.* Mexico . var. *fuscus.*[1]

b. Crown very distinctly rufous.

3. The ochraceous of posterior under parts spreading over whole lower part of abdomen and flanks. Ochraceous of the throat palest anteriorly, the chin and lores being almost white ; it spreads over the jugulum also, outside the series of rather scattered dusky

---

[1] *Pipilo fuscus,* Sw. Phil. Mag. I, 1827, 434 (Temiscaltepec). — Ib. Anim. in Menag. 1838, 347. — Bp. Consp. 1851, 487. — Sclater, P. Z. S. 1856, 304 (Cordova). *? Kieneria fusca,* Bp. C. R. XL, 1855, 356.

Sp. Char. Above dull olive-brown ; the top of head having the central portion of feathers tinged (inconspicuously and obscurely) with rufous. Chin and throat pale rufous, bordered by dusky streaks ; a single dusky spot in lower part of jugulum. Belly and flanks behind, anal region and crissum, rather darker rufous. Sides grayish-olive, lighter than the back, tingeing the breast, and leaving only a small patch in the centre of under parts white, shading into the surrounding ashy-brown. Fourth and fifth quills longest ; first shorter than ninth, or than secondaries.

Dimensions (prepared specimen) : Total length, 7.75 ; wing, 3.80 ; tail, 4.20 ; exposed portion of first primary, 2.30 ; of longest (measured from exposed base of first primary), 3.03. Bill : Length from forehead, .65 ; from nostril, .40. Legs : Tarsus, .95 ; middle toe and claw, 1.00 ; hind toe and claw, .68 ; claw alone, .36. *Hab.* Highlands of Mexico.

The specimen described is from the city of Mexico, and belongs to Mr. G. N. Lawrence ; others before us are from Temiscaltepec (the original locality of Swainson's type), Guadalaxara, and Tepic.

While admitting the strong probability that the different brown *Pipilos* with rufous throat bordered by black spots, *P. fuscus, crissalis, mesoleucus, albigula,* and probably even *albicollis,* are geographical modifications of the same original type, the large collection before us vindicates the action of those who have referred the California species to that described by Swainson as *fuscus,* and who have distinguished the *P. mesoleucus* from both. The original description of *fuscus* agrees almost exactly with *crissalis,* both actually scarcely separable ; while the *mesoleucus,* intermediate in geographical position, is decidedly different from either. The relationships of these different forms will be found expressed in the general diagnosis already given.

Two descriptions given by Swainson, copied below, of the *P. fuscus,* differ somewhat from each other, and may not have been taken from the same specimen. The identification of either with

spots. Whole breast white. Wing, 3.80; tail, 4.30. *Hab.*
Southern Middle Province of United States.   var. *mesoleucus.*
4. The ochraceous of under parts confined to crissum and anal
region; ochraceous of the throat palest posteriorly, where it is
nearly white, and confined within the encircling series of rather
coalesced dusky spots. Abdomen, only, white. Wing, 3.80; tail,
4.20. *Hab.* Cape St. Lucas.   .   .   .   .   var. *albigula.*

B. Middle coverts distinctly, and greater obsoletely, tipped with white.
Throat white crossed by an ochraceous band.
5. Crown without a trace of rufous. Dusky spots surrounding the
white gular patch, coalesced posteriorly into a narrow crescent.
Whole breast and abdomen white, somewhat broken anteriorly.
Flanks and lower tail-coverts ochraceous. Wing, 3.30; tail, 3.70.
Hab. Mexico.   .   .   .   .   .   .   (var.?) *albicollis.*[1]

Pipilo fuscus, var. crissalis, VIGORS.

BROWN TOWHEE; CAÑON FINCH.

Pipilo fusca, CASSIN, Illust. I, IV, 1853, 124, pl. xvii (the figure seems to be of the California species, the description more like *mesoleucus*). — NEWBERRY, Zoöl. Cal. & Or.
Route, Rep. P. R. R. VI, IV, 1857, 89. *Kieneria fusca*, BONAP. Comptes Rendus, XL,
1855, 356. *Fringilla crissalis*, VIGORS, Zoöl. Blossom, 1839, 19. *Orituras wrangeli*,
BRANDT, Bonap. Comp. Rend. 43, 1856, 413. *Pipilo fuscus*, BAIRD, Birds N. Am. 1858,
517. — HEERM. X, *S*, 51 (nest). — COOPER, Orn. Cal. I, 245.

SP. CHAR. Above dark olive-brown, the crown with a very slight tinge of scarcely
appreciable dark rufous. Under parts with the color somewhat similar, but of a lighter

P. mesoleucus would be a difficult matter; while the first one expresses the peculiar characters
of *crissalis* more nearly than any other. The statement of "white beneath," without any
qualification, applies better to *mesoleucus* than to others, but the "pale rufous tinge" observable
in *crissalis* and *fuscus* is very different from the abruptly defined chestnut cap of *mesoleucus*.

Pipilo fuscus, SWAINSON, Phil. Mag. I, 1827, 434. "Gray, beneath paler; throat obscure
fulvous, with brown spots; vent ferruginous. Length, 8.00; bill, .70; wings, 3.50; tail, 4.00;
tarsi, .90; hind toe and claw, .70." *Hab.* Table land; Temiscaltepec.

Pipilo fuscus, SWAINSON, Anim. in Men. 1838, 347. "Grayish-brown above; beneath white;
chin and throat fulvous, with dusky spots; under tail-coverts fulvous; tail blackish-brown,
unspotted. Bill and legs pale, the latter smaller, and the claws more curved than in any other
known species; crown with a pale rufous tinge. Length, 7.50; wings, 3.50; tail, 4.00; tarsus,
.90; middle toe and claw the same; hinder toe, .65. Rather smaller than *maculata*."

[1] *Pipilo albicollis*, SCLATER. Above uniform olivaceous-brown; the cap not differently colored.
Lores, chin, and throat white, the two last bordered and defined by dusky spots; jugulum and
breast white, the former clouded with olivaceous, and with a dusky blotch in middle; middle of
throat crossed by an olivaceous band which curves round on each side under the ear-coverts; sides
grayish. Flanks behind, anal region, and crissum, rufous. Middle wing-coverts with a whitish
bar across their tips. Fourth and fifth quills longest; first shorter than ninth and secondaries.
Length, 7.00; wing, 3.30; tail, 3.70. Bill and legs light. *Hab.* Central Mexico.
This "species" may fairly be considered as one extreme of the series of which *P. crissalis* is
the other; and differs from the rest merely in a greater amount of white, and the absence of
rufous tinge on top of head. The fulvous of throat is concentrated in a band across its middle
portion, leaving chin and lower throat white; this, however, is foreshadowed in the paler chin of
mesoleucus, and the whitish lower throat of *albigula*. The uniformity of coloring above is nearly
equalled by that of *P. crissalis*. The whitish band across the middle wing-coverts is the most
positive character.

shade, and washed with grayish; middle of the belly only whitish; the under tail-coverts pale rufous, shading into lighter about the vent and sides of lower belly; chin and throat well-defined pale rufous, margined all round by brown spots, a few of them scattered

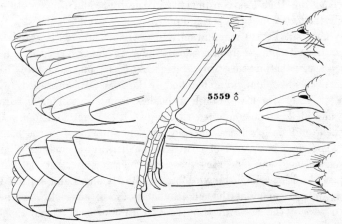

Pipilo fuscus, var crissalis.

within the margin. Eyelids and sides of head, anterior to the eye, rufous like the throat. One or two feathers on the lower part of the breast with a concealed brown blotch. Outer primary not edged with white. Fifth quill longest; first shorter than ninth, or even than secondaries. Bill pale brown, darker above; legs light. Length, 8.50 inches; wing, 4.00; tail, 4.60.

HAB. Coast region of California.

The bill is sinuated, as in *P. aberti*, differing from that of *P. erythrophthalmus.*

This race is very similar to the original *P. fuscus* of Mexico, the original description of Swainson answering almost exactly. It is, however, considerably larger; the proportions of wing are similar; and there is no decided indication of whitish in the middle of the body beneath, such as is always distinctly appreciable in *fuscus*, and still more in *mesoleucus.*

A young bird differs but little from the adult except in having obsolete dusky streaks below; the upper parts are uniform.

HABITS. The Brown, or Cañon Finch of California is found nearly throughout the State of California. Mr. Xantus obtained it at Fort Tejon, and Mr. Ridgway observed it among the chaparrals on the foothills of the western slope of the Sierras.

Dr. Cooper considers the name of Cañon Finch ill applied to this species, as it is equally plentiful in level districts, wherever trees and shrubbery exist. He regards it as one of the most abundant and characteristic birds of California, residing in all the lower country west of the Sierras, and extending up the slopes of the Coast Range to the height of three thousand feet. They are said to have habits very similar to those of all the other species, living much upon the ground, and seeking their food among the dead leaves, which they greatly resemble in color. This resemblance Dr. Cooper regards as a great protection to them from Hawks ; their hues also correspond with those of the earth and the dusky foliage during most of the year. They are thus less conspicuous in the light, and they venture more fearlessly forth and feed in open grounds.

They have but little song, and only utter a few faint chirps and hurried notes, as they sit perched upon some low bush, in the spring. At San Diego Dr. Cooper saw the first nest with eggs on April 17, but some birds had laid much earlier, as he found young hatched by the 20th. He afterwards observed other nests, all of which were built in bushes, from two to four feet from the ground, and all but one contained three eggs ; the other had four. He has found them built in low trees, and one in a vine growing over the porch of a house. The nest is formed of coarse twigs, bark, and grass, is thick and large, and is lined with fine root-fibres and finer grasses. The eggs are pale blue, spotted with purplish-brown blotches, mostly small and scattered. He gives the measurement of the eggs as .90 by .65 of an inch. In the more northern part of the State they are said to lay four eggs oftener than three. They are supposed by him to have two broods in a season.

Colonel McCall has no doubt that they are found throughout California, as he has met with them from the upper waters of the Sacramento to the mouth of the Gila ; the former having its origin in the extreme north, and the latter touching the extreme southern boundary of the State. It is most abundant south of Santa Barbara.

Colonel McCall states that its habits and manners differ somewhat from those of the common Towhee and the Arctic Finches. Its flight is more even and regular, and is without that violent jerking of the tail from side to side, which gives such a singular appearance of awkwardness to the movements of the Towhee. It is less shy and suspicious than the Arctic. It is also much less decidedly a Ground Finch than either of the others. Its favorite abode he found to be the vicinity of watercourses, where it is generally to be seen in pairs, though he has, at times, surprised eight or ten together under the shade of a large bush at noon in a summer day, when he has had no difficulty in procuring three or four specimens before the party dispersed. It is at all times a familiar bird, boldly coming into the roads to feed, and permitting a close approach. If compelled to retreat, it darts suddenly into the thicket, but returns as soon as the cause of alarm has disappeared. Near Santa Barbara he found thirty or forty of these birds, in the month of July, dispersed over an old field of some five acres in extent, contiguous to a sea-beach, through which flowed a small stream of fresh water. They were feeding on the ground, sheltered by a rank growth of weeds. When one was flushed it flew into a neighboring tree instead of seeking shelter again in the weeds. The young at that time were fully fledged, and scarcely differed in the color of their plumage from the adults.

Dr. Heermann once met with a nest of this bird built in a grapevine overhanging the Sacramento River. He describes the eggs of this species as differing entirely from any of this genus he had ever met with, and as having so great a resemblance to the eggs of the three different species of Blackbirds inhabiting California that they were liable to be confounded with them unless marked when taken from the nest.

Dr. Newberry, who found this bird very common in the Sacramento Valley, states that when he first met with it, a strange bird to him, its habit of scratching among the dry leaves under the bushes, as well as its long tail and jerking flight from one clump of bushes to another, at once indicated to him its affinities.

Among the memoranda made by Mr. Xantus at Fort Tejon are the following in reference to this species : " 474, nest and two eggs, found May 19 on a small thorn-bush in a very dark thicket, about six feet from the ground ; 1,675, nest and one egg, on a thick thorny bush, six feet from the ground ; 1,851, nest and two eggs, May 12, on a rose-bush, four feet from the ground, eggs already incubated."

The eggs of this species measure one inch by .75, have a light ground of robin-blue, and are spotted and blotched with varying shades of dark and light purple. In some the color of the blotches is so deep as not to be distinguishable from black, except in a strong light. The lighter shades are a faint lavender.

Pipilo fuscus, var. mesoleucus, BAIRD.

CAÑON BUNTING.

Pipilo mesoleucus, BAIRD, Pr. A. N. Sc. Ph. VII, June, 1854, 119 (Rocky Mountains). — IB. Birds N. Am. 1858, 518 ; pl. xxix. — KENNERLY, P. R. R. X, b. pl. xxix. — HEERM. X, c, p. 15. — COOPER, Orn. Cal. I, 247. ? *Pipilo fusca*, "SWAINS.," SCLATER & SALVIN, P. Z. S. 1869, 361 (city of Mexico).

SP. CHAR. Above very dull olivaceous-brown, with a grayish tinge; hood dull chestnut, conspicuously different from the back. Sides like the back, but paler; posteriorly, and about the vent and under tail-coverts, pale brownish-red. The ashy olive-brown of the sides scarcely meeting across the breast, the lower portion of which, with the upper belly, is rather pure white. The loral region, chin, throat, and upper part of the breast, pale yellowish-rufous, finely spotted on the sides and more coarsely across the breast with brown; an obscure spot in the middle of the breast; edge of outer primary white. Bill pale brown; legs flesh-color; first quill about equal to eighth, third and fourth longest. Length, 8.50 inches; wing, 3.80; tail, 4.70.

HAB. Valley of Upper Rio Grande and across to the Gila River. East to Santa Caterina, New Leon.

This race is similar in general appearance to *P. crissalis*, but the olive-brown and rufous are both of a lighter shade. The crown is of a decided rufous, conspicuously different from the back, instead of nearly the same tint. The light reddish under the head is wider throughout, and extends down to the upper part of the breast, blending with the colors of the breast and belly, instead of being narrower, more sharply defined, and restricted to the chin and throat; it is palest anteriorly, the chin and lore being almost white. The isolated larger spot on the breast is more conspicuous; the breast and belly are quite pure white, shaded with obsolete brownish blotches, instead of being uniform grayish-brown, with only an approach to whitish in the very middle. The edges of the wing and tail feathers are a good deal lighter, the outer web of the first primary being sharply edged with pure white, instead of obscure grayish-brown. The size generally is rather smaller, the wings more pointed.

Compared with *P. fuscus*, we find the tail decidedly longer; the wing more pointed; the first quill about equal to the eighth, instead of shorter than the secondaries. The colors generally are paler; the cap of head bright distinct rufous in strong contrast with the other plumage, instead of being only very obscurely tinged with that color. The white of belly is purer, and extends farther forward, displacing the ashy tinge almost to the buff of the throat.

If we consider all the brown *Pipilos* as modifications of one primitive species, it will be well to consider the Arizonan and New Mexican bird as the central figure around which the others are grouped. The common character will then be varied in the California race, *crissalis*, by the absence of decided rufous on crown, a darker shade of color, and an extension of the gray of sides over the whole under parts, almost entirely displacing the white. The wing is more rounded, and the general dimensions larger southward on the central plains of Mexico; the general tints are almost precisely as in the California bird, except that the white of belly is very evident; but the chestnut cap and extended whiteness of belly, together with the pointed wing of *mesoleucus*, are wanting. In *P. albigula* of Cape St. Lucas we have the general characters of *mesoleucus*, with paler colors, more restricted spots encircling throat, and a tendency to white in its lower part. In this it approaches *albicollis* of Southwestern Mexico.

HABITS. This little-known form was first obtained by Dr. Kennerly, naturalist to the Pacific Railroad Expedition on the 35th parallel, under Lieutenant Whipple. He met with it at Bill Williams Fork, in Arizona, February 5, 1854. It was described by Professor Baird the following June. Dr. Kennerly furnished at the time no information in regard to its habits.

Dr. Heermann, in his Report on the birds observed in Lieutenant Parke's expedition, mentions having met with this species in the vicinity of Tucson. Its habits, so far as he could judge of them from his opportunities, appeared very similar to those of *Pipilo aberti*.

Lieutenant Couch met with this species at Santa Catalina, Mexico, in April, 1853, but furnishes no information in reference to its manners. Mr. J. H. Clark, who obtained a specimen near the Copper Mines of the Mimbres, states that they were met with in abundance in the deep valleys or cañons of that region. They were almost always in or about the thick clumps of bushes, several usually being in company.

Dr. Kennerly, who met with them on a second trip, in June, 1855, near Los Nogales, in Mexico, speaks of them as not very common in that region. He found them preferring the dense bushes in the valleys. When approached, they became very restless, flying from one bush to another, accompanying their motions with very peculiar notes, which he does not describe.

Dr. Coues found this species abundantly distributed throughout the warmer portions of New Mexico and Arizona, from the valley of the Rio Grande to that of the Colorado. He did not observe any at Fort Whipple, though they were found breeding some twenty-five miles to the southward. He found them associating freely with *Pipilo aberti,* and inhabiting the same regions. The two birds have very similar habits.

Dr. Henry also states that this species is common in New Mexico both summer and winter, and, so far as he has observed, dwelling almost entirely among the mountains. It appeared to him very retiring in its habits, and seemed to prefer the cañons. He has seldom, if ever, observed it far from shady gorges, where, like its relative of the Eastern States, the Towhee Bunting, it passes the greater part of its time on the ground, and is generally accompanied by its congener, the Arctic Finch. When disturbed, it seeks the thickest cover, though it is by no means shy or difficult to approach. Its nest is usually constructed in the branches of a thick cedar or dwarf oak, and he has never known it to produce more than one brood in a season.

Dr. Cooper states that these birds are very abundant in Southern Arizona, that their habits closely resemble those of *P. aberti,* and that their eggs are similar to those of *Pipilo fuscus.*

Pipilo fuscus, var. albigula, BAIRD.

CAPE TOWHEE.

Pipilo albigula, BAIRD, P. A. N. S. Nov. 1859, 305 (Cape St. Lucas). — ELLIOT, Illust. Am. Birds, I, pl. xv (" = *P. mesoleucus* "). — COOPER, Orn. Cal. I, 248.

SP. CHAR. Similar to var. *mesoleucus,* having, like it, a distinctly rufous crown and white abdomen. Differing, however, in the following respects: The pale ochraceous gular area is more sharply defined, the buff being confined within the encircling series of dusky spots; the buff is palest posteriorly, instead of directly the opposite. The rufous of the crissal region is more restricted, only tingeing the anal region instead of invading the lower part of the abdomen, the white beneath also is shifted farther back, covering the abdomen alone, instead of the breast, the whole jugulum being distinctly ashy, like the sides. Wing, 3.80; tail, 4.25.

HAB. Cape St. Lucas.

A very large series of specimens from Cape St. Lucas agree in possession of the characters pointed out above, distinguishing them from *mesoleucus,* to which race the present one is most nearly related.

HABITS. The White-throated or Cape Towhee of Cape St. Lucas was first met with by Mr. Xantus in the southern extremity of the peninsula of Lower California, and described by Professor Baird in 1859. Its close resemblance to *P. mesoleucus* suggests an equal similarity as to its habits, in regard to which we possess no actual knowledge. Mr. Xantus has furnished us with no memoranda as to the manners of the bird. We have only the brief mention among his notes to the effect that No. 4,855 is the nest with four eggs of this *Pipilo*, found in a wild *Humulus* thicket ; and that No. 5,076 is a nest with eggs of the same, found in a thicket of wild roses in the garden fence.

Judging from the large number of the nests and eggs of this species collected by that gentleman at Cape St. Lucas, it would seem to be very abundant in that locality.

The eggs of this variety measure .95 of an inch in length and .72 in breadth. They bear a strong resemblance to those of the *P. fuscus*, but the markings are darker and more distinctly defined, standing out with a clear and striking effect, in marked contrast with the light background. The ground-color of the egg is a light tint of robin-blue. The markings of dots, dashes, and lines are all about the larger end, and are of a deep dark shade of purplish-brown, so dark as, except in a strong light, to be undistinguishable from black.

SECTION III.

Brown ; throat without light patch.

Pipilo aberti, BAIRD.

ABERT'S TOWHEE.

Pipilo aberti, BAIRD, Stansbury's Rep. Great Salt Lake, Zoölogy, June, 1852, 325 (New Mexico). — IB. Birds N. Am. 1858, 516, pl. xxx. — KENNERLY, P. R. R. X, b, pl. xxx. — HEERMANN, X, c, 15. — COOPER, Orn. Cal. I, 244. *Kieneria aberti*, BONAP. Comptes Rendus, XL, 1855, 356.

SP. CHAR. General color of upper parts pale brownish yellowish-red; beneath brighter,  and more ochraceous, especially on the under coverts, palest on the middle of the belly. Sides of head anterior to eyes, and chin dark brown. Bill and legs yellowish. Length, 9 inches; wing, 3.70 ; tail, 4.85.

6748 ♂

HAB. Base of Rocky Mountains in New Mexico. Valley of Gila and Colorado.

This plainly colored bird is perhaps the largest of the North American Finches, and is without any blotches, spots, or variations of importance from one color, except on the chin and sides of the head. The bill is similar to that of *P. erythrophthalmus*, but the cutting edge is less concave and more sinuated. The tail is more graduated; the claws thicker and stronger. The wings are short and much rounded; the first quill shorter than the secondaries; fifth and fourth longest.

It may be easily distinguished from all the varieties of *fuscus* by the blackish lores and chin, as well as by the absence of any colored gular area, there being, instead, a pinkish rufous tinge prevalent over the whole throat and jugulum. There are no dusky spots across the throat as in *fuscus*.

HABITS. Dr. Cooper assigns the base of the Rocky Mountains, in New Mexico, and the valleys of the Gila and Colorado Rivers, as the habitat of this species. Dr. Coues speaks of it as one of the most abundant and characteristic birds of those two valleys, and adds that it ranges northward to within a few miles of Fort Whipple, but is not found in the adjacent mountains. It was common at Fort Mohave, and particularly so at Fort Yuma.

Dr. Kennerly met with it at Camp No. 114, New Mexico, February 6, and again at Bill Williams Fork, February 12. He states that while travelling down the Big Sandy Creek and Bill Williams Fork, in the month of February, he found them very abundant. They confined themselves to the thick bushes near the water. Generally two or three were seen together. Their motions were very rapid, and their note was a peculiar, loud, chattering sound, sharp but not disagreeable. After leaving the Great Colorado he did not see it again.

On the borders of the Gila, east of Fort Yuma, Dr. Heermann found this bird in great abundance. It kept in the close sheltered thickets, where, secure from intrusion, it sought among the dead leaves for various seeds and insects and their larvæ, on which it feeds. In its habits it very much resembles the *Pipilo fuscus*, or Cañon Finch, diving into the bushes when alarmed, and repeating, at intervals, a short chirp. After leaving the Gila River he did not meet with any more, as he followed no longer the course of any large stream, for the borders of which these birds seem to have a decided preference.

Dr. Cooper regards this species as the almost exact counterpart of the *Pipilo fuscus*. The only difference he noticed in habits was in the character of its loud note of alarm, remarkably similar, however, to that of two very distinct birds of the same valley, namely, *Centurus uropygialis* and *Phainopepla nitens*. Like the Cañon Finch, this species is said to live almost constantly on the ground, but appears rather more gregarious, especially in winter.

About the first of April Dr. Cooper met with many of their nests. They were generally built in thorny shrubs, and were composed of a flooring of coarse twigs, or of green herbs, and strongly interwoven with strips of bark, grass, and leaves. One bird had taken advantage of the recent introduction of horses into the valley to obtain a lining of horse-hair for its nest. The eggs were in all cases only three, bluish-white, with brown spots and streaks in a ring near the large end, quite variable in number, and measuring one inch by .70. One of the nests was in a low mesquite-tree, another in a dense cluster of dead twigs hanging from a cottonwood. The time required for hatching was twelve or thirteen days, and in a fortnight more the young left the nest. Dr. Cooper found nests with eggs as late as May 25, and had no doubt that they raise two or more broods in a season. He adds that the song of the male, throughout April and May, is precisely like that of *P. fuscus*, and also reminded him of the notes of *P. oregonus* and of the eastern Black-throated Bunting (*Euspiza americana*).

Dr. Coues has kindly supplied me with the following interesting sketch of this species, as observed by him in Arizona: —

"This species appears to have a remarkably restricted geographical distribution. I never saw it at Fort Whipple, but on the Colorado bottom in the same latitude, and thence along the river to Fort Yuma, I found it to be one of the most abundant and characteristic birds of all. At the time I observed it, in September, it was generally in small flocks, and proved rather difficult to capture, partly because the dense underbrush it inhabited was almost impenetrable, and partly on account of its natural timidity. Everything along the river-bottom is scorched with the heat, and the dry dead twigs constantly snap at a touch, with such noise that it is almost impossible to force a passage through the underbrush without alarming all its inmates. The bird occurs everywhere along the river-side, but is particularly numerous on the patches of mesquite, and the extensive areas grown up to young willows and cottonwoods, and the arrowwood (*Tessaria borealis*). Its ordinary cry of alarm, if not its call-note, is a loud, clear chirp, very different from the mewing sound made under similar circumstances by its congener, the *P. megalonyx*. The latter, as is well known, is almost exactly like that of a Catbird. I never heard the song of this bird, which appears to sing only during the breeding-season, but Dr. Cooper says it resembles that of the western Black *Pipilos*, and I can indorse his observation, that this is curiously like the monotonous notes of the Black-throated Bunting, — *Chip, chip, chee-chee-chee;* the first two syllables deliberately pronounced, the others more rapidly enunciated, with greater emphasis. The associates of this species seem to be few, if indeed they be not confined to the *P. mesoleucus*, a very near ally. The moult seems to me unusually protracted, as many September specimens were still in poor plumage.

"Excepting my experience with this bird on the Colorado, I only met with it on the Hassayampa, a small stream a few miles from Fort Whipple, yet in a somewhat different region, across a slight mountain-ridge, lower and warmer. Two specimens were secured, adult and young, the first week in August."

Dr. Coues, on his way from Arizona to the Pacific (Ibis, 1866, p. 261), mentions that he was often startled by the loud, clear, sharp chirp of this bird, which, though fringilline in character, is more than usually powerful, and is its alarm-note. Everywhere in the Colorado Valley this was one of the most characteristic birds. Fort Yuma seemed to be its head-quarters. It is, like all its congeners, a retiring species, and keeps perseveringly in the almost impenetrable undergrowth. It is said to be more decidedly gregarious than most of the genus, often collecting in flocks of a dozen or more, wandering restlessly, yet in a cautious manner, through the thickets.

A nest with eggs, procured at Fort Mohave by Dr. Cooper, is in the Smithsonian Collection (No. 7,276). The egg measures .93 by .70 of an inch, is obovate in shape, being much rounded at the smaller end. Its ground-color is a dull white, without any perceptible tinge of blue, — though possibly bluish when fresh, — with heavy dots and occasional delicate, hair-like, zigzag markings of black. These markings are wholly confined to the larger end. One of the eggs has these markings much finer, consisting of minute dots, more dense, and upon the apex of the larger end. The nest is loosely built and very bulky. Its external diameter is about six inches, and its depth three. The cavity is three inches wide and two deep. It is constructed almost entirely of strips of inner bark, the coarser, ribbon-like pieces being used on the outer portion, and the finer shreds composing the lining. Externally are also a few sticks about one quarter of an inch in diameter.

SECTION IV.

Crown rufous ; body above, olive-green.

Pipilo chlorurus, BAIRD.

GREEN-TAILED BUNTING ; BLANDING'S FINCH.

Fringilla chlorura, (TOWNSEND,) AUD. Orn. Biog. V, 1839, 336 (Young). *Zonotrichia chlorura*, GAMBEL, J. A. N. Sc. Ph. 2d Series, I, 1847, 51. *Embernagra chlorura*, BONAP. Conspectus, 1850, 483. *Fringilla blandingiana*, GAMBEL, Pr. A. N. Sc. Ph. I, April, 1843, 260. *Embernagra blandingiana*, CASSIN, Illus. I, III, 1853, 70, pl. xii. *Pipilo rufipileus*, LAFRESNAYE, Rev. Zoöl. XI, June, 1848, 176. — BP. Conspectus, 1850, 487. *Kieneria rufipileus*, BON. Comptes Rendus, XL, 1855, 356. *Pipilo chlorura*, BAIRD, Birds N. Am., 1858, 519. — HEERM. X, c, 15. — COOPER, Orn. Cal. I, 248.

SP. CHAR. Above dull grayish olive-green. Crown uniform chestnut. Forehead with superciliary stripe, and sides of the head and neck, the upper part of the breast and sides of the body, bluish-ash. Chin and upper part of throat abruptly defined white, the former margined by dusky, above which is a short white maxillary stripe. Under tail-coverts and sides of body behind brownish-yellow. Tail-feathers generally, and exterior of wings, bright olive-green, the edge and under surface of the wings bright greenish-yellow ; edge of first primary white. First quill longer than eighth, fourth longest. Length, about 7 inches ; wing, 3.20 ; tail, 3.65.

HAB. Whole of the Middle Province, including the Rocky Mountains and eastern slope of the Sierra Nevada ; north to beyond the 40th parallel ; south to Mexico.

In this species the wing is considerably rounded, the tertials considerably shorter than the primaries, and not exceeding the secondaries ; the fourth quill longest, the first shorter than the sixth, the second and fifth quills considerably longer than the rest. The tail is long and considerably graduated, the outer feather half an inch shortest; the feathers broad and obtusely pointed, the corners rounded.

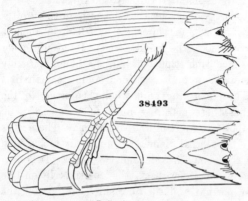

Pipilo chlorurus

The extent of the chestnut of the crown varies somewhat; more extended probably in the males. The region on the side of the head, adjoining the nostrils, is whitish; the small feathers under the eye are spotted with the same. The posterior outline of the ash of the breast is much less sharply defined than the anterior.

Specimens vary in the brightness of the olive above, which is never as pure as that of the wings and tail. The olive of the tail, too, is darker than that of the wings.

A very young bird (1,896) has the whole under parts dull white, streaked and spotted on the sides of the throat and on the breast with dark brown. The crown and back are also thickly spotted. In 5,734 the ash of the breast has made its appearance; the middle of the belly is white, spotted; the chin white, encircled by spots. The spots above are restricted to near the head, and there is a small central patch of chestnut on the crown.

No. 1,896 is the original "Green-tailed Sparrow" killed July 12, 1834, by Townsend, and described in an extract of a letter to Mr. Audubon, published page 336 of Vol. V. of the Ornithological Biography.

Pipilo chlorurus.

HABITS. Dr. Kennerly, who procured a specimen of this bird at San Elizario, Tex., December 16, states that it was obtained with some difficulty. For several successive days it was found in the same place, occupying a small clump of very thick weeds. When aroused, which was only accomplished with some effort, its flight was short, rapid, and decidedly irregular. Its motions on the ground were very awkward This species was found by Mr. Ridgway very generally distributed throughout the fertile mountain portions of the interior. It was not seen by him in California, and was first met with in the ravines at the base of the eastern slope of the Sierra Nevada. On the high mountain-ranges it was a characteristic and the best-known singer, as well as one of the most abundant of the *Fringillidæ*, being found in all bushy places, from the bases to the summits of the mountains. It is exclusively a summer species, arriving at Carson City about the middle of April. He describes the usual note of this bird as very peculiar, and, as nearly as can be described, a sweet laughing utterance of the syllables *keek-keek'*, a little resembling the *tweet* of a Canary, but very musical. This curious note was generally uttered when anything unusual attracted its attention, such as the approach of an intruder. Then, with elevated tail and its very conspicuous red cap raised, it would hop familiarly and unsuspiciously about. He adds that it is a songster of high merit, in power and variety ranking very little below the song of the *Chondestes grammaca*. The song varies in the modulations greatly with the individual, but the same general style is preserved. At times it seemed to have a slight resemblance to the song of Bewick's Wren, and at others to that of a *Cyanospiza*, and more rarely, to to be the reproduction of a passage from the song of the *Chondestes*.

In the early part of July, near Austin, in the cañons of the mountains, he found these birds breeding in the greatest abundance, and later in the same month a few of its nests were found on the East Humboldt Mountains. All of its nests, with hardly an exception, were placed from eighteen inches to two feet above the ground, among the thick bushes of a species of *Symphoricarpus*, or "snow-berry," which grows in great abundance upon the sides of the cañons of those mountains. The maximum number of eggs was four. It was also quite a common bird in the Wahsatch Mountains, though less abundant than the *P. megalonyx*.

Mr. Allen found this Finch quite numerous in Colorado Territory, and speaks of its song as very peculiar and very pleasing. It is said to resemble in no respect the eastern Towhee Finch, with which it is classed, but much more closely the group of Sparrows, so familiarly represented at the east by the White-throated, being like them in habits, song, and general aspect. It was more common among the foot-hills than on the plains. In Utah, according to Mr. Allen, this Finch begins to appear in numbers about September 20, from its breeding-haunts in the mountains.

Dr. Coues met with this species in Arizona, but only as a spring and autumn migrant. None remained there in summer to breed, and none were found there in the winter. In its migrations it passed rapidly by Fort Whipple, being found there only during the latter part of April and the beginning of May, and during the month of September. At those seasons it appeared to him the most silent and retiring of all the *Pipilos*. He found it very difficult to either observe its habits or to capture it. It winters sparingly at Fort Mohave.

Specimens of this bird were taken near Lookout Mountain by C. S. McCarthy, and at Gilmer, in Wyoming Territory, by Mr. Durkee.

Dr. Heermann, in his Report on the birds observed on the 32d parallel, under Lieutenant Parke, mentions first meeting with this species near Tucson. They were frequenting, in numbers, the thick undergrowth, and were seeking seeds and insects on the ground. They seemed inclined to shun observation, and always kept in the most retired situations. They were sociable among themselves, going about singly or in pairs, associated with the *Poospiza bilineata* and two or three other kinds of Finch. When started they fly low, diving into the bushes, and soon disappear from sight. Occasionally, until reaching El Paso, Texas, birds of this species were met with, mingling with the flocks of migrating *Fringillidæ*. He there procured a pair apparently just entering upon incubation.

Instead of being suited by color, like most of the other *Pipilos*, to inhabit dark thickets and among dry leaves, this species is clad in a gayer livery, and seems well adapted for concealment in its summer resorts, and also among the growing vegetation of the lower country during the rainy season. Dr. Heermann found a few wintering in the Colorado Valley, and yet more at San Diego, but they left both places in March. He found them silent and shy, hiding very closely in the bushes, and feeding altogether on the ground. The only note he heard, resembled the crowing note of the California Quail.

Among the memoranda of Mr. Xantus, made near Fort Tejon, are the two following : " 4,839, nest and two eggs (of *Pipilo chlorurus*) found in a dry hedge in Mr. Ritchie's garden ; 5,083, nest and eggs found in a dark garden-hedge."

The eggs of the *chlorurus* are like those of no other *Pipilo* that I have met with. They are peculiar in shape, being nearly of an exact oval, neither end being apparently much more rounded than the other. Their ground-color is white with a bluish tint, over which is profusely diffused a cloud of fine dottings of a pinkish-drab. These markings are occasionally so fine and so thickly distributed as to give to the egg the appearance of a uniform color, or as an unspotted pinkish drab-colored egg. Occasionally the dots are deeper and larger, and more sparsely diffused.

In considering the eggs of the *Pipilos* in general we find certain variations which deserve more than a passing notice. Those of *erythrophthalmus*, *oregonus*, *arcticus*, and *megalonyx* are all fringilline in their characters, and have a marked affinity to eggs of *Melospiza*, *Zonotrichia*, and many other genera of this order. The eggs of *aberti*, *fuscus*, *mesoleucus*, and *albigula* are also all closely alike, and exhibit a very close resemblance to those of the *Agelaii*, and even of the *Icteri*, while the eggs of *P. chlorurus*, though of a fringilline character, are unlike either style.

Family **ALAUDIDÆ.** — The Larks.

Char. First primary very short or wanting. Tarsi scutellate anteriorly and posteriorly, with the plates nearly of corresponding position and number. Hind claw very long and nearly straight. Bill short, conical, frontal feathers extending along side of the bill; the nostrils concealed by a tuft of bristly feathers directed forward. Tertials greatly elongate beyond the secondaries.

Subfamilies and Genera.

Alaudinæ. Bill stout, short, and conical ; nasal fossæ transverse and completely filled by the thick tuft of bristly feathers, and perforated anteriorly by a circular nasal opening. (Old and New World.)

Crown with a depressed soft crest of feathers, of normal structure ; a spurious primary ; tail deeply emarginate . . . . *Alauda.*

Crown without a crest, but occiput with an erectile tuft of narrow elongated feathers on each side. No spurious primary ; tail square, or slightly rounded . . . . *Eremophila.*

Calandritinæ. Bill broader, more depressed, and straighter at the base ; nasal fossæ longitudinal, large, elongated, the nasal opening rather linear. (Old World.)

Of the *Alaudidæ* only the two genera diagnosed above belong to the American continent ; and one of them is properly only a wanderer from the Old World, while the other is cosmopolitan.

The most characteristic feature of the Larks among other oscine families is seen in the scutellation of the tarsus. The anterior half of this is covered by divided scales lapping round on the sides, but instead of the two plates which go one on each side of the posterior half and unite ultimately behind as an acute ridge, there is but one which laps round on the sides, and is divided into scales like the anterior ones, but alternating with them. The posterior edge of the tarsus is as obtuse as the anterior, instead of being very acute. There is a deep separating groove on the inner side of the tarsus ; and there may be really but one plate divided transversely, the edges meeting at this place.

In the elongated hind claw and lengthened tertials, general style of coloration, mode of life, and manner of nesting, there is a decided approximation in the *Alaudidæ* to the *Anthinæ*, of the family *Motacillidæ;* but in these the posterior edge of the tarsus is sharp and undivided transversely, the toes more deeply cleft, the bill more slender, etc., — their relations being rather nearer to the *Sylvicolidæ* than to the present family.

Genus **ALAUDA**, Linn.

Alauda, Linn. S. N. 1735.

Gen. Char. Bill very small, less than half the length of the head, conical; nostrils exposed ; rictal bristles quite strong ; commissure without notch; tarsus much longer than middle toe; lateral toes equal; posterior toe about as long as the middle, its claw longer than the digit, and nearly straight; claws of anterior toe very small. Wing long, pointed, the third and fourth (apparently second and third) quills longest, the second and fifth sucessively, a little shorter; the first so small as to be almost concealed; tertials much elongated, reaching about half-way from end of secondaries to tip of primaries; their ends emarginated; tail rather deeply emarginated, and a little more than half the length of the wing.

Species.

A. arvensis. Above grayish-brown, beneath whitish, with a buffy tinge across jugulum and along sides; every feather above with a medial streak of dusky; sides of throat, sides, and across jugulum streaked with dusky; the outer tail-feathers partly white. Wing, 4.90; tail, 2.80; culmen, .40; tarsus, .80; hind claw, .50. *Hab.* Europe; accidental in Greenland and the Bermudas.

Alauda arvensis, LINN.

THE SKYLARK.

Alauda arvensis, LINN, Faun. Sue. p. 76. *Alauda vulgaris*, LEACH, Syst. Cat. Mamm. and Birds in B. M. p. 21. *Alauda cœlipeta*, PALL. Zoögr. I, 524. *Alauda segetum*, BREHM, Vög. Deutschl. 318. *Alauda montana*, BREHM, Vög. Deutschl. 319, t. 20, f. 1. *Alauda agrestis*, BREHM, Vög. Deutschl. 320. *Alauda italica*, GMEL. S. N. I, 793.

SP. CHAR. *Adult.* Above grayish umber-brown, beneath white, tinged across the breast with soft light ochraceous. Every feather above with a medial dusky streak, the shaft black; wing-feathers and upper tail-coverts bordered with white. Outer tail-feather mostly white, the next one edged with the same. A plain, light superciliary stripe; auriculars nearly uniform light brownish; sides of the throat, jugulum, and sides with short streaks of dusky brown.

Male. Wing, 4.90; tail, 2.80; culmen, .40; tarsus, .80; middle toe, .55; hind claw, .50.

Young. Above more yellowish-fulvous, the feathers with central spots, instead of medial stripes of dusky, and bordered terminally with whitish; jugulum washed strongly with ochraceous, and marked with dusky spots.

HAB. Europe; accidental in Greenland and the Bermudas; Aleutian Islands.

HABITS. The famed Skylark of the Old World can rest a twofold claim to be included in a complete list of North American birds. One of these is their occasional occurrence in the Bermudas, and in Greenland. The other is their probably successful introduction near New York.

A few years since an attempt was made to introduce these birds, for which purpose several individuals were set at liberty on Long Island. For a short time they did well, and succeeded in raising one or more broods, but, owing probably to the constant persecution of all small birds by the foreign population of the neighborhood, the experiment nearly failed, and none were noticed in that vicinity. Within the last year or two, however, several pairs of these birds have been observed in Westchester County, and also on Long Island, by parties competent to recognize them, and hopes are now entertained that these desirable birds have obtained a foothold in this country.

According to Messrs. Dresser and Sharpe, the Skylark is found throughout the polar Arctic regions, from the British Islands eastward to Siberia and Northern China. A smaller subspecies is met with in Southeastern Europe, which does not present any character by which it can be separated from it. In Eastern Europe the Lark has been found as far north as the Faroe Islands, but has not been observed in Iceland. It reaches Christiania in March, and leaves in October. It has been found breeding in Lapland as far north as latitude 65°, and is a common summer visitant in Finland. Pallas found it abundant throughout Russia and Siberia, and Steller found it not only in Kamtschatka, but equally in the Kurile Islands and in those between Asia and America, so that its occurrence in our Alaskan territories may be regarded as a not improbable event.

The same writers also state that the Skylark has been twice recorded as occurring in Greenland and in America ; and in another place they state that "the Skylark occasionally visits Greenland, and has been met with in the Bermudas." In the latter place a storm-tried waif was taken by Mr. J. M. Jones after an easterly gale.

The Lark is a universal favorite in the Old World, and as a vocalist enjoys a reputation hardly second even to the far-famed Nightingale. It is an inhabitant of all the countries of Europe, and is said to be most abundant in the cultivated districts.

We only know of its song from caged specimens and from the testimony of European writers. Yarrell speaks of its notes as cheerful and exhilarating, fresh as the season of spring, and the admiration of all hearers. Its voice is described as powerful to an extraordinary degree, and its song wild and joyous. They sing while they fly, rising, with quivering wings almost perpendicularly, until they gain so great an elevation that they can no longer be distinguished ; yet, while thus no longer visible, their wild music continues to be heard as that of some unseen spirits of the air. It is said that one familiar with their song can readily determine, by their notes, whether the singer is ascending, stationary, or descending. Occasionally, when at this great elevation, the Lark will close its wings and drop to the earth with the rapidity of a stone. At times it will sing while on the ground, but its most lively strains are poured forth during these flights. And though this bird will sing while in confinement, and is a favorite cage-bird, yet in singing they are said to flutter their wings, as if this motion were almost a necessary accompaniment to their song.

In regard to the song and its peculiarities writers are not quite in agreement. The general opinion seems to be that, while in the quality of its tone it is surpassed by the song of the Nightingale, the Bulfinch, and the Black-cap, it is unequalled in quantity, sprightliness, variety, and power. The Lark is in song eight months of the year, and during the summer months it sings from two in the morning, with very little intermission, until after sunset.

Mr. Macgillivray gives an excellent and graphic description of the habits of this bird, from which we extract a portion descriptive of its song. "It has been alleged," he writes, "that the Lark ascends in a spiral manner, but my observation does not corroborate the statement. In rising it often passes directly upward, but with the body always horizontal, or nearly so, then moves in a curve, and continues thus alternately, but without a continued spiral motion. At first, the motion of the wings is uniformly fluttering; but afterwards it shoots them out two or three times successively at intervals, and when at its greatest height exhibits this action more remarkably. When it descends, the song is not intermitted, but is continued until it approaches the ground, when it usually darts down headlong, and alights abruptly. Frequently it resumes its song after alighting, and continues it for a short time, but more commonly it stops when it has reached the ground. Often a Lark may be seen hovering over a field, in full song, for a considerable time, at a small height. On the 4th of May, 1837, I observed a Lark perched on a half-burnt whin branch, where it remained singing a long time. I have often seen it perch on a wall, and several times on a hawthorn bush in a hedge; but it never, I believe, alights on tall trees.

"The song of the Lark is certainly not musical, for its notes are not finely modulated, nor its tones mellow; but it is cheerful and cheering in the highest degree, and protracted beyond all comparison. In a sunny day in April or May, when the grass-fields have begun to resume their verdure, it is pleasant to listen to the merry songster that makes the welkin ring with its sprightly notes; in the sultry month of July, still more pleasant is it to hear its matin hymn while the dew is yet on the corn; and in winter, should you chance to hear the well-known voice on high, it reminds you of the bright days that have gone, and fills you with anticipation of those that are to come. No doubt much of the pleasure derived from the Lark's song depends upon association, but independently of circumstances and associations the song of the Lark imparts an elasticity to the mind, elevates the spirits, and suspends for a time the gnawing of corroding care. The carol of the Lark, like the lively fife, excites pure cheerfulness. In confinement this bird sings every whit as well as when at large, and when rapidly perambulating the square bit of faded turf in its cage, it enacts its part with apparently as much delight as when mounting toward heaven's gate."

This bird succeeds well in cages, and lives to a great age, Yarrell mentioning one that lived nearly twenty years in confinement. Its natural food is grain, the seeds of grasses, worms, and various kinds of insects. They begin to mate in April, and have two broods in a season. Their nest is always placed on the ground, often sheltered by a tuft of grass, or some other protection. The nests are woven of coarse grasses and stems of plants, and are lined with finer materials of the same. The eggs are five in number, have a grayish-white ground, occasionally a greenish-white, very generally sprinkled and blotched with markings of dark-gray and an ashy-brown, so profusely as to conceal the ground. They are oval in shape, slightly more pointed at one end, and measure .93 of an inch in length by .70 in breadth.

According to Selby, the young of the first brood are fully fledged by the end of June, and the second in August. The Lark evinces a very strong attachment to its young, and many interesting accounts are given by European writers of its intelligent endeavors to conceal and to protect its nest, — in one instance constructing an artificial dome of dry grass, where the natural protection had been cut away by mowers, and in another attempting to remove the young to a place of greater safety.

The Lark has, in several instances, been successfully induced to mate and rear her young in an aviary ; and Mr. W. P. Foster, of Hackney, is quoted by Mr. Yarrell as authority for the statement, that, during the period of producing the eggs, the female has been heard to sing with a power and a variety of tone equal to the voice of her mate.

While his mate is sitting on her eggs, the male Lark, apparently timid at all other times, is remarkably bold, and drives away other birds that venture too near their nest. He not only watches over her and seeks to protect her, but assiduously supplies her with food.

Genus **EREMOPHILA**, Boie.

Eremophila, Boie, Isis, 1828, 322. (Type, *Alauda alpestris*. Sufficiently distinct from *Eremophilus*, Humboldt, [Fishes,] 1805.)

Phileremos, Brehm, Deutschl. Vögel, 1831.

Otocoris, Bonaparte, 1839. (Type, *Alauda alpestris*, Gray.) (We are unable to find where the genus is named.)

Gen. Char. First primary wanting ; bill scarcely higher than broad ; nostrils circular, concealed by a dense tuft of feathers ; the nasal fossæ oblique. A pectoral crescent and cheek-patches of black.

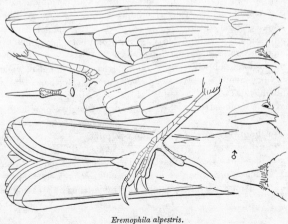

Eremophila alpestris.

This genus differs from *Melanocorypha* in having no spurious first primary, although the other characters are somewhat similar. *Calandritis* of Cabanis, with the same lack of first primary, has a much stouter bill. The spurious primary, more depressed bill, and differently constituted nostrils and nasal fossæ of *Alauda* are readily distinctive.

Eremophila alpestris.

The type of this genus is the *Alauda alpestris*, Linn., a well-known cosmopolitan species, though the birds of the New World have been distinguished under distinctive names, as *cornuta, chrysolœma, peregrina,* etc. The examination and critical comparison of more than a hundred specimens from all parts of North America, however, has convinced us of the identity with *alpestris* of the several forms mentioned above, though it may be advisable to retain one or more of them as geographical races.

Species and Varieties.

E. alpestris. *Adult.* Above pinkish-gray, varying to cinnamon, the pinkish deepest on nape and lesser wing-coverts ; tail black (except two middle feathers), the outer feather edged with white. Beneath white, the sides pinkish or grayish. A frontal band and superciliary stripe, the middle of auriculars, chin, and throat varying from white to deep Naples-yellow ; forepart of crown, and " ear-tufts," a patch on lores and cheeks, and a broad crescent across the jugulum, deep black ; end of auriculars ashy. *Female* and autumnal males, with the pattern less sharply defined, and the colors more suffused. *Young.* Brownish-black above, more or less mixed with clay-color, and sprinkled with whitish dots ; wing-feathers all bordered with whitish. Beneath white. Markings on head and jugulum just merely indicated by dusky cloudings.

Wing (of adult male), 4.20 to 4.60 ; tail, 2.90 to 3.16 ; culmen, .60 to .65. White frontal band, .25 to .30, wide ; the black prefrontal patch, .26 to .35 wide. The pinkish above of an ashy-lilac shade.

Throat and forehead white, with only a very faint tinge of yellow ; pinkish tinge above more rufous. *Hab.* Interior Northern Plains of the United States . . . . var. *occidentalis.*

Throat and forehead pale straw-yellow, or strongly tinged with it ; pinkish tinge above varying from ashy-lilacous to purplish-rufous. *Hab.* Northern regions of Old and New Worlds . . var. *alpestris.*

Wing (adult male), 3.80 to 4.10 ; tail, 2.75 to 2.90 ; culmen, .53 to .62. White frontal band, .13 to .16 wide ; the black prefrontal patch .35 to .50 wide. Pinkish above of a deep cinnamon shade. *Hab.* Desert plains of South Middle Province of United States, and table-lands of Mexico, south to Bogota . . . . var. *chrysolœma.*

Eremophila alpestris, Boie.

THE SHORE LARK.

Sp. Char. *Adult male;* spring. A frontal crescent, curving backward in a broad, sharply defined, superciliary stripe to the occiput; chin, throat and foreneck, and a crescent across middle of ear-coverts, whitish, either more or less tinged with yellow, or pure white. Lower parts, except laterally, white. A broad crescentic patch behind the frontal whitish crescent, running back on each side of the crown and terminating in an erectile tuft of narrow elongated feathers on each side of occiput, a patch covering the lores, nasal tufts, passing beneath the eye, and forming a broad "mustache" on the cheeks, with a convex outline behind and concave anteriorly, and a broad crescentic patch across the jugulum, deep black. A crescentic spot of grayish-drab across the ends of the auriculars. Posterior portion of the crown enclosed laterally between the "ear-tufts," occiput, nape, lateral lower parts, lesser and middle wing-coverts, and upper tail-coverts, pinkish-brown; the sides and flanks with obsolete dusky streaks. Back, scapulars, rump, wings, and two middle tail-feathers, ashy-drab, the feathers darker centrally, forming rather conspicuous broad streaks on lower part of back; middle and secondary coverts, secondaries and primaries bordered terminally, quite conspicuously, with white. Tail (except the *intermediæ*) black; outer web of lateral feather almost entirely white, that of the next edged with the same.

Adult female; spring. Similar, but markings rather less sharply defined; a tendency to streaking of nape and crown; these streaks often displacing the continuous black of the anterior portion of crown. The "ear-tufts" less developed.

Winter adult. Similar to the spring dress, but the black areas obscured, more or less, by whitish borders to the feathers; the frontal whitish band less sharply defined. Breast with numerous more or less distinct deltoid specks of plumbeous, and the pinkish of the sides much tinged with the same. The dusky streaks above are broader and more conspicuous.

Young. First plumage, entirely different from the adult. Above dusky, variegated with whitish dots, sprinkled over the whole surface; these specks terminal on each feather, and of a deltoid form, becoming more transverse and crescentic on the scapulars and rump; each feather of the wings broadly bordered with pale brownish, approaching white on the coverts. The blackish areas are but faintly indicated by a dusky suffusion, generally very indistinct, across the breast, and over the cheeks; and variegated with badly defined, more dusky spots; lower parts, including post-ocular stripe, dull white; sides spotted with dusky.

The *E. alpestris*, as restricted, is represented in the collection by three perfect specimens, in the several stages of plumage described; while there is also a fine specimen from Astrachan, representing a white-throated race ("var. *bei*" on MS. label) of Central Asia. The series of American specimens is all that could possibly be desired, there being numerous examples from nearly the whole northern continent, from the Arctic regions to as far south as Bogota, and from coast to coast.

The common Shore Lark of the northern parts of North America appears to be absolutely identical with the European bird, each of the specimens of the latter being easily matched from the American series. It therefore becomes necessary to reduce the name "*cornuta*" to a synonyme of *alpestris*, the former not affording characters to distinguish it as even a variety. To *alpestris* may also be referred the form known as " *occidentalis,* McCall," those specimens from the interior regions which are destitute of any yellow tinge on the throat. Were this feature a constant one in specimens from the region which it characterizes, it would be, of course, right to retain the name in the form of *alpestris* var. *occidentalis.* As it is, however, quite a large percentage of the specimens from every locality where *occidentalis* is found have more or less yellow throats, but it is possible that this mixture of the two may be the result of irregular migrations, those yellow-throated individuals being stragglers from their breeding habitat, — more to the eastward and northward. In its white instead of straw-yellow throat, and more lilaceous than vinaceous upper parts, this form bears a close resemblance to a race of the deserts of Western (and Central?) Asia, — the " *bei* "[1]; the latter, however, has these features more exaggerated than in the one of the central plains of North America. Breeding throughout the table-lands of Mexico, and in the Western Province of the United States, north to about the 40th parallel, is a more strongly marked race, maintaining also more constancy in its peculiar features; this race is the *E. chrysolœma,* Wagl., of which name *rufa,* Aud., and *minor,* Giraud, are synonymes. This race, which we propose to call *E. alpestris* var. *chrysolœma,* differs from both the northern styles in smaller size and longer bill, and in coloration is the opposite extreme from *occidentalis,* having the vinaceous tints deeper and browner, instead of paler and less brown, than in *cornuta* (i. e. typical *alpestris*). The black markings are also more extended, in proportion to the other colors, reducing the white on the forehead to a very narrow band, instead of a broad spot equalling, or exceeding, the black in width. Specimens from Bogota — about the southern limit of the genus on this continent — are, perhaps, referrible to *chrysolœma,* or at least not very different from it, though described by Sclater as distinct, under the name *peregrinus.*[2]

In fewer words, the variations, with the region, are about as follows. Starting with North America, north of the United States, we begin with a style absolutely undistinguishable from that of Europe ; this, to which the name *cornuta* belongs, visits the Eastern States only in winter, but breeds over the prairie region of Wisconsin, Illinois, and westward. West of the Rocky Mountains, especially south of about 40°, specimens referrible to this style are most numerous in winter, and in a large series a great percentage of the specimens entirely lack any yellow on the throat, while the pinkish-brown tints are lighter and less reddish ; this style represents, in these peculiar features, the " var. *bei* " of Western Asia (Astrachan), and has been distinguished by the name *occidentalis,* McCall, though it is doubtful whether McCall's description is of a specimen of this style or of one of *chrysolœma,* being

---

[1] The name in manuscript on the label of a specimen in the Schlüter collection, from Astrachan.

[2] *Otocorys peregrina,* SCLATER, P. Z. S. 1855, 110, pl. cii. *Eremophila per.* SCL. Cat. Am. Birds, 1862, 127.

taken from a young or immature bird. Breeding south of about 40°, from the Rocky Mountains to the Pacific coast, and throughout the table-lands of Mexico, — in winter sometimes resident at the northern limit assigned, and there mixed with northern-bred individuals, — is a kind which is smaller, and, generally, with a larger bill; the throat is deeper yellow than in the northern form, the pinkish tints deepened into cinnamon, and the frontal band narrower, caused by an encroachment of the black, which, in its several areas, is extended more in proportion to the other colors. This is the *E. chrysolæma* of Wagl., and of which *minor*, Giraud, and *rufa*, Aud., are synonymes, as already stated.

Along the coast of Oregon and Washington Territory is a very peculiar race, represented in the collection by several specimens. These differ essentially in having the dark streaks above very sharply defined, broad and clear blackish-brown,[1] while the lower parts are strongly tinged with yellow, even as deeply so as the throat. Additional specimens from the northwest coast may establish the existence of a race as distinct as any of those named above.

Var. alpestris.

Alauda alpestris, LINN. S. N. I, 289. — FORST. Phil. Trans. LXII, 1772, 383. — WILSON, — AUD. — JARD. — MAYNARD, B. E. Mass. 1870, 121. *Otocorys a.* FINSCH, Abh. Nat. 1870, 341 (synonymy and remarks). *Alauda cornuta*, WILS. Am. Orn. I, 1808, 85. — RICH. F. B. A. II. *Eremophila c.* BOIE, Isis, 1828, 322. — BAIRD, Birds N. Am. 1858, 403. — LORD, P. R. A. Inst. IV, 118 (British Col.). — COOPER & SUCKLEY, XII, 195. — DALL & BANNISTER, Tr. Ch. Ac. I, 1869, 218 (Alaska). — COOPER, Orn. Cal. I, 1870, 251. — SAMUELS, 280. *Phileremos c.* BONAP. List, 1838. *Otocoris c.* AUCT. *Otocoris occidentalis*, McCALL, Pr. A. N. Sc. V, June, 1851, 218 (Santa Fé). — BAIRD, Stansbury's Rep., 1852, 318.

CHAR. *Adult.* Frontal whitish crescent more than half as broad as the black patch behind it. Throat and forehead either tinged, more or less strongly, with yellow, or perfectly white. Pinkish tint above, a soft ashy-vinaceous.

Measurements. (56,583 ♂, North Europe,) wing, 4.40; tail, 2.90; culmen, .60; width of white frontal crescent, .25; of black, .30. (3,780 ♂, Wisconsin,) wing, 4.20; tail, 3.00; culmen, .60; width of white frontal crescent, .30; of black, .26. (16,768 ♂, Hudson's Bay Ter.,) wing, 4.55; tail, 3.10; culmen, .65; width of white frontal crescent, .35; of black, .36. (8,491 ♂, Fort Massachusetts,) wing, 4.35; tail, 3.15; culmen, .61; width of white frontal crescent, .27; of black, 27. (The three perfectly identical in colors.)

Young. On the upper parts the blackish greatly in excess of the whitish markings. Spots across jugulum distinct.

HAB. Northern Hemisphere; in North America, breeding in the Arctic regions and the open plains of the interior regions, from Illinois, Wisconsin, etc., to the Pacific, north of about 38°.

---

[1] A specimen from Cleveland, Ohio (7,429 ♀, April 1, Dr. Kirtland), and one from Washington, D. C. (28,246 ♂, Feb.), have nearly as distinct streaks above, but the white of lower parts is without any tinge of yellow.

Var. **chrysolæma.**

Alauda chrysolæma, WAGL. Isis, 1831, 350. — BONAP. P. Z. S. 1837, 111.   *Otocorys ch.*
FINSCH, Abh. Nat. 1870, 341.   *Alauda minor*, GIRAUD, 16 Sp. Tex. B. 1841.   *Alauda
rufa*, AUD. Birds Am. VII, 1843, 353, pl. ccccxcvii.   *Otocoris r.*, HEERM. X. s, 45.
? *Otocorys peregrina*, SCL. P. Z. S. 1855, 110, pl. cii.   *Eremophila p.*, SCL. Cat. Am. B.
1860, 127.

CHAR. *Adult.* Frontal crescent less than half as wide as the black. Throat and forehead deep straw-yellow ; pinkish tints above deep cinnamon.

a. Specimens from California and Mexico, streaks on back, etc., very obsolete; darker
central stripe to middle tail-feathers scarcely observable ; white beneath.

Measurements. (3,507, ♂, Tonila, Mexico,) wing, 3.80; tail, 2.75; bill, .53 — .15 — .42.
"   (9,115, ♂, Mexico,)   "   4.10; "   2.90; "   .63 — .13 — .50.
"   (3,939, ♂, California,)   "   3.85; "   2.75; "   .56 — .14 — .45.
"   (58,582, ♂, Gt. Salt Lake City,) " 4.10; "   2.80; "   .62 — .16 — .32.

b. Specimens from coast of Oregon and Washington Territory. Streaks on back, etc.,
very conspicuous; dark central stripe of tail-feathers distinct ; yellow beneath.

Measurements. (8,734 ♂, Fort Steilacoom,) wing, 3.75; tail, 2.60 ; bill, .61 — .15 — .40.

HAB. Middle America, from the desert regions of the southern Middle Province of
North America, south to Bogota.

HABITS. Assuming the Shore Lark of the Labrador coast and the rufous
Lark of the Western prairies to be one and the same species, but slightly
modified by differences of locality, climate, or food, we have for this species,
at all times, a wide range, and, during the breeding-season, a very unusual
peculiarity, — their abundant distribution through two widely distant and
essentially different regions.

During a large portion of the year, or from October to April, these birds
may be found in all parts of the United States. Dr. Woodhouse found them
very common throughout Texas, the Indian Territory, New Mexico, and California. Mr. Dresser states that he found the western variety — which he
thinks essentially different in several respects from the eastern — in great
numbers, from October to the end of March, in the prairies around San
Antonio. Afterwards, at Galveston, in May and June, 1864, he noticed and
shot several specimens. Although he did not succeed in finding any nests,
he was very sure that they were breeding there. It is common, during winter, on the Atlantic coast, from Massachusetts to South Carolina. In Maine
it is comparatively rare. In Arizona, Dr. Coues speaks of the western form
as a permanent resident in all situations adapted to its wants. The same
writer, who also had an opportunity of observing the eastern variety in
Labrador, where he found it very abundant on all the moss-covered islands
around the coast, could notice nothing in their voice, flight, or general manners, different from their usual habits in their southern migrations, except
that during the breeding-season they do not associate in flocks.

Richardson states that this Lark arrives in the fur countries in company
with the Lapland Bunting, with which it associates, and, being a shyer bird,
would act as sentinel and give the alarm on the approach of danger. As Mr.

Dall only obtained a single skin on the Yukon, it probably is not common there. Dr. Suckley states it to be a very abundant summer resident on the gravelly prairies near Fort Steilacoom, in Washington Territory. He describes it as a tame, unsuspicious bird, allowing a man to approach within a few feet of it. It is essentially a ground bird, rarely alighting on bushes or shrubs.

Dr. Cooper adds to this that the Shore Lark is common in the interior, but he only noticed one on the coast border. In ordinary seasons they seem to be permanent residents, and in winter to be both more gregarious and more common. He met with one as late as July 1, on a gravelly plain near Olympia, scratching out a hollow for its nest under a tussock of grass.

Dr. Cooper also found these birds around Fort Mohave in considerable flocks about the end of February, but all had left the valley by the end of March. About May 29 he found numbers of them towards the summits of the Providence range of mountains, west of the valley, and not far from four thousand feet above it, where they probably had nests. They were also common in July on the cooler plains towards the ocean, so that they doubt-less breed in many of the southern portions of California, as well as at Puget Sound and on the Great Plains. Dr. Cooper states that in May or June the males rise almost perpendicularly into the air, until almost out of sight, and fly around in an irregular circle, singing a sweet and varied song for several minutes, when they descend nearly to the spot from which they started. Their nests were usually found in a small depression of the ground, often under a tuft of grass or a bush. Mr. Nuttall started a Shore Lark from her nest, on the plains, near the banks of the Platte. It was in a small de-pression on the ground, and was made of bent grass, and lined with coarse bison-hair. The eggs were olive-white, minutely spotted all over with a darker tinge.

According to Audubon, these Larks breed abundantly on the high and desolate granite tracts that abound along the coast of Labrador. These rocks are covered with large patches of mosses and lichens. In the midst of these this bird places her nest, disposed with so much care, and the moss so much resembling the bird in hue, that the nests are not readily noticed. When flushed from her nest, she flutters away, feigning lameness so cunningly as to deceive almost any one not on his guard. The male at once joins her, and both utter the most soft and plaintive notes of woe. The nest is embedded in the moss to its edges, and is composed of fine grasses, circularly disposed and forming a bed about two inches thick. It is lined with the feathers of the grouse and of other birds. The eggs, deposited early in July, are four or five in number, and are described by Mr. Audubon as marked with bluish as well as brown spots.

About a week before they can fly, the young leave the nest, and follow their parents over these beds of mosses to be fed. They run nimbly, and squat closely at the first approach of danger. If observed and pursued, they open their wings and flutter off with great celerity.

These birds reach Labrador early in June, when the male birds are very pugnacious, and engage frequently in very singular fights, in which often several others besides the first parties join, fluttering, biting, and tumbling over in the manner of the European House Sparrow. The male is described as singing sweetly while on the wing, but its song is comparatively short. It will also sing while on the ground, but less frequently, and with less fulness. Its call-note is quite mellow, and is at times so altered, in a ventriloquial manner, as to seem like that of another bird. As soon as the young are hatched their song ceases. It is said to feed on grass-seeds, the blossoms of small plants, and insects, often catching the latter on the wing, and following them to a considerable distance. It also gathers minute crustaceans on the sea-shore.

Mr. Ridgway found this species abundant over the arid wastes of the interior, and, in many localities, it was almost the only bird to be found. In its habits he could observe no differences between this bird and the *alpestris*. He met with their nests and eggs in the Truckee Reservation, June 3. The nest was embedded in the hard, grassy ground, beneath a small scraggy sage-bush, on the *mesa*, between the river and the mountains.

Mr. J. K. Lord mentions that, having encamped at Cedar Springs on the Great Plains of the Columbia, where the small stream was the only water within a long distance, he became interested in watching the movements of these Larks. As evening approached they came boldly in among the mules and men, intense thirst overcoming all sense of fear. He found these handsome little birds very plentiful throughout British Columbia. They were nesting very early on those sandy plains, even before the snow had left the ground. He saw young fledglings early in May.

A single specimen of this species was taken at Godhaab, Greenland, in October, 1835.

Eggs from Labrador are much larger in size than those from Wisconsin. Two eggs from the first, one obtained by Mr. Thienemann, the other by Mr. George Peck, of Burlington, Vt., measure .93 and .94 of an inch in length by .71 in breadth ; while some from the West are only .83 in length and .63 in breadth, their greatest length being .90, and their largest breadth .69 of an inch. In their ground-color and markings, eggs from both localities vary about alike. The ground-color varies from a purplish-white to a dark gray, while the spots are in some a brownish-lavender, in others a brown, and, quite frequently, an olive-brown. In some they are in larger, scattered blotches ; while in others they are in very fine minute dots so thickly and so uniformly diffused as almost to conceal the ground.

Family ICTERIDÆ. — The Orioles.

Char. Primaries nine. Tarsi scutellate anteriorly; plated behind. Bill long, generally equal to the head or longer, straight or gently curved, conical, without any notch, the commissure bending downwards at an obtuse angle at the base. Gonys generally more than half the culmen, no bristles about the base of bill. Basal joint of the middle toe free on the inner side; united half-way on the outer. Tail rather long, rounded. Legs stout.

This family is strictly confined to the New World, and is closely related in many of its members to the *Fringillidæ*. Both have the angulated commissure and the nine primaries; the bill is, however, usually much longer; the rictus is completely without bristles, and the tip of the bill without notch.

The affinities of some of the genera are still closer to the family of *Sturnidæ* or Starlings, of which the *Sturnus vulgaris* may be taken as the type. The latter family, is, however, exclusively Old World, except for the occurrence of a species in Greenland, and readily distinguished by the constant presence of a rudimentary outer primary, making ten in all.

There are three subfamilies of the *Icteridæ*, — the *Agelainæ*, the *Icterinæ*, and the *Quiscalinæ*,[1] which may be diagnosed as follows, although it is difficult to define them with precision: —

Agelainæ. Bill shorter than, or about equal to, the head; thick, conical, both mandibles about equal in depth; the outlines all more or less straight, the bill not decurved at tip. Tail rather short, nearly even or slightly rounded. Legs longer than the head, adapted for walking; claws moderately curved.

Icterinæ. Bill rather slender, about as long as the head; either straight or decurved. Lower mandible less thick than the upper; the commissure not sinuated. Tarsi not longer than the head, nor than middle toe; legs adapted for perching. Claws much curved.

Quiscalinæ. Tail lengthened, considerably or excessively graduated. Bill as long as, or longer than, the head; the culmen curved towards the end, the tip bent down, the cutting edges inflexed, the commissure sinuated. Legs longer than the head, fitted for walking.

---

[1] It is an interesting fact in regard to the species of *Icteridæ*, that, as a general rule, female birds of West Indian representatives of the *Agelainæ* and *Quiscalinæ* are usually, or perhaps universally, uniformly black, where the continental are brown, either concolored or streaked. We know of no exception to the first part of this statement as to *Agelaius, Nesopsar, Scolecophagus*, and *Quiscalus*. The smaller North American species of *Quiscalus* have the females duller, but not otherwise very different from the males, except in size. The females of the large *Quiscalus*, all continental, are much smaller than the males, and totally different. In *Icterus* all the species in which the female is very different in color from the male are Northern Mexican or continental North American (*pustulatus, spurius, baltimore, bullocki, cucullatus*, etc.). Most West Indian *Icterus* also exhibit no difference in the sexes, *dominicensis, hypomelas, xanthomus, bonanæ*, etc.; in one alone (*leucopteryx*) is the difference appreciable. The South American species have the females pretty generally similar to the males, but smaller, as is the case in the entire family.

Subfamily AGELAINÆ.

CHAR. Bill stout, conical, and acutely pointed, not longer than the head; the outlines nearly straight, the tip not decurved. Legs adapted for walking, longer than the head. Claws not much curved. Tail moderate, shorter than the wings; nearly even.

The *Agelainæ*, through *Molothrus* and *Dolichonyx*, present a close relation to the *Fringillidæ* in the comparative shortness and conical shape of the bill, and, in fact, it is very difficult to express in brief words the distinctions which evidently exist. *Dolichonyx* may be set aside as readily determinable by the character of the feet and tail. The peculiar subfamily characteristics of *Molothrus* will be found under the generic remarks respecting it.

The following diagnosis will serve to define the genera : —

A. Bill shorter than the head. Feathers of head and nostrils as in B.
    Dolichonyx. Tail-feathers with rigid stiffened acuminate points. Middle toe very long, exceeding the head.
    Molothrus. Tail with the feathers simple ; middle toe shorter than the tarsus or head.
B. Bill as long as the head. Feathers of crown soft. Nostrils covered by a scale which is directed more or less downwards.
    Agelaius. First quill shorter than the second and third. Outer lateral claws scarcely reaching to the base of middle ; claws moderate.
    Xanthocephalus. First quill longest. Outer lateral claw reaching nearly to the tip of the middle. Toes and claws all much elongated.
C. Bill as long as, or longer than, the head. Feathers of crown with the shafts prolonged into stiffened bristles. Nostrils covered by a scale which stands out more or less horizontally.
    Sturnella. Tail-feathers acute. Middle toe equal to the tarsus.
    Trupialis. Tail-feathers rounded. Middle toe shorter than the tarsus.

Genus DOLICHONYX, Swainson.

Dolichonyx, SWAINSON, Zoöl. Journ. III, 1827, 351. (Type, *Emberiza oryzivora*, L.)

GEN. CHAR. Bill short, stout, conical, little more than half the head; the commissure slightly sinuated ; the culmen nearly straight. Middle toe considerably longer than the tarsus (which is about as long as the head) ; the inner lateral toe longest, but not reaching the base of the middle claw. Wings long, first quill longest. Tail-feathers acuminately pointed at the tip, with the shaft stiffened and rigid, as in the Woodpeckers.

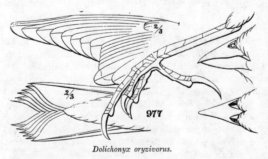

Dolichonyx oryzivorus.

The peculiar characteristic of this genus is found in the rigid scansorial tail and the very long middle toe, by means of which it is enabled to grasp the vertical stems of reeds or other slender plants. The color of the single species is black, varied with whitish patches on the upper parts.

Dolichonyx oryzivorus, SWAINSON.

BOBOLINK; REEDBIRD; RICEBIRD.

Emberiza oryzivora, LINN. Syst. Nat. I, 1766, 311. — GM. I, 1788, 850. — WILSON, Am. Orn. II, 1810, 48, pl. xii, f. 1, 2. *Passerina oryzivora*, VIEILLOT, Nouv. Dict. XXV, 1817, 3. *Dolichonyx oryzivora*, SWAINSON, Zoöl. Jour. III, 1827, 351. — IB. F. Bor.- Am. II, 1831, 278. — BON. List, 1838. — IB. Conspectus, 1850, 437. — AUD. Syn. 1839, 139. — IB. Birds Am. IV, 1842, 10, pl. ccxi. — GOSSE, Birds Jam. 1847, 229. — BAIRD, Birds N. Am. 1858, 522. — MAX. Cab. J. VI, 1858, 266. — COOPER, Orn. Cal. I, 1870, 255. — SAMUELS, 335. *Icterus agripennis*, BONAP. Obs. Wils. 1824, No. 87. AUD. Orn. Biog. I, 1831, 283 ; V, 1839, 486, pl. liv. — NUTT. Man. I, 1832, 185. *Icterus (Emberizoides) agripennis*, BON. Syn. 1828, 53. *Dolichonyx agripennis*, RICH. List, 1837. *Psarocolius caudacutus*, WAGLER, Syst. Av. 1827, 32.

SP. CHAR. General color of *male* in spring, black; the nape brownish cream-color; a patch on the side of the breast, the scapulars, and rump, white, shading into light ash on the upper tail-coverts and the back below the inter-scapular region. The outer primaries sharply margined with yellowish-white; the tertials less abruptly; the tail-feathers margined at the tips with pale brownish-ash. In autumn totally different, resembling the female.

Dolichonyx oryzivorus.

Female, yellowish beneath; two stripes on the top of the head, and the upper parts through-out, except the back of the neck and rump, and including all the wing-feathers generally, dark brown, all edged with brownish-yellow, which becomes whiter near the tips of the quills. The sides sparsely streaked with dark brown, and a similar stripe behind the eye. There is a super-ciliary and a median band of yellow on the head. Length of male, 7.70 ; wing, 3.83 ; tail, 3.15.

HAB. Eastern United States to the high Central Plains. North to Selkirk Settlement, and Ottawa, Canada; and west to Salt Lake Valley, Utah, and Ruby Valley, Nevada (RIDGWAY) ; Cuba, winter (CABAN.) ; Bahamas (BRYANT) ; Jamaica (GOSSE, SCL., Oct. ; MARCH, Oct., and in spring) ; James Island, Galapagos, Oct. (GOULD) ; Sombrero, W. I. (LAWRENCE) ; Brazil (PELZELN) ; Yucatan.

A female bird from Paraguay (Dec., 1859) is undistinguishable from the average of northern ones, except by the smaller size. Specimens from the western plains differ from those taken near the Atlantic Coast in having the light areas above paler, and less obscured by the grayish wash so preva-lent in the latter; the ochraceous of the nape being very pale, and at the same time pure.

HABITS. The well-known and familiar Bobolink of North America has, at different seasons of the year, a remarkably extended distribution. In its migrations it traverses all of the United States east of the high central plains to the Atlantic as far to the north as the 54th parallel, which is believed to be its most northern limit, and which it reaches in June. In the winter it reaches, in its wandering, the West Indies, Central America, the northern and even the central portions of South America. Von Pelzeln obtained Brazilian specimens from Matogrosso and Rio Madeira in November, and from Marabitanas, April 4th and 13th. Those procured in April were in their summer or breeding plumage, suggesting the possibility of their breeding in the high grounds of South America. Sclater received specimens from Santa Marta and from Bolivia. Other specimens have been reported as coming from Rio Negro, Rio Napo, in Brazil, Cuba, Jamaica, Porto Rico, Paraguay, Buenos Ayres, etc.

In North America it breeds from the 42d to the 54th parallel, and in some parts of the country it is very abundant at this season. The most southern breeding locality hitherto recorded is the forks of the Susquehanna River, along the west branch of which, especially in the Wyoming Valley, it was formerly very abundant.

Mr. Ridgway also observed this bird in Ruby Valley where, among the wheat-fields, small companies were occasionally seen in August. He was informed that, near Salt Lake City, these birds are seen in May, and again late in the summer, when the grain is ripe.

Of all our unimitative and natural songsters the Bobolink is by far the most popular and attractive. Always original and peculiarly natural, its song is exquisitely musical. In the variety of its notes, in the rapidity with which they are uttered, and in the touching pathos, beauty, and melody of their tone and expression, its notes are not equalled by those of any other North American bird. We know of none, among our native feathered songsters, whose song resembles, or can be compared with it.

In the earliest approaches of spring, in Louisiana, when small flocks of male Bobolinks make their first appearance, they are said, by Mr. Audubon, to sing in concert; and their song thus given is at once exceedingly novel, interesting, and striking. Uttered with a volubility that even borders upon the burlesque and the ludicrous, the whole effect is greatly heightened by the singular and striking manner in which first one singer and then another, one following the other until all have joined their voices, take up the note and strike in, after the leader has set the example and given the signal. In this manner sometimes a party of thirty or forty Bobolinks will begin, one after the other, until the whole unite in producing an extraordinary medley, to which no pen can do justice, but which is described as very pleasant to listen to. All at once the music ceases with a suddenness not less striking and extraordinary. These concerts are repeated from time to time, usually as often as the flock alight. This performance may also be witnessed early in April, in the vicinity of Washington, the Smithsonian grounds being a favorite place of resort.

By the time these birds have reached, in their spring migrations, the 40th parallel of latitude, they no longer move in large flocks, but have begun to separate into small parties, and finally into pairs. In New England the Bobolink treats us to no such concerts as those described by Audubon, where many voices join in creating their peculiar jingling melody. When they first appear, usually after the middle of May, they are in small parties, composed of either sex, absorbed in their courtships and overflowing with song. When two or three male Bobolinks, decked out in their gayest spring apparel, are paying their attentions to the same drab-colored female, contrasting so strikingly in her sober brown dress, their performances are quite entertaining, each male endeavoring to outsing the other. The female appears coy and retiring, keeping closely to the ground, but always attended by the several aspirants for her affection. After a contest, often quite exciting, the rivalries are adjusted, the rejected suitors are driven off by their more fortunate competitor, and the happy pair begin to put in order a new home. It is in these love-quarrels that their song appears to the greatest advantage. They pour out incessantly their strains of quaint but charming music, now on the ground, now on the wing, now on the top of a fence, a low bush, or the swaying stalk of a plant that bends with their weight. The great length of their song, the immense number of short and variable notes of which it is composed, the volubility and confused rapidity with which they are poured forth, the eccentric breaks, in the midst of which we detect the words "bob-o-link" so distinctly enunciated, unite to form a general result to which we can find no parallel in any of the musical performances of our other song-birds. It is at once a unique and a charming production. Nuttall speaks of their song as monotonous, which is neither true nor consistent with his own description of it. To other ears they seem ever wonderfully full of variety, pathos, and beauty.

When their contests are ended, and the mated pair take possession of their selected meadow, and prepare to construct their nest and rear their family, then we may find the male bird hovering in the air over the spot where his homely partner is brooding over her charge. All this while he is warbling forth his incessant and happy love-song; or else he is swinging on some slender stalk or weed that bends under him, ever overflowing with song and eloquent with melody. As domestic cares and parental responsibilities increase, his song becomes less and less frequent. After a while it has degenerated into a few short notes, and at length ceases altogether. The young in due time assume the development of mature birds, and all wear the sober plumage of the mother. And now there also appears a surprising change in the appearance of our gayly attired musician. His showy plumage of contrasting white and black, so conspicuous and striking, changes with almost instant rapidity into brown and drab, until he is no longer distinguishable, either by plumage or note, from his mate or young.

At the north, where the Bobolinks breed, they are not known to molest the crops, confining their food almost entirely to insects, or the seeds of valueless weeds, in the consumption of which they confer benefit, rather than harm. At the south they are accused of injuring the young wheat as they pass northward in their spring migrations, and of plundering the rice plantations on their return. About the middle of August they appear in almost innumerable flocks among the marshes of the Delaware River. There they are known as Reedbirds. Two weeks later they begin to swarm among the rice plantations of South Carolina. There they take the name of Ricebirds. In October they again pass on southward, and make another halt among the West India Islands. There they feed upon the seeds of the Guinea-grass, upon which they become exceedingly fat. In Jamaica they receive a new appellation, and are called Butterbirds. They are everywhere sought after by sportsmen, and are shot in immense numbers for the table of the epicure. More recently it has been ascertained that these birds feed greedily upon the larvæ of the destructive cotton-worm, and in so doing render an immense service to the cultivators of Sea Island cotton.

Dr. Bryant, in his visit to the Bahamas, was eye-witness to the migrations northward of these birds, as they passed through those islands. He first noted them on the 6th of May, towards sunset. A number of flocks — he counted nine — were flying to the westward. On the following day the country was filled with these birds, and men and boys turned out in large numbers to shoot them. He examined a quantity of them, and all were males in full plumage. Numerous flocks continued to arrive that day and the following, which was Sunday. On Monday, among those that were shot were many females. On Tuesday but few were to be seen, and on Wednesday they had entirely disappeared.

Near Washington, Dr. Coues observed the Bobolink to be only a spring and autumnal visitant, from May 1st to the 15th distributed abundantly about orchards and meadows, generally in flocks. In autumn they frequented in immense flocks the tracts of *Zizania aquatica*, along the Potomac, from August 20 to October.

The Bobolink invariably builds its nest upon the ground, usually in a meadow, and conceals it so well among the standing grass that it is very difficult of discovery until the grass is cut. The female is very wary in leaving or in returning to her nest, always alighting upon the ground, or rising from it, at a distance from her nest. The male bird, too, if the nest is approached, seeks to decoy off the intruder by his anxiety over a spot remote from the object of his solicitude. The nest is of the simplest description, made usually of a few flexible stems of grasses carefully interwoven into a shallow and compact nest. The eggs, five or six in number, have a dull white ground, in some tinged with a light drab, in others with olive. They are generally spotted and blotched over the entire egg with a rufous-brown, intermingled with lavender. They are pointed at one end, and measure .90 by .70 of an inch. They have but one brood in a season.

In some eggs, especially those found in more northern localities, the ground-color is drab, with a strong tinge of purple. Over this is diffused a series of obscure lavender-color, and then overlying these are larger and bolder blotches of wine-colored brown. In a few eggs long and irregular lines of dark purple, so deep as to be undistinguishable from black, are added. These eggs are quite pointed at one end.

Genus MOLOTHRUS, Swainson.

Molothrus, Swainson, F. Bor.-Am. II, 1831, 277 ; supposed by Cabanis to be meant for *Molobrus*. (Type, *Fringilla pecoris*, Gm.)

Gen. Char. Bill short, stout, about two thirds the length of head; the commissure straight, culmen and gonys slightly curved, convex, the former broad, rounded, convex, and running back on the head in a point. Lateral toes nearly equal, reaching the base of the middle one, which is shorter than tarsus; claws rather small. Tail nearly even; wings long, pointed, the first quill longest. As far as known, the species make no nest, but deposit the eggs in the nests of other, usually smaller, birds.

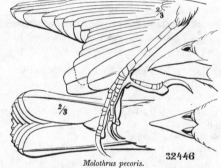

Molothrus pecoris. 32446

The genus *Molothrus* has the bill intermediate between *Dolichonyx* and *Agelaius*. It has the culmen unusually broad between the nostrils, and it extends back some distance into the forehead. The difference in the structure of the feet from *Dolichonyx* is very great.

Species of *Molothrus* resemble some of the *Fringillidæ* more than any other of the *Icteridæ*. The bill is,

Molothrus pecoris.

however, more straight, the tip without notch; the culmen running back farther on the forehead, the nostrils being situated fully one third or more of the total length from its posterior extremity. This is seldom the case in the American families. The entire absence of notch in the bill and of bristles along the rictus are strong features. The nostrils are perfectly free from any overhanging feathers or bristles. The pointed wings, with the first quill longest, or nearly equal to second, and the tail with its broad rounded feathers, shorter than the wings, are additional features to be specially noted.

Molothrus pecoris, Swainson.

COW BLACKBIRD; COWBIRD.

Fringilla pecoris, Gmelin, Syst. Nat. I, 1788, 910 (female). — Lath. Ind. Orn. I, 1790, 443. — Licht. Verzeich. 1823, Nos. 230, 231. *Emberiza pecoris*, Wils. Am. Orn. II, 1810, 145, pl. xviii, f. 1, 2, 3. *Icterus pecoris*, Bonap. Obs. Wilson, 1824, No. 88. — Aud. Orn. Biog. I, 1831, 493 ; V, 1839, 233, 490, pls. xcix and ccccxxiv. *Icterus (Emberizoides) pecoris*, Bon. Syn. 1828, 53. — Ib. Specchio comp. No. 41. — Nutt. Man. I, 1832, 178, (2d ed.,) 190. *Passerina pecoris*, Vieill. Nouv. Dict. XXV, 1819, 22. *Psarocolius pecoris*, Wagler, Syst. Av. 1827, No. 20. *Molothrus pecoris*, Swainson, F. Bor.-Am. II, 1831, 277. — Rich. List, 1837. — Bon. List, 1838. — Ib. Consp. 1850, 436. — Aud. Syn. 1839, 139. — Ib. Birds Am. IV, 1842, 16, pl. ccxii. — Cabanis, Mus. Hein. 1851, 193. — Baird, Birds N. Am. 1858, 524. — Cooper, Orn. Cal. I, 1870, 257. — Samuels, 339. — Allen, B. Fla. 284. *? Oriolus fuscus*, Gmelin, Syst. Nat. I, 1788, 393. *? Sturnus obscurus*, Gmelin, Syst. Nat. I, 1788, 804 (evidently a *Molothrus*, and probably, but not certainly, the present species). *Molothrus obscurus*, Cassin, Pr. Ph. Ac. 1866, 18 (Mira Flores, L. Cal.). — Cooper, Orn. Cal. I, 1870, 260. "*Icterus emberizoides*, Daudin." *? Sturnus junceti*, Lath. Ind. I, 1790, 326 (same as *Sturnus obscurus*, Gm.). *? Fringilla ambigua*, Nuttall, Man. I, 1832, 484 (young). *Sturnus nove-hispaniæ*, Briss. II, 448.

Sp. Char. Second quill longest; first scarcely shorter. Tail nearly even, or very slightly rounded. Male with the head, neck, and anterior half of the breast light chocolate-brown, rather lighter above; rest of body lustrous black, with a violet-purple gloss next to the brown, of steel blue on the back, and of green elsewhere. Female light olivaceous-brown all over, lighter on the head and beneath. Bill and feet black. Length, 8 inches ; wing, 4.42 ; tail, 3.40.

Hab. United States from the Atlantic to California; not found immediately on the coast of the Pacific? Orizaba (Scl. 1857, 213) ; Texas (Dresser, Ibis, 1865, 492) ; Fort Whipple, Arizona (Coues, P. A. N. S, 1866, 90) ; Nevada and Utah (Ridgway) ; Mazatlan, Tehuantepec, Cape St. Lucas.

The young bird of the year is brown above, brownish-white beneath ; the throat immaculate. A maxillary stripe and obscure streaks thickly crowded across the whole breast and sides. There is a faint indication of a paler superciliary stripe. The feathers of the upper parts are all margined with paler. There are also indications of light bands on the wings. These markings are all obscure, but perfectly appreciable, and their existence in adult birds of any species may be considered as embryonic, and showing an inferiority in degree to the species with the under parts perfectly plain.

Specimens from the west appear to have a rather longer and narrower bill than those from the east. Summer birds of Cape St. Lucas and the Rio Grande are considerably smaller (var. *obscurus*, Cassin). Length about 6.50 ; wing, 4.00 ; tail, 3.00. Some winter skins from the same region are equal in size to the average.

Birds of this species breeding south of the Rio Grande, as well as those from Cape St. Lucas, Mazatlan, etc., are very much smaller than those nesting within the United States ; but the transition between the extremes of size is so gradual that it is almost impossible to strike an average of characters for two races. The extremes of size in this species are as follows : —

Largest. (11,271, ♂, Fort Bridger.) Wing, 4.60; tail, 3.35; culmen, .72; tarsus, 1.03.
Smallest. (17,297, ♂, Mira Flores, L. C.) " 3.80; " 2.65; " .60; " .84.

HABITS. The common Cow Blackbird has a very extended distribution from the Atlantic to California, and from Texas to Canada, and probably to regions still farther north. They have not been traced to the Pacific coast, though abundant on that of the Atlantic. Dr. Cooper thinks that a few winter in the Colorado Valley, and probably also in the San Joaquin Valley.

This species is at all times gregarious and polygamous, never mating, and never exhibiting any signs of either conjugal or parental affections. Like the Cuckoos of Europe, our Cow Blackbird never constructs a nest of her own, and never hatches out or attempts to rear her own offspring, but imposes her eggs upon other birds ; and most of these, either unconscious of the imposition or unable to rid themselves of the alien, sit upon and hatch the stranger, and in so doing virtually destroy their own offspring, — for the eggs of the Cowbird are the first hatched, usually two days before the others. The nursling is much larger in size, filling up a large portion of the nest, and is insatiable in its appetite, always clamoring to be fed, and receiving by far the larger share of the food brought to the nest ; its foster-companions, either starved or stifled, soon die, and their dead bodies are removed, it is supposed, by their parents. They are never found near the nest, as they would be if the young Cow Blackbird expelled them as does the Cuckoo ; indeed, Mr. Nuttall has seen parent birds removing the dead young to a distance from the nest, and there dropping them.

For the most part the Cowbird deposits her egg in the nest of a bird much smaller than herself, but this is not always the case. I have known of their eggs having been found in the nests of *Turdus mustelinus* and *T. fuscescens, Sturnella magna* and *S. neglecta.* In each instance they had been incubated. How the young Cowbird generally fares when hatched in the nests of birds of equal or larger size, and the fate of the foster-nurslings, is an interesting subject for investigation. Mr. J. A. Allen saw, in Western Iowa, a female *Harporhynchus rufus* feeding a nearly full grown Cowbird, — a very interesting fact, and the only evidence we now have that these birds are reared by birds of superior size.

It lays also in the nests of the common Catbird, but the egg never remains there long after the owner of the nest becomes aware of the intrusion. The list of the birds in whose nests the Cow Blackbird deposits her egg and it is reared is very large. The most common nurses of these foundlings in New England are *Spizella socialis, Empidonax minimus, Geothlypis trichas,* and all our eastern *Vireos,* namely, *olivaceus, solitarius, noveboracensis, gilvus,* and *flavifrons.* Besides these, I have found their eggs in the nests of *Polioptila cærulea, Mniotilta varia, Helminthophaga ruficapilla, Dendroica virens, D.*

blackburniæ, D. pennsylvanica and *D. discolor, Seiurus aurocapillus, Setophaga ruticilla, Cyanospiza cyanea, Contopus virens,* etc. I have also known of their eggs having been found in the nests of *Vireo belli* and *V. pusillus,* and *Cyanospiza amœna.* Dr. Cooper has found their egg in the nest of *Icteria virens;* and Mr. T. H. Jackson of West Chester, Penn., in those of *Empidonax acadicus* and *Pyranga rubra.*

Usually not more than a single Cowbird's egg is found in the same nest, though it is not uncommon to find two; and in a few instances three and even four eggs have been met with. In one instance Mr. Trippe mentions having found in the nest of a Black and White Creeper, besides three eggs of the owner of the nest, no less than five of the parasite. Mr. H. S. Rodney reports having found, in Potsdam, N. Y., May 15, 1868, a nest of *Zonotrichia leucophrys* of two stories, in one of which was buried a Cowbird's egg, and in the upper there were two more of the same, with three eggs of the rightful owners. In the spring of 1869 the same gentleman found a nest of the *Sayornis fuscus* with three Cowbird's eggs and three of her own.

Mr. Vickary, of Lynn, found, in the spring of 1860, the nest of a *Seiurus aurocapillus,* in which, with only one egg of the rightful owner, there were no less than four of the Cowbird. All five eggs were perfectly fresh, and had not been set upon. In the summer of the preceding year the same gentleman found a nest of the Red-eyed Vireo containing three eggs of the Vireo and four of the Cow Blackbird.

How the offspring from these eggs may all fare when more than one of these voracious nurslings are hatched in the same nest, is an interesting problem, well worthy the attention of some patiently inquiring naturalist to solve.

The Cow Blackbird appears in New England with a varying degree of promptness, sometimes as early as the latter part of March, and as frequently not until the middle of April. Nuttall states that none are seen in Massachusetts after the middle of June until the following October, and Allen, that they are there all the summer. My own observations do not correspond with the statement of either of these gentlemen. They certainly do become quite rare in the eastern part of that State after the third week in June, but that all the females are not gone is proved by the constant finding of freshly laid eggs up to July 1. I have never been able to find a Cow Blackbird in Eastern Massachusetts between the first of July and the middle of September. This I attribute to the absence of sufficient food. In the Cambridge marshes they remain until all the seeds have been consumed, and only reappear when the new crop is edible.

This Blackbird is a general feeder, eating insects, apparently in preference, and wild seed. They derive their name of Cow Blackbird from their keeping about that animal, and finding, either from her parasitic insects or her droppings, opportunities for food. They feed on the ground, and occasionally scratch for insects. At the South, to a limited extent, they frequent the rice-fields in company with the Red-winged Blackbird.

Mr. Nuttall states that if a Cow Blackbird's egg is deposited in a nest alone it is uniformly forsaken, and he also enumerates the Summer Yellowbird as one of the nurses of the Cowbird. In both respects I think he is mistaken. So far from forsaking her nest when one of these eggs is deposited, the Red-eyed Vireo has been known to commence incubation without having laid any of her own eggs, and also to forsake her nest when the intrusive egg has been taken and her own left. The *D. œstiva*, I think, invariably covers up and destroys the Cowbird's eggs when deposited before her own, and even when deposited afterwards.

The Cow Blackbird has no attractions as a singer, and has nothing that deserves the name of song. His utterances are harsh and unmelodious.

In September they begin to collect in large flocks, in localities favorable for their sustenance. The Fresh Pond marshes in Cambridge were once one of their chosen places of resort, in which they seemed to collect late in September, as if coming from great distances. There they remained until late in October, when they passed southward.

Mr. Ridgway only met with this species in two places, the valley of the Humboldt in September, and in June in the Truckee Valley. Their eggs were also obtained in the Wahsatch Mountains, deposited in the nest of *Passerella schistacea*, and in Bear River Valley in the nest of *Geothlypis trichas*.

Mr. Boardman informs me that the Cow Blackbird is a very rare bird in the neighborhood of Calais, Me., so much so that he does not see one of these birds once in five years, even as a bird of passage.

The eggs of this species are of a rounded oval, though some are more oblong than others, and are nearly equally rounded at either end. They vary from .85 of an inch to an inch in length, and from .65 to .70 in breadth. Their ground-color is white. In some it is so thickly covered with fine dottings of ashy and purplish-brown that the ground is not distinguishable. In others the egg is blotched with bold dashes of purple and wine-colored brown.

On the Rio Grande the eggs of the smaller southern race were found in the nests of *Vireo belli*, and in each of the nests of the *Vireo pusillus* found near Camp Grant, Arizona, there was an egg of this species. At Cape St. Lucas, Mr. Xantus found their eggs in nests of the *Polioptila melanura*. We have no information in regard to their habits, and can only infer that they must be substantially the same as those of the northern birds.

The eggs of the var. *obscurus* exhibit a very marked variation in size from those of the var. *pecoris*, and have a different appearance, though their colors are nearly identical. Their ground-color is white, and their markings a claret-brown. These markings are fewer, smaller, and less generally distributed, and the ground-color is much more apparent. They measure .60 by .55 of an inch, and their capacity as compared with the eggs of the *pecoris* is as 33 to 70, — a variation that is constant, and apparently too large to be accounted for on climatic differences.

Genus AGELAIUS, Vieill.

Agelaius, Vieillot, "Analyse, 1816." (Type, *Oriolus phœniceus*, L.)

Gen. Char. First quill shorter than second; claws short; the outer lateral scarcely reach-

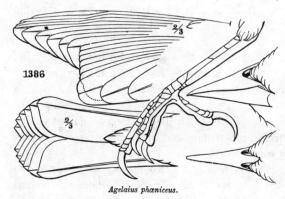

ing the base of the middle. Culmen depressed at base, parting the frontal feathers; length equal to that of the head, shorter than tarsus. Both mandibles of equal thickness and acute at tip, the edges much curved, the culmen, gonys, and commissure nearly straight or slightly sinuated; the length of bill about twice its height. Tail moderate, rounded, or very slightly graduated. Wings pointed, reaching to end of

Agelaius phœniceus.

lower tail-coverts. Colors black with red shoulders in North American species. One West Indian with orange-buff. Females streaked except in two West Indian species.

The nostrils are small, oblong, overhung by a membranous scale. The bill is higher than broad at the base. There is no division between the anterior tarsal scutellæ and the single plate on the outside of the tarsus.

The females of two West Indian species are uniform black. Of these the male of one, *A. assimilis* of Cuba, is undistinguishable from that of *A. phœniceus*; and in fact we may without impropriety consider the former as a melanite race of the latter, the change appreciable only in the female. The *A. humeralis*, also of Cuba, is smaller,

Agelaius phœniceus.

and black, with the lesser coverts brownish orange-buff.

Species and Varieties.

Common Characters. *Males* glossy black without distinct bluish lustre, lesser wing-coverts bright red. *Females* without any red, and either wholly black or variegated with light streaks, most conspicuous below.

A. **phœniceus.** Tail rounded. Red of shoulders a bright scarlet tint. Black of plumage without bluish lustre. *Females* with wing-coverts edged with brownish, or without any light edgings at all.

   a. Female continuous deep black, unvariegated.

Middle wing-coverts wholly buff in male.

Wing, 4.40; tail, 3.80; culmen, .95; tarsus, 1.00.   *Hab.* Cuba.

b. Females striped beneath .   .   .   .   .   .   var. *assimilis.*[1]

Wing, 4.90 ; tail, 3.85 ; culmen, .96 ; tarsus, 1.10.   *Female.*
White stripes on lower parts exceeding the dusky ones in width;
a conspicuous lighter superciliary stripe, and one strongly indicated
on middle of the crown. *Hab.* Whole of North America, south
to Guatemala .   .   .   .   var. *phœniceus.*

Middle wing-coverts black, except at base.

Wing, 5.00; tail, 3.90; culmen, .90; tarsus, 1.10. *Female.* White
stripes on lower parts narrower than dusky ones; the posterior
portion beneath being almost continuously dusky. No trace of
median stripe on crown, and the superciliary one indistinct. *Hab.*
Pacific Province of United States, south through Western Mexico.

var. *gubernator.*

Middle wing-coverts wholly white in male.

B. tricolor. Tail square. Red of the shoulders a brownish-scarlet, or
burnt-carmine tint. Black of the plumage (both sexes at all ages) with a
silky bluish lustre. *Female* with wing-coverts edged with pure white.

Wing, 4.90; tail, 3.70; culmen, .97; tarsus, 1.13. *Female.* Like
that of *gubernator,* but with scarcely any brownish tinge to the
plumage, and the lesser wing-coverts sharply bordered with pure
white. *Hab.* California (only ?).

Agelaius phœniceus, Vieillot.

SWAMP BLACKBIRD; REDWING BLACKBIRD.

Oriolus phœniceus, Linn. Syst. Nat. I, 1766, 161. — Gmelin, I, 1788, 386. — Lath. Ind.
Orn. I, 1790, 428. *Agelaius phœniceus,* "Vieillot, Anal. 1816." — Swainson, F.
Bor.-Am. II, 1831, 280. — Bonap. List, 1838. — Ib. Consp. 1850, 430. — Aud. Syn.
1839, 141. — Ib. Birds Am. IV, 1842, 31, pl. ccxvi. — Baird, Birds N. Am. 1858,
526. — Max. Cab. J. VI, 1858, 263. — Cooper & Suckley, 207. — Cooper, Orn. Cal.
I, 1870, 261. — Samuels, 341. — Allen, Birds E. Fla. 284. *Icterus phœniceus,*
Licht. Verz. 1823, No. 188. — Bon. Obs. Wils. 1824, No. 68. — Aud. Orn. Biog. I,
1831, 348 ; V, 1839, 487, pl. lxvii. *Psarocolius phœniceus,* Wagler, Syst. Nat. 1827,
No. 10. *Icterus (Xanthornus) phœniceus,* Bonap. Syn. 1828, 52. — Nuttall, Man. I,
1832, 167, (2d ed.,) 179. *Sturnus prædatorius,* Wilson, Am. Orn. IV, 1811, 30, pl.
xxx. *Red-winged Oriole,* Pennant, Arctic Zoöl. II, 255.

Sp. Char. Tail much rounded; the lateral feathers about half an inch shorter. Fourth
quill longest; first about as long as the fifth. Bill large, stout; half as high, or more
than half as high, as long.

Male. General color uniform lustrous velvet-black, with a greenish reflection. Shoulders and lesser wing-coverts of a bright crimson or vermilion-red. Middle coverts
brownish-yellow, or buff, and usually paler towards the tips.

Female. Brown above, the feathers edged or streaked with rufous-brown and

---

[1] *Agelaius assimilis,* Gundl. Cabanis, Journal, IX, 12 (nest). — Ib. Boston Journal, VI,
1853, 316.

yellowish; beneath white, streaked with brown. Forepart of throat, superciliary, and median stripe strongly tinged with brownish-yellow. Length of male, 9.50; wing, 5.00; tail, 4.15.

HAB. United States from Atlantic to Pacific; north to Great Slave Lake, Fort Resolution, Fort Simpson, Fort Rae, etc.; Guatemala (SCLATER, Ibis I, 19; breeding); Costa Rica (LAWRENCE, America, N. Y. Lyc. IX, 104); Bahamas (BRYANT, B. P. VII, 1859); Texas (DRESSER, Ibis, 65, 492); Arizona (COUES, P. A. N. S. 1866, 90; Fort Whipple); Yucatan.

There is some variation in the shade of red on the shoulders, which is sometimes of the color of arterial blood or bright crimson. It never, however, has the hæmatitic tint of the red in A. tricolor. The middle coverts are usually uniform brownish-yellow to the very tips; sometimes some of these middle coverts are tipped at the end with black, but these black tips are usually of slight extent, and indicate immaturity, or else a transition of hybridism or race to A. gubernator.

There is also some variation in the size and proportions of the bill. The most striking is in a series of three from the Red River Settlement, decidedly larger than more southern ones (wings, 5.15; tail, 4.40). The bill is about as long as that of Pennsylvania specimens, but much stouter, the thickness at the base being considerably more than half the length of the culmen. One specimen from San Elizario, Texas, has the bill of much the same size and proportions.

The male of A. assimilis of Cuba cannot be distinguished from small-sized males of phœniceus from the United States, the females, however, as in nearly all West Indian Icteridæ, are uniform though rather dull black. This we consider as simply a local variation of melanism, not indicating a specific difference. A young male is similar, but with the lesser coverts red, tipped with black. On the other extreme, streaked female and young birds from Lower California, Arizona, and Western Mexico are much lighter than in eastern birds, the chin, throat, jugulum, and superciliary stripe tinged with a peculiar peach-blossom pink; not buff, sometimes tinged with orange.

HABITS. The much abused and persecuted Redwinged Blackbird is found throughout North America as far north as the 57th parallel, from the Atlantic to the Pacific; and it breeds more or less abundantly wherever found, from Florida and Texas to the plains of the Saskatchewan. According to the observations of Mr. Salvin, it is resident all the year in Guatemala. It breeds among the reeds at the lake of Dueñas, deferring its incubation until the month of June. The females congregate in large flocks near the lake, feeding about the swampy grass on the edge of the water, the males keeping separate. At Orizaba, Mexico, Sumichrast regarded this species as only a bird of passage.

On the Pacific coast, it is only found, in any numbers, in Washington Territory and in Oregon, about cultivated tracts. Dr. Cooper thinks that none inhabit the bare and mountainous prairie regions east of the Cascade Mountains. Small flocks wintered at Vancouver about stables and haystacks. Dr. Suckley speaks of them as quite common west of the Cascade Mountains, arriving from the South in March. In all the marshy places of the entire West Mr. Ridgway met with this species and their nests in great abundance. In all respects he found the western birds identical with the eastern. Their nests were in low bushes in overflowed meadows.

Donald Gunn found this species common in the Red River Settlements; and Richardson met with them on the Saskatchewan, where they arrive in May, but do not breed until the 20th of June.

In New England this Blackbird is generally migratory, though instances are on record where a few have been known to remain throughout the winter in Massachusetts. They are among the earliest to arrive in spring, coming, in company with the Rusty Grakle, as early as the 10th of March. Those which remain to breed usually come a month later. They breed throughout New England, as also in New Brunswick and Nova Scotia.

It is equally abundant and resident in Arizona and Texas, and in the adjoining portions of Mexico. On the Rio Grande, Mr. Dresser found it very abundant, breeding on the banks of the rivers and streams. In the winter season these birds are found in immense flocks in the lower parts of Virginia, both the Carolinas, and all the Gulf States, particularly near the sea-coast and among old fields of rice and grain. Wilson states that once, passing, in January, through the lower counties of Virginia, he frequently witnessed the aerial evolutions of great bodies of these birds. Sometimes they appeared as if driven about like an enormous black cloud carried before the wind, varying every moment in shape. Sometimes they rose up suddenly from the fields with a noise like thunder, while the glittering of innumerable wings of the brightest vermilion, amid the black cloud, occasioned a very striking effect. At times the whole congregated multitude would suddenly alight in some detached grove and commence one general concert, that he could plainly distinguish at the distance of more than two miles, and when listened to at a distance of a quarter of a mile, the flow of its cadences was grand, and even sublime.

He adds that with the Redwings the whole winter season seems one continued carnival. They find abundant food in the old fields of rice, buckwheat, and grain, and much of their time is spent in aerial movements, or in grand vocal performances.

Early in March these large assemblies break up. A part separate in pairs and remain among the Southern swamps. The greater portion, in smaller flocks, the male bird leading the way, commence their movements northward. Late in April they have all re-established themselves in their chosen haunts, have mated, and are preparing to make their nests. In Pennsylvania this is done in May, in New England early in June, and farther north a fortnight later. For their nest they invariably select either the borders of streams or low marshy situations. These they usually place in low bushes, such as grow in moist situations, among thick bunches of reeds, or even on the ground. In one instance, in an island on the marshes of Essex River, Mr. Maynard found these nests placed in trees twenty feet from the ground. One nest was built on a slender sapling at the distance of fourteen feet from the ground. The nest was pensile, like that of the Baltimore Oriole. It was woven of bleached eel-grass.

When built in a bush, the outer, basket-like frame of the nest is carefully and strongly interwoven with, or fastened around, the adjacent twigs, and, though somewhat rudely put together, is woven firmly and compactly. Within this is packed a mass of coarse materials, with an inner nest of sedges and grasses. The outer framework is usually made of rushes and strong leaves of the iris. The male bird is a very attentive and watchful parent, constantly on the lookout for the approach of danger, and prompt to do all in his power to avert it, approaching close to the intruder, and earnestly remonstrating against the aggression. If the nest is pillaged, for several days he evinces great distress, and makes frequent lamentations, but soon prepares to remedy the disaster. So tenacious are they of a selected locality, that I have known the same pair to build three nests within as many weeks in the same bush, after having been robbed twice. The third time the pair succeeded in raising their brood.

In New England these birds have but one brood in a season. Farther south they are said to have three or more. In August they begin to collect in small flocks largely composed of young birds. The latter do not reach their full plumage until their third summer, but breed in their immature plumage the summer following their appearance. When the Indian corn is in the milk, these birds are said to collect in numbers, and to commit great depredations upon it. As soon, however, as the corn hardens, they desist from these attacks, and seek other food. In the grain-growing States they gather in immense swarms and commit great havoc, and although they are shot in immense numbers, and though their ranks are thinned by the attacks of hawks, it seems to have but little effect upon the survivors. These scenes of pillage are, for the most part, confined to the low sections, near the sea-coast, and only last during a short period, when the corn is in a condition to be eaten.

On the other hand, these Blackbirds more than compensate the farmer for these brief episodes of mischief, by the immense benefits they confer in the destruction of grub-worms, caterpillars, and various kinds of larvæ, the secret and deadly enemies of vegetation. During the months of March, April, May, June, and July, their food is almost wholly insects, and during that period the amount of their insect food, all of it of the most noxious kinds, is perfectly enormous. These they both consume themselves and feed to their young. Wilson estimated the number of insects destroyed by these birds in a single season, in the United States, at twelve thousand millions.

The notes of this bird are very various and indescribable. The most common one sounds like *con-cur-ee*. But there is also an almost endless mingling of guttural, creaking, or clear utterances that defy description.

Their eggs vary greatly in size; the largest measures 1.08 inches by .82 of an inch, the smallest .90 by .65. They average about an inch in length and .77 of an inch in breadth. They are oval in shape, have a light-bluish ground, and are marbled, lined, and blotched with markings of light and dark purple and black. These markings are almost wholly about the larger end, and are very varying.

Agelaius phœniceus, var. gubernator, Bon.

CRIMSON-SHOULDERED BLACKBIRD.

Psarocolius gubernator, WAGLER, Isis, 1832, IV, 281. *Agelaius gubernator*, BON. List, 1838. — IB. Conspectus, 1850, 430. — AUD. Syn. 1839, 141. — IB. Birds Am. IV, 1842, 29, pl. ccxv. — NEWBERRY, P. R. R. Rep. VI, IV, 1857, 86. — BAIRD, Birds N. Am. 1858, 529. — HEERM. X, S, 53 (nest). — COOPER, Orn. Cal. I, 1870, 263. *Icterus (Zanthornus) gubernator*, NUTTALL, Man. I, (2d ed.,) 1840, 187.

SP. CHAR. Bill rather shorter than the head, without any longitudinal sulci, but with faint traces of transverse ones at the base of the lower jaw. Tail rounded. First quill nearly equal to the fourth.

Male. Throughout of a lustrous velvety-black, with a greenish reflection. The lesser coverts rich crimson; the middle coverts brownish-yellow at the base, but the exposed portion black. Wing, 5.00; tail, 3.90; culmen, .90; tarsus, 1.10.

Female. Nearly uniform dark slaty-brown; an indistinct superciliary stripe, an indication of a maxillary stripe, and blended streaks on chin and throat delicate pale peach-blossom pink, this on the jugulum interrupted by dusky streaks running in longitudinal series; lesser wing-coverts tinged with dark wine-red. Wings with just appreciable paler edges to the feathers. Wing, 4.20; tail, 3.20.

HAB. Pacific Province of United States, and Western Mexico, to Colima; Western Nevada (RIDGWAY). ? Xalapa (SCLATER, 1859, 365).

In the female and all the immature stages, the dusky beneath is largely in excess of the light streaks; the superciliary light stripe is badly defined, and there is no trace of a median light stripe on the crown. These characters distinguish this race from *phœniceus;* while the rounded instead of square tail, and brown instead of pure white border to middle wing-coverts, distinguish it from corresponding stages of *tricolor.*

HABITS. The Crimson-shouldered Blackbird was first met with by Mr. Townsend, on the Columbia River, where two specimens were obtained, which were described by Mr. Audubon, in his Synopsis, in 1839. No information in regard to its habits, distribution, or nesting, was obtained by either Mr. Townsend or by his companion, Mr. Nuttall.

This species, or local race, whichever it is considered, occurs from the Columbia River south throughout California. It is given doubtingly as also from the Colorado River, but Dr. Cooper was only able to detect there the common *phœniceus.* According to the observations of that careful naturalist, this species is chiefly found in the warmer interior of California, Santa Cruz being the only point on the coast where he has met with it. He found it in scattered pairs, in May, throughout the Coast Range, even to the summits, where there are small marshes full of rushes, in which they build. He has not been able to detect any difference between the habits and notes of this bird and the common Redwing. The fact that specimens with entirely red shoulders seem limited to the middle of the State, or are rare along the coast, while most of those on the coast closely resemble the eastern bird, Dr. Cooper regards as suggestive of its being only a local race, though said to occur also in Mexico.

During the summer this species is said to emit a variety of sweet and liquid notes, delivered from some tree near its favorite marsh. These are also sometimes mingled with jingling and creaking sounds.

Dr. Suckley, in his Report on the Zoölogy of Washington Territory, expresses the opinion, that, although a specimen of this bird is reported as having been taken by Townsend on the Columbia, it is very rarely found so far north, as he never met with it in Washington Territory, and has never been able to hear of any other specimen having been found there.

Dr. Kennerly, in his Report on the birds observed in the survey of the 35th parallel, states that during the march along Bill Williams Fork, and along the Great Colorado and the Mohave Rivers, this species was found quite numerous. They were more abundant still along the creeks and swampy grounds that were passed as they approached the settlements of California. Large flocks could there be seen whirling around in graceful curves, like dark clouds, chattering joyfully as they moved along, or settling as a black veil on the topmost branches of some tree, indulging loudly in their harsh music.

In his Report of the birds observed in the survey under Lieutenant Williamson, Dr. Heermann mentions finding this species abundant, and, in the fall season, as associated with *Molothrus pecoris* and *A. tricolor*. Its nest he found built in the willow bushes and tussocks of grass above the level of the water, in the marshes. There were but a few pairs together, and in this respect they differ from the *tricolor*, which prefers dry situations near water, and which congregate by thousands while breeding. The nest was composed of mud and fine roots, and lined with fine grasses. The eggs, four in number, he describes as pale blue, dashed with spots and lines of black.

Neither this nor the *tricolor* was detected by Dr. Coues in Arizona.

These Blackbirds were found by Mr. Ridgway abundant in the marshy regions of California, but they were rarely met with east of the Sierra Nevada. A few individuals were collected in Nevada in the valley of the Truckee. A few pairs were found breeding among the *tulé* sloughs and marshes. The nests found in the Truckee Reservations were built in low bushes in wet meadows.

A nest procured by Dr. Cooper from the summit of the Coast Range was built of grass and rushes, and lined with finer grass. The eggs are described as pale greenish-white, with large curving streaks and spots of dark brown, mostly at the large end. They are said to measure one inch by .75 of an inch.

Eggs of this variety in my cabinet, taken in California by Dr. Heermann, are of a rounded-oval shape, nearly equally obtuse at either end, and varying in length from .90 of an inch to an inch, and in breadth from .70 to .80. Their ground-color is a light blue, fading into a bluish-white, marked only around the larger end with waving lines of dark brown, much lighter in shade than the markings of the *phœniceus* usually are.

Agelaius tricolor, Bonap.

RED AND WHITE SHOULDERED BLACKBIRD.

Icterus tricolor, "NUTTALL," AUD. Orn. Biog. V, 1839, I, pl. ccclxxxviii. — NUTTALL, Man. I, (2d ed.,) 1840, 186. *Agelaius tricolor*, BON. List, 1838. — AUD. Syn. 1839, 141. — IB. Birds Am. IV, 1842, 27, pl. ccxiv. — HEERM. X, S, 53 (nest). — BAIRD, Birds N. Am. 1858, 530. — COOPER, Orn. Cal. I, 1870, 265.

SP. CHAR. Tail nearly even. Second and third quills longest; first a little shorter than the fourth. Bill slender, not half as high as long.

Male. General color uniform lustrous velvet-black, with a strong silky-bluish reflection. Shoulders and lesser wing-coverts brownish-red, of much the color of venous blood; the median coverts of a well-defined and nearly pure white, with sometimes a brownish tinge. Wing, 4.90; tail, 3.70; culmen, .97; tarsus, 1.13.

Female. General color dusky slaty-brown, faintly variegated on head also by lighter streaks; middle wing-coverts broadly and sharply bordered with pure white. An obsolete superciliary and maxillary stripe of grayish-white. Beneath grayish-white for anterior half, with narrow streaks of dusky, this color gradually prevailing posteriorly, the sides, flanks, and crissum being nearly uniform dusky. Wing, 4.25; tail, 3.20.

HAB. Pacific Province of United States, from Columbia River southward, not yet found out of California and Oregon.

Immature males sometimes have the white on the wing tinged with brownish-yellow, as in *A. phœniceus.* The red, however, has the usual brownish-orange shade so much darker and duller than the brilliantly scarlet shoulders of the other species, and the black has that soft bluish lustre peculiar to the species. The relationships generally between the two species are very close, but the bill, as stated, is slenderer and more sulcate in *tricolor,* the tail much more nearly even ; the first primary longer, usually nearly equal to or longer than the fourth, instead of the fifth.

Two strong features of coloration distinguish the female and immature stages of this species from *gubernator* and *phœniceus.* They are, first, the soft bluish gloss of the males, both adult and immature ; and secondly, the clear white and broad, not brown and narrow, borders to the middle wing-coverts.

HABITS. The Red and White shouldered Blackbird was seen by Mr. Ridgway among the *tulé* in the neighborhood of Sacramento City, where it was very abundant, associating with the *A. phœniceus* and *gubernator,* and the Yellow-headed Blackbird. The conspicuous white stripe on the wings of this bird renders it easily recognizable from the other species, where they are all seen together. Mr. Ridgway is of the opinion that the notes of the white-shouldered species differ very considerably from those of the two other Blackbirds.

Dr. Heermann found this a very abundant bird in California. He states that during the winter of 1852, when hunting in the marshes of Suisan Valley, he had often, on hearing a dull, rushing, roaring noise, found that it was produced by a single flock of this species, numbering so many thousands as to darken the sky for some distance by their masses. In the northern part of California he met with a breeding-place of this species that occupied several acres, covered with alder-bushes and willow, and was in the immediate vicinity of water. The nests, often four or five in the same bush, were composed of mud and straw, and lined with fine grasses. The eggs he describes as dark blue, marked with lines and spots of dark umber and a few light purple dashes. Dr. Heermann, at different times, fell in with several other breeding-places of this species, similarly situated, but they had all been abandoned, from which he inferred that each year different grounds are resorted to by these birds for the purposes of incubation.

Dr. Kennerly obtained a specimen of this bird on the Colorado River, in California, December, 1854. Dr. Cooper is of the opinion that it is, nevertheless, a rare species in that valley. The latter found them the most abundant species near San Diego and Los Angeles, and not rare at Santa Barbara. North of the last place they pass more into the interior, and extend up as far as Klamath Lake and Southern Oregon.

They are to be seen in considerable flocks even in the breeding-season. Their song, Dr. Cooper states, is not so loud and is more guttural than are those of the other species. Their habits are otherwise very similar, and they associate, in fall and winter, in immense flocks in the interior, though often also found separate.

These birds were first obtained by Mr. Nuttall near Santa Barbara, in the month of April. They were very common there, as well as at Monterey. He observed no difference in their habits from those of the common Redwing, except that they occurred in much larger flocks and kept apart from that species. They were seldom seen, except in the near suburbs of the towns. At that time California was in the possession of Mexico, and its inhabitants were largely occupied in the slaughter of wild cattle for the sake of the hides. Mr. Nuttall found these birds feeding almost exclusively on the maggots of the flesh-flies generated in the offal thus created. They were in large whirling flocks, and associated with the *Molothri*, the Grakles, the Red-wings, and the Yellow-headed Blackbirds. They kept up an incessant chatter and a discordant, confused warble, much more harsh and guttural than even the notes of the Cow Blackbird.

Two eggs of this species, obtained by Dr. Heermann in California, and now in my cabinet, measuring an inch in length by .67 of an inch in breadth, are more oblong in shape than the preceding, but nearly equally obtuse at either end. They are similar in ground-color to the *phœniceus*, but are of a slightly deeper shade of blue, and are marked around one end with a ring of dark slaty-brown, almost black, lines, and irregular oblong blotches.

Genus **XANTHOCEPHALUS**, BONAP.

Xanthocephalus, BONAP. Conspectus, 1850, 431. (Type, *Icterus icterocephalus*, BONAP.)

GEN. CHAR. Bill conical, the length about twice the height; the outlines nearly straight. Claws all very long; much curved; the inner lateral the longest, reaching

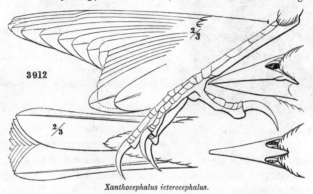

Xanthocephalus icterocephalus.

beyond the middle of the middle claw. Tail narrow, nearly even, the outer web scarcely widening to the end. Wings long, much longer than the tail; the first quill longest.

This genus differs from typical *Agelaius* in much longer and more curved claws, even tail, and first quill longest, instead of the longest being the second, third, or fourth. The yellow head and black body are also strong marks.

Xanthocephalus icterocephalus, BAIRD.

YELLOW-HEADED BLACKBIRD.

Icterus icterocephalus, BONAP. Am. Orn. I, 1825, 27, pl. iii. — NUTT. Man. I, 1832, 176. — IB., (2d ed.,) 187 (not *Oriolus icterocephalus*, LINN.). *Agelaius icterocephalus*, CABANIS, Mus. Hein. 1851, 188. *Icterus (Xanthornus) xanthocephalus*, BONAP. J. A. N. Sc. V, II, Feb. 1826, 222. — IB. Syn. 1828, 52. *Icterus xanthocephalus*, AUD. Orn. Biog. V, 1839, 6, pl. ccclxxxviii. *Agelaius xanthocephalus*, SWAINSON, F. Bor.-Am. II, 1831, 281. — BON. List, 1838. — AUD. Syn. 1839, 140. — IB. Birds Am. IV, 1842, 24, pl. ccxiii. — NEWBERRY, Zoöl. Cal. and Or. Route; Rep. P. R. R. Surv. VI, IV, 1857, 86. — MAX. Cab. J. VI, 1858, 361. — HEERM. X, S, 52 (nest). *Agelaius longipes*, SWAINSON, Phil. Mag. I, 1827, 436. *Psarocolius perspicillatus*, "LICHT." WAGLER, Isis, 1829, VII, 753. *Icterus perspicillatus*, "LICHT. in Mus." WAGLER, as above. *Xanthocephalus perspicillatus*, BONAP. Consp. 1850, 431. *Icterus frenatus*, LICHT. Isis, 1843, 59. — REINHARDT, in Kroyer's Tidskrift, IV. — IB. Vidensk. Meddel. for 1853, 1854, 82 (Greenland). *Xanthocephalus icterocephalus*, BAIRD, M. B. II, Birds, 18; Birds N. Am. 1858, 531. — COOPER, Orn. Cal. I, 1870, 267.

Sp. Char. First quill nearly as long as the second and third (longest), decidedly longer than the fourth. Tail rounded, or slightly graduated. General color black, including the inner surface of wings and axillaries, base of lower mandible all round, feathers adjacent to nostrils, lores, upper eyelids, and remaining space around the eye. The head and neck all round; the forepart of the breast, extending some distance down on the median line, and a somewhat hidden space round the anus, yellow. A conspicuous white patch at the

Xanthocephalus icterocephalus.

base of the wing formed by the spurious feathers, interrupted by the black alula.

Female smaller, browner; the yellow confined to the under parts and sides of the head, and a superciliary line. A dusky maxillary line. No white on the wing. Length of male, 10 inches; wing, 5.60; tail, 4.50.

Hab. Western America from Texas, Illinois, Wisconsin, and North Red River, to California, south into Mexico; Greenland (Reinhardt); Cuba (Cabanis, J. VII, 1859, 350); Massachusetts (Maynard, D. C. Mass. 1870, 122); Volusia, Florida (Mus. S. I.); Cape St. Lucas.

The color of the yellow in this species varies considerably; sometimes being almost of a lemon-yellow, sometimes of a rich orange. There is an occasional trace of yellow around the base of the tarsus. Immature males show every gradation between the colors of the adult male and female.

A very young bird (4,332, Dane Co., Wis.) is dusky above, with feathers of the dorsal region broadly tipped with ochraceous, lesser and middle wing-coverts white tinged with fulvous, dusky below the surface, greater coverts very broadly tipped with fulvous-white; primary coverts narrowly tipped with the same. Whole lower parts unvariegated fulvous-white; head all round plain ochraceous, deepest above.

Habits. The Yellow-headed Blackbird is essentially a prairie bird, and is found in all favorable localities from Texas on the south to Illinois and Wisconsin, and thence to the Pacific. A single specimen is recorded as having been taken in Greenland. This was September 2, 1820, at Nenortalik. Recently the Smithsonian Museum has received a specimen from New Smyrna, in Florida. In October, 1869, a specimen of this bird was taken in Watertown, Mass., and Mr. Cassin mentions the capture of several near Philadelphia. These erratic appearances in places so remote from their centres of reproduction, and from their route in emigration, sufficiently attest the nomadic character of this species.

They are found in abundance in all the grassy meadows or rushy marshes of Illinois and Wisconsin, where they breed in large communities. In swamps overgrown with tall rushes, and partially overflowed, they construct their nests just above the water, and build them around the stems of these water-plants, where they are thickest, in such a manner that it is difficult to discover them, except by diligent search, aided by familiarity with their habits.

In Texas Mr. Dresser met with a few in the fall, and again in April he found the prairies covered with these birds. For about a week vast flocks remained about the town, after which they suddenly disappeared, and no more were seen.

In California, Dr. Cooper states that they winter in large numbers in the middle districts, some wandering to the Colorado Valley and to San Diego. They nest around Santa Barbara, and thence northward, and are very abundant about Klamath Lake. They associate with the other Blackbirds, but always keep in separate companies. They are very gregarious, even in summer.

Dr. Cooper states that the only song the male attempts consists of a few hoarse, chuckling notes and comical squeakings, uttered as if it was a great effort to make any sound at all.

Dr. Coues speaks of it as less numerous in Arizona than at most other localities where found at all. He speaks of it as a summer resident, but in this I think he may have been mistaken.

In Western Iowa Mr. Allen saw a few, during the first week in July, about the grassy ponds near Boonesboro'. He was told that they breed in great numbers, north and east of that section, in the meadows of the Skunk River country. He also reports them as breeding in large numbers in the Calumet marshes of Northern Illinois.

Sir John Richardson found these birds very numerous in the interior of the fur countries, ranging in summer as far to the north as the 58th parallel, but not found to the eastward of Lake Winnipeg. They reached the Saskatchewan by the 20th of May, in greater numbers than the Redwings.

Through California, as well as in the interior, Mr. Ridgway found the Yellow-headed Blackbird a very abundant species, even exceeding in numbers the *A. phœniceus*, occurring in the marshes filled with rushes. This species he found more gregarious than the Redwing, and frequently their nests almost filled the rushes of their breeding-places. Its notes he describes as harsher than those of any other bird he is acquainted with. Yet they are by no means disagreeable, while frequently their attempts at a song were really amusing. Their usual note is a deep *cluck*, similar to that of most Blackbirds, but of a rather deeper tone. In its movements upon the ground its gait is firm and graceful, and it may frequently be seen walking about over the grassy flats, in small companies, in a manner similar to the Cow Blackbird, which, in its movements, it greatly resembles. It nests in the sloughs, among the *tulé*, and the maximum number of its eggs is four.

Mr. W. J. McLaughlin of Centralia, Kansas, writes (American Naturalist, III, p. 493) that these birds arrive in that region about the first of May, and all disappear about the 10th of June. He does not think that any breed there. During their stay they make themselves very valuable to the farmers by destroying the swarms of young grasshoppers. On the writer's land the grasshoppers had deposited their eggs by the million. As they began to hatch, the Yellow-heads found them out, and a flock of about two hundred attended about two acres each day, roving over the entire lot as wild pigeons feed, the rear ones flying to the front as the insects were devoured.

Mr. Clark met with these birds at New Leon, Mexico. They were always in flocks, mingled with two or three of its congeneric species. They were found more abundant near the coast than in the interior. There was a roost of these birds on an island in a lagoon near Fort Brown. Between sunset and dark these birds could be seen coming from all quarters. For about an hour they kept up a constant chattering and changing of place. Another similar roost was on an island near the mouth of the Rio Grande.

Dr. Kennerly found them very common near Janos and also near Santa Cruz, in Sonora. At the former place they were seen in the month of April in large flocks. He describes them as quite domestic in their habits, preferring the immediate vicinity of the houses, often feeding with the domestic fowls in the yards.

Dr. Heermann states that these birds collect in flocks of many thousands with the species of *Agelaius,* and on the approach of spring separate into smaller bands, resorting in May to large marshy districts in the valleys, where they incubate. Their nests he found attached to the upright stalks of the reeds, and woven around them, of flexible grasses, differing essentially from the nests of the *Agelaii* in the lightness of their material. The eggs, always four in number, he describes as having a ground of pale ashy-green, thickly covered with minute dots of a light umber-brown.

Mr. Nuttall states that on the 2d of May, during his western tour, he saw these birds in great abundance, associated with the Cowbird. They kept wholly on the ground, in companies, the sexes separated by themselves. They were digging into the earth with their bills in search of insects and larvæ. They were very active, straddling about with a quaint gait, and now and then whistling out, with great effort, a chuckling note, sounding like *ko-kuk kie-ait.* Their music was inferior even to the harsh notes of *M. pecoris.*

Several nests of this species, procured in the marshes on the banks of Lake Koskonong, in Southern Wisconsin, were sent me by Mr. Kumlien; they were all light, neat, and elegant structures, six inches in diameter and four in height. The cavity had a diameter of three and a depth of two and a half inches. The base, periphery, and the greater portion of these nests were made of interwoven grasses and sedges. The grasses were entire, with their panicles on. They were impacted together in masses. The inner portions of these nests were made of finer materials of the same. They were placed in the midst of large, overflowed marshes, and were attached to tall flags, usually in the midst of clumps of the latter, and these were so close in their growth that the nests were not easily discovered. They contained, usually, from five to six eggs. These are of an oblong-oval shape, and measure 1.02 inches in length by .70 of an inch in breadth. Their ground-color is of a pale greenish-white, profusely covered with blotches and finer dottings of drab, purplish-brown, and umber.

Genus **STURNELLA**, Vieillot.

Sturnella, Vieillot, Analyse, 1816. (Type, *Alauda magna*, L.)

Gen. Char. Body thick, stout; legs large, toes reaching beyond the tail. Tail short, even, with narrow acuminate feathers. Bill slender, elongated; length about three times

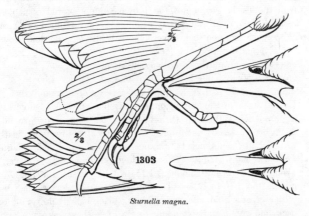

Sturnella magna.

the height; commissure straight from the basal angle. Culmen flattened basally, extending backwards and parting the frontal feathers; longer than the head, but shorter than tarsus. Nostrils linear, covered by an incumbent membranous scale. Inner lateral toe longer than the outer, but not reaching to basal joint of middle; hind toe a little shorter than the middle, which is equal to the tarsus. Hind claw nearly twice as long as the middle. Feathers of head stiffened and bristly; the shafts of those above extended into a black seta. Tertials nearly equal to the primaries. Feathers above all transversely banded. Beneath yellow, with a black pectoral crescent.

Sturnella magna.

The only species which we can admit is the *S. magna*, though under this name we group several geographical races. They may be distinguished as follows: —

Species and Varieties.

1. **S. magna.** Above brownish, or grayish, spotted and barred with black; crown divided by a median whitish stripe; side of the head whitish, with a blackish streak along upper edge of the auriculars. Beneath more or less yellowish, with a more or less distinct dusky crescent on the jugulum. Sides, flanks, and crissum whitish, streaked with dusky; lateral tail-feathers partly white. *Adult.* Supraloral spot, chin, throat, breast, and abdomen deep gamboge-yellow; pectoral crescent deep black. *Young.* The yellow only indicated; pectoral crescent obsolete. Length, about 9.00 to 10.50 inches. Sexes similar in color, but female much smaller.

A. In spring birds, the lateral stripes of the vertex either continuous black, or with black largely predominating; the black spots on the back extending to the tip of the feather, or, if not, the brown tip not barred (except in winter dress). Yellow of the throat confined between the maxillæ, or just barely encroaching upon their lower edge. White of sides, flanks, and crissum strongly tinged with ochraceous.

   a. Pectoral crescent much more than half an inch wide.

   Wing, 4.50 to 5.00; culmen, 1.20 to 1.50; tarsus, 1.35 to 1.55; middle toe, 1.10 to 1.26 (extremes of a series of four adult males). Lateral stripe of the crown continuously black; black predominating on back and rump (heavy stripes on ochraceous ground). Light brown serrations on tertials and tail-feathers reaching nearly to the shaft (sometimes the terminal ones uninterrupted, isolating the black bars). *Hab.* Eastern United States   .   . var. *magna*.

   Wing, 3.75 to 4.30; culmen, 1.15 to 1.30; tarsus, 1.50 to 1.75; middle toe, 1.10 to 1.25. (Ten adult males!) Colors similar, but with a greater predominance of black; black heavily prevailing on back and rump, and extending to tip of feathers; also predominates on tertials and tail-feathers. *Hab.* Mexico and Central America   .   .   .   . var. *mexicana*.[1]

   Wing, 4.45; culmen, 1.62; tarsus, 1.50; middle toe, 1.20. (One specimen). Colors exactly as in last. *Hab.* Brazil.

                                    var. *meridionalis*.[2]

   b. Pectoral crescent much less than half an inch wide.

   Wing, 3.90 to 4.10; culmen, 1.25 to 1.35; tarsus, 1.40 to 1.55; middle toe, 1.00 to 1.20. (Three adult males.) Colors generally similar to *magna*, but crown decidedly streaked, though black predominates; ground-color above less reddish than in either of the preceding, with markings as in *magna*. Pectoral crescent about .25 in breadth. *Hab.* Cuba   .   .   .   . var. *hippocrepis*.[3]

B. In spring birds, crown about equally streaked with black and grayish; black spots of back occupying only basal half of feathers, the terminal portion being grayish-brown, with narrow bars of black; feathers of the rump with whole exposed portion thus barred. Yellow of the throat extending over the maxillæ nearly to the angle of the mouth.

   Wing, 4.40 to 5.05; culmen, 1.18 to 1.40; tarsus, 1.30 to 1.45. (Six adult males.) A grayish-brown tint prevailing above; lesser

---

[1] *Sturnella mexicana*, SCLATER, Ibis, 1861, 179.

[2] *Sturnella meridionalis*, SCLATER, Ibis, 1861, 179.

[3] *Sturnella hippocrepis*, WAGLER, Ibis, 1832, 281. — LAWR. Ann. N. Y. Lyc. 1860.

wing-coverts concolor with the wings (instead of very decidedly more bluish); black bars of tertials and tail-feathers clean, narrow, and isolated. White of sides, flanks, and crissum nearly pure.

Hab. Western United States and Western Mexico   var. *neglecta.*

In *magna* and *neglecta,* the feathers of the pectoral crescent are generally black to the base, their roots being grayish-white; one specimen of the former, however, from North Carolina, has the roots of the feathers yellow, forbidding the announcement of this as a distinguishing character; *mexicana* may have the bases of these feathers either yellow or grayish; while *hippocrepis* has only the tips of the feathers black, the whole concealed portion being bright yellow.

In *mexicana,* there is more of an approach to an orange tint in the yellow than is usually seen in *magna,* but specimens from Georgia have a tint not distinguishable; in both, however, as well as in *hippocrepis,* there is a deeper yellow than in *neglecta,* in which the tint is more citreous.

As regards the bars on tertials and tail, there is considerable variation. Sometimes in either of the species opposed to *neglecta* by this character there is a tendency to their isolation, seen in the last few toward the ends of the feathers; but never is there an approach to that regularity seen in *neglecta,* in which they are isolated uniformly everywhere they occur. Two specimens only (54,064 California and 10,316 Pembina) in the entire series of *neglecta* show a tendency to a blending of these bars on the tail.

Magna, mexicana, meridionalis and *hippocrepis,* are most similar in coloration; *neglecta* is most dissimilar compared with any of the others. Though each possesses peculiar characters, they are only of degree; for in the most widely different forms (*neglecta* and *mexicana*) there is not the slightest departure from the pattern of coloration; it is only a matter of extension or restriction of the several colors, or a certain one of them, that produces the differences.

Each modification of plumage is attended by a still greater one of proportions, as will be seen from the diagnoses; thus, though *neglecta* is the largest of the group, it has actually the smallest legs and feet; with nearly the same general proportions, *magna* exceeds it in the latter respects (especially in the bill), while *mexicana,* a very much smaller bird than either, has disproportionally and absolutely larger legs and feet united with the smallest size otherwise in the whole series. *Meridionalis* presents no differences from the last, except in proportions of bill and feet; for while the latter is the smallest of the series, next to *neglecta,* it has a bill much exceeding that of any other.

The markings of the upper plumage of the young or even winter birds are different in pattern from those of the adult; the tendency being toward the peculiar features of the adult *neglecta;* the various species in these stages being readily distinguishable, however, by the general characters assigned. *Mexicana* and *neglecta* are both in proportions and colors the most widely different in the whole series; *hippocrepis* and *neglecta* the most similar. The relation of the several races to each other is about as follows : —

A. Yellow of throat confined within maxillæ.
　　Crown with black streaks predominating.
　　　　Smallest species, with reddish tints, and maximum amount of black.
　　　　　　Largest bill . . . . *meridionalis.*
　　　　　　Smallest bill; largest feet . . . . . . *mexicana.*
　　　　Next largest species, with less reddish tints, and smaller amount of
　　　　　　black. Bill and feet the standard of comparison . . . *magna.*
　　Crown with the light streaks predominating.
　　　　Narrowest pectoral crescent . . . . . . *hippocrepis.*
B. Yellow of throat covering maxillæ.
　　Crown with black and light streaks about equal.
　　　　Largest species, with grayish tints, and minimum amount of black.
　　　　Smallest feet . . . . *neglecta.*

Sturnella magna, Swainson.

MEADOW LARK; OLD FIELD LARK.

Alauda magna, Linn. Syst. Nat. I, 1758, 167, ed. 10 (based on *Alauda magna,* Catesby, tab. 33). — Ib., (12th ed.,) 1766, 289. — Gm. I, 1788, 801. — Wilson, Am. Orn. III, 1811, 20, pl. xix. — Doughty, Cab. I, 1830, 85, pl. v. *Sturnella magna,* Swainson, Phil. Mag. I, 1827, 436. — Baird, Birds N. Am. 1858, 535. — Samuels, 343. *Sturnus ludovicianus,* Linnæus, Syst. Nat. I, 1766, 290. — Gm. I, 802. — Lath. Ind. I, 1790, 323. — Bon. Obs. Wils. 1825, 130. — Licht. Verz. 1823, No. 165. — Aud. Orn. Biog. II, 1834, 216 ; V, 1839, 492, pl. cxxxvi. *Sturnella ludoviciana,* Swainson, F. Bor.·Am. II, 1831, 282. — Nuttall, Man. I, 1832, 147. — Bon. List, 1838. — Ib. Conspectus, 1850, 429. — Aud. Syn. 1839, 148. — Ib. Birds Am. IV, 1842, 70, pl. ccxxiii. — Cabanis, Mus. Hein. 1851, 192. — Allen, B. E. Fla. 288. *Sturnella collaris,* Vieill. Analyse, 1816. — Ib. Galerie des Ois. I, 1824, 134, pl. xc. *Sturnus collaris,* Wagler, Syst. Av. 1827, 1. — Ib. Isis, 1831, 527. "*Cacicus alaudarius,* Daudin," Cabanis.

Sp. Char. The feathers above dark brown, margined with brownish-white, and with a terminal blotch of pale reddish-brown. Exposed portions of wings and tail with dark brown bars, which on the middle tail-feathers are confluent along the shaft. Beneath yellow, with a black pectoral crescent, the yellow not extending on the side of the maxilla; sides, crissum, and tibiæ pale reddish-brown, streaked with blackish. A light median and superciliary stripe, the latter yellow anterior to the eye; a black line behind. *Female* smaller and duller. *Young* with pectoral crescent replaced by streaks; the yellow of under surface replaced more or less by ochraceous or pale fulvous. Length, 10.60; wing, 5.00 ; tail, 3.70 ; bill above, 1.35.

Hab. Eastern United States to the high Central Plains, north to Southern British Provinces. England (Sclater, Ibis, III, 176).

HABITS. The eastern form of the Meadow Lark is found in all the eastern portions of the United States, from Florida to Texas at the south, and from Nova Scotia to the Missouri at the north. Richardson met with it on the

Saskatchewan, where it arrives about the first of May. In a large portion
of the United States it is resident, or only partially migratory.

In Maine this species is not abundant. A few are found in Southern
Maine, even as far to the east as Calais, where it is very rare. It was not
found in Oxford County by Mr. Verrill. In New Hampshire and Vermont,
especially in the southern portions, it is much more abundant. Throughout
Massachusetts it is a common summer visitant, a few remaining all winter,
the greater number coming in March and leaving again in November, at
which time they seem to be somewhat, though only partially, gregarious.
South of Massachusetts it becomes more generally resident, and is only very
partially migratory, where the depth of snow compels them to seek food
elsewhere. Wilson states that he met a few of these birds in the month
of February, during a deep snow, among the heights of the Alleghanies,
near Somerset, Penn.

The favorite resorts of this species are old fields, pasture-lands, and meadows, localities in which they can best procure the insects, largely coleopterous, and the seeds on which they feed. They are not found in woods or
thickets, or only in very exceptional cases.

In New England they are shy, retiring birds, and are rarely seen in the
neighborhood of houses ; but in Georgia and South Carolina, Wilson found
them swarming among the rice plantations, and running about in the yards
and the out-buildings, in company with the Killdeer Plovers, with little
or no appearance of fear, and as if domesticated.

In Alabama and West Florida, Mr. Nuttall states, the birds abound during the winter months, and may be seen in considerable numbers in the salt
marshes, seeking their food and the shelter of the sea-coast. They are then
in loose flocks of from ten to thirty. At this season many are shot and
brought to market. By some their flesh is said to be sweet and good ; but
this is denied by Audubon, who states it to be tough and of unpleasant flavor.

Mr. Sclater records the occurrence of one or more individuals of this
species in England.

The song of the eastern Meadow Lark is chiefly distinguished for its
sweetness more than any other excellence. When, in spring, at the height
of their love-season, they alight on the post of a fence, a bush, or tree, or
any other high object, they will give utterance to notes that, in sweetness
and tenderness of expression, are surpassed by very few of our birds. But
they are wanting in variety and power, and are frequently varied, but not
improved, by the substitution of chattering call-notes, which are much inferior in quality. It is noticeable that at the West there is a very great improvement in the song of this bird as compared with that of their more
eastern kindred, though still very far from equalling, either in volume,
variety, or power, the remarkable song of the *neglecta*.

In the fall of the year these birds collect in small companies, and feed
together in the same localities, but keeping, individually, somewhat apart.

In New England these birds mate during the latter part of April, and construct their nests in May. They always place their nest on the ground, usually in the shelter of a thick tuft of grass, and build a covered passage to their hidden nest. This entrance is usually formed of withered grass, and so well conceals the nest that it can only be detected by flushing the female from it, or by the anxiety of her mate, who will frequently fly round the spot in so narrow a circuit as to betray its location.

The eggs of the Meadow Lark vary greatly in size and also in their markings, though the general character of the latter is the same. The smallest, from Florida, measure .95 by .68 of an inch. The largest, from Massachusetts, measure 1.20 inches by .90. They have a white ground, marked and dotted with irregular reddish-brown spots. Generally these are equally distributed, but occasionally are chiefly about the larger end. Their shape is oval, nearly equally rounded at either end.

The diversity in the characteristics of the eggs of this species has not unfrequently occasioned remarks, and even suggested conjectures as to specific differences. They are all, however, reconcilable with differences in the age of the parents, and are, to some extent, affected by the circumstances under which they are deposited. The eggs of old, mature birds, deposited in the early summer, or the first brood, are usually sub-globular or obtusely pointed at either end, large in size, and irregularly sprinkled over with fine bright red dots. Younger birds, breeding for the first time, birds that have been robbed of their eggs, or those depositing a third set, have smaller eggs, sometimes two thirds of the maximum size, more oblong and more pointed at one end, and are marked, at the larger end only, with plashes of dark purplish-brown.

Sturnella magna, var. neglecta, AUD.

WESTERN LARK.

Sturnella neglecta, AUD. Birds Am. VII, 1843, 339, pl. cccclxxxvii. — NEWBERRY, Zoöl. Cal. & Or. Route; Rep. P. R. R. Surv. VI, IV, 1857, 86. — BAIRD, Birds N. Am. 1858, 537. — HEERM. X, S, 54. — COOPER & SUCKLEY, 208. — COOPER, Orn. Cal. I, 1870, 270. *? Sturnella hippocrepis*, (WAGLER,) HEERMANN, J. A. N. Sc. Ph. 2d series, II, 1853, 269, Suisun.

SP. CHAR. Feathers above dark brown, margined with brownish-white, with a terminal blotch of pale reddish-brown. Exposed portion of wings and tail with transverse bands, which, in the latter, are completely isolated from each other, narrow and linear. Beneath yellow, with a black pectoral crescent. The yellow of the throat extending on the sides of the maxilla. Sides, crissum, and tibiæ very pale reddish-brown, or nearly white, streaked with blackish. Head with a light median and superciliary stripe, the latter yellow in front of the eye; a blackish line behind it. The transverse bars on the feathers above (less so on the tail) with a tendency to become confluent near the exterior margin. Length, 10 inches; wing, 5.25; tail, 3.25; bill, 1.25.

HAB. Western America from high Central Plains to the Pacific; east to Pembina, and perhaps to Wisconsin, on the north (Iowa, Allen), and Texas on the south; western Mexico, south to Colima.

HABITS. The differences of plumage between this species and our eastern Meadow Lark are so slight that we might hesitate to allow the existence of any specific distinctness between the two forms, were it not for the very strongly marked differences between them in other respects. Whether we regard them as races or as different species, their history diverges as we cross the Missouri River, though both are found on either bank.

The existence of this variety was first made known by Messrs. Lewis and Clark, in their memorable expedition to the Rocky Mountains. They refer especially to the difference, in the notes, between this bird and the old Field Lark of the east. It remained unnoticed by our ornithologists until 1844, when Mr. Audubon included it in the appendix to his seventh volume. He met with it in his voyage to the Yellowstone, and it would have escaped his notice had not the attention of his party been called to its curious notes. In its flight, manners on the ground, or general habits, he could perceive no difference between it and the common species. None of its nests that he found were covered over, in the manner of the *magna*, and the eggs were differently marked.

Mr. J. A. Allen, in his interesting paper on the birds observed in Western Iowa, while he does not admit any specific difference between these two forms, presents with impartial exactness the very striking dissimilarity between them, both in habits and in song. In regard to the diversity in habits we quote his words : —

" At the little village of Denison, where I first noticed it in song, it was particularly common, and half domestic in its habits, preferring the streets and grassy lanes, and the immediate vicinity of the village, to the remoter prairie. Here, wholly unmolested and unsuspicious, it collected its food ; and the males, from their accustomed perches on the housetops, daily warbled their wild songs for hours together." These traits of familiarity, so totally different from anything ever observed in our eastern birds, he does not concede, however, as establishing necessarily specific difference. Yet he does admit that its song was so new to him that he did not at first have the slightest suspicion that its utterer was the western Meadow Lark, as he found it to be. He adds : " It differs from that of the Meadow Lark in the Eastern States, in the notes being louder and wilder, and at the same time more liquid, mellower, and far sweeter. They have a pensiveness and a general character remarkably in harmony with the half-dreamy wildness of the primitive prairie, as though the bird had received from its surroundings their peculiar impress. It differs, too, in the less frequency of the harsh, complaining chatter so conspicuous in the eastern bird."

The value of these marked differences, both in song and character, between the eastern and western birds, we will not argue, but will only add that they are none too strikingly presented by Mr. Allen. During the writer's brief visit to the Plains he was strongly impressed by the natural, confiding trustfulness of this species and its wonderful beauty of song, both in such remarkable contrast with the habits of our eastern birds. At Antelope Station a pair of these birds had built their nest under the window of the office, and seemed to enjoy the society of the family, while the depot-master, familiar with the song and habits of our eastern birds, appreciated the great differences between the two forms, and called my attention to them.

Mr. Allen also found this Lark everywhere abundant in Colorado, but its notes appeared to him quite different from those of the representatives of this species living to the eastward, in the prairie States, being less varied and ringing, and more guttural.

Dr. Cooper says this bird is abundant in California, and resident nearly throughout the entire State, breeding in the Colorado Valley and in all other districts not quite waterless. Their songs are lively, sweet, and varied. They sing at all seasons, early and late, from the ground, from the tree-top, or in the air, and when unmolested are so tame as to make the house-top their favorite perch. Even the female has considerable musical power, and cheers her mate by singing to him while he relieves her by sitting on the eggs. She also has a harsh, petulant chirp, frequently repeated as if in anger. He states that they build their nest in a slight depression under a bunch of grass, and usually more or less arched over and artfully concealed. The female, when flushed, usually skulks off some distance before she flies. The eggs he describes as white, with a few large purplish-brown blotches and dots towards the larger end, and measuring 1.15 inches by .85. They are very obtuse in shape.

They feed chiefly on insects, seeds, and grain, do no damage to the crops, and destroy a vast number of noxious insects.

Dr. Suckley found this bird common everywhere in Oregon and Washington Territory, some remaining throughout every winter. In 1855 a few were seen at Fort Dalles as early as March 5. On the 7th he found them quite abundant on the ploughed fields near Fort Vancouver. Some of these had probably remained all the winter. In February, 1856, he found them quite abundant at Fort Steilacoom. At Fort Dalles, by the 2d of May, he obtained young birds nearly fledged.

Mr. Dresser found it very common during winter near San Antonio, where a few remain to breed.

In Arizona, according to Dr. Coues, it is resident, but quite rare.

Lieutenant Couch found these birds from the Rio Grande to the high bottoms of the Lower Bolson de Mapimi. Its notes he speaks of as highly musical, contending even with the Mocking Bird for a supremacy in song.

Mr. Ridgway found the western Meadow Lark one of the most abundant and characteristic birds of California and all fertile portions of the interior as far east as the Missouri, and remarks that, although closely resembling the eastern bird in appearance, its song is totally different, not a note uttered by it having more than a very distant resemblance to any of the well-known *magna* of the eastern meadows. In the depth of its tone and the charms of its articulation its song is hardly excelled, resembling very nearly the song of the Wood Thrush. Mr. Ridgway describes its modulations as expressed by the syllables *tung-tung-tungah-til′lah-til′lah-tung*, each note powerful and distinct. The difference between the other notes of the two birds is still greater than in their song, and even in character these are not alike. In the *neglecta* the call-note of watchfulness or alarm is a loud, deep-toned *tuck*, similar to the *chuck* of the Blackbird, but much louder and more metallic. That of sympathy for the young, or anxiety when the nest is approached, is a loud, liquid *tyur*, slightly resembling the complaining note of the eastern Bluebird, and also of the Orchard Oriole. All of its notes are of a power corresponding to the size of the bird.

Mr. Ridgway also notices important differences in their flight. That of the eastern species is carried on by an occasional spasmodic beat or jerk of the wings, which are then extended, the bird sailing a short distance. The flight of the western Lark is much more irregular, the bird flitting along by a trembling flutter of the wings, never assuming these peculiar features.

An egg of this species, collected by Dr. Cooper in Washington Territory, June 19, 1856, measures 1.20 inches in length and .86 in breadth. It is of an oblong-oval shape, obtuse ; the ground white, sparingly spotted with a very dark purple, most of the markings being at the larger end. Three eggs from Arizona, collected by Dr. Palmer, measure 1.10 inches by .80. The markings are of much lighter shades of lilac, purple, and purplish and reddish-brown. The markings are more generally diffused, but predominate at the larger end. An egg from the Yellowstone, collected by Mr. Audubon, is unusually pointed at one end, measures 1.13 inches by .82. The spots are a dark purplish-brown, intermingled with smaller and lighter dottings of reddish-brown. Eggs from California do not vary essentially in their markings from those of Arizona, and have an average measurement of 1.10 inches by .85. As a general rule, the mottling of the eggs of the western bird is finer than that of the eastern.

Subfamily ICTERINÆ.

Genus ICTERUS, Auct.

Icterus, Brisson, R. A. 1760. — Gray, Genera.
Xanthornus, Cuvier, Leç. Anat. Comp. 1800. — Gray, Genera.
Pendulinus, Vieillot, Analyse, 1816.
Yphantes, Vieillot, Analyse, 1816. — Gray, Genera.

Gen. Char. Bill slender, elongated, as long as the head, generally a little decurved, and very acute. Tarsi not longer than the middle toe, nor than the head ; claws short, much curved ; outer lateral toe a little longer than the inner, reaching a little beyond base of middle toe. Feet adapted for perching. Tail rounded or graduated. Prevailing colors yellow or orange, and black.

The species of this subfamily are all as strikingly characterized by diversity and brilliancy of plumage as the others are (with few exceptions) for their uniform sombre black, scarcely relieved by other colors. Of the four genera of this subfamily, recognized by Gray, all but *Cacicus* are well represented in the United States. This differs from all the rest in having the culmen widened and much depressed towards the base, where it advances in a crescent on the forehead, separating the frontal plumes. In the other genera the culmen advances somewhat on the forehead, but it is in a narrow acute point, and not dilated.

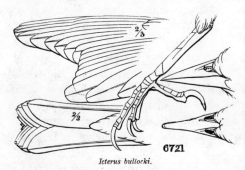

Icterus bullocki.

6721

In studying the North American Orioles we have found it exceedingly difficult to arrange them in any sharply defined sections, as whatever characters be taken as the basis of classification, the other features will not correspond. Thus, species with the bill of the same proportions and amount of curvature differ in the shape and graduation of the tail, while tails of the same form are accompanied by entirely dissimilar bills and wings. The bill is sometimes much attenuated and decurved, as in *I. cucullatus*, while in *melanocephalus* and *baltimore* it is stouter and straighter. The tail is usually much graduated; in *I. baltimore* and *bullocki* it is only moderately rounded. These last-mentioned species constitute the genus *Hyphantes*. Many of the species have a naked space round the eye, very evident in *I. vulgaris*, less so in *melanocephalus*.

Icterus bullocki.

I. vulgaris is peculiar in having the feathers of the throat pointed and lanceolate, as in the ravens.

In view of the difficulties attendant upon the definition of subordinate groups among the United States *Icterinæ*, we propose to consider them all under the single genus *Icterus*, leaving it for some one with more ingenuity to establish satisfactory divisions into sub-genera.[1]

---

[1] An attempt at division into subgenera is as follows : —

Icterus, bill stout, conical, the culmen and gonys nearly straight. Tail graduated. Species: *vulgaris, auduboni, melanocephalus*.

Xanthornus, bill slender, slightly decurved. Tail graduated. Species : *wagleri, parisorum, spurius, cucullatus*.

Hyphantes, bill stout, conical ; the culmen and gonys straight. Tail slightly rounded. Species : *baltimore, bullocki, abeillei*.

We do not find, however, that these subgenera are very tangible, excepting *Hyphantes*, which

The colors of the Orioles are chiefly black and yellow, or orange, the wing sometimes marked with white. The females are generally much duller in plumage, and the young male usually remains in immature dress till the third year. In all the North American species the rump is of the same color with the belly ; the chin, throat, and tail, black.

In the North American Orioles the *baltimore* and *bullocki* have the tail but little graduated ; *spurius*, more so; the others very decidedly graduated. The bills of the two first mentioned are stout and nearly straight; that of *I. melanocephalus* quite similar. *I. parisorum* has the bill more attenuated, but scarcely more decurved ; in *spurius* it is attenuated and decurved, much as in *wagleri ;* this character is strongest in *I. cucullatus.* The much graduated tail is combined with a slender decurved bill in *I. cucullatus* and *wagleri ;* with a straighter one in *parisorum ;* with a thick, nearly straight, one in *melanocephalus.* The arrangement, according to the graduation of the tail, would be *baltimore, bullocki, spurius, parisorum, wagleri, melanocephalus,* and *cucullatus.* According to stoutness and curvature of bill, it would be *baltimore, melanocephalus, bullocki, parisorum, spurius, wagleri,* and *cucullatus.*

All the species have the rump and under parts yellow or orange. All have the head entirely black, except *bullocki,* in which its sides are orange, and *cucullatus,* which has an orange crown. All have black on the throat. In the species with black head and neck, all have the tails black towards the end, except *bullocki* and *baltimore.*

The females and young males are so entirely different in colors from the adult males, and so similar in the different species, that they can best be distinguished by the details of form and size. The *I. prosthemelas* and *I. melanocephalus* are placed, according to the above arrangement, in different subgenera, yet the young male of the former and the adult male of the latter are so perfectly similar in colors as to be undistinguishable in this respect, and require careful examination of points of external structure to be separated (see description of *I. melanocephalus,* p. 782).

The following synopsis may help to distinguish the North American Orioles and their nearest allies, as far as color is concerned.

Species and Varieties.

ICTERUS. Head all round deep black, sharply defined against the yellow of the nape ; wings black, with or without white markings. Body generally, including lesser wing-coverts, deep greenish-yellow (intense orange-red in some South American species).

    I. vulgaris. Feathers of the throat elongated and lanceolate. Bill longer than head. Back and scapulars black; greater coverts and tertials with much white on outer webs ; middle wing-coverts white. Rest of plumage, including lesser coverts, chrome-yellow. Sexes alike. *Hab.* Northern South

is rather well marked by square tail and straight outlines of the bill, as indicated above. The differences are really so minute, and the characters so variable with the species, that it seems entirely unnecessary to subdivide the genus.

America. Jamaica? Accidental in southeastern United States?? Several races.

I. melanocephalus. Feathers of the throat not elongate and lanceolate, but soft and normal; bill shorter than head. Back and scapulars greenish-yellow. Rest of plumage, including lesser wing-coverts, gamboge-yellow. Sexes alike.

Wings without any white. Wing, 4.00; tail, 4.00; culmen, .95; tarsus, .96. *Hab.* Southern Mexico. . .   var. *melanocephalus.*

Wings with white edgings to greater coverts, secondaries and tertials. Wing, 4.25; tail, 4.40; culmen, 1.10; tarsus, 1.10. *Hab.* Northern Mexico and Rio Grande Valley of United States. . . var. *auduboni.*

XANTHORNUS. Back, scapulars, wings, tail, and throat, black; wings and tail with, or without, white. Rest of plumage greenish-yellow, gamboge-yellow, orange, orange-red, or chestnut-rufous.

A. Head and neck, all round, deep black.

     a. Tail-feathers wholly black.

         I. dominicensis. Head, neck, back, scapulars, wings, tail, and jugulum, deep black; lesser and middle wing-coverts, lining of the wing, anal region, tibiæ, and rump, deep gamboge-yellow. No white on wings or tail. Sexes similar (in all the races?).

Abdomen and sides yellow.

Tail-coverts partially or wholly yellow. Wing, 3.25 to 3.50; Tail, 3.75 to 4.00; culmen, .80; tarsus, .85. *Hab.* South Mexico to Costa Rica . . . . var. *prosthemelas.*[1]

Tail-coverts uniform black. Wing, 3.75; tail, 4.50; culmen, .80; tarsus, .90. *Hab.* Mexico and Guatemala   var. *wagleri.*

Abdomen and sides black.

Flanks and crissum yellow; upper tail-coverts yellow. Wing, 3.50; tail, 3.50; culmen, .80; tarsus, .85. *Hab.* Hayti.

                    var. *dominicensis.*[2]

Flanks black; crissum mostly yellow; upper tail-coverts black. Wing, 3.75; tail, 4.00; culmen, .93; tarsus, .85. *Hab.* Porto Rico . . . . . . var. *portoricensis.*[3]

Flanks black; crissum mostly black; upper tail-coverts black. Wing, 3.75; tail, 3.90; culmen, .80; tarsus, 86. *Hab.* Cuba.

                    var. *hypomelas.*[4]

---

[1] *Icterus dominicensis,* var. *prosthemelas. Icterus prosthemelas,* STRICKLAND, Jard. Cont. Orn. 1850, 120, pl. lxii. *Pendulinus p.* CASSIN, Icteridæ, P. A. N. S. 1867, 56. *Pendulinus lessoni,* BONAP. Consp. I, 432, 1850.

[2] *Icterus dominicensis,* var. *dominicensis. Oriolus dominicensis,* LINN. S. N. I, 163, 1766. *Pendulinus d.* CASSIN. P. A. N. S. 1867, 58. *Pendulinus flavigaster,* VIEILL. Nouv. Dict. V, 317, 1816. *Pendulinus viridis,* VIEILL. Nouv. Dict. V, 321, 1816?

[3] *Icterus dominicensis,* var. *portoricensis,* BRYANT, Pr. Bost. Soc. 1866, 254. *Pendulinus portoricensis,* CASS. P. A. N. S. 1867, 58. *Turdus ater,* GM. S. N. I, 830, 1788? *Turdus jugularis,* LATH. Ind. Orn. I, 351, 1790?

[4] *Icterus dominicensis,* var. *hypomelas. Pendulinus hypomelas,* BONAP. Consp. I, 433, 1850. — CASS. P. A. N. S. 1867. 59,

There seems to be no reason for not referring all the above forms to one species, the differences being merely in the relative amount of black and yellow. The greater predominance of the former color we should expect in specimens from the West Indies, where in this family the melanistic tendency is so marked.

I. spurius. Head, neck, back, scapulars, wings, and tail, deep black; other portions, including lesser and middle wing-coverts, lining of wing, and the tail-coverts, above and below, chestnut-rufous; greater coverts and secondaries edged with dull white, and tail-feathers margined terminally with the same. *Female* greenish-yellow, darker above. *Young male* in second year similar, but with a black patch covering face and throat. Wing, 3.20; tail, 3.20, its graduation, .45; culmen, .73; tarsus, .92. *Hab.* Eastern Province of United States; south throughout Middle America, to New Granada.

b. Tail-feathers (except the two middle ones) with their basal half yellow.

I. parisorum. Head, neck, jugulum, back, scapulars, wings, and terminal half of tail, deep black; rest of plumage, including lesser and middle wing-coverts, bright lemon-yellow, approaching white on the middle coverts; greater coverts tipped with white, and tertials edged with the same; tail-feathers margined terminally with the same. Sexes very different. *Hab.* Mexico: Rio Grande Valley and Cape St. Lucas.

B. Crown, occiput, nape, and auriculars, orange; frontlet, lores, cheeks, chin, throat, and jugulum, deep black.

I. cucullatus. Back, scapulars, wings, and tail, and patch covering jugulum and throat, extending up over lores, around eyes and across frontlet, deep black. Other portions orange. Sexes very different.

Lesser coverts black; middle coverts white; greater coverts tipped with white, and secondaries, primaries, and tertials edged with the same; tail-feathers with narrow white tips. Wing, 3.30; tail, 4.00; culmen, .80; tarsus, .90. Sexes very unlike. *Hab.* Southern border of Western United States (San Bernardino, California, Camp Grant, Arizona and Rio Grande of Texas), south through Mexico to Guatemala; Cape St. Lucas . . . var. *cucullatus.*

Lesser coverts gamboge-yellow; middle coverts yellow; no white on wings or tail. Wing, 3.50; tail, 3.90; culmen, .85; tarsus, .90. *Hab.* New Granada, Venezuela, and Trinidad . var. *auricapillus.*[1]

HYPHANTES. Crown, back, scapulars, wings, and part of tail, deep black; wing with much white. Other portions orange or yellow. Sexes very different.

I. baltimore. Head entirely deep black; tail orange, the feathers black at base; greater coverts broadly tipped with white; secondaries and primaries skirted with the same. Other portions rich, mellow orange, the rump as intense as the breast. Wing, about 3.75; tail, 3.50; culmen, .80; tarsus, .97.

(Specimens from Eastern United States and Middle America with middle coverts deep orange.)

(Specimens from the Plains of Kansas, Nebraska, etc., with middle coverts pure white. Some eastern specimens similar.)

I. bullocki. Head mainly black, with an orange or yellow superciliary stripe, and a broader one beneath the eye, cutting off the black of the throat into a narrow strip; tail orange or yellow, the feathers with black

---

[1] *Icterus cucullatus,* var. *auricapillus. Icterus auricapillus,* CASS. P. A. N. S. 1847, 382. — IB. Journ. A. N. S. I, pl. xvi, f. 2. — IB. P. A. N. S. 1867, 60.

at ends; greater coverts with outer webs wholly white, and middle coverts entirely white, producing a large conspicuous longitudinal patch on the wing; tertials and secondaries broadly edged with white, and primaries more narrowly skirted with the same. Other portions rich orange or yellow.

Rump grayish-orange; sides and flanks deep orange; forehead and auriculars orange; a broad supraloral stripe of the same. Xanthic tints deep orange, with a reddish tinge on the breast. Wings, 4.00; tail, 3.50; culmen, .80; tarsus, .90. *Hab.* Western Province of United States . . . . var. *bullocki*.

Rump black; sides and flanks black; forehead and auriculars black; no yellow or orange supraloral stripes. Xanthic tint a very intense gamboge, without any shade of orange. Wing, 4.00; tail, 3.50; culmen, .75; tarsus, .85. *Hab.* Mexico . . . . var. *abeillei*.[1]

Icterus vulgaris, DAUDIN.

TROUPIAL.

Oriolus icterus, LINN. Syst. Nat. I, 1766, 161. *Icterus vulgaris*, "DAUDIN." — AUD. Birds Am. VII, 1844, 357, pl. ccccxcix. — BP. Conspectus Av. 1850, 434. — BAIRD, Birds N. Am. 1858, 542. — CASS. P. A. N. S. 1867, 46. *Le troupiale vulgaire*, BUFFON, Pl. enl. "532" (535, BP.).

SP. CHAR. Bill curved. Throat and chin with narrow pointed feathers. A naked space around and behind the eye. Tail-feathers graduated. Head and upper part of neck all round, and beneath from tail to upper part of breast, interscapular region of back, wings, and tail, black. Rest of under parts, a collar on the lower hind neck, rump, and upper tail-coverts, yellow-orange. A broad band on the wing and outer edges of secondaries, white. Length, 10 inches; wing, 4.50; tail, 4.50; bill above, 1.35.

HAB. Northern South America and West Indies? Accidental on the southern coast of the United States?

This is the largest Oriole said to be found in the United States, and differs from the rest in its longer bill, and pointed, elongated feathers on the throat. The bill is attenuated, and somewhat decurved. The third quill is longest, the first quill almost the shortest of all the primaries. The outer tail-feather is about .60 of an inch less than the middle.

There is only a trace of whitish on the edges of the primaries. The broad white edges to the secondaries are continuous in the folded wing with the white on the greater coverts, the lowest row of which, however, is black. The extreme and concealed base of the tail is white.

One specimen has the light markings yellow, instead of orange.

This species is given by Mr. Audubon as North American, on the strength of occasional stragglers from South America. One of the specimens before us was received from Mr. Audubon (2,842), and is, possibly, North Ameri-

---

[1] *Icterus bullocki*, var. *abeillei*. *Xanthornus abeillei*, LESS. Rev. Zoöl. 1839, 101. *Hyphantes a.* CASS. P. A. N. S. 1867, 62. *? Oriolus costototl*, GM. Syst. Nat. I, 385, 1788.

The only essential difference from *I. bullocki* is in the greater amount of black, it being merely more extended, while the pattern is the same.

can, although we doubt very much whether the species was ever taken within our limits, except as escaped from captivity.

An allied race (*I. longirostris*) from New Grenada has a longer and more slender bill, and a paler, lemon-yellow color. The *I. aurantius* of Brazil lacks the long, pointed, distinct feathers of the throat, and is of an intensely rich orange-red color, with much the same pattern as the present bird.

HABITS. The common Troupial of South America and some of the West India Islands is probably only an imported species, or an accidental visitant. It is given by Mr. Audubon in the appendix to his seventh volume, on the strength of a specimen shot in Charleston, S. C., by his son, John W. The bird, when first seen, was perched on the point of the lightning-rod of Dr. Bachman's house. A few days after others were seen, one of which was shot, though it fell into the river and was lost. Mr. Audubon was afterwards informed that small groups of four or five subsequently made their appearance in the same city and among the islands. If his information was correct, it precludes the supposition that those which have been procured are caged birds. Yet the Troupial is so common and so popular a bird in the cage, that its accidental occurrence is possible in many localities it never visits of its own accord.

This bird is common in all the northern countries of South America, Venezuela, Guiana, Rio Negro, Northern Brazil, etc. Its occurrence in Jamaica and the West Indies may be only accidental. It is said by Daudin to be a common species in South America, where it associates in large flocks, and constructs a large and pensile nest. In confinement it becomes very easily tamed, is reconciled to a life of imprisonment, and is very fond of those who feed and care for it. It has a loud, clear, and ringing whistle, and a great variety of call-notes and single or brief utterances, but rarely indulges in a continuous song. One kept in confinement several years answered readily to the name of *Troopy*, and always promptly responded, when thus addressed by his mistress, in notes of unmistakable and affectionate recognition. He was very fond of his liberty, and used his sharp bill with such effect that it was difficult to keep him in his cage. When at large he never attempted to escape, but returned upon being called. He, however, acquired such a mortal antipathy to children, attacked them so fiercely when at large, and his sharp bill was so dangerous a weapon, that it was found very necessary to keep him a close prisoner.

The eggs of this species measure 1.02 inches in length by .88 of an inch in breadth; they are a rounded, obtuse oval in shape. Their ground-color is a reddish-drab, and they are very generally blotched with markings of a deep claret-brown and faint purple, the markings being deeper and larger at one end.

Icterus melanocephalus, var. auduboni, GIRAUD.

AUDUBON'S ORIOLE.

Icterus auduboni, GIRAUD, Sixteen New Species Texas Birds, 1841 (not paged). — BAIRD,
Birds N. Am. 1858, 542. — CASSIN, Pr. A. N. S. 1867, 53. *Xanthornus melanocepha-
lus*, BON. Consp. 1850, 434 (not the description of the young). *Icterus melanocephalus*,
CASSIN, Ill. I, v, 1854, 137, pl. xxi (the description, but perhaps not the figure).

SP. CHAR. Bill stout; upper and lower outlines very little curved downwards. Tail
much graduated. Head and neck all round (this color extending down on the throat),
tail, and wings black; rest of body, under wing-coverts, and middle and lesser upper
coverts, yellow; more olivaceous on the back. An interrupted band across the ends of
the greater wing-coverts, with the terminal half of the edges of the quills, white. Supposed female similar, but the colors less vivid. Length, 9.25; wing, 4.00; tail, 4.65;
tarsus, 1.10.

HAB. Valley of the Lower Rio Grande of Texas, southward; Oaxaca (SCL. 1859, 38);
Xalapa (SCL. 132); Vera Cruz (temperate regions; SUMICHRAST, M. B. S.).

This bird is perhaps rather a local race (larger as more boreal) of *I.
melanocephalus*[1] of Southern Mexico. The differences are indicated in the
foot-note.

The adult male of this species can be distinguished from the young male
of *I. prosthemelas* only by stouter and less decurved bill, stronger feet, and
black instead of yellow middle wing-coverts.

HABITS. This handsome and rather recent addition to our fauna is a
Northern Mexican species, which extends north to the valley of the Rio
Grande and into Texas, from various localities in which it has been procured.
Lt. D. N. Couch, who found this species common from the Lower Rio Grande
to the Sierra Madre, speaks of the strong mutual attachment shown by the
sexes. He describes its song as soft and melancholy, and the notes as resembling *peut-pou-it*. The sweetness of its notes renders it a favorite as a
caged bird. In the State of Vera Cruz this bird is given by Sumichrast as
inhabiting the temperate regions, and as there having exclusively their centre
of propagation. They are very common in the district of Orizaba, where they

---

[1] *Icterus melanocephalus*, GRAY. *Psarocolius melanocephalus*, WAGLER, Isis, 1829, 756.
Icterus melanocephalus, GRAY, Genera. — SCLATER, Pr. Zoöl. Soc. 1858, 97. — CASSIN, Pr. A.
N. S. 1867, 53. — BAIRD, Birds N. Am. 1858, 543. *Xanthornus melanocephalus*, BON. Consp.
1850, 434 (description of young only). *? Icterus graduacauda*, LESSON, Rev. Zoöl. 1839, 105.

SP. CHAR. Similar to *I. auduboni*, but without any white whatever on the wing. Head and
neck all round, wings, scapulars, and tail, uniform pure black. Rest of body, including inside of wing and tibia and the lesser wing-coverts, orange-yellow; clouded with olivaceous-
green on the back, less so on the rump. Bill and legs plumbeous, the former whitish at base.
Length, 7.70; wing, 3.75; tail, 4.80. *Hab.* Warm parts of Mexico.

Very like the *auduboni*, but smaller, the bill much stouter, shorter, and the culmen more
curved. The third quill is longest; the fourth, fifth, and second successively a little shorter;
the first and seventh about equal. The black of the head and neck comes farther behind and
on the sides than in *auduboni*. The wings are totally destitute of the white edges of quills and
coverts as seen in *auduboni*, and the middle coverts are black instead of pure yellow. The tail,
too, is entirely black.

breed. Their common name is *Calandria*, a name also given, without discrimination, to four or five other species of *Icteri* common in Vera Cruz. Mr. Pease, in 1847, observed either this species or the *melanocephalus* at Jalapa, and in the neighborhood of the city of Mexico, in considerable numbers. This bird was first described and brought to notice as belonging to our fauna, by Mr. Giraud, in 1841. Since then, Mr. John H. Clark, zoölogist on the Mexican Boundary Survey, obtained several specimens from the Lower Rio Grande. It was first seen by him near Ringgold Barracks. It was not abundant, and its quiet manners and secluded habits prevented it from being very conspicuous. It was most frequently observed by him feeding on the fruit of the hackberry, but whenever approached, while thus feeding, it always showed signs of uneasiness, and soon after sought refuge in some place of greater concealment.

Usually pairs were to be seen keeping close together, apparently preferring the thick foliage found on the margin of ponds, or in the old bed of the river. They did not communicate with each other by any note, and Mr. Clark was struck with their remarkable silence. Their habits seemed to him very different from those of any other Oriole with which he was acquainted.

From the papers of Lieutenant Couch, quoted by Mr. Cassin, we learn that these birds were seen by him, March 3, at Santa Rosalio, eight leagues from Matamoras. They were in pairs, and both sexes were very shy and secluded, seeking insects on the prickly pear, or among the low mimosa-trees, seeming to be never at rest, but ever on the lookout for their favorite food.

While at Charco Escondido, farther in the interior of Tamaulipas, Lieutenant Couch met with a pair of these birds, and having brought down the male bird with his gun, the female flew to a neighboring tree, apparently unaware of her loss. She soon, however, observed his fall, and endeavored to recall him to her side with notes uttered in a strain of such exquisite sadness that he could scarcely believe them uttered by a bird; and so greatly did they excite his sympathy, that he almost resolved to desist from further ornithological collections. He adds that he never heard the lay of any songster of the feathered tribe expressed more sweetly than that of the present species. At Monterey he found it a favorite cage-bird. The female also sings, but her notes are less powerful than those of the male. Generally the flight of this bird was low and rapid, and it seemed to prefer the shade of trees. It was observed almost invariably in pairs, and the male and female showed for each other great tenderness and solicitude.

The eggs of this species measure .90 of an inch in length by .70 in breadth. Their ground-color is a light drab or a dull purplish-white, scattered over which are faint markings of a subdued purple, blending imperceptibly with the ground, and above these markings are dots and irregular zigzag lines of dark brown, and darker purple, almost running into black.

Icterus parisorum, BONAP.

SCOTT'S ORIOLE.

Icterus parisorum, ("BON. Acad. Bonon. 1836.") — BP. Pr. Zoöl. Soc. V, 1837, 109. — BAIRD, Birds N. Am. 1858, 544, pl. lvii, f. 1; Mex. B. II, Birds, 19, pl. xix, f. 1. — CASSIN, Pr. 1867, 54. — COOPER, Orn. Cal. I, 1870, 276. *Xanthornus parisorum,* IB. Conspectus, 1850, 434. *Icterus melanochrysura,* LESSON, Rev. Zoöl. 1839, 105. — *Icterus scotti,* COUCH, Pr. A. N. Sc. Phil. VII, April, 1854, 66 (Coahuila).

SP. CHAR. Bill attenuated; not much decurved; tail moderately graduated. Head and neck all round, breast, interscapular region, wings, and tail, black. Under parts generally, hinder part of back to the tail, middle and lesser upper, and whole of lower wing-coverts, and base of the tail-feathers, gamboge-yellow; a band across the ends of the greater coverts, with the edges of the inner secondaries and tertiaries, white. Length, 8.25; extent, 11.75; wing, 4.00; tail, 3.75; tarsus, .95.

Female. Olivaceous above, the back with obsolete dusky streaks; rump and under parts yellowish, clouded with gray. Tail brownish-olive on upper surface, more yellow beneath; wings with two white bands.

HAB. Valley of the Rio Grande; south to Guatemala. In Texas, found on the Pecos. Cape St. Lucas. Oaxaca, winter (SCL. 1858, 303); Orizaba (SCL. 1860, 251); Vera Cruz, temp. and alpine (SUM. M. B. S. I, 553).

The bill is slender and attenuated, very little decurved, much less so than in *I. cucullatus,* slenderer and a little more decurved than in *I. baltimore.* The tail is moderately graduated, the outer feather .45 of an inch less than the middle.

In this species the black feathers of the neck, except below, have a sub-terminal bar of yellow; elsewhere it is wanting. The black of the breast comes a little posterior to the anterior extremity of the folded wing. The posterior feathers in the yellow patch on the shoulders are tinged with white. The white in the bar across the ends of the greater coverts is confined mainly to the terminal quarter of an inch of the outer web. In the full plumage, there is only a faint trace of white on the edges of the primaries. The yellow of the base of the tail only extends on the middle feather as far as the end of the upper tail-coverts; on the three outer, it reaches to within an inch and a quarter of the end of the tail.

An immature male has the yellow more tinged with green, the black feathers of the head and back olivaceous with a black spot.

Specimens vary much in size; the more northern being the larger.

Icterus wagleri [1] is an allied species found just south of the Rio Grande by Lieutenant Couch, but not yet detected within our limits.

---

[1] *Icterus wagleri,* SCLATER, Pr. Zoöl. Soc. 1857, 7. — BAIRD, Birds N. Am. 1858, 545, pl. lvii, f. 2. — IB. Mex. B. II, Birds, 19, pl. xix, f. 2. — CASS. Pr. 1867, 55. *Psarocolius flavigaster,* WAGLER, Isis, 1829, 756 (not of VIEILLOT). *Pendulinus dominicensis,* BP. Consp. 1850, 432 (not of LINN.).

SP. CHAR. Bill much attenuated and considerably decurved. Tail considerably graduated. Head and neck all round, back (the color extending above over the whole interscapular region),

HABITS. Notwithstanding the apparent abundance of the species at Cape St. Lucas, and also in Northern Mexico along our entire border, as far as New Mexico and Texas, our knowledge of its history still remains quite incomplete. A single specimen was obtained in Western Texas on the Pecos River, by Captain Pope, in 1856. Others were obtained by Lieutenant Couch, April, 1853, at Santa Catarina, in Mexico. They were first seen by him in the vicinity of Monterey. They were found to be generally of secluded habits. Their song, consisting of three or four notes, is said to be both rich and melodious.

In the State of Vera Cruz, this species is given by Sumichrast as occurring in both the temperate and the alpine regions. Its common name is *Calandria india*. They are said by him to occur chiefly in the temperate parts, where they breed, but not to be exclusively confined there, for they are also found in the alpine region to the height of at least five thousand feet, near Orizaba, and on the plateau at even a higher elevation. Dr. Cooper saw a bird at Fort Mohave, in April, which he supposed to be this bird, but he was not able to assure himself of the fact, by obtaining it.

Mr. Xantus found this species very abundant during his stay at Cape St. Lucas, and procured a number of specimens of the birds and of their nests and eggs. From his brief notes we gather that the nests are open, and are not pensile. One, found May 22, was built in a bunch of moss hanging

wings, and tail, including the whole of the lower coverts and the tips of the upper, black. Lesser and middle upper, with lower wing-coverts, hinder part of back, rump, and under parts generally (except tail-coverts), orange-yellow. Length, 9.50 ; extent, 12.00 ; wing, 4.50 ; tail, 4.25 ; tarsus, 1.15.

Young or female. Above yellowish-green ; more yellow on head ; throat black ; sides of neck and body beneath dull yellow. Wings dark brown, the coverts edged with white ; middle tail-feathers brownish-black ; outer yellowish-green. Length about 8 inches.

Younger birds are entirely dull olive-green above ; beneath greenish-yellow.

Hab. Northeastern Mexico to Rio Grande Valley ; south to Guatemala. Oaxaca, Jan. and March (SCL. 1859, 381) ; Guatemala (SCL. Ibis, I, 20) ; Vera Cruz, hot region, resident (SUMICHRAST, M. B. S. I, 552).

A close ally, and perhaps only a race, of this species, is the *I. prosthemelas*, STRICKL., which differs in smaller size, and in having the lower tail-coverts yellow instead of black (see synoptical table, p. 778).

HABITS. This fine species appears to be an abundant bird from Northern Mexico throughout that republic and Central America to Costa Rica. I am not aware that any specimens have been procured actually within our territory. It was met with at Saltillo, in the state of Coahuila, Mexico, by Lieutenant Couch, where only a single specimen was obtained. It was taken at the rancho of *Ojo Caliente*, or Hot Springs. It was quite shy and difficult of approach. Like all the other Orioles, it appeared to be quite fond of the palm-tree known as the Spanish bayonet. It is given by Sumichrast as occurring in the department of Vera Cruz, where it appears to be confined to the hot region. It is quite common in the district of Cordova, to the height of about three thousand feet.

Mr. Salvin states this to be the only *Icterus* found by him about Dueñas, where it was not uncommon. In a letter written by this naturalist, published in the Ibis of October, 1859, he mentions having taken the nest and eggs of this species. The structure, though of the same character, — a hanging nest, — is very different from that of *I. gularis*, the common species on the Yzabal road. The nest has none of the depth of the other, but is comparatively shallow.

down from an old cactus. Another was made in a bunch of hops, suspended from a cactus. A third was placed in a bunch of weeds growing out from a crevice in a perpendicular rock. Another, found May 29, was built in a small dead tree, overhung with vines. This nest was about five feet from the ground. A nest containing four young birds was found placed in a bunch of moss, hanging out of a crevice in a rock. These instances serve to show the general character of the position of their nests. Without being pensile they are usually resting upon pendent branches, and are not placed at great elevations.

The eggs measure .90 of an inch in length by .65 in breadth. Their shape is an oblong-oval, and they are obtuse at either end. Their ground-color is a dull white, with a purplish or a bluish tint. They are variously marked, in different eggs, with small blotches and finer dottings of a light purple, purplish-brown, darker purple, and even black.

Icterus spurius, BON.

ORCHARD ORIOLE.

Oriolus spurius, LINN. Syst. Nat. I, 1766, 162. — GM. I, 1788, 389 (very inaccurate description; only identified by the references). *Icterus spurius*, BON. Obs. on Nom. Wils. 1825, No. 44. — AUD. Orn. Biog. I, 1831, 221 ; V, 485, pl. xlii. — IB. Birds Am. IV, 1842, 46, pl. ccxix. — BAIRD, Birds N. Am. 1858, 547. — SAMUELS, 346. *Oriolus varius*, GMELIN, Syst. Nat. I, 1766, 390. *Turdus ater*, GM. Syst. 1788, I ; 1788, 83. *Oriolus castaneus*, LATHAM, Ind. Orn. I, 1790, 181 (same citations as *O. varius*, GM.). *Turdus jugularis*, LATHAM, Ind. Orn. I, 1790, 361 (same citations as *Turdus ater*, GM.). *Yphantes solitaria*, VIEILLOT ♂. "*Pendulinus nigricollis*, VIEILL. ♀. — *viridis*, IB." *Oriolus mutatus*, WILSON, Am. Orn. I, 1808, 64, pl. iv, f. 1–4. *Xanthornus affinis*, LAWRENCE, Ann. N. Y. Lyc. N. H. V, May, 1851, 113 (small race from Texas). *Pendulinus s.*, CASS. Pr. 1867, 61. *Pendulinus affinis*, CASS. Pr. 1867, 61.

SP. CHAR. Bill slender, attenuated, considerably decurved; tail moderately graduated. *Male*, three years. Head and neck all round, wings, and interscapular region of back, with tail-feathers, black. Rest of under parts, lower part of back to tail, and lesser upper wing-coverts, with the lower one, brownish-chestnut. A narrow line across the wing, and the extreme outer edges of quills, white. *Female*. Uniform greenish-yellow beneath, olivaceous above, and browner in the middle of the back; two white bands on the wings. Young male of two years like the female, but with a broad black patch from the bill to the upper part of the breast, this color extending along the base of the bill so as to involve the eye and all anterior to it to the base of the bill, somewhat as in *I. cucullatus*. Length of Pennsylvania male specimens, 7.25; wing, 3.25.

HAB. United States from the Atlantic to the high Central Plains, probably throughout Texas; south to Guatemala. Xalapa (SCL. 1859, 365); Cordova (SCL. 1856, 301); Guatemala (SCL. Ibis, I, 20 ; LAWR. N. Y. Lyc. IX, 104); Rio Atrato (CASS. P. A. N. S., 1860, 140); Costa Rica (CABAN. J. 1861, 8); Panama (LAWR. N. Y. Lyc. 1861, 331); Cuba (GUNDLACH); Veragua (SALVIN, 1867, 142); Vera Cruz, winter (SUM. M. B. S. I,); Mazatlan.

This species varies greatly in size with its geographical distribution.

Winter specimens from Mexico have the black obscured by brownish borders to the feathers.

HABITS. The Orchard Oriole is found abundant throughout most of the United States, from the Atlantic to the Missouri Valley, and on the south-west to the valley of the Rio Grande. Mr. J. A. Allen met with individuals of this species as far west as the base of the Rocky Mountains, in Colorado, which he regards as the extreme western limit. It is a very rare summer visitant in New England, though found even as far eastward as Calais, Me. It was not found in Western Maine by Verrill, nor am I aware of its having been met with in either New Hampshire or Vermont. Mr. Allen states that a few pairs breed every season near Springfield, in Western Massachusetts. I have never met with it in the eastern part of the State, but others have been more fortunate, and it is probable that a few visit us each season.

In Texas Mr. Dresser found this species very common at San Antonio during the summer, arriving there quite early in April. He procured a num-ber of their nests, all of which were made of light-colored flexible grasses, and suspended from the upper branches of the mesquite-trees. He also found them breeding near Houston, and on Galveston Island. He describes them as much smaller than birds from the Northern States. This smaller race Mr. Lawrence has regarded as a distinct species, to which he gives the name of *affinis*. It has been traced as far to the west as Fort Riley in Kan-sas, and Fort Lookout in Nebraska. It winters in Guatemala, where it is very abundant at that season. Mr. James McLeannan killed it as far south as Panama.

Dr. Elliott Coues considers this bird as rare and chiefly migrant in South Carolina ; but Mr. H. S. Rodney (Naturalist, Jan., 1872) found them quite numerous at Camden, in that State, in the summer of 1871. He met with five nests between June 28 and July 19, and has no doubt he could have taken many more, as he counted at least fifteen different pairs. From the fact that Dr. Coues did not meet with any nest at Columbia, only thirty miles distant, Mr. Rodney infers that this Oriole is very partial to certain favored localities, as is also the Baltimore.

The Orchard Oriole is an active, sprightly, and very lively species, and possesses a very peculiar and somewhat remarkable song. Its notes are very rapidly enunciated, and are both hurried and energetic. Some writers speak of the song as confused, but this attribute is not in the utterance of the song, the musician manifesting anything but confusion in the rapid and distinct enunciation of his gushing notes. These may be too quick in their utterance for the listener to follow, but they are wonderful both for their rapidity and their harmony. His performance consists of shrill and lively notes, uttered with an apparent air of great agitation, and they are quite as distinct and agreeable, though neither so full nor so rich, as are those of the more celebrated Golden Robin.

In the Central States, from New York to North Carolina, these birds are not only very abundant, but very generally diffused. Hardly an orchard or a garden of any size can be found without them. They seem to prefer apple-trees for their abode, and for the construction of their nests. These structures, though essentially different, are, in their style of architecture, quite as curiously wrought and ingenious as those of the Baltimore. They are suspended from small twigs, often at the very extremity of the branches. In Pennsylvania they are usually formed externally of a peculiar kind of long, tough, and flexible grass. This material is woven through and through in a very wonderful manner, and with as much neatness and intricacy as if actually sewed with a needle. They are hemispherical in shape, open at the top, and generally about four inches in breadth and three deep. The cavity has a depth and a width of about two inches.

Wilson states that, having had the curiosity to detach one of these fibres of dried grass from the nest, he found it thirteen inches in length, and that, in that distance, it had been hooked through and returned no less than thirty-four times ! In this manner it was passed entirely around the nest. The nests are occasionally lined with wool or the down of seeds. The external portions are strongly fastened to several twigs, so that they may be blown about by the wind without being upset.

Wilson also remarks that he observed that when these nests are built in the long pendent branches of the weeping-willow, where they are liable to much greater motion, though formed of the same materials, they are always made much deeper and of slighter texture. He regards this as a manifestation of a remarkable intelligence, almost equivalent to reason. The willow, owing to the greater density of its foliage, affords better shelter, and is preferred on that account, and owing to the great sweep, in the wind, of the branches, the eggs would be liable to be rolled out if the nest were of the usual depth ; hence this adaptation to such positions.

The food of the Orchard Oriole is almost exclusively insects. Of these it consumes a large number, and with them it also feeds its young. Most of these are of the kinds most obnoxious to the husbandman, preying upon the foliage, destroying the fruit, and otherwise injuring the trees, and their destroyers render an incalculable amount of benefit to the gardens they favor with their presence. At the same time they are entirely innocent of injury to crops of any description, and I cannot find that any accusations or expressions of suspicion have been raised against them. They seem to be, therefore, general favorites, and, wherever protected, evince their appreciation of this good-will by their familiarity and numbers.

The female sits upon her eggs fourteen days, and the young remain in the nest about ten days longer. They are supposed to have occasionally two broods in a season, as nests with eggs are found the last of July. They are said to arrive in Pennsylvania about the first of May, and to leave before the middle of September.

According to Wilson they are easily raised from the nest, and become very tame and familiar. One that he kept through the winter, when two months old whistled with great clearness and vivacity.

All the nests of this species that I have seen from Georgia, Florida, Louisiana, or Texas, have no lining, but are wholly made of one material, a flexible kind of reed or grass.

The sociability of this species is one of its most marked characteristics. Audubon says that he has known no less than nine nests in the same enclosure, and all the birds living together in great harmony.

A nest of this bird, taken in Berlin, Conn., by Mr. Brandigee, has a diameter and a height of four inches. Its cavity is three inches in depth, and varies from three to three and a half in diameter, being widest at the centre, or half-way between the top and the base. It is entirely homogeneous, having been elaborately and skilfully woven of long green blades of grass. The inside is lined with animal wool, bits of yarn, and intermingled with a wooly substance of entirely vegetable origin. It was built from the extremity of the branch of an apple-tree.

An egg of this species, from Washington, measures .85 of an inch in length by .62 in breadth. The ground is a pale bluish-white, blotched with a pale purple, and dashed, at the larger end, with a few deep markings of dark purplish-brown. An egg from New Mexico is similar, but measures .79 of an inch by .54. Both are oblong oval, and pointed at one end.

Icterus cucullatus, Swainson.

HOODED ORIOLE.

Icterus cucullatus, Swainson, Philos. Mag. I, 1827, 436. — Lawrence, Ann. N. Y. Lyc. V, May, 1851, 116 (first introduced into fauna of United States). — Cassin, Ill. I, II, 1853, 42, pl. viii. — Cooper, Orn. Cal. I, 1870, 275. — Baird, Birds N. Am. 1858, 546. *Pendulinus cucullatus,* Bon. Consp. 1850, 433. — Cass. Pr. 1867, 60.

Sp. Char. Both mandibles much curved. Tail much graduated. Wings, a rather narrow band across the back, tail, and a patch starting as a narrow frontal band, involving the eyes, anterior half of cheek, chin, and throat, and ending as a rounded patch on the upper part of breast, black. Rest of body orange-yellow. Two bands on the wing and the edges of the quills white. *Female* without the black patch of the throat; the upper parts generally yellowish-green, brown on the back, beneath yellowish. Length, 7.50; wing, 3.25.

Hab Valley of Lower Rio Grande, southward; Tucson, Arizona (Dr. Palmer); Lower California, Cordova (Scl. 1856, 300); Guatemala? (Scl. Ibis I, 20); Cuba? (Lawr. Ann. VII, 1860, 267); San Bernardino, California (Cooper, P. Cal., etc. 1861, 122); Vera Cruz hot region (Sum. M. B. S. I, 553); Mazatlan.

The orange varies greatly in tint and intensity with the individual; sometimes it is deep orange-red; often clear dull yellow, but more frequently of an oily orange.

This species is closely allied to the *I. aurocapillus* of South America, but differs in having black, not yellow, shoulders, and in the white markings on the wings.

HABITS. The Hooded Oriole is essentially a Mexican species, though it also extends northward into Texas at the Rio Grande, and into Southern California and Arizona. It was not noticed by Dr. Coues in Arizona, but Lieutenant Charles Bendire found it breeding near Tucson in the summer of 1872. It is abundant at Cape St. Lucas. Dr. Cooper found that this species arrived at San Diego about April 22, where they were not rare for a fortnight afterwards, and all then retired into the warmer interior valleys, where he has seen them as far to the north as Los Angeles. While migrating, they were generally silent.

Captain McCown found it quite common on the Rio Grande, where it rears its young. When met with in the woods and far away from the abodes of men, it seemed shy and disposed to conceal itself. Yet a pair of these birds were his constant visitors, morning and evening. They came to the vicinity of his quarters — an unfinished building — at Ringgold Barracks, and at last became so tame and familiar that they would pass from some ebony-trees, that stood near by, to the porch, clinging to the shingles and rafters, frequently in an inverted position, prying into the holes and crevices, apparently in search of spiders and such insects as could be found there. From this occupation they would occasionally desist, to watch his movements. He never could induce them to partake of the food he offered them.

Lieutenant Couch found this species common in the states of Tamaulipas and New Leon. He found their nests generally on or under the tops of the palm known as the Spanish bayonet.

This species is given by Mr. Sumichrast as one of the birds of Vera Cruz, where it is exclusively an inhabitant of the hot region, and where it is rarely found above an elevation of eighteen hundred feet.

These birds were found quite abundant at Cape St. Lucas, Lower California, by Mr. Xantus, by whom a number of their nests and eggs were obtained. The following brief memoranda in regard to a few of these nests will serve to show their general position : — " Nest and two eggs, found May 20, about ten feet from the ground, woven to a small aloe, in a bunch of the *Acacia prosopis*. Nest and two eggs, found May 22, on a dry tree overhung with hops. Nest and one egg, found May 30, on an acacia, about fifteen feet from the ground. Nest with young, found on an aloe four feet high. Nest and eggs, found on a moss hanging out of a perpendicular bluff, on the sea-coast. Nest and eggs found on a *Yucca angustifolia*, on its stem, six feet from the ground. Nest and two eggs, found in a convolvulus, on a perpendicular rock fifty feet high. Nest and three eggs, found on an acacia, twenty-five feet high."

The eggs of this species vary somewhat in shape, some being obtuse and more spherical, others more pointed and oblong. They vary in length from

.92 to .88 of an inch, and from .68 to .65 of an inch in breadth. They have a clear white ground, marbled and blotched with large dashes, dots, and irregular zigzag lines of purple, brown, and black, chiefly disposed around the larger end. In those where the spots are more diffused they are blended with obscure blotches of a faint lavender.

Icterus baltimore, DAUDIN.

BALTIMORE ORIOLE; GOLDEN ROBIN; HANG-NEST.

Oriolus baltimore, LINN. Syst. Nat. I, 1766, 162. — WILSON, Am. Orn. I, 1808, 23, pl. i. — IB. VI, 1812, pl. liii. "*Icterus baltimore*, DAUD." — AUD. Orn. Biog. I, 1831, 66 ; V, 1839, 278, pls. xii. and ccccxxiii. — IB. Birds Am. IV, 1842, 37, pl. ccxvii. — BAIRD, Birds N. Am. 1858, 548. — SCLATER & SALVIN, Ex. Orn. I, 69, 188 (diagnosis). — SAMUELS, 348. *Yphantes baltimore*, VIEILLOT, Gal. des Ois. I, 1824, 124, pl. lxxxvii. *Psarocolius baltimore*, WAGLER, Syst. Av. 1825, No. 26. *Le Baltimore*, BUFF. pl. enl. 506, f. 1. *Hyphantes b.*, CASS. Pr. 1867, 62.

SP. CHAR. Tail nearly even. Head all round and to middle of back, scapulars, wings, and upper surface of tail, black ; rest of under parts, rump, upper tail-coverts, and lesser wing-coverts, with terminal portion of tail-feathers (except two innermost), orange-red. Edges of wing-quills, with a band across the tips of the greater coverts, white. Length, 7.50 inches ; wing, 3.75.

The female much less brilliant in color ; the black of the head and back generally replaced by brownish-yellow, purer on the throat ; each feather with a black spot.

HAB. From Atlantic coast to the high Central Plains, and in their borders ; south to Panama. Xalapa (SCL. 1856, 365) ; Guatemala (SCL. Ibis, I, 20) ; Cuba (CABAN. J. IV, 10) ; Costa Rica (CABAN, J. 1861, 7 ; LAWR. IX, 104) ; Panama (LAWR. N. Y. Lyc. 1861, 331) ; Veragua (SALV. 1867, 142) ; Mosquito Coast (SCL. & SALV. 1867, 279) ; Vera Cruz (autumn, SUM. M. B. S. I, 553).

A young bird is soft, dull orange beneath, palest on the throat, and tinged along the sides with olive ; above olive, with an orange cast on the rump and tail, the latter being without any black ; centres of dorsal feathers blackish ; wings blackish, with two broad white bands across coverts, and broad edges of white to the tertials.

Specimens collected in Western Kansas, by Mr. J. A. Allen, have the middle wing-coverts pure white instead of deep orange, and, according to that naturalist, have more slender bills than Eastern birds. Mr. Allen thinks they form a race peculiar to the plains ; but in examining the series of specimens in the museum of the Smithsonian Institution, we have failed to discover any constancy in this respect. A male (5,356, Farm Isl., May 30) from Nebraska has the middle wing-coverts pure white, — the lesser, clear orange ; the black throat-stripe is almost separated from the black of the cheeks by the extension forward of the orange on each side of it, only the tips of the feathers being black.

No. 61,192 ♂, Mount Carmel, Ill. (August 12), has the throat-stripe even more isolated, being connected anteriorly for only about a quarter of an inch with the black of the jaw ; there is also a distinct indication of an orange superciliary stripe, mostly concealed, however, by the black tips of the feathers. The middle coverts, like the lesser, are pure plain orange.

A male from Cape May, N. J. (59,458, May), has the middle coverts white, and the lesser wholly uniform black. The head, however, is as in typical specimens.

In a series of twenty adult spring males from Carlisle, Penn., seven have the middle coverts more or less white. But it is noticed that all these specimens with white middle coverts have invariably less intense colors than those with orange shoulders, while in the Kansas specimens the other colors are of the brightest character.

A male from Washington (12,317, May 6) is exactly similar.

HABITS. The familiar Baltimore Oriole, the Golden Robin of the New England States, is found throughout eastern North America, at various seasons, from Texas to the British Possessions, and from the Atlantic to the plains. It is, however, for the most part, not common beyond the Mississippi River. It has been traced as far to the north as the 55th parallel of latitude, and probably breeds more or less abundantly in every State east of the Mississippi River. It is rare in Florida, and is not given by Mr. Allen as known to that State, but I have received its nest and eggs from Monticello in West Florida. The Smithsonian Museum embraces specimens from as far west as Powder River and the Yellowstone.

Mr. J. A. Allen (Am. Naturalist, June, 1872) mentions finding this species at the base of the Rocky Mountains, in Colorado, which he regards as its extreme western limit. In Kansas he found this species, as well as the Orchard Oriole, abundant, the Baltimore indulging in a dialect so different from that of its northern relatives as often to puzzle him to make out to what bird its strange notes belonged. Its colors were also unusually bright in all the specimens he examined.

Mr. Boardman gives it as very rare at Calais, but Professor Verrill thinks it common in Western Maine. It is abundant throughout the southern and central portions of Vermont and New Hampshire, and in all New York. It is a common summer resident at Hamilton, Ontario, where it arrives the second week in May. It was found on the plains of the Saskatchewan by Captain Blakiston.

Mr. Dresser states it to have been abundant at Matamoras, where it was breeding, though he was too late for its eggs. He saw none at San Antonio, but Mr. J. H. Clark was more fortunate. Numbers of them, he states, were seen nesting in the mesquite-trees on the prairies, at which time they were very musical, having sometimes as many as three nests in the same tree. These were all built of fine grass, among the top branches, and interwoven with the leaves. Dr. Woodhouse found it quite common in the Indian Territory and in Eastern Texas. Specimens of this species were taken by Mr. James M. Leannan, at Panama, which is presumed to be the most southern locality on record for this bird.

The Baltimore Oriole is one of the most common birds nearly throughout New England. Gay and brilliant in plumage, interesting and lively in manners and habits, and a vocalist of rare power, with pathos, beauty, and variety in his notes, this bird has been, and would still be, a great favorite, but for its transgressions among the pea-vines of our gardens. He makes his appearance with exemplary punctuality, seeming regardless of the prematureness or tardiness of the season. Rarely does the 10th of May pass without the sound of his welcome notes, and rarely, if ever, does he come sooner.

Their period of song is not a long one, but soon terminates, as family cares increase and the tender broods require an undivided attention. Early in July this Oriole ceases to favor the world with those remarkable notes that seldom fail to attract attention by their peculiarity, and to excite admiration by their rich and full-toned melody.

When the male Baltimores first arrive, they come unaccompanied by their mates. At this time their notes are unusually loud, and their voices seem shrill. Their song appears to partake somewhat of the nature of tender lamentations and complaining. At this period they are very active and restless, moving rapidly through the branches of the trees, just opening into leaf and blossom, searching busily for the insects which then form their principal food. When, a few days after their arrival, they are joined by the females, the whole character of their song changes, which becomes a lower-toned, richer, and more pleasing refrain. During their love-season their resonant and peculiarly mellow whistle resounds in every garden and orchard, along the highways of our villages, and in the parks and public squares of our cities.

Nuttall, generally very felicitous in expressing by verbal equivalents the notes of various species of our song-birds, describes the notes of its song as running thus, *Tshippe-tshayia-too-too-tshippe-tshippe-too-too*, with several other very similar modifications and variations. But these characters give a very inadequate idea of their song. It must be heard to be appreciated, and no description can do justice to its beauties. The notes are of an almost endless variety, and each individual has his own special variations. The female, too, has her own peculiar and very pretty notes, which she incessantly warbles as she weaves her curiously elaborate nest.

To agriculturists this Oriole renders immense service in the destruction of vast numbers of highly injurious insects; among the most noteworthy of these are the common canker-worm and the tent caterpillars, both great pests to orchards. These benefits far more than compensate for its annoying attacks on the pods of esculent peas, the only sin that can rightfully be brought against it, except, perhaps, the acts of theft committed against other birds, in seizing upon and appropriating to it materials collected by smaller birds for their nests.

The Baltimore Orioles are devoted, faithful, and courageous parents, resolutely defending their young when in danger, and exposing themselves fearlessly to danger and to death rather than forsake them. If their young are taken and caged, the parents follow them, and, if permitted, will continue to feed them.

Mr. Ridgway mentions an instance where the female entered her nest while he was in the act of severing the limb from which it was suspended, and persisted in remaining there until the nest had been cut off and taken into the house. One of these birds, reared from the nest by a family in Worcester, Mass., became perfectly domesticated, was allowed full liberty, and even when taken by the married daughter of its mistress, perched on her finger, through the open grounds to her own house, made no attempt to escape. It delighted in occasional acts of mischief, especially in putting its pointed bill through the meshes of the lace curtains, and then opening its beak, seeming to enjoy the sound produced by tearing the threads.

In the construction of its nest the Oriole displays great skill and ingenuity. This structure is a pendulous and nearly cylindrical pouch, suspended from the extremity of some hanging branch. It is constructed by means of the interweaving of the natural filaments of several flaxlike plants into a homogeneous fabric of great strength, and admirably adapted to its purpose. A nest of this species from West Florida, as well as the one figured by Audubon, was made entirely of the long moss (*Tillandsia usneoides*) so abundant in Southern forests.

The young birds, before they can fly, climb to the edge of the nest, and are liable, in sudden tempests, to be thrown out. If uninjured, they are good climbers, and by means of wings, bill, and claws, are often able to reach places of safety. In one instance a fledgling, which had broken both legs, and was placed in a basket to be fed by its parents, managed, by wings and bill, to raise itself to the rim, and in a few days took its departure.

The parents feed their young chiefly with caterpillars, which they apparently swallow and then disgorge for this purpose. In confinement they feed readily on soaked bread and fruit, and are especially fond of figs. They are soon reconciled to confinement, become very docile and even playful, sing readily, and will even come at a given signal and alight on the finger of their master.

The eggs of the Baltimore are usually five and rarely six in number. They are of an oblong-oval shape, pointed at one end, and measure .91 of an inch in length by .60 in breadth. Their ground-color is white, with a slight roseate tinge when fresh, fading into a bluish shade in time. They are all variously marked, dotted, and marbled, with spots, blotches, and irregular waving lines of purplish-brown. These markings are of greatly varying shades, from a light purple to almost complete blackness, only perceptibly purplish in a strong light.

Icterus bullocki, BON.

BULLOCK'S ORIOLE.

Xanthornus bullocki, Sw. Syn. Mex. Birds, Taylor's Phil. Mag. I, 1827, 436. *Agelaius bullocki*, RICH. Rep. Brit. Assoc. 1837. *Icterus bullocki*, BON. List. 1838. — AUD. Orn. Biog. V, 1839, 9, pls. ccclxxxviii and ccccxxxiii. — IB. Birds Am. IV, 1842, 43, pl. ccxviii. — NEWBERRY, Rep. P. R. R. VI, IV, 1857, 87. — BAIRD, Birds N. Am. 1858, 549. — MAX. Caban. J. VI, 1858, 259. — LORD, Pr. R. A. Inst. IV, 121. — COOPER & SUCKLEY, 209. — SCLATER & SALVIN, Ex. Orn. I, 1869, 188 (diagnosis). — COOPER, Orn. Cal. I, 1870, 273. *Psarocolius auricollis*, MAXIM. Reise Nordam. I, 1839, 367 (Fort Pierre, Neb.). *Hyphantes b.*, CASS. Pr. A. N. S. 1867, 62. — HEERM. X, *S*, 52 (nest).

SP. CHAR. Tail very slightly graduated. Upper part of the head and neck, back, wings, two central tail-feathers, line from base of bill through the eye to the black of the nape, and a line from the base of the bill running to a point on the throat, black. Under parts generally, sides of head and neck, forehead and line over the eye, rest of tail-feathers, rump, and upper tail-coverts, yellow-orange. A broad band on the wings, involving the greater and middle coverts, and the outer edges of the quills, white. Young male with the black replaced by greenish-yellow, that on the throat persistent; female without this. The first plumage of the young differs from that of *baltimore* in being more whitish beneath; lighter olive above, and without dark spots on back; white of middle and greater coverts connected by white edges of the latter. Length, about 7.50 inches; wing, 3.80.

HAB. High Central Plains to the Pacific; rare on Upper Missouri; south into Mexico. City of Mexico (SCL. & SALV. 1869, 362).

A closely allied Mexican species is *I. abeillei* of Lesson, differing principally in having the sides and rump black.

HABITS. Bullock's Oriole, the western counterpart of the eastern Baltimore, is found throughout the Pacific shore, from the great Central Plains to the ocean, and from Washington Territory to Mexico. It is not given by Sumichrast as occurring in Vera Cruz, where its place is taken, as a migrant, by the Baltimore. It was not noticed by Mr. Dresser on the Rio Grande, but in Arizona it was found by Dr. Coues to be a common summer resident. It was there seen to frequent, almost exclusively, the willows and cotton-woods of the creek-bottoms. To the small twigs of these trees its pensile nests were usually attached. It is said to arrive in Arizona late in April, and to remain there nearly through September.

In the survey of the Mexican boundary Dr. Kennerly met with this species in passing through Guadaloupe cañon, where it was often seen, but it was observed at no other point on the route. It seemed to prefer the low bushes on the hillside to the large trees. In its motions it was quick and restless, passing rapidly from bush to bush.

In Washington Territory this species is stated by Dr. Suckley to be more abundant in the sparsely wooded districts of the eastern base of the Cascade Mountains than in the Coast Range. He found it exceedingly abundant at Fort Dalles and along the eastern base of Mt. Adams. They arrive about the 15th of May, and were very common among the low oaks of that region. He speaks of its song as very pleasant, and especially melodious early in the morning, when the bird is generally perched on the sunny side or top of an oak.

At Puget Sound, according to Dr. Cooper, these birds do not arrive until the beginning of June, and are at no time very common there. He describes their habits as similar to those of the *spurius*, they being shy and difficult to discover among the foliage. Their song is more like that of the Baltimore, loud, clear, and varied.

In his Report on the birds of California, Dr. Cooper states that these birds arrive at San Diego, from the south, about March 1; but at Fort Mohave, one hundred and sixty miles farther north, he saw none until a month later. Like the Baltimore Oriole, they resort to the open roads, gardens, and orchards, putting themselves under the protection of man, and repaying him both by their sweet melody and their usefulness in destroying insects. They keep chiefly in the trees and rarely descend to the ground, except to collect materials for their nests. These are suspended from the end of a branch, and are constructed of fibrous grasses, horse-hairs, strings, bits of rags, wool, hempen fibres of plants, etc. At times only a single material is used, such as horse-hair. These nests are neatly and closely interwoven in the form of a deep bag or purse, and are suspended by the edges from the forks of a branch, near its end. They have usually a depth of about four or five inches, and a diameter of about three or three and a half. In most cases they are largely made of the flaxen fibres of wild hempen plants, and by strings of this are firmly bound around the ends of the twigs to which they are suspended. They are lined within with fine, soft vegetable down. In some nests the inner bark of the silkweed largely predominates.

Dr. Cooper states that the eggs of Bullock's Oriole are, in number, from four to six. He describes them as bluish-white, with scattered, winding streaks and hair-lines of black and reddish-brown near the larger end, measuring .98 by .60 of an inch. In the southern half of California they are laid in the first or second week of May. At Santa Cruz, in 1866, he did not observe any of this species until April 3.

Mr. Allen did not meet with this species in Western Kansas, and it is not included in his list of birds observed by him near Fort Hays. At Ogden and Salt Lake City, in Utah, which he reached the first of September, Bullock's Oriole had already migrated southward.

In all the fertile portions of the country west of the plains, Mr. Ridgway found Bullock's Oriole — the western representative of the Baltimore — extremely abundant. In May, when the valley of the Truckee, near Pyramid Lake, was visited, he observed great numbers feeding upon the buds of the grease-wood, in company with the Louisiana Tanager and the Black-headed Grosbeaks. In certain localities there was scarcely a tree that did not contain one or more nests of these birds, and as many as five have been found in a single tree. Although constructed in a manner almost precisely similar to those of the common eastern species, its nest is less frequently pendulous, being in many cases fixed between the upright twigs near the top of the tree. It is, however, not unfrequently suspended, like that of the Baltimore, from the extremity of a drooping branch, though very rarely in so beautiful a manner. The notes of this Oriole, which are similar to those of the Baltimore, are neither so distinct, so mellow, nor so strong, and their effect is quite different from that produced by the splendid mellow whistling of the eastern species; and the mellow, rolling chatter so characteristic of the latter is not so full in the western species, and generally ends in a sharp *chow*, much like the curious mewing of an *Icteria*. He regards Bullock's Oriole as altogether a less attractive species.

Mr. Lord found this bird by no means an abundant species in British Columbia. Those that were seen seemed to prefer the localities where the scrub-oaks grew, to the pine regions. He found their long, pendulous nests suspended from points of oak branches, without any attempt at concealment. He never met with any of these birds north of Fraser's River, and very rarely east of the Cascades. A few stragglers visited his quarters at Colville, arriving late in May and leaving early in September, the males usually preceding the females three or four days.

On the Shasta Plains Mr. Lord noticed, in the nesting of this bird, a singular instance of the readiness with which birds alter their habits under difficulties. A solitary oak stood by a little patch of water, both removed by many miles from other objects of the kind. Every available branch and spray of this tree had one of the woven nests of this brilliant bird hanging from it, though hardly known to colonize elsewhere in this manner.

Dr. Coues, in an interesting paper on the habits of this species in the Naturalist for November, 1871, states that its nests, though having a general resemblance in their style of architecture, differ greatly from one another, usually for obvious reasons, such as their situation, the time taken for their construction, and even the taste and skill of the builders. He describes one nest, built in a pine-tree, in which, in a very ingenious manner, these birds bent down the long, straight, needle-like leaves of the stiff, terminal branchlets, and, tying their ends together, made them serve as the upper portion of the nest, and a means of attachment. This nest was nine inches long and four in diameter.

Another nest, described by the same writer, was suspended from the forked twig of an oak, and draped with its leaves, almost to concealment. It had an unusual peculiarity of being arched over and roofed in at the top, with a dome of the same material as the rest of the nest, and a small round hole on one side, just large enough to admit the birds.

The eggs of this Oriole are slightly larger than those of the Baltimore, and their ground-color is more of a creamy-white, yet occasionally with a distinctly bluish tinge. They are marbled and marked with irregular lines and tracings of dark umber-brown, deepening almost into black, but never so deep as in the eggs of the eastern species. These marblings vary constantly and in a remarkable degree; in some they are almost entirely wanting. They measure .90 of an inch in length by .65 in breadth.

Subfamily QUISCALINÆ.

CHAR. Bill rather attenuated, as long as or longer than the head. The culmen curved,

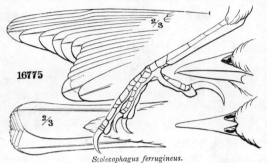

16775

⅔

Scolecophagus ferrugineus.

the tip much bent down. The cutting edges inflected so as to impart a somewhat tubular appearance to each mandible. The commissure sinuated. Tail longer than the wings, usually much graduated. Legs longer than the head, fitted for walking. Color of males entirely black with lustrous reflections.

The bill of the *Quiscalinæ* is very different from that of the other *Icteridæ*, and is readily recognized by the tendency to a rounding inward along the cutting edges, rendering the width in a cross section of the bill considerably less along the commissure than above or below. The culmen is more curved than in the *Agelainæ*. All the North American species have the iris white.

The only genera in the United States are as follows: —

Scolecophagus. Tail shorter than the wings; nearly even. Bill shorter than the head.

Quiscalus. Tail longer than the wings; much graduated. Bill as long as or longer than the head.

Genus SCOLECOPHAGUS, SWAINSON.

Scolecophagus, SWAINSON, F. Bor.-Am. II, 1831. (Type, *Oriolus ferrugineus*, GMELIN.)

GEN. CHAR. Bill shorter than the head, rather slender, the edges inflexed as in *Quiscalus*, which it otherwise greatly resembles; the commissure sinuated. Culmen rounded, but not flattened. Tarsi longer than the middle toe. Tail even, or slightly rounded.

The above characteristics will readily distinguish the genus from its allies. The form is much like that of *Agelaius*. The bill, however, is more attenuated, the culmen curved and slightly sinuated. The bend at the base of the commissure is shorter. The culmen is angular at the base posterior to the nostrils, instead of being much flattened, and does not extend so far behind. The two North American species may be distinguished as follows: —

Synopsis of Species.

S. ferrugineus. Bill slender; height at base not .4 the total length. Color of male black, with faint purple reflection over whole body; wings, tail, and abdomen glossed slightly with green. Autumnal specimens with feathers broadly edged with castaneous rusty. *Female* brownish dusky slate, without gloss; no trace of light superciliary stripe.

S. cyanocephalus. Bill stout; height at base nearly .5 the total length. Color black, with green reflections over whole body. Head only glossed with purple. Autumnal specimens, feathers edged very indistinctly with umber-brown. *Female* dusky-brown, with a soft gloss; a decided light superciliary stripe.

Cuba possesses a species referred to this genus (*S. atroviolaceus*), though it is not strictly congeneric with the two North American ones. It differs in lacking any distinct membrane above the nostril, and in having the bill not compressed laterally, as well as in being much stouter. The plumage has a soft silky lustre; the general color black, with rich purple or violet lustre. The female similarly colored to the male.

Scolecophagus ferrugineus, Swainson.

RUSTY BLACKBIRD.

Oriolus ferrugineus, GMELIN, Syst. Nat. I, 393, No. 43. — LATH. Ind. I, 1790, 176. *Gracula ferruginea*, WILSON, Am. Orn. III, 1811, 41, pl. xxi, f. 3. *Quiscalus ferrugineus*, BON. Obs. Wils. 1824, No. 46. — NUTTALL, Man. I, 1832, 199. — AUD. Orn. Biog. II, 1834, 315 ; V, 1839, 483, pl. cxlvii. — IB. Synopsis, 1839, 146. — IB. Birds Am. IV, 1842, 65, pl. ccxxii. — MAX. Caban. J. VI, 1858, 204. *Scolecophagus ferrugineus*, SWAINSON, F. Bor.-Am. II, 1831, 286. — BON. List, 1838. — BAIRD, Birds N. Am. 1858, 551. — COUES, P. A. N. S. 1861, 225. — CASS. P. A. N. S. 1866, 412. — DALL & BANNISTER, Tr. Ch. Ac. I, 1869, 285 (Alaska). ? ? *Oriolus niger*, GMELIN, I, 1788, 393, Nos. 4, 5 (perhaps *Quiscalus*). — SAMUELS, 350. — ALLEN, B. E. Fla. 291. *Scolecophagus niger*, BONAP. Consp. 1850, 423. — CABANIS, Mus. Hein. 1851, 195. ? ? *Oriolus fuscus*, GMELIN, Syst. I, 1788, 393, No. 44 (perhaps *Molothrus*). *Turdus hudsonius*, GMELIN, Syst. Nat. I, 1788, 818. — LATH. Ind. *Turdus noveboracensis*, GMELIN, I, 1788, 818. *Turdus labradorius*, GMELIN, Syst. Nat. I, 1788, 832. — LATH. Ind. I, 1790, 342 (*labradorus*). "*Pendulinus ater*, VIEILLOT, Nouv. Dict." *Chalcophanes virescens*, WAGLER, Syst. Av. (Appendix, *Oriolus* 9). ? *Turdus* No. 22 from Severn River, Forster, Phil. Trans. LXII, 1772, 400.

SP. CHAR. Bill slender; shorter than the head; about equal to the hind toe; its height not quite two fifths the total length. Wing nearly an inch longer than the tail; second quill longest; first a little shorter than the fourth. Tail slightly graduated; the lateral feathers about a quarter of an inch shortest. General color black, with purple reflections; the wings, under tail-coverts, and hinder part of the belly, glossed with green. In autumn the feathers largely edged with ferruginous or brownish, so as to change the appearance entirely. Spring female dull, opaque plumbeous or ashy-black; the wings and tail sometimes with a green lustre. Young like autumnal birds. Length of male, 9.50; wing, 4.75; tail, 4.00. Female smaller.

HAB. From Atlantic coast to the Missouri. North to Arctic regions. In Alaska on the Yukon, at Fort Kenai, and Nulato.

HABITS. The Rusty Blackbird is an eastern species, found from the Atlautic to the Missouri River, and from Louisiana and Florida to the Arctic regions. In a large portion of the United States it is only known as a migratory species, passing rapidly through in early spring, and hardly making a longer stay in the fall. Richardson states that the summer

range of this bird extends to the 68th parallel, or as far as the woods extend. It arrives at the Saskatchewan in the end of April, and at Great Bear Lake, latitude 65°, by the 3d of May. They come in pairs, and for a time frequent the sandy beaches of secluded lakes, feeding on coleopterous insects. Later in the season they are said to make depredations upon the grain-fields.

They pass through Massachusetts from the 8th of March to the first of April, in irregular companies, none of which make any stay, but move hur-

Scolecophagus ferrugineus.

riedly on. They begin to return early in October, and are found irregularly throughout that month. They are unsuspicious and easily approached, and frequent the streams and edges of ponds during their stay.

Mr. Boardman states that these birds are common near Calais, Me., arriving there in March, some remaining to breed. In Western Massachusetts, according to Mr. Allen, they are rather rare, being seen only occasionally in spring and fall as stragglers, or in small flocks. Mr. Allen gives as their arrival the last of September, and has seen them as late as November 24. They also were abundant in Nova Scotia. Dr. Coues states that in South Carolina they winter from November until March.

These birds are said to sing during pairing-time, and become nearly silent while rearing their young, but in the fall resume their song. Nuttall has heard them sing until the approach of winter. He thinks their notes are quite agreeable and musical, and much more melodious than those of the other species.

During their stay in the vicinity of Boston, they assemble in large numbers, to roost in the reed marshes on the edges of ponds, and especially in those of Fresh Pond, Cambridge. They feed during the day chiefly on grasshoppers and berries, and rarely molest the grain.

According to Wilson, they reach Pennsylvania early in October, and at this period make Indian corn their principal food. They leave about the middle of November. In South Carolina he found them numerous around the rice plantations, feeding about the hog-pens and wherever they could procure corn. They are easily domesticated, becoming very familiar in a few days, and readily reconciled to confinement.

In the District of Columbia, Dr. Coues found the Rusty Grakle an abundant and strictly gregarious winter resident, arriving there the third week in October and remaining until April, and found chiefly in swampy localities, but occasionally also in ploughed fields.

Mr. Audubon found these birds during the winter months, as far south as Florida and Lower Louisiana, arriving there in small flocks, coming in company with the Redwings and Cowbirds, and remaining associated with them until the spring. At this season they are also found in nearly all the Southern and Western States. They appear fond of the company of cattle, and are to be seen with them, both in the pasture and in the farm-yard. They seem less shy than the other species. They also frequent moist places, where they feed upon aquatic insects and small snails, for which they search among the reeds and sedges, climbing them with great agility.

In their habits they are said to resemble the Redwings, and, being equally fond of the vicinity of water, they construct their nests in low trees and bushes in moist places. Their nests are said to be similarly constructed, but smaller than those of the Redwings. In Labrador Mr. Audubon found them lined with mosses instead of grasses. In Maine they begin to lay about the first of June, and in Labrador about the 20th, and raise only one brood in a season.

The young, when first able to fly, are of a nearly uniform brown color. Their nests, according to Audubon, are also occasionally found in marshes of tall reeds of the *Typha*, to the stalks of which they are firmly attached by interweaving the leaves of the plant with grasses and fine strips of bark. A friend of the same writer, residing in New Orleans, found one of these birds, in full plumage and slightly wounded, near the city. He took it home, and put it in a cage with some Painted Buntings. It made no attempt to molest his companions, and they soon became good friends. It sang during its confinement, but the notes were less sonorous than when at liberty. It was fed entirely on rice.

The memoranda of Mr. MacFarlane show that these birds are by no means uncommon near Fort Anderson. A nest, found June 12, on the branch of a spruce, next to the trunk, was eight feet from the ground. Another nest, containing one egg and a young bird, was in the midst of a branch of a pine, five feet from the ground. The parents endeavored to draw him from their nest, and to turn his attention to themselves. A third, found June 22, contained four eggs, and was similarly situated. The eggs contained large embryos. Mr. MacFarlane states that whenever a nest of this species is approached, both parents evince great uneasiness, and do all in their power, by flying from tree to tree in its vicinity, to attract one from the spot. They are spoken of as moderately abundant at Fort Anderson, and as having been met with as far east as the Horton River. He was also informed by the Eskimos that they extend along the banks of the Lower Anderson to the very borders of the woods.

Mr. Dall states that these Blackbirds arrive at Nulato about May 20, where they are tolerably abundant and very tame. They breed later than some other birds, and had not begun to lay before he left, the last of May. Eggs were procured at Fort Yukon by Mr. Lockhart, and at Sitka by Mr. Bischoff.

Besides these localities, this bird was found breeding in the Barren Grounds of Anderson River in 69° north latitude, on the Arctic coast at Fort Kenai, by Mr. Bischoff, and at Fort Simpson, Fort Rae, and Peel River. It has been found breeding at Calais by Mr. Boardman, and at Halifax by Mr. W. G. Winton.

Eggs sent from Fort Yukon, near the mouth of the Porcupine River, by Mr. S. Jones, are of a rounded-oval shape, measuring 1.03 inches in length by .75 in breadth. In size, shape, ground-color, and color of their markings, they are hardly distinguishable from some eggs of Brewer's Blackbird, though generally different. All I have seen from Fort Yukon have a ground-color of very light green, very thickly covered with blotches and finer dottings of a mixture of ferruginous and purplish-brown. In some the blotches are larger and fewer than in others, and in all these the purple shading predominates. One egg, more nearly spherical than the rest, measures .98 by .82. None have any waving lines, as in all other Blackbird's eggs. Two from near Calais, Me., measure 1.02 by .75 of an inch, have a ground of light green, only sparingly blotched with shades of purplish-brown, varying from light to very dark hues, but with no traces of lines or marbling.

According to Mr. Boardman, these birds are found during the summer months about Calais, but they are not common. Only a few remain of those that come in large flocks in the early spring. They pass along about the last of April, the greater proportions only tarrying a short time; but in the fall they stay from five to eight weeks. They nest in the same places with the Redwing Blackbirds, and their nests are very much alike. In early summer they have a very pretty note, which is never heard in the fall.

Scolecophagus cyanocephalus, Cab.

BREWER'S BLACKBIRD.

Psarocolius cyanocephalus, WAGLER, Isis, 1829, 758. *Scolecophagus cyanocephalus*, CABANIS, Mus. Hein. 1851, 193. — BAIRD, Birds N. Am. 1858, 552. — CASS. P. A. N. S. 1866, 413. — HEERM. X, S, 53. — COOPER & SUCKLEY, 209. — COOPER, Orn. Cal. I, 1870, 278. *Scolecophagus mexicanus*, SWAINSON, Anim. in Men. 2¼ cent. 1838, 302. — BON. Conspectus, 1850, 423. — NEWBERRY, Zoöl. Cal. and Or. Route ; Rep. P. R. R. Surv. VI, IV, 1857, 86. *Quiscalus breweri*, AUD. Birds Am. VII, 1843, 345, pl. ccccxcii.

SP. CHAR. Bill stout, quiscaline, the commissure scarcely sinuated; shorter than the head and the hind toe; the height nearly half length of culmen. Wing nearly an inch longer than the tail; the second quill longest; the first about equal to the third. Tail rounded and moderately graduated; the lateral feathers about .35 of an inch shorter. General color of male black, with lustrous green reflections everywhere except on the head and neck, which are glossed with purplish-violet. *Female* much duller, of a light brownish anteriorly; a very faint superciliary stripe. Length about 10 inches; wing, 5.30; tail, 4.40.

HAB. High Central Plains to the Pacific; south to Mexico. Pembina, Minn.; S. Illinois (Wabash Co.; R. RIDGWAY); Matamoras and San Antonio, Texas (breeds; DRESSER, Ibis, 1869, 493); Plateau of Mexico (very abundant, and resident; SUMICHRAST, M. B. S. I, 553).

Autumnal specimens do not exhibit the broad rusty edges of feathers seen in *S. ferrugineus.*

The females and immature males differ from the adult males in much the same points as *S. ferrugineus,* except that the "rusty" markings are less prominent and more grayish. The differences generally between the two species are very appreciable. Thus, in *S. cyanocephalus,* the bill, though of the same length, is much higher and broader at the base, as well as much less linear in its upper outline; the point, too, is less decurved. The size is every way larger. The purplish gloss, which in *ferrugineus* is found on most of the body except the wings and tail, is here confined to the head and neck, the rest of the body being of a richly lustrous and strongly marked green, more distinct than that on the wings and tail of *ferrugineus.* In one specimen only, from Santa Rosalia, Mexico, is there a trace of purple on some of the wing and tail feathers.

HABITS. This species was first given as a bird of our fauna by Mr. Audubon, in the supplementary pages of the seventh volume of his Birds of America. He met with it on the prairies around Fort Union, at the junction of the Yellowstone and the Missouri Rivers, and in the extensive ravines in that neighborhood, in which were found a few dwarfish trees and tall rough weeds or grasses, along the margin of scanty rivulets. In these localities he met with small groups of seven or eight of these birds. They were in loose flocks, and moved in a silent manner, permitting an approach to within some fifteen or twenty paces, and uttering a call-note as his party stood watching their movements. Perceiving it to be a species new to him, he procured several specimens. He states that they did not evince the pertness so usual to birds of this family, but seemed rather as if dissatisfied with their abode. On the ground their gait was easy and brisk. He heard nothing from them of the nature of a song, only a single *cluck,* not unlike that of the Redwing, between which birds and the *C. ferrugineus* he was disposed to place this species.

Dr. Newberry found this Blackbird common both in California and in Oregon. He saw large flocks of them at Fort Vancouver, in the last of October. They were flying from field to field, and gathered into the large spruces about the fort, in the manner of other Blackbirds when on the point of migrating.

Mr. Allen found this Blackbird, though less an inhabitant of the marshes than the Yellow-headed, associating with them in destroying the farmers' ripening corn, and only less destructive because less numerous. It appears to be an abundant species in all the settled portions of the western region, extending to the eastward as far as Wisconsin, and even to Southeastern Illinois, one specimen having been obtained in Wisconsin by Mr. Kumlien, and others in Wabash Co., Ill., by Mr. Ridgway.

In the summer, according to Mr. Ridgway, it retires to the cedar and piñon mountains to breed, at that time seldom visiting the river valley. In the winter it resorts in large flocks to the vicinity of corrals and barn-yards, where it becomes very tame and familiar. On the 3d of June he met with the breeding-ground of a colony of these birds, in a grove of cedars on the side of a cañon, in the mountains, near Pyramid Lake. Nearly every tree contained a nest, and several had two or three. Each nest was saddled on a horizontal branch, generally in a thick tuft of foliage, and well concealed. The majority of these nests contained young, and when these were disturbed the parents flew about the heads of the intruders, uttering a soft *chuck*. The maximum number of eggs or young was six, the usual number four or five. In notes and manners it seemed to be an exact counterpart of the *C. ferrugineus*.

Dr. Suckley found these birds quite abundant at Fort Dalles, but west of the Cascade Mountains they were quite rare. At Fort Dalles it is a winter resident, where, in the cold weather, it may frequently be found in flocks in the vicinity of barn-yards and stables. Dr. Cooper also obtained specimens of this Grakle at Vancouver, and regards it as a constant resident on the Columbia River. He saw none at Puget Sound. In their notes and habits he was not able to trace any difference from the Rusty Blackbird of the Atlantic States. In winter they kept about the stables in flocks of fifties or more, and on warm days flew about among the tree-tops, in company with the Redwings, singing a harsh but pleasant chorus for hours.

Dr. Cooper states it to be an abundant species everywhere throughout California, except in the dense forests, and resident throughout the year. They frequent pastures and follow cattle in the manner of the *Molothrus*. They associate with the other Blackbirds, and are fond of feeding and bathing along the edges of streams. They have not much song, but the noise made by a large flock, as they sit sunning themselves in early spring, is said to be quite pleasing. In this chorus the Redwings frequently assist. At Santa Cruz he found them more familiar than elsewhere. They frequented the yards about houses and stables, building in the trees of the gardens, and collecting daily, after their hunger was satisfied, on the roofs or on neighboring trees, to sing, for an hour or two, their songs of thanks. He has seen a pair of these birds pursue and drive away a large hawk threatening some tame pigeons.

This species has an extended distribution, having been met with by Mr. Kennicott as far north as Pembina, and being also abundant as far south as Northern Mexico. In the Boundary Survey specimens were procured at

Eagle Pass and at Santa Rosalie, where Lieutenant Couch found them living about the ranches and the cattle-yards.

Mr. Dresser, on his arrival at Matamoras, in July, noticed these birds in the streets of that town, in company with the Long-tailed Grakles *Q. macrurus* and *Molothrus pecoris.* He was told by the Mexicans that they breed there, but it was too late to procure their eggs. In the winter vast flocks frequented the roads near by, as well as the streets of San Antonio and Eagle Pass. They were as tame as European Sparrows. Their note, when on the wing, was a low whistle. When congregated in trees, they kept up an incessant chattering.

Dr. Coues found them permanent residents of Arizona, and exceedingly abundant. It was the typical Blackbird of Fort Whipple, though few probably breed in the immediate vicinity. Towards the end of September they become very numerous, and remain so until May, after which few are observed till the fall. They congregate in immense flocks about the corrals, and are tame and familiar. Their note, he says, is a harsh, rasping squeak, varied by a melodious, ringing whistle. I am indebted to this observing ornithologist for the following sketch of their peculiar characteristics : —

"Brewer's Blackbird is resident in Arizona, the most abundant bird of its family, and one of the most characteristic species of the Territory. It appears about Fort Whipple in flocks in September; the numbers are augmented during the following month, and there is little or no diminution until May, when the flocks disperse to breed.

"The nest is placed in the fork of a large bush or tree, sometimes at the height of twenty or thirty feet, and is a bulky structure, not distantly resembling a miniature Crow's nest, but it is comparatively deeper and more compactly built. A great quantity of short, crooked twigs are brought together and interlaced to form the basement and outer wall, and with these is matted a variety of softer material, as weed-stalks, fibrous roots, and dried grasses. A little mud may be found mixed with the other material, but it is not plastered on in any quantity, and often seems to be merely what adhered to the roots or plant-stems that were used. The nest is finished inside with a quantity of hair. The eggs are altogether different from those of the *Quiscali* and *Agelœi,* and resemble those of the Yellow-headed and Rusty Grakles. They vary in number from four to six, and measure barely an inch in length by about three fourths as much in breadth. The ground-color is dull olivaceous-gray, sometimes a paler, clearer bluish or greenish gray, thickly spattered all over with small spots of brown, from very dark blackish-brown or chocolate to light umber. These markings, none of great size, are very irregular in outline, though probably never becoming line-tracery ; and they vary indefinitely in number, being sometimes so crowded that the egg appears of an almost uniform brownish color.

"In this region the Blackbirds play the same part in nature's economy that the Yellow-headed Troupial does in some other parts of the West, and

the Cowbird and Purple Grakle in the East. Like others of their tribe they
are very abundant where found at all, and eminently gregarious, except
whilst breeding. Yet I never saw such innumerable multitudes together as
the Redwinged Blackbird, or even its Californian congener, *A. tricolor*, shows
in the fall, flocks of fifty or a hundred being oftenest seen. Unlike the
Agelæi, they show no partiality for swampy places, being lovers of the woods
and fields, and appearing perfectly at home in the clearings about man's
abode, where their sources of supply are made sure through his bounty or
wastefulness. They are well adapted for terrestrial life by the size and
strength of their feet, and spend much of their time on the ground, betaking
themselves to the trees on alarm. On the ground they habitually run with
nimble steps, when seeking food, only occasionally hopping leisurely, like a
Sparrow, upon both feet at once. Their movements are generally quick,
and their attitudes varied. They run with the head lowered and tail somewhat elevated and partly spread for a balance, but in walking slowly the
head is held high, and oscillates with every step. The customary attitude
when perching is with the body nearly erect, the tail hanging loosely down,
and the bill pointing upward; but should their attention be attracted, this
negligent posture is changed, the birds sit low and firmly, with elevated and
wide-spread tail rapidly flirted, whilst the bright eye peers down through
the foliage. When a flock comes down to the ground to search for food,
they generally huddle closely together and pass pretty quickly along, each
one striving to be first, and in their eagerness they continually fly up and
re-alight a few paces ahead, so that the flock seems, as it were, to be rolling
over and over. When disturbed at such times, they fly in a dense body to
a neighboring tree, but then almost invariably scatter as they settle among
the boughs. The alarm over, one, more adventurous, flies down again, two
or three follow in his wake, and the rest come trooping after. In their behavior towards man, they exhibited a curious mixture of heedlessness and
timidity; they would ramble about almost at our feet sometimes, yet the
least unusual sound or movement sent them scurrying into the trees. They
became tamest about the stables, where they would walk almost under the
horses' feet, like Cowbirds in a farm-yard.

"Their hunger satisfied, the Blackbirds would fly into the pine-trees and
remain a long time motionless, though not at all quiet. They were 'at sing-
ing-school,' we used to say, and certainly there was room for improvement
in their chorus; but if their notes were not particularly harmonious, they
were sprightly, varied, and on the whole rather agreeable, suggesting the
joviality that Blackbirds always show when their stomachs are full, and the
prospect of further supply is good. Their notes are rapid and emphatic, and,
like the barking of coyotes, give an impression of many more performers
than are really engaged. They have a smart chirp, like the clashing of pebbles, frequently repeated at intervals, varied with a long-drawn mellow
whistle. Their ordinary note, continually uttered when they are searching

for food, is intermediate between the guttural *chuck* of the Redwing and the metallic *chink* of the Reedbird.

"In the fall, when food is most abundant, they generally grow fat, and furnish excellent eating. They are tender, like other small birds, and do not have the rather unpleasant flavor that the Redwing gains by feeding too long upon the *Zizania*.

"These are sociable as well as gregarious birds, and allied species are seen associating with them. At Wilmington, Southern California, where I found them extremely abundant in November, they were flocking indiscriminately with the equally plentiful *Agelaius tricolor*."

Dr. Heermann found this Blackbird very common in New Mexico and Texas, though he was probably in error in supposing that all leave there before the period of incubation. During the fall they frequent the cattle-yards, where they obtain abundance of food. They were very familiar, alighting on the house-tops, and apparently having no cause for fear of man. Unlike all other writers, he speaks of its song as a soft, clear whistle. When congregated in spring on the trees, they keep up a continual chattering for hours, as though revelling in an exuberance of spirits.

Under the common Spanish name of *Pajaro prieto*, Dr. Berlandier refers in MSS. to this species. It is said to inhabit the greater part of Mexico, and especially the Eastern States. It moves in flocks in company with the other Blackbirds. It is said to construct a well-made nest about the end of April, of blades of grass, lining it with horse-hair. The eggs, three or four in number, are much smaller than those of *Quiscalus macrurus*, obtuse at one end, and slightly pointed at the other. The ground-color is a pale gray, with a bluish tint, and although less streaked, bears a great resemblance to those of the larger Blackbird.

Dr. Cooper states that these birds nest in low trees, often several in one tree. He describes the nest as large, constructed externally of a rough frame of twigs, with a thick layer of mud, lined with fine rootlets and grasses. The eggs are laid from April 10 to May 20, are four or five in number, have a dull greenish-white ground, with numerous streaks and small blotches of dark brown. He gives their measurement at one inch by .72. They raise two and probably three broods in a season.

Four eggs of this species, from Monterey, collected by Dr. Canfield, have an average measurement of 1.02 inches by .74. Their ground-color is a pale white with a greenish tinge. They are marked with great irregularity, with blotches of a light brown, with fewer blotches of a much darker shade, and a few dots of the same. In one egg the spots are altogether of the lighter shade, and are so numerous and confluent as to conceal the ground-color. In the other they are more scattered, but the lines and marbling of irregularly shaped and narrow zigzag marking are absent in nearly all the eggs.

Mr. Lord found this species a rare bird in British Columbia. He saw a few on Vancouver Island in the yards where cattle were fed, and a small number frequented the mule-camp on the Sumas prairie. East of the Cascades he met none except at Colville, where a small flock had wintered in a settler's cowyard. They appeared to have a great liking for the presence of those animals, arising from their finding more food and insects there than elsewhere, walking between their legs, and even perching upon their backs.

Captain Blakiston found this species breeding on the forks of the Saskatchewan, June 3, 1858, where he obtained its eggs.

Genus **QUISCALUS**, Vieillot.

Quiscalus, Vieillot, Analyse, 1816 (Gray). (Type, *Gracula quiscala*, L.)

Sp. Char. Bill as long as the head, the culmen slightly curved, the gonys almost straight; the edges of the bill inflected and rounded; the commissure quite strongly

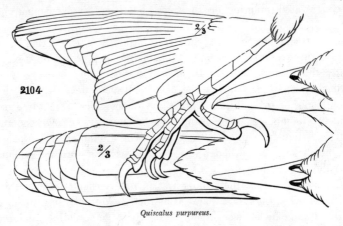

Quiscalus purpureus.

sinuated. Outlines of tarsal scutellæ well defined on the sides; tail long, boat-shaped, or capable of folding so that the two sides can almost be brought together upward, the feathers conspicuously and decidedly graduated, their inner webs longer than the outer. Color black.

The excessive graduation of the long tail, with the perfectly black color, at once distinguishes this genus from any other in the United States. Two types may be distinguished: one *Quiscalus*, in which the females are much like the males, although a little smaller and perhaps with rather less lustre; the other, *Megaquiscalus*, much larger, with the tail more graduated, the females considerably smaller, and of a brown or rusty color. The *Quiscali* are all from North America or the West Indies (including Trinidad); none having been positively determined as South American. The *Megaquiscali* are Mexican and Gulf species entirely, while a third group, the *Holoquiscali*, is West Indian.

Synopsis of Species and Varieties.

A. QUISCALUS. Sexes nearly similar in plumage. Color black; each species glossed with different shades of bronze, purple, violet, green, etc. Lateral tail-feathers about .75 the length of central. *Hab.* Eastern United States. Proportion of wing to tail variable.

Q. purpureus. *a.* Body uniform brassy-olive without varying tints. Head and neck steel-blue, more violaceous anteriorly.

1. Length, 13.50; wing, 5.50 to 5.65; tail, 5.70 to 5.80, its graduation, 1.50; culmen, 1.35 to 1.40. Vivid blue of the neck all round abruptly defined against the brassy-olive of the body. *Female.* Wing, 5.20; tail, 4.85 to 5.10. *Hab.* Interior portions of North America, from Texas and Louisiana to Saskatchewan and Hudson's Bay Territory; New England States; Fort Bridger, Wyoming Territory . . . var. *aeneus.*

b. Body variegated with purple, green, and blue tints. Head and neck violaceous-purple, more blue anteriorly.

2. Length, 12.50; wing, 5.60; tail, 5.30, its graduation, 1.20; culmen, 1.32. Dark purple of neck all round passing over the breast, and appearing in patches on the lower parts. Wing and tail purplish; tail-coverts reddish-purple. *Female.* Wing, 5.10; tail, 4.50. *Hab.* Atlantic coast of United States . . . . . var. *purpureus.*

3. Length, 11.75; wing, 4.85 to 5.60; tail, 4.60 to 5.50, its graduation, .90; culmen, 1.38 to 1.66. Dark purple of neck sharply defined against the dull blackish olive-green of the body. Wings and tail greenish-blue; tail-coverts violet-blue. *Female.* Wing, 4.65 to 4.90; tail, 3.80 to 4.60. *Hab.* South Florida; resident . . . . var. *agelaius.*

B. HOLOQUISCALUS. (CASSIN.) Tail shorter than wings; sexes similar. Color glossy black, but without varying shades of gloss; nearly uniform in each species. Tail moderately graduated. *Hab.* West India Islands, almost exclusively; Mexico and South America.

Q. baritus. Black, with a soft bluish-violet gloss, changing on wings and tail into bluish-green.

Culmen decidedly curved; base of mandibles on sides, smooth.

1. Bill robust, commissure sinuated; depth of bill, at base, .54; culmen, 1.33; wing, 6.15; tail, 5.50, its graduation, 1.30. *Female.* Wing, 5.20; tail, 4.70; other measurements in proportion. *Hab.* Jamaica. var. *baritus.*[1]

2. Bill slender, commissure scarcely sinuated; depth of bill, .43; culmen, 1.35; wing, 5.40; tail, 5.10, its graduation, 1.20. *Female.* Wing, 4.60; tail, 4.20. *Hab.* Porto Rico . . var. *brachypterus.*[2]

Culmen almost straight; base of mandibles on sides corrugated.

3. Depth of bill, .51; culmen, 1.44; wing, 6.00; tail, 5.50, its graduation, 1.50. *Female.* Wing, 5.15; tail, 4.80. *Hab.* Cuba. var. *gundlachi.*[3]

4. Depth of bill, .40; culmen, 1.35; wing, 5.00; tail, 4.50, its graduation, .85. *Hab.* Hayti . . . . var. *niger.*[4]

---

[1] *Quiscalus baritus* (LINN.), CASS. Proc. Ac. Nat. Sc. Phila., 1866, p. 405. (*Gracula barita*, LINN. S. N. I, 165, 1766). *Q. crassirostris*, SWAINSON.

[2] *Quiscalus brachypterus*, CASS. Pr. A. N. S. 1866, 406.

[3] *Quiscalus gundlachi*, CASS. Pr. A. N. S. 1866, 406.

[4] *Quiscalus niger* (BODDAERT), CASS. Pr. A. N. S. 1866, 407. (*Oriolus niger*, BODD. Tab. Pl. Enl. p. 31, 1783.)

None of the continental forms are in the collection, and therefore their relationship to each other and to the West Indian species cannot be here given. They are : (1) *Q. lugubris*, SWAINS.

C. MEGAQUISCALUS. (Cassin.) Tail longer than wings. Sexes very unlike. Female much smaller, and very different in color, being olivaceous-brown, lightest beneath. Male without varying shades of color; lateral tail-feather about .60 the middle, or less.

Q. major. Culmen strongly decurved terminally; bill robust. *Female* with back, nape, and crown like the wings; abdomen much darker than throat.

Lustre of the plumage green, passing into violet anteriorly on head and neck.

1. Length, 15.00; wing, 7.50; tail, 7.70, its graduation, 2.50; culmen, 1.60. *Female*. Wing, 5.10. *Hab*. South Atlantic and Gulf coast of United States . . . . var. *major*.

Lustre, violet passing into green posteriorly.

2. Length, 14.00; wing, 6.75; tail, 7.20, its graduation, 2.40; culmen, 1.57. *Female*. Wing, 5.30; tail, 5.00. *Hab*. Western Mexico. (Mazat-lan, Colima, etc.) . . . . var. *palustris*.[1]
3. Length, 18.00; wing, 7.70; tail, 9.20, its graduation, 3.50; culmen, 1.76. *Female*. Wing, 5.80; tail, 6.30. *Hab*. From Rio Grande of Texas, south through Eastern Mexico; Mazatlan (accidental?).

var. *macrurus*

Q. tenuirostris.[2] Culmen scarcely decurved terminally; bill slender. *Female* with back, nape, and crown very different in color from the wings; abdomen as light as throat.

1. *Male*. Lustre purplish-violet, inclining to steel-blue on wing and upper tail-coverts. Length, 15.00; wing, 7.00; tail, 8.00, its gradua-tion, 3.00. *Female*. Crown, nape, and back castaneous-brown; rest of upper parts brownish-black. A distinct superciliary stripe, with the whole lower parts as far as flanks and crissum, deep fulvous-ochraceous, lightest, and inclining to ochraceous-white, on throat and lower part of abdomen; flanks and crissum blackish-brown. Wing, 5.10; tail, 5.35, its graduation, 1.80; culmen, 1.33; greatest depth of bill, .36. *Hab*. Mexico (central?).

Quiscalus purpureus, BARTR.

THE CROW BLACKBIRD.

Sp. Char. Bill above, about as long as the head, more than twice as high; the com-missure moderately sinuated and considerably decurved at tip. Tail a little shorter than the wing, much graduated, the lateral feathers .90 to 1.50 inches shorter. Third quill

(Cabinet Cyclopædia, p. 299, 1838. — Cass. Pr. A. N. S. 1866, 408). *Hab*. S. Am., Trinidad. (2) *Q. mexicanus*, Cass. (Pr. A. N. S. 1866, 408). *Hab*. Mexico. Besides these are the two fol-lowing, whose habitats are unknown : *Q. inflexirostris*, Swains. (Cab. Cyc. p. 300, 1838), and *Q. rectirostris*, Cass. (Pr. A. N. S. 1866, 409).

[1] *Quiscalus palustris* (Swains.), Cassin, Pr. A. N. S., Phila., 1866, p. 411. (*Scaphidurus pal.*, Swains. Phil. Mag. 1827, 437).

[2] *Quiscalus tenuirostris*, Swains. Cabinet Cyclopædia, 1838, p. 299. — Cassin, Pr. A. N. S. 1866, 411. The *Q. assimilis*, Scl. Cat. Am. B. 1862, 141, from Bogota, and *Q. peruvianus*, Swains. Cab. Cyc. 1838, 354, of Peru, are not in the collection ; they are probably referrible to the *major* type.

longest; first between fourth and fifth. Color black, variously glossed with metallic reflections of bronze, purple, violet, blue, and green. *Female* similar, but smaller and duller, with perhaps more green on the head. Length, 13.00; wing, 6.00; ill above, 1.25.

HAB. From Atlantic to the high Central Plains.

Of the Crow Blackbird of the United States, three well-marked races are now distinguished in the species: one, the common form of the Atlantic States; another occurring in the Mississippi Valley, the British Possessions, and the New England States, and a third on the Peninsula of Florida. The comparative diagnoses of the three will be found on page 809.

Quiscalus purpureus.

Var. **purpureus,** BARTRAM.

PURPLE GRAKLE.

Gracula quiscala, LINN. Syst. Nat. I, (ed. 10,) 1758, 109 (*Monedula purpurea,* Cal.) ; I, (ed. 12,) 1766, 165. — GMELIN, I, 1788, 397. — LATHAM, Ind. I, 1790, 191. — WILSON, Am. Orn. III, 1811, 44, pl. xxi, f. 4. *Chalcophanes quiscalus,* WAGLER, Syst. Av. 1827 (*Gracula*). — CAB. Mus. Hein. 1851, 196. *? ? Oriolus ludovicianus,* GMELIN, Syst. Nat. I, 1788, 387 ; albino var. *? ? Oriolus niger,* GMELIN, Syst. Nat. I, 1788, 393. *? Gracula purpurea,* BARTRAM, Travels, 1791, 290. *Quiscalus versicolor,* VIEILLOT, Analyse ? 1816. — IB. Nouv. Dict. XXVIII, 1819, 488. — IB. Gal. Ois. I, 171, pl. cviii. — BON. Obs. Wils. 1824, No. 45. — IB. Am. Orn. I, 1825, 45, pl. v. — IB. List, 1838. — IB. Conspectus, 1840, 424. — SW. F. Bor.-Am. II, 1831, 485. — NUTTALL, Man. I, 1832, 194. — AUD. Orn. Biog. I, 1831, 35 ; V, 1838, 481 (not the pl. vii.). — IB. Syn. 1839, 146. — IB. Birds Am. IV, 1842, 58 (not the pl. ccxxi.). — BAIRD, Birds N. Am. 1858, 575. *Gracula barita,* ORD, J. A. N. Sc. I, 1818, 253. *"Quiscalus purpureus,* LICHT." — CASSIN, Pr. A. N. Sc., 1866, 403. — RIDGWAY, Pr. A. N. S. 1869, 133. — ALLEN, B. E. Fla. 291 (in part). *Quiscalus nitens,* LICHT. Verz. 1823, No. 164. *Quiscalus purpuratus,* SWAINSON, Anim. in Menag. 1838, No. 55. *Purple Grakle,* PENNANT, Arctic Zoöl. II.

SP. CHAR. Length about 12.50 ; wing, 5.50 ; tail, 4.92 ; culmen, 1.24 ; tarsus, 1.28. Second quill longest, hardly perceptibly (only .07 of an inch) longer than the first and third, which are equal ; projection of primaries beyond secondaries, 1.56 ; graduation of tail, .92. General appearance glossy black ; whole plumage, however, brightly glossed with reddish-violet, bronzed purple, steel-blue, and green ; the head and neck with purple prevailing, this being in some individuals more bluish, in others more reddish: where most blue this is purest anteriorly, becoming more violet on the neck. On other portions of the body the blue and violet forming an iridescent zone on each feather, the blue first, the violet terminal; sometimes the head is similarly marked. On the abdomen the blue generally predominates, on the rump the violet; wings and tail black, with violet reflection, more bluish on the latter; the wing-coverts frequently tipped with steel-blue or violet. Bill, tarsi, and toes pure black; iris sulphur-yellow.

HAB. Atlantic States, north to Nova Scotia, west to the Alleghanies.

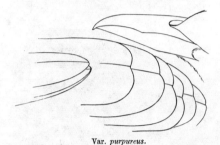

This form is more liable to variation than any other, the arrangement of the metallic tints varying with the individual; there is never, however, an approach to the sharp definition and symmetrical pattern of coloration characteristic of the western race.

Var. *purpureus.*

The female is a little less brilliant than the male, and slightly smaller. The young is entirely uniform slaty-brown, without gloss.

An extreme example of this race (22,526, Washington, D. C. ?) is almost wholly of a continuous rich purple, interrupted only on the interscapulars, where, anteriorly, the purple is overlaid by bright green, the feathers with terminal transverse bars of bluish. On the lower parts are scattered areas of a more bluish tint. The purple is richest and of a reddish cast on the neck, passing gradually into a bluish tint toward the bill; on the rump and breast the purple has a somewhat bronzy appearance.

HABITS. The common Crow Blackbird of the eastern United States exhibits three well-marked and permanently varying forms, which we present as races. Yet these variations are so well marked and so constant that they almost claim the right to be treated as specifically distinct. We shall consider them by themselves. They are the Purple Grakle, or common Crow Blackbird, *Quiscalus purpureus;* the Bronzed Grakle, *Q. æneus;* and the Florida Grakle, *Q. aglæus.*

The first of these, the well-known Crow Blackbird of the Atlantic States, so far as we are now informed, has an area extending from Northern Florida on the south to Maine, and from the Atlantic to the Alleghanies. Mr. Allen states that the second form is the typical form of New England, but my observations do not confirm his statement. Both the eastern and the western forms occur in Massachusetts, but the *purpureus* alone seems to be a summer resident, the *æneus* occurring only *in transitu,* and, so far as I am now aware, chiefly in the fall.

The Crow Blackbirds visit Massachusetts early in March and remain until the latter part of September, those that are summer residents generally departing before October. They are not abundant in the eastern part of the State, and breed in small communities or by solitary pairs.

In the Central States, especially in Pennsylvania and New Jersey, they are much more abundant, and render themselves conspicuous and dreaded by the farmers through the extent of their depredations on the crops. The evil deeds of all birds are ever much more noticed and dwelt upon than their beneficial acts. So it is, to an eminent degree, with the Crow Blackbird. Very few seem aware of the vast amount of benefit it confers on the farmer, but all know full well — and are bitterly prejudiced by the knowledge — the extent of the damages this bird causes.

They return to Pennsylvania about the middle of March, in large, loose flocks, at that time frequenting the meadows and ploughed fields, and their food then consists almost wholly of grubs, worms, etc., of which they destroy prodigious numbers. In view of these services, and notwithstanding the havoc they commit on the crops of Indian corn, Wilson states that he should hesitate whether to consider these birds most as friends or as enemies, as they are particularly destructive to almost all the noxious worms, grubs, and caterpillars that infest the farmer's fields, which, were they to be allowed to multiply unmolested, would soon consume nine tenths of all the productions of his labor, and desolate the country with the miseries of famine.

The depredations committed by these birds are almost wholly upon Indian corn, at different stages. As soon as its blades appear above the ground, after it has been planted, these birds descend upon the fields, pull up the tender plant, and devour the seeds, scattering the green blades around. It is of little use to attempt to drive them away with the gun. They only fly from one part of the field to another. And again, as soon as the tender corn has formed, these flocks, now replenished by the young of the year, once more swarm in the cornfields, tear off the husks, and devour the tender grains. Wilson has seen fields of corn in which more than half the corn was thus ruined.

These birds winter in immense numbers in the lower parts of Virginia, North and South Carolina, and Georgia, sometimes forming one congregated multitude of several hundred thousands. On one occasion Wilson met, on the banks of the Roanoke, on the 20th of January, one of these prodigious armies of Crow Blackbirds. They rose, he states, from the surrounding fields with a noise like thunder, and, descending on the length of the road before him, they covered it and the fences completely with black. When they again rose, and after a few evolutions descended on the skirts of the high timbered woods, they produced a most singular and striking effect. Whole trees, for a considerable extent, from the top to the lowest branches, seemed as if hung with mourning. Their notes and screaming, he adds, seemed all the while like the distant sounds of a great cataract, but in a more musical cadence.

A writer in the American Naturalist (II. 326), residing in Newark, N. Y., notes the advent of a large number of these birds to his village. Two built their nest inside the spire of a church. Another pair took possession of a martin-house in the narrator's garden, forcibly expelling the rightful owners. These same birds also attempted to plunder the newly constructed nests of the Robins of their materials. They were, however, successfully resisted, the Robins driving the Blackbirds away in all cases of contest.

The Crow Blackbird nests in various situations, sometimes in low bushes, more frequently in trees, and at various heights. A pair, for several years, had their nest on the top of a high fir-tree, some sixty feet from the ground, standing a few feet from my front door. Though narrowly watched by unfriendly eyes, no one could detect them in any mischief. Not a spear of corn was molested, and their food was exclusively insects, for which they diligently searched, turning over chips, pieces of wood, and loose stones. Their nests are large, coarsely but strongly made of twigs and dry plants, interwoven with strong stems of grasses. When the Fish Hawks build in their neighborhood, Wilson states that it is a frequent occurrence for the Grakles to place their nests in the interstices of those of the former. Sometimes several pairs make use of the same Hawk's nest at the same time, living in singular amity with its owner. Mr. Audubon speaks of finding these birds generally breeding in the hollows of trees. I have never met with their nests in these situations, but Mr. William Brewster says he has found them nesting in this manner in the northern part of Maine. Both, however, probably refer to the var. *æneus*.

The eggs of the Grakle exhibit great variations in their ground-color, varying from a light greenish-white to a deep rusty-brown. The former is the more common color. The eggs are marked with large dashes and broad, irregular streaks of black and dark brown, often presenting a singular grotesqueness in their shapes. Eggs with a deep brown ground are usually marked chiefly about the larger end with confluent, cloudy blotches of deeper shades of the same. The eggs measure 1.25 inches by .90.

Var. æneus, RIDGWAY.

BRONZED GRAKLE.

Quiscalus versicolor, AUD. Orn. Biog. pl. vii ; Birds Am. IV, pl. ccxxi (figure, but not
description). — BAIRD, Birds N. Am. 1858, 555 (western specimens). — SAMUELS, 352.
Quiscalus æneus, RIDGWAY, Pr. Phil. Acad., June, 1869. 134.

SP. CHAR. Length, 12.50 to 13.50 ; wing, 6.00 ; tail, 6.00 ; culmen, 1.26 ; tarsus, 1.32.

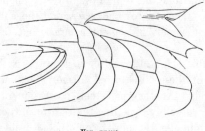

Var. *æneus*.

Third and fourth quills longest and equal ; first shorter than fifth ; projection of primaries beyond secondaries, 1.28 ; graduation of tail, 1.48.

Metallic tints rich, deep, and uniform. Head and neck all round rich silky steel-blue, this strictly confined to these portions, and abruptly defined behind, varying in shade from an intense Prussian blue to brassy-greenish, the latter tint always, when present, most apparent on the neck, the head always more violaceous ; lores velvety-black. Entire body, above and below, uniform continuous metallic brassy-olive, varying to burnished golden olivaceous-bronze, becoming gradually uniform metallic purplish or reddish violet on wings and tail, the last more purplish; primaries violet-black ; bill, tarsi, and toes pure black; iris sulphur-yellow.

HAB. Mississippi region of United States, east to Alleghany Mountains, west to Fort Bridger; Saskatchewan Region, Hudson's Bay Territory; Labrador? and Maine (52,382, Calais, Me., G. A. Boardman). More or less abundant in all eastern States north of New Jersey.

This species may be readily distinguished from the *Q. purpureus* by the color alone, independently of the differences of proportions.

The impression received from a casual notice of a specimen of the *Q. purpureus* is that of a uniformly glossy black bird, the metallic tints being much broken or irregularly distributed, being frequently, or generally, arranged in successive bands on the feathers over the whole body, producing a peculiar iridescent effect. In the *Q. æneus* nothing of this character is seen; for, among a very large series of western specimens, not one has the body other than continuous bronze, the head and neck alone being green or blue, and this sharply and abruptly defined against the very different tint of the other portions. These colors, of course, have their extremes of variation, but the change is only in the shade of the metallic tints, the precise pattern being strictly retained. In the present species the colors are more vivid and silky than in the eastern, and the bird is, in fact, a much handsomer one. (Ridgway.)

Just after moulting, the plumage is unusually brilliant, the metallic tints being much more vivid.

HABITS. The Bronzed Blackbird has been so recently separated from the *purpureus* that we cannot give, with exactness or certainty, the area over which it is distributed. It is supposed to occupy the country west of the Alleghanies as far to the southwest as the Rio Grande and Fort Bridger, extending to the Missouri plains on the northwest, to the Saskatchewan in the north, and to Maine and Nova Scotia on the northeast. Subsequent explorations may somewhat modify this supposed area of distribution. It is at least known that this form occurs in Texas, in all the States immediately west of the Alleghanies, and in the New England States, as well as the vicinity of New York City.

In regard to its habits, as differing from those of *purpureus*, we are without any observations sufficiently distinctive to be of value. It reaches Calais about the first of April, and is a common summer visitant.

In the fall of 1869, about the 10th of October, several weeks after the *Quiscali* which had been spending the summer with us had disappeared, an unusually large number of these birds, in the bronzed plumage, made their appearance in the place; they seemed to come all together, but kept in smaller companies. One of these flocks spent the day, which was lowering and unpleasant, but not rainy, in my orchard. They kept closely to the ground, and seemed to be busily engaged in searching for insects. They had a single call-note, not loud, and seemingly one of uneasiness and watchfulness against danger. Yet they were not shy, and permitted a close approach. They remained but a day, and all were gone the following morning. On the day after their departure, we found that quite a number of apples had been bitten into. We had no doubt as to the culprits, though no one saw them in the act.

Audubon's observations relative to the Crow Blackbird are chiefly made with reference to those seen in Louisiana, where this race is probably the only one found. The only noticeable peculiarity in his account of these birds is his statement that the Blackbirds of that State nest in hollow trees, a manner of breeding now known to be also occasional in the habits of the *purpureus*. The eggs of this form appear to exhibit apparently even greater variations than do those of the *purpureus*. One egg, measuring 1.10 inches by .85, has a bright bluish-green ground, plashed and spotted with deep brown markings. Another has a dull gray ground, sparingly marked with light brown; the measurement of this is 1.13 inches by .85. A third has a greenish-white ground, so profusely spotted with a russet-brown that the ground-color is hardly perceptible. It is larger and more nearly spherical, measuring 1.16 inches by .90. A fourth is so entirely covered with blotches, dots, and cloudings of dark cinnamon-brown that the ground can nowhere be traced.

Mr. Gideon Lincecum, of Long Point, Texas, writes, in regard to this species, that, in his neighborhood, they nest in rookeries, often on a large live oak. They build their nests on the top of large limbs. In favorable situations four or five nests can be looked into at once. They are at this time full of song, though never very melodious. The people of Texas shoot them, believing them to be injurious to their crops ; but instead of being an injury they are an advantage, they destroy so many worms, grasshoppers, caterpillars, etc. They are migratory, and very gregarious. They all leave Texas in the winter, and the same birds return in the spring to the same nesting-places. They lay five eggs in a nest.

In Southern Illinois, as Mr. Ridgway informs me, these birds are resident throughout the year, though rather rare during the winter months. They breed in the greatest abundance, and are very gregarious in the breeding-season. On a single small island in the Wabash River, covered with tall willows, Mr. Ridgway found over seventy nests at one time. These were placeed indifferently on horizontal boughs, in forks, or in excavations, — either natural or made by the large Woodpeckers (*Hylotomus*), — nests in all these situations being sometimes found in one tree. They prefer the large elms, cottonwoods, and sycamores of the river-bottoms as trees for nesting-places, but select rather thinly wooded situations, as old clearings, etc. In the vicinity of Calais, according to Mr. Boardman, they nest habitually in hollow stubs in marshy borders of brooks or ponds.

Var. **aglæus,** BAIRD.

FLORIDA GRAKLE.

Quiscalus baritus, BAIRD, Birds N. Am. 1858, 556, pl. xxxii (not of LINN.). *Quiscalus aglæus,* BAIRD, Am. Jour. Sci. 1866, 84. — CASSIN, Pr. A. N. S. 1866, 44. — RIDGWAY, Pr. A. N. S. 1869, 135. *Q. purpureus,* ALLEN, B.' E. Fla. 291.

SP. CHAR. Length, 10.60; wing, 5.20; tail, 5.12; culmen, 1.40; tarsus, 1.40. Second and third quills equal and longest; first shorter than fourth; projection of primaries beyond secondaries, 1.12; graduation of tail, 1.00.

Bill very slender and elongated, the tip of upper mandible abruptly decurved; commissure very regular.

Metallic tints very dark. Head and neck all round well defined violaceous steel-blue, the head most bluish, the neck more purplish and with a bronzy cast in front; body uniform

Var. *aglæus.*

soft, dull, bronzy greenish-black, scarcely lustrous; wings, upper tail-coverts, and tail blackish steel-blue, the wing-coverts tipped with vivid violet-bronze; belly and crissum glossed with blue.

HAB. South Florida.

This race is quite well marked, though it grades insensibly into the var. *purpureus.* It differs from both that and *æneus* in much smaller size, with more slender and more decurved bill.

The arrangement of the colors is much as in the larger western species, while the tints are most like those of the eastern. All the colors are, however, darker, but at the same time softer than in either of the others.

In form this species approaches nearest the western, agreeing with it in the primaries, slender bill, and more graduated tail, and, indeed, its relations in every respect appear to be with this rather than the eastern.

This race was first described from specimens collected at Key Biscayne by Mr. Wurdemann, in April, 1857, and in 1858, and is the smallest of the genus within our limits. The wing and tail each are about an inch shorter than in the other varieties of *purpureus.* The bill, however, is much longer and more slender, and the tip considerably more produced and decurved. The feet are stouter and much coarser, the pads of the toes very scabrous, as if to assist in holding slippery substances, a feature scarcely seen in *purpureus.*[1]

[1] A series of twenty-nine specimens of *Q. purpureus* from Florida, has been kindly furnished for examination by Mr. C. J. Maynard, chiefly from the northern and middle portions of the State, and consequently intermediate between the varieties *aglæus* and *purpureus.* In color, however, they are nearly all essentially, most of them typically, like the former; but in size and proportions they scarcely differ from more northern specimens of the latter. Their common and nearly constant features of coloration are, uniform soft dark greenish body, with blue tinge on belly, and bluish-green tail-coverts and tail, violet head, more blue anteriorly and more bronzy

HABITS. This race or species seems to be confined exclusively to the peninsula of Florida. We have no notes as to any of its peculiarities, nor do we know that it exhibits any differences of manners or habits from those of its more northern relatives.

Of its eggs I have seen but few specimens. These do not exhibit much variation. The ground-color shades from a light drab to one with a greenish tinge. They average 1.17 inches in length by .85 in breadth, are more oblong in shape, and are very strikingly marked with characters in black and dark brown, resembling Arabic and Turkish letters.

Quiscalus major, VIEILL.

BOAT-TAILED GRAKLE; JACKDAW.

Gracula barita, WILSON, Index Am. Orn. VI, 1812 (not of LINNÆUS). *Gracula quiscala*, ORD. J. A. N. Sc. I, 1818, 253 (not of LINNÆUS). *Quiscalus major*, VIEILLOT, Nouv. Dict. XXVIII, 1819, 487. — BON. Am. Orn. I, 1825, 35, pl. iv. — IB. List, 1838. — IB. Consp. 1850, 424. — AUD. Orn. Biog. II, 1834, 504; V, 1838, 480, pl. clxxxvii, IB. Syn. 1839, 146. — IB. Birds Am. IV, 1842, 52, pl. ccxx. — BAIRD, Birds N. Am. 1858, 555. — CASSIN, Pr. A. N. S. 1867, 409. — ALLEN, B. E. Fla. 295. — COUES, Ibis, N. S. IV, No. 23, 1870, 367 (Biography). *Chalcophanes major*, "TEMM." CAB. Mus. Hein. 1851, 196.

SP. CHAR. (1,563.) Form rather lengthened, but robust; bill strong, about the length of head; wing rather long, second and third quills usually longest, though the first four quills are frequently nearly equal; tail long, graduated; lateral feathers about 2.50 inches shorter than the central; legs and feet strong.

Adult male. Black; head and neck with a fine purple lustre, rather abruptly defined on the lower part of the neck behind, and succeeded by a fine green lustre which passes into a purple or steel-blue on the lower back and upper tail-coverts. On the under parts the purple lustre of the head and neck passes more gradually into green on the abdomen; under tail-coverts usually purplish-blue, frequently plain black. Smaller wing-coverts with green lustre; larger coverts greenish-bronze; quills frequently plain black, with a greenish or bronzed edging and slight lustre. Tail usually with a slight bluish or greenish lustre, frequently plain black. Bill and feet black. Iris yellow. Total length about 15 inches; wing, 7.00; tail, 6.50 to 7.00.

on the foreneck, and with this color abruptly defined posteriorly against the peculiar uniform blackish dull green of the body; the wing-coverts usually tipped with vivid violet and green spots. One male is a typical example of the var. *purpureus*, distinguished by the blending of the similar metallic tints on the body and head, the broken tints on the body arranged in transverse bars on the back, more purple tail-coverts, and lack of the vivid metallic tips to the wing-coverts. There are also four nearly typical specimens of the var. *aglœus*, these probably from farther south on the peninsula, but with the characteristics of the race less exaggerated than in the types from the keys. The measurements of this series are as follows : —

Var. *purpureus* (one specimen). ♂. Wing, 5.30 ; tail, 4.65 ; culmen, 1.38.

Intermediate specimens. Typical *aglœus* in colors, but like *purpureus* in size. (16 males, and 17 females). ♂. Wing, 4.85 to 5.50 ; tail, 4.60 to 5.50 ; culmen, 1.25 to 1.50. ♀. Wing, 4.65 to 4.90 ; tail, 3.80 to 4.50 ; culmen, 1.10 to 1.30.

Var. *aglœus* (four specimens). ♂. Wing, 5.30 to 5.60 ; tail, 5.00 to 5.30 ; culmen, 1.38 to 1.40.

Adult female. Smaller. Upper parts dark brown, lighter on the head and neck behind; darker and nearly a dull black on the lower part of the back and upper tail-coverts; under parts lighter, dull yellowish-brown; tibiæ and under tail-coverts darker; wings and tail dull brownish-black; upper parts frequently with a slight greenish lustre. Total length, about 12.50; wing, 5.50 to 6.00; tail, 5.50. (CASSIN.)

HAB. Coast region of South Atlantic and Gulf States of North America. Galveston and Houston, Texas (DRESSER, Ibis, 1865, 494).

HABITS. The Boat-tailed Grakle, or Jackdaw, of the Southern States, is found in all the maritime portions of the States that border both on the Atlantic and the Gulf of Mexico, from North Carolina to Rio Grande. In Western Texas it does not seem to be abundant. Lieutenant Couch met with only a single specimen at Brownsville, in company with *Q. macrurus.* Mr. Dresser, when at Houston and at Galveston in May and June, 1864, noticed several of these birds. Mr. Salvin mentions finding them as far south as the Keys of the Belize coast.

We learn from the observations of Mr. Audubon that this species is more particularly attached to the maritime portions of the country. It rarely goes farther inland than forty or fifty miles, following the marshy banks of the larger streams. It occurs in great abundance in the lower portions of Louisiana, though not found so high up the Mississippi as Natchez. It also abounds in the Sea Islands on the coast of the Carolinas, and in the lowlands of South Carolina, Georgia, and Florida.

Dr. Coues states that this species hardly occurs in any abundance north of the Carolinas, and that it is restricted to a narrow belt along the coast of the ocean and gulf, from North Carolina throughout our entire shore to Mexico. He supposed it to stop there, and to be replaced by the *macrurus.* Though the larger proportion of these birds pass beyond our southern boundaries to spend the winter, a few, chiefly old males, are resident in North Carolina throughout the year. In the spring the females are the first to appear. Just before the mating has taken place, the flocks of these birds are said to execute sudden and unaccountable evolutions, as if guided by some single commanding spirit; now hovering uncertain, then dashing impulsive, now veering in an instant, and at last taking a long, steady flight towards some distant point. During this period, Dr. Coues further informs us, their voices crack, and they utter a curious medley of notes from bass to falsetto, a jingling, unmusical jargon that is indescribable.

The laying-season is said to be at its height during the latter part of April. He found in no instance more than six eggs in a nest, nor less than three. He thinks that they have two, and perhaps three, broods in a season, as he found it not uncommon to meet with newly fledged birds in September.

These birds are eminently gregarious at all seasons of the year, and at certain seasons assemble in large flocks. They are omnivorous, eating both insects and grain, and are alternately benefactors and plunderers of the planters. In the early season they seek their food among the large salt marshes of the seaboard, and along the muddy banks of creeks and rivers. They do great damage to the rice plantations, both when the grain is in the soft state and afterwards when the ripened grain is stacked. They also feed very largely upon the small crabs called fiddlers, so common in all the mud flats, earthworms, various insects, shrimps, and other aquatic forms of the like character.

A few of these birds are resident throughout the year, though the greater part retire farther south during a portion of the winter. They return in February, in full plumage, when they mate. They resort, by pairs and in companies, to certain favorite breeding-places, where they begin to construct their nests. They do not, however, even in Florida, begin to breed before April. They build a large and clumsy nest, made of very coarse and miscellaneous materials, chiefly sticks and fragments of dry weeds, sedges, and strips of bark, lined with finer stems, fibrous roots, and grasses, and have from three to five eggs.

It is a very singular but well-established characteristic of this species, that no sooner is their nest completed and incubation commenced than the male birds all desert their mates, and, joining one another in flocks, keep apart from the females, feeding by themselves, until they are joined by the young birds and their mothers in the fall.

These facts and this trait of character in this species have been fully confirmed by the observations of Dr. Bachman of Charleston. In 1832 he visited a breeding-locality of these birds. On a single Smilax bush he found more than thirty nests of the Grakles, from three to five feet apart, some of them not more than fifteen inches above the water, and only females were seen about the nests, no males making their appearance. Dr. Bachman also visited colonies of these nests placed upon live-oak trees thirty or forty feet from the ground, and carefully watched the manners of the old birds, but has never found any males in the vicinity of their nests after the eggs had been laid. They always keep at a distance, feeding in flocks in the marshes, leaving the females to take charge of their nests and young. They have but one brood in a season.

As these birds fly, in loose flocks, they continually utter a peculiar cry, which Mr. Audubon states resembles or may be represented by *kirrick, crick, crick*. Their usual notes are harsh, resembling loud, shrill whistles, and are frequently accompanied with their ordinary cry of *crick-crick-cree*. In the love-season these notes are said to be more pleasing, and are changed into sounds which Audubon states resemble *tirit, tirit, titiri-titiri-titireē*, rising from low to high with great regularity and emphasis. The cry of the young bird, when just able to fly, he compares to the whistling cry of some kind of frogs.

The males are charged by Mr. Audubon with attacking birds of other species, driving them from their nests and sucking their eggs.

Dr. Bryant, who found this species the most common bird in the neighborhood of Lake Monroe, adds that it could be seen at all times running along the edge of the water, almost in the manner of a Sandpiper. They were breeding by hundreds in the reeds near the inlet to the lake. On the 6th of April some of the birds had not commenced laying, though the majority had hatched, and the young of others were almost fledged.

The eggs of this species measure 1.25 inches in length by .92 in breadth. Their ground-color is usually a brownish-drab, in some tinged with olive, in others with green. Over this are distributed various markings, in lines, zigzags, and irregular blotches of brown and black.

Quiscalus major, var. macrurus, Sw.

GREAT-TAILED GRAKLE.

Quiscalus macrourus, SWAINSON, Anim. in Menag. 2¼ centen. 1838, 299, fig. 51, a. — BAIRD, Birds N. Am. 1858, pl. lviii. — IB. Mex. B. II, Birds, 20, pl. xx. — CASSIN, Pr. A. N. S. 1867, 410. *Chalcophanes macrurus*, CAB. Mus. Hein. 1851, 196.

SP. CHAR. (The largest species of this genus.) Form lengthened but robust, bill strong, longer than the head; wing long, third quill usually longest; tail long, graduated, outer feathers three to five inches shorter than those in the middle; legs and feet strong.

Adult male. Black; head, neck, back, and entire under parts with a fine bluish-purple lustre; lower part of back and the upper tail-coverts, and also the abdomen and under tail-coverts, frequently with green lustre, though in specimens apparently not fully adult those parts are sometimes bluish-brown, inclining to dark steel-blue. Wings and tail with a slight purplish lustre, smaller coverts with bluish-green, and larger coverts with greenish-bronze lustre. Bill and feet black. Iris yellow. Total length, 17.50 to 20.00; wing, about 8.00; tail, 8.00 to 10.50.

Female. Smaller, and generally resembling that of *Q. major*, but rather darker colored above. Entire upper parts dark brown, nearly black, and with a green lustre on the back; wings and tail dull brownish-black. Under parts light, dull yellowish-brown; paler on the throat, and with a trace of a narrow dark line from each side of the lower mandible. Tibiæ and under tail-coverts dark brown. Total length about 13.00; wing, 6.00; tail, 6.50. (CASSIN.)

HAB. Eastern Texas to Panama and Carthagena. Cordova (SCL. 1856, 300); Guatemala (SCL. Ibis. I, 20, eggs); Honduras (SCL. II, 112); Carthagena, N. 9 (CASS. R. A. S., 1860, 138); Costa Rica (CABAN. Journ. IX, 1861, 82; LAWR. IV, 104); Nicaragua (LAWR. N. Y. Lyc. VIII, 181); Rio Grande of Texas (DRESSER, Ibis, 1865, 493, breeds); Vera Cruz (from hot to alpine regions; resident. SUMICHRAST, M. B. S. I, 553).

HABITS. The Great-tailed or Central American Grakle is an abundant species throughout Mexico and Central America, and probably extends to some distance into South America. In Vera Cruz, Sumichrast states it to be one of the few birds that are found in nearly equal abundance throughout the three regions, hot, temperate, and alpine, into which that department is physically divided. It is abundant everywhere throughout that State, and also nests there. In the neighborhood of Cordova and Orizaba it lives in large communities, a single tree being often loaded with the nests.

On the Rio Grande it extends into Texas, and thus qualifies itself for a place within our fauna. A few specimens were procured at Eagle Pass and elsewhere by the Mexican Boundary Survey party. It is more abundant on the western banks of the Rio Grande, especially at Matamoras. Among the MS. notes left by Dr. Kennerly is a part of the memoranda of the late Dr. Berlandier of that place. Under the name of *Pica elegans* the latter refers to what is evidently this species. He describes it as found in all parts of the Republic of Mexico, where it is known as *Uraca, Pajaro negro*, and, in Acapulco, *Papate*. It is found, he adds, abundantly throughout the State of Tamaulipas. It lives upon grain, especially corn, devouring the planted seeds and destroying the crops. It builds its nest in April, laying its eggs in the same month, and the young birds are hatched out by the beginning of May. The nests are large, the edges high, and the cavity correspondingly deep. They are constructed of dry plants and small bits of cloth, which the birds find about the settlements, and the bottom of the nest is plastered with clay, which gives it great firmness. This is covered with grasses and pieces of dry weeds. The eggs are described as large, of a pale leaden-gray or a rusty color, over which are black marks, stripes, lines, and spots without order or regularity. They are generally four in number. The nests are built on the tops of the highest trees, usually the willows or mesquites.

Mr. G. C. Taylor, in his notes on the birds of Honduras, states that he found this Blackbird common, and always to be met with about the villages. It appeared to be polygamous, the males being generally attended by several females. A fine male bird, with his accompanying females, frequented the court-yard of the Railroad House at Comayagua, where Mr. Taylor was staying. They generally sat on the roof of the house, or among the upper branches of some orange-trees that grew in the yard. They had a very peculiar cry, not unlike the noise produced by the sharpening of a saw, but more prolonged.

Mr. Salvin found the bird very abundant in Central America. In one of his papers relative to the birds of that region, he states that this species, in Guatemala, plays the part of the European House Sparrow. It seeks the abode of man, as does that familiar bird, and is generally found frequenting larger towns as well as villages. Stables are its favorite places of resort, where it scratches for its food among the ordure of the horses. It will even perch on the backs of these animals and rid them of their ticks, occasionally picking up stray grains of corn from their mangers. At Duenas he found it breeding in large societies, usually selecting the willows that grow near the lake and the reeds on the banks for its nest. The breeding season extends over some length of time. In May, young birds and fresh eggs may be found in nests in the same trees. On the coast, young birds, nearly capable of flying, were seen in the early part of March. Mr. Salvin adds that the nests are usually made of grass, and placed among upright branches, the grass being intwined around each twig, to support the structure. The eggs in that region were seldom found to exceed three in number.

Mr. Dresser found the Long-tailed Grakles very common at Matamoras, where they frequented the streets and yards with no signs of fear. They were breeding there in great quantities, building a heavy nest of sticks, lined with roots and grass. They were fond of building in company, and in the yard of the hotel he counted seven nests in one tree. At Eagle Pass, and as far east as the Nueces River, he found them not uncommon, but noticed none farther in the interior of Texas. Their usual note is a loud and not unmelodious whistle. They have also a very peculiar guttural note, which he compares to the sound caused by drawing a stick sharply across the quills of a dried goose-wing.

Captain McCown states that he observed these Blackbirds building in large communities at Fort Brown, Texas. Upon a tree standing near the centre of the parade-ground at that fort, a pair of the birds had built their nest. Just before the young were able to fly, one of them fell to the ground. A boy about ten years old discovered and seized the bird, which resisted stoutly, and uttered loud cries. These soon brought to its rescue a legion of old birds, which vigorously attacked the boy, till he was glad to drop the bird and take to flight. Captain McCown then went and picked up the young bird, when they turned their fury upon him, passing close to his head and uttering their sharp caw. He placed it upon a tree, and there left it, to the evident satisfaction of his assailants. These birds, he adds, have a peculiar cry, something like tearing the dry husk from an ear of corn. From this the soldiers called them corn-huskers. He often saw other and smaller birds building in the same tree. They were very familiar, and would frequently approach to within ten feet of a person.

The eggs measure 1.32 inches in length by .92 of an inch in breadth, and exhibit great variations both in ground-color and in the style and character of their marking. In some the ground-color is of a light grayish-white with a slight tinge of green or blue; in others it is of a light drab, and again many have a deep brownish-drab. The markings are principally of a dark brown, hardly distinguishable from black, distributed in the shape of drops, or broad irregular narrow plashes, or in waving zigzag lines and markings. Intermingled with these deeper and bolder markings are suffused cloud-like colorations of purplish-brown.

Family STURNIDÆ. — The Starlings.

Char. General characters of the Icteridæ, but with a rudimentary first primary, making the total number ten.

The introduction of this family into the present work is required by the occurrence of the typical species, *Sturnus vulgaris*, in Greenland, although it otherwise characterizes the Old World exclusively. There are several subfamilies, principally African and East Indian (*Lamprotornithinæ, Buphaginæ, Sturninæ,* and *Graculinæ*), some of them of very brilliant plumage.

The *Sturnidæ* in many respects constitute a natural stage of transition from the *Icteridæ* to the *Corvidæ*, through the Jays.

Genus STURNUS, Linnæus.

Sturnus, Linn. Syst. Nat., I, (ed. 10,) 1758, 167. (Type, *S. vulgaris.*)

Gen. Char. Bill long, conical, much depressed; the culmen, gonys, and commissure nearly straight, the latter angulated at base. Wings, twice length of tail; much pointed,

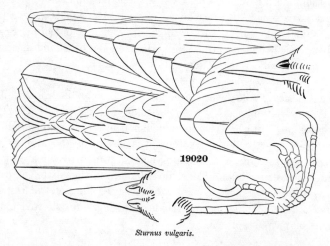

19020

Sturnus vulgaris.

the primaries graduating rapidly from the second, the first being rudimentary, the secondaries much shorter. Tail nearly even ; the feathers acuminate. Tarsi short; about equal to middle toe; lateral toes equal. Plumage coarse and stiff, each feather distinctly outlined.

The bill of *Sturnus* is very similar to that of *Sturnella*, although less inflected at the edges. The shorter tarsi, much longer wings, with the innermost secondaries much less than the primaries, etc., readily distinguish the two families.

Sturnus vulgaris, Linn.

THE STARLING.

Sturnus vulgaris, Linn. Syst. Nat. I, (ed. 10,) 1758, 167 ; (ed. 12,) 1766, 290. — Degland
& Gerbe, Orn. Europ. I, 1867, 232. — Reinhardt, Ibis, 1861, 7 (Greenland).

Sp. Char. Feathers principally lustrous-black, with purple and green reflections,
except at their extremities, which are dull and opaque ; brownish above, silvery-white
beneath. Bill yellow in spring, brown in autumn. Legs flesh-color. Length about
8.51 ; wing, 5.11 ; tail, 2.81 ; bill above, 1.11, from nostril, .75 ; gape, 1.15 ; tarsus, 1.15 ;
middle toe and claw, 1.15. *Female* similar, but less brilliant.

Hab. Europe and North Africa, most abundant in Holland. One specimen killed in
Greenland, in 1851, and preserved in the Royal Zoölogical Museum of Copenhagen.

The preceding description will serve to distinguish the Starling from any
North American species, although it is subject to considerable variation.
A second form, scarcely distinguishable as a species (*S. unicolor*, De la
Marmora), of a prevailing black color, without terminal spots, and with the
feathers of the under part elongated, is found in Sardinia and Sicily.

Habits. We give a place to the common Starling of Europe in the fauna
of North America, as an occasional and rare visitant of Greenland. Only a
single instance is on record of its actual capture, — a female taken by Holböll in 1851, and now in the Royal Museum of Copenhagen.

The well-known Starling of Europe is handsome in plumage and of graceful shape. It is numerous, as a species, is very generally distributed, and
therefore very well known. With many it is a great favorite, and is also
familiar as a caged bird. Its sprightly habits, retentive memory, and flexibility of voice, commend it as an interesting and entertaining pet. It has
been taught to whistle tunes, and even to imitate the human voice, with
facility and correctness. In its natural state it is a very social bird, and
lives in flocks the greater part of the year.

Mr. Waterton, who was a great admirer of the Starling, sought to induce
these birds to frequent his grounds, and with this view made various cavities in the walls of an old tower near his residence. His wishes were grati-
fied, and soon every cavity he had made was taken possession of by a pair,
and many more would have been thus domiciled had provision been made
for them.

A similar instance is on record in Hamburg, where, within a few years,
a well-known horticulturist induced nearly two hundred pairs of Starlings
to occupy and to breed in wooden boxes put up in his grounds for their
accommodation. His plants had been destroyed by the attacks of hosts of
subterranean larvæ, and the Starlings were invited in the hope that they
would remove this evil, which they did quite effectually.

Dr. Beverley Morris gives a very interesting account of a female Starling
that he observed building a nest in a hollow tree. The male looked on, but

took no part, except to drive away other intrusive birds. The female made on an average three trips a minute, with small twigs and bits of dry grass, taking sometimes three or four at a time. He estimated that in the space of six hours she had taken to her nest not less than a thousand sticks.

The Starling is said to select for its nest suitable places in church-steeples, the eaves of houses, and holes in walls, especially of old towers and ruins; occasionally it builds in hollow trees, in cliffs or in high rocks overhanging the sea, and also in dovecotes. The nests are made of slender twigs, straw, roots, and dry grasses. The birds incubate sixteen days. The old birds are devoted to their offspring.

Almost as soon as the nestlings are able to fly, different families unite to form large flocks, which may be seen feeding on commons and grass-grounds, in company with the Rooks and other birds. Their chief food consists of larvæ, worms, insects in various stages, and, at times, berries and grain. In confinement they are very fond of raw meat.

Mr. Yarrell, quoting Dr. Dean of Wells, gives an account of an extraordinary haunt of Starlings on an estate of a gentleman who had prepared the place for occupation by Pheasants. It was in a plantation of arbutus and laurustinus, covering some acres, to which these birds repaired, in the evening, almost by the million, coming from the low grounds about the Severn. A similar instance is given by Mr. Ball, of Dublin, of an immense swarm of several hundred thousand Starlings sleeping every night in a mass of thorn-trees at the upper end of the Zoölogical Garden in Phœnix Park.

The Starlings are found throughout Great Britain, even to the Hebrides and the Orkneys, where they are great favorites, and holes are left in the walls of the houses for their accommodation. They are common throughout Norway, Sweden, and the north of Europe, and as far east as the Himalayas and even Japan. They are also found in all the countries on both sides of the Mediterranean, and Mr. Gould states that they occur in Africa as far south as the Cape of Good Hope.

The eggs of the Starling are five in number, of a uniform delicate pale blue, oval in shape and rounded at one end; they measure 1.20 inches in length by .88 in breadth.

Family **CORVIDÆ**. — The Crows.

CHAR. Primaries ten; the first short, generally about half as long as the second (or a little more); the outer four sinuated on the inner edge. The nasal fossæ and nostrils usually more or less concealed by narrow, stiffened bristles (or bristly feathers), with short appressed lateral branches extending to the very tip, all directed forwards (these bristles occasionally wanting). Tarsi scutellate anteriorly, the sides undivided (except sometimes below), and separated from the anterior plates by a narrow naked strip, sometimes filled up with small scales. Basal joint of middle toe united about equally to the lateral, generally for about half the length. Bill generally notched.

The preceding characters distinguish the family of Crows quite markedly from all others. The features of the bristles on the bill, and the separation of the lateral and anterior scales by a narrow interval, are worthy of particular attention. The commissure is without the obtusely angular bend near the base, seen in the *Icteridæ*.

There are two sub-families of *Corvidæ* represented in America, one embracing the true Crows, the other the Jays. They pass very insensibly into each other, and it is difficult to mark the dividing line. We may, however, distinguish these, as found in the United States, by the following characters : —

Corvinæ. Bill as long as the head. Tail short, nearly even; wings long and pointed, longer than tail, and nearly reaching its tip; projecting beyond the under tail-coverts, which reach the middle of tail. Tip of wing formed by the third, fourth, and fifth quills, which are longest.

Garrulinæ. Bill usually shorter than head. Tail lengthened, rounded, and generally longer than the wings, which are short, rounded, and extend scarcely beyond the lower tail-coverts; these not reaching the middle of the tail. Tip of wing formed by the fourth, fifth, and sixth quills, which are longest.

The row of small scales is usually present on both sides of the tarsi in the *Corvinæ*, but in the Jays is generally restricted to the inner face.

Subfamily **CORVINÆ.**

CHAR. Wings long and pointed; longer than the tail, and, when closed, reaching nearly to its tip, extending far beyond the under tail-coverts; the third, fourth, and fifth quills forming the tip of the wing.

The following diagnosis may serve to distinguish the three genera of North American *Corvinæ* : —

A. (*Corveæ*). Bill compressed, much higher than broad; its tip compressed. Size large (i. e. over 15 inches long), color black, or mainly black.

Color black throughout; bill much compressed, the culmen much arched, and the gonys convex; nasal bristles strong . . . *Corvus*

B. (*Nucifrageæ.*) Bill cylindrical, scarcely or not at all higher than broad; its tip depressed. Size small (i. e. less than 15 inches long). Color uniform blue or with ashy on body, and black wings and tail.

Color ashy, with wings and tail mainly black. Culmen convex, gonys slightly concave. Nostrils covered by the short nasal tuft   . *Picicorvus.*

Color uniform blue, brighter on the head; the throat streaked with whitish. Culmen straight; gonys slightly convex. Nostrils completely exposed; no nasal tufts .   .   .   .   *Gymnokitta.*

Genus CORVUS, Linnæus.

Corvus, Linnæus, Syst. Nat. 1735. (Type, *Corvus corax*, L.)

Gen. Char. The nasal feathers lengthened, reaching to or beyond the middle of the bill. Nostrils large, circular, overhung behind by membrane, the edges rounded elsewhere. Rictus without bristles. Bill nearly as long as the tarsus, very stout; much

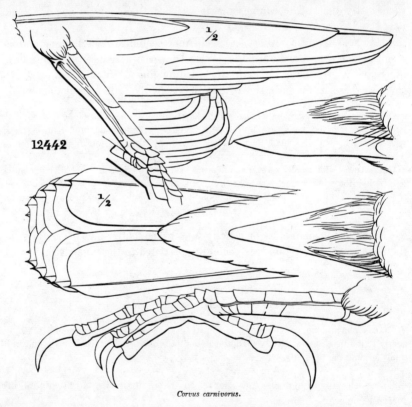

12442

Corvus carnivorus.

higher than broad at the base; culmen much arched. Wings reaching nearly or quite to the tip of the tail, the outer four primaries sinuated internally. Tarsi longer than the middle toe, with a series of small scales on the middle of each side separating the anterior scutellate portion from the posterior continuous plates. Sides of the head occasionally with nearly naked patches. Tail graduated or rounded.

Species and Varieties.

RAVENS. Feathers of the chin and throat stiffened, elongated, narrow and lanceolate, with their outlines very distinct.

    1. **C. corax** var. **carnivorus.** Length about 25.00; wing, 17.00; tail, 10.00; graduation of tail, 1.60 to 2.40. Feathers of the neck and breast light gray beneath surface. *Hab.* Whole of North America; Guatemala and Mexico. Rare in Eastern United States.

    2. **C. cryptoleucus.** Length about 21.00; wing, 14.00; tail, 8.50; graduation of tail, about 1.25. Feathers of neck and breast snowy-white beneath surface. *Hab.* Llano Estacado, or Staked Plain of Texas; Arizona; Colorado.

CROWS. Feathers of chin and throat soft, short, broad, obtuse, and with their webs blended.

    A. Angle of mouth feathered — North American Crows.

      a. Tarsus longer than the bill. First quill not longer than tenth.

      3. **C. americanus.** The gloss of the plumage purplish-violet, and hardly perceptible on head and neck, middle toe and claw rather shorter than tarsus, measured from beginning of scutellæ.

        Wing, 12.25; tail, 7.20; culmen, 1.85; tarsus, 2.00; middle toe, 1.45; wing-formula, 4, 3, 5, 6, 2; first quill equal to tenth. *Hab.* North America generally   var. *americanus.*[1]

        Wing, 12.50; tail, 7.20; culmen, 2.10; tarsus, 2.30; middle toe, 1.60. Wing-formula? (moulting). *Hab.* South Florida.

                                var. *floridanus.*

      4. **C. ossifragus.** The gloss of plumage violaceous-blue, almost green on the head, neck, and breast, where very perceptible. Middle toe and claw longer than tarsus, as above. Wing, 10.50; tail, 6.50; culmen, 1.55; tarsus, 1.65; middle toe, 1.35. Wing-formula, 4, 3, 5; first quill slightly shorter than tenth. *Hab.* Atlantic Coast of the United States.

      b. Tarsus shorter than the bill. First quill longer than tenth.

      5. **C. caurinus.** Gloss of the plumage as in *americanus,* but deeper. Wing, 10.50; tail, 6.40; culmen, 1.95; tarsus, 1.70; middle toe, 1.25. Wing-formula, 4, 3, 5. *Hab.* Northwestern coast of North America.

      6. **C. mexicanus.**[2] Plumage highly lustrous, blended. Soft burnished steel-blue, changing to violet on the crown, and with a greenish cast on lower parts. Wing, 9.00; tail, 6.50; culmen, 1.60; tarsus, 1.20; middle toe, 1.10. Wing-formula, 4, 3, 5. First quill very much longer than tenth. *Hab.* Western Mexico (Mazatlan, etc.).

    B. Angle of mouth naked — West Indian Crows.

      a. Tarsus much shorter than the bill.

---

[1] The measurements given are of a California specimen, in order the better to show the great distinction to be made between this species and *caurinus,* which is probably not found in California, being a more northern species, and having the coast of Washington Territory, or perhaps Oregon, as about its southern limit.

[2] *C. mexicanus,* GMEL. Syst. Nat. p. 375. This species is perfectly distinct from all the others. The plumage has a silky blended character, and very high lustre, almost exactly as in the larger Grakles (*Quiscalus major,* etc.).

7. **C. nasicus.**[1] Nostrils scarcely concealed by the short nasal bristles. Entirely violaceous-black, the feathers smoky-gray beneath the surface. Wing, 11.00; tail, 7.75; culmen, 2.45; depth of bill, .80; tarsus, 1.95; middle toe, 1.50; graduation of tail about 1.00; wing-formula, 4, 3, 5, 6, 2; first quill shortest. *Hab.* Cuba.

8. **C. leucognaphalus.**[2] Nostrils well concealed by the longer, but rather scant, nasal bristles. Entirely violaceous-black, the feathers of the neck all round, breast and sides, pure white below the surface. Wing, 12.50; tail, 9.00; culmen, 2.45; depth of bill, .95; tarsus, 2.15; middle toe, 1.50; graduation of tail about 1.25. Wing-formula, 4, 5, 3, 6, 2; first quill much the shortest. *Hab.* Porto Rico.

  b. Tarsus about equal to bill.

9. **C. jamaicensis.**[3] Nostrils just covered by the short but dense tuft of nasal bristles. Entirely dark sooty-plumbeous, inclining to black on the head, wings, and tail, where is a very faint violaceous gloss. Wing, 9.50; tail, 6.50; culmen, 2.00; depth of bill, 1.70; tarsus, 2.05; middle toe, 1.35; graduation of tail, about .60. Wing-formula, 5, 4, 3, 6, 2; first shortest. *Hab.* Jamaica.

Corvus corax, var. carnivorus, BARTRAM.

AMERICAN RAVEN.

Corvus carnivorus, BARTRAM, Travels in E. Florida, 1793, 290. — BAIRD, Birds N. Am. 1858, 560, pl. xxi. — COOPER & SUCKLEY, 210, pl. xxi. — COUES, P. A. N. S. 1866, 225. — LORD, Pr. R. A. Inst. IV, 1864, 121 (British Columbia). — DALL & BANNISTER, Tr. Ch. Ac. I, 1869, 285 (Alaska). — COOPER, Orn. Cal. I, 1870, 282. — SAMUELS, 355. *Corvus corax*, WILSON, Am. Orn. IX, 1825, 136, pl. lxxv. f. 3. — BONAP. Obs. Wils. 1825, No. 36. — IB. Syn. 1828, 56. — DOUGHTY, Cab. N. H. I, 1830, 270, pl. xxiv. — RICH. F. B. Am. II, 1831, 290. — NUTTALL, Man. I, 1832, 202. — AUD. Orn. Biog. II, 1834, 476, pl. ci. — IB. Syn. 1839, 150. — IB. Birds Am. IV. 1842, 78, pl. ccxxiv. — HEERM. X, *S*, 54. — FINSCH, Abh. Nat. III, 1872, 40 (Alaska). *Corvus cacalotl*, "WAGLER,"? BONAP. Pr. Zoöl. Soc. 1837, 115 (perhaps true *cacalotl*). — IB. List, 1838 (probably not of Wagler). — IB. Conspectus, 1850, 387. — MAXIMILIAN, Reise innere Nord Amer. II, 1841, 289 (does not consider it different from European). — NEWBERRY, P. R. R. Rep. VI, IV, 1857, 82. *Corvus lugubris*, AGASSIZ, Pr. Bost. Soc. N. H. II, Dec. 1846, 188. — IB. Caban. J. VI, 1858, 195. — BAIRD, Birds N. Am. 1858, 563, pl. xx. — KENNERLY, P. R. R. X, b. pl. xxii. *Corvus*, var. *littoralis* "HOLBÖLL, Kroger Tidsk. IV, 1843, 390." — SCHLEGEL, note on *Corvus*.

---

[1] *C. nasicus*, TEMM. Pl. Col. 413. — GUNDL. Rev. y Catal. de las Aves de Cuba, 1865, 290. *Corvus americanus*, LEMB. Aves de Cuba, 1830, 65. *Hab.* Cuba.

[2] *C. leucognaphalus*, DAUD. Tr. d'Orn. II, 231. — SALLÉ, P. Z. S. 1857, 232. — BRYANT, Pr. Bost. Soc. 1866, XI, 94. *Hab.* Porto Rico and Santo Domingo.

[3] *C. jamaicensis*, GM. S. N. I, 367. — GOSSE, B. Jam. 209. — SCL. Catal. Am. B. 1860, 146. BONAP. Consp. 385. — SALLÉ, P. Z. S. 1857, 232. — MARCH, P. A. N. S, 1863, 300. — BRYANT, Pr. Bost. Soc. 1866, XI, 94. *Hab.* Jamaica and Santo Domingo.

The *C. minutus* of Cuba we have not seen; it seems, however, to be rather nearly related to *C. ossifragus*, and possesses more lengthened nasal plumes than the three West Indian species diagnosed above. Its synonymy is as follows: —

　Corvus minutus, GUNDL. Cab. J. 1856, 20, p. 97. — IB. Rev. y Catal. de las Aves de Cuba. *Hab.* Cuba.

Sp. Char. Fourth quill longest; third and fifth about equal; second between fifth and sixth; first nearly equal to the eighth. Length, about 24.00 or 25.00; extent, 50.00 to 51.00; wing, about 17.00; tail, 10.00. Tail moderately graduated; the outer feather about 1.60 to 2.40 inches less than the middle. Entirely glossy black, with burnished violet reflections.

Hab. Entire continent of North America. Rare east of the Mississippi. South to Guatemala.

Though easily distinguishable from the European bird, the American Raven is so nearly related to it as to be beyond doubt referrible to it as a variety. The differences presented in a very large series of both forms are, however, very constant and tangible. In the American bird the bill is always longer and less deep, and the plumage is more highly burnished, while the wings, especially the secondaries, are perceptibly of a more reddish violet than the other portions. Though in an immense series of American specimens many differences of form and size are noted, yet there is nothing sufficiently characteristic of any particular region to indicate more than one variety.

As a rule, however, specimens from the high north exceed in size those from elsewhere, and have the bill more robust, though not so short as in the European bird; while those from the Middle Province and Mexico to Guatemala (= " *cacalotl*," Baird et Auct.) have the plumage more brilliant than others, and frequently the bill very narrow.

Corvus carnivorus.

Habits. Assuming that we must consider as but one species the two differing forms of Raven found in North America, we find this bird more or less common throughout nearly the whole continent. It is much more abundant in some regions than in others, and, as a general rule, is much more common and also more generally distributed in the western portion, where also its habits are remarkably different from the manners of its eastern representative.

It seems to be more or less common throughout the Arctic regions. Mr. Kennicott met with Ravens at Lake Winnipeg. Mr. MacFarlane found them abundant at Lockhart River, at Fort Anderson, and on the Lower Anderson River. Mr. Ross obtained them at Fort Simpson, Mr. Reid at

Big Island, Mr. Clarke at Fort Rae, Mr. Lockhart at Fort Resolution, and Mr. Dall at Nulato, in Alaska.

Richardson speaks of it as abounding in the fur countries, where it frequents the barren grounds even in the intense winter cold, and where its movements are regulated by those of reindeer, musk-oxen, and other animals, which it follows, to assist in devouring whatever may be killed. Ravens are seen to collect from various quarters wherever any animal is slain, in order to feast on the offal, and considerable numbers are in constant attendance upon the several fishing-stations. He mentions a singular instance of the disposition of this bird to appropriate glittering objects of no value to it for food or anything else. A Raven was seen flying off with something in its claws, pursued by a number of its clamorous companions. Having been fired at, it dropped the object of contention, which proved to be the lock of a chest.

Mr. MacFarlane's notes in regard to the nesting of these birds describe certain variations as to position, etc. One nest was on a ledge of a cliff of shale, and was composed of dry willow sticks, lined with pieces of rabbit skin and the hair of moose. Both parents were seen,— one on the nest, the other on a tree, — but both flew away on being approached. A second nest was in the top crotch of a tall pine on the river-bank. It was made of dry sticks, and thickly lined with reindeer hair. There were eight eggs in this nest. A third was in a tall pine, and was forty-five feet from the ground. It was constructed in a manner precisely similar to the preceding. A fourth was on the top of a tall pine, and only differed in having been lined with dry grass, moss, and a few reindeer hairs. The other nests appear to have been similarly situated and constructed. Nearly all were in high trees, built of dry sticks, and lined with dry grasses, mosses, and the hair of various quadrupeds. The maximum number of eggs was eight, their average six.

Mr. MacFarlane states that the Raven is found throughout the winter in the Arctic regions, and that, though he has met with it north of latitude 69°, he has never known it to breed north of that line. He informs us that it is seldom that more than a single pair is to be seen at a time, and occasionally they may be noted singly, flying alone, or feeding on garbage. Sometimes a dead fox or wolf will attract quite a number to the spot. On one occasion he observed as many as twenty Ravens amicably associated together around the carcasses of two wolves that had been poisoned with strychnine. In many cases he has known the partaking of a poisoned animal prove fatal to them, as also the eating of bait laid for foxes and wolves.

According to this same correspondent, one of these birds became almost domesticated at Fort Anderson, during February and March, 1865. At first it fed about the fort with a companion ; soon after, coming alone, it grew bolder and bolder, alighted within the square, allowed itself to be closely approached, where the young dogs soon became familiar with it, and would even frolic and gambol with it, the Raven joining heartily in the sport in its own way.

It was never known to attempt to injure even the smallest of the young dogs, nor did any of the dogs ever offer to annoy it. It at length came to be considered by all as an inmate of the establishment. While it seemed to have full confidence in the people of the fort, it kept at a careful distance from all Indian or Esquimaux visitors.

Mr. B. R. Ross speaks of Ravens as common as far north as the Arctic Ocean. They feed on carrion, and act as scavengers to the establishments. Their sight is remarkably keen, and the sagacity with which they follow the trapper is wonderful. Early as the hunter may start, these harpies will have been before him, and torn out the eyes and entrails of each hare. They will break into marten-traps for the sake of the bait or the captured animal, thrusting aside or pulling out with their beaks the sticks that compose the enclosure. Sometimes they are caught in steel traps that are set for foxes, or eat the strychnine baits laid for the same animals, and slowly succumb to this powerful poison. Their flesh is so rank that even a fox, unless sorely pressed by hunger, will not eat it. They pair in April, and usually construct their nests in the loftiest trees. They have various call-notes, one of which is like that of the Canada Goose, and another is said by Mr. Ross to be very liquid and musical.

Mr. Dall states that these birds were abundant all the year at Nulato, and indeed everywhere throughout Alaska, but much more common near the Indian villages and trading-posts than elsewhere. They build on the sandstone cliffs at Nulato, in cavities that have been occupied for years. They lay about the 20th of April, and the young are hatched before open water. He also speaks of them as very intelligent, and states that on several expeditions made to obtain their eggs, the instant he stopped at the foot of the bluff the whole colony would arrange themselves on the edge of the rock in anxious consultation, uttering repeated cries of warning. On one occasion, where the nest was inaccessible and the party went back unsuccessful, their departure was announced by significant and joyous croaks and derisive screeches. Ravens were also found by Mr. Bannister common all the year on the small islands lying off the northeast point of St. Michaels.

In the Eastern States the Raven is a comparatively rare bird, except in a few special localities. These are usually mountain-ranges, high precipitous banks of rivers and lakes and of the ocean, and among wild and lonely islands. It occurs on the Labrador coast, at Grand Menan in the Bay of Fundy, the Adirondacks, Lake George, the Hudson River, etc. Mr. Lawrence speaks of it as quite common on the coast of New Jersey. It is found among the mountains of Buncombe and other counties in North Carolina, and Mr. Audubon mentions its occurrence at Table Mountain, in the district of Pendleton, South Carolina. Dr. Coues found Ravens not rare at Labrador, where the almost inaccessible cliffs afford them safe and convenient retreats. They were so excessively wary that it was found impossible to shoot them. They descended in pairs to the sea-shore to feed on dead fish, crabs, and other animal substances thrown up by the sea.

Mr. Ridgway informs me of the presence of this bird in the heavy forests of the bottom-lands in Southern Illinois. It is there quite rare, however, as he has met with but a few pairs. These were resident, and nested in the tall timber of the Big Creek bottoms, in Richland Co.

Audubon's party found it equally impossible to obtain a specimen at Labrador. One afternoon Mr. Audubon hid himself under a nest several hours, to no purpose. The old Ravens would not show themselves while he was within gunshot, though the young clamored for food. As soon as he had left the spot the female alighted on the nest, fed her young, and was off again before she could be approached.

At Grand Menan, where they are not rare, and where they breed among the high cliffs, I found them so wild that it was almost impossible even to obtain sight of them. Passing high in the air above our heads, their loud, hoarse croak attested their alarm at the sight of their enemy, man. They are looked upon with aversion by the islanders, and are persecuted by them without mercy. They rob the nests of the Herring Gulls, interfering with the islanders in this privilege, and are, wrongfully I believe, charged with destroying young lambs.

Years afterwards, when I again encountered individuals of this species at Cheyenne, on the Plains, I could not but notice the immense difference in their character. There perfect confidence in man took the place of dread. Unmolested by the people, who regard them as desirable scavengers, valueless for food and useful in removing nuisances, they were as tame and familiar as the European Sparrow in the parks of New York or Boston. On one occasion I found one engaged in eating the remains of a dead cow just outside the city. It allowed me to approach to within five or six feet, when with a very stately and dignified stride it moved out of my way, and kept me at about this distance. I could not compel it to fly to any distance, even when I hastened my steps.

In New England these birds are very rare, and their occurrence is only accidental. One has been shot on the Connecticut, and another on the Merrimack, in Massachusetts. They are not unfrequently met with in Northern New York.

On the Pacific Coast the Raven is common from Sitka to San Diego. Throughout Washington Territory it is said to be plentiful, more scattered in the summer, and in the winter congregating about settlements and the sea-shore. At Vancouver, during the winter, it was observed amicably associating with the Crows, and on the coast with the Fish Crows, but during the spring, when the latter had nests, they boldly attacked the Ravens, and drove them away.

In California and in all the adjacent regions, Dr. Cooper states, the Raven is found everywhere in pairs, more numerous than in the Atlantic States, and abundant even in the most barren desert districts. It follows trains and herds of cattle, and keeps on the lookout for anything befalling them. It is omnivorous, eating snakes, lizards, eggs, carrion, and even grain, though the last very rarely. It is accused of destroying young chickens and lambs.

In Arizona Dr. Coues speaks of it as resident, and very abundant about the cattle enclosures, where it congregates in immense numbers during the autumn and winter. During the severe winter of 1864 – 65 great numbers perished of cold and hunger at Fort Whipple. Dr. Coues has favored us with the following interesting sketch of the habits of this bird as observed by him in that Territory.

" The geographical distribution of the Raven seems to be in great measure complementary to that of the Crow. On the prairies, in the desert, among the mountains, of the Western States and Territories, where the Ravens and their congenial companions, the coyotes, abound, the Crows are rare or wanting altogether. In travelling westward, I saw no Crows after leaving the settlements this side of the Plains, while the Ravens were conspicuous, until in some parts of Southern California Crows reappeared, but no Ravens amongst them. I saw a fair number of Ravens along the Arkansas River, and they were frequent in the valley of the Rio Grande; after crossing the river, while traversing the wild region thence to the Colorado, they were our inseparable companions; hundreds, if not thousands, of them lived about Fort Whipple all the year, seemingly attracted from miles around by probabilities of finding abundant food. Throughout the Western wilds they hang on the footsteps of man, needy adventurers, claiming their share of his spoils, disputing with the wolves and vultures for the refuse of his camp, and polishing the skeletons of the buffalo, with which he sometimes strews the plain. The more desolate the land, the closer the Raven follows in the trail of the emigrant, till its dismal croaking sounds ominous of hardship, and its plumage seems to foreshadow days as dark.

" One accustomed to the shrewdness and prudence of Crows in populous districts is at first surprised at an apparent familiarity the Raven often shows in the West. There no one would think of wasting ammunition on the worthless bird, and it comes to look upon man more as its provider than as an enemy. Nevertheless, like the rest of its tribe, the Raven is a sagacious bird, not likely to be twice deceived, and very ready to take a hint; he always has his wits about him, and keeps a bright lookout when anything stranger than a coyote is near. This wariness is something altogether different from the childlike timidity of little birds like Sparrows, that scurry away in terror from any unusual sight or sound, and unquestionably implies keen powers of observation coupled with no small degree of reasoning faculty. Almost every day during the winter of 1864 – 65 I must have passed within a few paces of Ravens stalking about the fort; and yet, when I wanted a specimen, it was not an easy matter to secure one. The birds assuredly knew the difference between a person going quietly about his business and one "on mischief bent," and their intelligent watchfulness rendered it quite impossible to approach them openly with gun in hand.

"Ravens are resident in the region about Fort Whipple, and their apparently diminished number in summer is simply due to the fact that they are then spread over a greater surface, are less restless, and better provided for in the matter of food. In winter, and especially when snow covered the ground, their numbers at the fort were simply incalculable. They dotted the ground everywhere during the day, and roosted in crowds on the neighboring pines by night. One patriarchal tree, that stood somewhat isolated, was a favorite resting-place for the Ravens and Buzzards, and gradually assumed a singular appearance, as if it had been whitewashed. This great pine overlooked a little open space where our beeves were slaughtered, and the banqueting there was never ended. All night long the wolves howled and barked as they tugged at the offal, till daylight sent them reluctant to their rocky fastnesses, when the great dark birds, with a premonitory stretching of the wings, flapped down to renew the feast. The Ravens and Buzzards seemed to get along very well together, quarrelling no more with each other than each species did with its own kind ; but in the occasional disputes the smaller birds seemed to have rather the advantage of the heavier and clumsier gluttons. This comparative good-fellowship was in striking contrast to the behavior of Crows towards Turkey Buzzards.

"The Raven is not, on the whole, so noisy a bird as the Crow, though he croaks vigorously on occasion, and his caw may claim to be impressive, if not agreeable. But the queer sounds that the bird can utter, if he be so minded, are indescribable ; even his ordinary cawing is susceptible of considerable modulation. A favorite amusement of his, when, his hunger appeased for the time, he feels particularly comfortable, is to settle snugly on the top of a pine-tree, and talk to himself. The performance generally begins with a loud caw, self-asserting, followed by a complacent chuckle ; and then comes a series of comical syllables, so low as to be scarcely audible from the ground below, as if he were musing aloud, and tickled with his own fancies. Then he will raise his voice again, and file away at some old saw for a while, finishing with the inimitable 'cork-drawing' for which his tribe is famous.

"A Raven that I had slightly wounded in the wing and captured soon became quite tame, and developed a variety of amusing traits. Proving rather obtrusive and inconvenient in my narrow quarters, I undertook to tie him in a corner with a string round his leg. This he objected to, and it was astonishing to see the perseverance he showed in untying any number of knots I might make. It was a task that sometimes took him hours, but he never rested until it was done. I had no chain light enough for the purpose, but I finally got the better of him by twisting a wire with the cord. His intelligence did not reach in that direction more than six inches from his leg."

Mr. Dresser observed the Raven common at San Antonio, frequenting the slaughter-houses. In November, in the Baudera Hills, several came to his camp to feast on the offal of deer. Dr. Woodhouse also found them very abundant in Texas, the Indian Territory, and New Mexico, and especially so on the buffalo plains. In the Mexican Boundary Survey, Dr. Kennerly observed these birds everywhere in Northern Mexico, flocks of them following the train from point to point. They were not at all shy, but often came into camp in search of food.

Captain Blakiston, having enjoyed unusual opportunities for observing the habits of the American Raven during his residence in high northern regions, characterizes the species as anything but solitary. During the day they are usually met with in pairs, except when drawn together in large numbers around the carcass of a dead animal. At night, during the winter, they repair to some chosen resting-place, usually a clump of trees on the edge of a prairie, and there roost in one immense body. One of these roosting-places was about a mile from Fort Carlton, and Captain Blakiston's attention was first drawn to it by noticing that about sunset all the Ravens, from all quarters, were flying towards this point. Returning to the fort in the evening by that quarter, he found a clump of aspen-trees, none of them more than twenty-five feet high, filled with Ravens, who, at his approach, took wing and flew round and round. He also noted the wonderful regularity with which they repaired to their roosting-place in the evening and left it again in the morning, by pairs, on their day's hunt. They always left in the morning, within a minute or two of the same time, earlier and earlier as the days grew longer, on cold or cloudy mornings a little later, usually just half an hour before sunrise. In April they all paired off, and their roosting-place became deserted. During an excursion about one hundred and fifty miles southwest of Fort Carlton, Captain Blakiston found several nests of Ravens with eggs, one of which was in a small tree near a lake, and was not more than fifteen feet above it. It contained six eggs, was about a foot in diameter, composed of sticks, and was lined with buffalo-hair and pieces of scarlet cloth, evidently picked up about an Indian camping-ground.

Dr. Heermann states that while in California he always found the nests of the Raven placed high on bold precipitous cliffs, secure against danger; in the vast desolate plains of New Mexico he saw these birds building on low trees, and even on cactus-plants, less than three feet from the ground, showing how much circumstances and localities affect the habits of birds regarding incubation.

A Raven, probably this species, is abundant on the plateau of Mexico. The Cerro Colorado, near Tehuacan, is the rendezvous of a large number of these birds, where, according to Sumichrast, at the time of the flowering of the *maguey*, they gather in great abundance, to feed on the blossoms of this plant, which are their favorite food.

Mr. Boardman writes me that he has several times collected Ravens' eggs at Grand Menan, but always found the nest a hard one to take, as they usually build it under some high cliff. They make a very large and bulky nest, and, where not disturbed, use it several years in succession. They also breed very early. He once took a nest with eight eggs on the 10th of April, when the snow all around was quite deep. This was sent to the Smithsonian Institution. Its contents nearly filled a bushel basket. He does not regard the Ravens as migratory. Though they are apparently more numerous in winter than in summer, this is probably because they forsake the woods and come about the open fields and the banks of rivers for dead fish, and thus are more noticed. They are very shy, sagacious, and vigilant, so much so that it is almost impossible for one to get a shot at them. Crows avoid them, and the two are never seen together. The farmers of Grand Menan accuse them of pecking the eyes out of young lambs, and always try to destroy them, and they grow less and less numerous every year. The Ravens, he adds, appear to be on good terms with the Duck Hawks, as he has known a nest of the former within a few rods of one of the latter.

An egg of this species, from Anderson River, measures 1.96 inches in length by 1.32 in breadth. Two from Grand Menan measure, one 2.05 inches by 1.30, the other 1.95 by 1.25. The ground-color of two of these is a soiled sea-green, that of the third is a light bluish-green. This is more sparingly marked with dots, blotches, and cloudings of faint purple and purplish-brown, chiefly at the larger end. The others are marked over the entire egg with blotches of varying size and depth of coloring, of a deep purple-brown ; some of the markings are not readily distinguishable from black.

Corvus cryptoleucus, Couch.

WHITE-NECKED CROW.

Corvus cryptoleucus, Couch, Pr. A. N. Sc. VII, April, 1854, 66 (Tamaulipas, Mexico). — BAIRD, Birds N. Am. 1858, 565, pl. xxii. — COOPER, Orn. Cal. I, 1870, 284.

SP. CHAR. The fourth quill is longest; the third and fifth equal; the second longer than the sixth; the first about equal to the seventh. Glossy black, with violet reflections; feathers of neck all round, back, and breast, snow-white at the base. Length, about 21.00; wing, 14.00; tail, 8.50. Feathers of throat lanceolate; bristly feathers along the base of the bill covering it for nearly two thirds its length.

HAB. Valley of Rio Grande and Gila. Abundant on the Llano Estacado, and at Eagle Pass, Texas (DRESSER, Ibis, 1865, 494). Colorado (AIKEN).

In the white bases to the feathers of the neck, etc., there is a resemblance in this species to the *C. leucognaphalus* of Porto Rico ; but the latter has entirely different proportions, blended instead of lanceolate feathers on the throat, exceedingly short instead of unusually long nasal plumes, and many other differences, and is in every feature totally distinct.

HABITS. Of the distinctive habits or the extent of the distribution of the

White-necked Raven we have very little knowledge. It was first described by Lieutenant Couch, in 1854, from specimens obtained by him at Charco Escondido, Mexico, in May, 1853. Other specimens were afterwards procured by Dr. Kennerly, at Janos, Mexico, in 1855, and by Mr. Dresser at Eagle Pass, Texas, in March, 1864. The latter gives no notes as to its habits.

Dr. Kennerly's note in regard to it is that it was not very common, and when seen was generally associated with the larger species of Raven. Lieutenant Couch merely mentions it as found in small numbers in Eastern Tamaulipas, generally near ranches.

Mr. J. H. Clark writes that this species does not seem to possess the cunning or wariness of its congeners. It was met with, in the greatest abundance, about watering-places. It was not found habitually in great flocks, though at the head of the Limpia many were congregated and flying about the face of an immense rocky mountain wall, where they were probably nesting. Their note he describes as coarse, and less shrill than that of the common Crow. He met with the supposed nest in an arborescent cactus.

Dr. Coues does not appear to have met with this species in Arizona, but Lieutenant Bendire writes to Professor Baird from Tucson, April 12, 1872, that it is the most common Crow or Raven there. This he discovered accidentally, finding that three fourths of the Ravens he shot proved to be of this species; the others were the Colorado race of the Raven. Specimens of this Crow were obtained at Fort Buchanan by Dr. Irwin, at Pecos River by Dr. Anderson, and in the Indian Territory by Mr. McCarthy.

An egg of this species, from Trout Creek, Texas, obtained June 20 by Charles S. McCarthy, measures 1.75 inches in length by 1.25 in breadth. The ground-color is a light grayish-green, and is pretty uniformly marked with fine dottings of mingled purple and brown.

Corvus americanus, Aud.

COMMON CROW.

Corvus corone, WILSON, Am. Orn. IV, 1811, 79, pl. xxv, f. 3. — BON. Obs. Wils. 1824, No. 37. — IB. Syn. 1828, 56. — RICH. F. B. Am. II, 1831, 291. — NUTTALL, Man. I, 1832, 209 (not *Corvus corone* of LINN.). *Corvus americanus,* AUD. Orn. Biog. II, 1834, 317 ; V, 477, pl. clvi. — IB. Syn. 1839, 150. — IB. Birds Am. IV, 1842, 87, pl. ccxxv. — BON. List, 1838. — IB. Consp. 1850, 385. — NUTTALL, Man. I, (2d ed.,) 1840, 221. — MAXIM. Reise, I, 1839, 140. — NEWBERRY, Zoöl. Cal. & Or. Route, P. R. R. Rep. VI, IV, 1857, 82. — BAIRD, Birds N. Am. 1858, 566, pl. xxiii. — MAX. Caban. J. VI, 1858, 198. — SCHLEGEL, Notice sur les Corbeaux, 10, pl. i, f. 16. — COUES, P. A. N. S. 1861, 226. — SAMUELS, 357. — ALLEN, B. E. Fla. 297 (in part).

SP. CHAR. Fourth quill longest; second shorter than sixth; first shorter than ninth. Glossy black with violet reflections, even on the belly. Length, 19.00 to 20.00 ; wing, 13.00 to 13.50 ; tail about 8.00. Tarsus longer than the middle toe and claw.

HAB. United States, from Atlantic to Pacific; rare in the Middle Province and on Missouri Plains, and on northwest coast. N. E. Texas (DRESSER, Ibis, 1865, 494). North to Great Slave Lake, Fort Rae, and Nelson River, H. B. T.

The *C. americanus* has no analogue in Europe, though the *C. corone* somewhat resembles it. The most important feature of distinction appears to lie in the structure of the feathers of the head and neck, which in *C. corone* are narrow, with the tips distinct, while in the American bird these tips are blended together and do not maintain their individuality. The feathers on the fore-neck in *corone* are also lanceolate and distinct, showing the outline of each one as in the Raven, while in the American Crow they are three times as broad, rounded, and entirely blended. Mr. Audubon further remarks that the neck of the European bird is glossed with green and blue, while that of the American has a decided purplish-brown tinge.

Prince Maximilian states, in addition, that the note differs in the two species.

HABITS. The Common Crow of North America is found in great abundance in all the Eastern States, from Texas to Florida, and from the Missouri to Nova Scotia. A few are found beyond the Great Plains, and they also extend their migrations, in summer, into high Arctic regions. Richardson found them as far north as the 55th parallel, but was in error when he stated that beyond this they do not go. He adds that none approach within five or six hundred miles of Hudson's Bay. They were observed at Cross Lake and at Lake Winnepeg by Mr. Kennicott, at Big Island by Mr. Reid, at Fort Rae by Mr. Clarke, and at Fort Anderson and on the Lower Anderson River by Mr. MacFarlane, who also found them breeding even at this high latitude. They were not seen in Russian America, and Dr. Cooper thinks that the species does not occur in California, or, if at all, only rarely, but that it is there replaced by *C. caurinus*.

Mr. Ridgway found the Crow of very rare occurrence in the interior. A very few were seen in the Truckee meadows, in November, and others at the Humboldt marshes, in October. These western birds were exceedingly unsuspicious and familiar, so much so that those seen in the Humboldt marshes were walking about with all the familiarity of domestic pigeons, only hopping aside as they were approached. None were seen either in spring or summer.

In Western Iowa Mr. Allen states that he saw but very few of this species, and even in Northern Illinois it was not very common. At the West this bird is reported to be held in better estimation than at the East, by the farmers. It is not known to pull corn, and seems to be entirely unsuspicious. It is regarded generally as a benefactor, and not only deserves, but receives, good treatment. In Indiana he found it more common.

Dr. Coues met with a single individual on the Labrador coast. In Nova Scotia it is much more abundant, and there, as on the Western prairies, being unmolested by the inhabitants, it is exceedingly unsuspicious, and will permit a very near approach before it will fly, and even then will not move to a distance. In all of the United States east of the Mississippi it is very abundant. In Texas, between San Antonio and the Mexican frontier, it is not common ; but Mr. Dresser found it very common in the northeast part of the State during the whole year.

Probably no one of our birds, so wholly worthless for food, has been more hunted and destroyed than this species. In certain parts of the country it is held in great aversion by the farmers, and in some States bounty-laws have been enacted by legislatures to promote its destruction. Had not these birds been possessed of an extraordinary intelligence, they must long since have been exterminated or driven from a large part of the country. In some sections their numbers have been of late much diminished by the use of strychnine. During the month of May the Crow is very destructive in the cornfield, pulling up the grains as soon as they begin to vegetate, and compelling the farmer to replant perhaps several times. Wilson remarks that in the State of Delaware these birds collect in immense flocks and commit great devastation upon crops of standing corn. They also occasionally commit depredations in the barnyard, robbing hens'-nests of their eggs, and even destroying young chickens. They also destroy the eggs and young of other birds. The mischief they thus do is doubtless very great, and the ground for the prevalent prejudice against them is quite apparent. Yet it is equally demonstrable that this bird is surpassed, and probably is equalled, by no other in the vast amount of the benefits conferred upon agriculturalists. The evil it perpetrates is very limited, and is confined to but a short period, but during all the time it is resident the Crow is constantly engaged in the destruction of injurious insects and rodent quadrupeds. In the early spring it feeds almost wholly upon the most destructive grubs, and in extensive districts of Massachusetts, where these birds have been largely destroyed, the ravages of the May-bugs and the grasshoppers in pasturelands have been a natural consequence of so short-sighted a policy.

The persecutions to which the Crow is subjected have developed in them a wariness and a distrust that is foreign to their nature. They can only live by keeping on a constant lookout for dangers, and by learning to distinguish the weapons that threaten their destruction. As soon as anything is seen that causes alarm, the signal is at once given, and the warning passed from one to another.

In New Jersey and in Pennsylvania, during the winter months, the Crows assemble in immense flocks, and their movements appear to be regulated by the guidance of a few chosen leaders. I received from the lips of the late John Cassin, an ornithologist hardly less remarkable for his outdoor observations than for his researches in the closet, only a few days before his death, a very surprising account of the movements of a large army of Crows, witnessed by himself, in the spring of 1868.

On a Sunday morning in April, when Philadelphia was enveloped in a fog so dense and impenetrable that it was hardly possible to distinguish objects across its streets, Mr. Cassin's attention was called to an immense accumulation of these birds in Independence Square. The whole park he found, to his utter astonishment, occupied by an immense army of Crows. They filled all the trees, bending down the overloaded branches, and swarmed over and covered the ground. The entire space seemed alive with Crows. They had evidently become bewildered in the fog, and had strangely taken refuge in this small park in the very heart of Philadelphia. As if aware of their close proximity to danger, the whole assembly was quiet, orderly, and silent. A few birds, evidently acting as leaders, moved noiselessly back and forth through their ranks, as if giving tacit signals. These movements were followed by the departure of a few scouts, as if sent to make explorations, but they soon returned unsuccessful. Again were repeated the uneasy movements of their leaders, passing slowly and cautiously through their close ranks. After an apparently much longer consultation, another small party ascended to explore, wheeling round and round in wider and wider zones. At length, satisfied with their observations, they quietly returned, and made their report in a manner evidently understood, though not audibly expressed; for immediately the leaders passed again among the crowd, and, as if signals were given for a general movement, the whole of this immense congregation, numbering, Mr. Cassin estimated, hundreds of thousands, rose slowly and silently, preceded by their scouts, and, moving off in a westerly direction, were soon lost to view.

When taken young, the Crow can be easily domesticated, and becomes a very entertaining, but a very mischievous pet. It is very secretive, hiding objects of no value to itself, and seems to delight in mischief. It displays often a wonderful intelligence, appears to understand and to obey certain directions, and manifests also remarkable quickness of vision. A tame Crow belonging to a family resident near Boston, and permitted to go at large, manifested all the attachment of a dog. It especially enjoyed the society of the children, and played with them in their games of hide and seek, surpassing them by its readiness in finding the secreted object. It was especially attached to the mistress of the house, flying to her whenever she approached, hovering over her head, and alighting on her shoulder.

In a few instances the Crow has been taught to imitate articulate sounds. In one of these, in Grafton, Mass., the Crow not only vociferated a single monosyllable repeatedly, but at other times enunciated a short sentence of five syllables.

A few are resident in Massachusetts during the year, but the greater portion move south in November and return in March. Those who remain during the winter are chiefly resident near the sea-shore. The Crow breeds from April to June, varying with the latitude of its residence. In Massachusetts it has full-grown young by June 1. It builds, usually in March, a large rudely constructed nest of sticks, moss, and bark, lined with finer mosses, and sometimes with hair. The parent birds are very watchful and vigilant if their nest is in danger, and often expose their lives in their anxiety for their young. The male bird is attentive to his mate during incubation, and assists in feeding the young. The young are fed chiefly on insects, frogs, mice, and similar food.

The eggs of the Crow vary from 1.60 to 1.55 inches in length, and from 1.20 to 1.10 in breadth. In their markings they exhibit surprising variations. They usually have a ground of a light sea-green, over which are scattered, more or less thickly, blotches, some of them quite large, of a dark-brown, almost black, with purplish reflections. These are chiefly about the larger end. Another quite common variety is of a deeper ground of green, very uniformly and thickly sprinkled with fine dottings of a sepia-brown. Others have a ground nearly white, slightly tinged with green, more sparingly spotted with small blotches of light purplish-brown. A nest found near Springfield contained eggs having the ground-color on one side a pinkish-gray, the rest being greenish-white, all spotted with brown. Another set of eggs from Hudson, Mass., were of a light bluish-green, entirely unspotted, resembling large Robin's eggs; and Dr. Wood mentions another four, the ground of which was flesh-color, and the spots red.

Corvus americanus, var. floridanus, BAIRD.

FLORIDA CROW.

Corvus americanus, var. *floridanus*, BAIRD, Birds N. Am. 568, pl. lxvii, f. 1. *C. americanus*, ALLEN, B. E. Fla. 297.

Sp. Char. About the size of *C. americanus*, but bill and feet larger. Tail less rounded. Third, fourth, and fifth quills nearly equal; third rather longer than fifth. Color less violet above. Length, 19.50; wing, 12.00; tail, 7.70; tarsus, 2.60.

Hab. Southern peninsula of Florida.

This resident Crow of Florida differs in some marked features from that of the more northern localities in several characters. Although perhaps rather smaller, the bill and feet, especially the latter, are very considerably larger. The nasal feathers extend over the basal two fifths of the bill, instead of the half. The proportions of the bill are about the same; in the Florida bird it is rather the longer. The greatest difference is in the feet. The tarsal joint of the tibia is bare, the feathers scarcely coming below it, even anteriorly, instead of projecting some distance. The tarsus is almost a quarter of an inch longer, covered anteriorly by nine scutellæ, instead of eight. The outer lateral toe is shorter, not reaching the base of the middle claw. The middle toe and claw are considerably shorter than the tarsus; the middle claw is shorter than in the northern bird.

The wing-formula differs somewhat; the third, fourth, and fifth quills are nearly equal, the third even longer than the fifth, instead of shorter. The tail is short and very nearly even, the difference in length of feathers being less than half an inch, instead of an inch. This, however, may in part be owing to the absence of the middle pair.

The colors differ somewhat from those of the common Crow. There is less violet, and the feathers of the back have almost a brassy gloss on their margins, as in *Crotophaga*.

The specimen upon which these remarks are based, though apparently perfectly mature, is changing some of its feathers, such as the inner primaries, the middle tail-feathers, and the greater coverts. The long primaries and ten tail-feathers, however, are of full length. It is possible that the bird is really as large as the northern Crow, although this is hardly probable. It was killed on the mainland of the extreme southern portion of Florida, not far from Fort Dallas.

No comparison of this bird is required with the Fish Crow, which has the middle toe and claw longer than the tarsus, not shorter, and the proportions much less.

HABITS. The common resident Crow of Florida exhibits so many peculiarities differing from the northern species, that Professor Baird, in his Birds of America, deemed it worthy of mention at least as a race, if not a distinct species. We have no account of its habits, and do not know if, in any respects, they differ from those of the common Crow. Dr. J. C. Cooper, in his brief manuscript notes on the birds of Florida, made in the spring of 1859, speaks of the Florida Crow as very common, as being quite maritime in its habits, and as having full-fledged young on the 20th of April. Three eggs of this race, obtained in Florida in the spring of 1871, by Mr. Maynard, differ not more from those of the Crow than do those of the latter occasionally from one another. They measure 1.73 by 1.20 inches ; 1.70 by 1.20 ; and 1.54 by 1.25. Their ground-color is a bright bluish-green, and they are all more or less marked, over the entire egg, with blotches of a mingled bronze and brown with violet shadings. The latter tints are more marked in one egg than in the others, and in this the spots are fewer and more at one end, the larger end being nearly free from markings. Their average capacity, as compared with the average of the *C. americanus*, is as 5.1 to 4.2.

Corvus caurinus, BAIRD.

NORTHWESTERN FISH CROW.

Corvus caurinus, BAIRD, Birds N. Am. 1858, 569, pl. xxiv. — COOPER & SUCKLEY, 211, pl. xxiv. — DALL & BANNISTER, Tr. Chic. Ac. I, 1869, 286 (Alaska). — FINSCH, Abh. Nat. III, 1872, 41 (Alaska). — COOPER, Orn. Cal. I, 1870, 285.

SP. CHAR. Fourth quill longest; fifth and third about equal; second longer than sixth; first shorter than ninth. Color black, glossed with purple. Tail nearly even. Tarsus longer than middle toe and claw. Length about 16.50; wing about 11.00; tail about 7.00.

HAB. Northwestern coast, from Columbia River to Sitka.

This species is readily distinguished from the eastern Fish Crow by the larger size ; the absence of green gloss on the belly ; the tarsi longer than the middle toe and claw, instead of shorter ; and the second quill being generally shorter than the sixth instead of longer, and considerably shorter than the culmen, instead of longer.

It is rather to be compared with *C. americanus*, with which it agrees in colors, but from which it differs, essentially, in having the wing and tail very much shorter, while the bill is considerably longer, and in having the tarsus shorter than the culmen, instead of longer, as in all the other North American species. In this last respect it agrees with *C. mexicanus* (see synopsis, p. 829) of Western Mexico ; in this, however, the color and proportions are entirely different.

HABITS. This species appears to be confined to the seaboard of the Pacific, from Alaska to California inclusive. Smaller than the common Crow, in its more essential features it closely resembles that bird, while in all its habits it appears the exact counterpart of the Fish Crow, from which it is specifically and essentially distinct.

It is found as far north as Sitka, several specimens having been procured at that point by Mr. Bischoff.

In the opinion of Dr. Suckley, the marked differences in the habits of this species from those of the common Crow, even more than the great difference in size, sufficiently mark them as entirely distinct. The western Fish Crow is never wary or suspicious, like the common species, but in its impudent familiarity with man resembles the English Jackdaw, and hardly learns to be shy even after having been annoyed with the gun. In Oregon and Washington Territory, he states, this Crow is very abundant, and is one of the marked ornithological features of the country. The great abundance of fish, especially of salmon, in both of these divisions, amply supplies this species with food. At Puget Sound it is abundant throughout the year. During the winter it subsists principally upon the refuse food and offal thrown out by the natives from their lodges. He describes it as cunning, but very tame and impudent, allowing a very near approach, and retiring but a short distance when pursued. Like the Raven and the Herring Gull, these birds are in the habit of carrying clams high into the air and then dropping them, in order to break the shell. Dr. Suckley observed one fruitlessly trying to break the shell of a clam by letting it drop on soft ground. In this effort he persisted perseveringly as long as he was watched.

Dr. Suckley found a nest of this species at Fort Dalles. It was situated in a dense willow-thicket, near a lagoon on the Columbia, and contained three eggs. He describes them as about an inch and a half long, and very wide in their short diameter, of a dirty green ground with brown spots.

Dr. Cooper speaks of it as much more gregarious and familiar than the common Crow, but otherwise resembling that bird in habits, being very sagacious, feeding upon almost everything animal and vegetable, differing rather in the tone than in the character of its cries. Its chief dependence for food being on the sea, it is generally found along the beach, devouring dead fish and other objects thrown up by the waves. At high tide the birds leave the shore and resort to dwellings near the sea, where they devour the offal and any refuse, vegetable or animal. As soon as the tide changes they are sure to notice it and to return to their favorite feeding-ground. They are very troublesome to the Indians, stealing their fish exposed for drying, and other articles of food. From some superstitious awe of them the Indians never molest these birds, but set their children to watch and drive them away. They build in trees near the shore, and the young are fledged in May.

In the southern half of California, Dr. Cooper states, these birds are rarely seen near the sea, preferring inland districts, and only occasionally coming to the shores of the bays to feed. During most of the year they associate in large flocks, feeding in company, and are gregarious even in the breeding-season, building in close proximity to one another. Frequently several nests may be found on the same tree. In this respect they are very unlike the eastern species, which never permit another pair near their nest.

These birds were found by Dr. Cooper breeding as far south as San Diego, where they selected for their breeding-places the groves of evergreen oaks growing in ravines. Their nests were from twelve to forty feet from the ground. In the north they generally build in spruces. He describes their nests as strongly built of sticks, coarse on the outside, but finer on the inside, where they are mingled with roots, grasses, moss, horse-hair, etc., to form a soft lining. The eggs, four in number, have a ground-color of a dark shade of green, thickly marked with dark brown and olive. He gives their average measurement as 1.60 by 1.10 inches. At San Diego they are laid about April 15.

Where unmolested, these birds have not yet become so shy as in the older districts, but they soon learn to apprehend the danger of a gun, and to evince the cunning characteristics of their tribe. They have not, as yet, manifested any disposition to disturb the growing crops, and the small depredations they commit are far more than counterbalanced by their destruction of immense numbers of grubs, grasshoppers, and other injurious insects. They obtain a large supply of food around the cattle-ranches.

In northern California they feed largely on fish, and on the Columbia on clams and oysters.

For reasons not well understood, they avoid particular districts during the breeding-season. Dr. Cooper has never noticed one, during this season, on the coast south of Santa Clara, has never seen one in the Colorado Valley, nor in the Sierra Nevada.

At Visalia, where an extensive forest of oaks forms an oasis in the great Tulare plain, he met with large flocks of these birds, with the same gregarious habits as were observed on the coast.

During the month of July, 1866, a large number of these Crows came every evening to roost in an alder-grove near the town of Santa Cruz. They gathered in long, continuous flocks from the neighboring fields, flying rather high. All at once they would descend, with zigzag turns, to the low trees, sportively chasing and pecking at one another, and chattering in the air.

Mr. John K. Lord, who enjoyed an unusually good opportunity of comparing the habits of our common Crow with those of this species, has not the slightest doubt as to their distinctness, though so very like in all essential respects, as far as color, form of bill, and other details are concerned. The smaller size of this bird, the difference in voice, and their habit of building with mud a domed nest, sufficiently demonstrate their difference. This Crow he found principally near the sea-coast; retiring to the trees at high tide, following out its ebb and retreating before its flood, they feed on any marine food they can find. The caw of this species reminded him of the Jackdaws of Europe. During the breeding-season they abandoned the coast, from early May resorting by pairs to the interior. Selecting patches of open prairie, they build their nests in the bushes of the crab-apple or wild thorn, and something in the manner of the Magpie, arching over the top with sticks, with two openings for entrance and exit on either side. The inside is plastered with mud, and lined with a few loose grass-stalks. The eggs he found generally small, and of a lighter color than those of the common Crow. After nesting, they return with their young to the sea-coast, and remain in large flocks. During the breeding-season they feed on small reptiles, fresh-water mollusks, insects, grubs, etc. Mr. Lord noticed them capturing butter-flies flying near their nests. Their eggs range in number from five to seven.

An egg of this species from Sitka measures 1.62 inches in length by 1.12 in breadth. It is of an oblong-oval shape, pointed at one end. The ground-color is a light sea-green, with marks and blotches of olive-brown, of varying size and different shades.

Corvus ossifragus, WILSON.

FISH CROW.

Corvus ossifragus, WILSON, Am. Orn. V, 1812, 27, pl. xxxvii, f. 2. — BON. Obs. Wils. 1825, No. 39. — IB. Syn. 1828, 57. — IB. Conspectus, 1850, 385. — WAGLER, Syst. Avium, 1827, *Corvus*, No. 12. — NUTTALL, Man. I, 1832, 216. — AUD. Orn. Biog. II, 1834, 268 ; V, 479, pl. cxlvi. — IB. Syn. 1839, 151. — IB. Birds Am. IV, 1842, 94, pl. ccxxvi. — BAIRD, Birds N. Am. 1858, 571, pl. lxvii, f. 2. — SAMUELS, 363. — ALLEN, B. E. Fla. 297.

SP. CHAR. Fourth quill longest; second rather longer than seventh; first shorter than the ninth. Glossy black, with green and violet reflections; the gloss of the belly greenish. Length, about 15.50; wing, 10.50; tail, less than 7.00; tarsus shorter than the middle toe and claw.

HAB. Atlantic coast, from New Jersey to Florida.

The Fish Crow of the Atlantic States is readily distinguishable from the common Crow by the much smaller size (16 inches instead of 20; wing, about 11 inches instead of 13) ; the bill is broader at the base and tapers more rapidly to the end ; the middle toe and claw are longer than the scutellate portion of the tarsus, not shorter, the inner claw not reaching to the base of the middle one. The tail is less rounded. The gloss on the belly is green instead of violet ; that on the back is mixed with green, not entirely violet.

HABITS. The Fish Crow of Eastern North America has a distribution restricted to the Southern Atlantic and the Gulf shore. It is found in the States of New Jersey, Pennsylvania, Maryland, Delaware, Virginia, the Carolinas, Georgia, and Florida, and, according to Audubon, thence to the mouth of the Mississippi. West of that river it appears to be very rarely met with. Dr. Würdemann obtained it at Calcasieu, La. Mr. Allen, in a list of the birds of Massachusetts, published in 1864, names this species as an occasional visitor along the southern coast of that State, but I am not able to find any corroboration of the statement, and believe it to be a mistake. Dr. De Kay, in his Report on the birds of New York, states that this Crow is occasionally seen on the shores of Long Island, but Mr. Lawrence is confident that it never occurs farther north than Squaw Beach, in New Jersey. So, too, Mr. Townsend is quoted by both Audubon and Nuttall as authority for its occurrence on the Columbia River, of which we have no confirmation.

This species was first described by Wilson, who met with it and observed its habits on the sea-coast of Georgia. In some respects its habits were the exact reverse of those of the common Crow, as the former regularly retired at evening into the interior to roost, and came down to the shores of the river Savannah, on the first appearance of day, to feed. Its voice first attracted his notice ; there was something in it very different from the utterances of the Crow, being more hoarse and guttural, and more varied in its modulations. The mode of flight was also observed to be quite different, as the Fish Crow occasionally soars about in the manner of the Raven and of Hawks, without flapping its wings, — a flight which the Crow is never observed to make, and is probably not able to execute.

The food was also observed to be unlike, as well as the manner of procuring it. The favorite haunt of this species seemed to be the banks of the river, up and down which they soared, and in a very dexterous manner snatched up with their claws dead fish, or other garbage found floating on the surface. This Crow was also seen to perch frequently on the back of cattle, in the manner of the Jackdaw of Europe. It was never seen to mingle with the common Crows ; and never, like the latter, roosts among the reeds and marshes near the water, but always seeks the shelter of the woods, in which to pass the night.

Afterwards, in his journey near the Mississippi, Wilson observed the same birds frequenting the borders of rivers and ponds, and feeding on the reptiles found in those waters. They were close attendants upon the cow-yards, and were more solitary, but much less shy and suspicious, than the common Crow. This species was also observed by Wilson in Cape May County, New

Jersey, and in the regions bordering on the Schuylkill and the Delaware, near Philadelphia, during the shad and herring fishing, or from March till June.

During the breeding-season they were observed to separate into pairs, and to build their nests in tall trees near the sea or the river shore. One of their nests was in a tall wood at Great Egg Harbor, and they were presumed to have four or five young at a time.

In the District of Columbia, Dr. Coues found the Fish Crow to be an abundant resident throughout the year, less wary and suspicious than the common Crow, and more confined to the borders of rivers. It was generally confounded with *C. americanus.*

The Fish Crow appears to have received, even if it does not merit, an exemption from the general unpopularity of its race. It is generally believed to be at least a harmless species, and in its destruction of reptiles and vermin to be even beneficial. This belief, we apprehend, is for the most part well founded. Yet Mr. Audubon accuses these Crows of entering gardens and feeding upon the best fruits. He also states that, near Charleston, they commit such depredations upon the ripe figs, and become so troublesome generally in the gardens, that it is often found necessary to station a man near the fig-trees to shoot and destroy them.

The Fish Crow is confined either to the maritime districts or to the banks of rivers branching from them. Audubon states that they ascend the Delaware to quite a distance, and that some breed in New Jersey every year, but that all retire to the South on the approach of cold weather. Some go up the Mississippi to the distance of five hundred miles, but return to the sea-shore in the winter. In East Florida, where they were very abundant, Mr. Audubon found them breeding in February, in South Carolina on the 20th of March, and in New Jersey a month later. On the St. John's River, during February, he saw them in flocks of several hundred, but all seemed mated and to move in pairs, sailing high in the air in the manner of Ravens. After these aerial excursions the whole body descended to the water's edge to feed. When their fishing was over, they would alight in flocks on the live-oaks near the shore, and there keep up their gabbling, while they plumed themselves, for hours. They then returned to their fishing-grounds, where they remained until near sunset, moving into the interior to great distances, to roost on the loblolly-pines. These retreats were made in silence, but their return to the sea-shore in the early morning was made with noisy and lively demonstrations. They were then to be seen among the bays, rivers, salt ponds, and marshes, searching for small fry, and picking up any garbage they might find.

Mr. Audubon also accuses them of robbing other birds of their eggs and young. This was especially observed on the Florida Keys, where they even dared to plunder the nests of the Cormorants and White Ibis. They feed largely on the small crabs called fiddlers, which they pursue and easily capture in their burrows. He has also seen them attack and pursue small Gulls and Terns, and attempt to make them disgorge the fish they have caught; but as the flight of the latter is swifter, they are frequently unsuccessful in these attempts at robbery.   This Crow can catch living fish with considerable dexterity, but cannot feed while on the wing.

During the winter and early spring, Mr. Audubon states that these birds feed on various kinds of berries, especially those of the *Ilex cassina* and of the common holly, and those of the exotic tallow-tree, now so common near Charleston (*Stillingia sebifera*).   In January and February these trees are much resorted to by the Crows, who greedily devour their white and oily seeds.

Mr. Audubon found these birds breeding generally on moderate-sized trees of the loblolly-pine, building their nests towards the extremities of the branches, about twenty feet from the ground.   The nests are smaller than those of the Crow, and are built of sticks, lined with dry grasses and moss, and neatly finished with fine fibrous roots.   The eggs are five or six in number, and resemble those of the Crow, but are smaller.

Two eggs of this species, from St. Simon's Island, measure, one 1.50 in length by 1.10 in breadth, the other 1.52 by 1.09.   Their ground-color is a light blue with a slight greenish tinge, marked over the entire egg with small blotches of a light brown.   An egg from Great Egg Harbor, obtained by Wilson, from the old Peale Museum, and which may be a faded specimen, has no tinge of blue or green, but a ground of pinkish-gray, marked with smaller blotches and cloudings of dark drab.   It measures 1.46 inches in length by one inch in breadth.

<hr>

Genus PICICORVUS, Bonap.

Picicorvus, Bonaparte, Consp. Av. 1850, 384.   (Type, *Corvus columbianus*, Wils.)

Gen. Char.   Leaden-gray color, with black wings and tail.   Bill longer than the head, considerably longer than the tarsus, attenuated, slightly decurved; tip without notch.   Culmen and commissure curved; gonys straight or slightly concave, as long as the tarsi.   Nostrils circular, completely covered by a full tuft of incumbent white bristly feathers.   Tail much shorter than the wings, nearly even or slightly rounded.   Wings pointed, reaching to the tip of tail.   Third, fourth, and fifth quills longest.   Tarsi short, scarcely longer than the middle toe, the hind toe and claw very large, reaching nearly to the middle of the middle claw, the lateral toe little shorter.   A row of small scales on the middle of the sides of tarsus.

Picicorvus columbianus.

Color of the single species leaden-gray, with black wings and tail.

This genus is so similar to *Nucifraga* as to be hardly separable ; the principal difference being in the slender and more decurved and attenuated

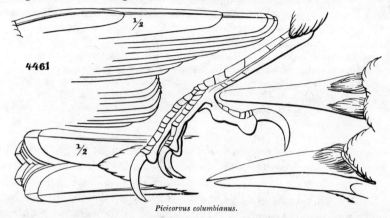

Picicorvus columbianus.

bill, with a slightly concave, instead of convex, culmen, and plain instead of spotted plumage. The differences of form are expressed by the accom-

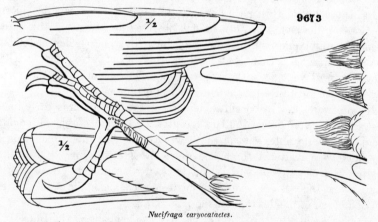

Nucifraga caryocatactes.

panying outlines of the generic features of the two. But one species is known, this being peculiar to Western North America.

Picicorvus columbianus, BONAP.

CLARKE'S CROW.

Corvus columbianus, WILSON, Am. Orn. III, 1811, 29, pl. xx. — BON. Obs. Wilson, 1824, No. 38. — IB. Syn. 1828, 57. — NUTTALL, I, 1832, 218. *Nucifraga columbiana,* AUD. Orn. Biog. IV, 1838, 459, pl. ccclxii. — IB. Syn. 1839, 156. — IB. Birds Am. IV, 1842, 127, pl. ccxxxv. — BON. List, 1838. — NUTTALL, Man. I, (2d. ed.,) 251. *Picicorvus columbianus,* BONAP. Consp. 1850, 384. — NEWBERRY, P. R. R. Rep. VI, IV, 1837, 83. — BAIRD, Birds N. Am. 1858, 573. — LORD, Pr. R. A. Inst. IV, 121 (British Columbia). — DALL & BANNISTER, Tr. Chic. Ac. I, 1869, 286. — COOPER, Orn. Cal. I, 1870, 289. *"Corvus megonyx,* WAGLER."

Sp. Char. Tail rounded or moderately graduated, the closed wings reaching nearly to its tip. Fourth quill longest; second considerably shorter than the sixth. General color bluish-ash, changing on the nasal feathers, the forehead, sides of head (especially around the eye), and chin, to white. The wings, including their inner surface, greenish-black, the secondaries and tertials, except the innermost, broadly tipped with white; tail white, the inner web of the fifth feather and the whole of the sixth, with the upper tail-coverts, greenish-black. The axillars plumbeous-black. Bill and feet black. Young similar in color, without additional markings of any kind. The gonys, however, convex, and the bill generally more like that of the Jays. Length of male (fresh), 12.00; wing, 7.00; tail, 4.30; tarsus, 1.20.

Hab. From Rocky Mountains to Pacific. East to Fort Kearney, north to Sitka, south to Arizona.

Habits. Clarke's Crow was first met with by the parties composing the celebrated exploring party to the Rocky Mountains under the direction of Lewis and Clarke. It was described by Wilson in 1811, who was informed by individuals belonging to the expedition that these birds were found inhabiting the shores of the Columbia and the adjacent country in great numbers, frequenting the rivers and sea-shore, and that it seemed to have all the noisy and gregarious habits of the common Crow of Europe.

In his account of this species, Mr. Nuttall states that during his journey westward in the month of July, he first observed individuals of this bird in a small grove of pines on the borders of Bear River, near where it falls into Lake Timpanagos. This was at a height of about seven thousand feet above the sea level, and in the 42d parallel. Their habits appeared to him to correspond with those of the Nutcrackers of Europe.

He afterwards saw a considerable flock of the young birds early in August, in a lofty ravine near the Three Buttes, a remarkable isolated mountain group about forty miles west of the Lewis River. They appeared somewhat shy, and were scattered through a grove of aspens, flying, with a slight chatter, from the tops of bushes and trees, to the ground. He was of the opinion that this species never descends below the mountain plains, but that it has a constant predilection for the pine forests.

Mr. Townsend afterwards found this species abundant on the Blue Mountains of Oregon. He describes its flight as very unlike that of a Crow, being performed in jerks, in the manner of a Woodpecker. At times, when sitting, it is said to keep up a constant scream, in a very harsh and grating voice, and in an unvaried and prolonged tone. He states that it breeds in very high pine-trees, and that he did not meet with it within five hundred miles of the Columbia River.

Mr. Ridgway found this species one of the most abundant birds of the pine forests of the Sierra Nevada. East of this range it was also met with, though only in smaller numbers, in the cedar and piñon woods of the East Humboldt Mountains. He adds that it is a bird so curiously striking as at once to attract attention. It bears but very little resemblance to any bird of its family, and in its general appearance, flight, and notes approaches so nearly to the Woodpeckers as to be usually known to the settlers as a bird of that tribe.

He further remarks that its flight much resembles that of *Melanerpes torquatus*, and, as it alights from the top of a tall dead tree, and sits quietly gazing around, it might readily be mistaken for one of the *Picidæ*. He describes them as being very active in their movements, now flying from a tree to the ground to pick up some article of food, now examining the excavations of an old dead stump or snag, or, on being approached, as flying up and alighting upon the extreme summit of a tree, out of gunshot. It is a very noisy bird, and its notes are harsh and discordant, though less so than are those of the Steller's Jay, which is generally seen in the same localities. Its usual note is a harsh guttural *churr-churr*, generally uttered when two or more alight on the same tree. Occasionally an individual takes up a peculiar piping strain, which is immediately answered by all the others in the neighborhood, thus awakening the echoes of the surrounding solitude with their discordant cries. In regard to its nest he can give no positive information, but thinks that they breed in cavities in old dead trees and stumps, having found a nest in such a situation in the East Humboldt Mountains, which he thinks belonged to a pair of these birds which were flying about, and seen to enter this cavity.

Dr. Newberry, in his Report on the zoölogy of his route, states that he found this species rather common along a large portion of it, and was thus enabled to study its habits at leisure. He found it strictly confined to the highlands and mountains, never, where he saw it, descending to a lower altitude than about four thousand feet. On the other hand, while crossing the Cascade Mountains at the line of perpetual snow, seven thousand feet above the sea-level, he has seen this bird, in company with the *Melanerpes torquatus*, flying over the snow-covered peaks three thousand feet above him.

He first met with this bird on the spur of the Sierra Nevada, near Lassen's Butte, and found it constantly, when in high and timbered regions, from there to the Columbia. He describes its habits as a compound, in about equal parts of those of the Jays and of the Woodpeckers. Its cry he speaks of as particularly harsh and disagreeable, something like that of Steller's Jay, but louder and more discordant. It seems to combine the shrewdness with all the curiosity of the Jays and Crows, and from its shyness is a very difficult bird to shoot, the Doctor never being able to get directly within killing distance of one of them, but only obtaining specimens by concealing himself and waiting for them to approach him. Apparently from excess of caution, it almost invariably alights on a dry tree. Even when going to a living tree for its food, it always flies first into a dry one, if one is near, to reconnoitre, and, if the coast is clear, it begins to feed. At the first movement of an intruder, without uttering a note, it puts a safe distance between itself and its enemy.

The food of this bird, at the time when Dr. Newberry visited its haunts, consisted exclusively of the seeds of the yellow pine (*P. ponderosa*), in dislodging which from the cones the bird displays great dexterity. Both Maximilian's Jay and Steller's Jay were, at that time, feeding on the same seeds, but not so exclusively.

Dr. Suckley obtained a specimen of this bird as far east as Milk River, in Nebraska, about two hundred miles east of the Rocky Mountains.

In crossing the Cascade Mountains, in 1853, Dr. Cooper found these birds quite abundant on the banks of the Yakima River, and from thence north wherever there were trees of the long-leaved pine, the seeds of which were its principal food. On returning to Vancouver during the severe cold weather of the following January, these birds appeared there in considerable numbers. At no other season of the year has he met with them west of the Cascade Mountains, and believes these migrations westward are only made in the severest weather. They extend eastward throughout Washington Territory, as Dr. Cooper has shot them at Fort Laramie, and met with a straggling pair even as far east as Fort Kearney. Dr. Cooper has never known these birds to eat anything except seeds and berries. They rarely descend to the ground, and never frequent river-banks, or other places, for fish or carrion. They may be seen on the tops of trees extracting seeds from cones, hanging head downwards, like a Chickadee. Dr. Cooper has observed this bird pecking at dead bark, in quest of insects. When feeding they are very shy, flying off, if approached, to a great distance before alighting. They are not known to visit the Coast Mountains south of San Francisco, but abound in the Rocky Mountains throughout our limits.

Mr. J. K. Lord notes the arrival of this species at Fort Colville, in May, in large flocks. They were hopping busily from branch to branch, amidst pine-trees.

The statement made to Wilson that this species frequents rivers and seashores, and his inference that its formidable claws indicated that they feed on living animals, is controverted by Mr. Lord. They never frequent riverbanks, never by any chance eat fish, and never capture any living thing. Their habits are strictly arboreal, and their food the seeds of pine-trees. These noisy seed-hunters use their formidable claws to enable them to hang on to the pine cones while they are extracting the seed, which they are obliged to get out from under scaly coverings. For this nature has given them feet and claws that serve the purpose of hands, and a powerful bill, like a small crowbar. The cone must be steadied when they pry it open, or it would snap and fall. One foot clasps it, and the powerful claws hold it firmly. The other foot, encircling a branch, supports the bird in every possible position, the long grasping claws being equal to any emergency. The cone is thus fixed, and the seeds are forced out from under the scales. Mr. Lord collected a large packet of seeds of the *Abies douglassi* from the crops of these birds.

On their arrival they assemble in immense flocks, and the noise they make he describes as a most discordant, continuous, grating clatter, intensified at times into a perfect shriek. These assemblies last about a week, after which they separate in pairs.

A nest of this bird was found by Mr. Lord in the top of a lofty pine at least two hundred feet high, — felled in cutting the boundary line. By chance he discovered the nest, about which the old birds were hovering, leaving no doubt of its identity. This nest was very large and composed of fir twigs, bits of bark, the leaves of the pine, fine root-fibres, with small pieces of moss, and gray lichens mixed carelessly with the other materials. It was shallow and round, and presented a large extent of surface beyond the margins of the hollow containing the eggs. The eggs were in fragments, much like the eggs of Steller's Jay in color, but of a lighter shade of bluish-green. He thinks that their habit is to build in the very tallest pines.

Dr. Kennerly also met with this Crow west of Albuquerque, in New Mexico, in the thick pine woods skirting the eastern slope of the Rocky Mountains, where it was quite abundant. He rarely saw more than two or three together. None were met with after leaving the mountains.

A single specimen of this crow was obtained at Sitka, by Bischoff.

GENUS **GYMNOKITTA**, PR. MAX.

Gymnorhinus, PR. MAX. Reise Nord. Amer. II, 1841, 21. (Type, *G. cyanocephala.*)
Gymnokitta, PR. MAX. "1850," GRAY.
Cyanocephalus, BONAP. "1842," preoccupied in Botany.

GEN. CHAR. Bill elongated, depressed, shorter than the tarsus, longer than the head, without notch, similar to that of *Sturnella* in shape. Culmen nearly straight; commissure curved; gonys ascending. Nostrils small, oval, entirely exposed, the bristly

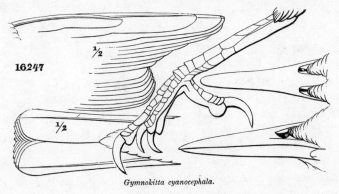

16247

Gymnokitta cyanocephala.

feathers at the base of the bill being very minute. Tail short, nearly even, much shorter than the pointed wings, which cover three fourths of the tail. Tarsi considerably longer than the middle toe. Color of the single species blue, most intense anteriorly; the throat streaked with white.

The bill in this genus is not unlike that of *Sturnus* and *Sturnella,* and conspicuous among *Corvinæ* by its uncovered nostrils.

Gymnokitta cyanocephala, Pr. Max.

MAXIMILIAN'S JAY

Gymnorhinus cyanocephalus, Pr. Maximilian, Reise in das innere Nord-Amerika, II, 1841, 21. — Ib. Voyage dans l'Am. du Nord, III, 1843, 296. *Gymnokitta cyanocephala,* "Pr. Max. 1850," Bp. Conspectus, 1850, 382. — Cassin, Illust. I, vi, 1854, 165, pl. xxviii. — Newberry, Rep. P. R. R. VI, iv, 1857, 83. — Baird, Birds N. Am. 1858, 574. — Max. Cab. J. VI, 1858, 193. — Cooper, Orn. Cal. I, 1870, 292. *Psilorhinus cyanocephalus,* Gray, Genera. *Cyanocorax cassini,* M'Call, Pr. A. N. Sc. V, June, 1851, 216.

Sp. Char. Wings considerably longer than the tail, and reaching to within an inch of

Gymnokitta cyanocephala.

its tip. Tail nearly even. General color dull blue, paler on the abdomen, the middle of which is tinged with ash; the head and neck of a much deeper and more intense blue, darker on the crown. Chin and forepart of the throat whitish, streaked with blue. Length, 10.00; wing, 5.90; tail, 4.50; tarsus, 1.50. Young bird not differing in markings.

Hab. Rocky Mountains of Colorado, to Cascade Mts. of California and Oregon. Not on the Pacific coast? South to New Mexico and Arizona.

The female is appreciably different from the male, both in size and plumage, being smaller, and of a light bluish-ash tint. This difference is readily appreciable when the birds are seen flying.

Habits. Maximilian's Jay was discovered and first described by that eminent naturalist, Maximilian, Prince of Wied, in his book of travels in North America, published in 1841. Mr. Edward Kern, who was connected with Colonel Fremont's exploring expedition in 1846, was the first to bring specimens of this interesting and remarkable bird to the notice of American naturalists, transmitting them to the Philadelphia Academy. The specimens procured by its discoverer were met with by him on Maria's River, one of the tributaries of the Upper Missouri, in the extreme northern portion of our northwestern territory, a point much farther north than it has been met with by any other naturalist. As this species has since been seen in large numbers in New Mexico, it may be presumed to extend its movements over quite an extended area of distribution in the region of the Rocky Mountains.

According to the more recent observations of Mr. Ridgway, the Maximilian Jay inhabits exclusively the nut-pine and cedar woods on the interior mountain ranges, and is one of the most characteristic birds of those regions. This species he states to be eminently gregarious, even breeding in colonies, and in winter congregating in flocks, sometimes of thousands. Ever restless and in motion, as it moves it is constantly uttering its curious, querulous notes. It is a very conspicuous bird, and is one well worthy of particular attention. Its blue color is the only thing suggestive of its affinity to the Jay. All its habits are different, and its appearance is quite peculiar. It is as essentially migratory as the *Ectopistes migratoria*, its coming and its going being quite as sudden and uncertain. On one occasion, in visiting a nut-pine wood, Mr. Ridgway found it full of roving, noisy troops of these birds, but upon visiting the same locality the next day not one could be seen.

He also states that these birds are exceedingly early in their nesting, as he met with companies of fully fledged young flying about on the 21st of April. Near Carson City, April 20, 1868, he found these birds abundant among the scattered cedars and nut-pines on the lower slopes of the hills. They were in pairs, often three or four pairs in company.

The notes of this bird are both peculiar and curious. The usual ones are said to have some resemblance to the querulous wailings of the Screech Owl; but none, in his opinion, have any resemblance to the cry of the Catbird.

It flies very swiftly, but with a gentle floating motion, very much in the manner of the Robin. In its movements among the small cedars, it generally alighted upon the summit of a tree, and, quietly sitting there, would look about in the manner of the *Picicorvus columbianus*. In flying, it continually uttered a very peculiar querulous note, resembling very much one of the notes of the Magpie, — the peculiarly soft note of that bird uttered during the love-season, or when its nest is approached. In searching among the cedars, Mr. Ridgway found several of its nests. Nearly all had been deserted, and there were several families of fully fledged young flying about. One nest contained four fully feathered young. When these had been taken, and placed in a hat, they all jumped out, squalling vociferously. These nests were all saddled upon horizontal branches of cedars, and, except in their greater bulk they closely resembled the nest of the eastern Blue Jay.

In autumn and in winter the large flocks of these birds, as they fly back and forth over the hills, present a very peculiar appearance. Their flight is then very swift.

Dr. Kennerly, in November, 1853, frequently saw large flocks of these birds between the Puebla of Laguna and the Sierra Madre, about a hundred miles west of Albuquerque, in New Mexico. They were found chiefly frequenting the watercourses, and when startled would circle around, rising higher above their heads, uttering their singular cries; then suddenly descending they would alight in the top of some tree on the adjoining cliffs. He compares its voice to that of the common Catbird.

Dr. T. C. Henry also repeatedly noticed these birds in the vicinity of Fort Webster, in New Mexico. He first met with them near San Miguel, in July, 1852, where he observed a party of about thirty flitting through the cedars along the roadside. They were chiefly young birds, and were constantly alighting on the ground for the purpose of capturing lizards, which they killed with great readiness, and devoured. After that he repeatedly, in winter, saw these birds near Fort Webster, and usually in flocks of about forty or fifty. They evinced great wariness, and were very difficult of approach.

The flocks would usually alight near the summit of a hill and pass rapidly down its sides, all the birds keeping quite near to each other, and frequently alighting on the ground. They appeared to be very social, and kept up a continual twittering note. This bird, so far as Dr. Henry observed it, is exclusively a mountain species, and never seen on the plains or bottom-lands, and was never observed singly, or even in a single pair, but always in companies.

Dr. Newberry met with this species in the basin of the Des Chutes, in Oregon. He first noticed it in September. Early every morning flocks of from twenty-five to thirty of these birds came across, in their usual straggling flight, chattering as they flew to the trees on a hill near the camp, and then, from tree to tree, they made their way to the stream to drink. He describes their note, when flying or feeding, as a frequently repeated *ca-ca-că*. Sometimes, when made by a straggler separated from mate or flock, it was rather loud and harsh, but was usually soft and agreeable. When disturbed, their cry was harsher. They were very shy, and could only be shot by lying in wait for them. Subsequently he had an opportunity of seeing them feed, and of watching them carefully as they were eating the berries of the cedars, and in their habits and cries they seemed closely to resemble Jays. A specimen, previously killed, was found with its crop filled with the seeds of the yellow pine.

Dr. Cooper has seen specimens of this bird from Washoe, just east of the California State line, and he was informed by Mr. Clarence King that they frequent the junipers on mountains near Mariposa.

From Dr. Coues we learn that this bird is very abundant at Fort Whipple, where it remains all the year. It breeds in the retired portions of the neighboring mountains of San Francisco and Bill Williams, the young leaving the nest in July. As the same birds are ready to fly in April, at Carson City, it may be that they have two broods in Arizona. During the winter they collect in immense flocks, and in one instance Dr. Coues estimates their number at a thousand or more. In a more recent contribution to the Ibis (April, 1872), Dr. Coues gives a more full account of his observations in respect to this bird. In regard to geographical range he considers its distribution very nearly the same with that of the *Picicorvus*. Mr. Aiken has recently met with these birds in Colorado Territory, where, however, Mr. Allen did not obtain specimens. General McCall found these birds abundant near Santa Fé, in New Mexico, at an altitude of seven thousand feet; and the late Captain Feilner obtained specimens at Fort Crook, in Northeastern California. Dr. Coues considers its range to be the coniferous zone of vegetation within the geographical area bounded eastward by the foot-hills and slopes of the Rocky Mountains; westward by the Cascade and Coast ranges; northward, perhaps to Sitka, but undetermined; and somewhat so southward, not traced so far as the *tierra fria* of Mexico.

Dr. Coues adds that, like most birds which subsist indifferently on varied animal or vegetable food, this species is not, strictly speaking, migratory, as it can find food in winter anywhere except at its loftiest points of distribution. A descent of a few thousand feet from the mountains thus answers all the purposes of a southward journey performed by other species, so far as food is concerned, while its hardy nature enables it to endure the rigors of winter. According to his observations, this bird feeds principally upon juniper berries and pine seeds, and also upon acorns and other small hard fruits.

Dr. Coues describes this bird as garrulous and vociferous, with curiously modulated chattering notes when at ease, and with extremely loud harsh cries when excited by fear or anger. It is also said to be restless and impetuous, as if of an unbalanced mind. Its attitudes on the ground, to which it frequently descends, are essentially Crow-like, and its gait is an easy walk or run, very different from the leaping manner of progress made by the Jays. When perching, its usual attitude is stiff and firm. Its flight resembles that of the *Picicorvus*. After breeding, these birds unite in immense flocks, but disperse again in pairs when the breeding-season commences.

Nothing, so far, has been published in regard to the character of the eggs.

Subfamily GARRULINÆ.

Char. Wings short, rounded; not longer or much shorter than the tail, which is graduated, sometimes excessively so. Wings reaching not much beyond the lower tail-coverts. Bristly feathers at base of bill variable. Bill nearly as long as the head, or shorter. Tarsi longer than the bill or than the middle toe. Outer lateral claws rather shorter than the inner.

The preceding diagnosis may perhaps characterize the garruline birds, as compared with the Crows. The subdivisions of the group are as follows : —

A. Nostrils moderate, completely covered by incumbent feathers.
  a. Tail much longer than the wings; first primary attenuated, falcate.
    Pica. Head without crest.
  b. Tail about as long as the wings; first primary not falcate.
    Cyanura. Head with lengthened narrow crest. Wing and tail blue, banded with black.
    Cyanocitta. Head without crest. Above blue, with a gray patch on the back. No bands on wing and tail.
    Xanthoura. Head without crest. Color above greenish; the head blue; lateral tail-feathers yellow.
    Perisoreus. Head full and bushy. Bill scarcely half the head, with white feathers over the nostrils. Plumage dull.
B. Nostrils very large, naked, uncovered by feathers.
    Psilorhinus. Head not crested; tail broad; wings two thirds as long as the tail.
    Calocitta. Head with a recurved crest; wings less than half as long as the tail.

There is a very close relationship between the Jays and the Titmice, the chief difference being in size rather than in any other distinguishing feature. The feathers at the base of the bill, however, in the Jays, are bristly throughout, with lateral branches reaching to the very tip. In *Paridæ* these feathers are inclined to be broader, with the shaft projecting considerably beyond the basal portion, or the lateral branches are confined to the basal portion, and extended forwards. There is no naked line of separation between the scutellæ on the outer side of the tarsi. The basal joint of the middle toe is united almost or quite to the end to the lateral, instead of half-way. The first primary is usually less than half the second, instead of rather more; the fourth and fifth primaries nearly equal and longest, instead of the fifth being longer than the fourth.

Genus **PICA**, Cuvier.

Coracias, Linnæus, Syst. Nat. 1735 (Gray).
Pica, Brisson, Ornithologia, 1760, and of Cuvier (Agassiz). (Type, *Corvus pica*, L.)
Cleptes, Gambel, J. A. N. Sc. 2d Ser. I, 1847, 47.

Gen. Char. Tail very long, forming much more than half the total length; the feathers much graduated; the lateral scarcely more than half the middle. First primary falcate, curved, and attenuated. Bill about as high as broad at the base; the culmen and gonys much curved, and about equal; the bristly feathers reaching nearly to the middle of the bill. Nostrils nearly circular. Tarsi very long; middle toe scarcely more than two thirds the length. A patch of naked skin beneath and behind the eye.

The peculiar characteristic of this genus, in addition to the very long graduated tail, lies in the attenuated, falcate first primary. *Calocitta*, which has an equally long or longer tail, has the first primary as in the Jays generally (besides having the nostrils exposed).

A specimen of *P. nuttalli* has the lateral tarsal plates with two or three

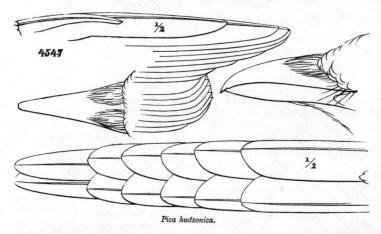

½

4547

½

Pica hudsonica.

transverse divisions on the lower third. This has not been observed by us to occur in *P. hudsonica.*

Species and Varieties.

P. caudata. Head, neck, breast, interscapulars, lining of wing, tail-coverts and tibiæ, deep black: wings metallic greenish-blue; tail rich metallic green, the feathers passing through bronze and reddish-violet into violet-blue, at their tips. Scapulars, abdomen, sides, flanks, and inner webs of primaries, pure white. Sexes alike; young similar.

  a. Bill and bare space around the eye black.

   Wing, 7.50; tail, 9.50 or less, its graduation less than half its length, 4.50; culmen, 1.20; tarsus, 1.75; middle toe, 1.05. *Hab.* Europe.

var. c a u d a t a.[1]

   Wing, over 8.00 (8.50 maximum); tail over 10.00 (13.50, max., its graduation more than half its length, 7.70); culmen, 1.55; tarsus, 1.75; middle toe, 1.05. *Hab.* Northern and Middle North America, exclusive of the Atlantic Province of United States and California.

var. h u d s o n i c a.

  b. Bill and bare space around the eye yellow.

   Wing, 7.50; tail, 10.50; its graduation, 5.00; culmen, 1.50; tarsus, 1.75; middle toe, 1.05. *Hab.* California .   .   .   .   var. *n u t t a l l i.*

---

[1] *Pica caudata,* FLEM. Brit. An. p. 87. *Corvus pica,* LINN. Fuan. Suec. p. 31. *Pica mela-noleuca,* VIEILL. N. D. XXVI, 121. *Pica albiventris,* VIEILL. Faun. Franc. p. 119, t. 55, f. 1. *Pica european* (CUV.) BOIE, Isis, 1822, 551. *Pica rusticorum,* LEACH, Syst. Cat. Mamm. and Birds in Brit. Mus. p. 18.

Pica caudata, var. hudsonica, BONAP.

MAGPIE.

Corvus pica, FORSTER, Phil. Trans. LXXII, 1772, 382. — WILSON, Am. Orn. IV, 1811, 75,
pl. xxxv. — BON. Obs. Wils. 1825, No. 40. — IB. Syn. 1828, 57. — NUTTALL, Man. I,
1832, 219. — AUD. Orn. Biog. IV, 1838, 408, pl. ccclvii (not of LINNÆUS). *Corvus
hudsonica*, JOS. SABINE, App. Narr. Franklin's Journey, 1823, 25, 671. *Picus hudsonica*, BONAP. List, 1838. — IB. Conspectus, 1850, 383. — MAXIM. Reise Nord Amer.
I, 1839, 508. — IB. Cabanis, Journ. 1856, 197. — NEWBERRY, Zoöl. Cal. & Or. Route,
Rep. P. R. R. VI, IV, 1857, 84. — BAIRD, Birds N. Am. 1858, 576, pl. xxv. — LORD,
Pr. R. A. Inst. IV, 121 (British Columbia). — COOPER & SUCKLEY, 213, pl. xxv. —
DALL & BANNISTER, Tr. Chic. Ac. I, 1869, 286 (Alaska). — FINSCH, Abh. Nat. III,
1872, 39 (Alaska). — COOPER, Orn. Cal. I, 1870, 296. *Cleptes hudsonicus*, GAMBEL,
J. A. N. Sc. 2d Ser. I, Dec. 1847, 47. *Pica melanoleuca*, "VIEILL." AUD. Syn. 1839,
157. — IB. Birds Am. IV, 1842, 99, pl. ccxxvii.

SP. CHAR. Bill and naked skin behind the eye black. General color black. The

Pica nuttalli.

belly, scapulars, and inner webs of the primaries white; hind part of back grayish; exposed portion of the tail-feathers glossy green, tinged with purple and violet near the end; wings glossed with green; the secondaries and tertials with blue; throat-feathers spotted with white in younger specimens. Length, 19.00; wing, 8.50; tail, 13.00. Young in color and appearance similar generally to the adult.

HAB. The northern regions of North America. The middle and western Provinces of the United States exclusive of California; Wisconsin, Michigan, and Northern Illinois, in winter.

The American Magpie is almost exactly similar to the European, and differs only in larger size and disproportionably longer tail. According to Maximilian and other authors, the iris of the American bird has a grayish-blue outer ring, wanting in the European bird, and the voice is quite different. It is, however, difficult to consider the two birds otherwise than as geographical races of one primitive stock.

HABITS. The American Magpie has an extended western distribution from Arizona on the south to Alaska on the northwest. It has been met with as far to the east as the Missouri River, and is found from there to the Pacific. It is abundant at Sitka; it was observed at Ounga, one of the Shumagin Islands, and was obtained by Bischoff at Kodiak.

Richardson observed these birds on the Saskatchewan, where a few remain even in winter, but are much more frequent in summer.

Mr. Lord, the naturalist of the British branch of the Northwest Boundary Survey, characterizes our Magpie as murderous, because of its cruel persecution of galled and suffering mules, its picking out the eyes of living animals, and its destruction of birds. These birds caused so much trouble to the party, in winter, at Colville, as to become utterly unbearable, and a large number were destroyed by strychnine. They were then so tame and impudent that he repeatedly gave them food from his hand without their showing any evidence of fear. He says they nest in March.

Dr. Suckley states that this Magpie is abundant throughout the central region of Oregon and Washington Territory. He first met with it a hundred miles west of Fort Union, at the mouth of the Yellowstone. It became more abundant as the mountains were approached, and so continued almost as far west as the Cascade Mountains, where the dense forests were an effectual barrier. On Puget Sound he saw none until August, after which, during the fall, it was tolerably abundant. It breeds throughout the interior. He obtained a young bird, nearly fledged, about May 5, at Fort Dalles. At this place a few birds remain throughout the winter, but a majority retire farther south during the cold weather. One of its cries, he says, resembles a peculiar call of Steller's Jay.

Mr. Ridgway regards this Magpie as one of the most characteristic and conspicuous birds of the interior region, distinguished both for the elegance of its form and the beauty of its plumage. While not at all rare in the fertile mountain cañons, the principal resort of this species is the rich bottomland of the rivers. The usual note of the Magpie is a frequently uttered chatter, very peculiar, and, when once heard, easily recognized. During the nesting-season it utters a softer and more musical and plaintive note, sounding something like *kay-e-ehk-kay-e*. It generally flies about in small flocks, and, like others of its family, is very fond of tormenting owls. In the winter, in company with the Ravens, it resorts to the slaughter-houses to feed on offal. The young differ but little in plumage from the adult, the metallic colors being even a little more vivid ; the white spotting of the throat is characteristic of the immature bird.

The nests were found by Mr. Ridgway in various situations. Some were in cedars, some in willows, and others in low shrubs. In every instance the nest was domed, the inner and real nest being enclosed in an immense thorny covering, which far exceeded it in bulk. In the side of this thorny protection is a winding passage leading into the nest, possibly designed to conceal the very long tail of the bird, which, if exposed to view, would endanger its safety.

Dr. Cooper first met this bird east of the Cascade Mountains, near the Yakima, and from there in his journey northward as far as the 49th degree it was common, as well as in all the open unwooded regions until the mountains were passed on his return westward.

Dr. Kennerly met with these birds on the Little Colorado in New Mexico, in December. He found them in great numbers soon after leaving the Rio Grande, and from time to time on the march to California. They seemed to live indifferently in the deep cañons among the hills or in the valleys, but were only found near water.

Dr. Newberry first met with these birds on the banks of one of the tributaries of the Des Chutes, one hundred miles south of the Columbia, afterwards on the Columbia, but nowhere in large numbers. He regards them as much less gregarious in their habits than *Pica nuttalli*, as all the birds he noticed were solitary or in pairs, while the Yellow-bills were often seen in flocks of several hundreds.

All accounts of this bird agree in representing it as frequently a great source of annoyance to parties of exploration, especially in its attacks upon horses worn down and galled by fatigue and privations. In the memorable narrative of Colonel Pike's journey in New Mexico, these birds, rendered bold and voracious by want, are described as assembling around that miserable party in great numbers, picking the sore backs of their perishing horses, and snatching at all the food they could reach. The party of Lewis and Clark, who were the first to add this bird to our fauna, also describe them as familiar and voracious, penetrating into their tents, snatching the meat even from their dishes, and frequently, when the hunters were engaged in dressing their game, seizing the meat suspended within a foot or two of their heads.

Mr. Nuttall, in his tour across the continent, found these birds so familiar and greedy as to be easily taken, as they approached the encampment for food, by the Indian boys, who kept them prisoners. They soon became reconciled to their confinement, and were continually hopping around and tugging and struggling for any offal thrown to them.

Observers have reported this bird from different parts of Arizona and New Mexico; but Dr. Coues writes me that he never saw it at Fort Whipple, or elsewhere in the first-named Territory. He found it breeding, however, in the Raton Mountains, in June, under the following circumstances, recorded at the time in his journal.

"Yesterday, the 8th, we were rolling over smooth prairie, ascending a little the while, but so gradually that only the change in the flora indicated the difference in elevation. The flowery verdure was passed, scrubby junipers came thicker and faster, and pine-clad mountain-tops took shape before us. We made the pass to-day, rounding along a picturesque ravine, and the noon halt gave me a chance to see something of the birds. Troops of beautiful Swallows were on wing, and as their backs turned in their wayward flight, the violet-green colors betrayed the species. A colony of them were breeding on the face of a cliff, apparently like *H. lunifrons*, but the nests were not accessible. Whilst I was watching their movements, a harsh scream attracted my attention, and the next moment a beautiful Magpie flew swiftly past with quivering wings, and with a flirt of the glittering tail and a curious evolution dashed into a dense thicket close by In the hope of seeing him again, and perhaps of finding his nest, I hurried to the spot where he had disappeared, and pushed into the underbrush. In a few moments I stood in a little open space, surrounded on all sides and covered above with a network of vines interlacing the twigs and foliage so closely that the sun's rays hardly struggled through. A pretty shady bower! and there, sure enough, was the nest, not likely to be overlooked, for it was as big as a bushel basket, — a globular mass, hung in the top of one of the taller saplings, about twelve feet from the ground. The mother bird was at home, and my bustling approach alarmed her; she flew out of the nest with loud cries of distress, which brought the male to her side in an instant. As I scrambled up the slender trunk, which swayed with my weight, both birds kept flying about my head with redoubled outcry, alighting for an instant, then dashing past again so close that I thought they would peck at me. As I had no means of preserving the nest, I would not take it down, and contented myself with such observations as I could make whilst bestriding a limb altogether too slender for comfort. It was nearly spherical in shape, seemed to be about eighteen inches in diameter, arched over, with a small hole on one side. The walls, composed entirely of interlaced twigs bristling outwardly in every direction, were extremely thick, the space inside being much less than one would expect, and seemingly hardly enough to accommodate the bird's long tail, which I suppose must be held upright. The nest was lined with a little coarse dried grass, and contained six young ones nearly ready to fly. Authors state that the American Magpie lays only two eggs; but I suppose that this particular pair lived too far from scientific centres to find out what was expected of them. Other birds, noticed to-day, were Steller's Jays among the pines and cedars, a flock of *Chrysomitris*, apparently *pinus*, feeding on willow-buds along the rivulet that threaded the gorge, and some Robins."

The eggs of this Magpie are somewhat larger than any I have seen of *P. nuttalli*, and are differently marked and colored. Six specimens from the Sierra Nevada exhibit the following measurements: 1.40 × 0.98, 1.22 × 1.00, 1.41 × 0.95, 1.28 × 0.95, 1.26 × 0.92, 1.32 × 0.96. Their ground-color is a grayish-white, or light gray with a yellowish tinge, spotted with blotches, dottings, and dashes of a purplish or violet brown. In some they are sparsely distributed, showing plainly the ground, more confluent at the larger end. In others they are finer, more generally and more thickly distributed. In others they are much larger and of deeper color, and cover the whole of the larger end with one large cloud of confluent markings. None of these closely resembles the eggs of *P. nuttalli*. The usual number of eggs in a nest, according to Mr. Ridgway, varies from six to nine, although it is said that ten are sometimes found.

Pica caudata, var. nuttalli, AUD.

YELLOW-BILLED MAGPIE.

Pica nuttalli, AUD. Orn. Biog. IV, 1838, 450, pl. ccclxii. — IB. Syn. 1839, 152. — IB. Birds
Am. IV, 1842, 104, pl. ccxxviii. — BON. List, 1838. — IB. Conspectus, 1850, 383. —
NUTTALL, Man. I, (2d ed.,) 1840, 236. — NEWBERRY, Rep. P. R. R. VI, iv, 1857, 84.
— BAIRD, Birds N. Am. 1858, 578, pl. xxvi. — HEERM. X, *S,* 54. — COOPER, Orn.
Cal. I, 1870, 295. *Cleptes nuttalli,* GAMBEL, J. A. N. Sc. Ph. 2d Series, I, 1847, 46.

SP. CHAR. Bill, and naked skin behind the eye, bright yellow ; otherwise similar to *P.
hudsonica.* Length, 17.00 ; wing, 8.00 ; tail, 10.00.
HAB. California (Sacramento Valley, and southern coast region).

We cannot look upon the Yellow-billed Magpie otherwise than as a local
race of the common kind, since it is well known that among the Jays many
species have the bill either black or yellow according to sex, age, or locality ;
and as the Yellow-billed Magpie occupies a more southern locality than
usual, and one very different from that of the black-billed species, it well
may exhibit a special geographical variation. The great restriction in range
is another argument in favor of its being a simple variety.

HABITS. The Yellow-billed Magpie seems to be exclusively a bird of
California, where it is very abundant, and where it replaces almost entirely
the more eastern form. Mr. Ridgway, who met with this variety only in
the valley of the Sacramento, states that he there found it very abundant
among the oaks of that region. It differed from the common Magpie in
being exceedingly gregarious, moving about among the oak groves in small
companies, incessantly chattering as it flew, or as it sat among the branches
of the trees. He saw many of their nests in the tops of the oaks, — indeed,
all were so situated, — yet he never met with the nests of the other species
in a high tree, not even in the river valleys. The young of this Magpie
have the white of the scapulars marked with rusty triangular spots.

Dr. Cooper found this Magpie abundant in the valleys of California, especially near the middle of the State, except during the spring months, when
none were seen in the Santa Clara Valley, the supposition being that they
had retired eastward to the mountains to build their nests. At Santa Barbara he found them numerous in April and May, and saw their nests in oak-
trees. The young were already fledged by the 25th of April. The nest, he
states, is composed of a large mass of coarse twigs twisted together in a
spherical form, with a hole in the side. The eggs he saw resembled those
of the other species, and are described as being whitish-green, spotted with
cinereous-gray and olive-brown. They also breed abundantly about Monterey. They have not been traced to the northern border of the State.

Their food, Dr. Cooper adds, consists of almost everything animal and
vegetable that they can find, and they come about farms and gardens to pick
up whatever they can meet with. They have a loud call that sounds like

pait-pait, with a variety of chattering notes, in tone resembling the human voice, which, indeed, they can be taught to imitate.

An egg of this species from Monterey, California, is of a rounded oval shape, a little less obtuse at one end than the other. The ground-color is a light drab, so closely marked with fine cloudings of an obscure lavender color as nearly to conceal the ground, and to give the egg the appearance of an almost uniform violet-brown. It measures 1.20 inches in length by .90 in breadth.

Genus **CYANURA**, Swainson.

Cyanurus, Swainson, F. Bor.-Am. II, 1831, 495, Appendix. (Type, *Corvus cristatus,* Linn.)
Cyanocitta, Cabanis, Mus. Hein. 1851 (not of Strickland, 1845).

Gen. Char. Head crested. Wings and tail blue, with transverse black bars; head and back of the same color. Bill rather slender, somewhat broader than high at the base;

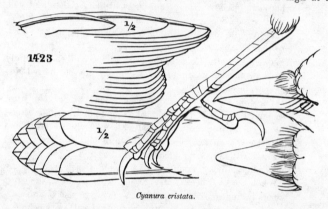

Cyanura cristata.

culmen about equal to the head. Nostrils large, nearly circular, concealed by bristles. Tail about as long as the wings, lengthened, graduated. Hind claw large, longer than its digit.

Species and Varieties.

Common Characters. Wings and tail deep blue, the latter, with the secondaries and tertials, sometimes also the greater coverts, barred with black.

A. Greater coverts, tertials, secondaries, and tail-feathers tipped broadly with white; lower parts generally, including lateral and under parts of head, whitish.

C. cristata. Head above, back, scapulars, lesser wing-coverts, rump and upper tail-coverts, light ashy purplish-blue; a narrow frontal band, a loral spot, streak behind the eye, and collar round the neck, commencing under the crest, passing down across the end of the auriculars and expanding into a crescent across the jugulum, black; throat tinged with purplish-gray, the breast and sides with smoky-gray; abdomen, anal region, and crissum pure white. Wing, 5.70; tail, 6.00; bill, 1.25; tarsus, 1.35; middle toe, .85; crest, 2.20. *Hab.* Eastern Province of North America.

B. No white on wing or tail; lower parts deep blue.

C. stelleri. Color deep blue, less intense than on wings and tail, except dorsal region, which may be deep blue, ashy-brown, or sooty-black. Head and neck dark grayish-brown, dusky-blue, or deep black, the throat more grayish.

a. No white patch over the eye; throat and chin not abruptly lighter than adjacent parts; secondary coverts not barred with black.

Whole head, neck, jugulum, and dorsal region plain sooty-black; no blue streaks on forehead, or else these only faintly indicated. The blue everywhere of a uniform dull greenish-indigo shade. Depth of bill, .45; crest, 2.60; wing, 6.00; tail, 6.00; culmen, 1.35; tarsus, 1.75; middle toe, 1.00. *Hab.* Northwest coast, from Sitka to the Columbia . var. *stelleri.*

Whole head, neck, jugulum, and dorsal region plumbeous-umber; the forehead conspicuously streaked with blue, and the crest washed with the same. The blue of two very different shades, the wings and tail being deep indigo, the body and tail-coverts greenish cobalt-blue. Depth of bill, .35; crest, 2.80; wing, 6.00; tail, 6.00; culmen, 1.25; tarsus, 1.55; middle toe, .90. *Hab.* Sierra Nevada, from Fort Crook to Fort Tejon . . . . . . var. *frontalis.*

b. A patch of silky white over the eye; throat and chin abruptly lighter than the adjoining parts; secondary coverts barred distinctly with black.

Whole crest, cheeks, and foreneck deep black; the crest scarcely tinged with blue; dorsal region light ashy-plumbeous; forehead conspicuously streaked with milk-white. The blue contrasted as in var. *frontalis.* Depth of bill, .35; crest, 3.00; wing, 6.10; tail, 6.10; culmen, 1.25; tarsus, 1.65; middle toe, .90. *Hab.* Rocky Mountains of United States var. *macrolopha.*

Whole crest, cheeks, and foreneck deep black, the crest strongly tinged with blue; dorsal region greenish plumbeous-blue. The blue nearly uniform; forehead conspicuously streaked with bluish-white. Depth of bill, .35; crest, 2.80; wing, 5.90; tail, 5.90; culmen, 1.30; tarsus, 1.60; middle toe, .90. *Hab.* Highlands of Mexico . . . var. *diademata.*[1]

Whole crest, cheeks, and foreneck deep blue, lores black; dorsal region deep purplish-blue; forehead conspicuously streaked with light blue. The blue of a uniform shade — deep purplish-indigo — throughout. Depth of bill, .40; length of crest, 2.50; wing, 5.80; tail, 5.80; culmen, 1.30; tarsus, 1.60; middle toe, .95. *Hab.* Southeastern Mexico (Xalapa, Belize, etc.) . . . . . . var. *coronata.*[2]

The different varieties just indicated under *Cyanura stelleri,* namely, *stelleri, frontalis, macrolopha, diademata,* and *coronata,* all appear to represent

---

[1] *Cyanura diademata* (BONAP.), *Cyanogarrulus diadematus,* BONAP. Consp. p. 377. *Cyanocitta diad.,* SCLATER, Catal. Am. B. 1862, 143. The *C. galeata,* CAB., from Bogota, we have not seen.

[2] *Cyanura coronata,* SWAINS. Phil. Mag. I, 1827, 437.

well-marked and easily defined races of one primitive species, the gradation from one form to the other being very regular, and agreeing with the general variation attendant upon geographical distribution. Thus, beginning with *C. stelleri*, we have the anterior part of head and body, including interscapular region, black, without any markings on the head. In *frontalis* the back is lighter, and a glossy blue shows on the forehead. In *macrolopha* the blue of posterior parts invades the anterior, tingeing them very decidedly, leaving the head black, with a blue shade to the crest; the forehead is glossed with bluish-white; the upper eyelids have a white spot. In *coronata* the blue tinge is deeper, and pervades the entire body, except the side of the head. The shade of blue is different from *macrolopha*, and more like that of *stelleri; diademata*, intermediate in habitat between *macrolopha* and *coronata*, is also intermediate in colors. The tail becomes rather more even, and the bill more slender, as we proceed from *stelleri* to *coronata*. The bars on the secondary coverts become darker in the same progression.

Cyanura cristata, SWAINSON.

BLUE JAY.

Corvus cristatus, LINN. Syst. Nat. I, (10th ed.,) 1758, 106 ; (12th ed.,) 1766, 157. — GMELIN, Syst. Nat. I, 1788, 369. — WILSON, Am. Orn. I, 1808, 2, pl. i, f. 1. — BON. Obs. Wilson, 1824, No. 41. — DOUGHTY, Cab. N. H. II, 1832, 62, pl. vi. — AUD. Orn. Biog. II, 1834, 11 ; V, 1839, 475, pl. cii. *Garrulus cristatus,* "VIEILLOT, Encyclop. 890." — IB. Dict. XI, 477. — BON. Syn. 1828, 58. — SW. F. Bor.-Am. II, 1831, 293. — VIEILLOT, Galerie, I, 1824, 160, pl. cii. — AUD. Birds Am. IV, 110, pl. ccxxxi. — MAX. Caban. J. 1858, VI, 192. *Pica cristata*, WAGLER, Syst. Av. 1827, *Pica*, No. 8. *Cyanurus cristatus,* SWAINSON, F. Bor.-Am. II, 1831, App. 495. — BAIRD, Birds N. Am. 1858, 580. — SAMUELS, 364. — ALLEN, B. E. Fla. 297. *Cyanocorax cristatus*, BON. List, 1838. *Cyanocitta cristata,* STRICKLAND, Ann. Mag. N. H. 1845, 261. — CABANIS, Mus. Hein. 1851, 221. *Cyanogarrulus cristatus*, BON. Consp. 1850, 376.

SP. CHAR. Crest about one third longer than the bill. Tail much graduated. General color above light purplish-blue; wings and tail-feathers ultramarine-blue; the secondaries and tertials, the greater wing-coverts, and the exposed surface of the tail, sharply banded with black and broadly tipped with white, except on the central tail-feathers. Beneath white; tinged with purplish-blue on the throat, and with bluish-brown on the sides. A black crescent on the forepart of the breast, the horns passing forward and connecting with a half-collar on the back of the neck. A narrow frontal line and loral region black; feathers on the base of the bill blue, like the crown. Female rather duller in color, and a little smaller. Length, 12.25; wing, 5.65; tail, 5.75.

HAB. Eastern North America, west to the Missouri. Northeastern Texas (DRESSER, Ibis, 1865, 494). North to Red River and Moose Factory.

Specimens from north of the United States are larger than more southern ones. A series of specimens from Florida, brought by Mr. Boardman, are quite peculiar in some respects, and probably represent a local race resident there. In these Florida specimens the wing and tail are each an inch or more shorter than in Pennsylvania examples, while the bill is not any smaller. The crest is very short; the white spaces on secondaries and tail-feathers more restricted.

Cyanura cristata.

HABITS. The common Blue Jay of North America is found throughout the continent, from the Atlantic coast to the Missouri Valley, and from Florida and Texas to the fur regions nearly or quite to the 56th parallel. It was found breeding near Lake Winnepeg by Donald Gunn. It was also observed in these regions by Sir John Richardson. It was met with by Captain Blakiston on the forks of the Saskatchewan, but not farther west.

The entire family to which this Jay belongs, and of which it is a very conspicuous member, is nearly cosmopolitan as to distribution, and is distinguished by the remarkable intelligence of all its members. Its habits are striking, peculiar, and full of interest, often evincing sagacity, forethought, and intelligence strongly akin to reason. These traits belong not exclusively to any one species or generic subdivision, but are common to the whole family.

When first met with in the wild and unexplored regions of our country, the Jay appears shy and suspicious of the intruder, man. Yet, curious to a remarkable degree, he follows the stranger, watches all his movements, hovers with great pertinacity about his steps, ever keeping at a respectful distance, even before he has been taught to beware of the deadly gun. Afterwards, as he becomes better acquainted with man, the Jay conforms his own conduct to the treatment he receives. Where he is hunted in wanton sport, because of brilliant plumage, or persecuted because of unjust prejudices and a bad reputation not deserved, he is shy and wary, shuns, as much as possible, human society, and, when the hunter intrudes into his retreat, seems to delight to follow and annoy him, and to give the alarm to all dwellers of the woods that their foe is approaching.

In parts of the country, as in Iowa, Illinois, Indiana, and other Western States, where the Jay is unmolested and exempt from persecution, we find him as familiar and confiding as any of the favored birds of the Eastern States. In the groves of Iowa Mr. Allen found our Blue Jay nearly as unsuspicious as a Black-capped Titmouse. In Illinois he speaks of them as very abundant and half domestic. And again, in Indiana, in one of the principal streets of Richmond, the same gentleman found the nest of these birds in a lilac-bush, under the window of a dwelling. In the summer of 1843 I saw a nest of the Jay, filled with young, in a tree standing near the house of Mr. Audubon, in the city of New York. The habits of no two species can well be more unlike than are those which persecution on the one hand and kind treatment on the other have developed in this bird.

The Blue Jay, wherever found, is more or less resident. This is especially the case in the more southern portions of its area of reproduction. In Texas, Dr. Lincecum informs us, this Jay remains both summer and winter. It is there said to build its nest of mud, a material rarely if ever used in more northern localities; and when placed not far from dwelling-houses, it is lined with cotton thread, rags of calico, and the like. They are, he writes, very intelligent and sensible birds, subsisting on insects, acorns, etc. He has occasionally known them to destroy bats. In Texas they seem to seek the protection of man, and to nest near dwellings as a means of safety against Hawks. They nest but once a year, and lay but four eggs. In a female dissected by him, he detected one hundred and twelve ova, and from these data he infers that the natural life of a Jay is about thirty years.

Mr. Allen mentions finding the Blue Jay in Kansas equally at home, and as vivacious and even more gayly colored than at the North. While it seemed to have forgotten none of the droll notes and fantastic ways always to be expected from it, there was added to its manners that familiarity which characterizes it in the more newly settled portions of the country, occasionally surprising one with some new expression of feeling or sentiment, or some unexpected eccentricity in its varied notes, perhaps developed by the more southern surroundings.

The Blue Jay is arboreal in its habits. It prefers the shelter and security of thick covers to more open ground. It is omnivorous, eating either animal or vegetable food, though with an apparent preference for the former, feeding upon insects, their eggs and larvæ, and worms, wherever procurable. It also lays up large stores of acorns and beech mast for food in winter, when insects cannot be procured in sufficient abundance. Even at this season it hunts for and devours in large quantities the eggs of the destructive tent caterpillar.

The Jay is charged with a propensity to destroy the eggs and young of the smaller birds, and has even been accused of killing full-grown birds. I am not able to verify these charges, but they seem to be too generally conceded to be disputed. These are the only serious grounds of complaint that can be brought against it, and are more than outweighed, tenfold, by the immense services it renders to man in the destruction of his enemies. Its depredations on the garden or the farm are too trivial to be mentioned.

The Blue Jay is conspicuous as a musician. He exhibits a variety in his notes, and occasionally a beauty and a harmony in his song, for which few give him due credit. Wilson compares his position among our singing birds to that of the trumpeter in the band. His notes he varies to an almost infinite extent, at one time screaming with all his might, at another warbling with all the softness of tone and moderation of the Bluebird, and again imparting to his voice a grating harshness that is indescribable.

The power of mimicry possessed by the Jay, though different from, is hardly surpassed by that of the Mocking-Bird. It especially delights to imitate the cries of the Sparrow Hawk, and at other times those of the Red-tailed and Red-shouldered Hawks are given with such similarity that the small birds fly to a covert, and the inmates of the poultry-yard are in the greatest alarm. Dr. Jared P. Kirtland, of Cleveland, on whose grounds a large colony of Jays took up their abode and became very familiar, has given me a very interesting account of their habits. The following is an extract: "They soon became so familiar as to feed about our yards and corn-cribs. At the dawn of every pleasant day throughout the year, the nesting-season excepted, a stranger in my house might well suppose that all the axles in the country were screeching aloud for lubrication, hearing the harsh and discordant utterances of these birds. During the day the poultry might be frequently seen running into their hiding-places, and the gobbler with his upturned eye searching the heavens for the enemy, all excited and alarmed by the mimic utterances of the adapt ventriloquists, the Jays, simulating the cries of the Red-shouldered and the Red-tailed Hawks. The domestic circle of the barn-yard evidently never gained any insight into the deception by experience; for, though the trick was repeated every few hours, the excitement would always be re-enacted."

When reared from the nest, these birds become very tame, and are perfectly reconciled to confinement. They very soon grow into amusing pets, learning to imitate the human voice, and to simulate almost every sound that they hear. Wilson gives an account of one that had been brought up in a family of a gentleman in South Carolina that displayed great intelligence, and had all the loquacity of a parrot. This bird could utter several words with great distinctness, and, whenever called, would immediately answer to its name with great sociability.

The late Dr. Esteep, of Canton, Ohio, an experienced bird-fancier, assured Dr. Kirtland that he has invariably found the Blue Jay more ingenious, cunning, and teachable than any other species of bird he has ever attempted to instruct.

Dr. Kirtland has also informed me of the almost invaluable services rendered to the farmers in his neighborhood, by the Blue Jays, in the destruction of caterpillars. When he first settled on his farm, he found every apple and wild-cherry tree in the vicinity extensively disfigured and denuded of its leaves by the larvæ of the *Clisiocampa americana*, or the tent caterpillar. The evil was so extensive that even the best farmers despaired of counteracting it. Not long after the Jays colonized upon his place he found they were feeding their young quite extensively with these larvæ, and so thoroughly that two or three years afterwards not a worm was to be seen in that neighborhood; and more recently he has searched for it in vain, in order to rear cabinet specimens of the moth.

The Jay builds a strong coarse nest in the branch of some forest or orchard tree, or even in a low bush. It is formed of twigs rudely but strongly interwoven, and is lined with dark fibrous roots. The eggs are usually five, and rarely six in number.

The eggs of this species are usually of a rounded-oval shape, obtuse, and of very equal size at either end. Their ground-color is a brownish-olive, varying in depth, and occasionally an olive-drab. They are sparingly spotted with darker olive-brown. In size they vary from 1.05 to 1.20 inches in length, and in breadth from .82 to .88 of an inch. Their average size is about 1.15 by .86 of an inch.

Cyanura stelleri, SWAINSON.

STELLER'S JAY.

Corvus stelleri, GMELIN, Syst. Nat. I, 1788, 370. — LATH. Ind. Orn. I, 1790, 158. — PALLAS, Zoog. Rosso-As. I, 1811, 393. — BONAP. Zoöl. Jour. III, 1827, 49. — IB. Suppl. Syn. 1828, 433. — AUD. Orn. Biog. IV, 1838, 453, pl. ccclxii. *Garrulus stelleri*, VIEILLOT, Dict. XII, 1817, 481. — BONAP. Am. Orn. II, 1828, 44, pl. xiii. — NUTTALL, Man. I, 1832, 229. — AUD. Syn. 1839, 154. — IB. Birds Am. IV, 1842, 107, pl. ccxxx (not of SWAINSON, F. Bor.-Am. ?). *Cyanurus stelleri*, SWAINSON, F. Bor.-Am. II, 1831, 495, App. *Pica stelleri*, WAGLER, Syst. Av. 1827, *Pica*, No. 10. *Cyanocorax stelleri*, BON. List, 1838. FINSCH, Abh. Nat. III, 1872, 40 (Alaska). *Cyanocitta stelleri*, CAB. Mus. Hein. 1851, 221. NEWBERRY, P. R. R. Rep. VI, IV, 1857, 85. *Cyanogarrulus stelleri*, BONAP. Conspectus, 1850, 377. *Steller's Crow*, PENNANT, Arctic Zoöl. II, Sp. 139. LATH. Syn. I, 387. *Cyanura s.* BAIRD, Birds N. Am. 1858, 581 (in part). LORD, Pr. R. A. Inst. IV, 122 (British Columbia ; nest). — DALL & BANNISTER, Tr. Chic. Ac. I, 1869, 486 (Alaska). — COOPER, Orn. Cal. I, 1870, 298 (in part).

SP. CHAR. Crest about one third longer than the bill. Fifth quill longest; second about equal to the secondary quills. Tail graduated; lateral feathers about .70 of an inch shortest. Head and neck all round, and forepart of breast, dark brownish-black. Back and lesser wing-coverts blackish-brown, the scapulars glossed with blue. Under parts, rump, tail-coverts, and wings greenish-blue; exposed surfaces of lesser quills dark indigo-blue ; tertials and ends of tail-feathers rather obsoletely banded with black. Feathers of the forehead streaked with greenish-blue. Length, about 13.00; wing, 5.85; tail, 5.85; tarsus, 1.75 (1,921).

HAB. Pacific coast of North America, from the Columbia River to Sitka; east to St. Mary's Mission, Rocky Mountains.

HABITS. Dr. Suckley regarded Steller's Jay as probably the most abundant bird of its size in all the wooded country between the Rocky Mountains and the Pacific. He describes it as tame, loquacious, and possessed of the most impudent curiosity. It is a hardy, tough bird, and a constant winter resident of Washington Territory. It is remarkable for its varied cries and notes, and seems to have one for every emotion or pursuit in which it is engaged. .It also has a great fondness for imitating the notes of other birds. Dr. Suckley states that frequently when pleasantly excited by the hope of obtaining a rare bird, in consequence of hearing an unknown note issuing from some clump of bushes or thicket, he has been not a little disappointed by finding that it had issued from this Jay. It mimics accurately the principal cry of the Catbird.

Dr. Cooper also found it very common in all the forests on both sides of the Cascade Mountains. While it seemed to depend chiefly upon the forest for its food, in the winter it would make visits to the vicinity of houses, and steal anything eatable it could find within its reach, even potatoes. In these forages upon the gardens and farm-yards, they are both silent and watchful, evidently conscious of the peril of their undertaking, and when discovered they instantly fly off to the concealment of the forests. They also make visits to the Indian lodges when the owners are absent, and force their way into them if possible, one of their number keeping watch. In the forest they do not appear to be shy or timid, but boldly follow those who intrude upon their domain, screaming, and calling their companions around them. Hazel-nuts are one of their great articles of winter food ; and Dr. Cooper states that, in order to break the shell, the Jay resorts to the ingenious expedient of taking them to a branch of a tree, fixing them in a crotch or cavity, and hammering them with its bill until it can reach the meat within. Their nest he describes as large, loosely built of sticks, and placed in a bush or low tree.

At certain seasons of the year its food consisted almost entirely of the seeds of the pine, particularly of *P. brachyptera,* which Dr. Newberry states he has often seen them extracting from the cones, and with which the stomachs of those he killed were usually filled. He found these birds ranging as far north as the line of the British Territory, and from the coast to the Rocky Mountains.

In his Western journey Mr. Nuttall met with these birds in the Blue Mountains of the Oregon, east of Walla-walla. There he found them scarce and shy. Afterwards he found them abundant in the pine forests of the Columbia, where their loud trumpeting clangor was heard at all hours of the day, calling out with a loud voice, *djay-djay,* or chattering with a variety of other notes, some of them similar to those of the common Blue Jay. They are more bold and familiar than our Jay. Watchful as a dog, no sooner does a stranger show himself in their vicinity than they neglect all other employment to come round him, following and sometimes scolding at him with great pertinacity and signs of irritability. At other times, stimulated by curiosity, they follow for a while in perfect silence, until something seems to arouse their ire, and then their vociferous cries are poured out with unceasing volubility till the intruder has passed from their view.

In the month of May, Mr. Nuttall found a nest of these birds in a small sapling of the Douglas fir, on the borders of a dense forest, and, some time after, a second nest with young, in an elevated branch of another fir, on the border of a rocky cliff. The first nest contained four eggs, of a pale green, marked with small olive-brown spots, varied with others inclining to a violet hue. The parents flew at him with the utmost anger and agitation, almost deafening him with their cries ; and although he took only two of their eggs, the next day he found they had forsaken their nest. This nest was bulky, made of interlaced twigs and roots, with a stout layer of mud, and lined with black rootlets. One of the eggs taken by Mr. Nuttall is in my cabinet, and is as he describes it, except that the obscure markings of violet have nearly faded out. It measures 1.20 inches in length, and .90 in breadth, is oval in shape, and a little more obtuse at one end than at the other.

This Jay was obtained by Steller at Nootka, on the west coast of Vancouver Island, in latitude 50°. It was also found in abundance by Mr. Dall at Sitka, in British Columbia, where a number of specimens were obtained by Mr. Bischoff and by Mr. Elliot.

Mr. J. K. ·Lord states that this Jay ever makes its presence known by the constant utterance of discordant screams. It is continually hopping from bough to bough, darting down to catch an insect, performing short, erratic flights, and jerking up and down its crest of bright feathers. Its noisy song seems to be everywhere. It is the embodiment of restlessness, and, by dint of sheer impudence, attracts attention even from the hunter. He adds that it seemed fond of frequenting the haunts of man, and is always plentiful near Indian lodges or white men's shanties. It is by no means epicurean in taste, but readily devours anything, whether seeds or salmon, grasshoppers or venison. Its nest he found artfully concealed amidst the thick foliage of a young pine-tree. It was composed of moss, small twigs, lichens, and fir fronds, and lined with deer's hair. The average number of eggs laid appears to be seven.

Cyanura stelleri, var. frontalis, RIDGWAY.

SIERRA JAY.

Cyanura stelleri, AUCT. All reference to Steller's Jay as occurring in California, excepting on the northern Coast Range, relate to this variety.

SP. CHAR. Head, neck, and dorsal region plumbeous-umber, darker on the head, and posteriorly changing gradually into the light greenish-blue of the rest of the body ; wings and tail deep indigo-blue, the tertials, secondaries, and tail conspicuously marked with broad and rather distant bars of black ; primaries greenish light-blue, like the rump, abdomen, etc. Whole forehead conspicuously streaked with blue (the streaks forming two parallel series, where the feathers are not disarranged), and the crest strongly tinged with blue. ♂ (53,639, Carson City, Nevada, April 30, 1868) : wing, 6.00; tail, 6.00; culmen, 1.25; depth of bill, .35; tarsus, 1.55; middle toe, .90; crest, 2.80. ♀ (53,640, Carson City, Nevada, April 30, 1868) : wing, 5.70; tail, 5.50. *Young* with the blue of the body and head entirely replaced by a sooty grayish; and that of the wings and tail duller, and less distinctly barred.

HAB. Whole length of the Sierra Nevada, from Fort Crook (where it approaches var. *stelleri*) to Fort Tejon.

In the colors of the body, wings, and tail, this well-marked race resembles *C. macrolopha* in every respect, except that the greater coverts are not barred with black ; there being the same abrupt contrast between the deep blue of the wings and tail, and the light greenish-blue of the body, tail-coverts, and primaries, — seen only in these two forms. The variety is confined to the mountains of California and Western Nevada, extending along the Sierra Nevada about the entire length of the State, there being specimens in the collection from Fort Crook and Fort Tejon, and intermediate localities.

HABITS. The Blue-fronted Jay, so far as it was observed by Mr. Ridgway, was found to be exclusively an inhabitant of the pine woods of the Sierra Nevada, and is, with Clarke's Nutcracker, one of the most characteristic birds of that region. In its general habits and manners, it greatly resembles the eastern Blue Jay, but is rather more shy, while its notes are very different, and do not possess the variety and flexibility of the *cristata*, but are in comparison harsh and discordant. The usual note is a hoarse, deep-toned monosyllabic squawk. Sometimes it utters a hollow sonorous chatter.

Near Carson City one of these birds had been winged by a shot, and, in falling, alighted on the lower branches of a pine-tree. Upon an attempt to capture it, the bird began to ascend the tree limb by limb, at the same time uttering a perfect imitation of the cry of the Red-tailed Hawk, evidently in the hope of frightening away his tormentors. Dr. Newberry regards this Jay as the western counterpart of the *C. cristata*. By its more conspicuous crest, its bold, defiant air, and its excessively harsh and disagreeable cry, it challenges and secures attention. He found it almost exclusively confined to the hilly and mountainous districts, choosing in preference those covered with pines.

Dr. Heermann found these Jays abundant and resident as far south as Warner's Ranch, where, though common, they were for some reason so unusually wild and vigilant as not to be easily procurable. In feeding, he observed that they seemed always to begin in the lower branches and ascend, hopping from twig to twig, to the topmost point, and, while thus employed, utter a harsh screaming note that can be heard to a considerable distance.

This species, Dr. Cooper states, is numerous in the mountains of California, inhabiting the whole length of the Sierra Nevada, and the Coast Range as far south, at least, as Santa Cruz. Though showing a decided preference for the pine forests, they sometimes in winter frequent those of oaks. They are omnivorous, eating seeds, acorns, nuts, insects, and in winter even potatoes and dead fish. They are at times bold and prying, and at others very cautious and suspicious. They soon learn to appreciate a gun, and show great sagacity in their movements to avoid its peril. On the Columbia they lay in May, and in California about a month earlier.

Cyanura stelleri, var. macrolopha, BAIRD.

LONG-CRESTED JAY.

Cyanocitta macrolopha, BAIRD, Pr. A. N. Sc. Phila. VII, June, 1854, 118 (Albuquerque). *? Garrulus stelleri,* SWAINSON, F. Bor.-Am. II, 1831, 294, pl. liv (head-waters of Columbia; figure of a bird intermediate between *C. stelleri* and *macrolopha*). *Cyanura macrolopha,* BAIRD, Birds N. Am. 1858, 582. — ELLIOT, Illust Am. B, I, xvii. — COOPER, Orn. Cal. I, 1870, 300.

SP. CHAR. Crest nearly twice the length of the bill. Tail moderately graduated; the lateral feathers about .60 of an inch shorter than the middle. Fourth and fifth quills longest; second shorter than the secondaries. Head all round, throat, and forepart of the breast, black, the crest with a gloss of blue; rest of back dark ashy-brown with a gloss of greenish. Under parts, rump, tail-coverts, and outer surfaces of primaries, greenish-blue; greater coverts, secondaries, and tertials, and upper surface of tail-feathers bright blue, banded with black; forehead streaked with opaque white, passing behind into pale blue; a white patch over the eye. Chin grayish. Length, 12.50; wing, 5.85; tail, 5.85; tarsus, 1.70 (8,351).

HAB. Central line of Rocky Mountains from northern border of the United States to table-lands of Mexico; Fort Whipple, Arizona.

Young birds have the bright blue of body and black of head replaced by a dull slate; the head unvaried.

An apparent link between this variety and *C. stelleri* is represented in the Smithsonian collection by three specimens from the region towards the head-waters of the Columbia, where the respective areas of distribution of the two overlap. In this the anterior parts of the body are nearly as black as in *stelleri* (much darker than *macrolopha*), with the short crest; but the forehead (except in one specimen) is streaked with blue, and there is a white patch over the eye. As in *stelleri,* there are no black bars on the greater wing-coverts. As this is an abundant form, whether permanent race or hybrid, it may be called var. *annectens.*

HABITS. The Long-crested Jay appears to occur throughout the central range of the Rocky Mountains from British Columbia to Mexico, where it is replaced by a closely allied species or race, the *Cyanura coronata* of Swainson.

Mr. Ridgway met with this Jay only among the Wahsatch and the Uintah Mountains. They appeared to be rather common in those regions, though far from being abundant. In their manners and in their notes they are described as having been almost an exact counterpart of the Sierra Nevada form. Their notes, however, are said to be not so loud nor so coarse as those of the more western species. A nest, found by Mr. Ridgway, June 25, 1869, in Parley's Park, Wahsatch Mountains, was in a small fir-tree on the edge of a wood. It was saddled on a horizontal branch about fifteen feet from the ground, and contained six eggs. The base of the nest was composed of coarse strong sticks, rudely put together. Upon this was constructed a solid, firm plastering of mud of a uniform concave shape, lined with fine wiry roots. The external diameter is about nine inches, and the height of the nest four. The interior is five inches in diameter, and three in depth.

The species was first described by Professor Baird, from specimens obtained by Dr. Kennerly, who writes that he first saw this bird among the lofty pines of the Sierra Madre in November, 1853. Leaving that range, he did not meet with it again until his party crossed the Aztec Mountains, in January, 1854, where it was less abundant than when first met with. It was, for the most part, found among the cedars on the high grounds, though occasionally seen among the clumps of large pines that were scattered along the valley. The party did not meet with it again.

Dr. Coues found this species a common and a resident bird in Arizona. It was observed to be almost exclusively an inhabitant of pine woods, and was generally to be met with only in small companies, never congregating in the manner of Woodhouse's Jay. He describes it as very shy, vigilant, noisy, and tyrannical.

The eggs of *C. macrolopha* measure 1.30 inches in length and .91 in breadth. Their ground-color is a light sea-green. They are somewhat sparingly spotted with fine markings of dark olive-brown, and lighter cloudings of a purplish or violet brown. They are oblong oval in shape, obtuse at either end, but more tapering at one end. They appear to be a little larger than the eggs of *stelleri*, and the ground-color is brighter, and the markings deeper and more of an olive hue.

Genus CYANOCITTA, Strickland.

Cyanocitta, Strickland, Annals and Mag. N. H. XV, 1845, 260. (Type, *Garrulus californicus*, Vigors.)
Aphelocoma, Cabanis, Mus. Hein. 1851, 221. (Same type.)

Char. Head without crest. Wings and tail blue, without any bands. Back usually with a gray patch, different from the head. Bill about as broad as high at the base, and the culmen a little shorter than the head. Nostrils large, nearly circular, and concealed. Tail nearly equal to the wings, lengthened, graduated, or else shorter and nearly even.

This genus is readily distinguished from the preceding by the entire absence of crest and of black bars on the blue of wings and tail. The species and races hitherto described will be found detailed in the accompanying synopsis. The characters indicated above are of no very great generic value, but as the group is a very natural one it will be as well to retain it. As in *Cyanura*, the species are peculiar to the United States and Mexico, one indeed being apparently confined to the Peninsula of Florida.

It would perhaps be not very far out of the way to consider Sections A

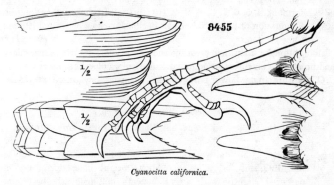

8455

½

½

Cyanocitta californica.

and B as representing in their general characters, respectively, the types from which their subdivisions have sprung.

A. Tail longer than wings. A superciliary stripe of whitish streaks; jugular and pectoral feathers faintly edged with bluish, posteriorly forming an indistinct collar, interrupted medially. Ear-coverts dusky, except in var. *woodhousei.*

a. Forehead and nasal tufts hoary white; the superciliary stripe a continuous wash of the same. Scapulars blue like the wings; dorsal region (the interscapulars) as light-colored as the lower parts.

C. floridana. Back and lower parts pale ashy-brown; lower tail-coverts bright blue. Wing, 4.50; tail, 5.70; bill, 1.20 and .35; tarsus, 1.40; middle toe, .85. Wing-formula, 4, 5, 6, 7, 3, 8, 9, 2, 10; first, 1.80 shorter than longest. Graduation of tail, 1.50. *Hab.* Florida (only).

b. Forehead and nasal tufts bright blue; superciliary stripe composed of narrow streaks; scapulars ashy like the back; back much darker than the lower parts.

C. californica.

Lower tail-coverts bright blue, dorsal region not well-defined ashy; auriculars bluish, beneath continuous pure ash. Superciliary streak well defined. Wing, 5.15; tail, 6.00; bill, 1.35 and .30; tarsus, 1.40; middle toe, .85. Wing-formula, fourth, fifth, and sixth equal; 7, 3, 8, 9 = 2; first, 1.80 shorter than longest. Graduation of tail, .90. *Hab.* Rocky Mountains and Middle Province of United States . . . . var. *woodhousei.*

Lower tail-coverts pure white; dorsal region well-defined ashy; auriculars blackish; beneath dull white, approaching ash on breast. Superciliary streak indistinct. Wing, 5.65; tail, 6.00; bill, 1.20 and .35; tarsus, 1.42; middle toe, .90. Wing-formula, 5, 6, 7, 4, 8, 3, 9, 10 = 2; first, 2.20 shorter than longest. Graduation of tail, .80. *Hab.* Mexico (Orizaba; City of Mexico) var. *sumichrasti.*[1]

[1] *Cyanocitta sumichrasti*, RIDGWAY, Rep. U. S. Geol. Expl. 40th Par. All Mexican *Cyanocittas* with a whitish superciliary streak, blue edgings to jugular feathers, etc., are to be referred to this strongly marked race. A very conspicuous character of this variety is the strong "hook" to the upper mandible; the tip beyond the notch being much elongated, or unusually "produced." In the collection is a specimen (60,058 ♀, Mexico, A. BOUCARD) which we have re-

Superciliary streak sharply defined, conspicuous. Wing, 5.00; tail, 5.60; bill, 1.20 and .37; tarsus, 1.55; middle toe, .95. Wing-formula, 4, 5, 6, 7, 3, 8, 9, 2, 10; first, 2.10 shorter than longest. Graduation of tail, 1.15. *Hab.* Pacific Province of United States; Cape St. Lucas . . . . var. *c a l i f o r n i c a.*

B. Tail not longer than wings, or considerably shorter. No superciliary stripe, and no streaks on throat or jugulum. Auriculars blue like the crown.

C. ultramarina. Lower parts whitish, conspicuously different from the upper.

Tail nearly, or perfectly even.

Length, 13.00; tail even; bill, 1.50; tail, 7.00. *Hab.* Mexico.

var. *u l t r a m a r i n a.*[1]

Length, 11.50; tail very slightly rounded (graduation, .25 only); bill, 1.28 and .35; tail, 50. Above bright blue, dorsal region obscured slightly with ashy; beneath dull pale ash, becoming gradually whitish posteriorly, the crissum being pure ash. Lores blue. Tarsus, 1.45; middle toe, .95. Wing-formula, 5, 4 = 6, 7, 3, 8, 9, 10, 2; first, 2.10 shorter than longest. Graduation of tail, .25. *Hab.* Lower Rio Grande . . . . . var. *c o u c h i.*

Tail considerably rounded.

Colors as in *couchi*, but dorsal region scarcely obscured by ashy. Lores black. Wing, 7.50; tail, 7.50; bill, 1.30 and .40; tarsus, 1.60; middle toe, .90. Wing-formula, 5, 4, 6, 3 = 7, 8, 9, 2; first, 2.75, shorter than longest. Graduation of tail, 1.15. *Hab.* Mexico (Orizaba, Mirador, etc.) . . . . . . var. *s o r d i d a.*[2]

Graduation of the colors as in *sordida*, but the blue, instead of being a bright ultramarine, is very much paler and duller, and with a greenish cast, the whole dorsal region decidedly ashy; ash of the pectoral region much paler, and throat similar, instead of decidedly whitish, in contrast; pure white of posterior lower parts covering whole abdomen instead of being confined to crissum. Wing, 6.20; tail, 5.70; bill, 1.30 and .40; tarsus, 1.50; middle toe, .97. Wing-formula, fourth, fifth, and sixth equal; 7, 3, 8, 9, 2; first, 2.20, shorter than longest. Graduation of tail, .50. *Hab.* Southern Rocky Mountains (Fort Buchanan, and Copper Mines, Arizona).

var. *a r i z o n œ.*

C. unicolor.[3] Lower parts bright blue, like the upper. Entirely

ferred to this race, but which differs in such an important respect from all other specimens of the several races referrible to *californica*, as extended, that it may belong to a distinct form. Having the precise aspect of *sumichrasti* in regard to its upper plumage, it lacks, however, any trace of the blue edgings and pectoral collar, the whole lower parts being continuously uninterrupted dull white, purer posteriorly. The appearance is such as to cause a suspicion that it may be a link between *sumichrasti* and one of the races of *ultramarina*. It measures: wing, 5.50; tail, 6.00; graduation of tail, .70.

[1] *Cyanocitta ultramarina,* (BONAP.) STRICKLAND. — *Garrulus ultramarinus,* BONAP. J. A. N. S. IV, 1825, 386 (not of Audubon).

[2] *Cyanocitta sordida,* (SWAINS.) (not of BAIRD, Birds N. Am., which is *arizonæ*). — SCLATER, Cat. Am. B. 1862, 143. *Garrulus sordidus,* SWAINS. Phil. Mag. 1827, i, 437.

[3] *Cyanocitta unicolor,* (DU BUS) BONAP. Consp. p. 378. — *Cyanocorax unicolor,* DU BUS, Bull. Acad. Brux. XIV, pt. 2, p. 103.

uniform rich ultramarine-blue; lores black. Wing, 6.70; tail, 6.70; bill, 1.30 and .50; tarsus, 1.45; middle toe, .95. Wing-formula, 5, 6, 4, 7, 3, 8, 9, 2; first, 2.60 shorter than longest. Graduation of tail, 1.50. *Hab.* Southern Mexico (Cordova, Mirador, etc.); Guatemala.

In the first section of this group we see the same indication of variation from a common type with the region that is so evident in *Cyanura.* Thus, *Cyanocitta woodhousei* differs from *californica,* much as *Cyanura macrolopha* does from *C. stelleri* (var. *frontalis*), in more slender bill and a greater percentage of blue; this invading the back and under parts, the lower tail-coverts especially. But here the parallel of modification ends, for the Mexican representative of the species (*C. sumichrasti*) appears to revert back to the characters of *californica,* having like it a minimum amount of blue, though this almost obliterates the superciliary stripe of white. In this respect there is more resemblance to the case of *Pipilo fusca* and its three races in the three regions inhabited by these representative forms of *Cyanocitta californica;* for, while the Mexican (*P. fusca*) and Californian (*P. crissalis*) are very much alike, the one from the intervening region (*P. mesoleuca*) is more different from the two extreme races than they are from each other.

In the other section of the genus the relation between *arizonæ* and *sordida* is a parallel to that between *Cyanura macrolopha* and *C. coronata;* the southern forms (*sordida* and *coronata*) differing principally in the greater intensity and prevalence or amount of the blue. The relations of *couchi* and *ultramarina* to the two above mentioned are yet obscure, owing to the small material at command, — there being only two specimens of the former, and none of the latter, in the National Museum at Washington.

Cyanocitta floridana, BONAP.

FLORIDA JAY.

Corvus floridanus, BARTRAM, Travels, 1791, 291. — AUD. Orn. Biog. I, 1831, 444, pl. lxxxvii. *Garrulus floridanus,* BON. Am. Orn. II, 1828, 11, pl. xi. — NUTTALL, Man. I, 1832, 230. — AUD. Syn. 1839, 154. — IB. Birds Am. IV, 1842, 118, pl. ccxxxiii. *Cyanurus floridanus,* SWAINSON, F. B. A. II, 1831, 495. *Cyanocorax floridanus,* BON. List, 1838. *Cyanocitta floridana,* BON. Consp. 1850, 377. — BAIRD, Birds N. Am. 1858, 586. — ALLEN, B. E. Fla. 298. *Aphelocoma floridana,* CABANIS, Mus. Hein. 1851, 22. *Garrulus cyaneus,* VIEILLOT, Nouv. Dict. XII, 1817, 476 (not described). *? Garrulus cærulescens,* VIEILLOT, Nouv. Dict. XII, 1817, 480. — ORD. J. A. N. Sc. I, 1818, 347. *Pica cærulescens,* WAGLER, Syst. Av. 1827, *Pica,* No. 11.

SP. CHAR. Tail much graduated; lateral feathers nearly 1.50 inches shortest. Tail an inch longer than the wings. Above blue, including scapulars; interscapular region and back brownish-ash, the former lighter. Forehead and sides of the crown, including the nasal feathers, hoary white. Sides of head and neck blue; the former tinged with blackish, the latter sending a streaked collar of the same entirely across the breast; region anterior to this collar dirty white, streaked on the edges of the feathers with blue; rest of under parts dirty whitish-brown; under tail-coverts blue, the tibia tinged with the same. Length, 11.00; wing, 4.50; tail, 5.70; tarsus, 1.45.

HAB. Florida only, and quite local.

HABITS. This beautiful species appears to be exclusively confined to the peninsula of Florida, and there is no authentic evidence that it has ever been found outside of the limits of that State. The statement of Bonaparte, that these birds are found in the States of Louisiana and Kentucky, has never been confirmed, and Mr. Audubon, who was for many years a resident of both States and familiar with the birds of each, was very positive the statement was without foundation. It has never been observed even in Georgia or Alabama, and Mr. Nuttall states that it is not found in any part of West Florida.

Mr. Allen, in his recent paper on the winter birds of East Florida, speaking of this species, states that it is numerous in the scrub, but does not appear to frequent the pine woods, the hummocks, or the swamps. He saw none along the St. John's, except at Blue Springs, but they occur in numbers a few miles back from the river.

Dr. Bryant, in his Notes on the birds of Florida, mentions that this species is tolerably plentiful in the vicinity of Enterprise. He regarded it as exceedingly interesting on account of its limited geographical distribution. With no apparent obstacle to its movements, it is yet confined to a small part of the peninsula of Florida, its area of distribution north and south not exceeding three degrees of latitude, if so much. He saw none north of St. Augustine, and none south of Jupiter's Inlet. So far as he observed them, they were exclusively confined to the growth of scrub-oak, which in many places is so entangled with creeping plants that it is impossible to walk through without cutting a path. This growth is generally found on elevated ridges running parallel to the sea-coast. The most extensive of these, near Enterprise, is about three miles wide, and eighty feet above the lake.

The flight of this species is said by Mr. Audubon to be performed at a short distance from the ground, and to consist either of a single sailing sweep, as it passes from one tree to another, or of continuous flappings with a slightly undulating motion, in the manner of the Canada Jay. Its notes are described as softer than those of the Blue Jay, and more frequently uttered. Its motions are also quicker and more abrupt. Its food is said to consist of snails, which it collects on the ground, insects, and various kinds of fruits and berries. It is also charged with being very destructive of eggs and young birds.

The Florida Jay is said to be easily kept in confinement, feeding readily on dried or fresh fruit and the kernels of various nuts, and soon appears to be reconciled to its loss of liberty. It secures its food between its feet, and breaks it into pieces before swallowing it. In this way it feeds on the acorn of the live-oak, snails, and the seeds of the sword-palmetto.

The nest of this Jay is formed of dry sticks, placed across each other, and, although rounded in form, is so lightly made that the birds may be seen through its interstices. It is lined with fibrous rootlets. Only one brood is raised in a season. Audubon's descriptions of its eggs are inaccurate, and only applicable to those of the Blue Jay.

Mr. Audubon observed a pair of these birds in confinement in New Orleans. They were fed upon rice and dry fruit. At dessert they were allowed their liberty, when they would fly to the table, feed on the almonds given them, and drink claret diluted with water. They attempted to mimic various sounds, but did so very imperfectly.

Mr. Nuttall states that at the approach of winter these birds retire to the south of St. Augustine. He regards their voice as less harsh than that of the Blue Jay, and states that they have a variety of notes, some of which are probably imitations, and are said to resemble the song of the Wood Thrush and the calls of the common Jay.

An egg of the Florida Jay before me is of a rounded oval shape, being nearly equally obtuse at either end. The ground-color is a light bluish-gray, marked almost exclusively at the larger end with a few small spots of a light rufous-brown. It has no near resemblance to the eggs of the California Jay, nor to those of any other Jay that I have seen. It measures 1.05 inches by .80.

In its flight and action, Dr. Bryant thought the Florida Jay resembled the Mocking-Bird. It has none of the restless, suspicious manner of the Blue Jay. He never heard it utter more than a single note, this being much softer than the usual cry of the Blue Jay; its song he regarded as rather monotonous. It seldom flies more than a short distance at a time, and seems to trust for protection to the difficulty of access to its abode. It also evinces a great partiality for particular localities. Generally only a single pair is seen at a time, though in one place he has seen three pairs together. It is not fond of civilization, and is seldom known to frequent the vicinity of dwellings.

A nest found by Dr. Bryant on the 15th of April was built in a scrub-oak about three feet from the ground. It was made of small twigs, compactly and carefully lined with fibres of the dwarf palmetto, that had apparently been brought a distance of half a mile. The cavity measured about five inches in breadth and one and a half in depth. The nest contained three eggs of a light blue, sparingly sprinkled with rufous, the spots being larger and more numerous towards the larger end. Another nest, found a few days later, contained five eggs of a more neutral tint, with the spots darker, larger, and more evenly distributed.

Cyanocitta californica, STRICKLAND.

CALIFORNIA JAY.

Garrulus californicus, VIGORS, Zoöl. Beechey's Voyage, 1839, 21, pl. v. *Cyanocitta californica*, STRICKLAND, Ann. Mag. XV, 1845, 342. — GAMBEL, J. A. N. Sc. 2d series, I, Dec. 1847, 45. — BON. Conspectus, 1850, 377. — NEWBERRY, P. R. R. Rep. VI, IV, 1857, 85. — BAIRD, Birds N. Am. 1858, 584. — HEERM. X, *S*, 55. — COOPER, Orn. Cal. I, 1870, 302. *Cyanocorax californicus*, GAMBEL, Pr. A. N. Sc. III, Ap. 1847, 201. *Aphelocoma californica*, CABANIS, Mus. Hein. 1851, 221. — BON. Comptes Rendus, XXXVII, Nov. 1853, 828 ; Notes Orn. Delattre. *Corvus ultramarinus*, AUD. Orn. Biog. IV, 1838, 456, pl. ccclxii (not *Garrulus ultramarinus*, BON.). *Garrulus ultramarinus*, AUD. Syn. 1839, 154. — IB. Birds Am. IV, 1842, 115, pl. ccxxxii (not of BONAPARTE). *Cyanocitta superciliosa*, STRICKLAND, Ann. Mag. XV, 1845, 260 (type of genus *Cyanocitta*). "*Corvus palliatus*, DRAPIEZ," BONAP.

SP. CHAR. Width of bill at base of lower mandible rather more than half the length of culmen. Lateral tail-feathers about an inch the shortest. Tail an inch longer than the wings. General color above, including the surface of the wings, bright blue, without bars. The whole back, including to some extent the scapulars, brownish-ash, very faintly glossed with blue in the adult. A streaked white superciliary line from a little anterior to the eye as far as the occiput. Sides of the head and neck blue, the region around and behind the eye, including lores and most of ear-coverts, black. The blue of the sides of the neck extends across the forepart of the breast, forming a crescent, interrupted in the middle. The under parts anterior to the crescent white, the feathers edged with blue ; behind it dull white ; the sides tinged with brown. Length, 12.25 ; wing, 5.00 ; tail, 6.15 ; tarsus, 1.55. (No. 2,841.)

HAB. Pacific Province from Columbia River to Cape St. Lucas ; Carson City, Nevada (RIDGWAY).

Specimens from Cape St. Lucas are rather smaller and perhaps whiter beneath than elsewhere ; those from the eastern slope of Sierra Nevada are

Cyanocitta californica.

very large. Upon a careful comparison, we find that the supposed specimens of *C. californica* in the Smithsonian collection from Mexico (Orizaba, etc.) constitute a quite different form, characterized by very indistinct superciliary white and bluish edges to throat and jugular feathers, and especially by the lengthened wings, which average 5.75 inches instead of 5.00. In general respects the resem-

blance, as suggested by Sclater, is to *californica,* and not to *woodhousei.* The dorsal patch is very distinct.

One Mexican specimen (8,465 from Real del Monte ?), presented by Mr.

John Gould, differs again in having the dorsal patch obscured by a bluish wash; an unusual amount of blue edging to the throat and jugular feathers, and a dull brownish tinge to the belly. It almost suggests the possibility of a hybrid form between *sumichrasti* and *ultramarina*.

HABITS. The California Jay appears to be a Pacific coast species, occurring from the Columbia River southward to Cape St. Lucas, but not found in the interior at any considerable distance from the coast. Mr. Ridgway speaks of it as the Valley Jay of California, having been observed by him in abundance only among the oaks of the Sacramento Valley, the brushwood of the ravines, and the scattered pines of the foot-hills along the western base of the Sierra Nevada. It was also quite common, in April, in the vicinity of Carson City, where he found it breeding. Its notes and manners, he adds, are very similar to those of the Woodhouse Jay, belonging to the wooded regions of the interior, but the shrill cries of this species are even more piercing. There is, moreover, something in its appearance, caused by the sharp contrast of the bright blue, the light ash, and the pure white colors, by which it may be distinguished at a glance from the more uniformly colored *woodhousei*.

Dr. Heerman speaks of it as frequenting to some extent the same districts as Steller's Jay, but also found in greater abundance throughout the valleys. He likewise describes it as noisy, alert, and cunning in its habits, wild and wary, and yet often seeking the habitations of man, near which to rear its young, drawn thither by the abundance of food found in such localities. Their nests, he states, are built in a thick-leaved bush, or on the lower branches of an oak, at but little height from the ground. They are constructed of twigs, and are lined with fine rootlets. The eggs, four in number, are, he says, emerald-green in color, profusely dotted with umber-brown spots.

Dr. Newberry states that he found the trees and the thickets bordering the streams in the valleys the favorite haunts of the California Jay. As his party ascended among the evergreen forests of the higher grounds, and passed northeasterly from the Sacramento Valley, these birds were no longer met with, and long before reaching the Oregon line they lost sight of it altogether. Nor did they meet with it again until their return to California. This Jay, he adds, has all the sprightliness and restlessness of the family, but is less noisy, and its notes are far more agreeable than those of Steller's Jay, by which it is replaced at the north.

The Smithsonian Museum has a specimen of this species obtained on the Columbia by Townsend, and Mr. Nuttall mentions that early in October, on arriving at the forests of the Columbia, near Fort Vancouver, he met with it in company with Steller's Jay. They were breeding in the dark pine woods, and by the 15th of June they were feeding their fully fledged young. He also states that they were found as far north as Fraser's River, migrating to the south at the approach of winter. Without questioning the correctness of this statement, it is worthy of mention that these birds have not been met there by more recent collectors, and that Dr. Newberry nowhere met with them in Oregon. Dr. Cooper suggests that, since then, the increased severity of the winters may have driven them permanently farther south.

Mr. Nuttall describes its habits as very much like those of the Blue Jay. It usually flies out to the tops of the tallest pines, jerks its tail, and perches playfully on some extreme branch, where, as if in anger, it calls *woit, woit-woit*, with an occasional recognition note of *twee-twee*. When pursued, it retreats to the shade of the loftiest branches. It feeds on insects, acorns, which it breaks up, and pine seeds. He describes it as a graceful, active, and shy bird, with a note much less harsh and loud than that of Steller's Jay.

Dr. Cooper remarks that this species is one of the most common and conspicuous of the birds of the State of California. They frequent every locality in which oak-trees are found, even within the limits of large towns, where they enter gardens and audaciously plunder the fruit. They have all the usual cunning of their tribe, and when alarmed become very quiet, and conceal themselves in the thick foliage. They are usually noisy and fearless, and their odd cries, grotesque actions, and bright plumage make them general favorites in spite of their depredations. They are also said to have a talent for mimicry, besides notes to express their various wants and ideas.

They breed abundantly throughout the western parts of California, and construct a large and strong nest of twigs, roots, and grass. These are placed in a low tree or bush. They lay about five eggs, which Dr. Cooper describes as dark green marked with numerous pale brown blotches and spots, and measure 1.80 by 1.04 inches. At San Diego he found these eggs laid as early as April 5.

This Jay inhabits the Coast Range of mountains to their summit, south of San Francisco, and the Sierra Nevada as far as the oaks extend, or to an elevation of from 1,000 to 5,000 feet. Dr. Cooper saw none on the east side of the Sierra Nevada in latitude 39°.

He describes their flight as slow and laborious, on account of their short wings, and states that they never fly far at a time. He also accuses them of being very destructive to the eggs of smaller birds, hunting for them in the spring, and watching the movements of other birds with great attention.

Mr. Xantus found these birds very abundant at Cape St. Lucas, being, like all the other resident species there, much smaller than those occurring in more northern localities. Their habits are said to be very much the same.

This species was taken in winter near Oaxaca, Mexico, by Mr. Boucard.

Four eggs of this species from different parts of California present the following measurements: 1.20 × 0.85; 1.10 × 0.80; 1.13 × 0.80; 1.05 × 0.80. The measurements given by Dr. Cooper we are confident must be a mistake.

Their ground-color is a bright, but not a dark, emerald-green; and they are marked and blotched with faint purplish-brown, and deeper spots of dark umber. These spots are sparingly distributed, and are chiefly about the larger end. In one they are wholly of a light violet-brown. These eggs are of a perfectly oval shape.

Mr. Charles D. Gibbes, of Stockton, writes that he found in a garden in that city a nest built by a pair of these birds that had become half domesticated. It was placed in a very thick arbor of honeysuckle. The body of the nest was composed of clippings from a hedge of osage orange, with thorns on them half an inch long. These twigs were tied and interlaced with twine and bits of cotton strings. Within this frame was a layer of fine weeds and grasses nicely arranged, the whole lined with horse-hair. The nest was found in May, and contained five eggs. The parents kept a good deal about the kitchen door, and would steal anything they had an opportunity to take. They made use of an old nest in the same garden as a receptacle for their stolen goods; among other things was found a large slice of bread-and-butter.

Cyanocitta californica, var. woodhousei, BAIRD.

WOODHOUSE'S JAY.

Cyanocitta woodhousei, BAIRD, Birds N. Am. 1858, 585, pl. lix. — IB. Mex. B. II, Birds, 20, pl. xxi. — COOPER, Orn. Cal. I, 1870, 304.

SP. CHAR. Size and general appearance of *C. californica*. Bill slender. Graduation of tail one inch. Blue, with a very obscure ashy patch on the back. Sides of the head and neck and incomplete pectoral collar, blue; throat streaked with the same. Breast and belly uniform brownish-ash, glossed with blue; under tail-coverts bright blue. Sides of head, including lores, black, glossed with blue below; a streaked white superciliary line. Length, 11.50; wing, 5.35; tail, 6.10; tarsus, 1.60. *Young.* All the blue, except that of the wings and tail, replaced by dull ash.

HAB. Rocky Mountains and Middle Province of United States; north to Idaho and Wyoming (RIDGWAY); south to Northern Mexico; east to Wyoming and Colorado.

The bluish wash on the back nearly obscuring the dorsal patch, the general ashy tinge of the under parts, the decided blue under tail-coverts, and the longer and much slenderer bill, distinguish this form from *californica*, although probably both are geographical races of the same species.

HABITS. This bird was first met with by Dr. Woodhouse among the San Francisco Mountains of New Mexico, and was given by him, in his Report of the Sitgreaves Expedition, as the California Jay. He states in regard to it, that wherever he found the piñon, or nut-pine (*Pinus edulis*), growing in New Mexico, this bird was sure to be there in great numbers, feeding upon the fruit of those trees. Among the men it was known as the piñon bird. Its notes are said to be harsh and disagreeable. It was extremely restless, and was continually in motion, flying from tree to tree, uttering its well-known cries.

Mr. Ridgway calls this a very interesting species, and states that it was found very abundant in the fertile cañons of the West Humboldt Mountains, as well as in all the extensive nut-pine and cedar woods to the eastward. On the Toyaba and East Humboldt Mountains, and the extensive piñon woods in Southern Idaho, it was equally common. In Utah, in the cañons of the Wahsatch Mountains, it was occasionally seen, though oftener observed in the valley of the Weber. When unmolested, this bird is, he states, very unsuspicious, and anything unusual at once excites its curiosity. Often when at work, in camp, skinning birds, on the edge of bushes, one of them would approach within a few feet, and quietly watch every movement. At Unionsville they were quite common in the gardens and around the door-yards of the town, and were very familiar and unsuspicious. Their cries greatly resembled those of the California Jay, and consisted of a repetition of harsh screeching notes.

This species, according to Dr. Coues, is a resident and a very abundant species in Arizona, where it is one of the most characteristic species. It was found in all situations, but seemed to shun dense pine woods, and to prefer to keep on the open hillsides, among the scrub-oaks, etc. In winter it collects in rather large flocks, sometimes as many as fifty together. They are, however, usually seen in small groups of six or seven individuals. They are said to be a restless, vigilant, shy, and noisy species.

Mr. C. E. Aiken found this bird a common and resident species in Colorado. He met with it along the foot of the mountains, in brush thickets, in which they also breed. The base and periphery of a nest found by him were composed of dead twigs, intermingled within with fine rootlets and horse-hair. The eggs, four or five in number, are said to be laid about the first of May. They have a ground-color of a light bluish-green, and marked with reddish-brown specks, thickest at the larger end. They are of a rounded oval shape, much more pointed at one end, and rounded at the other, and average 1.06 inches in length by .80 of an inch in breadth.

Cyanocitta ultramarina, var. arizonæ, RIDGWAY.

Cyanocitta sordida (not of SWAINS.!), BAIRD, Birds N. Am. 1858, 587, pl. lx. f. 1. — IB. Mex. B. II, Birds, 21, pl. xxii, f. 1. — COOPER, Orn. Cal. I, 1870, 305. *Cyanocitta sordida* var. *arizonæ*, RIDGWAY, Rep. U. S. Geol. Expl. 40th Par.

SP. CHAR. Bill short, thick; half as high as long. Wing considerably longer than the tail, which is slightly graduated (.50 of an inch). Upper surface (including whole side of head to the throat) light sky-blue, the whole dorsal region inclining to pure bluish-ashy. Beneath fine, uniform, pale ash for anterior half (including the throat), this gradually fading into white on the posterior portions (including whole abdomen), the lower tail-coverts being pure white. Lores blue. Length, 13.00; wing, 6.20; tail, 5.70; culmen, 1.30; depth of bill, .40; tarsus, 1.50; middle toe, .97. Fourth, fifth, and sixth quills equal and longest, second shorter than ninth; first 2.20 shorter than longest. (18,279, Fort Buchanan, Arizona, December; Dr. Irwin.) *Immature* (8,469 ♂, Copper Mines, Arizona). The blue, except that of the wings and tail, replaced by dull ash; the blue feathers appearing in scattered patches.

HAB. Arizona (Copper Mines, J. H. Clark; and Fort Buchanan, Dr. Irwin, U. S. A.).

The nearest ally of this race is the var. *sordida* of Mexico, which, however, differs in many important respects; the differences between the two being giving in the synopsis (page 880), it is unnecessary to repeat them here. In both there is a tendency towards a party-colored bill; each example of the northern style, and most of those of the southern, having more or less whitish on the lower mandible.

Nothing definite is known as to the habits or reproduction of this bird.

Cyanocitta ultramarina, var. couchi, BAIRD.

ULTRAMARINE JAY.

Garrulus ultramarinus, BONAP. J. A. N. Sc. IV, 1825, 386 (not of AUDUBON). — TEMM. Pl. Col. II, 439. *Cyanocitta ultramarina*, STRICKLAND, Ann. & Mag. XV, 1845, 260. — GAMBEL, J. A. N. Sc. 2d Ser. I, 1847, 45. — BAIRD, Birds N. Am. 588, pl. 60, f. 2. — IB. Mex. B. II, Birds 21, pl. xxii. *Cyanogarrulus ultramarinus*, BON. Consp. 1850, 378. *Cyanocitta couchi*, BAIRD, Birds N. Am. 1858, 588.

SP. CHAR. Tail rounded, but little graduated; lateral feather about a quarter of an inch shortest. Wings longer than the tail; when closed, reaching nearly to its middle. Above and on sides of head and neck bright blue; the lores blackish; the middle of the back slightly duller, the tips of some of the feathers dark brown. Beneath brownish-ash, paler on the chin and towards the anal region, which, with the crissum, is white. No trace of white or black on the sides of the head, nor of any streaks or collar on the breast. Length, (fresh,) 11.50; wing, 6.00; tail, (dried,) 5.40; tarsus, 1.50.

HAB. South side of valley of Rio Grande, near the coast, and southward.

This well-marked species is quite different in form from the *C. californica*, having a shorter, more even tail, much longer wings, and stouter feet. The absence of any collar or streaks on the breast and throat, of black or white on the side of the head, and of decided ash on the back, are very well marked features. There is also much more green in the blue of the head.

As suggested in the P. R. R. Report, the birds collected by Lieutenant Couch at Monterey, Mexico, although agreeing almost exactly with the original description of Bonaparte, are much smaller, and perhaps entitled to recognition as a separate form. The tail is nearly two inches less, 5.40 instead of 7.00, or over.

HABITS. The Ultramarine Jay is a well-marked species, and is specifically quite distinct from the *C. californica*. It is found in the valley of the Rio Grande, and thence southward and eastward in the northern provinces of

Mexico. Though we know of no specimens having been procured on this side of the boundary line, their occurrence is quite probable. Lieutenant Couch met with this species near Monterey, Mexico, and from thence west to Parras. He describes it as being gregarious and eminently Jay-like in its habits. They are very noisy and vociferous in their outcries, and three or four of them suffice to keep a whole forest in an uproar. Near Guyapuco a large snake (*Georgia obsoleta*) was seen pursued by three or four of this species. The reptile was making every effort to escape from their combined attacks, and would, no doubt, have been killed by them, had they not been interfered with. The cause of so much animosity against the snake was explained when, on opening its stomach, three young of this species, about two thirds grown, were found.

In the Department of Vera Cruz, Sumichrast found what he calls *C. ultramarina* in company with *Cyanura coronata* and *Cyanocitta nana*, "*californica*" (*Sumichrasti*), and *sordida*, occurring in the alpine region, and with the three first named restricted to that locality. The limit of their extension is about that of the alpine region, that is, from an elevation of about 4,500 feet to the height of 10,500 feet. The *sordida* is also found on the plateau.

Genus **XANTHOURA**, Bonap.

Xanthoura, Bonaparte, Consp. Av. 1850. (Type, "*Corvus peruvianus*, Gm.")

Char. Head without crest. Throat black. Lateral tail-feathers bright yellow. Bill very stout, rather higher than broad; culmen curved from the base. Nostrils rather small,

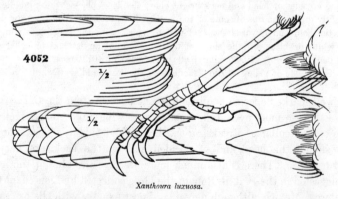

Xanthoura luxuosa.

oval, concealed by a nasal tuft varying in length with species. Tail longer than the wings; graduated. The wings concave, rounded; the secondaries nearly as long as the primaries. Legs very stout; hind claw about half the total length of the toe.

The genus *Xanthoura* is composed of three so-called species, of different geographical distribution, and exhibits a progressive change from one to the other, with variation of latitude that enforces assent to the hypothesis of their all belonging to one primitive form. These differences may be expressed as follows : —

COMMON CHARACTERS. Nasal tufts, patch on side of lower jaw and one above eye, (both eyelids,) bright blue; remainder of face and throat black. Back, and upper surface of wings and tail (the four central feathers), green, the latter tinged with blue at end; the rest of tail-feathers bright yellow. Belly and crissum varying from bright yellow to green. Forehead yellowish or whitish.

a. Nasal tufts short, only covering the nostrils; whole top of head (except anteriorly) and nape bright blue.

1. Body beneath, and crissum, green. *Hab.* Mexico and South Texas.

var. *luxuosa.*

2. Body beneath, and crissum, yellow, sides more greenish. *Hab.* Guatemala and Honduras . . . . . var. *guatemalensis.*

b. Nasal tuft elongated, forming an anterior crest, the feathers reaching far beyond nostrils. Whole top of head pale heavy yellow, glossed behind with bluish.

3. Body beneath, and crissum, very bright gamboge-yellow. *Hab.* Colombia, Ecuador, Bogota, and Bolivia . . . . var. *incas.*

Thus, starting with the green-bellied *luxuosa* of the Rio Grande, we come to the yellow-bellied *guatemalensis;* but intermediate localities show different proportions of the two colors. The nasal tufts in the first do not extend beyond the nasal fossæ; and the frontal yellowish is very narrow. In the second these tufts reach beyond the fossæ, and the frontal yellowish is more extended. In *incas* again the nasal tufts have reached their maximum, while the frontal yellowish extends over the whole cap, leaving only a trace of blue on the nape.

Xanthoura incas, var. luxuosa, BONAP.

GREEN JAY.

Garrulus luxuosus, LESSON, Rev. Zoöl. April, 1839, 100. *Cyanocorax luxuosus,* DU BUS, Esquisses Ornithologiques, IV, 1848, pl. xviii. — CASSIN, Illust. I, 1853, I, pl. i. *Xanthoura luxuosa,* BON. Consp. 1850, 380. — CABANIS, Mus. Hein. 1851, 224. — BAIRD, Birds N. Am. 1858, 589. *Pica chloronota,* WAGLER, Isis, 1829, 750 (young male ; name belongs to *Corvus peruvianus,* GM.). *Cyanocorax cyanicapillus,* CABANIS, Fauna Peruana, 1844 – 46, 233 (note). *Cyanocorax yncas,* "BODDÆRT," LAWRENCE, Ann. N. Y. Lyc. V, April, 1851, 115 (first added here to fauna of United States).

SP. CHAR. Wings shorter than the tail, which is much graduated, the lateral feathers 1.25 inches shorter. Above green; beneath yellow, glossed continuously with green; inside of wings and outer four tail-feathers straw-yellow; rest of tail feathers green, glossed with blue. Sides of the head, and beneath from the bill to the forepart of the breast, velvet-black. Crown, nape, and a short maxillary stripe running up to the eye and involving the upper eyelid, brilliant blue; the nostril-feathers rather darker; the sides of the forehead whitish. Bill black; feet lead-color. Length, 11.00; wing, 4.75; tail, 5.40; tarsus, 1.65.

HAB. Valley of Rio Grande, of Texas, and southward.

As remarked above, the passage into the yellow-bellied *guatemalensis* is gradual as we proceed south; and the latter, and perhaps even the *incas*, can only be considered as fellow races of a common original species.

HABITS. Within the limits of the United States this beautiful species

has thus far been only met with in Southeastern Texas in the lower valley of the Rio Grande. It was first described in 1839, by M. Lesson, a French naturalist, from a Mexican specimen, and in 1851 was first brought to our notice as a bird of the United States by Mr. Geo. N. Lawrence of New York. Specimens of this bird were obtained by the party of the Mexican Boundary Survey, and by Lieutenant Couch on the Rio Grande, at Matamoras, New Leon, and San Diego, Mexico. The only note

Xanthoura luxuosa.

as to its habits by Lieutenant Couch is to the effect that it eats seeds and insects.

The late Dr. Berlandier of Matamoras obtained specimens of this bird in the vicinity of that city, which were found among his collections. Among his manuscript notes occurs a description of the plumage and habits of this species, which he had described under the name of *Pica cervantesii*. In this he states that this bird inhabits the whole eastern coast of Mexico, but that he has only met with it on the banks of the Rio Bravo del Norte, in the vicinity of Matamoras. It is said to be both carnivorous and graminivorous, and comes about the houses in search of the refuse. Although it can swallow whole grains of corn, before eating it breaks them with its beak, holding them between its claws, in the manner of birds of prey, and biting with great force. It is commonly known as *Pajaro verde*, or Greenbird.

Mr. Dresser states that this species was common on the lower Rio Grande during the winter, but was not found on the Upper Rio Grande or in Texas, except as a straggler from Mexico.

This bird, Mr. Sumichrast states, is common throughout the Department of Vera Cruz, where it is generally known by the name of *Verde detoca* and *Sonaja*. It is said to be one of the birds most generally diffused throughout the whole department. It inhabits both the hot and the temperate regions, and is found even at the foot of the alpine, to the altitude of nearly six thousand feet above the sea. It is also said to be abundant in other parts of Mexico. It was observed to be quite numerous on the *Tierra templada*, or table-lands, and also among the hills that bound the plains of Perote and Puebla on the east, by Mr. William S. Pease, a naturalist who was with General Scott's army in its campaign in Mexico. Mr. Pease stated that it lived on the sides of the hills throughout the year, and that its local name was *Pepe verde.*

Colonel George A. McCall, Inspector-General of the United States Army, was the first person to collect these birds within our limits. He obtained them in the forests that border the Rio Grande on the southeastern frontier of Texas. There he found them all mated in the month of May, and he felt no doubt that they had their nests in the extensive and almost impenetrable thickets of mimosa, commonly called chaparral. From the jealousy and pugnacity which these birds manifested on the approach, or appearance even, of the large boat-tailed Blackbirds of that country (*Quiscalus macrurus*), which were nesting in great numbers in the vicinity, Colonel McCall was satisfied that the Jays were at that time also engaged in the duties of incubation and rearing their young. In character and temperament these birds appeared to be very active and lively, though less noisy than some other species of the family. Their gay plumage was exhibited to great advantage as they flitted from tree to tree, or dashed boldly in pursuit of such of their more plainly attired neighbors as ventured to intrude upon their domain.

Captain J. P. McCown, also quoted by Mr. Cassin, furnishes some additional observations in regard to these birds. He states that during the several years that he was in Texas, he frequently saw these Jays, but never met with them above Ringgold Barracks, or north of the woods that skirt the Rio Grande. They seemed to prefer the acacia groves which have sprung up where the ground has been overflowed. He regards it as a rather cautious bird. He observed nests high up in the trees above mentioned, which he supposes belong to this species, though this was never positively ascertained. He had no doubt that they breed in Texas.

Genus **PERISOREUS**, Bonap.

Perisoreus, Bonap. Saggio di una dist. met. 1831. (Type, *Corvus canadensis ?*)
Dysornithia, Swainson, F. B. Am. II, 1831, 495. (Same type.)

Char. Feathers lax and full, especially on the back, and of very dull colors, without any blue. Head without distinct crest. Bill very short; broader than high. Culmen scarcely half the length of the head; straight to near the tip, then slightly curved; gonys more curved than culmen. Bill notched at tip. Nostrils round, covered by bristly feathers. Tail about equal to the wings; graduated. Tarsi rather short; but little longer than the middle toe. Plumage very soft, and without any lustre.

The Canada Jay has a near ally in a species of northern Europe and Siberia, — the Siberian Jay (*P. infaustus*). In size and proportions the two are quite identical, there being about the same proportionate length of wing and tail, and a general correspondence in the minutiæ of external anatomy.

In colors, however, they differ entirely; the *P. infaustus* having the head darker than the body, and uniform (instead of the contrary), and in having the lower primary and lower feathers of the greater coverts, as well as the greater part of the tail, bright rufous.

A. Dusky nuchal hood reaching forward to, or in front of, the eyes; plumbeous-black.

Dorsal feathers with white shafts in old and young. Tail-feathers not distinctly paler at ends.

1. White frontal patch narrower than length of the bill; blending gradually with the blackish of the crown. Upper parts umber-brownish. Wing, 5.50; tail, 5.40; bill, .90 and .30. *Young.* Entirely plumbeous-brown, feathers of head above bordered with paler. Beneath paler, whitish brown. *Hab.* Oregon, Washington Teritory, British Columbia, etc.   .   .   var. *obscurus.*

Dorsal feathers without white shafts in old or young. Tail-feathers broadly tipped with dull white.

2. White frontal patch much broader than length of bill; abruptly defined, with a convex outline behind, against the dusky of the occiput. Upper parts plumbeous, with a slight brownish cast. Wing, 5.25; tail, 5.80; bill, .95 and .35. *Young.* Entirely uniform dark plumbeous. *Hab.* Canada, Maine, and Labrador to the Yukon .   .   .   .   .   . var. *canadensis.*

B. Dusky nuchal hood not reaching to the eyes, but confined to the nape; bluish-plumbeous.

3. White frontal patch covering whole crown, melting gradually into the ashy of the nape; upper parts bluish-ashy. Wing, 6.00; tail, 6.00; bill, 1.00 and .31. *Young.* Bluish-plumbeous, inclining to ashy-white on the crown and cheeks. *Hab.* Rocky Mountains of United States   .   . var. *capitalis.*

In the more slender form, longer and narrower bill, and paler tints

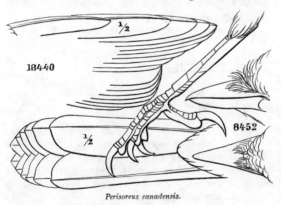

18440

8452

with a predominance of the light colors, of the var. *capitalis,* compared with the typical, or standard, var. *canadensis,* we see the peculiar impression of the middle region; while in the var. *obscurus,* the more dusky tints, and predominance of darker colors, the influence of the well-known law affecting colors in birds of the northwest coast region is seen.

Perisoreus canadensis.

Perisoreus canadensis, BONAP.

CANADA JAY; WHISKEY-JACK; MOOSE-BIRD.

Corvus canadensis, LINN. Syst. Nat. I, 1766, 158. — FORSTER, Phil. Trans. LXII, 1772, 382. — WILSON, Am. Orn. III, 1811, 33, pl. xxi. — BON. Obs. 1824, No. 42. — AUD. Orn. Biog. II, 1834, 53 ; V, 1839, 208, pl. cvii. *Garrulus canadensis,* BON. (Saggio, 1831 ?) Syn. 1828, 58. — SWAINSON, F. Bor.-Am. II, 1831, 295. — NUTTALL, Man. I, 1832, 232. — AUD. Syn. 1839, 155. — IB. Birds Am. IV, 1842, 121, pl. ccxxxiv. *Dysornithia canadensis,* SWAINSON, F. Bor.-Am. II, 1831, Appendix. *Perisoreus canadensis,* BON. List, 1838. — IB. Conspectus, 1850, 375. — CAB. Mus. Hein. 1851, 219. — NEWBERRY, Rep. P. R. R. Surv. VI, IV, 1857, 85. — BAIRD, Birds N. Am. 1858, 590. — COUES, P. A. N. S. 1861, 226. — SAMUELS, 366. *Garrulus fuscus,* VIEILLOT, Nouv. Dict. XII, 1817, 479. *Pica nuchalis,* WAGLER, Syst. Av. 1827 (Pica No. 14). *Garrulus trachyrrhynchus,* SWAINSON, F. Bor.-Am. II, 1831, 296, pl. lv (young). "*Coracias mexicanus,* TEMMINCK," GRAY.

SP. CHAR. Tail graduated ; lateral feathers about one inch shortest. Wings a little shorter than the tail. Head and neck and forepart of breast white. A rather sooty plumbeous nuchal patch, becoming darker behind, from the middle of the cap to the back, from which it is separated by an interrupted whitish collar. Rest of upper parts dark ashy-plumbeous ; the outer primaries margined, the secondaries, tertials, and tail-feathers obscurely tipped with white. Beneath smoky-gray. Crissum whitish. Bill and feet black. Length, 10.70 ; wing, 5.75 ; tail, 6.00 ; tarsus, 1.40.

HAB. Eastern Northern America into the northern part of United States ; British America to Upper Yukon.

Perisoreus canadensis.

The young of this species are everywhere of a dull sooty-plumbeous, lighter on the middle of the belly, and more bluish-plumbeous on the wings and tail. With increasing age the region about the base of the bill whitens.

There is a decided bluish cast to the plumbeous of the tail. The white frontal patch has a convex posterior outline, and is abruptly defined against the blackish of the occiput and nape.

All specimens from Canada and the Northeastern United States, to the interior of British America, are referrible to this variety ; in the Yukon Territory specimens show a tendency to var. *obscurus* of the northwest coast, having a narrower whitish frontal patch.

HABITS. The Canada Jay was procured at Fort Simpson by Mr. Kennicott in August, September, and December, and at the same point by Mr. Ross in March and April, in the years 1860 and 1861. It was found breeding in May at Anderson River Fort by Mr. MacFarlane. It was also procured at Big Island by Mr. Reid, at Nulato and Unalakleet by Mr. Dall, at St. Michael's by Colonel Bulkley, at Fort Kenai by Bischoff, and at Fort Rae by Mr. Clarke. From the memoranda of Mr. MacFarlane, we have valuable information in regard to the nesting and breeding habits of this species. May 24, at Fort Anderson, an Indian lad discovered a nest of this Jay. It was built in a tree, was composed of hay and feathers, and contained, with two young birds a few days old, an egg that was perfectly fresh. This bird, Mr. MacFarlane states, is tolerably numerous in that quarter. During the severe cold of winter it is not quite so common as at other seasons. It is by no means a difficult bird to shoot, as it will always venture into close proximity to man. Flesh or fish are certain to attract numbers of them, and they also cause great annoyance to the marten-hunter, by eating the bait placed in the traps used for capturing those animals. None of this species were observed on the Arctic coast, nor east of Horton River, Fort Anderson being the most northern point where Mr. MacFarlane saw any, in his journeys across the barren grounds.

Other nests found in the same region were usually built in spruce-trees, on branches near the trunk, well concealed from view, and about ten feet from the ground. They were constructed of hay and feathers, supported underneath by a few willow sticks laid crosswise.

Mr. Dall characterizes this species as a very bold and familiar bird, that will frequently fly down and steal away his dinner from some hungry dog, if he is not on the alert, or devour the fish hung up in camp by the Indians to dry. They breed very early, and occupy the same nest year after year. The nest is very large, and composed entirely of soft materials, moss, hair, and the like. On the 20th of April, Mr. Dall received a nest of this Jay containing four half-fledged young, so that they must lay in March. The bird was abundant everywhere on the Yukon River.

These birds are known throughout the fur countries by the name of Whiskey-Jack, not from any supposed predilection for that beverage, but probably, as Mr. Kennicott has suggested, from a corruption of the Indian name for these birds, Wiss-ka-chon, which has been contorted into Whiskey-John and thence into Whiskey-Jack. Richardson observed these birds from Canada to the fur countries as far as latitude 69°. Throughout that region it is a constant attendant at the fur-posts and fishing-stations, and becomes so tame in the winter as to feed from the hand. Yet it is impatient of confinement, and soon pines away if deprived of its liberty. Its voice is said to be plaintive and squeaking, though it occasionally makes a low chattering. It hoards berries, pieces of meat, etc., in hollow trees, or between layers of bark, by which it is enabled to feed its young while the ground is still covered with snow.

Dr. Newberry found this Jay as far to the south, in California, as the upper end of the Sacramento Valley, in latitude 40°. The fact that the isothermal line of this region passes south of Cincinnati, shows that climate and temperature do not regulate the range of this species. As observed in the summer months among the forests of Oregon, the Canada Jay appeared as a rather shy bird, exhibiting none of the familiarity and impudence exhibited in winter when made bold by hunger.

Wilson mentions the St. Lawrence as the southern boundary of this bird, a few only wintering in Northern New York and Vermont. But this is inexact. They are found resident throughout the year in a large part of Maine and in all the highlands of New Hampshire and Vermont. They are resident at Calais, where they breed in March at about latitude 45°, and descend in the winter to the southwest corner of Vermont, whence it is quite probable a few cross into Massachusetts, at Williamstown and Adams, though none have been detected, that I am aware. Wilson himself states that he was informed by a gentleman residing near Hudson, N. Y., that these birds have been observed in that neighborhood in the winter.

Dr. Coues met with these birds in Labrador. The first he saw were in a dense spruce forest. These were very shy, alighting only on the tops of the tallest trees, and flying off with loud harsh screams on his approach. Subsequently, at Rigolet, he found them abundant and very familiar. One or more were always to be seen hopping unconcernedly in the garden-patches around the houses, not in the least disturbed by the near presence of man, and showing no signs of fear even when very closely approached. He describes their voice as a harsh, discordant scream.

Mr. Edward Harris, of Moorestown, N. J., informed Mr. Audubon, that once, when fishing in a canoe in one of the lakes in the interior of Maine, these Jays were so fearless as to light on one end of his boat while he sat in the other, and helped themselves to his bait without taking any notice of him.

A nest of the Canada Jay, found by Mr. Boardman near St. Stephen's, New Brunswick, measures four and a half inches in diameter and three inches in height. The cavity is about three inches wide and two deep. The nest is woven above a rude platform of sticks and twigs crossed and interlaced, furnishing a roughly made hemispherical base and periphery. Upon this an inner and more artistic nest has been wrought, made of a soft felting of fine mosses closely impacted and lined with feathers. The nest contained three eggs.

The egg of the Canada Jay measures 1.20 inches in length, by .82 of an inch in breadth. They are of an oblong-oval shape, and are more tapering at the smaller end than are most of the eggs of this family. The ground-color is of a light gray, with a slightly yellowish tinge over the entire egg, finely marked, more abundantly about the larger end, with points and blotches of slate-color and brown, and faint cloudings of an obscure lilac.

Perisoreus canadensis, var. obscurus, RIDGWAY.

ALASKAN GRAY JAY.

Perisoreus canadensis, COOPER & SUCKLEY, 216. — DALL & BANNISTER, Tr. Chic. Ac. I, 1869, 286 (Alaska). — FINSCH, Abh. Nat. III, 1872, 40 (Alaska). — COOPER, Orn. Cal. I, 1870, 307.

SP. CHAR. (8,454 Shoalwater Bay, W. T., March 10, 1854; Dr. J. G. Cooper.) Above plumbeous-umber, inclining to grayish-plumbeous on wings and tail; shafts of the dorsal feathers conspicuously white. Whole crown and nape, above the lores and auriculars, sooty-black; separated from the brown of the back by a whitish tint. Forehead (narrowly), nasal tufts, lores, whole lateral and under side of head, with jugulum, pure white, rest of lower parts a duller and more brownish white. Wing, 5.50; tail, 5.30; culmen, .93; tarsus, 1.20. *Young* (5,904, Shoalwater Bay). Entirely plumbeous-brown, inclining to brownish-white beneath. Dorsal feathers with white shafts, and those of the forehead, crown, and nape, as well as the wing-coverts, with obsolete whitish borders.

This form, as described above, seems to be peculiar to the northwest coast, reaching its extreme development in Washington Territory and Oregon. North of Sitka, and in the Yukon Territory, specimens incline toward the var. *canadensis*, in broader frontal white, and purer plumbeous colors.

HABITS. Dr. Cooper met with this variety at the mouth of the Columbia River in March in small scattered flocks, industriously seeking insects and seeds among the spruce-trees, occasionally whistling in a loud melodious tone like that of the Cardinal Grosbeak. He also states that the notes of this bird differ much from the other Jays in being clear and musical, and they sometimes show a considerable variety of song.

This Jay, Mr. Lord states, is so familiar and confiding, and so fond of being near the habitations of man, that the settlers never harm it. In the cold weather he has seen it hop by the fire, ruffle up its feathers and warm itself without the least fear, keeping a sharp lookout for crumbs, and looking so beseechingly with its glittering gray eyes, that no one could refuse such an appeal for a stray morsel. It winters in British Columbia and Vancouver Island.

Perisoreus canadensis, var. capitalis, BAIRD.

ROCKY MOUNTAIN GRAY JAY.

SP. CHAR. (61,084, Henry's Fork, Wyoming Teritory, F. V. Hayden.) Above fine light bluish-plumbeous, becoming much lighter on the anterior portion of the back; tertials, secondaries, wing-coverts, primaries, and tail-feathers passing into whitish terminally, on the latter forming quite broad and distinct tips. A nuchal patch of a slightly darker tint than the back, and separated from it by the hoary whitish of the anterior dorsal region. Whole of the head (except the nuchal patch), with the anterior lower parts, as far as the breast, pure white; rest of lower parts ashy-white, becoming gradually more ashy posteriorly. Wing, 5.80; tail, 6.00; culmen, 1.00. *Young* (18,440,

Fort Benton, April 23, J. A. Mullan). Generally ashy-plumbeous, with a decided bluish cast to wings and tail; orbital region, lores, forehead, and nasal tufts blackish; crown, a broad space below the eye from the bill across the auriculars, with the middle of the abdomen, pale hoary-ashy. Wings and tail as in the adult.

This race, very different from the two styles found to the westward and eastward of it, is peculiar to Rocky Mountain regions, and apparently only occurring south of the northern boundary of the United States. A very large series of specimens, brought in at various times from numerous localities, substantiate the constancy of the characters pointed out above.

GENUS **PSILORHINUS**, RÜPPELL.

Psilorhinus, RÜPPELL, Mus. Senck. 1837, 188. (Type, *Pica morio*, WAGLER.)

CHAR. Color very dull brown above. Bill very stout, compressed, without notch; higher than broad at the nostrils; culmen curved from the base. Nostrils rounded; the

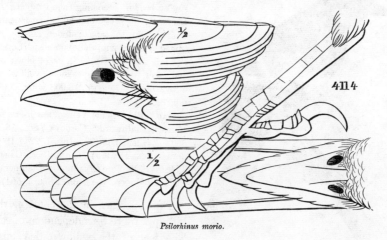

Psilorhinus morio.

anterior extremity rounded off into the bill; not covered by bristles, but fully exposed. Tail rather longer than the wings, graduated; the lateral feather three fourths the longest; secondaries and tertials nearly as long as the primaries. Legs stout and short, not equal to the head, and little longer than the bill from base.

This genus embraces Jays of large size and very dull plumage. The thick bill, with the much curved culmen, the moderate tail, and the open nostrils, may serve to distinguish it from its allies. The nostril is very large, and its anterior portion is bevelled off to a greater degree than in any genus, except in *Calocitta*. This last-mentioned genus has the same form of bill and of nostrils, but the head has a long recurved crest; the tail is twice as long as the wings; the lateral feather nearly half the middle; the lateral tarsal plates scutellate for the inferior half, etc.

In the shape of the bill and the shortness of the primaries, compared with the broad tertials and secondaries, there is much resemblance to *Xanthoura*. The nostrils are, however, uncovered, the legs much stouter and shorter, being shorter than the head instead of longer; the tail-feathers are broader, etc.

Psilorhinus morio, GRAY.

BROWN JAY.

Pica morio, WAGLER, Isis, 1829, VII, 751. — IB. Isis, 1831, 527. — Voyage de la Favorite, V, 1839, 54 (said to have been killed at San Francisco, Cal., by Botta). *Psilorhinus morio*, GRAY, List, genera, 1841, 51. — BONAP. Consp. 1850, 381. — CAB. Mus. Hein. 1851, 226. — BAIRD, Birds N. Am. 1858, 592, pl. lxviii, f. 1, 2. *"Pica fuliginosa*, LESSON, Traite d'Orn. 1831, 333." *Psilorhinus mexicanus*, RÜPPELL, Mus. Senck, 1837, pl. xi, f. 2.

Psilorhinus morio.

SP. CHAR. Tail much graduated; the lateral feathers about two inches shortest. Second quill equal to the secondaries; third and fourth longest. General color dark smoky-brown, becoming almost black on the head; the breast brownish-gray; nearly white about the anus; under tail-coverts tinged with brown; the exposed portion of the tail with a decided gloss of blue; bill and feet, in some specimens yellow, in others black. Length, 16.00; wing, 8.00; tail, 8.25; tarsus, 1.80.

HAB. Rio Grande Valley, north-eastern Mexico, southward. Cordova (SCL. 1856, 300); ? Guatemala (SCL. Ibis, I, 22); Honduras (SCL. II, 113); Costa Rica (CABAN. J. 1861, 83); Vera Cruz, hot and temperate regions (SUMICH. Mem. Bost. Soc. I, 554).

The difference in the color of the bill appears to be independent of sex. The feet of the yellow-billed birds are not of the same pure yellow.

The *Psilorhinus mexicanus* of Rüppell is described as having white tips to the tail-feathers; of these there is no trace in the adult specimens, male and female, from the Rio Grande, before us. He speaks of a supposed young bird sent from Tamaulipas, by Lindheimer, as being without these white tips.

A series of specimens of this species exhibits considerable diversities. Some skins from Mirador, Mex., not far from Vera Cruz, perhaps best represent the species as first described by Wagler. In these the head and neck are sooty-brown, becoming lighter on the jugulum and on the back. The wings and tail show a trace of dull bluish. In No. 23,915 the under parts are sooty-gray, the bill and legs black; in 23,916 the colors are similar, with a fulvous tinge on the breast, the bill and feet yellow. In both the under surface of tail is brown to the end. In 23,917 the under parts, from breast to crissum inclusive, with the tibiæ, are brownish-white, the tail-feathers (excepting the two median) tipped with white for over an inch, the bill and feet black. This one also has an obscure dull bluish wash or patch along the feathers of the ramus of lower jaw not observed in other specimens.

The specimens collected by Lieutenant Couch, and described in the Pacific Railroad Report are considerably smaller, and exhibit other differences which may prove of specific importance. In this case they will appropriately bear Rüppell's name of *P. mexicanus*.

HABITS. This is a Mexican species, occasionally extending its movements as far north as the valley of the Rio Grande, and probably crossing our lines into Texas, although of this there is as yet no positive evidence.

Specimens of this species were procured by Lieutenant Couch at Boquillo, San Diego, and at China, in north-eastern Mexico, and were found by him living in forests of high trees. It is Jay-like in its habits, being decidedly gregarious, and having harsh and loud notes. Though making more noise than any other bird in the neighborhood, if one of their number is brought down by the discharge of a gun, the noise hushes them at once, and the rest move off in perfect silence.

Mr. Sumichrast, in his paper on the Distribution of the Birds of Vera Cruz, states that this species abounds in both the hot and the temperate regions of that department, and, indeed, the greater portions of Vera Cruz. He speaks of it as a bird well known and generally detested on account of its troublesome and noisy habits. It is found everywhere except in the alpine region, and it does not appear ever to go beyond a vertical elevation of 4,500 feet. This gentleman has been assured that the bird never makes any nest of its own, but invariably lays its eggs in those belonging to other birds. He does not so state, but we infer that he means to convey the idea that this Jay appropriates the nests of other birds in which to hatch its own young, not that, like the Cowbird, it leaves its eggs to be brought up by strangers.

This Jay was met with by Mr. G. C. Taylor at Taulevi, in Honduras; and from that place eastward, as far as the Atlantic, he found it very common. It was generally seen or heard shrieking in the bushes by the roadsides. It was also found by Mr. Salvin to occur on the eastern road between Quiriqua and Iguana, on the road to Guatemala.

Mr. Joseph Leyland found this species common both in Honduras and the Belize. It occurred in small flocks, which were very noisy, and annoyed the hunter by always giving the alarm.

FAMILY **TYRANNIDÆ.** — TYRANT FLYCATCHERS.

PRIMARY CHARACTERS. Primaries ten. Bill in typical forms broad, triangular, much depressed, abruptly decurved and notched at tip, with long bristles along gape. Tarsi with scutellæ extending round the outer face of tarsus from the front to back; sometimes divided on the outer side. Bill with culmen nearly as long as the head, or shorter; straight to near the tip, then suddenly bent down into a conspicuous hook, with a notch behind it; tip of lower jaw also notched. Commissure straight to near the notch; gonys slightly convex. Nostrils oval or rounded, in the anterior extremity of the nasal groove, and more or less concealed by long bristles which extend from the posterior angle of the jaws along the base of the bill, becoming smaller, but reaching nearly to the median line of the forehead. These bristles with lateral branches at the base. Similar bristles are mixed in the loral feathers and margin the chin. Tarsí short, generally less than middle toe, completely enveloped by a series of large scales, which meet near the posterior edge of the inner side, and are separated either by naked skin or by a row of small scales. Sometimes a second series of rather large plates is seen on the posterior face of the tarsus, these, however, usually on the upper extremity only. Basal joint of middle toe united almost throughout to that of the outer toe, but more than half free on the inner side; outer lateral toe rather the longer. Wings and tail variable; first quill always more than three fourths the second. The outer primaries sometimes attenuated near the tip.

The primary characters given above will serve to distinguish the North American *Tyrannidæ* from their allies; the essential features consisting in the peculiarity of the scales of the tarsus and the ten primaries. In the *Sylvicolidæ* there are species as truly "flycatching," and with a depressed bristly bill, but the nine (not ten) primaries, and the restriction of the scales to the anterior face of the tarsus, instead of extending entirely round the outer side, will readily separate them.

The relationships of the *Tyrannidæ* are closest to the *Cotingidæ*. These last differ mainly in having the tarsus more or less reticulated, or covered in part at least with small angular scales, instead of continuous broad ones; and in the greater adhesion of the toes. The legs are shorter, and the body broader and more depressed. The bill is less abundantly provided with bristles, and the species do not appear to be strictly flycatchers, feeding more on berries and on stationary insects and larvæ, rather than capturing them on the wing. Two species of this family, *Hadrostomus affinis*[1] and *Pachyramphus major*,[2] were introduced into the Birds of North America, from specimens collected by Lieutenant Couch in the valley of the Rio

---

[1] *Hadrostomus affinis. Platypsaris affinis*, ELLIOT, Ibis, 1859, 394, pl. xiii. *Pachyramphus aglaiæ*, BAÍRD, Birds N. Am. 1858, 164, pl. xlvii, f. 1. — IB. Rep. Mex. Bound. II, Birds, 7, pl. xix, f. 1. *Hadrostomus aglaiæ*, CABANIS, Mus. Hein, II, 85 (Xalapa). — IB. Journ. 1861, 252. — SCLATER, P. Z. S. 1864, 176 (City Mex.). *Hab.* Northern Mexico, Jalapa, Nicaragua (SCL. Catalogue, p. 240) ; Yucatan (LAWRENCE).

[2] *Pachyramphus major. Bathmidurus major*, CAB. Orn. Nat. 1847, I, 246. — CAB. ET HEIN. Mus. Hein. II, 89. — BAIRD, Birds N. Am. 1858, 165, pl. xlvii, f. 2 ♀. — IB. Rep. Mex. Bound. II, Birds, 7, pl. xix, f. 2. *Pachyramphus major*, SCLATER, P. Z. S. 1857, 78 ; 1864, 176 (City of Mex.). *Hab.* Mexico and Guatemala.

Grande, not far from the border of the United States, but as they have not yet been detected within our limits, we have concluded to omit them in the present work.

The bird fauna of America may be said to have one of its chief features in the great number and variety of its *Tyrannidæ*, the family being strictly a New World one. Nearly every possible diversity of form is exhibited by different members; the size, however, usually varying from that of our common Robin to that of the Kinglet, our smallest bird with exception of the Humming-Bird. Of the numerous subfamilies, however, only one, the *Tyranninæ* proper, belongs to North America, and will be readily distinguished from other of our land birds by the family characters given at the head of this article, and which, as drawn up, apply rather to the subfamily than to the *Tyrannidæ* generally.

The North American species of the *Tyranninæ* may, for our present purposes, be divided into *Tyranni* and *Tyrannuli*. The former are large, generally with bright color, pointed wings, with attenuated primaries and a colored crest in the middle of the crown. The others are plainer, smaller, without colored crest; the primaries not attenuated.

The genera of our Flycatchers may be arranged as follows: —

TYRANNI. Size large; colors generally brilliant; crown with a brightly colored crest, usually concealed; outer primaries abruptly contracted or attenuated near the tip; upper scales of tarsus usually continuing round on the outside and behind. Nest in trees, very bulky, containing much downy material; eggs white or pinkish, with ovate dots of rich brown, of various shades.

> **Milvulus.** Tail excessively forked and lengthened; more than twice as long as the wings.
>
> **Tyrannus.** Tail moderate; nearly even or slightly forked; less than the wings.

TYRANNULI. Size generally small; colors usually plain; crown without any colored crest concealed by the tips of the feathers; primaries normal; scales of the upper part of the tarsus usually continuing only to the middle of the outer face, and a second series opposite to them behind.

1. Tail lengthened; about equal to the wings, which reach scarcely to its middle.

> **Myiarchus.** Tarsus equal to the middle toe, which is decidedly longer than the hinder one. Tail even or rounded. Throat pale ash, rest of lower parts yellow generally, the primaries edged with rufous, and inner webs of tail-feathers with more or less of the same color. Nest in a cavity of a tree, of loose material; eggs whitish, with intricate tangled lines and streaks of dark brown, the general effect salmon-color.
>
> **Sayornis.** Tarsus rather longer than the middle toe, which is scarcely longer than the hind toe. Tail slightly forked. Bill very narrow. No light orbital ring, nor distinct bands on wings; both mandibles black. Nest attached to rocks or parts of buildings, very compact and bulky, containing much mud in its composition; eggs pure white, immaculate, or with very minute sparse dots near larger end.

2. Tail decidedly shorter than the wings, which reach beyond its middle. Tarsus shorter than the middle toe.

Contopus. Hind toe much longer than the lateral. Tail considerably forked. Wings long, pointed; much longer than the tail, reaching beyond the middle of the latter; first quill about equal to the fourth. Bill broad. Color olive-gray, and white, sometimes with a yellowish tinge beneath. Lower mandible pale-colored. Nest saucer-shaped, compact, and very small, saddled very securely upon a thick branch; eggs cream-colored, with a zone of lilac and rich brown blotches round the larger end.

3. Tail shorter than the wings, as in the last. Tarsus considerably longer than the middle toe; hind toe much longer than lateral. Tail nearly even, sometimes slightly rounded, but little shorter than the wings; first primary much shorter than the fourth.

Empidonax. Head moderately crested; tail about even. Bristles of bill reaching about half-way to tip. Legs stout. A conspicuous light orbital ring, and distinct bands on the wing. More or less tinged with sulphur-yellow on lower parts. Nest variously constructed, deeply cup-shaped, compact or loose, entirely of either grassy or fibrous and downy material, and fixed to slender twigs or lodged in a crotch between thick branches; eggs white, immaculate, or with blotches of brown round larger end.

Mitrephorus. Head decidedly crested. Tail forked. Bristles of bill reaching nearly to tip. Legs very weak and slender. Beneath more or less tinged with fulvous or ochraceous.

Pyrocephalus. Head with a full crest. Tarsus but little longer than the middle toe; hind toe not longer than the lateral. Tail broad, even; first quill shorter than the fifth. Beneath, with whole crown bright red (except in *P. obscurus*). Female very different, lacking the red, except posteriorly beneath, and with the breast obsoletely streaked.

Genus **MILVULUS**, Swainson.

Milvulus, Swainson, Zoöl. Jour. III, 1827, 165.
Despotes, Reichenbach, Avium Syst. Naturale, 1850 (in part).

Sp. Char. Bill shorter than the head, and nearly equal to the tarsus. Tail nearly twice as long as the wing, excessively forked; the middle feathers scarcely half the lateral. First primary abruptly attenuated at the end, where it is very narrow and linear. Head with a concealed crest of red.

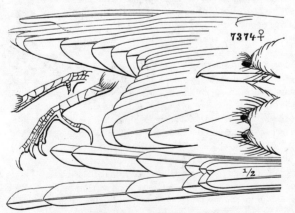

7374 ♀

½

Milvulus forficatus (tail abnormal).

This group is distinguished from *Tyrannus* by the very long tail, but the two species assigned by authors to North America, although agreeing in many respects, differ in some parts of their structure. The peculiarities of coloration are as follows : —

M. forficatus. Whitish-ash above; rump black. Tail-feathers rose-white with black tips; shoulders, axillars, and belly light vermilion. *Hab.* Middle America, and open portions of Texas, Indian Territory, etc.; accidental in New Jersey.

M. tyrannus.[1] Head above and tail black; the latter edged externally with white. Back ashy. Beneath pure white. *Hab.* Middle America, accidental in Eastern United States.

Milvulus tyrannus, BON.

FORK-TAILED FLYCATCHER.

Muscicapa tyrannus, LINN. Syst. Nat. I, 1766, 325. *Milvulus tyrannus*, BONAP. Geog. List, 1838. — AUDUBON, Synopsis, 1839, 38. — IB. Birds Am. I, 1840, 196, pl. lii. — BAIRD, Birds N. Am. 1858, 168. — CABAN. Journ. 1861, 251. — SCL. List. 1862, 237. — FINSCH, P. Z. S. 1870, 572 (Trinidad ; considers *violentus*, *tyrannus*, and *monachus* as identical). *Despotes tyrannus*, BONAP. Comptes Rendus, 1854, 87. *Tyrannus savana*, VIEILLOT, Ois. Am. Sept. I, 1807, 72, pl. xliii. — SWAINSON, Mon. Ty. Shrikes ; Quarterly Jour. XX, Jan. 1826, 282. *Muscicapa savana*, BONAP. Am. Orn. I, 1825, 1, pl. i, f. 1. — AUD. Orn. Biog. II, 1834, 387, pl. clxviii. *Milvulus savanus*, GRAY, List, 1841. *Tyrannus milvulus*, NUTTALL, Man., (2d ed.,) I, 1840, 307. *Fork-tailed Flycatcher*, PENNANT, LATHAM. *Tyran a queue fourchue*, BUFFON, pl. enl. 571.

SP. CHAR. Outer four primaries abruptly attenuated at the end, the sides of the attenuated portion parallel. Second and third quills longest; fourth little shorter, and not much exceeding the first. Tail very deeply forked; the external feather linear, and twice as long as the head and body alone. Top and sides of the head glossy black. Rump, upper tail-coverts, and tail almost black; the outer web of outer tail-feather yellowish-white for more than the basal half; rest of upper parts ash-gray. Under parts generally pure white. Wings dark brown; the outer primary and tertials edged with white. Crown with a concealed patch of yellow. Length, 14.00; wing, 4.75; tail, 10.00; depth of fork, 7.00. *Young.* No colored patch on crown; wing-coverts (including the lesser) and tail-feathers, with their upper coverts, bordered with rusty ochraceous. Black of head, tail, etc., duller than in adult.

HAB. Mexico to South America. Accidental in the United States. (New Jersey, Kentucky, and Mississippi, AUDUBON.)

This species claims a place in the fauna of the United States on account of two specimens captured in New Jersey, at long intervals, and one or two seen by Mr. Audubon in the southwest. It is, however, hardly proper to include it in our work on so slight a basis, and we only retain it for the purpose of referring to the notice of it by Mr. Audubon.

HABITS. The Fork-tailed Flycatcher is of purely accidental occurrence in the United States. Two specimens, taken at long intervals, are said to have been captured in the United States. One of these was shot by Mr. Audubon, in June, 1832, near the city of Camden, N. J. It was first observed

---

[1] *M. tyrannus*, var. *violentus* (*Tyrannus violentus*, VIEILL. N. D. xxxv, p. 89. *Milvulus v.*, SCL. Catal. Am. B. 1862, 237), is the South American race of this species. It is exceedingly similar, but differs slightly, though constantly, in certain characters. We have not at present the means of comparing the two.

flying over a meadow, in pursuit of insects. It afterwards alighted on the top of a small detached tree, when it was secured. The bird appeared to have lost its way, was unsuspicious, and paid no attention. when approached. On the wing, it seemed to make use of its long tail whenever it sought to suddenly turn in pursuit of its prey. On the ground, it vibrated its tail in the manner of a Sparrow-Hawk.

When the bird fell to the ground severely wounded, it uttered a sharp squeak, which it repeated, accompanied by a smart clicking of the bill, when Mr. Audubon approached it. It lived only a few moments, and from this specimen he made his drawing.

Several years previous to this, one of these birds had been shot near Henderson, Ky., but it was so far decayed when given to Mr. Audubon that it could not be preserved. It had been obtained among the Barrens late in October. Near Natchez, Miss., in August, 1822, Mr. Audubon was confident he saw two others of this species. They were high in the air, and were twittering in the manner of a Kingbird. He was, however, unable to secure them.

Another straggler was obtained near Bridgton, N. J., early in December. From this specimen was made the engraving in Bonaparte's Ornithology. It was given to Titian Peale by Mr. J. Woodcraft of that place.

This Flycatcher is a resident in tropical South America from Guiana to La Plata, and in its habits resembles the swallow-tailed species of our southern fauna. It is said to be a solitary bird, remaining perched on the limb of a tree, from which, from time to time, it darts after passing insects; while standing, it is said to vibrate its long tail in the manner of the European Wagtail. It also occasionally utters a twitter not unlike the common note of the Kingbird. Besides insects, this bird also feeds on berries, as the bird obtained near Bridgton had its stomach distended with the fruit of the poke-weed.

This species, according to Sumichrast, is found abundantly in winter in the savannas of the hot lands of Vera Cruz, and occurs to the height of about two thousand feet. He is not aware of its being resident.

Mr. Leyland found this species frequenting Old River and the pine ridges of Belize. They were also plentiful on the flats near Peten, and were occasionally found at Comayagua and Omoa, Honduras.

Mr. C. W. Wyatt met with this Flycatcher in Colombia, South America, on the savanna in the neighborhood of Aquachica. When at Ocaña, he used to see them congregated in considerable numbers just before sunset, whirling round high up in the air, and darting down like rockets to the ground. He only found it frequenting the open part of the country, and he never met with it at a greater elevation than five thousand feet.

An egg of this species obtained by Dr. Baldamus, from Cayenne, exhibits a strong resemblance to the egg of the common Kingbird. It has a clear white ground, and is spotted with deep and prominent marking of red and red-brown. They are of an oblong-oval shape, are tapering at one end, and measure .90 by .68 of an inch.

Milvulus forficatus, SWAIN.

SCISSOR-TAIL; SWALLOW-TAIL FLYCATCHER.

Muscicapa forficata, GMELIN, Syst. Nat. I, 1788, 931. — VIEILLOT, Ois. Am. Sept. I, 1807, 71. — STEPHENS, in Shaw's Zoöl. X, II, 413, pl. iii. — BONAP. Am. Orn. I, 1825, 15, pl. ii, f. 1. — AUD. Orn. Biog. IV, 1838, 426, pl. ccclix, f. 3. *Tyrannus forficatus*, SAY, Long's Exped., II, 1823, 224. — NUTTALL's Manual, I, (2d ed.,) 1840, 309. *Milvulus forficatus*, "SWAINS." RICH. List, 1837. — AUDUBON, Synopsis, 1839, 38. — IB. Birds Am. I, 1840, 197, pl. liii. — CABAN. Mus. Hein. II, 79. — SCL. List, 1862, 237. — BAIRD, Birds N. Am. 1858, 169. — IB. Mex. B. II, Zoöl. 7. — HEERM. X, c. p. 11. *Tyrannus mexicanus*, STEPHENS, Shaw, Gen. Zoöl. Birds, XIII, II, 1826, 135. *Moucherolle a queue fourchue du Mexique*, BUFFON, pl. enl. 677. *Bird of Paradise* of the Texans.

SP. CHAR. Wing with the outer primary only abruptly attenuated, and narrowly linear (for about .85 of an inch); the second but slightly emarginate; second quill longest; first and third equal. Tail very deeply forked; the lateral feathers twice as long as the body, all narrow and linear or subspatulate. Top and sides of the head very pale ash; the back a little darker, and faintly tinged with light brick-red; under parts nearly pure white, tinged towards the tail with light vermilion, rather more rose on the under wing-coverts; a patch on the side of the breast and along the fore-arm dark vermilion-red. Tail-feathers rosy white, tipped at the end for two or three inches with black. Rump dark brown, turning to black on the coverts. Wings very dark brown; the coverts and quills, excepting the primaries (and including the outer of these), edged with whitish. Crown with a concealed patch of white, having some orange-red in the centre. Length, 13.00; wing, 4.75; tail, 8.50; depth of fork, 5.80.

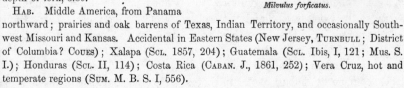
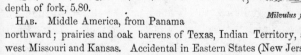

Milvulus forficatus.

HAB. Middle America, from Panama northward; prairies and oak barrens of Texas, Indian Territory, and occasionally Southwest Missouri and Kansas. Accidental in Eastern States (New Jersey, TURNBULL; District of Columbia? COUES); Xalapa (SCL. 1857, 204); Guatemala (SCL. Ibis, I, 121; Mus. S. I.); Honduras (SCL. II, 114); Costa Rica (CABAN. J., 1861, 252); Vera Cruz, hot and temperate regions (SUM. M. B. S. I, 556).

This exquisitely beautiful and graceful bird is quite abundant on the prairies of Southern Texas, and is everywhere conspicuous among its kindred

species. It is usually known as the Scissor-tail from the habit of closing
and opening the long feathers of the tail like the blades of a pair of scissors.
The adult female is very similar, though rather smaller. The young is not
conspicuously different, only lacking the concealed patch of the head.

HABITS. The Swallow-tailed Flycatcher appears to be a common species
from Central Texas to the Rio Grande, and thence throughout Mexico to
Central America, as far south at least as Guatemala. It is also found in
the Indian Territory, where it breeds, specimens of the nest and eggs having
been obtained at the Kioway Agency by Dr. E. Palmer.

It was found very plentiful at Langui, in Honduras, by Mr. G. C. Taylor,
and also in fewer numbers in other localities. In the evening, just before
roosting time, they were in the habit of assembling on the tops of certain
favorite trees, where they remained until nearly dark. They then all went
off to the woods. He generally met with them on open ground, not much
encumbered by trees or brushwood.

Mr. Dresser states that he found this very graceful bird quite abundant at
Matamoras and in Western Texas, where it is known by the name of
" Texan Bird of Paradise." He found it as far east as the river Guadaloupe.
It arrives, he states, in the neighborhood of San Antonio, late in March, and
remains until the middle or latter end of October. It breeds abundantly
near San Antonio, building its nest in a mesquite or other tree, and lays
from three to four eggs, which, as he states, are pure white, blotched with
large spots of a dark red color.

He adds that these birds are of a quarrelsome and fearless disposition,
rarely brooking intruders near their homes. During the breeding-season
Mr. Dresser has often, when travelling, stopped to admire four or five of
them fighting on the wing. They show their long tail-feathers and the
rich scarlet color under their wings to the fullest advantage. After passing
Guadaloupe River, he saw none of these birds to the eastward, though he
was told they have occasionally been seen on Galveston Island.

This Flycatcher was met with at Eagle Pass, in Lower Texas, and in
Tamaulipas by Mr. Clark and Lieutenant Couch, in the Mexican Boundary
Survey. None were found occurring west of the valley of the Rio Pecos.
Mr. Clark states that he always saw them either following one another
through the air, or perched upon some solitary twig. In their gyrations the
scissors were always more or less expanded, suggesting the idea of bal-
ancers. Their nests were built of sticks, lined on the inside, though not
very softly, with grass, and were placed almost invariably on dry limbs
of the mesquite. They contained from three to five eggs, and, what was
quite remarkable, more than one pair always seemed to have an interest in
the same nest, over which they were all very watchful, and gave proofs of
their courage by darting at the intruders. He describes their notes as short
and sharp, without much variation, and they can be heard at quite a distance.
The Mexicans imagine that this Flycatcher lives on the brains of other birds.

Lieutenant Couch describes the Scissor-tail as shy, but of a very lively disposition. Usually four or more are seen in company, and seem to prefer the thinly wooded prairies to close thickets. In beauty, Lieutenant Couch considers it the queen of all the birds found in Northern Tamaulipas. This superiority is not owing so much to the brilliancy of its plumage, for in that it is excelled by several species, but to the inimitable grace and charm of its flight. Rising from the topmost branch of some acacia, it seems to float, rather than to fly; then descending perpendicularly, it retakes its position, uttering its usual note. He did not see it west of the Cadereita. Dr. Kennerly, in his march from the Gulf of Mexico into Western Texas, frequently met with these Flycatchers along his route. He usually saw them in the open prairie, or among the mesquite-bushes. When perched, they were generally on the top of a bush or a tall weed, and their tails were constantly in motion. When they darted off after some passing insect, they usually circled around, displaying the singular bifurcation of their tail, but seldom alighting again on the same bush. It was occasionally seen on the open prairie, flying for a long distance near the earth, as if in search of insects.

In Vera Cruz this species is an inhabitant of the hot lands. A few individuals ascend, though very rarely, to the height of the city of Orizaba, or about 3,700 feet.

Mr. Nuttall states that he met with this Flycatcher rather common along the banks of the Red River, near the confluence of the Kiamesha. He again met them, even more frequently, near the Great Salt River of Arkansas, in August. They seemed to be preying upon grasshoppers.

Dr. Woodhouse not only found this species abundant in Texas, in the vicinity of San Antonio, but in the Indian Territory also it was quite common, particularly near the Cross Timbers. He found them breeding in the beginning of the month of July, on the Great Prairie. Its nest was built on the horizontal branch of a small scrub-oak, about six feet from the ground, and was composed of coarse dry grass and sticks. It contained four young birds nearly able to fly. On his approach the female flew from the nest to a bush near by. The male bird flew to a great height above him, circling round in the air, apparently watching his movements, and at the same time uttering a coarse scolding chirp.

Dr. Gideon Lincecum, of Texas, writes that the Scissor-tail Flycatchers have greatly increased in numbers in that State since 1848. They are severe hunters of insects, and make great havoc among honey-bees. They are exclusively prairie birds. He adds that they construct their nests far out on the top branches of the live-oak or any other lone tree on the prairies. They seem to be a very playful bird, and delight in shooting rapidly upwards, cutting the air with their strong wings with such force that the sound may be heard to the distance of three hundred yards or more. Their notes are harsh and inharmonious. They leave Texas late in autumn, and return again about the first of April. The resounding strokes of their wings and their oft-repeated cries are heard just before the dawn of day. They usually have but three eggs.

A single individual of *Milvulus*, and supposed to be one of this species, was seen by Mr. C. Drexler, May 6, 1861, but was not obtained, in the vicinity of Washington. Another bird of this species is mentioned by Mr. Abbott as having been taken near Trenton, N. J., April 15, 1872. It was a male bird in full health and feather. Its stomach was found to be full of small coleoptera, insects' eggs, flies, etc.

The eggs of this species vary greatly in size, from .92 by .75 to .80 by .60 of an inch. They are in shape a rounded oval, and tapering at one end. The ground-color is white, marked with a few very large dark red spots, and occasionally of an obscure purple.

GENUS **TYRANNUS**, CUVIER.

Tyrannus, CUVIER, Leçons Anat. Comp. 1799, 1800 (AGASSIZ).

GEN. CHAR. Tail nearly even, or moderately forked; rather shorter than the wings; the feathers broad, and widening somewhat at the ends. Wings long and pointed; the outer primaries rather abruptly attenuated near the end, the attenuated portion not linear, however. Head with a concealed patch of red on the crown.

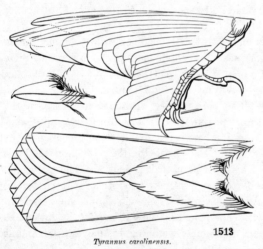

1513

Tyrannus carolinensis.

The species of this genus are especially characterized by their long, attenuated primaries, their moderately forked or nearly even tail, and the concealed colored crest in the crown. Their affinities are nearest to *Milvulus*, from which the tail, shorter than the wings, instead of twice as long, or more, will always serve as a point of distinction. The attenuation of the primary differs in being less abrupt, and not truly linear, sloping gradually, and not bounded behind by a notch. We are unable to appreciate any other differences of importance.

The character and extent of the attenuation of the primaries, the depth of the fork of the tail, with the size of the legs and bill, all vary considerably, and may, perhaps, serve as ground for further subdivisions. The bill, in particular, varies much in size in the North American species, from that of

T. carolinensis, where the culmen is but little more than half the head, to that of *T. dominicensis* (genus *Melittarchus* of Cabanis), where it is decidedly longer than the head, and almost as stout as that of *Saurophagus.*

The North American species of *Tyrannus* (with their nearest Mexican allies) may be arranged by colors, accordingly as they are white beneath or yellow, in the following manner : —

A. Under parts whitish, without any shade of yellow. A faint grayish-plumbeous pectoral band.

> 1. **T. carolinensis.** Tail slightly rounded. Bill much shorter than the head. Above black, shading into dark plumbeous on the back. Tail abruptly and broadly margined and tipped with pure white. (*Tyrannus.*) *Hab.* Whole of North America, north to the British Provinces, and south to Panama. Rare in the Western Province of North America.
>
> 2. **T. dominicensis.** Tail moderately forked. Bill longer than the head. Above gray; the tail and wings brownish. The edges and tips of the tail narrowly margined with soiled white. (*Melittarchus.*) *Hab.* West Indies, New Granada, Panama, Florida, Georgia, and South Carolina.

B. Above ashy-olive, becoming purer ash on the head. Tail brown or black. Beneath yellow; the chin paler; the breast strongly shaded with olivaceous or ashy. (*Laphyctes.*)

> *a.* Tail nearly black; the outer edges of the outer webs of the feathers with the fibres united closely throughout, and colored similarly to the rest of the feathers; beneath sulphur-yellow.
>
> 3. **T. verticalis.** Tail slightly forked; external feather with the entire outer web and the outer half of the shaft abruptly yellowish-white. Pectoral band pale ashy, lighter than the back. *Hab.* Western Province of United States.
>
> 4. **T. vociferans.** Tail nearly even or slightly rounded; external feather with the shaft brown; the outer edge only of the outer web obscurely yellowish-white, and all the feathers fading into paler at the tip. Throat and breast broadly tinged with dark ashy-olive like the back. *Hab.* Plains and southern Middle Province of United States, south into Middle America.
>
> *b.* Tail brown, scarcely darker than the wings; outer edges of the outer webs of the tail-feathers olivaceous like the back, in contrast with the brown; the fibres loosened externally; shafts of tail-feathers white beneath. Beneath bright gamboge-yellow.
>
> 5. **T. melancholicus.**[1] Tail quite deeply forked (.70 of an inch), brownish-black, the lighter edgings obsolete, and those on wings indistinct. Throat ashy. *Hab.* South America . . var. *melancholicus.* Tail moderately forked (.30 of an inch), grayish-brown, the light edges conspicuous, as are also those of the wings. Throat white. *Hab.* Middle America, north to southern boundary of United States . . var. *couchi.*

In the Birds of North America a supposed new species, *T. couchi,* was mentioned as coming so close to the boundary line of the United States in

---

[1] *Tyrannus melancholicus,* VIEILLOT, Nouv. Dict. xxxv, 1819, 84. — BAIRD, Birds N. Am. 1858, 176. — SCLATER, Catal. Am. Birds, 1862, 235. *Hab.* South America. A more northern race scarcely distinguishable (Panama, Costa Rica, etc.), separated as *T. satrapa,* LICHT.

Texas as to warrant its introduction into our fauna. We have, however, concluded to give in the present work nothing but what has actually been found within its prescribed limits.

Tyrannus carolinensis, BAIRD.

KINGBIRD; BEE MARTIN.

? *Lanius tyrannus*, LINN. Syst. Nat. I, 1766, 136. This belongs to the Cuban *T. matutinus*, according to Bonaparte. *Muscicapa tyrannus*, (BRISSON ?) WILSON, Am. Orn. I, 1808, 66, pl. xiii. — AUD. Orn. Biog. I, 1832, 403 ; V, 1839, 420, pl. lxxix. — IB. Birds Am. I, 1840, 204, pl. lvi. *Lanius tyrannus*, var. γ, *carolinensis*, δ, *ludovicianus*, GMELIN, Syst. Nat. I, 1788, 302. *Muscicapa rex*, BARTON, Fragments N. H. Penna. 1799, 18. *Tyrannus pipiri*, VIEILLOT, Ois. Am. Sept. I, 1807, 73, pl. xliv. — CAB. Journ. Orn. III, 1855, 478. — SCL. List, 1862, 236. *Tyrannus intrepidus*, VIEILLOT, Galerie Ois. I, 1824, 214, pl. cxxxiii. — SWAINSON, Mon. Ty. Shrikes, Quart. Jour. 1826, 274. *Muscicapa animosa*, LICHT. Verz. Doubl. 1823, No. 558. *Gobe Mouche de la Caroline*, BUFFON, Ois. V, 281, enl. pl. 676. *Tyrannus leucogaster*, STEPHENS, Shaw, Gen. Zoöl. XIII, II, 1826, 132. *Tyrannus carolinensis*, BAIRD, Birds N. Am. 1858, 171. — CABAN. Mus. Hein. II, 79. — LORD, Pr. R. A. Inst. IV, 64, 113. — COOPER & SUCKLEY, 167. — SAMUELS, 128. — COOPER, Orn. Cal. I, 1870, 311.

SP. CHAR. Two, sometimes three, outer primaries abruptly attenuated at the end. Second quill longest ; third little shorter ; first rather longer than fourth, or nearly equal.

Tyrannus carolinensis.

Tail slightly rounded. Above dark bluish-ash. The top and sides of the head to beneath the eyes bluish-black. A concealed crest on the crown vermilion in the centre, white behind, and before partially mixed with orange. Lower parts pure white, tinged with pale bluish-ash on the sides of the throat and across the breast ; sides of the breast and under the wings similar to, but rather lighter than, the back. Axillaries pale grayish-brown tipped with lighter. The wings dark brown, darkest towards the ends of the quills ; the greater coverts and quills edged with white, most so on the tertials ; the lesser coverts edged with paler. Upper tail-coverts and upper surface of the tail glossy black, the latter very dark brown beneath ; all the feathers tipped, and the exterior margined externally with white, forming a conspicuous terminal band about .25 of an inch broad. Length, 8.50 ; wing, 4.65 ; tail, 3.70 ; tarsus, .75.

HAB. Eastern North America to Rocky Mountains. Occasional in various parts of the Western Province (Washington Territory, Salt Lake Valley, Truckee River, Nevada, etc.). South to Panama. Oaxaca, lowlands, March (SCL. P. Z. S. 1858, 302) ; Honduras (MOORE, P. Z. S. 1859, 55) ; Guatemala (SCL. Ibis I, 120) ; Cuba (CAB. J. III, 476 ; GUNDL. Rep. 1865, 239, " *T. pipiri*") ; Panama, (MUS. S. I. ; LAWR. Ann. N. Y. Lyc. VII, 295) ; Greytown, Nic. (LAWR. Ann. VIII, 183) ; East of San Antonio, Texas (DRESSER, Ibis, 1865, 472 ; breeds) ; Upper Amazon, Peru, Nauta (SCL. and SALV. P. Z. S., 1866, 189) ; Vera Cruz, hot region, resident (SUMICHRAST, M. B. S. I, 557).

The young of the year is similar ; the colors duller, the concealed colored patch on the crown wanting. The tail more rounded; the primaries not attenuated.

Specimens vary in the amount of white margining the wing-feathers; the upper tail-coverts are also margined sometimes with white.

HABITS. The common Kingbird or Bee Martin of North America is found throughout the continent, from Texas and Florida, on the south, as far to the north as the 57th parallel of north latitude. Westward, north of the 44th parallel, it is found from the Atlantic to the Pacific, but south of this it has not been found west of the Rocky Mountains. It is included by Dr. Cooper among the birds of California, but I am not aware that it has ever been taken within the limits of that State. Mr. Allen regards the eastern slope of the Rocky Mountains its extreme western limit; but Mr. Ridgway states that this species was met with by him in various portions of the Great Basin, though always in less abundance than the *T. verticalis*. Among the cottonwoods of the Truckee Valley, in Western Nevada, two or three pairs were seen in July and August. In the fertile Salt Lake Valley it was nearly or quite as common as the *T. verticalis*, and was also met with in the fertile " parks " of the Wahsatch Mountains.

This species not only has this widely extended area, but is also quite abundant wherever found. It is apparently as abundant throughout Nova Scotia as it is in the State of Florida. Richardson even found it common on the banks of the Saskatchewan, where he traced its northern migrations beyond the 57th parallel of latitude. It was found at the Carlton House early in May, and retired southward in September. It winters in Central and South America, and has been received by Mr. Lawrence from Panama.

Dr. Suckley found this species quite plentiful at the eastern base of the Rocky Mountains, in Washington Territory, and more sparingly at Puget Sound, where he obtained several specimens. They appeared to shun the dense forests near Puget Sound, but were moderately plentiful in the groves of low oaks, and among the cottonwood-trees fringing the lakes on Nisqually Plains, where, August 5, he obtained a nest with newly fledged young.

Mr. Joseph Leyland found this species near Omoa, in Honduras, migratory. They came in flocks of two or three hundred, but remained only a short time before departing farther south. They flew high, and seemed very wild. This species was also met with, in May, at Playa Vicente, in the low lands of the State of Oaxaca, Mexico, by Mr. Boucard, and during the winter months is found throughout Mexico.

No one of our common birds possesses more strongly marked characteristics of manners and habits than this species. Its pugnacious disposition during the breeding-season, the audacious boldness with which it will attack any birds larger than itself, the persistent tenacity with which it will continue these attacks, and the reckless courage with which it will maintain its unequal warfare, are well-known peculiarities of this interesting and familiar species. Its name, Kingbird, is given it on the supposition that it is superior to all other birds in these contests. My own observations lead me to the conclusion that writers have somewhat exaggerated the quarrelsome disposition of this bird. I have never, or very rarely, known it to molest or attack any other birds than those which its own instinct prompts it to drive away in self-defence, such as Hawks, Owls, Eagles, Crows, Jays, Cuckoos, and Grakles. These it will always attack and drive off to quite a distance from their nests. Nothing can be more striking than the intrepidity with which one of these birds will pounce upon and harass birds vastly larger and more powerful than itself. The Kingbird is always prompts to perceive the approach of one of these enemies, and always rushes out to meet it. Mounting in the air high above, it pounces down upon its back, upon which it will even rest, furiously pecking at the exposed flanks of its victim, and only leaving it to descend again and again with the same unrelenting animosity. In these encounters it always comes off conqueror.

Wilson states that his jealous affection for his mate and for his nest and young makes him suspicious of every bird that happens to pass near his residence. But this is not the case in all instances. A pair of these birds nested, in the summer of 1871, and peacefully reared their young, in an apple-tree near my residence, within four feet of the nest of the Baltimore Oriole, and not more than eight or ten feet from the nest of a Robin, all in the same tree. The three pairs were on evident terms of amity and mutual good-will. The male Kingbird kept a sharp lookout for danger from the topmost bough, and seemed to have all under his special guardianship, but showed no disposition to molest or annoy them.

The Purple Martin is said to be the implacable enemy of the Kingbird, and one of the few birds with which the latter maintains an unequal contest. Its superiority in flight gives the former great advantages, while its equal courage and strength render it more than a match. Audubon relates an instance in which the Kingbird was slain in one of these struggles.

Wilson also narrates an encounter, of which he was an eyewitness, between one of this species and a Red-headed Woodpecker, in which the latter, while clinging on the rail of a fence, seemed to amuse itself with the violence of the Kingbird, playing bo-peep with it round the rail, while the latter became greatly irritated, and made repeated but vain attempts to strike at him.

The Kingbird feeds almost exclusively upon winged insects, and consumes a vast number. It is on this account one of our most useful birds, but, unfortunately for its popularity, it is no respecter of kinds, and destroys large numbers of bees. In districts where hives of honey-bees abound, the Kingbird is not in good repute. Wilson suggests that they only destroy the drones, and rarely, if ever, meddle with the working bees. But this discrimination, even if real, is not appreciated by the raisers of bees, who regard this bird as their enemy.

The Kingbirds arrive in Pennsylvania the latter part of April, and in New

England early in May, and leave for the South in September. They nest in May, selecting an upper branch; usually of an isolated tree, and often in an exposed situation. Their nests are large, broad, and comparatively shallow, and coarsely, though strongly, made of rude materials, such as twigs, withered plants, bits of rags, strings, etc. These are lined with fine rootlets, horse-hair, and fine grasses.

The Kingbird has no song, but, instead, utters an incessant monotonous succession of twitterings, which vary in sharpness and loudness with the emotions that prompt them.

The flight of the Kingbird when on the hunt for insects is peculiar and characteristic. It flies slowly over the field, with rapid vibrations of the wings, in the manner of Hawks, and soars or seems to float in the air in a manner equally similar. At other times it flies with great rapidity, and dives about in the air in the manner of a Swallow. It also exhibits great power and rapidity of flight when rushing forth to encounter a Hawk or an Eagle.

As they are known occasionally to plunge into the water, and, emerging thence, to resume their seat on a high branch, to dry and dress their plumage, it has been conjectured that they feed on small fish, but this is unsupported by any positive evidence.

Though the Kingbird usually builds in trees, it does not always select such situations. In the summer of 1851, passing over a bridge near the village of Aylesford, in Nova Scotia, I observed a Kingbird fly from a nest built on the projecting end of one of the planks of which the bridge was made. So remarkably exposed a position, open to view, and on a level with and within a few feet of a highway, must be quite unusual.

The eggs of this bird are five, sometimes six, in number, and vary considerably in size. Their ground-color is white with a more or less decided roseate tinge, beautifully spotted with blotches and markings of purple, brown, and red-brown. In some, these are disposed in a confluent crown around the larger end; in others they are irregularly distributed over the entire egg. In length they vary from 1.05 to .86 of an inch, and in breadth from .72 to .70 of an inch.

Tyrannus dominicensis, Rich.

GRAY KINGBIRD.

Tyrannus dominicensis, Brisson, Ois. II, 1760, 394, pl. xxxviii. fig. 2. — Rich. List, 1837. — Baird, Birds N. Am. 1858, 172. *Lanius tyrannus*, var. β, *dominicensis*, Gmelin, Syst. Nat. I, 1788, 302. *Muscicapa dominicensis*, Aud. Orn. Biog. II, 1834, 392, pl. xlvi. — Ib. Birds Am. I, 1840, 201, pl. lv. *Melittarchus dominicensis*, Cabanis, Journal für Ornith. III, Nov. 1855, 478. *Tyrannus griseus*, Vieillot, Ois. Am. Sept. I, 1807, 76, pl. xlvi. — Swainson, Mon. Shrikes, Quart. Jour. XX, 1826, 276. — Bp. Consp. 1850, 192 (Bonaparte makes two species). — Scl. List, 1862, 236. *Tyrannus matutinus*, Vieill. De La Sagra, pl. xiv.

Sp. Char. Bill very large and stout. Tail conspicuously forked. Wings long; the first six quills attenuated abruptly, much longer than the seventh. Tertials much developed, nearly intermediate in length between the longest primaries and the shortest secondary. Above, and on the sides of the head and neck, ash-gray, shaded in places with brown, which forms the middle portion of each feather. Downy portion at the base of each feather above light ash, then light brown, tipped and edged with darker ash-gray. The mottled appearance is caused by the brown showing from under the feathers; the ear-coverts darker. A concealed colored patch on the crown, formed by the base of the feathers, white before and behind, orange in the middle. Lower parts grayish-white, tinged with ash across the breast, deepest anteriorly. Sides of the breast similar to, but lighter than, the back. Under wing-coverts and axillars pale sulphur-yellow. The wings brown, darker to the tips; the secondaries narrowly, the tertials more broadly, edged with dull white. Edges of the coverts paler. Alula dark brown. Tail similar in color to the quills. Upper tail-coverts brown. Bill and feet black. Length, 8.00; wing, 4.65; tail, 4.00; tarsus, .76.

Young. Lesser wing-coverts and upper tail-coverts distinctly bordered with pale ochraceous; tail-feathers bordered all round with a deeper shade of the same. No colored patch on the crown.

Hab. South Carolina coast, accidental; Florida Keys and West Indies; Nicaragua; New Granada. Santa Cruz (Newton, Ibis I, 146, eggs); Carthagena, N. G. (Cass. P. A. N. S. 1860, 143); Cuba (Cab. J. III, 478, breeds; Gundl. Rep. 1865, 238, "*Mel. griseus*"); Jamaica (Gosse, B. J. 169, breeds; March, P. A. N. S. 1863, 287); St. Thomas (Cass. P. A. N. S. 1860, 375); Sombrero (Lawr. Ann. N. Y. Lyc. VIII, 1864, 99, "*griseus*"); Greytown, Nicar. (Lawr. Ann. 183); Sta. Bartholemy (Sund. 1869, 584); Massachusetts (Maynard, B. E. Mass. 1870, 124).

This species, though about the same size as the *T. carolinensis*, is much more powerfully built, the bill and feet being much stronger, the former considerably longer than the head, and as large as that of *Saurophagus sulphuratus*, though less compressed.

Specimens from Nicaragua and New Granada appear to be almost perfectly identical with those from Florida and the West Indies, differing only in being just appreciably smaller, which, however, might be expected from their more southern habitat.

Habits. The Gray Kingbird — the Pipiry Flycatcher of Audubon, or Gray Petchary of Jamaica — is, except in Florida, of scarcely more than occasional occurrence within the limits of the United States. A single specimen has been taken in Massachusetts. This was shot in Lynn, October 23, 1868, and was in immature plumage. The bird was shot on a tree near one of the streets of that city by Mr. Charles Goodall. Mr. Audubon also found these birds quite common on the Florida Keys, almost every Key, however small, having its pair. A pair was observed breeding in the college yard at Charleston, S. C., by Dr. Bachman; and for at least three years in succession they regularly returned each year, and raised two broods in a season. This Flycatcher is abundant in St. Croix, Cuba, Jamaica, and in the other West India Islands. In the first-named locality Mr. Alfred Newton found it one of the most conspicuous and commonest birds over the entire island. Its favorite station, he states, was the top of the spearlike unexpanded frond of a tall mountain-cabbage tree, from which place, in the breeding-season, it darted down to attack almost any animal that passed near. Its favorite object of attack was the Green Heron (*Butorides virescens*), at which it would make several well-directed swoops, never leaving it until it had driven it into some shelter, when, much pleased with its prowess, it would return to its lookout station and celebrate its victory with cries of triumph. On one occasion Mr. Newton observed a Gray Kingbird pursue a Green Heron out to sea for a quarter of a mile and back. It is described as a very clamorous bird, even when there is apparently no need; taking alarm from the domestic poultry, its oft-repeated notes were heard every morning before the dawn. This noise it continued pertinaciously till sundown. Its food consists of insects, which are caught with great dexterity on the wing. It also feeds very largely on the black berries of a myrtle-leaved parasite that grows abundantly on the orange-trees. The nest is often placed under the fronds or among the spathes of a cocoanut or mountain-cabbage tree, and sometimes in any ordinary situation. It is described as flat in construction and large for the size of the bird, being nearly a foot in diameter, composed of a platform of twigs, in the midst of which is hollowed a cup lined with fine roots. In St. Croix the eggs rarely exceeded three in number, and are spoken of as exceedingly beautiful when fresh, of a delicate creamy white, marked at the larger end with blotches and spots of pink or orange-brown, often disposed in a zone. He found their eggs from May till August.

Mr. Richard Hill, of Spanishtown, Jamaica, in some interesting notes furnished to Mr. Gosse, states that along the seaside savannas of that island migrant flocks of these birds swarm early in September. Numbers then congregate on the trees around the cattle ponds and about the open meadows, pursuing the swarms of insects which fill the air at sundown. These throngs are immediately joined by resident birds of this species, which gather about the same places, and do not return to their usual abodes until the breeding-season is at hand.

The Jamaica bird is not exclusively an insect-feeder, but eats very freely of the sweet wild berries, especially those of the pimento. These ripen in September, and in groves of these this bird may always be found in abundance. By the end of September most of the migrant birds have left the island.

This is among the earliest to breed of the birds of Jamaica. As early as January the mated pair is said to be in possession of some lofty tree, sounding at day-dawn a ceaseless shriek, which is composed of a repetition of three or four notes, sounding like *pē-chēē-ry*, according to Mr. Hill, and from which they derive their local name. In these localities they remain until autumn, when they quit these haunts and again congregate about the lowland ponds. In feeding, just before sunset, they usually sit, eight or ten in a row, on some exposed twig, darting from it in pursuit of their prey, and returning to it to devour whatever they have caught. They are rapid in their movements, ever constantly and hurriedly changing their positions in flight. As they fly, they are able to check their speed suddenly, and to turn at the smallest imaginable angle. At times they move off in a straight line, gliding with motionless wings from one tree to another. When one descends to pick an insect from the surface of the water, it has the appearance of tumbling, and, in rising again, ascends with a singular motion of the wings, as if hurled into the air and endeavoring to recover itself.

In the manner in which the male of this species will perch on the top of some lofty tree, and from that vantage-height scream defiance to all around him, and pursue any large bird that approaches, as described by Mr. Hill, all the audacity and courage of our Kingbird is exhibited. At the approach of a Vulture or a Hawk, he starts off in a horizontal line, after rising in the air to the same height as his adversary, and, hovering over him for a moment, descends upon the intruder's back, rising and sinking as he repeats his attack, and shrieking all the while. In these attacks he is always triumphant.

This Flycatcher is also charged by Mr. Hill with seizing upon the Humming-Birds as they hover over the blossoms in the garden, killing its prey by repeated blows struck on the branch, and then devouring them.

The nest, according to Mr. Hill, is seldom found in any other tree than that of the palm kind. Among the web of fibres around the footstalk of each branch the nest is woven of cotton-wool and grass. The eggs, he adds, are four or five, of an ivory color, blotched with deep purple spots, intermingled with brown specks, the clusters thickening at the greater end. Mr. Gosse, on the contrary, never found the nest in a palm. One, taken from an upper limb of a bitterwood-tree that grew close to a friend's door, at no great height, was a cup made of the stalks and tendrils of a small passion flower, the spiral tendrils very prettily arranged around the edge, and very neatly and thickly lined with black horse-hair. The other, made in a spondias bush, was a rather loose structure, smaller and less compact, almost entirely composed of tendrils, with no horse-hair, but a few shining black frond-ribs of a fern.

Mr. March states that the migrant birds of this species return to Jamaica about the last of March, gradually disperse, and, like the resident birds, occupy their selected trees in solitary pairs, and immediately set about preparing their nests. At St. Catharine's the first nest found was on the 14th of April, and the latest in the middle of July. They seldom build in the tree in which they perch, but select a lower tree near it. Some make their nests high, others low, usually at the extremity of a lateral branch. He describes them as loose structures of twigs and the stems of trailing plants, with the cup of grass, horse-hair, and vegetable fibre. The eggs are three, rarely four, of a long oval, with a ground of light cream-color, dashed around the larger end more or less thickly with blotches of burnt sienna, and with cloudings of pale bistre underneath.

Mr. Audubon states that this Flycatcher reaches the Florida Keys about the first of April. He describes their usual flight as performed by a constant flutter of the wings, except when in chase, when they exhibit considerable power and speed. He noticed them pursue larger birds, such as Herons, Crows, Cuckoos, Grakles, and Hawks, following them quite a distance. They did not molest the Doves. They built their nests in a manner similar to the Kingbird, on the horizontal branches of the mangrove, almost invariably on the western side of the tree and of the island. Some were not more than two feet above the water, others were twenty feet. On one of the keys, although of small size, he saw several of their nests, and more than a dozen of the birds living amicably together.

Dr. J. G. Cooper, who visited Florida in the spring of 1859, informed me, by letter, on his return, that when he reached Cape Florida, March 8, none of this species were to be seen on any of the keys. The first he noticed were about the first of May, near Fort Dallas on the mainland. As, however, it rarely appears at this place, he supposes they reached the keys some weeks sooner. About May 14 he found several pairs at the Cape, and, going up the coast to New Smyrna, he found them abundant about the marshy islands. On the first of June, with a companion, he went in a small boat for the express purpose of finding their nests ; and, pushing the boat about among the islands which almost filled Mosquito Lagoon, he discovered three in one afternoon. They were all built among the small branches of low dead mangrove-trees, about ten feet from the ground, formed of a loose, open flooring of small twigs, with scarcely any lining of a finer material. One contained four eggs half hatched, another three young and one egg, the third four young just hatched. He preserved one nest and all the eggs, and presented them to the National Museum in Washington. The old birds showed no resentment, and neither came near nor followed him, differing very much in this respect from the fearless and devoted Kingbird. The only notes this bird was heard to utter were loud and harsh rattling cries. Dr. Bachman informed Dr. Cooper that these birds had become quite regular summer visitants of Charleston, where they continued to breed each season. Dr. Cooper saw none away from the Florida coast, and thinks that none go inland.

The eggs of this species measure from 1 to 1.05 inches in length, and from .70 to .72 of an inch in breadth. They are of an oblong oval shape, variously marked with large blotches and smaller spots of purple, red-brown, and a dark purplish-brown. The latter color, in a few cases, is found in large masses, covering nearly a fifth of the entire surface of the egg ; not inaptly compared by Mr. Gosse to the sinuous outlines of lands, as represented on a terrestrial globe.

Tyrannus verticalis, SAY.

ARKANSAS FLYCATCHER.

Tyrannus verticalis, SAY, Long's Exped. II, 1823, 60. — NUTTALL, Man. II, (2d ed.,) 1840, 306. — BAIRD, Birds N. Am. 1858, 173. — SCL. Catal. 1862, 235. — LORD, Pr. R. A. Inst. IV, 113 (Br. Col.). — COOPER & SUCKLEY, 168. — COOPER, Orn. Cal. I, 1870, 312. *Muscicapa verticalis,* BONAP. Am. Orn. I, 1825, 18, pl. xi. — AUD. Orn. Biog IV, 1838, 422, pl. ccclix. — IB. Birds Am. I, 1840, 199, pl. liv. *Laphyctes verticalis,* CABAN. Mus. Hein. II, 1859, 77. — HEERM. X. *S,* 37.

SP. CHAR. The four exterior quills attenuated very gently at the end, the first most so; third and fourth quills longest, second and fifth successively a little shorter. Tail slightly forked; bill shorter than the head. Crown, sides of head above the eyes, nape, and sides of neck pale lead-color, or ash-gray; a concealed crest on the crown, vermilion in the centre, and yellowish before and behind. Hind neck and back ash-gray, strongly tinged with light olivaceous-green, the gray turning to brown on the rump; upper tail-coverts nearly black, lower dusky; chin and part of ear-coverts dull white; throat and upper part of breast similar to the head, but lighter, and but slightly contrasted with the chin; rest of lower parts, with the under wing-coverts and axillars, yellow, deepening to gamboge on the belly, tinged with olivaceous on the breast. Wing brown, the coverts with indistinct ashy margins; secondaries and tertials edged with whitish; inner webs of primaries whitish towards the base. Tail nearly black above and glossy, duller brownish beneath; without olivaceous edgings. Exterior feather, with the outer web and the shaft, yellowish-white; inner edge of latter brown. Tips of remaining feathers paler. Bill and feet dark brown. *Female* rather smaller and colors less bright. Length of male, 8.25; wing about 4.50.

HAB. Western North America, from the high Central Plains to the Pacific; Colima, Mexico. Accidental in Eastern States (New Jersey, TURNBULL; Plymton, Maine, Oct. 1865, BRYANT, Pr. Bost. Soc, X, 1865, 96).

The young bird is, in general, quite similar, with the exception of the usual appearance of immaturity, the colored patch on the crown wanting. In one specimen the first primary only is attenuated, in others none exhibit this character.

A specimen of this bird, shot at Moorestown, N. J., is in the museum of the Philadelphia Academy, but this locality can only be considered as very exceptional.

HABITS. The Arkansas Flycatcher was first discovered by the party in Long's Expedition in 1823, and described by Mr. Say. It is a bird of western North America, found from the great plains to the Pacific, and only accidentally occurring east. A single specimen is said to have been shot in Moorestown, N. J., near Philadelphia. It has been met with in Texas as far east as the river Mimbres, and in Nebraska nearly to the Missouri River. The specimen from which the first description was made was obtained in the beginning of July, near the Platte River.

Mr. Nuttall, in his Western tour, first met with this species early in July, among the scanty wood on the banks of the northwest branch of the Platte River. He characterizes it as a bold and querulous bird. He found it all the way from thence to the forests of the Columbia and the Wahlamet, and throughout California to latitude 32°. He speaks of them as remarkably noisy and quarrelsome with each other, and, like the Kingbird, suffering nothing of the bird kind to approach them without exhibiting their predilection for dispute. He describes their note as a discordant, clicking warble, resembling *tsh'k-tsh'k-tshivait,* — sounding not unlike the creaking of a rusty door-hinge, something in the manner of a Kingbird, with a blending of the notes of the common Purple Grakle.

Mr. Townsend mentions finding this bird numerous along the banks of the Platte, particularly in the vicinity of trees. From that river to the banks of the Columbia, and as far as the ocean, it was a very common species. The males were wonderfully belligerent, fighting almost constantly and with great fury.

Dr. J. G. Cooper states that in California this is an abundant species, arriving in that State about the 20th of March. None are known to remain within the State during the winter. Small parties of males come first, and are very quarrelsome until each one has selected its mate. This is not done for several weeks, and the earliest nest with eggs that he has found was on the 12th of May at Santa Barbara. The nest, built on a branch of a low oak near the town, was five inches wide, constructed of lichens, twigs, coarse grass, and wool, lined with hair. It contained four eggs, measuring .94 by .70 of an inch. He describes them as creamy-white, spotted with purple of two shades near the larger end.

These birds are said to be almost an exact counterpart of the Kingbird, exhibiting the same courage in defence of their nests. Their notes are more varied and noisy, and they utter them almost constantly during the spring, often when flying and fighting. They are very destructive to bees, but compensate for this damage by destroying great quantities of noxious insects. They leave the State in October. At Puget Sound, early in June, Dr. Cooper found this species associating with the common Kingbird without any signs of disagreement, though their similar habits would naturally lead to disputes. He has even seen them together in parties of four about the period of mating. They do not approach the coast in Washington Territory.

Dr. Suckley found this species abundant in the central and western portions of Oregon and Washington Territory. He first noted their arrival from the South about May 15. The first notification of their presence is given by the skirmishes and quarrels incident to the love-season. Their battles are generally fought in the air, and present ludicrous alternations of pursuit and flight. At Fort Dalles their favorite breeding-places were oak-trees for the most part.

Mr. Charles D. Gibbes, of Stockton, informs us that these birds occasionally build their nests in the shrubbery about the gardens, but more frequently in large oak-trees, fifteen or twenty feet from the ground. They are constructed of weeds and grass firmly woven together, and lined with cotton, feathers, strings, and other soft materials. They are usually secured to the limb on which they are placed by a portion of the string. The diameter of the cavity of the nest is about three inches, depth one and a half. Their eggs are laid in May and June, and are four, five, or six in number. They are described as white, marked with dark brown spots on the larger end. In some the spots, decreasing in size, extend to the smaller end.

Dr. Hoy informs me that he has never detected this bird within the limits of Wisconsin, though he has no doubt that they may occasionally straggle into its limits, as have many of the birds peculiar to the Missouri region.

Mr. Ridgway gives it as one of the most abundant and familiar of the *Tyrannidœ* in the Sacramento Valley and the fertile portions of the Great Basin. He notes their excessively quarrelsome disposition, which far exceeds that of the eastern Kingbird, for fighting among themselves seems to be their chief amusement. As many as half a dozen of these birds were sometimes noticed pitching at one another promiscuously, in their playful combats; and when a nest was disturbed, the cries of the parents invariably brought to the vicinity all the birds of this species in the neighborhood, which, as soon as gathered together, began their aerial battles by attacking each other without regard apparently to individuals, accompanying the fight by a shrill twitter, very different from the loud rattling notes of the *T. carolinensis.* Indeed, all the notes of the western Kingbird are very conspicuously different from those of the eastern species, being weaker, and more twittering in their character. The nesting habits, the construction of the nest, and appearance of the eggs, are, however, almost perfectly identical.

Mr. Ridgway gives an interesting account (Am. Nat., Aug., 1869) of a young bird of this species which became quite domesticated with his party in the geological survey of the 40th parallel. It had been taken about the middle of July, fully fledged, from the nest, by some Indians, and was fed with grasshoppers and flies until able to catch them for itself. When not in quest of food it remained quietly perched on Mr. Ridgway's shoulder or his hat, or would perch on a rope extending from the top of the tent to a stake. At night it frequently roosted under an umbrella which hung outside of the tent. If permitted, it would have preferred to keep on its master's shoulder, snuggling against his neck. In the morning it was sure to come fluttering about his head, singling him out from a dozen or more persons who lay around upon the ground. It had an insatiable appetite, and was ascertained by actual count to consume one hundred and twenty fat grasshoppers in a day. It soon learned its own name, Chippy, and always answered to the call. It followed Mr. Ridgway when on horseback, occasionally leaving to sport with other birds, but always returning to his shoulder or hat. It evidently preferred the society of the camp to that of his own race. It was once, by accident, nearly shot, and ever after held the gun in great dread. It went with Mr. Ridgway from camp to camp, continuing perfectly tame and domesticated, until, as was supposed, it fell a prey to a Hawk.

The eggs of this species are not easily distinguishable from those of the common Kingbird. They have a ground-color of a crystalline whiteness, marked with bold dashes of reddish and purplish brown, the latter fewer and faint. They are oblong in shape, are pointed at one end, and measure 1 inch in length by .70 of an inch in breadth.

Tyrannus vociferans, SWAINSON.

CASSIN'S FLYCATCHER.

Tyrannus vociferans, SWAINSON, Mon. Tyrant Shrikes in Quarterly Journal Sc. XX, Jan. 1826, 273. — IB. Philos. Mag. I, 1827, 368. — BAIRD, Birds N. Am. 1858, 174, pl. xlviii. — IB. M. B. II, Birds 8, pl. x. — SCL. Catal. 1862, 235. — COOPER, Orn. Cal. I, 1870, 314. *Laphyctes vociferans*, CABAN. Mus. Hein. II, 77. *Tyrannus cassini*, LAWRENCE, Ann. N. Y. Lyc. N. H. V, 1852, 39, pl. iii, fig. 2 (Texas).

SP. CHAR. Bill from the forehead about as long as the head. Tail even or slightly rounded. Outer five primaries attenuated; the first four abruptly and deeply emarginated; third quill longest, second and fourth a little less, first shorter than the sixth, and half an inch less than the longest. Head and neck above and on the sides rather dark bluish-ash; the throat and breast similar, and only a little paler. Rest of upper parts olive-green tinged with gray, mixed with brown on the rump; the upper tail-coverts and surface of the tail nearly black; the outer web of the external feather and the tips of all pale brown. The chin is white, in strong contrast to the dark ash of the throat; the rest of the under parts bright sulphur-yellow (the sides olivaceous), palest on the under tail-coverts and inside of wing. A concealed vermilion patch in the crown, bordered by straw-yellow. Wing-feathers brown, tinged with olive, becoming paler towards the edge. Length, 8.80; wing, 5.25; tail, 4.25.

HAB. Valley of Gila and southern California, eastward to Pecos River, Texas, and into Mexico, on table-lands; north along the Plains to Fort Laramie, south to Costa Rica. Oaxaca (SCL. P. Z. S. 1859, 383); Vera Paz (SCL. Ibis I, 121); W. Arizona (COUES, P. A. N. S. 1866, 59); Vera Cruz, hot and temp. regions, and Plateau (SUM. M. Bost. Soc. I, 557.)

The table of specific characters presented under the generic head will readily serve to distinguish this species from its near ally, *T. verticalis*. The white outer web of the exterior tail-feather in *verticalis*, compared with the brown web, only edged with whitish of the present bird, is always sufficient to separate them; while the deep ash of the jugulum, and the much lighter, more brownish shade of the wings, are entirely peculiar features.

HABITS. This bird is abundant in Vera Cruz, where it is known by the name of *Portuguéz*. According to Sumichrast, it belongs to the hot and temperate regions, rather than the alpine. It is also common in the Plateau, and is found in all parts of Mexico.

In Arizona Dr. Coues states this bird to be an abundant summer resident, arriving in that Territory during the third week in April, and remaining until the latter part of September. It was found in every kind of locality. He furnishes no information as to its habits.

During the Mexican Boundary Survey this species was taken on the

Colorado River, in California, by Dr. A. Schott, and at Los Nogales, Mexico, by Dr. Kennerly. It was also met with in the Sacramento Valley by Dr. Heermann; at Fort Thorn, New Mexico, by Dr. Henry; on the Pecos, Texas, by Captain Pope; and specimens from Mexico have been received from Mr. Gould. It does not appear to have been observed in Southwestern Texas by Mr. Dresser.

This species Dr. Cooper states to be quite common throughout the southern half of California, and resident throughout the year at least as far north as Los Angeles. In color they greatly resemble the *T. verticalis*, but are less lively and not so quarrelsome in their habits. During the early part of the year they begin to sing by daylight, generally from the top of some high tree. Their notes are said to be loud and much more musical than those of the other species, and their song exhibits considerable variety for a bird of this family. During the middle of the day they are rather quiet, and sit much of the time on their perch, occasionally catching an insect that comes very near, but they are supposed by Dr. Cooper to feed mostly in the very early morning. This observer found them breeding at San Diego as early as March 28, as well as subsequently. Their nest is said to be much larger and more firmly built than are those of others of the genus, being five and a half inches in external diameter and about two and a half in height. The cavity is three inches wide at the rim. The eggs, which he describes as white, with large scattered reddish-brown and umber blotches, measure .96 of an inch in length and .70 in breadth. He found some of these birds in Santa Clara Valley in May, 1864. They appeared to be smaller and greener on the back than those from the South. They winter in large numbers at Santa Clara, in latitude 37°.

Dr. Coues found this a very abundant summer resident at Fort Whipple, breeding there in considerable numbers, and all leaving early in October.

Mr. Ridgway did not meet with this species anywhere in the Great Basin, nor in the Sacramento Valley. On the plains it is found as far north as Cheyenne and Laramie Peak, and in the southern portion of the Western Provinces extends westward to California.

Specimens were obtained by Mr. George M. Skinner from Salamá, Vera Paz, in Central America. It was also taken, in February, near Oaxaca, Mexico, by Mr. Boucard.

A nest of this bird (No. 1,828), in the Smithsonian Museum, was taken at Volcan de Colima, June, 1863, by Mr. John Xantus. It is a slight structure composed chiefly of wiry grass, mixed with bits of wool, and lined with finer grasses. The eggs are two in number, having a pure-white ground, freckled on the larger end with purplish-brown and grayish-lilac. These markings are more sparse and are finer than those of the eggs of any other species of this genus, so far as I am aware. One of the eggs has a few blotches of umber on the larger end. They measure, one .93 by .68 of an inch, the other .93 by .65.

Tyrannus melancholicus, var. couchi, BAIRD.

COUCH'S KINGBIRD.

Tyrannus couchi, BAIRD, Birds N. Am. 1858, 175, pl. xlix, f. 1. — SCL. Catal. Am. B. 1862, 235.

SP. CHAR. Bill long as the head. Feet stout. Five outer primaries abruptly attenuated at the end; the third and fourth longest; the first a little longer than the sixth. Tail considerably forked (depth of fork about .30 of an inch, or more). Head, neck, and jugulum bluish-ashy, becoming nearly white on the throat, and shaded with yellow on the breast. Rest of lower parts gamboge-yellow. Rest of upper parts olive-green, tinged with ash anteriorly. Tail and primaries grayish-brown, the tail not the darker. Wing-coverts passing externally into pale, the tertials edged with almost white. Crown with a concealed patch of bright orange-red. Length, 9.00; wing, 5.00; tail, 4.70.

HAB. Middle America (both coasts), from southern border of United States, south to Guatemala; Tucson, Arizona (BENDIRE).

All specimens of *T. melancholicus* from regions north of Guatemala are referrible to var. *couchi;* all from Costa Rica southward, to *melancholicus.*

It is only by comparing specimens from near the extreme northern and southern limits of the range of the species, that differences are readily discernible; and between these two extremes there is so gradual a transition that it is impossible to draw a line separating two well-marked varieties, so that it is necessary to assume an arbitrary geographical line, and determine specimens from the middle regions by their position, whether to the north or south of the line established. Specimens from Buenos Ayres, the Parana, and Brazil, to Peru and New Granada, are identical. Costa Rica specimens (*T. satrapa*, LICHT.) have the dark tail of var. *melancholicus* and white throat of *couchi.*

GENUS MYIARCHUS, CABANIS.

Myiarchus, CABANIS, Fauna Peruana, 1844–46, 152. — BURMEISTER, Thiere Brasiliens, II, Vögel, 1856, 469.

GEN. CHAR. Tarsus equal to or not longer than the middle toe, which is decidedly longer than the hinder one. Bill wider at base than half the culmen. Tail broad, long, even, or slightly rounded, about equal to the wings, which scarcely reach the middle of the tail; the first primary shorter than the sixth. Head with elongated lanceolate distinct feathers. Above brownish-olive, throat ash, belly yellow. Tail and wing feathers varied with rufous.

This genus is well marked among the American Flycatchers, and constitutes what Bonaparte called *Ultimi Tyrannorum sive Tyrannularum primæ.* The type is the *Muscicapa ferox* of Gmelin, (*M. tyrannulus,*) which, as identified by Cabanis and Burmeister as above, appears to resemble our species very closely.

For an elaborate discussion of the various forms of this exceedingly difficult genus, we are indebted to a recent monograph by Dr. Coues, in the

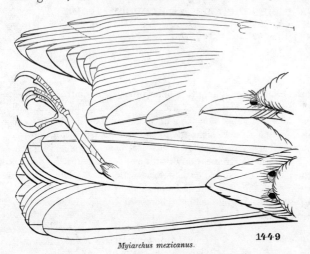
Myiarchus mexicanus.

1449

Proceedings of the Philadelphia Academy, for June and July, 1872 (pp. 56 – 81). With the same material for our investigations, we have been led, after a very careful perusal of the valuable paper mentioned, and tedious critical comparison of the large material at our command, to adopt a somewhat difficult view of the

relationship of the forms characterized. The following synopsis expresses their affinity as at present understood : —

COMMON CHARACTERS. Above olivaceous, usually uniform, sometimes darker, sometimes more ashy, on the head above. Head and jugulum more or less ashy, though the latter is sometimes very pale. Rest of lower parts sulphur-yellow, sometimes almost or quite white. Primaries, secondaries, and rectrices usually more or less edged on either web with rufous; but sometimes entirely destitute of this color.

Species and Varieties.

A. Bill sub-conical; sometimes nearly terete, its depth equal to, or exceeding, its breadth in the middle portion; its lateral outlines moderately divergent basally; terminal hook abrupt, strong. (*Myionax.*)

  1. **M. tyrannulus.** No trace of rufous edgings on either wings or tail. Above ashy-olive, the pileum similar, the outer webs of wing-coverts and secondaries edged with whitish. Head, laterally and beneath, ashy, the throat and jugulum more whitish   rest of lower parts sulphur-yellow. Tail slightly rounded.

  Pileum and nape umber-brown; upper surface umber-grayish. Bill dark brown. Wing, 3.50 – 3.70; tail, 3.60 – 3.90; culmen, .90 – .95; tarsus, .80 – .90. *Hab.* South and Central America, from Bolivia and Southern Brazil to Costa Rica   .   .   .   .   .   var. *tyrannulus.*[1]

  Whole head and neck pure ash, paler on the throat, and darker on the pileum; upper surface greenish-ash. Bill black. Wing, 3.70; tail, 4.00; culmen, .82; tarsus, .91. *Hab.* Ecuador and Guayaquil.

var. *phaeocephalus.*[2]

[1] *Myiarchus tyrannulus* (MÜLL.), COUES. *Muscicapa tyrannulus*, MÜLL. (G. R. GR. Hand List, No. 5,527). *Myiarchus t.* COUES, P. A. N. S. Phila. July, 1872, 71. (*M. aurora*, BODD.; *flaviventris*, STEPH.; *ferox*, GM.; *swainsoni*, CABAN.; *panamensis*, LAWR.; *venezuelensis*, LAWR.)

[2] *Myiarchus tyrannulus*, var. *phæocephalus* (SCLATER). *Myiarchus phæocephalus*, SCL. P. Z. S. 1860, 481. — COUES, P. A. N. S. 1872, 73.

2. **M. validus.**[1] All the wing-coverts, tertials, secondaries, primaries, and rectrices distinctly edged with rufous (the latter on both webs). Above olivaceous, more ashy anteriorly; the upper tail-coverts more rufescent; remiges broadly rufous on exterior edges; rectrices with the whole inner web (except a narrow streak along the shaft) and edge of outer web rufous. Head beneath, and entire throat and breast, deep ash; rest of lower parts sulphur-yellow, the junction of the two colors not well defined. Wing, 3.80 – 4.20 ; tail, 3.80 – 4.20 ; culmen, 1.00 ; tarsus, .80 – 91 ; tail even ; third and fourth quill longest. *Hab.* Jamaica.

3. **M. crinitus.** Outer webs of primaries distinctly edged with rufous (no other rufous on wings); inner webs of rectrices broadly, sometimes entirely, rufous, none on outer webs (except in young). Above olivaceous, varying from a greenish to an ashy cast, the pileum more brownish. Wing-coverts (both rows) broadly tipped with brownish ashy-whitish; tertials, secondaries, and lateral tail-feather broadly edged on outer web with the same. Head laterally and beneath ashy, paler on the throat and jugulum; rest of lower parts delicate yellow, varying from a rich lemon to a pale sulphur tint. *Hab.* Continental America.

Bill dark brown (never black). Upper parts decidedly greenish; ash of throat and jugulum, and yellow of abdomen, etc., very deep.

Inner webs of rectrices wholly rufous, or with only a narrow strip of dusky along the shaft. Wing, 3.75 – 4.25 ; tail, 3.75 – 4.20; culmen, .95 – 1.00; tarsus, .85 – .90. *Hab.* Eastern Province of North America ; in winter south through Eastern Mexico to Guatemala (grading into var. *irritabilis* in Nicaragua) . var. *crinitus.*

Bill deep black ; upper parts without a greenish, but, instead, an ashy-brownish cast ; ash of throat and jugulum, and yellow of abdomen, etc., very pale.

Inner webs of rectrices broadly (but not entirely) rufous to the extreme tip, with a broad dusky stripe next the shaft.

Wing, 4.10 – 4.50 ; tail, 4.00 – 4.70 ; culmen, 1.10 – 1.20 ; tarsus, 1.00 – 1.05. *Hab.* Southern and Western Mexico (Tehuantepec, Yucatan, Mazatlan, etc.) . . var. *cooperi.*[2]

Wing, 3.60 – 3.90; tail, 3.50 – 3.75; culmen, .90 – 1.00; tarsus, .80 – .85. *Hab.* Eastern South America, and Central America, from Paraguay to Costa Rica (grading into var. *cooperi* in Guatemala, and into var. *cinerascens* in Tehuantepec) var. *irritabilis.*[3]

---

[1] *Myiarchus validus*, CABANIS. *Tyrannus crinitus*, GOSSE, B. Jam. 186 (nec Auct.). *Myiarchus validus*, CABAN. Orn. Nat. II, 351, et Auct. COUES, P. A. N. S. July, 1872, 62.

[2] *Myiarchus crinitus*, var. *cooperi* (KAUP.) BAIRD. *Tyrannula cooperi*, KAUP. P. Z. S. 1851, 51. *Myiarchus cooperi*, BAIRD, Birds N. Am. 1858, 180. *Myiarchus crinitus*, var. *cooperi*, COUES, P. A. N. S. July, 1872, 67.

[3] *Myiarchus crinitus*, var. *irritabilis* (VIEILL.), COUES. *Tyrannus irritabilis*, VIEILL. Enc. Meth. 1823, II, 847. *Myiarchus crinitus*, var. *irritabilis*, COUES, P. A. N. S. July, 1872, 65. (*M. erythrocercus*, SCL. ; *M. mexicanus*, KAUP, LAWR. ; *M. yucatanensis*, LAWR.)

Obs. — It is, perhaps, probable that in Yucatan this race grades into the *M. stolidus* (var. *stolidus*), since there is a specimen in the collection from Merida (39,213, April 9, 1865, A. Schott) which seems to be very nearly intermediate in every way between the two. It has the very black bill, restricted rufous on inner webs of rectrices, and pale yellow of lower parts of *M. stolidus*, and the brown pileum and more robust proportions of *irritabilis*. The specimen, however, is in poor condition, being of worn and faded plumage, and much distorted, so that its true characters cannot be ascertained satisfactorily.

Inner webs of rectrices almost entirely rufous to near the extreme tip, the end of the web, however, being brownish-dusky like the outer.

Wing, 3.35 – 4.10; tail, 3.35 – 4.10; culmen, .80 – 1.00; tarsus, .80 – .91.   *Hab.*   Western Province of United States, and Western Mexico (grading into var. *irritabilis* in Tehuantepec, and in winter migrating into Eastern Mexico)   var. *cinerascens.*

4. **M. stolidus**   Colors essentially nearly as the varieties of *M. crinitus.* Primaries more or less distinctly edged with rufous, especially on inner quills; rectrices with inner webs more or less edged with rufous (found only terminally in var. *antillarum*).   Wing-coverts broadly tipped with dull ashy-whitish.   Above brownish-slaty, with an olivaceous cast, the pileum more or less appreciably darker.   Beneath ashy-white, without distinct yellow (except in var. *stolidus*, in which the abdomen, etc., are pale sulphury yellow).   Tail varying in shape from slightly rounded to distinctly emarginated.   *Hab.*   West Indies.

Beneath entirely white, only faintly, or hardly appreciably, tinged with sulphur-yellow on the flanks.

Inner web of rectrices broadly edged with rufous for the whole length.   Crown scarcely darker than the back.   Tail distinctly emarginated.   Wing, 3.15 – 3.50; tail, 3.30 – 3.60; culmen, .85 – .95; tarsus, .80 – 85.   (Bahaman specimens the larger).   *Hab.* Bahamas and Cuba . . . . var. *phœbe.*[1]

Inner web of rectrices not edged with rufous except at extreme tip, where sometimes also absent.   Crown decidedly darker than the back.   Tail slightly rounded.   Wing, 3.25 – 3.50; tail, 3.20 – 3.60; culmen, .85 – 95; tarsus, .85 – 90.   *Hab.* Porto Rico.

var. *antillarum.*[2]

Beneath white only on throat and jugulum, the abdomen, etc., being sulphur-yellow.

Inner webs of rectrices more or less distinctly edged with rufous for whole length.   Pileum very much darker than the back.   Wing, 3.35 – 3.50; tail, 3.35 – 3.65; culmen, .90 – .95; tarsus, .80 – .85.   Tail faintly doubly-rounded.   *Hab.*   Hayti, Jamaica, (and Yucatan ?)

var. *stolidus.*[3]

B. Bill much depressed, its depth only about half its width, in the middle portion; lateral outlines widely divergent basally; terminal hook weak. (*Myiarchus.*)

5. **M. tristis.**   Colors very variable, and amount of rufous exceedingly different in the different races.   Inner webs of rectrices seldom edged with rufous; rufous sometimes entirely absent on both wings and tail, and sometimes the whole wing and both webs of rectrices distinctly edged with it. Above ashy-olive, usually with more or less of a greenish cast, the pileum

---

[1] *Myiarchus stolidus*, var. *phœbe* (D'ORB.), COUES. *Tyrannus phœbe*, D'ORB. Sagra's Cuba, Ois. p. 84. *Myiarchus stolidus*, var. *phœbe*, COUES, P. A. N. S. July, 1872, 78. (*Sagræ*, GUNDL. ; *stolida*, var. *lucaysiensis*, BRYANT).

[2] *Myiarchus stolidus*, var. *antillarum* (BRYANT), COUES. *Tyrannus* (*Myiarchus*) *antillarum*, BRYANT, P. B. S. N. H. 1866, p. 2. *Myiarchus stolidus*, var. *antillarum*, COUES, P. A. N. S. July, 1872, 79.

[3] *Myiarchus stolidus*, var. *stolidus* (GOSSE), CABANIS. *Myiobius stolidus*, GOSSE. B. Jam. p. 168. *Myiarchus s.* CABANIS, J. für Orn. 1855, 479. — COUES. P. A. N. S. 1872, 77. (*Stolidus* var. *dominicensis*, BRYANT.)

decidedly darker (except in var. *lawrencei*); throat and jugulum ashy-white; rest of lower parts sulphur-yellow. *Hab.* Central and South America, and Jamaica.

Pileum sooty-brown, decidedly darker than the back; wings and tail entirely destitute of rufous edgings, except a faint tinge on outer webs of inner secondaries and rectrices, towards the base. Tail faintly rounded. Wing, 3.00; tail, 3.10; culmen, .80; tarsus, .65. *Hab.* Jamaica . . . . var. *tristis.*[1]

Pileum grayish-brown, not appreciably darker than the back; outer webs of inner secondaries and primaries and rectrices faintly edged with rufous. Wing, 2.80 – 3.40; tail, 2.85 – 3.45; culmen, .85 – .90; tarsus, .75 – .80. *Hab.* Northern Mexico, from northern boundary, south to Colima, Tehuantepec, Yucatan, and Salvador . var. *lawrencei.*[2]

Pileum sooty-blackish, decidedly and abruptly darker than the back. Outer webs of wing-coverts, primaries, secondaries, and rectrices distinctly edged with rufous. Yellow beneath brighter than in *lawrencei.* Wing, 3.20 – 3.30; tail, 3.15 – 3.30; culmen, .80 – .85; tarsus, .75 – .80. *Hab.* Central America from Panama to Guatemala (grading into var. *lawrencei* in Tehuantepec, and Orizaba) . . . var. *nigricapillus.*[3]

Pileum deep black, abruptly different from the greenish-olive of the back, and separated from it by a more ashy shade. Wings and tail wholly destitute of rufous edgings. Yellow beneath brighter than in var. *nigricapillus.* Wing, 3.20; tail, 3.20; culmen, .85; tarsus, .78. Tail about even. *Hab.* Northwest South America, from Ecuador northward (grading into *nigricapillus* on Isthmus of Panama).

var. *nigriceps.*[4]

---

[1] *Myiarchus tristis* (Gosse), Coues. *Myiobius tristis,* Gosse, B. Jam. 167, pl. xli. *Myiarchus t.* Coues, P. A. N. S. July, 1872, 80.

[2] *Myiarchus tristis,* var. *lawrencei* (Giraud), Baird. *Tyrannula lawrencei,* Giraud, 16 sp. Tex. B. pl. ii. *Myiarchus l.* Baird, Birds N. Am. 1858, 181, pl. xlvii, f. 3. — Coues, P. A. N. S. July, 1872, 74.

Obs. — The most typical specimens are from Mazatlan and northward, across the northern portion of Mexico. On the eastern coast, specimens from Mirador and Orizaba already strongly incline toward var. *nigricapillus.*

[3] *Myiarchus tristis,* var. *nigricapillus,* Cabanis. "*Myiarchus nigricapillus,* Caban." Scl. Cat. Am. B. 1862, 233, et Auct. *M. lawrencei,* Coues, P. A. N. S. 1872, 74 (in part).

Obs. — A very strongly differentiated form, but unquestionably grading into var. *lawrencei* on the one hand, and var. *nigriceps* on the other.

[4] *Myiarchus tristis,* var. *nigriceps,* Sclater. *Myiarchus nigriceps,* Scl. P. Z. S. 1860, 68, 295. — Coues, P. A. N. S., July, 1872, 75.

Obs. — The last three races appear to be all reducible to one species, as, taking the large series of specimens before us (over 30 skins), we find it impossible to draw the line between them. Specimens from Southern Mexico are referrible, with equal propriety, to *lawrencei* or to *nigricapillus,* while skins from Panama of *nigriceps* are less typical than those from Ecuador. This case of gradually increasing melanistic tendency as we proceed southward affords an exact parallel to that of *Vireosylvia gilvus* and *V. josephœ, Sayornis nigricans* and *S. aquaticus,* and many other cases.

Myiarchus crinitus, CABANIS.

GREAT CRESTED FLYCATCHER.

Muscicapa crinita, LINN. Syst. Nat. I, 1766, 325. — WILSON, Am. Orn. II, 1810, 75, pl. xiii. — LICHT. Verzeichniss Doubl. 1823, No. 559. — AUD. Orn. Biog. II, 1834, 176; V, 423, pl. cxxix. — IB. Birds Am. I, 1840, 209, pl. lvii. *Tyrannus crinitus*, SWAIN-SON, Mon. Tyrant Shrikes in Quarterly Journal, XX, Jan. 1826, 271. — NUTTALL, Man. I, (2d ed.,) 1840, 302. — MAX. Cab. J. VI, 1858, 182. *Myiobius crinitus*, GRAY, Genera, I, 248. ·*Tyrannula crinita*, BONAP. Consp. 1850, 189. — KAUP, Pr. Zoöl. Soc. 1851, 51. *Myiarchus crinitus*, CABANIS, Journ. für Ornith. III, 1855, 479. — BAIRD, Birds N. Am. 1858, 178. — SCL. Catal. 1862, 232. — SAMUELS, 131. *Myionax crinitus*, CABAN. Mus. Hein. 1859, 73 (type, Journ. 1861, 250). *Muscicapa ludovici-ana*, GM. Syst. Nat. I, 1788, 934. — LATHAM, Ind. *Tyrannus ludovicianus*, VIEILLOT, Ois. Am. Sept. I, 1807, pl. xlv. *Muscicapa virginiana cristata*, BRISSON, II, 1760, 412. *Crested Flycatcher*, PENNANT, LATHAM.

Figure : BUFFON, pl. enl. 569, fig. 1.

SP. CHAR. Head with a depressed crest. Third quill longest; fourth and second successively but little shorter; first a little longer than seventh; much shorter than sixth. Tail decidedly rounded or even graduated; the lateral feather about .25 of an inch shorter. Upper parts dull greenish-olive, with the feathers of the crown and to some extent of the back showing their brown centres; upper tail-coverts turning to pale rusty-brown. Small feathers at the base of the bill, ceres, sides of the head as high as the upper eyelid, sides of the neck, throat, and forepart of the breast, bluish-ashy; the rest of the lower parts, including axillaries and lower wing-coverts, bright sulphur-yellow. A pale ring round the eye. Sides of the breast and body tinged with olivaceous. The wings brown; the first and second rows of coverts, with the secondary and tertial quills, margined externally with dull white, or on the latter slight-

Myiarchus cinerascens.

ly tinged with olivaceous-yellow. Primaries margined externally for more than half their length from the base with ferruginous; great portion of the inner webs of all the quills very pale ferruginous. The two middle tail-feathers light brown, shafts paler; the rest have the outer web and a narrow line on the inner sides of the shaft brown, pale oliva-ceous on the outer edge; the remainder ferruginous to the very tip. Outer web of ex-terior feather dull brownish-yellow. Feet black. Bill dark brown above and at the tip below; paler towards the base. Length, 8.75; wing, 4.25; tail, 4.10; tarsus, .85.

HAB. Eastern North America to the Missouri and south to Eastern Texas (not yet observed farther west). Guatemala (SCL. Ibis, I, 121); Cuba (GUNDL. Repert. 1865, 239; CAB. J. III, 479); ? Jamaica (GOSSE, B. J. 186); Panama (LAWR. N. Y. Lyc. 1861, 329); Costa Rica (CABAN. J. 1861, 250; LAWR. N. Y. Lyc. IX, 115); San Antonio, Texas (DRESSER, Ibis, 1865, 473, rare).

The female appears to have no brown on the inner web of the quills along the shaft, or else it is confined chiefly to the outer feathers.

The young is hardly appreciably different, having merely the wing-coverts tinged with rusty at the ends.

HABITS. The common Great-crested Flycatcher of eastern North America has a much more extended northern distribution than has been generally given it by earlier writers. Wilson speaks of it only as a bird of Pennsylvania. Audubon mentions their occurring as far as Massachusetts, but as confined to the mountains, and as entirely unknown farther eastward. Mr. Nuttall refers to it as nearly unknown in New England, and as never appearing near the coast.

It is now known to be a regular though a somewhat rare summer resident, at least as far to the northeast as St. Stephen, New Brunswick, latitude 45° north, longitude 67° west, and as far to the north in Vermont as Randolph, and Hamilton in Canada, both in about latitude 44°. Mr. Boardman mentions it as a regular summer visitant, and as breeding near Calais. Professor Verrill gives it as a rare summer visitant of Western Maine. Mr. McIlwraith states it to be a common summer resident of Hamilton, Canada West, where it arrives about the 10th of May, after which its harsh cry is heard in all parts of the woods. It winters in Central America and Panama.

In a letter dated June 17, 1865, Mr. C. S. Paine of Randolph, Vt., informed me that he had, within a few days, found a nest of this Flycatcher. It was built in the hollow of a decayed apple-tree, in one of its limbs. The nest was built up from the bottom of the cavity some eight inches, and contained six eggs. Though not very abundant in that neighborhood, Mr. Paine had been aware, for several years, of the occurrence of this Flycatcher, but had never before been able to ascertain its manner of nesting. He has since informed me that these Flycatchers have continued to occur every summer, as they always make their presence known by their harsh notes, which may be heard to quite a distance, and he knows that they breed there regularly every year. They are shy, and do not come about the buildings, but are generally seen in the woods and orchards.

In Eastern Massachusetts they are not common, but scattered pairs have been met with in Concord, Acton, Newton, Hingham, and in other places.

Dr. Coues states that the Great-crested Flycatcher reaches Washington the third week in April, and leaves the last of September. It is a common summer resident, but is most numerous in the spring and autumn. It is found on the edge of open woods, and betrays its presence by its peculiar notes. In the western part of Massachusetts, Mr. Allen gives it as a rare summer visitant, having been taken by him from May 15 to September 17, and having been found breeding on Mount Tom by Mr. C. W. Bennett. It is found abundantly in the Middle and Southern States as far south as Florida and Texas, and occurs as far to the west as the Missouri River. Dr. Woodhouse found it very abundant in Texas and in the Indian Territory, and Mr. Dresser obtained specimens at San Antonio in the month of April.

In speaking of the habits of this species, Wilson accuses it of being addicted to eating bees equally with the Kingbird; but as this bird is known to feed largely on berries, and to feed its young to some extent with the same, the extent of such propensity may well be doubted. It is not so prone to attack birds larger than itself as is the Kingbird, which Wilson characterizes as cowardice, but which it would be more charitable to call prudence. It is said to be harsh, cruel, and vindictive to smaller birds and to weaker individuals of its own species.

In its flight it moves with power, steadiness, and swiftness, and when in pursuit of insects follows its prey with great zeal and perseverance. When it captures a large insect, it retires to its perch and beats it against the limb. These birds are not in the least gregarious. They occur in isolated pairs, and appear to have no interest or sympathy with others than those of their own household. To each other, however, they are attentive and considerate, and they are devoted in their solicitude for their young.

Their usual call-note is a sharp disagreeable squeak, which, once known, is easily recognized. Besides this it has a monotonous succession of squeaking, harsh notes, only a little less unpleasant. They raise but one brood in a season, and remain together in a family group of from six to eight until they leave, in the middle of September.

During the early summer this species feeds chiefly upon insects of various kinds, which it catches with great facility, skill, and assiduity; afterwards, as if from choice, it chiefly eats ripe berries of various kinds of shrubs and plants, among which those of the poke-weed and the huckleberry are most noticeable. It nests altogether in hollows in trees, stumps, or limbs. It lines the bottoms of these hollows with a great variety of miscellaneous materials, and in quantities that vary with the size and shape of the place to be occupied. These beds are composed of loose hay, feathers, the hair of various small quadrupeds, etc., while the exuviæ of snakes are almost always to be met with.

The eggs, four, five, or six in number, are peculiar and noticeably varied and beautiful in their style of markings, varying also somewhat in shape. Generally they are nearly spherical, and equally obtuse at either end. Occasionally they are an oblong oval, one end a very little more tapering than the other. Their ground-color is a beautiful light buff, rather than a cream-color, over which are waving lines, marblings, markings, and dots of a brilliant purple, and others of a more obscure shading. The lines are variously distributed, generally running from one pole of the egg to the other with striking effect, as if laid on with the delicate brush of an artist. In some eggs the whole surface is so closely covered with these intercrossing and waving lines, blending with the obscure cloudings of lilac, as nearly to conceal the ground. Usually the buff color is conspicuously apparent, and sets off the purple lines with great effect.

An oblong-oval egg from New Jersey measures 1.10 inches in length by .70 of an inch in breadth. A more nearly spherical egg from Florida measures .90 by .75 of an inch. These well represent the two extremes. Their average is about 1 inch by .75 of an inch.

The eggs of all the members of this genus have a remarkable similarity, and can scarcely be mistaken for those of any other group.

Myiarchus crinitus, var. cinerascens, LAWR.

ASH-THROATED FLYCATCHER.

Tyrannula cinerascens, LAWRENCE, Ann. N. Y. Lyc. N. Hist. V, Sept. 1851, 109. *Myiarchus cinerascens*, SCL. List, 1862, 133. — IB. P. Z. S. 1871, 84. — COUES, Pr. A. N. S. July, 1872, 69. *Myiarchus mexicanus*, BAIRD, Birds N. Am. 1858, 179, pl. 5. — HEERM. X, *S*, 37, pl. v. — COOPER, Orn. Cal. I, 1870, 316. *Myiarchus mexicanus*, var. *pertinax*, BAIRD, P. A. N. S. 1859, 303 (Cape St. Lucas).

SP. CHAR. Bill black, the width opposite the nostrils not half the length of culmen. Head crested. Tail even, the lateral feathers slightly shorter. Second, third, and fourth quills longest; first rather shorter than the seventh. Above dull grayish-olive; the centres of the feathers rather darker; the crown, rump, and upper tail-coverts tinged with brownish. The forehead and sides of the head and neck grayish-ash; the chin, throat, and forepart of the breast ashy-white; the middle of the breast white; the rest of the under parts very pale sulphur-yellow; wings and tail brown. Two bands across the wing, with outer edges of secondaries and tertials, dull white; the outer edges of the primaries light chestnut-brown (except towards the tip and on the outer feather); the inner edges tinged with the same. Whole of middle tail-feathers, with the outer webs (only) and the ends of the others brown; the rest of the inner webs reddish-chestnut, the outer web of exterior feather yellowish-white. Legs and bill black; lower mandible brownish at the base. Length about 8.00; wing, 4.00; tail, 4.10; tarsus, .90.

HAB. Coast of California, to Cape St. Lucas, and across by the valley of Gila and Rio Grande to Northeastern Mexico. Seen as far north in Texas as San Antonio. Oaxaca (SCL. 1859, 384); ? Guatemala (SCL. Ibis, I, 129); Vera Cruz hot regions, resident (SUM. M. Bost. Soc. I); San Antonio, Texas (DRESSER, Ibis, 1865, 473).

In a young specimen the crown is more tinged with brown; the upper tail-coverts and the middle tail-feathers are chestnut, and, in fact, all the tail-feathers are of this color, except along both sides of the shaft on the central feathers, and along its outer side in the lateral ones.

This species is easily distinguished from *T. crinitus* and *T. cooperi* by the brown tip of the tail; the colors paler than in the former, bill slenderer, and tarsi longer.

A variety of this species (*pertinax*[1]) is found at Cape St. Lucas, and distinguished chiefly by the considerably larger and stouter bill.

HABITS. The Ash-throated or Mexican Flycatcher appears to be a common species, from San Antonio, Texas, its extreme northeastern point, southwesterly throughout Mexico as far south as Guatemala, and westward to the Pacific coast. It has been obtained in various parts of California by Mr. Cutts, Mr. Schott, Dr. Heermann, and others, as also on the Gila

---

[1] *Myiarchus mexicanus*, var. *pertinax*, BAIRD, Pr. Phil. Acad. 1859, 303.

River. Dr. Kennerly procured specimens at Los Nogales, Mexico, and others have met with it near the city of Mexico, at Saltillo, and in different parts of Western Texas. It was found breeding at Cape San Lucas by Mr. Xantus.

In the Department of Vera Cruz, Mr. Sumichrast found this species apparently confined to the hot region. He did not meet with it anywhere else.

Mr. Dresser thinks that this Flycatcher does not reach San Antonio before the latter part of April. The first that came under his notice was one that he shot, on the 23d of that month, on the Medina River. It breeds near the Medina and the San Antonio Rivers, making its nest in a hollow tree, or taking possession of a deserted Woodpecker's hole. Mr. Dresser observed these birds as far to the east as the Guadaloupe River, where they were common. Farther east he saw but very few. Their eggs he speaks of as peculiarly marked with a multitude of purple and brown dashes and lines on a dull yellowish-brown ground, and very similar to those of *Myiarchus crinitus*.

In the Mexican Boundary Survey, individuals of this species were taken by Mr. A. Schott, March 31, on the Colorado Bottom; near the Gila River, New Mexico, December 31; and also at Eagle Pass, in Texas, date not given. Mr. J. H. Clark obtained a specimen at Frontera, Texas, where he mentions finding it in great abundance in damp places, or near the water. In May, 1853, Lieutenant Couch secured several near Saltillo, and notes its occurrence among mesquite-bushes. In the following June, Dr. Kennerly found them very abundant at Los Nogales. Where two were found together, they were generally noticed to be uttering a loud chattering noise.

Dr. Heermann, in his Report on the birds observed in the survey of Lieutenant Williamson's route between the 32d and the 35th parallels, mentions finding this species abundant. His specimens were obtained near Posa Creek. He describes them as of shy and retiring habits, preferring the deep and shady forests where its insect food abounds. The nests, found in hollows of trees or in a deserted squirrel's or Woodpecker's hole, were composed of grasses and lined with feathers. The eggs, five in number, he describes as cream-colored, marked and speckled with purplish-red dashes and faint blotches of a neutral tint.

Dr. Coues found them a common summer resident in Arizona, where they arrived in the third week in April and remained until the middle of September. They were seldom found among pine-trees, but appeared to prefer ravines, hillsides, and creek bottoms. Some wintered as high up in the Colorado Valley as Fort Mohave. At Fort Whipple young birds were first observed early in July.

Dr. Cooper obtained one of this species at Fort Mohave, January 15, and is of the opinion that some may habitually winter in the Colorado Valley. In California they begin to arrive about March 10, and extend their range through very nearly the whole of the State. He describes their notes as few, loud, and harsh, but little varied, and uttered from time to time as they fly after an insect from an accustomed perch, usually a lower dead limb of a forest tree. They prefer shady situations, and are said to feed late in the evening.

Mr. Ridgway met with this species in all suitable localities, from the Sacramento Valley eastward to the Wahsatch Mountains. It was most abundant among the oaks of the plains between the Sacramento River and the Sierra Nevada; but in the wooded river valleys of the interior, as well as in the cedar and piñon or mahogany woods on the mountains of the latter region, it was also more or less frequently met with. In its manners it is described as a counterpart of the eastern *M. crinitus*, but its notes, though generally similar in character, have not that strength which makes the vociferous screaming whistles of the eastern species so noticeable.

This species, or a very closely allied race of it (var. *pertinax*) was procured at Cape St. Lucas by Mr. Xantus. It had the peculiarities of a southern race, stronger feet, stouter bill, and a generally smaller size.

A few individuals of this species were found by Mr. Grayson inhabiting the islands of the Three Marias, on the Pacific coast of Mexico. He usually saw them among low bushes, darting from their perch after flies and other winged insects. They were very silent, and seldom uttered a note.

Four eggs of this species from Matamoras, collected by the late Dr. Berlandier, have the following measurements: .82 by .75, .91 by .71, .95 by .75, .98 by .75 of an inch. Though having a very close resemblance to the eggs of *M. crinita*, there are noticeable certain constant variations. The ground-color is a little lighter, and has a tinge of pinkish not found in the eggs of the eastern species. The markings are more in oblong plashes of irregular shape, and rarely exhibit the waving lines. There are more and larger blotches of a light purplish-brown. The eggs are a little more spherical in their general shape, and the markings are less abundant. The eggs of *M. cooperi* have a still more roseate tint in the buff of the ground-color, are marked with smaller blotches of bright purple and much larger ones of lilac-brown. They measure .92 by .75 of an inch.

Genus **SAYORNIS**, BONAP.

Sayornis, BONAP. ? Ateneo italiano, 1854. — IB. Comptes Rendus, 1854, Notes Orn. Delattre.
Aulanax, CABANIS, Journal für Orn. 1856, 1 (type, *nigricans*).

GEN. CHAR. Head with a blended depressed moderate crest. Tarsus decidedly longer than middle toe, which is scarcely longer than the hind toe. Bill rather narrow; width at base about half the culmen. Tail broad, long, slightly forked; equal to the wings, which are moderately pointed, and reach to the middle of the tail. First primary shorter than the sixth.

This genus agrees with the preceding in the length of the broad tail, but has a longer tarsus and a different style of coloration.   The species are distinguished as follows : —

S. nigricans. Sooty black ; abdomen and edge of outer web of lateral tail-feather pure white.

 a. Lower tail-coverts pure white.

  Greater wing-coverts paler toward tips of outer webs. Wing, 3.60 ; tail, 3.45. *Hab.* Pacific Province, United States, and Mexico . . . . var. *nigricans.*

 b. Lower tail-coverts blackish.

  Greater coverts not appreciably paler at ends. Wing, 3.35 ; tail, 3.30. *Hab.* Middle America, north of Panama . var. *aquaticus.*[1]

  Both rows of wing-coverts distinctly tipped with white ; white edgings of secondaries very conspicuous. Wing, 3.35 ; tail, 3.30.

  Hab. New Granada ; Venezuela . . . var. *cinerascens.*[2]

S. fuscus. Grayish-olive above, and on sides of breast ; beneath (including throat) white, tinged with sulphur-yellow. Wing, 3.40 ; tail, 3.20. *Hab.* Eastern Province United States ; Eastern Mexico.

S. sayus. Brownish-ashy, the tail and upper tail-coverts black ; abdomen and crissum deep ochraceous. *Hab.* Western Province of United States, and whole of Mexico.

Sayornis nigricans, BONAP.

BLACK PEWEE.

Tyrannula nigricans, SWAINSON, Syn. Birds Mex. Taylor's Phil. Mag. I, 1827, 367. — NEWBERRY, Zoöl. Cal. & Or. Route, Rep. P. R. R. Surv. VI, IV, 1857, 81. *Muscicapa nigricans,* AUD. Orn. Biog. V, 1839, 302, pl. cccclxxiv. — IB. Birds Am. I, 1840, 218, pl. lx. *Tyrannus nigricans,* NUTTALL, Man. I, (2d ed.,) 1840, 326. *Myiobius nigricans,* GRAY. *Myiarchus nigricans,* CABANIS, Tschudi Fauna Peruan. 1844 – 46, 153 (Peru). *Sayornis nigricans,* BONAP. Comptes Rendus XXVIII, 1854, notes Orn. 87. — BAIRD, Birds N. Am. 1858, 183. — HEERM. X, *S,* 38. — COOPER, Orn. Cal. I, 1870, 319. *Aulanax nigricans,* CABANIS, Cab. Journ. für Ornith. IV, Jan. 1856, 2 (type of genus). — IB. M. H. II, 68. *Muscicapa semiatra,* VIGORS, Zoöl. Beechey Voy. 1839, 17.

---

[1] *Sayornis nigricans,* var. *aquaticus.* *Sayornis aquaticus,* SCLATER & SALVIN, Ibis, 1859, p. 119 (Guatemala).

[2] *Sayornis nigricans,* var. *cineracens.* *Sayornis cineracea,* LAFR. Rev. Zoöl. 1848, p. 8. — SCL. Catal. Am. Birds, 1862, 200. The above races are clearly shown to be merely modifications, with latitude, of one type, by the series of specimens before us. Thus, specimens of *S. nigricans* from Orizaba show more or less dusky on the lower tail-coverts, while in more northern specimens (i. e. typical var. *nigricans*) there is not a trace of it. Typical specimens of *aquaticus,* from Guatemala, show merely a more advanced melanism, the lighter markings on the wings becoming greatly restricted ; there is still, however, a decided presence of white on the lower tail-coverts. Specimens from Costa Rica (typical *aquaticus*) exhibit the maximum degree of melanism, the white beneath being confined to a central spot on the abdomen. In *cineraceus* (from New Granada) the white beneath is similarly restricted, but on the wings is very conspicuous, showing a reversion back to the character of *nigricans,* though surpassing the latter in the amount of white on the coverts and secondaries.

The *S. latirostris (Aulanax l.* CAB. & HEIN. Mus. Hein. ii, p. 68 ; *Sayornis l.* SCL. Cat. Am. B. 1862, 200), from Ecuador, we have not seen. It is probably also referrible to the same type.

Sp. Char. Wings rounded; second, third, and fourth longest; first rather shorter than sixth. Tarsi with a second row of scales behind. The head and neck all round, forepart and sides of the breast, dark sooty-brown; the rest of the upper parts similar, but lighter; faintly tinged with lead-color towards the tail. The middle of the breast, abdomen, and lower tail-coverts white; some of the latter, with the shafts and the centre, brown. The lower wing-coverts grayish-brown, edged with white. Wings dark brown; the edges of secondary coverts rather lighter; of primary coverts dull white. Edge of the exterior vane of the first primary and of secondaries white. Tail dark

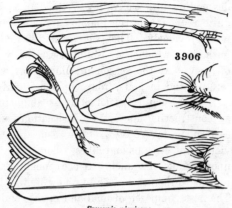

3906

Sayornis nigricans.

brown, with the greater part of the outer vane of the exterior tail-feather white; this color narrowing from the base to the tip. Bill and feet black. The tail rounded, rather emarginate; feathers broad; more obliquely truncate than in *sayus*. The bill slender; similar to that of *S. fuscus*. Length, nearly 7 inches; wing, 3.60; tail, 3.45.

Hab. California coast (Umpqua Valley, Oregon, Newberry), and across by valley of Gila and Upper Rio Grande to New Leon, and south; Mazatlan. Oaxaca (Scl. 1859, 383); Cordova (Scl. 1856, 296); Vera Cruz, temp. and alp. regions, breeding (Sum. M. B. Soc. I, 557); W. Arizona (Coues, P. A. N. S., 1866, 60).

The female appears to differ only in the smaller size. A young bird from San Francisco has two bands of rusty on the wing; the shoulders and hinder part of the back tinged with the same.

Habits. Within our limits the Black Flycatcher has a distribution very nearly corresponding with that of *Myiarchus cinerascens.* It is found from Oregon and California on the Pacific coast, to the valley of the Rio Grande, and thence south throughout Mexico. It also occurs as a resident in Guatemala. Specimens in the Smithsonian Museum are from various parts of Mexico, from New Mexico, and California.

During his explorations in Northern Mexico, Lieutenant Couch first met with this species at Cadereita, Mexico, in April, occurring in abundance under the high banks of the stream which supplies the town with water. Its habits appeared to him to be much the same with those of the common Phœbe-Bird (*Sayornis fuscus*). Its nest was supposed to be in the bank. Dr. Kennerly, who found it at Espia, Mexico, could not observe any difference in the habits from those of the *Pyrocephalus rubineus.* They were both observed in the same vicinity, feeding alike on insects and having the same movements.

In the Department of Vera Cruz, Mr. Sumichrast says that this species is known by the common name of *Aguador.* It is very common in both the temperate and the colder regions of that State. It nests within the dwelling-houses in the city of Orizaba.

Dr. Kennerly states that after passing the mountains of California, and descending into the valley of the San Gabriel River, he found these birds quite abundant on the Pueblo Creek in New Mexico, though he had noticed none previously. They were generally found perched upon the summit of a bush, from which they would occasionally make short excursions in search of prey. At the season in which they were observed, March, they were rarely found in pairs, from which he inferred they were already hatching.

Dr. Heermann speaks of it as abundant throughout all California, and as constructing its nests in situations similar to those of the common eastern species (*S. fuscus*). It seems to have a marked predilection for the vicinity of streams and lakes, where it is nearly always to be seen, perched upon a stake or branch. It occasionally darts into the air for an insect, and returns to the same place to renew its watch and to repeat these movements. The nest, composed of mud and mosses and lined with hair, is placed against the rocks, the rafters of a house ·or bridge, or against the inside of a large hollow tree, and the eggs, four or five in number, are pure white, speckled with red.

Dr. Coues found this Flycatcher a very abundant and permanent resident in the valleys of the Gila and Colorado, and the more southern portions of the Territory of Arizona generally. It was not observed in the immediate vicinity of Fort Whipple, though it was detected a few miles south of that locality. As it has been found on the Pacific coast so much farther north than the latitude of Fort Whipple, he thinks it may yet be met with, at least as a summer visitant to that place. In his journey from Arizona to the Pacific, he ascertained that it is common throughout Southern Arizona, being, among land birds, his most constant companion on the route. Perched generally in pairs upon the dense verdure that in many places overhangs the river, it pursued its constant vocation of securing the vagrant insects around it, constantly uttering its peculiar unmelodious notes. In all its movements the Pewee of the Eastern States was unmistakably reproduced. It was rather shy and wary. In Southern Arizona and California it remains throughout the winter. It seems to delight not only in river bottoms, but also in deep mountain gorges and precipitous cañons with small streams flowing through them.

Dr. Newberry found this species quite common in Northern California, and specimens were also obtained as far to the north as the Umpqua Valley in Oregon. According to Dr. Cooper it is an abundant and resident species in all the lower parts of California, except the Colorado Valley, where he found none later than March 25, as they had all evidently passed on farther north. At San Diego, at that date, the following year (1862), all these birds had nests and eggs, and were there, as elsewhere, the first birds to build. Their nest, he states, is formed of an outer wall of mud about five and a quarter inches wide and three and a half high. It is built like that of the Barn Swallow, in little pellets, piled successively, as they dry, in the shape of a half-cup. They are fastened to a wall, or sometimes placed on a shelf, beam, or ledge of a rock, but are always under some protecting cover, often under a bridge. They are lined with fine grass or moss, and horse or cow hair. The eggs, four or five in number, he describes as pure white, measuring .74 by .55 of an inch.

This bird is said to prefer the vicinity of human habitations, and also to keep about water, on account of the numerous flies they find in such situations. It will often sit for hours at a time on the end of a barn, or some other perch, uttering a monotonous but not unpleasant ditty, which resembles, according to Dr. Cooper, the sound of *pittic pittit,* alternately repeated, and quite like the cry of the eastern *Sayornis fuscus,* which is its exact counterpart in habits. It is said to fly only a short distance at a time, turning and dodging quickly in pursuit of its prey, which it captures with a sharp snap of the bill.

This species was met with by Mr. Ridgway only in the vicinity of Sacramento City, Cal., where it seemed to replace our eastern Pewee, having the same familiarity and general habits, and with notes not distinguishable from some belonging to *S. fuscus.*

The eggs of this species, as described by Dr. Cooper and by Dr. Heermann, are either pure white unspotted, or else white with fine red dots, in this respect resembling the eggs of the *S. fuscus,* which present the same variations. The measurements of those in my cabinet vary from .75 by .56 of an inch to .78 by .60.

Mr. Salvin says that *Sayornis nigricans* is a resident species at Dueñas, in Guatemala, where it may always be found at a short distance from the village, up the stream of the river Guacatate. It also occurs about the lake. In its actions it is described as a lively and restless species, in this respect having but little resemblance to the Tyrant Flycatchers. It may always be found near water, generally sitting on a stone on the margin, from which it constantly darts to seize a fly or an insect from the surface. His remarks may, however, refer to the var. *aquaticus.*

Sayornis fuscus, BAIRD.

PEWEE; PHŒBE-BIRD.

Muscicapa fusca, GMELIN, Syst. Nat. I, 1788, 931. — LATHAM, Index, Orn. II, 1790, 483. — VIEILLOT, Ois. Am. Sept. I, 1807, 68, pl. xl. — BONAP. Obs. Wilson, 1825, no. 115. — IB. Synopsis, 68. — AUD. Orn. Biog. II, 1834, 122 ; V, 1839, 424, pl. cxx. — IB. Synopsis, 1839, 43. — IB. Birds Am. I, 1840, 223, pl. lxiii. — GIRAUD, Birds L. Island, 1844, 42. *Tyrannula fusca,* RICH. List, 1837. — BONAP. List, 1838. *Tyrannus fuscus,* NUTTALL, Man. I, (2d ed.,) 1840, 312. ? *Aulanax fuscus,* CABANIS, Cab. Journ. IV, 1856, 1. *Muscicapa atra,* GMELIN, Syst. Nat. I, 1788, 946. — NUTTALL, Man. I, 1832, 278. *Muscicapa phœbe,* LATHAM, Index Orn. II, 1790, 489. *Muscicapa nunciola,* WILSON, Am. Orn. II, 1810, 78, pl. xiii. *Myiobius nunciola,* GRAY, Genera,

I, 248. *Muscicapa carolinensis fusca*, Brisson, Orn. II, 1760, 367. *Black-headed Flycatcher*, Pennant, Arc. Zoöl. II, 389, 269. *Black-cap Flycatcher*, Latham, Synopsis, I, 353. *Empidias fuscus*, Caban. M. H. II, Sept. 1859, 69 (type). — Scl. Catal. 1862, 234. *Sayornis fuscus*, Baird, Birds N. Am. 1858, 184. — Samuels, 133. — Allen, B. Fla. 1871, 299.

Sp. Char. Sides of breast and upper parts dull olive-brown, fading slightly towards

Sayornis nigricans.

the tail. Top and sides of head dark brown. A few dull white feathers on the eyelids. Lower parts dull yellowish-white, mixed with brown on the chin, and in some individuals across the breast. Quills brown, the outer primary, secondaries, and tertials edged with dull white. In some individuals the greater coverts faintly edged with dull white. Tail brown; outer edge of lateral feather dull white; outer edges of the rest like the back. Tibiæ brown. Bill and feet black. Bill slender, edges nearly straight. Tail rather broad and slightly forked. Third quill longest; second and fourth nearly equal; the first shorter than sixth. Length, 7 inches; wing, 3.42; tail, 3.30.

Hab. Eastern North America; Eastern Mexico to Mirador and Orizaba. Cuba (Caban. J. IV, 1); Xalapa, (Scl. List, 234); Vera Cruz, winter (Sumichrast, M. B. S. I, 557); San Antonio, Texas (Dresser, Ibis, 1865, 773, rare).

In autumn, and occasionally in early spring, the colors are much clearer and brighter. Whole lower parts sometimes bright sulphur-yellow; above, greenish-olive; top and sides of the head tinged with sooty. In the young of the year the colors are much duller; all the wing-coverts broadly tipped with light ferruginous, as also the extreme ends of the wings and tail-feathers. The brown is prevalent on the whole throat and breast; the hind part of the back, rump, and tail strongly ferruginous.

Habits. The Pewee, or Phœbe-Bird, a well-known harbinger of early spring, is a common species throughout the whole of eastern North America, from the Rio Grande, on the southwest, to the provinces of Nova Scotia and New Brunswick on the northeast, and as far west as the Missouri River.

Dr. Woodhouse found it common both throughout Texas and in the Indian Territory. It was taken by Sumichrast in the Department of Vera Cruz, but he was in doubt whether it occurs there as a resident or is only migratory. It was observed at San Antonio, Texas, but only as a migrant, by both Dresser and Heermann; but at Houston, in that State, it evidently remains and breeds, as individuals were seen there in June by Dresser. Specimens were taken in February at Brownsville, Texas, by Lieutenant Couch, and afterwards in March on the opposite side of the river, — in Tamaulipas, Mexico.

In South Carolina, Dr. Coues found these birds most common in the months of February and March, and again in October and November. He had no doubt that some remain and pass the winter, and that others are resident in the State during the summer months, but believes the great majority go farther north to breed.

In Western Maine it is a common summer visitant, breeding there in considerable numbers. Professor Verrill states that it is frequently seen there the first of March, becoming quite common by the first of April. It is also a summer visitant about Calais, where it breeds, but is rather rare. At Hamilton, Canada, Mr. McIlwraith reports it as a common summer resident, arriving about April 15.

In Pennsylvania this species arrives among the earliest spring visitants, sometimes as early as the first week in March, and continues in that region until late in October. Wilson has seen specimens as late as the 12th of November. He states that in the month of February he met with them feeding on the smilax berries in the low, swampy woods of North and South Carolina. They were already chanting their simple, plaintive notes. In Massachusetts they usually arrive from the 15th to the 25th of March. In the warm spring of 1870 they were already abundant by the 10th. They were nesting early in April, and their first brood was ready to fly by the middle of May. They have two broods in a season, and occasionally perhaps three, as I have known fresh eggs in the middle of August. They leave late in October, unless the season be unusually open, when a few linger into November.

Their well-known and monotonous, though not unpleasing, note of *pē-wēē*, or, as some hear it, *phœ-bēē*, is uttered with more force and frequency in early spring than later in the season, though they repeat the note throughout their residence north. It usually has some favorite situation, in which it remains all the morning, watching for insects and continually repeating its simple song. As he sits, he occasionally flirts his tail and darts out after each passing insect, always returning to the same twig.

This species is attracted both to the vicinity of water and to the neighborhood of dwellings, probably for the same reason,—the abundance of insects in either situation. They are a familiar, confiding, and gentle bird, attached to localities, and returning to them year after year. They build in sheltered situations, as under a bridge, under a projecting rock, in the porches of houses, and in similar situations. I have known them to build on a small shelf in the porch of a dwelling; against the wall of a railroad-station, within reach of the passengers; and under a projecting window-sill, in full view of the family, entirely unmoved by the presence of the latter at meal-time.

Their nests are constructed of small pellets of mud, placed in layers one above the other, in semicircular form, covered with mosses, and warmly lined with fine straw and feathers. When the nest is placed on a flat surface, — a shelf or a projecting rock,— it is circular in form, and mud is not made use of. A nest of this description, taken by Mr. Vickary in Lynn, and containing five eggs, was constructed on a ledge, protected by an overhanging rock, only a few feet from the ground. It measured four and a half inches in diameter and three in height. The cavity was nearly three inches wide and one and a half deep. Its base was constructed of layers of fine leaves, strips of bark, roots of plants, and other miscellaneous materials. The great mass of the nest itself was made up of fine mosses closely interwoven, and strengthened by an intermixture of firmer plant fibres. The whole was carefully and softly lined with strips of the inner bark of various deciduous shrubs, fine roots, and finer grasses. The semicircular nests are usually placed out of reach of the weather under some projecting shelter.

Wilson states that they often nest in eaves, and occasionally in an open well, five or six feet down, among the interstices of the side-walls. Nuttall has known them to nest in an empty kitchen.

Their attachment to a locality, when once chosen, is remarkable, and is often persevered in under the most discouraging circumstances. In one instance, Nuttall states that a nest was built in the boathouse at Fresh Pond, Cambridge, — a place so common as to be almost a thoroughfare. Although with its young brood this nest was torn down by ruffian hands, the female immediately built a new one in the same spot, and laid five additional eggs. This was lined with the silvery shreds of a manilla rope, taken from the loft over the boathouse.

Besides the common call-note, from which these birds derive their name, they have, during the love-season, a low twittering song with which they entertain their mates, but which is heard only when the birds are in company, and for a brief season.

The flight of the Pewee is an alternation of soaring and a succession of light fluttering motions, more rapid when pursuing its prey than in its ordinary movements. Its crest is usually erected when it is in motion, or on the lookout for insects.

Mr. Audubon found these birds in full song in Florida during the winter, and as lively as in spring, but met with none breeding south of Charleston. They leave Louisiana in February, and return to it in October. They feed largely on berries, especially during the winter, and Mr. Maynard found some in the spring of 1868 with hawthorn berries in their stomachs.

The eggs of the Pewee measure .80 of an inch in length and .60 in breadth. They are of a rounded oval shape, pointed at one end and much larger at the other. Their ground-color is a pure bright white, and generally unspotted; but a certain proportion, one set in every five or six, is distinctly marked with reddish-brown dots at the larger end.

Sayornis sayus, BAIRD.

SAY'S PEWEE.

Muscicapa saya, BONAP. Am. Orn. I, 1825, 20, pl. xi, fig. 3. — AUD. Orn. Biog. IV, 1838,
428, pl. ccclix. — IB. Birds Am. I, 1840, 217, pl. lix. *Tyrannus saya*, NUTTALL,
Man. I, (2d ed.,) 1840, 311. *Myiobius saya*, GRAY, Genera, I, 1844–49, 249. *Ochthœca
sayi*, CABANIS, Wiegmann Archiv, 1847, I, 255 (not type). *Tyrannula saya*, BONAP.
Conspectus, 1850. — MAX. Cab. J. VI, 1858, 183. *Aulanax sayus*, CABANIS, Journ.
Orn. 1856, 2. *Tyrannula pallida*, SWAINSON, Syn. Birds Mex. No. 15, in Taylor's
Phil. Mag. I, 1827, 367. *Sayornis pallida*, BONAP. — SCL. P. Z. S. 1857, 204. *Say-
ornis sayus*, BAIRD, Birds N. Am. 1858, 185. — IB. M. B. II, Birds, 9. — COOPER,
Orn. Cal. I, 1870, 320. *Theroinyias saya*, CABAN. M. H. II, Sept. 1859, 68 (type).

SP. CHAR. Above and on the sides of the head, neck, and breast, grayish-brown,
darker on the crown; region about the eye dusky. The chin, throat, and upper part of
the breast similar to the back, but rather lighter and tinged with the color of the rest of
the lower parts, which are pale cinnamon. Under wing-coverts pale rusty-white. The
wings of a rather deeper tint than the back, with the exterior vanes and tips of the quills
darker. Edges of the greater and secondary coverts, of the outer vane of the outer
primary, and of the secondaries and tertials, dull white. The upper tail-coverts and tail
nearly black. Edge of outer vane of exterior tail-feather white. Bill dark brown,
rather paler beneath. The feet brown. Second, third, and fourth quills nearly equal;
fifth nearly equal to sixth; sixth much shorter than the fifth. Tail broad, emarginate.
Tarsi with a posterior row of scales. Length, 7 inches; wing, 4.30; tail, 3.35.

HAB. Missouri and central High Plains, westward to the Pacific and south to Mexico.
Xalapa (SCL. 1859, 366); Orizaba (SCL. List, 199); Vera Cruz, winter? (SUM. M. Bost.
Soc. I, 557); S. E. Texas (DRESSER, Ibis, 1865, 473, breeds); W. Arizona (COUES, P. A.
N. S. 1866, 60).

The young of the year have the upper parts slightly tinged with ferruginous; two broad (ferruginous) bands on the wings formed by the tips of the
first and second coverts. The quills and tail rather darker than in an adult
specimen.

Autumnal specimens are simply more deeply colored than spring examples,
the plumage softer and more blended.

HABITS. Say's Flycatcher has an extended distribution throughout western North America, from Mexico, on the south, to the plains of the Saskatchewan on the north, and from the Rio Grande and the Missouri to the Pacific
Ocean.

It was first discovered by Mr. Titian Peale on the Arkansas River, near
the Rocky Mountains, and described by Bonaparte. Mr. Peale noticed a
difference in its voice from that of the common *S. fuscus*, and found it nesting
in a tree, building a nest of mud and moss, lined with dried grasses. Its
young were ready to fly in July. Richardson obtained individuals of this
species at the Carlton House, May 13. It is not given by Cooper and
Suckley in their Zoölogy of Washington Territory, but Dr. Newberry found
it not uncommon throughout both Oregon and California.

Mr. Sumichrast ascertained the presence of this bird within the Department of Vera Cruz, but whether there as resident or as exclusively migratory he was not able to state. It has also been found in winter throughout Mexico. Mr. J. H. Clark met with it near Fort Webster, in New Mexico, and describes it as particularly abundant about the copper mines. One of the shafts near the fort, and which was partially filled up, served as a sinkhole for the offal of the town, and around this quite a number of these birds could always be seen in pursuit of flies and insects attracted to the place. Mr. Clark observed that their sudden darting from their perch and their instantaneous return were not always attended with the capture of an insect, but seemed at times to be done only for amusement or exercise. Mr. Dresser first noticed these birds in November, when walking in the gardens of the arsenal at San Antonio. On his journey to Eagle Pass in December, he saw several daily, generally in pairs. They would perch on a bush by the roadside, occasionally darting off after some insect, and, as soon as he drew near, would fly off to a convenient perch some distance ahead, thus keeping in advance for miles. During the months of January and February they were not uncommon, but after that he lost sight of them altogether. They seemed to prefer the open country, as he generally found them on the prairies, and never in the mesquite thickets. Their stomachs were found to contain small insects.

Dr. Woodhouse frequently met with these birds in Western Texas and in New Mexico. They seemed more silent and more shy than the *fuscus*, but otherwise similar in their habits.

Dr. Kennerly met with this species at Bill Williams's Fork, New Mexico, February 10, 1854. He states that he found them common in Texas, and as far to the westward as the Great Colorado River. They built their nests under the cliffs along the stream, and in notes and in every other respect closely resembled the common Pewee.

Dr. Heermann mentions finding this species abundant in Southern California. It was more especially plentiful in the fall, at the time of its migration southward. He also found it in New Mexico, in the northern part of Texas, near El Paso, and in Sacramento Valley, though somewhat rare. In migrating, it prefers the deep valleys bordered by high hills, but also occurs on the open plains, where, perched on the stalk of some dead weed, or on a prominent rock, it darts forth in pursuit of its prey, to return to the same point.

In Arizona, Dr. Coues found this Flycatcher common throughout the Territory. At Fort Whipple it was a summer resident. It was one of the first of the migratory birds to make its appearance in spring, arriving early in March, and remained among the last, staying until October. It winters in the Colorado Valley and the southern portions of the Territory generally. He found it frequenting almost exclusively open plains, in stunted chaparral and sage brush. In some other points of habits it is said to differ remarkably from our other Flycatchers. It does not habitually frequent cañons, rocky gorges, and secluded banks of streams, as does *S. fuscus,* nor does it inhabit forests, like other Flycatchers.

Dr. Cooper regards this bird as mostly a winter visitor in the southern and western parts of California, where he has seen none later than March. In summer it is said to migrate to the great interior plains as far to the north as latitude 60°. It arrives from the north at Los Angeles in September, and perhaps earlier in the northern part of the State, and possibly breed there east of the Sierras. Mr. Allen found it common in Colorado Territory, among the mountains.

In the arid portions of the Great Basin this species was often seen by Mr. Ridgway. In its natural state it preferred rocky shores of lakes or rivers, or similar places in the cañons of the mountains, where it attached its bulky down-lined nests to the inside of small caves or recesses in the rocks, usually building them upon a small projecting shelf. Wherever man has erected a building in those desert wastes, — as at the stage-stations along the road, or in the mining towns, — it immediately assumed the familiarity of our eastern Pewee, at once taking possession of any outbuilding or any abandoned dwelling. Its notes differ widely from those of the *S. fuscus* and *S. nigricans,* the common one consisting of a wailing *peer,* varied by a tremulous twitter, and more resembling certain tones of the Wood Pewees (*Contopus virens* and *richardsoni*), with others which occasionally call to mind the *Myiarchus cinerascens.*

This species has been observed as far to the east as Racine, Wisconsin, where it was taken by Dr. P. R. Hoy. The specimen was sent to Mr. Cassin, and its identity fully established. Dr. Palmer found it breeding near Fort Wingate, in Arizona, June 11, 1869, and Mr. Ridgway obtained its nests and eggs at Pyramid Lake, Nevada, May 23, 1868. One of these nests (No. 13,588) he describes as a nearly globular mass, more flattened on top, 3.50 inches in depth by 4.00 in diameter, and composed chiefly of spiders' webs, with which is mixed very fine vegetable fibres, of various descriptions. This composition forms the bulk of the nest, and makes a closely matted and tenacious, but very soft structure; the neat but rather shallow cavity is lined solely with the grayish-white down of wild ducks. The nest was placed on a shelf inside a small cave on the shore of the island, at about ten or twelve feet from the water.

Their eggs are rounded at one end and pointed at the other, measure .82 of an inch in length by .65 in breadth. They are of a uniform chalky white, and, so far as I am aware, entirely unspotted.

Genus **CONTOPUS**, Cabanis.

Contopus, Cabanis, Journ. für Ornith. III, Nov. 1855, 479.   (Type, *Muscicapa virens*, L.)

Gen. Char. Tarsus very short, but stout; less than the middle toe and scarcely longer than the hinder; considerably less than the culmen. Bill quite broad at the base; wider

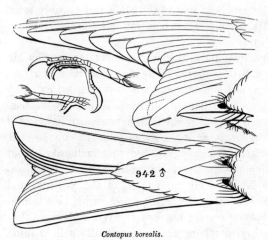

than half the culmen. Tail moderately forked. Wings very long and much pointed, reaching beyond the middle of the tail; the first primary about equal to the fourth. All the primaries slender and rather acute, but not attenuated. Head moderately crested. Color olive above, pale yellowish beneath, with a darker patch on the sides of the breast. Under tail-coverts streaked in most species. A tuft of cottony-white feathers on each side of the rump (concealed in most species).

Contopus borealis.

This genus is pre-eminently characterized among North American Fly-catchers by the very short tarsi, and the long and much pointed wings.

In most other genera, as *Sayoris, Myiarchus,* and *Empidonax,* a trace of a cottony tuft may be discovered by careful search on the flanks; but in the present genus, there is, in addition, the tufts on the rump, not found in the others. The species are as follows: —

Species and Varieties.

A. Cottony patch of white feathers on sides of the rump greatly developed, and conspicuous. Rictal bristles very short (about one fourth the length of the bill). Lower parts distinctly and abruptly white medially (somewhat interrupted on the breast).

    1. **C. borealis.** First quill longer than the fourth, generally exceed-ing the third. Wing, 4.00 to 4.40; tail, 2.90 to 3.00; culmen, .90; tarsus, .60. Above dark olive-plumbeous, the tertials edged with whitish; lower parts a lighter shade of the same, laterally and across the breast (narrowly), the throat and middle line of the abdomen being abruptly white. Young not different. *Hab.* Northern parts of North America, to the north border of United States; on the mountain-ranges, farther south, on the interior ranges, penetrating through Mexico to Costa Rica.

B. Cottony patch on side of rump rudimentary and concealed. Rictal bristles strong (one half, or more, the length of the bill). Lower parts not distinctly white medially.

    a. First primary shorter than fifth, but exceeding the sixth. Tail shorter than wings.

2. C. pertinax. Wing more than 3.50. Grayish-olive, becoming lighter on the throat (indistinctly) and abdomen (decidedly). No distinct light bands on the wing. Rictal bristles about half the length of bill.

The olive of a grayish cast, and not darker on the crown. Wing, 4.45; tail, 3.90; depth of its fork, .35; culmen, .92; tarsus, .70. *Hab.* Mexico, generally north into Arizona (Fort Whipple, COUES).

var. p e r t i n a x.

The olive of a sooty cast, and darker on the crown. Wing, 3.60; tail, 3.10; its fork, .20; culmen, .83; tarsus, .61. *Hab.* Costa Rica . . . . var. *l u g u b r i s.*[1]

3. C. brachytarsus. Wing less than 3.00; colors much as in *pertinax*, var. *pertinax*, but wing-bands distinct, breast less grayish, and pileum decidedly darker than the back. Rictal bristles two thirds as long as the bill.

Wing, 2.65; tail, 2.55; culmen, .60; tarsus, .53. *Hab.* Panama.

var. b r a c h y t a r s u s.[2]

Wing, 2.90; tail, 2.55; culmen, .67; tarsus, .53. *Hab.* Yucatan.

var. s c h o t t i.[3]

b. First primary shorter than the sixth. Tail variable.

4. C. caribæus. Bill much depressed, very long and broad, the sides more nearly parallel on the basal than on the terminal half; rictal bristles very strong (two thirds, or more, the length of the bill). Above olivaceous, generally rather dark, but varying in tint. Beneath whitish, or dull light-ochraceous, more brownish along the sides and (more faintly) across the breast. Axillars and lining of the wing deep light-ochraceous.

Tail longer than wings; bill moderately depressed; rictal bristles three fourths as long as the bill.

Dark greenish-olive above; beneath dingy ochrey-yellowish. Wing, 2.80; tail, 2.90; culmen, .78; tarsus, .58. *Hab.* Cuba.

var. c a r i b æ u s.

Dark olive-gray above; beneath whitish, with scarcely any yellowish tinge. Wing, 3.00; tail, 3.05; culmen, .70; tarsus, .59. *Hab.* Hayti . . . . . . var. *h i s p a n i o l e n s i s.*[5]

Brownish-olive above; beneath deep dingy ochrey-yellowish. Wing, 2.85; tail, 2.90; culmen, .66; tarsus, .56. *Hab.* Jamaica . . . . var. *p a l l i d u s.*[6]

Tail shorter than wing; bill excessively depressed; rictal bristles only one half as long as the bill.

---

[1] *Contopus lugubris,* LAWR. Ann. N. Y. Lyc. VIII, 1865, 134 (Costa Rica, Baranca).

[2] *Contopus brachytarsus,* SCLATER, Cat. Am. B. 1862, 231. (*Empidonax brachyt.* SCL. Ibis, 1859, p. 441.) A strongly marked race, but distinguishable from *schotti* only by just appreciable differences in color (being paler beneath), and shorter wing and bill, the latter broader at the tip.

[3] *Contopus* (*brachytarsus* var. ?), var. *schotti,* LAWR. Ann. N. Y. Lyc. IX, 1869, 202 (Yucatan). Very nearly related to *C. richardsoni,* but easily distinguished by the very different proportions.

[4] *Contopus caribæus* (D'ORB.) *Muscipeta caribæa,* D'ORB. (R. de la Sagra), Hist. Cuba, 1839, 77.

[5] *Contopus caribæus,* var. *hispaniolensis,* BRYANT. *Tyrannula caribæa,* var. *hispaniolensis,* BRYANT, Pr. Bost. Soc. XI, 1866, 91.

[6] *Contopus caribæus,* var. *pallidus* (GOSSE). *Myiobius pallidus,* GOSSE, Birds Jam. 166. *Blacicus pallidus,* SCL. P. Z. S. 1861, 77. *Contopus p.* SCL. Catal. Am. B. 1862, 231. — MARCH, Pr. Ph. A. N. Sc. 1863, 290.

Olive-plumbeous above; beneath dingy white (not interrupted on the breast); tinged posteriorly with sulphury (not
ochrey) yellow; wing-bands pale ash. Wing, 2.80; tail, 2.65;
culmen, .79; tarsus, .63. *Hab.* Bahamas.   . var. *b a h a m e n s i s.*[1]

C. First quill much longer than fifth (sometimes equal to fourth). Tail much
shorter than the wing. Bill much smaller, less depressed, and more triangular;
rictal bristles about one half the bill.

    5. **C. virens.** Colors of *caribæus* var. *bahamensis*, but rather more
olivaceous above, and more distinctly tinged with sulphur-yellow posteriorly beneath. Lining of the wings, and axillars, without any
ochraceous tinge; lower tail-coverts distinctly grayish centrally.

    Whitish of the lower parts not interrupted on the breast. Wing,
3.40; tail, 2.90; culmen, .67; tarsus, .54. *Hab.* Eastern Province
of United States . . . . var. *v i r e n s.*
    Whitish of medial lower parts interrupted by a grayish wash
across the breast. Wing, 3.40; tail, 2.65 to 2.70; culmen, .70;
tarsus, .54 to 56. *Hab.* Western Province of United States, south
throughout Middle America to Ecuador . . var. *r i c h a r d s o n i.*[2]

---

[1] *Contopus (caribæus* var. ?) *bahamensis*, BRYANT. *Empidonax bahamensis*, BRYANT, List of
Birds of the Bahamas, 1859, p. 7. Young with the colors more ashy above, and less yellowish
beneath; the upper parts with feathers faintly tipped with paler, causing an obsolete transverse
mottling; two distinct bands on wing of pale ochraceous.

    Of the above, *caribæus*, *hispaniolensis*, and *pallidus* are clearly to be referred to one species;
the *C. bahamensis* also has many characters in common with them, and no violence would be
done by referring it, also, to the same type; it is, however, more modified from the standard
than any of the others, though the modifications are not of importance.

[2] These measurements are not only those of United States and Mexican examples, but also of
Middle American examples ("*sordidulus*," SCLATER, and "*plebeius*," CABANIS), and of a series
from Ecuador and New Granada (= "*bogotensis*," SCLATER). In comparing a quite large
number of such Middle American and Equatorial specimens with the large series of Northern
examples, we have been utterly unable to appreciate even the slightest difference between them.

    The *C. punensis* (LAWR. Ann. N. Y. Lyc. IX, 1869, 237; Puna Island, Guayaquil) is founded
upon an immature specimen, so the characters of the species cannot be given with exactness.
The relationship appears very close to the *C. caribæus*, there being the same large, very depressed
bill, with the long bristles reaching nearly to its tip, and the tail about as long as the wing;
while the upper plumage has the light faint transverse mottling seen in the young *caribæus*, var.
bahamensis, and the lining of the wing ochraceous. In colors, however, the two are very different, the young of *punensis* being ashy-green, instead of pure ash, on the back, the crown very
much darker, instead of not appreciably so; the wing-bands are white instead of ochraceous,
while the breast and sides are dull sulphur-yellowish, instead of ashy, without any yellow tinge.
The measurements are as follows: Wing, 2.60; tail, 2.60; culmen, .72; tarsus, .56.

    The *C. ochraceus*, SCLATER & SALVIN (P. Z. S. 1869, 419; SALV. Ibis, 1870, 115), of Costa
Rica, we have not seen. From the description, however, it seems to be scarcely different from
C. lugubris, and it is probably the same. The size (wing, 3.30) appears to be a little smaller,
and the belly more deeply yellowish.

Contopus borealis, BAIRD.

OLIVE-SIDED FLYCATCHER.

Tyrannus borealis, Sw. & RICH. F. Bor.-Am. II, 1831, 141, plate. *Myiobius borealis*, GRAY, Genera, I, 248. *Muscicapa cooperi*, NUTTALL, Man: I, 1832, 282. — AUD. Orn. Biog. II, 1834, 422 ; V, 1839, 422, pl. clxxiv. — IB. Synopsis, 1839, 41. — IB. Birds Am. I, 1840, 212, pl. lviii. *Tyrannus cooperi*, BONAP. List, 1838. — NUTTALL, Man. I, (2d. ed.,) 1840, 298. *Contopus cooperi*, CABANIS, Journal für Ornithol. III, Nov. 1855, 479. *Muscicapa inornata*, NUTTALL, Man. I, 1832, 282. *Contopus borealis*, BAIRD, Birds N. Am. 1858, 188. — COOPER & SUCKLEY, 169. — SCLATER, Catal. 1862, 230. — SAMUELS, 135. — COOPER, Orn. Cal. I, 1870, 323. *Contopus mesoleucus*, SCLA-TER, P. Z. S. 1859, 43. — IB. Ibis, 1859, 122, 151. *Tyrannus nigricans*, MAX. Cab. J. VI, 1858, 184.

SP. CHAR. Wings long, much pointed ; the second quill longest ; the first longer than the third. Tail deeply forked. Tarsi short. The upper parts ashy-brown, showing darker brown centres of the feathers ; this is emi-nently the case on the top of the head ; the sides of the head and neck, of the breast and body, resem-bling the back, but with the edges of the feathers tinged with gray, leaving a darker central streak. The chin, throat, narrow line down the middle of the breast and body, abdomen, and lower tail-coverts white, or sometimes with a faint tinge of yellow. The lower tail-coverts somewhat streaked with brown in the centre. On each side of the rump, generally concealed by the wings, is an elongated bunch of white silky feathers. The wings and tail very dark brown, the former with the edges of the secondaries and tertials edged with dull white. The lower wing-coverts and axillaries grayish-brown. The tips of the primaries and tail-feathers rather paler. Feet and upper mandible black, lower mandible brown. The young of the year similar. but the color duller ; edges of wing-feathers dull rusty instead of grayish-white. The feet light brown. Length, 7.50 ; wing, 4.33 ; tail, 3.30 ; tarsus, .60.

Contopus borealis.

HAB. Northern portions of whole of North America, throughout Rocky Mountains, south through elevated regions of Mexico to Costa Rica. Localities : Oaxaca, high regions, Oct. (SCL. 1858, 301) ; Xalapa (SCL. 1859, 366) ; Guatemala (SCL. Ibis, I, 122) ; Costa Rica (LAWR. IX, 115) ; Veragua (SALV. 1870, 199) ; San Antonio, Texas (DRESSER, Ibis, 1865, 474, winter).

There is wonderfully little variation in this species, both in coloration and size, with different regions ; in fact none other than individual can be observed. Contrary to the usual rule, spring specimens have a more appreciable sulphur-yellow tinge below.

HABITS. This still comparatively rare species was first obtained by Rich-ardson and described by Swainson. The specimen was shot on the Sas-katchewan. No other was taken, and no information was obtained in reference to its habits. It appears to have been next met with by Mr. John Bethune, in Cambridge, June 7, 1830, in the woods of Mount Auburn. This and a second specimen, obtained soon after, were females, on the point of incubation. A third female was shot in the following year, June 21. Supposed to be a new species, it was described by Mr. Nuttall as *Tyrannus cooperi*. All the specimens procured had their stomachs filled with torn fragments of bees, wasps, and similar insects.

Mr. Nuttall, who watched the motions of two other living individuals of this species, states that they appeared tyrannical and quarrelsome even with each other. Their attacks were always accompanied with a whining, querulous twitter. The disputes seemed to be about the occupancy of certain territories. One bird, a female, appeared to confine herself to a small clump of red cedars, in the midst of a sandy piece of forest. From the tree-tops she kept a sharp lookout for passing insects, and pursued them, as they appeared, with great vigor and success, sometimes chasing them to the ground, and returning to her perch with a mouthful which she devoured at her leisure. When she resumed her position, she would occasionally quiver her wings and tail, erect her crest, keeping up a whistling call of *pŭ-pŭ*, uttered with variations. Besides this call the male had a short song which sounded like *ch'-phe'bēē*.

The nest of this pair Mr. Nuttall discovered in the horizontal branch of a tall red cedar, fifty feet from the ground. It was made externally of interlaced dead twigs of the cedar, lined with wiry stems, and dry grasses, and fragments of lichens. It contained three young, which remained in the nest twenty-three days, and were fed on beetles and other insects. Before they left their nests they could fly as well as their parents. The male bird was very watchful, and would frequently follow Mr. Nuttall half a mile. They were in no way timid, and allowed him to investigate them and their premises without any signs of alarm.

In 1832 the same pair, apparently, took possession of a small juniper, near the tree they had occupied the year before, in which, at the height of fifteen feet, they placed their nest. It contained four eggs which, except in their superior size, were precisely similar to those of the Wood Pewee, yellowish cream-color, with dark brown and lavender-purple spots, thinly dispersed. After removing two of these eggs, the others were accidentally rolled out of the nest. The pair constructed another nest, again in a cedar-tree, at a short distance. The next year they did not return to that locality. Mr. Nuttall afterwards met with individuals of this species in the fir woods on the Columbia.

On the 8th of August, 1832, Mr. Audubon, in company with Mr. Nuttall, obtained the specimen of this species in Brookline, Mass., from which his drawing was made. In the course of his journey farther east, Audubon found it in Maine, on the Magdeleine Islands, and on the coast of Labrador. He afterwards met with it in Texas.

Mr. Boardman reports the Olive-sided Flycatcher as having of late years been very abundant during the summer in the dead woods about the lakes west of Calais, where formerly they were quite uncommon. Mr. Verrill mentions it as a summer visitant in Oxford County, in the western part of the State, but not very common, and as undoubtedly breeding there. It was never observed there before the 20th of May. It is said to be more abundant at Lake Umbagog.

In Western Massachusetts Mr. Allen regards this bird as a not very rare summer visitant. It arrives about May 12, breeds in high open woods, and is seldom seen at any distance from them. It leaves about the middle of September.

Mr. William Brewster, who resides in Cambridge, in the neighborhood in which this species was first observed by Mr. Nuttall, informs me that these birds still continue to be found in that locality. He has himself met with five or six of their nests, all of which were placed near the extremity of some long horizontal branch, usually that of a pitch-pine, but on one occasion in that of an apple-tree. The eggs were laid about the 15th of June, in only one instance earlier. The females were very restless, and left their nest long before he had reached it, and, sitting on some dead branch continually uttered, in a complaining tone, notes resembling the syllables *pill-pill-pill*, occasionally varying to *pu-pu-pu*. The males were fierce and quarrelsome, and attacked indiscriminately everything that came near their domain, sometimes seeming even to fall out with their mates, fighting savagely with them for several seconds. When incubation was at all far advanced, the birds evinced considerable courage, darting down to within a few inches of his head, if he approached their nest, at the same time loudly snapping their bills.

A nest of this Flycatcher was found in Lynn, Mass., by Mr. George O. Welch, in June, 1858. It was built on the top of a dead cedar, and contained three eggs. It was a flat, shallow structure, five inches in its external diameter, and with a very imperfectly defined cavity. The greatest depth was less than half an inch. It was coarsely and loosely built of strips of the bark and fine twigs of the red cedar, roots, mosses, dry grasses, etc. The nest was so shallow, that, in climbing to it, two of the eggs were rolled out and broken.

Mr. Charles S. Paine has found this bird breeding in Randolph, Vt. On one occasion he found its nest on the top of a tall hemlock-tree, but was not able to get to it.

In Philadelphia, Mr. Trumbull found this species very rare. It passed north early in May, and south in September. Near Hamilton, Canada, it is very rare, none having been seen ; and two specimens obtained near Toronto are all that Mr. McIlwraith is aware of having been taken in Canada West.

Dr. Hoy informs me that this species used to be quite common near Racine, frequenting the edges of thick woods, where they nested. They have now become quite scarce. Some years since, he found one of their nests, just abandoned by the young birds, which their parents were engaged in feeding. It was on the horizontal branch of a maple, and was composed wholly of *usneæ*.

In Washington Territory this bird appears to be somewhat more common than in other portions of the United States. Dr. Suckley obtained a specimen at Fort Steilacoom, July 10, 1856. It was not very abundant about Puget Sound, and showed a preference for shady thickets and dense foliage, where it was not easily shot. Dr. Cooper speaks of it as very common, arriving early in May and frequenting the borders of woods, where, stationed on the tops of tall dead trees, it repeats a loud and melancholy cry throughout the day, during the whole of summer. It frequents small pine groves along the coast, and also in the interior, and remains until late in September.

In California Dr. Cooper found this species rather common in the Coast Range towards Santa Cruz, where they had nests in May; but as these were built in high inaccessible branches, he was not able to examine them. He also found it at Lake Tahoe in September.

This species was only met with by Mr. Ridgway in the pine woods high up on the East Humboldt, Wahsatch, and Uintah Mountains. There it was breeding, but was nowhere abundant, not more than two pairs being observed within an area of several miles. They preferred the rather open pine woods, and were shot from the highest branches. Their common note was a mellow *puer*, much like one of the whistling notes of the Cardinal Grosbeak (*Cardinalis virginianus*).

Mr. Dresser states it to be not uncommon near San Antonio in the winter season. Dr. Heermann mentions that two specimens of this species were obtained, to his knowledge, on the Cosumnes River, in California. It has been taken in winter, in the State of Oaxaca, Mexico, by Mr. Boucard, and has been met with at Jalapa, and even as far south as Guatemala.

A single specimen of this bird was taken, August 29, 1840, at Nenortalik, Greenland, and sent to Copenhagen.

The eggs of this species measure .86 of an inch in length by .62 in breadth, and are rounded at one end and sharply tapering at the other. The ground-color is a rich cream-color with a roseate tint. They are beautifully marked around the larger end with a ring of confluent spots of lilac, purple, and red-brown. These vary in number and in the size of this crown, but the markings are invariably about the larger end, as in *Contopus virens*.

Contopus pertinax, CABANIS & HEINE.

MEXICAN OLIVE-SIDED FLYCATCHER.

Contopus pertinax, CAB. et HEIN. Mus. Hein. II, p. 72. — SCLATER, Catal. Am. B. 1862, 231. — COUES, Pr. Ac. Phil. 1866, 60. — ELLIOT, Illust. B. Am. I, pl. viii. — COOPER, Geol. Surv. Calif. Orn. I, 324. — COOPER, Orn. Cal. I, 1870, 324. *Contopus borealis*, SCLATER, P. Z. S. 1858, 301 ; 1859, 43 ; Ibis, 1859, 122, 440.

SP. CHAR. Nearly uniformly olive-gray, lighter on the throat and abdominal region, where is a strong tinge of ochraceous-yellow ; feathers of the wings with faintly lighter edges. Length about 8.00; wing, 4.45; tail, 3 90; depth of its fork, .35; culmen, .92; tarsus, .70. Rictal bristles long, about half the bill; lower mandible whitish. *Young.* Similar, but with a stronger ochraceous tinge on the abdomen and lining of the wings, and two distinct ochraceous bands across the wing.

HAB. Mexico generally, into southern borders of United States (Fort Whipple, Arizona; DR. COUES).

HABITS. Dr. Coues found this species a rare summer resident at Fort Whipple, where a single specimen was taken August 20, in good plumage. This was its first introduction into the fauna of the United States. It is one of several Mexican and peninsular birds found in Upper Arizona, probably following the course of the valley of the Great Colorado River. No observations were made in reference to its habits.

This species is abundant in the Department of Vera Cruz, according to Mr. Sumichrast, who gives it as confined to the alpine region. He found both it and *C. virens* common in the mountains of Orizaba, between the height of 3,600 and 7,500 feet.

Contopus virens, CABANIS.

WOOD PEWEE.

Muscicapa virens, LINN. Syst. Nat. I, 1766, 327. — GMELIN, Syst. Nat. I, 1788, 936. — LATHAM, Index Orn. — LICHT. Verz. 1823, 563. — NUTTALL, Man. I, 1832, 285. — AUD. Orn. Biog. II, 1834, 93 ; V, 1839, 425, pl. cxv. — IB. Synopsis, 1839, 42. — IB. Birds Am. I, 1840, 231, pl. lxiv. — GIRAUD, Birds L. Island, 1844, 43. *Muscicapa querula,* VIEILLOT, Ois. Am. Sept. I, 1807, 68, pl. xxxix (not of WILSON). *Muscicapa rapax,* WILSON, Am. Orn. II, 1810, 81, pl. xiii, f. 5. *Tyrannula virens,* RICH. App. Back's Voyage. — BONAP. List. 1838. *Myiobius virens,* GRAY. *Tyrannus virens,* NUTTALL, Man. I, (2d ed.,) 1840, 316. *Contopus virens,* CABANIS, Journal für Ornithologie, III, Nov. 1855, 479. — BAIRD, Birds N. Am. 1858, 190. — SCLATER, Catal. 1862, 231. — SAMUELS, 137.

SP. CHAR. The second quill longest; the third a little shorter; the first shorter than the fourth; the latter nearly .40 longer than the fifth. The primaries more than an inch longer than the secondaries. The upper parts, sides of the head, neck, and breast, dark olivaceous-brown, the latter rather paler, the head darker. A narrow white ring round the eye. The lower parts pale yellowish, deepest on the abdomen ; across the breast tinged with ash. This pale ash sometimes occupies the whole of the breast, and even occasionally extends up to the chin. It is also sometimes glossed with olivaceous. The wings and tail dark brown; generally deeper than in *S. fuscus.* Two narrow bands across the wing, the outer edge of first primary and of the secondaries and tertials, dull white. The edges of the tail-feathers like the back; the outer one scarcely lighter. Upper mandible black ; the lower yellow, but brown at the tip. Length, 6.15; wing, 3.50 ; tail, 3.05.

HAB. Eastern North America to the borders of the high Central Plains. Localities : ? Guatemala (SCL. Ibis, I, 122) ; Mexico (SCL. Ibis, I, 441); Cuba? (CAB. J. III, 479; GUNDL. Rep. 1865, 239); Costa Rica (CAB. J. 1861, 248; LAWR. IX, 115); Coban (SCL. List) ; Vera Cruz, alpine region, breeds (SUM. M. Bost. Soc. I, 557) ; San Antonio, Texas and Eastern Texas (DRESSER, Ibis, 1865, 474, breeds).

Young birds are duller in plumage; the whitish markings of wing tinged with ferruginous; the lower mandible more dusky.

HABITS. The common Wood Pewee of eastern North America occurs in abundance from the Atlantic to the great plains, and from Texas to New Brunswick. It breeds from South Carolina and Texas north. It is found in Central and Southern Maine, but is not so abundant as it is farther south. It is found near St. Stephens, N. B., and breeds in that vicinity, but is not common. It is a summer visitant at Norway, Me., but Professor Verrill states that it is much less common than in Massachusetts, where it arrives the last of May. At Hamilton, in Canada, Mr. McIlwraith records this species as abundant in the summer, arriving there the middle of May. I am not aware of its having been taken north of the 45th parallel of latitude, with the exception of one at Red River, Minnesota, and another at Fort William by Mr. Kennicott. It is said by Dr. Coues to be a summer resident of South Carolina from the middle of April to the middle of October, and Mr. Dresser states that he found it very common in the wooded river-bottoms near San Antonio during the summer, not arriving there until late in April or early in May. Their call-note, he states, is a low prolonged whistle. Their stomachs were found to contain minute coleopterous insects. Dr. Woodhouse also speaks of it as common in Texas and in the Indian Territory. In the Department of Vera Cruz, Mr. Sumichrast found this species, as well as the *Contopus pertinax*, common in the mountains of Orizaba, between the height of 3,600 and 7,500 feet.

In Pennsylvania, Wilson states that the Wood Pewee is the latest of the summer birds in arriving, seldom coming before the 12th or 15th of May. He found it frequenting the shady high-timbered woods, where there is little underwood and an abundance of dead twigs and branches. It was generally found in low situations. He adds that it builds its nest on the upper side of a limb or branch, formed outwardly of moss and lined with various soft materials, and states that the female lays five white eggs, and that the brood leave the nest about the middle of June. Probably the last statement is correct as applied to Pennsylvania, but the intimation as to the color of the egg and some of the characteristics of the nest is so inaccurate as to make it doubtful whether Wilson could have ever seen the nest for himself.

This species, like all its family, is a very expert catcher of insects, even the most minute, and has a wonderfully quick perception of their near presence, even when the light of day has nearly gone and in the deep gloom of thick woods. It takes its station on the end of a low dead limb, from which it darts out in quest of insects, sometimes for a single individual, which it seizes with a peculiar snap of its bill; and, frequently meeting insect after insect, it keeps up a constant snapping sound as it passes on, and finally returns to its post to resume its watch. During this watch it occasionally is heard to utter a low twitter, with a quivering movement of the wings and tail, and more rarely to enunciate a louder but still feeble call-note, sounding like *pēē-ē*. These notes are continued until dark, and are also uttered throughout the season.

Mr. Nuttall states that this species at times displays a tyrannical disposition, and that it has been observed to chase a harmless Sparrow to the ground, because it happened to approach his station for collecting insects.

According to Mr. Audubon, some of these birds spend the winter months in the extreme Southern States, Louisiana and Florida, where they feed upon berries as well as insects.

In Massachusetts the Wood Pewee is a very abundant species, and may usually be found in any open woods, or in an orchard of large spreading trees. In the latter situation it frequently breeds. It usually selects a lower dead limb of a tree, from ten to thirty feet from the ground, and occasionally, but more seldom, a living moss-grown branch. It always chooses one that is covered with small lichens, and saddles its nest upon its upper surface, so closely assimilated by its own external coating of lichens as not to be distinguishable from a natural protuberance on the limb. This structure is extremely beautiful, rivalling even the artistic nests of the Humming-Bird. It is cup-shaped, and a perfect segment of a sphere in shape. The periphery of the nest is made of fine root fibres, small lichens, and bits of cobwebs and other similar materials. The outer sides are entirely covered with a beautiful coating of mosses and lichens, glued to the materials with the saliva of the builder. The eggs are usually four in number, measure .78 of an inch in length and .55 in breadth. They are obtuse at one end and tapering at the other, have a ground of a rich cream-color, and are marked about the larger end with a wreath of blended purple, lilac, and red-brown in large and confluent spots. They hatch about the middle of June, leave the nest in July, and have but a single brood.

A nest of this species, taken in Lynn by Mr. Welch, and built on the dead branch of a forest tree, has a diameter of three and a height of one and a half inches. The cavity has a depth of one inch, and a diameter, at the rim, of two and a half inches. The base is flattened by its position. Its walls are strongly woven of fine dry stems, intermingled with vegetable down, covered externally with lichens, cemented to the exterior, apparently by the secretions of the bird. The base is thinner, and made of softer materials.

During the winter months this species is present as a migrant in various parts of Mexico, south to Guatemala.

Contopus virens, var. richardsoni, BAIRD.

SHORT-LEGGED PEWEE; WESTERN WOOD PEWEE.

Tyrannula richardsoni, SWAINSON, F. Bor.-Am. II, 1831, 146, plate. *Muscicapa richardsoni,* AUD. Orn. Biog. V, 1839, 299, pl. ccccxxxiv. *Tyrannula phœbe,* BON. List, 1838, 24. *Muscicapa phœbe,* AUDUBON, Synopsis, 1839, 42. — IB. Birds Am. I, 1840, 219, pl. lxi (not of LATHAM). *Tyrannus phœbe,* NUTTALL, Man. I, (2d ed.,) 1840, 319. *Tyrannus atriceps,* D'ORBIGNY (fide G. R. GRAY). *Contopus richardsoni,* BAIRD, Birds N. Am. 1858, 189. — SCLATER, Catal. 1862, 231. — COOPER, Orn. Cal. I, 1870, 325. *Contopus sordidulus,* SCLATER, Catal. 1862, 231. *Contopus plebeius,* (CABAN.) SCLATER, Cat. 1862, 231. *Contopus bogotensis,* (BONAP.) SCLATER, P. Z. S. 1858, 459. (*Tyrannula b.* BONAP. Comp. Rend. p. 196.)

SP. CHAR. General appearance of *C. virens.* Bill broad. Wings very long and much pointed, considerably exceeding the tail; second quill longest; third a little shorter; first shorter than fourth, and about midway between distance from second to fifth (.60 of an inch). Primaries 1.20 inches longer than secondaries. Tail moderately forked. Above dark olive-brown (the head darker); the entire breast and sides of head, neck, and body of a paler shade of the same, tingeing strongly also the dull whitish throat and chin. Abdomen and under tail-coverts dirty pale-yellowish. Quills and tail dark blackish-brown; the secondaries narrowly, the tertials more broadly edged with whitish. Two quite indistinct bands of brownish-white across the wings. Lower mandible yellow; the tip brown. Length, 6.20; wing, 3.65; tail, 3.10.

HAB. High central dry plains to the Pacific; Rio Grande Valley, southward to Mexico; Labrador (AUDUBON). Localities: Orizaba, Guatemala, Coban (SCL. Catal. 1862, 231); Costa Rica (LAWR. IX, 115); Matamoras, Texas (DRESSER, Ibis, 1865, 474, breeds); San Antonio, Texas (DRESSER, one spec.); W. Arizona (COUES, P. A. N. S. 1866, 61).

This species has a very close relationship to *C. virens,* agreeing with it in general shape of wings and in color. The wings are, however, still longer and more pointed; the primaries exceeding the secondaries by nearly 1.25 inches. The proportions of the quills are nearly the same in both; the primaries, too, are similarly a little emarginated or attenuated towards the end. The tail is rather more deeply forked, the feathers broader. The bills are similar; the feet are larger and stouter.

The general colors are almost precisely the same. The outer primary, however, lacks the decidedly white margin. The under parts are much darker anteriorly, the entire breast being nearly a uniform olive-brown, but little paler than the back; the throat, too, in some specimens, being scarcely paler. There is little or none of the pale sulphur-yellow of *C. virens* on the abdomen, and the under wing-coverts and axillaries are much darker olivaceous. In *C. virens* the middle line of the breast is always paler than the sides, or at least the connecting space is short.

The lower mandible is generally yellow; in a few specimens, however, it is quite dusky, especially on its terminal half.

The young bird has the darker head and broader light edgings, with the ferruginous tinge on the wing-markings, usually seen in young of the *Tyrannulas.*

A large series shows considerable variations; autumnal specimens have a more appreciable tinge of yellow on the lower parts, while summer individuals are more grayish.

HABITS. This species was first obtained by Richardson in the Arctic regions, and described by Swainson. It was found in the neighborhood of the Cumberland House, where it frequented moist shady woods by the banks of rivers and lakes. It was supposed likely to travel in summer as far as the shores of the Great Slave Lake.

Since its discovery by Richardson, this Flycatcher has been found to have a widely extended geographical range, as far to the south as Guatemala, and even Panama, and northward as far as the 60th parallel of latitude, and from the great plains to the Pacific.

During the survey of the Mexican Boundary, specimens of this bird were obtained by Mr. J. H. Clark in El Paso, Texas, and in the month of May by Lieutenant Couch in Monterey, Mexico.

Mr. Dresser found that this bird was very common near Matamoras during the summer, and that they were breeding there. He also shot one specimen near San Antonio in May. Its stomach contained small insects. Dr. Coues thinks this Flycatcher an exceedingly abundant summer resident in the Territory of Arizona. It arrives there in spring about the first of May, the latest of the Flycatchers, and is deemed by the Doctor a counterpart of the eastern *Contopus virens*. It departs from that Territory about the third week in September. It is found in all situations, but most especially in open forests.

This species arrives in California, according to Dr. Cooper, at least a fortnight earlier than the date of its earliest advent in Arizona as given by Dr. Coues, or about the 15th of April, and spends its summers in the most mountainous parts of the State. It is said to perch mainly on the lower dead limbs, watching for the passing insects, uttering occasionally a plaintive *pe-ah*. It is usually very silent, and seems to prefer the dark, solitary recesses of the forests.

Dr. Hoy informs me that this Flycatcher is occasionally found in the neighborhood of Racine, but that it is rare. It keeps in the deep forest, and never comes near dwellings in the manner of *C. virens*.

This bird was found breeding at Fort Tejon by Mr. Xantus, at Napa Valley by Mr. A. J. Grayson, and both in the Sacramento Valley and at Parley's Park, among the Wahsatch Mountains, by Mr. Ridgway.

A nest of this bird in the Smithsonian Museum (10,076) from California, collected by W. Vuille, had been apparently saddled on the limb of a tree, in the manner of *C. virens*, having a broad flattened base, and a general resemblance to the nests of that species. It differs, however, somewhat in regard to materials, and most especially in having no lichens attached to the exterior. It has a diameter of three inches and a height of one and a half. The cavity is about one inch deep and two wide at the rim. The base and sides of this nest are largely composed of the exuviæ of chrysalides, intermingled with hemp-like fibres of plants, stems, and fine dry grasses. The rim is firmly wrought of strong wiry stems, and a large portion of the inner nest is of the same material. The whole is warmly and thoroughly lined with the soft fine hair of small quadrupeds and with vegetable fibres.

According to Mr. Ridgway, this is the most abundant and generally diffused of all the *Tyrannuli* of the Great Basin, as well as of California. It inhabits every grove of the lowest valleys, as well as the highest aspen copses on the mountains in the alpine region, and breeds abundantly in all these places. Resembling the eastern *C. virens* in its general habits, its appearance, and its every motion, it yet differs most widely from it in notes, the common one being a disagreeable weird squeak, very unlike the sad, wailing, but not unpleasant one of the eastern Wood Pewee. Mr. Ridgway relates that having shot a female bird, and taken her nest and eggs, he was surprised, a few days afterwards, to find the male with another mate, and a new nest built in precisely the same spot from which the other had been taken. Upon climbing to the nest, it was found to contain one egg; and the parents exhibited very unusual distress. When visited two or three days after, it was found to be deserted and the egg broken.

The eggs, three in number, measure .69 of an inch in length and .53 in breadth. They have a ground of beautiful cream-color slightly tinged with a roseate tint, surrounded at the larger end with a wreath of purple and reddish-brown spots. A few smaller markings are sparingly distributed, but nearly all are about the larger end.

Genus **EMPIDONAX**, Cabanis.

Empidonax, Cabanis, Journal für Ornithologie, III, Nov. 1855, 480. (Type, *Tyrannula pusilla*.) *Tyrannula* of most authors.

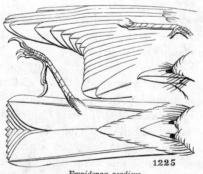

1225

Empidonax acadicus.

Gen. Char. Tarsus lengthened, considerably longer than the bill, and exceeding the middle toe, which is decidedly longer than the hind toe. Bill variable. Tail very slightly forked, even, or rounded; a little shorter only than the wings, which are considerably rounded; the first primary much shorter than the fourth. Head moderately crested. Color olivaceous above, yellowish beneath; throat generally gray.

The lengthened tarsi, the short toes, the short and rounded wings, and the plain dull olivaceous of the plumage, readily distinguish the species of this genus from any other North American Flycatchers. The upper plates of the tarsi in a good many species do not encircle the outside, but meet there a row on the posterior face.

There are few species of North American birds more difficult to distinguish than the small Flycatchers, the characters, though constant, being very slight and almost inappreciable, except to a very acute observer.

The following synopsis may aid in distinguishing the species : —

Species and Varieties.

A. Inner webs of secondaries edged with pinkish-buff.

   a. Olive-brown above, whitish beneath ; tibiæ ochraceous.

      E. brunneus.[1] Third quill longest, first equal to seventh ; tail slightly rounded. Russet-olive above, the crown, wings, and tail with a reddish-brown tinge ; a yellowish-gray shade across the breast, and a faint sulphur-yellow tinge to posterior lower parts. Wing-bands broad, sharply defined, deep ochraceous ; lining of wing and tibiæ slightly tinged with the same. Wing, 2.35 ; tail, 2.30 ; bill, .57 and .27 ; tarsus, .56 ; middle toe, .33. *Hab.* Parana.

      E. axillaris.[2] Third quill longest, first equal to seventh ; tail ? Dark grayish-brown above, nearly uniform, breast ochraceous-olive ; a just appreciable tinge of sulphur-yellow on abdomen. Wing-bands narrow, badly defined, in color nearly like the back ; lining of the wing and tibiæ very deep ochraceous. Wing, 2.40 ; tail, 2.50 ; bill, .60 and .30 ; tarsus, .60 ; middle toe, .43. Hab. Orizaba.

   b. Olive-green above, yellow beneath ; tibiæ greenish.

      E. flavescens.[3] Third, or third and fourth quills longest ; first equal to eighth. Tail decidedly emarginated. Intense greenish-olive above, the crown with a decided russet tinge ; beneath bright lemon-yellow, with a shade of fulvous-brown across the breast. Wing, 2.35 to 2.70 ; tail, 2.20 to 2.40 ; bill, .59 and .30 ; tarsus, .66 ; middle toe, .35. *Hab.* Costa Rica.

      E. bairdi.[4] Fourth quill longest, first shorter than eighth. Tail slightly emarginated. Dull greenish-olive above, nearly uniform ; beneath clear sulphur-yellow, with a greenish-olive shade across the breast. Wing, 2.60 ; tail, 2.50 ; bill, .62 and .29 ; tarsus, .65 ; middle toe, .35. *Hab.* Eastern Mexico (MIRADOR).

B. Inner webs of secondaries edged with yellowish or grayish white.

   a. Olive-green above, yellowish beneath.

§. *Young not mottled above.*

   E. flaviventris. Bill broad, twice as wide as deep, and the culmen less than twice the breadth. Outer web of lateral tail-feather dusky, like the inner. Wing-bands narrow, whitish. Tail square.

      Clear olive-green above, sulphur-yellow beneath ; wing-bands sulphur-yellowish ; lining of wing clear sulphury-yellow. Wing,

---

[1] *Empidonax brunneus,* RIDGWAY. A very distinct species, not needing comparison with any other.

[2] *Empidonax axillaris,* RIDGWAY.

[3] *Empidonax flavescens,* LAWR. May be the southern form of *bairdi,* but differ in some apparently essential features.

[4] *Empidonax bairdi,* SCLATER, P. Z. S. 1858, 301 ; Ibis, 1859, 442 ; Catal. Am. B. 1862, 230. — SCLATER & SALVIN, Ibis, 1860, 36. (*Hab.* Cordova, Coban, Mazatlan, Mirador, etc.)

2.60; tail, 2.35, or less; bill, .57 and .27 : tarsus, .66; middle toe,
.37. *Hab.* Eastern Province North America, south through Eastern Mexico to Guatemala . . . . . var. *flaviventris*.
Dull olive-gray above, pale, somewhat ochraceous, yellow beneath;
wing-bands grayish-white; lining of wing strongly tinged with
fulvous. Wing, 2.75; tail, 2.60 to 2.75. *Hab.* Western Province
of North America, south, through Western Mexico, to Colima.
                                                        var. *difficilis*.
E. fulvipectus.[1] Bill narrow, the width but little more than the
depth, and the culmen considerably more than twice the breadth at
base. Outer web of lateral tail-feather distinctly whitish, very different
from the dusky of the inner web. Tail deeply emarginated. Colors
of *flaviventris* var. *difficilis*, but wing-bands broad and buffy olive, and
a deep shade of fulvous-olive across the breast. Wing, 3.00; tail, 2.90;
bill, .61 and .22; tarsus, .60; middle toe, .37. *Hab.* City of Mexico.
b. Grayish or greenish olive above, whitish beneath.

¶. *Tail deeply emarginated.*

E. obscurus. Exact form and proportions of *fulvipectus*, but tarsus
much longer proportionally. Ashy above, with a slight olive tinge;
white beneath with no yellow tinge, and without distinct ashy shade
across breast; sides of breast like the back. Orbital ring, wing-
markings, and outer web of lateral tail-feather pale clear ashy. Wing,
3.00; tail, 2 80; bill, .64 and .24; tarsus, .77; middle toe, .42.
E. hammondi. Very similar, but bill much smaller and less elongated.
Color of upper parts the same as in *obscurus;* but anterior lower parts
nearly uniform ashy, the throat only indistinctly paler, and the posterior
portions distinctly uniform pale sulphur-yellow. Outer web of lateral
tail-feather less distinctly whitish. Wing, 2.85; tail, 2.55; bill, .50 and
.20; tarsus, .64; middle toe, .34.
E. minimus Very similar to *hammondi,* but bill much larger, broader,
and the lateral outlines less straight. Outer web of lateral tail-feather
not appreciably paler than the inner; whole throat distinctly whitish;
wing-bands only about half as wide as in *hammondi.*
Wing, 2.70; tail, 2.60; bill, .57 and .27; tarsus, .66; middle toe,
.35. *Hab* Eastern Province of North America, and Eastern
Mexico . . . . var. *minimus*.

¶. *Tail doubly rounded.*

Wing, 2.35; tail, 2.20; bill, .54 and .25; tarsus, .62; middle toe,
.33. Colors of *minimus,* but wing-markings whiter. *Hab.*
Panama . . . . (var. ?) *pectoralis.*[2]

---

[1] *Empidonax fulvipectus,* LAWR. Ann. N. Y. Lyc. Feb. 1871, 11. (Type examined.) A very
distinct species, most nearly related to *obscurus,* from which it differs totally in color and in
much shorter tarsus.

[2] *Empidonax minimus,* var. *pectoralis. Empidonax pectoralis,* LAWR. It seems but reasonable to consider this bird as the southern race of *minimus,* as the differences — i. e. smaller size
and whiter wing-bands — are just what we find in several other species of the same region,
compared with allied and probably co-specific northern types, — as *griseigularis* and *acadicus,*
southern specimens of *trailli* var. *pusillus* in which the wing-bands are much whiter than in
northern specimens of the same bird.

E. griseipectus.[1] Colors of *hammondi*, but wing-bands whiter and narrower, very sharply defined; sides tinged with clear greenish; jugulum and sides of throat clear ashy. Wing, 2.40; tail, 2.40; bill, .56 and .27; tarsus, .60; middle toe, .35. *Hab.* Guayaquil, Ecuador.

¶. *Tail square, or slightly rounded; feathers acute at tips.*
E. pusillus. Brownish-olive or olive-gray above, wing-bands olive or gray; beneath whitish, with a grayish shade across the breast, and a sulphur-yellow tinge posteriorly.

Olive-grayish above, wing-bands much lighter, or whitish-gray. Wing, 2.90; tail, 2.70; bill, .69 and .26; tarsus, .67; middle toe, .40. *Hab.* Western Province of North America, and Middle and Western Mexico . . . . . . var. *pusillus.*

Brownish-olive above, wing-bands but little lighter. Wing, 2.90; tail, 2.50; bill, .64 and .27; tarsus, .66; middle toe, .38. *Hab.* Eastern Province of North America, and Eastern Mexico . var. *trailli.*

§. *Young with upper plumage transversely mottled. Wing-bands with a pale buff tinge; upper mandible brown.*

E. acadicus. Grayish-green above, greenish-white beneath; throat purer white. Wing, 3.10; tail, 2.80; bill, .67 and .30; tarsus, .60; middle toe, .34. *Hab.* Eastern Province of United States, and Eastern Mexico . . . . var. *acadicus.*

Wing, 2.65; tail, 2.50; bill, .66 and .30; tarsus, .62; middle toe, .33. Wing-bands whiter. *Hab.* Panama . var. *griseigularis.*[2]

In *Empidonax,* as well as *Contopus,* autumnal birds have the plumage softer and the colors brighter than in spring; the brilliancy of the yellow shades is especially enhanced. The young of the year resemble the parents, but there is a greater tendency to light bands on the wings, which with the other markings of this region show an ochraceous tinge. The lower mandible is also usually tinged with dusky. In the young of *E. acadica,* alone, there are light transverse bars over upper surface, as in the young of some species of *Contopus* (*C. bahamensis* and *C. punensis*).

---

[1] *Empidonax griseipectus,* LAWR. May possibly be another seasonal plumage of the same species as *pectoralis,* but differs in some seemingly important respects.

[2] *Empidonax acadicus,* var. *griseigularis. Empidonax griseigularis,* LAWR. Differing from *acadicus* only in smaller size and whiter wing-bands.

The remaining described American species of *Empidonax,* which we have not seen, are the following : —

Empidonax magnirostris, GOULD, Voy. Beagle, pl. 8. — GRAY, Hand List.

Empidonax albigularis, SCLATER & SALVIN, Ibis, 1859, p. 122 (Orizaba). — SCLATER, Catal. Am. B. 1862, 229. This may possibly be the species described above as *E. axillaris.*

Empidonax pusillus, CABANIS.

LITTLE FLYCATCHER.

? *Platyrhynchus pusillus*, SWAINSON, Phil. Mag. I, May, 1827, 366. *Tyrannula pusilla*, Sw. F. B. Am. II, 1831, 144, pl. — RICH. App. Back's Voyage, 1834–36, 144. — GAMBEL, Pr. A. N. Sc. III, 1847, 156. *Muscicapa pusilla*, AUD. Orn. Biog. V, 1839, 288 ; pl. ccccxxxiv. — IB. Birds Am. I, 1840, 236, pl. lxvi. *Tyrannus pusilla*, NUT-TALL, Man. I, (2d ed.,) 1840. *Empidonax pusillus*, BAIRD, Birds N. Am. 1858, 194. COOPER & SUCKLEY, 176. — SCLATER, Catal. 1862, 229. *Empidonax trailli*, COOPER, Orn. Cal. I, 1870, 327 (Colorado River).

Empidonax pusillus.

SP. CHAR. Second, third, and fourth quills longest; first shorter than the sixth. Bill rather broad ; yellow beneath. Tail even. Tarsi rather long. Above dirty olive-brown, paler and more tinged with brown towards the tail. Throat and breast white, tinged with grayish-olive on the sides, shading across the breast ; belly and under tail-coverts very pale sulphur-yellow. Wings with two dirty narrow brownish-white bands slightly tinged with olive ; the secondaries and tertials narrowly and inconspicuously margined with the same. First primary faintly edged with whitish ; the outer web of first tail-feather paler than the inner, but not white. Under wing-coverts reddish ochraceous-yellow. A whitish ring round the eye. Length, 5.50 ; wing, 2.80 ; tail, 2.75. *Young.* Wing-bands ochraceous instead of grayish. HAB. High Central Plains to the Pacific. Fur countries. Southward into Mexico. Fort Whipple, Arizona (COUES, P. A. N. S. 1866, 61) ; Vera Cruz, temp. reg. resident (SUM. Mem. Bost. Soc. I, 557).

This race represents the var. *trailli* in the region west of the Rocky Mountains. The present bird is paler colored than *trailli*, the olivaceous above much more grayish anteriorly, and more brownish posteriorly, the olive being thus less greenish and less uniform in tint ; the brownish shade across the breast is lighter and more ashy, and the yellow tinge posteriorly beneath more faint ; the wing-bands lighter and more grayish. In color, *pusillus* thus approximates somewhat to *E. minimus*, which, however, is a very distinct species, and more closely related to *E. hammondi ; minimus* may be distinguished by much smaller size (the bill especially), the wing-bands grayish-white instead of olive-gray, and the tail emarginated instead of appreciably rounded ; *minimus* lays a white egg like *E. obscurus*, while *pusillus* and *trailli* lay distinctly spotted ones, and build a very different nest.

HABITS. Professor Baird, in his Birds of North America, assigns to this species an area of distribution extending from the Great Plains to the Pacific, southward into Mexico, and north to the fur country. Dr. Hoy cites it as of Wisconsin in his List of the birds of that State, but without positive data for this claim ; it has, however, since been actually taken, a summer resident breeding in Jefferson County, in that State. This is its most eastern known occurrence. In the Smithsonian Museum are skins from Fort Steilacoom, Fort Tejon, and Mexico. This species is probably identical with the Little Tyrant Flycatcher, described by Swainson in the Fauna Boreali as both from Mexico and from the Arctic regions. Dr. Richardson was not able to supply anything in regard to its habits. They were first seen by him at the Carlton House on the 19th of May. For a few days they were found flitting about among low bushes on the banks of the river, after which they retired to moist shady woods lying farther north.

Mr. Ridgway mentions the *E. pusillus* as the most common of the *Empidonaces* in the Great Basin, as well as in California and the Rocky Mountains. It is chiefly, if not entirely, confined to the willows along streams, but it is as common in the river valleys as in the mountain "parks." In all respects it is a counterpart of the *E. trailli*; its notes, as well as its manners, being the same. In Parley's Park, in the Wahsatch Mountains, at an elevation of over 7,000 feet, they were breeding abundantly; about nightfall they became particularly active, chasing each other, with a merry twitter, through the willow thickets, or, as they perched upon a dry twig, uttered frequently, with swelling throats and raised crest, their odd but agreeable enunciation of *pretty dear*, as their notes were translated by the people of the locality.

In the Department of Vera Cruz, Mexico, Mr. Sumichrast gives this species as a summer resident within the temperate region. He found it quite common around Orizaba in the months of June and July.

It was also met with on the Mexican Boundary Survey in summer, having been taken in June at Los Nogales by Dr. Kennerly, and at Rio Nasas, in Duvango, by Lieutenant Couch, the same month.

Dr. Coues mentions it as moderately plentiful as a summer resident in Arizona. None of this genus were very common at Fort Whipple, but this one was by far the most characteristic species. It arrives there about the middle of April, and remains through September.

Dr. Suckley found this species quite abundant in the vicinity of Fort Steilacoom, where it arrives early in May. It seems to prefer the vicinity of bushes and low trees at the edges of dense forests. This species, he adds, is rather less pugnacious than others of the group, and in habits generally more resembles the Vireo family. Its notes are said to be short but sweet, and just after sundown on warm summer evenings particularly low, plaintive, and soothing.

Dr. Cooper speaks of it as found by him frequenting the dark and gloomy spruce forests, which it seems to prefer to more open places. He found it most numerous near the coast, but also saw a few at Puget Sound, where it arrived about the 25th of April. He speaks of its song as lively but monotonous. He found it very difficult to get a sight of this bird among the upper branches of the tall spruces, its color making it almost invisible in the shade. One of these birds was observed to keep constantly on the border of a small pond and to drive away a Kingbird from the place. He adds that it has a peculiar short and lisping song of three notes, very different from those of the other species. In the fall the young birds uttered a very different call-note.

Mr. Ridgway found this species breeding, June 23, at Parley's Park, Utah. One nest was built on the horizontal branch of a willow, over a stream, about four feet from the ground. It was partly pensile. It was three inches deep and four in diameter; the cavity was two inches wide and one and a half deep. Externally the nest was somewhat loosely constructed of flaxen fibres of plants, soft strips of inner bark and straw, and lined more firmly with fine roots of plants. This structure was firmly bound around the smaller branches of the limb. The inner nest was much more compactly interwoven than the periphery. The eggs, four in number, were of a chalky whiteness, more pinkish when unblown, finely sprinkled at the larger end with reddish-brown dots. Length, .77 of an inch; breadth, .51.

Another nest from the same locality was built in the upright fork of a wild rose, in the undergrowth of a willow thicket, and about four feet from the ground. It is a much more compact and homogeneous nest. Its external portion was almost wholly composed of the interweaving of the fine inner bark of deciduous shrubs, blended with a few stems of grasses, feathers, etc., and is lined with a few fine grass stems and fibrous roots. The eggs, four in number, have a pinkish-white ground, and are spotted at the larger end with reddish-brown and chestnut spots, in scattered groups.

In the summer of 1870 a son of Mr. Thure Kumlien, of Jefferson Co., Wisconsin, found the nest and eggs of this species. Both parents were obtained, and were fully identified by Professor Baird. The nest was placed in a thick mass of coarse marsh grasses, near the ground, and firmly interwoven with the tops of the surrounding herbage. The grass and reeds, among which it was made, grew in the midst of water, and it was discovered by mere accident in a hunt for rail's eggs. It was found, June 28, on the edge of Lake Koskonong. It is a large nest for the bird; its base and sides are made of masses of soft lichens and mosses, and within this a neat and firm nest is woven of bits of wool and fine wiry stems of grasses, and lined with the same. The eggs measure .70 by .54 of an inch, are white with a pinkish tinge, and are marked with reddish-brown and fainter lilac blotches at the larger end.

Empidonax pusillus, var. trailli, BAIRD.

TRAILL'S FLYCATCHER.

Muscicapa trailli, AUD. Orn. Biog. I, 1832, 236 ; V, 1839, 426, pl. xlv. — IB. Syn. 1839, 43. — IB. Birds Am. I, 1840, 234, pl. lxv. *Tyrannula trailli*, RICH. List, 1837. — BONAP. List, 1838. *Tyrannus trailli*, NUTTALL, Man. I, (2d ed.,) 1840, 323. *Empidonax trailli*, BAIRD, Birds N. Am. 1858, 193. — SCLATER, Catal. 1862, 231. — SAMUELS, 140.

SP. CHAR. Third quill longest; second scarcely shorter than fourth ; first shorter than fifth, about .35 shorter than the longest. Primaries about .75 of an inch longer than secondaries. Tail even. Upper parts dark olive-green; lighter under the wings, and duller and more tinged with ash on nape and sides of the neck. Centre of the crown-feathers brown. A pale yellowish-white ring (in some specimens altogether white) round the eye. Loral feathers mixed with white. Chin and throat white ; the breast and sides of throat light ash tinged with olive, its intensity varying in individuals, the former sometimes faintly tinged with olive. Sides of the breast much like the back. Middle of the belly nearly white; sides of the belly, abdomen, and the lower tail-coverts, sulphur-yellow. The quills and tail-feathers dark brown, as dark (if not more so) as these parts in *C. virens*. Two olivaceous yellow-white bands on the wing, formed by the tips of the first and second coverts, succeeded by a brown one ; the edge of the first primary and of secondaries and tertials a little lighter shade of the same. The outer edge of the tail-feathers like the back; that of the lateral one rather lighter. Bill above dark brown ; dull brownish beneath. Length, nearly 6.00 ; wing, 2.90 ; tail, 2.60. *Young* with the wing-bands ochraceous instead of grayish-olive.

HAB. Eastern United States and south to Mexico. Localities : ? Isthmus of Panama (LAWR. VIII, 63) ; ? San Antonio, Texas (DRESSER, Ibis, 1865, 474, breeds); ? Costa Rica (LAWR. IX, 114) ; Yucatan (LAWR. IX, 201). All these localities, except perhaps the last, are to be questioned, as being more properly in the habitat of var. *pusillus*.

This species is most closely related to *E. minimus,* but differs in larger size and the proportions of quills. The middle of the back is the same color in both, but instead of becoming lighter and tinged with ash on the rump and upper tail-coverts, these parts very rarely differ in color from the back. The markings on the wings, instead of being dirty white, are decidedly olivaceous-grayish. The yellow of the lower parts is deeper. The tail-feathers are rather broad, acuminate, and pointed ; in *minimus* they are narrow and more rounded, while the tail itself is emarginated, instead of square, as in the present bird. The bill is larger and fuller. The legs are decidedly shorter in proportion.

HABITS. Traill's Flycatcher was first described by Mr. Audubon as a western bird, procured from Arkansas. In his subsequent reference to this species he also speaks of it as identical with several birds obtained by Townsend near the Columbia River, but which our present knowledge as to the distribution of this species compels us to presume to have been specimens of the *Empidonax pusillus,* a closely allied species or race. That Traill's Flycatcher does occur in Arkansas, on the other hand, is rendered probable by its abundance in other parts of the country, making this region directly within its range of migration. Dr. Woodhouse found it very common both in Texas and in the Indian Territory. Mr. Dresser found it common during the summer season near San Antonio, and to the eastward, breeding there, and building a small hanging nest. He also had its eggs sent to him from Systerdale. The stomach of the specimen he procured contained minute insects. It is mentioned by Dr. E. Coues as found in South Carolina, but whether as a migrant or as a resident is not stated. Dr. William P. Turnbull refers to it as rare near Philadelphia, and as only a spring and autumnal migrant. Mr. McIlwraith cites it as a rare summer visitant near Hamilton, Canada West. It is mentioned by Mr. Boardman as found near Calais, but has not been recorded as occurring in Nova Scotia, as far as I am aware. In Western Maine, Professor Verrill found it a regular but not a common summer visitant, arriving there the third week in May. And Mr. Brewster found it breeding in considerable abundance near Lake Umbagog in the summer of 1872.

In Massachusetts it has been found to occur very irregularly, and so far chiefly as a migrant, at least I am not aware that it has been known, except in a single instance, to breed within the limits of that State. It passes through the State about the middle of May, is rare some seasons, much more abundant for a few days in others. Near Springfield Mr. Allen regarded it as a rather rare summer visitant, arriving from the 10th to the 15th of May, and also mentioned it as probably breeding. A number have been taken in Lynn by Mr. Welch, but none have been observed to remain more than a day or two. Mr. Maynard once met with it on the 1st of June, 1869, in a swampy thicket. It was very shy, and he heard no note.

This species was observed by Mr. Paine, at Randolph, Vt., where it was found to be a not uncommon, though very retiring and shy species. It was found frequenting shady thickets, on the borders of the mountain streams, and several of its nests were procured. The bird was thoroughly identified, specimens of the parents having been sent to Professor Baird for verification. Mr. Paine was not able to obtain much insight into the manners and habits of this species, on account of its shyness. The nests were always placed in low alder-bushes, near running streams, and not more than three or four feet from the ground.

Mr. Paine has since informed me that Traill's Flycatcher reaches Central Vermont from the 20th to the 25th of May, and is one of the last birds to arrive, coming in company with *Contopus virens* and *C. borealis*. They all leave before the close of September. Mr. Paine has met with a great many nests of this species, but has only found one containing more than three eggs. It has a very simple song, consisting of but two notes. It has also a sort of twitter as it plays with its mate. They are usually found in thickets, for the most part near water, but not always, and are never seen in tall woods. They are occasionally seen chasing one another in the open fields.

Mr. William Brewster informs me that he found Traill's Flycatcher moderately common and breeding at the foot of Mount Washington, in the Glen, in August, 1869, and in the township of Newry, Me., in June, 1871. Their favorite haunts were the dense alder thickets along the runs and small streams, over these dark retreats, perched on some tall dead branch, full in the rays of the noonday sun. The male sang vigorously, occasionally darting out after some insect, and returning to the same perch. His song consisted of a single dissyllabic refrain, *ke'wing*, uttered in a harsh peevish tone at an interval of about thirty seconds, varied occasionally to *ke'wink*, or *ki-winch*. At each utterance his head is thrown upwards with a sudden jerk. They were retiring, but not shy, were easily approached, and were apparently not so restless as most Flycatchers.

Near Washington, Dr. Coues found Traill's Flycatcher a rare spring and fall visitant, a few possibly remaining to breed. They came about the last of April, and passed south the last of September. Professor Baird frequently met with them about Carlisle, Pa.'

In Southern Illinois, Mr. Ridgway has found this species a rather common summer resident, chiefly met with in the open woods. It was found nesting in Northwestern Massachusetts by Mr. A. Hopkins, in Illinois by Mr. Tolman, in New Brunswick by Mr. Barnstow, and at Fort Resolution by Messrs. Kennicott, Ross, and Lockhart.

I have myself found this species on the banks of the Androscoggin and Peabody Rivers in Gorham, and met with several of their nests. They were all in similar situations, and it was quite impossible to obtain a glimpse of the bird after she had left her nest. The nests were all made like those of the Indigo-Bird, externally of dry grasses and fine strips of bark, and lined with finer stems of grasses. The eggs were five in number, and incubation commenced about the first of June. I have discovered their nests at the same time among the foot-hills at the base of Mount Washington, its wooded sides being, at the time, covered with snow to the depth of several feet.

Among the memoranda of Mr. Kennicott I find one dated Fort Resolution, July 9, mentioning the procuring of the parent nest and egg of this species. The nest was three feet from the ground, in a small spruce among thick low bushes. The female was shot on the nest, which contained two young and two eggs. Eggs of this species from Gorham, N. H., and Coventry and Randolph, Vt., do not essentially vary in size or shape. They measure .63 of an inch in length, by .56 in breadth. Their ground-color is white, with a distinctly roseate tinge. They are oval in shape, a little less obtuse at one end, and marked almost entirely about the larger end with large and well-defined spots and blotches of purplish-brown.

Empidonax minimus, BAIRD.

LEAST FLYCATCHER.

Tyrannula minima, WM. M. and S. F. BAIRD, Pr. A. N. Sc. I, July, 1843, 284. — IB.
Sillim. Am. Jour. Sc. July, 1844. — AUD. Birds Am. VII, 1844, 343, pl. ccccxci.
Empidonax minimus, BAIRD, Birds N. Am. 1858, 195. — SCLATER, Catal. 1862, 229.
— SAMUELS, 141.

SP. CHAR. Second quill longest; third and fourth but little shorter ; fifth a little less; first intermediate between fifth and sixth. Tail even. Above olive-brown, darker on the head, becoming paler on the rump and upper tail-coverts. The middle of the back most strongly olivaceous. The nape (in some individuals) and sides of the head tinged with ash. A ring round the eye and some of the loral feathers white; the chin and throat white. The sides of the throat and across the breast dull ash, the color on the latter sometimes nearly obsolete ; sides of the breast similar to the back, but of a lighter tint; middle of the belly very pale yellowish-white, turning to pale sulphur-yellow on the sides of the belly, abdomen, and lower tail-coverts. Wings brown ; two narrow white bands on the wing, formed by the tips of the first and second coverts, succeeded by one of brown. The edge of the first primary, and of the secondaries and tertials, white. Tail rather lighter brown, edged externally like the back. Feathers narrow, not acuminate, with the ends rather blunt. In autumn the white parts are strongly tinged with yellow. Length, about 5.00 ; wing, 2.65 ; tail, 2.50. Young with ochraceous, instead of grayish-white wing-bands.

HAB. Eastern United States to Missouri Plains; Mirador; Orizaba; Belize. Localities : Oaxaca (SCL. 1859, 384) ; Guatemala (SCL. Ibis, I, 122) ; Orizaba (SCL. Ibis, I, 441, and Mus. S. I.) ; Coban, Escuintla, Dueñas (SCL. Catal. 1862, 229) ; San Antonio, Texas (DRESSER, Ibis, 1865, 474, common, summer).

HABITS. The distinctness of this species from the *acadica*, with which it had been previously confused, was first pointed out by the Messrs. Baird in 1843, but it was some time before the complete differences between the two species and their distinctive habits and distribution were fully appreciated and known. This species, one of the commonest birds in the State of Massachusetts, where the *E. acadica* is nearly or quite unknown, was supposed by Mr. Nuttall to be the latter species, and under that name is treated and its history given. Wilson contributed to cause this error. For although his account of the *acadica* is in part correct, it is not wholly free from error, and probably the nest and eggs described as belonging to the latter were those of the *minima*. The discovery, by Professor Baird, of the nest and eggs of the *acadica*, and their marked difference in all respects from those of the *minima*, which had hitherto been attributed to it, at once pointed out the errors that had prevailed, and permitted the real facts to be appreciated.

This bird is an abundant species throughout Eastern North America, occurring as a migrant in all the States between the Atlantic and the Great Plains, and breeding from the 40th parallel northward over an extent not fully defined, but probably to within the Arctic Circle. It occurs in great numbers from Maine to Nebraska, and, unlike all the other species of this genus, is not shy or retiring, but frequents the open grounds, visits gardens, is found in the vicinity of dwellings, and breeds even in the vines that half conceal their windows and doors.

This Flycatcher reaches Washington, according to Dr. Coues, the last of April, and remains about two weeks. It returns in autumn the third week in August, and remains till the last of September. It is only a spring and autumnal visitant, none breeding, and is rather common. It frequents the margins of small streams and brooks.

I am not aware that the nest of this species has ever been procured farther south than New York City, yet it is given by Mr. Dresser as having been found common by him, through the summer, near San Antonio. It is not, however, mentioned by Dr. Woodhouse, nor by the Mexican Survey, nor was it met with by Sumichrast in Vera Cruz. It is cited by Dr. Coues as only a migrant in South Carolina. Near Philadelphia Mr. Turnbull gives it as a somewhat rare migrant, passing north in April and returning in September, but adds that a few remain to breed. I did not find it breeding in the vicinity of Newark, nor, among a very extensive collection of nests and eggs made in that neighborhood, were there any eggs of this species. It is mentioned by Mr. Boardman as occurring at Calais, and in the western part of the State Mr. Verrill found it a very common summer visitant, arriving there about the middle of May and breeding there in numbers. It is also an exceedingly frequent summer visitant at Hamilton, Canada West, according to Mr. McIlwraith. It is found during the winter months near Oaxaca, Mexico, according to Mr. Boucard, and has been met with throughout Mexico and south to Guatemala.

In Massachusetts this Flycatcher is one of the most abundant and familiar species, arriving from about the 20th of April to the 1st of May. It is found most frequently in orchards, gardens, and open grounds, and very largely on the edges of woods, remaining until October. They are much addicted to particular localities, and return to the same spot year after year, if undisturbed. A pair that had established their hunting-grounds in an open area north of a dwelling in Roxbury returned to the same spot for several successive years, and would come regularly to the piazza of the house, where bits of cotton were exposed for the benefit of such of the whole feathered tribe as chose to avail themselves of it. Each year they drew nearer and nearer the house, until at last the nest was made in a clump of honeysuckle on the corner of the piazza, from which they would sally forth in quest of insects, entirely unmindful of the near presence of the family. I never observed the quarrelsome disposition that Nuttall speaks of, nor have I ever seen them molest other birds, even when the summer Yellow-Birds and the Chipping Sparrows have nested in the same clump. They are very silent birds, having no song and no other cry or note than a very feeble, guttural utterance, given out either as a single sound or as a succession of twitters. Their nest is a very common receptacle for the eggs of the Cow Blackbird.

This species was found breeding at Fort Resolution, latitude 62°, by Mr. Kennicott, the nest being in an alder-bush, and about five feet from the ground. It was also found nesting in the same locality by Mr. Ross and by Mr. Lockhart. Its nest was found at Lake Manitobah by Mr. McTavish, and at Fort Simpson by Mr. Ross.

This species has been gradually undergoing certain modifications of habits and manners in consequence of its contact with civilization and becoming familiarized to the society of man. In nothing is this made more apparent than in the construction of its nests. Those made on the edge of woodlands or in remote orchards are wrought almost entirely of fine deciduous bark, hempen fibres of vegetables, feathers, dried fragments of insect cocoons, and other miscellaneous substances felted and impacted together; within this is a lining of fine strips of vegetable bark, woody fibres, fine lichens, and soft downy feathers. In some the lining is exclusively of fine pine leaves, in others with the seeds or pappus of compositaceous plants. The nests are always quite small, rarely measuring more than three inches in diameter or two in height. Those made in the vicinity of dwellings indicate their neighborhood by the variety of miscellaneous and convenient materials, such as bits of paper, rags, cotton, wool, and the larger and more conspicuous feathers of the poultry-yard. Where raw cotton was abundantly provided, I have known this material, strengthened with a few straws and woody fibres, with a lining of feathers, constitute the whole substance of the nest.

One nest, constructed in a thick tamarack swamp in Wisconsin, is composed of a dense, impacted mass of a dirty white vegetable wool, intertwined at the base with shreds of bark, vegetable stems, and small black roots. The inner rim and frame of the nest are made of black, shining rootlets, intermingled with slender leaves and stems of dry sedges, and lined with the pappus of a small composite plant and a few feathers.

The eggs of this species are pure white, never, so far as I am aware, spotted, of a rounded-oval shape, nearly equally obtuse at either end, and measuring about .60 of an inch in length by .50 in breadth.

Empidonax acadicus, BAIRD.

SMALL GREEN-CRESTED FLYCATCHER.

? Muscicapa acadica, GMELIN, Syst. Nat. I, 1788, 947. — LATHAM, Index Orn. II, 1790, 489. — VIEILLOT, Ois. Am. Sept. I, 1807, 71 (from LATHAM). — AUD. Orn. Biog. II, 1834, 256; V, 1839, 429, pl. cxliv. — IB. Birds Am. I, 1840, 221, pl. lxii. — NUTTALL, Man. I, 1832, 208. — GIRAUD, Birds L. Island, 1844, 40. *Muscicapa querula*, WILSON, Am. Orn. II, 1810, 77, pl. xiii, f. 3 (not of VIEILLOT). "*Platyrhynchus virescens*, VIEILLOT." *Tyrannula acadica*, RICHARDSON, ? Bon. List. *Tyrannus acadica*, NUTTALL, Man. I, (2d ed.,) 1840, 320. *Empidonax acadicus*, BAIRD, Birds N. Am. 1858, 197. — SCLATER, Catal. 1862, 229. — SAMUELS, 143.

SP. CHAR. The second and third quills are longest, and about equal; the fourth a little shorter; the first about equal to the fifth, and about .35 less than the longest. Tail even.

The upper parts, with sides of the head and neck, olive-green; the crown very little if any darker. A yellowish-white ring round the eye. The sides of the body under the wings like the back, but fainter olive; a tinge of the same across the breast; the chin, throat, and middle of the belly white; the abdomen, lower tail and wing coverts, and sides of the body not covered by the wings, pale greenish-yellow. Edges of the first primary, secondaries, and tertials margined with dull yellowish-white, most broadly on the latter. Two transverse bands of pale yellowish (sometimes with an ochrey tinge) across the wings, formed by the tips of the secondary and primary coverts, succeeded by a brown one. Tail light brown, margined externally like the back. Upper mandible light brown above; pale yellow beneath. In autumn the lower parts are more yellow. Length, 5.65; wing, 3.00; tail, 2.75. *Young* (60,892 Mt. Carmel, Ill., August 11, 1870; R. Ridgway.) Whole upper surface with indistinct transverse bars of pale ochraceous; wing-markings light ochraceous.

Hab. Eastern United States to the Mississippi; Yucatan. Localities: Cuba (Lawr. VII, 1860, 265; Gundl. Rept. 1865, 240); San Antonio, Texas, summer (Dresser, Ibis, 1865, 475).

This species is very similar to *E. trailli,* but the upper parts are of a brighter and more uniform olive-green, much like that of *Vireo olivaceus.* The feathers of the crown lack the darker centre. There is less of the olivaceous-ash across the breast. The bands across the wing are light yellowish, instead of grayish-olive. There is much more yellow at the base of the lesser quills. The wings are longer, both proportionally and absolutely. The primaries exceed the secondaries by nearly an inch, instead of by only about .70; the proportions of the quills are much the same.

Habits. This species belongs to Eastern North America, but its distribution north and east is not determined with entire certainty. I have never met with or received any evidence of its breeding northeast of Philadelphia. Nuttall's account of this bird so blends what he had ascertained in regard to the habits of a different species with what he derived from other writers, that his whole sketch must be passed as unreliable. It is shy and retiring in its habits, frequenting only lonely places, and would readily escape notice, so that its presence in New Jersey, New York, and even New England, may not be uncommon, although we do not know it. Mr. Lawrence mentions its occurring in the vicinity of New York City; but I can find no evidence whatever that a single specimen of this bird has ever been procured in any part of New England, except Mr. Allen's mention of finding it near Springfield. That it is found in the immediate neighborhood of Philadelphia I have positive evidence, having received its nest and eggs, found in West Philadelphia. Mr. Turnbull gives it as of frequent occurrence from the beginning of May to the middle of September. He generally met with it in the most secluded parts of woods. Mr. McIlwraith calls it a rare summer resident near Hamilton, Canada West.

I am informed by Mr. Thomas H. Jackson, an accurate observer, resident in Westchester, Pa., that this Flycatcher arrives in that neighborhood early in May, constructing its nest about the first of June. This is generally placed on a drooping limb of a beech or dogwood tree at the height of from six to ten feet from the ground. It is never saddled on a limb like that of a Wood Pewee, neither is it pensile like those of the Vireos, but is built in the fork of a small limb, and securely fastened thereto by a strip of bark. The nest itself is mostly made of fine strips of bark or weedstalks, woven together without much care as to neatness or strength, and so very slight is the structure that you may often count the eggs in the nest from below. Occasionally this bird constructs its nest of the blossoms of the hickory-tree, and when thus made is very neat and pretty.

The eggs are generally three in number (Mr. Jackson has never known more in a nest), and they are said to be of a rich cream-color, thinly spotted near the greater end. The Cow-Bird sometimes imposes on this species with its parasitic offspring, but not so often as upon other birds.

Mr. Jackson also informs me that this is quite a common bird in some localities. In one piece of woodland, half a mile east of West Chester, he can every season meet with six or eight of their nests, while in another direction, in a wood apparently similar in every respect, he has never met with any.

Mr. J. A. Allen mentions finding this Flycatcher as a rare summer visitant in Western Massachusetts, where, as he states, it breeds in swamps and low moist thickets, which are its exclusive haunts. He characterizes it as one of the most spirited and tyrannical of this genus. It is said to have a short quick note, sounding like *quequeal,* which it utters hurriedly and sharply, and to have an erect, hawk-like attitude. He adds that it is very quarrelsome with its own species, a battle ensuing whenever two males meet. They pursue each other fiercely, with snapping bills and sharp, querulous, twittering notes. He found it a very shy bird, and difficult to collect, frequenting exclusively, so far as he was able to observe, thick alder-swamps and swampy thickets, keeping concealed among the thick bushes, or at a great distance.

Wilson's history of this species is quite brief, and he expressly states that it is a bird but little known. His account of its nest and eggs is inaccurate, and refers probably to that of the *minimus,* as also the statement that it extends its migrations as far as Newfoundland. He found it inhabiting only the deepest solitary parts of the woods, stationed among the lower branches, uttering at short intervals a sudden, sharp squeak, heard at considerable distance through the woods. As it flies, it utters a low, querulous note, which it changes, on alighting, to its usual sharp cry. He adds that it is a rare and very solitary bird, always haunting the most gloomy, moist, and unfrequented parts of the forest, feeding on flying insects, devouring wild bees and huckleberries in their season.

To this account Audubon furnishes but little additional that is reliable. He evidently confounded with it the *minimus,* repeats Wilson's description of its eggs, and is incorrect as to its northern distribution. He speaks of it as extremely pugnacious, chasing from its premises every intruder, and when once mated seldom leaving the vicinity of its nest except in pursuit of food. His description of the nest applies to that of the *minimus*, but not to that of this species.

Mr. Ridgway writes me that in Southern Illinois it is the most abundant of the *Empidonaces*, breeding in the same woods with *E. trailli*. It is so exceedingly similar to that species in manners and general habits that they are hard to distinguish, and it requires a long acquaintance with the two in the woods to learn to distinguish them when seen or heard. A close attention, however, shows that the notes of the two are quite distinct.

Mr. Dresser mentions finding this species not uncommon near San Antonio, Texas, during the summer. Its stomach was found to contain small insects. Dr. Woodhouse also speaks of it as common in Texas, New Mexico, and the Indian Territory, but at what season is not mentioned.

Dr. Hoy writes me that this bird, quite common about Racine some twenty-five years ago, has now almost entirely disappeared.

Near Washington Dr. Coues found this Flycatcher a common summer resident, the most abundant of the kind, and the only one that breeds there in any numbers. They arrive the last of April, and remain until the last of September.

A beautiful nest of this species was found by Mr. George O. Welch near Indianapolis, Indiana. It was fully identified, and the parent shot. This nest has a diameter of four inches, and a height of two. Its base is composed to a large extent of dried grasses, intermingled with masses of withered blossoms of different herbaceous plants. Above this is constructed a somewhat rudely interwoven nest, composed entirely of long, fine, wiry stems of grasses. The cavity is two inches wide and less than one in depth. The eggs, three in number, are exceedingly beautiful, and differ from all the eggs of this genus, having more resemblance to those of *Contopi*. They have an elongated oval shape, and are quite pointed at one end. They measure .78 by .56 of an inch. Their ground is a rich cream-color, tinged with a reddish-brown shading, and at the larger end the eggs are irregularly marked with scattered and vivid blotches of red and reddish-brown. The nest was found on the 3d of June.

Empidonax flaviventris, BAIRD.

YELLOW-BELLIED FLYCATCHER.

Tyrannula flaviventris, WM. M. and S. F. BAIRD, Pr. Ac. Nat. Sc. Phila. I, July, 1843,
    283. — IB. Am. Journ. Science, April, 1844. — AUD. Birds Am. VII, 1844, 341, pl.
    ccccxc.   *Tyrannula pusilla* (SWAINSON), REINHARDT, Vidensk. Meddel. for 1853,
    1854, 82. — GLOGER, Cab. Jour. 1854, 426.   *Empidonax hypoxanthus,* BAIRD (pro-
    visional name for eastern specimens).   *Empidonax difficilis,* BAIRD (provisional name
    for western).   *Empidonax flaviventris,* BAIRD, Birds N. Am. 1859, 198. — SCLATER,
    Catal. 1862, 229. — MAYNARD, B. E. Mass. 1870, 126.

SP. CHAR. Second, third, and fourth quills nearly equal; first intermediate between
fifth and sixth. Tail nearly even, slightly rounded. Tarsi long. Above bright olive-
green (back very similar to that of *Vireo noveboracensis*); crown rather darker. A
broad yellow ring round the eye. The sides of the head, neck, breast and body, and a
band across the breast like the back, but lighter; the rest of the lower parts bright
greenish sulphur-yellow ; no white or ashy anywhere on the body. Quills dark brown;
two bands on the wing formed by the tips of the primary and secondary coverts, the
outer edge of the first primary and of the secondaries and tertials pale yellow, or greenish-
yellow. The tail-feathers brown, with the exterior edges like the back. The bill dark
brown above, yellow beneath. The feet black. In the autumn the colors are purer, the
yellow is deeper, and the markings on the wings of an ochrey tint. Length, 5.15 ; wing,
2.83 ; tail, 2.45.

HAB. Eastern United States, and Eastern Middle America, south to Costa Rica. Localities: Guatemala (SCL. Ibis, I, 122); Xalapa (SCL. Ibis, I, 441); Choctun, Dueñas,
(SCL. Catal. 1862, 230); Costa Rica (LAWR. IX, 114); Panama (LAWR. VIII, 63); Vera
Cruz, winter, resident? (SUM. M. B. S. I, 557) ; San Antonio, Texas (DRESSER, Ibis, 1865,
475).

Specimens from the eastern regions of North and Middle America,
though varying slightly among themselves, all agree in the characters which
distinguish them from the western series.

HABITS. This well-marked species was first obtained in Carlisle, Penn.,
and described by the Bairds in 1843. It has since remained a comparatively
rare and scattered species, and has been only seldom met with. I found it
breeding in the vicinity of Halifax, and also among the Grand Menan
Islands, and in both cases was so fortunate as to be able to obtain its nest
and eggs. It has been found near Calais by Mr. Boardman, and its nest
also procured. It has also been found breeding near Trenton, N. J., by
Dr. Slack, and in a not distant locality in the same State by Dr. Abbott.

Dr. Coues observed the Yellow-bellied Flycatcher to be a rather rare
spring and autumnal visitant at Washington. As specimens were taken there
July 28, undoubtedly they occasionally breed there. They appear early in
May, and go south the latter part of September.

Two specimens of Flycatcher, identified as of this species, are recorded
by Professor Reinhardt as having been taken at Godthaab, Greenland, in
1853.

Sumichrast met with this species in Vera Cruz, but whether as a resident

or only as a migrant he could not determine. Mr. Dresser states that it is
common in the summer near San Antonio, arriving there in April. Dr.
Coues met it in its migrations through South Carolina. Dr. Turnbull speaks
of it as rare in the neighborhood of Philadelphia, where it arrives in the
middle of April on its way north. It has been found throughout Eastern
Mexico and Guatemala, and as far south as Panama.

Mr. Verrill regarded this species as a summer resident in Western Maine,
though he never met with its nest, and at no time very common. Specimens were procured between the last of May and the middle of June. It
was found, though very rare, by Mr. McIlwraith, at Hamilton, where it was
supposed to be a summer resident. Specimens were taken about the middle
of May.

Dr. Hoy detected this species in the summer of 1869, in the vicinity of
Racine, and although he had no doubt that they had a nest in the vicinity,
he was not able to discover it. He was surprised to find that the male of
this species has quite a pretty song. This fact has since been confirmed by
the observations of Mr. Boardman, who has heard this bird give forth quite
a pleasing, though somewhat monotonous trill. This, according to Dr. Hoy,
resembles *Pēa-wāyk-pēa-wāyoc*, several times repeated in a soft and not unpleasant call or song.

In Western Massachusetts Mr. Allen has found this species rather rare.
Those met with have all been taken from May 15 to June 5. Dr. Coues,
in his List of the birds of New England, expresses his conviction that this
species is probably much less rare than collectors have generally supposed.
It harbors very closely in shady woods and thickets, and is very rarely to be
met with anywhere else. In the distance it is not easily distinguished from
other species of this genus, and may have been allowed to go unsought,
mistaken for a much more common species. Mr. Allen has generally met
with quite a number each year in May, sometimes several in a single excursion. Mr. Maynard took eight specimens in a few hours, May 31, in Eastern
Massachusetts, and Mr. Welch obtained an unusual number in a single season.
Dr. Coues has also met with them near Washington during their breeding-
season.

At Grand Menan I found the nest of this species in a low alder-bush, on
the edge of a thicket, but within a few feet of the shore. The nest was
about two feet from the ground, placed in the fork of the bush, and bearing
a close resemblance to the nest of the *Cyanospiza cyanea*. It was loosely
made of soft strips of the inner bark of deciduous trees, and lined with
yellow stems of grasses. It was not large for the bird, but the conspicuous
color of the materials at once betrayed the nest as we chanced to land within
a few feet of it. The female immediately slid from it, and was not seen
again, but her mate was undisturbed by our presence. Afterwards other
nests were obtained at Halifax, on the edge of swampy woods, made of
stubble, and placed in low bushes. All the eggs I obtained were white, of a

slightly more chalky hue than those of the *minimus*, and more oblong. Those procured by Mr. Boardman were sprinkled with minute dots of reddish-brown. Their measurement is .68 by .52 of an inch.

Empidonax flaviventris, var. difficilis, BAIRD.

WESTERN YELLOW-BELLIED FLYCATCHER.

Empidonax difficilis, BAIRD, Birds N. Am. 1858, 198 (under *E. flaviventris*), pl. lxxvi, f. 2.
— SCLATER, Catal. 1862, 230. *Empidonax flaviventris*, COOPER, Orn. Cal. I, 1870, 328.

SP. CHAR. Similar to *flaviventris*, but tail much longer, and colors lighter and duller. The olive above less green, and the sulphur-yellow beneath less pure, having an ochraceous cast, this especially marked on the edge of the wing; wing-bands grayish rather than yellowish white. Measurements, ♂ (58,550, Parley's Park, Wahsatch Mountains, Utah, August 5, 1869; C. KING, R. RIDGWAY): Wing, 2.90; tail, 2.80; wing-formula, 3, 4, 2, 5, 6, 1. *Young*. Wing-bands ochraceous, instead of grayish-white, with a sulphur-yellow tinge.

HAB. Western Province of United States, and Western Mexico. (Mazatlan, Colima, etc.) Fort Whipple, Arizona (COUES, P. A. N. S. 1866, 62).

HABITS. This Flycatcher is a western form, closely allied to our eastern *E. flaviventris*. It was met with by Dr. Coues in Arizona, where it was rather rare, and appeared to be a summer resident. It arrives in that Territory about the middle of April, and remains there until the latter part of September. Dr. Coues found it difficult to distinguish this form from our eastern *flaviventris*.

Dr. Cooper obtained at Monterey, Cal., specimens of the western types of this bird, having darker markings on the wing, which, however, he regards as only indicative of a young plumage, and not of specific distinctness. He found these birds chiefly frequenting woods of *Coniferæ*, and very silent, which, so far as the observation has any value, indicates a marked difference between the eastern and the western birds.

The eggs of this species are also different from any of the eastern *E. flaviventris* that I have ever seen, and are more like the eggs of *E. trailli* than of the other species of *Empidonax*. They measure .73 of an inch in length, by .58 in breadth, have a creamy-white ground, marked at the larger end with reddish-brown and purplish markings. They are of an oblong-oval shape. Mr. Ridgway met with this species only once in his western explorations, when he obtained a pair in a thick pine woods on the Wahsatch Mountains, in June. They were exceedingly retiring, and frequented dark woods, whose solitudes were shared besides only by the *Turdus auduboni* and *Myiadestes townsendi*. Their note was a *pit*, much more like that of some Warblers than like the notes of the other *Empidonaces*.

This species, called by Mr. Grayson "The Lonely Flycatcher," was found by him quite common in the Three Marias, islands off the Pacific coast of Mexico, as well as on the main coast, and also in California. The accustomed places of resort of this solitary little bird were, he states, the most retired and secluded dells of the forest. He there met with it beneath the canopy of the natural and shady grottos formed by the overlapping branches, intermingled with innumerable creeping plants, sitting upon some low twig watching for a passing fly. At other times it might be seen frequenting some secluded and shady little brook, near the surface of which it often darted upon the flies that skimmed over the surface of the water, ever and anon uttering a low and plaintive one-syllabled note.

Empidonax obscurus, BAIRD.

WRIGHT'S FLYCATCHER.

? *Tyrannula obscura*, SWAINSON, Syn. Mex. Birds, in Philos. Mag. I, 1827, 367. *Empidonax obscurus*, BAIRD, Birds N. Am. 1858, 200, pl. xlix, f. 3. — IB. M. B. II, Birds 9, pl. xi, f. 3. — SCL. Catal. 1862, 230. — COOPER, Orn. Cal. I, 1870, 329. *Empidonax wrighti*, BAIRD, Birds N. Am. 1858, 200 (name proposed in case this should prove not to be the *T. obscura* of Swainson).

SP. CHAR. Bill very narrow. Tarsi long. Wing rounded. Second, third, and fourth quills longest; first shorter than sixth, sometimes than seventh and eighth. Tail rounded. Above dull brownish-olive, paler on the rump, tinged with gray on the head. Loral region and space round the eye whitish. Throat and forepart of the breast grayish-white, slightly tinged with olive across the latter; the rest of the under parts pale yellowish. Wings and tail brown; the former with two conspicuous bands of brownish-white; the outer primary edged, the secondaries and tertials edged and tipped with the same. The outer web of the external tail-feather white, in strong contrast. Length, 5.75; wing, 2.75; tail, 2.55; tarsus, .70. *Young.* Wing-bands yellowish-gray, or grayish-buff (not ochraceous); upper parts with a brownish wash; abdomen tinged with dull buff.

HAB. Rocky Mountains and Middle Province of United States, and table-lands of Mexico. Localities: La Parada, Mexico (SCL. Catal. 1862, 230); Vera Cruz, winter, perhaps resident (SUM. M. B. S. I, 557); Fort Whipple, Arizona (COUES, P. A. N. S. 1866, 63).

The most decided character of this species is seen in the combination of the narrow bill and the white outer margin of the external tail-feather, together with the long tarsi. The bill measured across opposite the middle of the nostrils is less than half its length from the forehead, instead of being considerably more, as in nearly all the other North American species, except *hammondi*. From this, however, the longer tail, edged externally with white; the longer bill and tarsus, the more rounded wings, the paler throat, etc., will distinguish it. Some specimens (spring and summer individuals) are very pale, showing scarcely any yellow beneath; the upper parts more tinged with gray. Sometimes there is a decidedly hoary frontlet.

A young specimen (53,303, ♀, Upper Humboldt Valley, Nev., September

16, 1868; C. King, R. Ridgway) is remarkable for its pale and unusually grayish colors. There is nowhere any tinge of yellow, and scarcely any of brown, the colors being simply clear ash and pure dull white, except the dusky of wings and tail. In these respects it differs from all others in the collection; there can be no doubt, however, that it is the same species as the brownish individuals obtained in the same locality.

HABITS. This Flycatcher appears to have been first described as a Mexican species by Swainson in 1827. Since then it has been obtained by Sumichrast in the Department of Vera Cruz, but whether resident or only migratory he was unable to decide. Specimens were obtained at El Paso, in Texas, by Mr. C. Wright, on the Mexican Boundary Survey. Dr. Coues found this bird a summer resident in Arizona, but rare. It arrives there early in April, and remains until October. Dr. Cooper first observed this species at Fort Mohave about April 1, and a few afterwards until May 25. They kept among low bushes, were generally silent, or with only a single lisping chirp. Occasionally they flew a short distance after insects in the general manner of this genus. We are indebted to Mr. Ridgway for all the knowledge we possess in reference to the habits and nesting of this rare species.

He met with them in all the aspen groves and thickets of the high mountain regions, from the Sierra Nevada to the Wahsatch and Uintah Mountains. The aspen copses at the head of the cañons of the highest and well-watered ranges of the Great Basin were their favorite resort; but they were sometimes seen in the "mahogany" woods on the spurs, and occasionally, even, on the willows in the river valleys. Their common note was a weird *sweer*, much like the call of *Chrysomitris pinus*, but very often, especially when the nest was approached, they uttered a soft liquid *whit*. In the Toyabe Mountains, where these little Flycatchers were breeding abundantly in the aspen copses, Mr. Ridgway found them to be so unsuspicious that several were taken from the nest with his hand; and one which was shot at and slightly wounded returned to her nest and suffered herself to be taken off without showing any alarm.

A nest obtained by Mr. Ridgway near Austin, in Nevada, July 3, 1868, was built in the crotch of a small aspen, about five feet from the ground. This nest is a very neat, homogeneous, compact structure, cup-like in shape, three inches in diameter, and two and a half in height. Its cavity is one and a half inches in depth, and three inches across the rim. It is composed almost entirely of strips of soft and bleached fragments of the inner bark of deciduous trees and shrubs, and hempen fibres of various plants. The inner nest is a lining made of finer materials of the same, with a few fine roots and feathers.

The eggs, three in number, are of a uniform creamy white, unspotted, and not unlike the eggs of *Empidonax minimus*. They measure .73 of an inch in length, and .60 in breadth.

The nest and eggs of this species were also found by Mr. C. S. McCarthy, in Dodge Valley, July 2, 1859. The nest was in a low flowering bush, and was a few feet from the ground. It was likewise found breeding at Camp Grant, Arizona, by Dr. Palmer.

Empidonax hammondi, BAIRD.

HAMMOND'S FLYCATCHER.

Tyrannula hammondi, DE VESEY (XANTUS), Pr. A. N. Sc. May, 1858. *Empidonax hammondi*, BAIRD, Birds N. Am. 1858, 199, pl. lxxvi, f. 1. — SCLATER, Catal. 1862, 230. —COOPER, Orn. Cal. I, 1870, 330.

SP. CHAR. Tail moderately forked; the feathers acutely pointed. Third quill longest; second and then fourth a little shorter. First much shorter than fifth, a little longer than sixth. Bill very slender; dark brown. Above dark olive-green, considerably darker on the head. Breast and sides of the body light olive-green, the throat grayish-white; the rest of under parts bright sulphur-yellow. A whitish ring round the eye. Wings and tail dark brown; the former with two olivaceous gray bands across the coverts; the latter with the outer edge a little paler than elsewhere, but not at all white. Length, 5.50; wing, 2.80; tail, 2.50; tarsus, .67.

HAB. Mexico and Western Province of United States (Clark's Fork; Fort Laramie; Fort Tejon, Orizaba, and numerous intermediate points). North to Lesser Slave Lake, where breeding abundantly (S. JONES, Mus. S. I.). Localities: Vera Cruz, winter, perhaps resident (SUM. M. B. S. I, 557); W. Arizona (COUES, P. A. N. S. 1866, 62).

In this species the olive-green on the sides is scarcely distinguishable from that on the back, although becoming more yellow on the middle of the breast. There is a decided ashy shade on the whole head. The only light edging to the quills is seen on the terminal half of the secondaries. The upper mandible and feet are black; the tip of the lower (and in one specimen the whole) dark brown. The fork of the tail measures a quarter of an inch in depth; the longest quill exceeds the first by .40.

This species is at once distinguishable from all the North American *Tyrannulas*, except *obscurus*, by the extreme narrowness as well as shortness of the bill. This is only .25 of an inch wide at the posterior angle of the mouth, and only .19 at the nostrils. Its colors above are those of *acadicus*, while the general effect is much more that of *flaviventris*, although less brightly olive. The throat is grayish, not of the same yellow with the belly; the ring round the eye white, not yellow; the olive of the breast much more continuous and distinct; the bands on the wings dull grayish instead of clear greenish-yellow. The tail, instead of being nearly even, is quite deeply forked. The bill is scarcely half as wide, and brownish, not yellow, beneath. The tarsus has the same peculiar scutellation.

The differences from *T. obscurus* are less easily expressed. It is, however, considerably smaller, and more olivaceous above and below, the tarsi very much shorter; the most tangible character is seen in the absence of the white on the outer web of the external tail-feather, which is only a little paler brown than elsewhere. The abdomen is much more distinctly yellowish.

HABITS. This species was first discovered in the vicinity of Fort Tejon, Cal., by Mr. Xantus, in 1858, and described by him in the Proceedings of the Philadelphia Academy. It has since been taken in other parts of California and Mexico. Sumichrast found it in the Department of Vera Cruz; and Dr. Coues has taken it in Arizona, where he regarded it as a rather rare summer resident, arriving late in April and remaining until the third week in October.

Dr. Cooper obtained a single specimen of this species at Fort Mohave, May 20. It closely resembled *E. obscurus* in its habits at that time, and he mistook it for that species. He afterwards met with others, as supposed, of these birds, on Catalina Island, in June. They kept in low trees, and uttered a few faint lisping notes. The first of this species arrived at Santa Cruz, March 13, and they were numerous during the summer, disappearing in September. April 27, Dr. Cooper found the first nest. It was built on the horizontal branch of a negundo-tree, about eighteen feet from the ground. He found four others afterwards, from four to ten feet high, either on horizontal branches or on forks of small trees. They contained three or four eggs each, or young. The last one with eggs was found as late as June 29, probably a second nest of a pair that had been robbed. These nests were all thick walled, composed externally of dry mosses and downy buds, with a few strips of bark and leaves, and slender woody fibres, and often with a few hairs or feathers lining the inside. Externally the nests were about four inches wide and two and a half high. The cavity was two inches wide and one and a half deep. The eggs were white with brown blotches and specks near the larger end, disposed mostly in a circle. They measured .68 by .52 of an inch.

These birds, he further states, frequented only the darkest groves along the river, and had a very few simple call-notes of a monotonous character. They were so very shy that he could not get near enough to determine the species, which in all probability was not this species, but the *E. pusillus*.

The *E. hammondi* was met with by Mr. Ridgway only in the East Humboldt Mountains, where, in September, it was found in the thickest groves of tall aspens. It seemed to be confined to these localities, and was much more secluded than the *E. obscurus*. Its common note was a soft *pit*.

A number of nests and eggs sent, with the parent birds, from Lesser Slave Lake, by Mr. Strachan Jones, show that its eggs are unspotted creamy-white, like those of *E. minimus* and *E. obscurus*. Indeed, a number of nests and eggs of the former of these two species, also accompanied by the parent birds, could not be distinguished, except by their apparently just appreciably larger size, on the average.

Genus **MITREPHORUS**, Sclater.

Mitrephorus, Sclater, P. Z. S. 1859, 44.   (Type, *M. phæocercus*.)

Gen. Char.   Similar in general character to *M. empidonax*, but with fulvous, fulvous-olive and rufous tints, instead of clear olive, gray, white, and sulphur-yellow. Head crested; bristles of gape reaching nearly to tip of bill. Feet very weak.

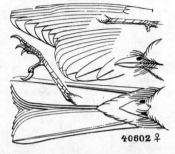

40602 ♀

The type of this genus (*M. phæocercus*) is quite different in form from *Empidonax*, the nearest North American ally, but both *M. pallescens* and *fulvifrons* could with little violence be placed in it.   There is no positive character to separate the latter from the average of species of *Empidonax*, except it be the color.   The crest is not at all conspicuous, nor is there any appreciable difference of form; while in the form of the bill these species are much nearer *Empidonax* than *Mitrephorus*.   The legs, however, are weaker, and the rictal bristles longer.

There are two forms of the group, as defined by Sclater: one embracing *E. phæocercus*, Sclater (Mexico and Guatemala), and *E. aurantiiventris*, Lawr. (Costa Rica); the other *E. fulvifrons*, Giraud, and *pallescens*, Coues.   The differences between the last two, which are probably merely races of one species, may be expressed as follows: —

M. fulvifrons.   Olivaceous above; beneath ochraceous-fulvous; darkest on the breast, paler on throat and crissum.   External edge of outer tail-feathers whitish.

> Olive of back fulvous; under parts decided ochrey-fulvous.   Wing-bands tinged with ochraceous; wing rather pointed.   First quill equal to sixth; third, longest.   Wing, 2.65; tail, 2.40; tarsus, .61.   *Hab.* Northern Mexico.
>
> <div align="right">var. <i>fulvifrons</i>.[1]</div>
>
> Olive of back grayish; beneath obscurely ochrey-fulvous and much paler; wing-bands grayish-white; wing rather rounded.   First quill shorter than sixth; fourth longest.   Length, 4.75; wing, 2.15; tail, 2.00; tarsus, .55.   *Hab.* Arizona   .   .   .   .   var. *pallescens*.

[1] *Mitrephorus fulvifrons.*   *Muscicapa fulvifrons*, Giraud, 16 species Texas birds, 1841, pl. ii (Mexico ?).   *Empidonax fulvifrons*, Sclater, P. Z. S. 1858, 301.   *Mitrephorus fulvifrons*, Sclater, P. Z. S. 1859, 45.   *Empidonax rubicundus*, Cabanis, Mus. Hein. ii, 1859, 70 (Mexico).   *Hab.* Northern Mexico.

Mitrephorus fulvifrons, var. pallescens, Coues.

BUFF-BREASTED LEAST FLYCATCHER.

Mitrephorus pallescens, Coues, Pr. Philad. Ac. 1866, 63 (Fort Whipple, Arizona). — Cooper, Orn. Calif. I, 334. *Mitrephorus fulvifrons*, Elliot, Illust. B. Am. I, pl. xix.

Sp. Char. Above fulvous-gray, with an ashy cast on the tail and crown; lighter across the nape. Two grayish-white bands across the wings, and the terminal half of the secondaries and outer web of lateral tail-feather broadly edged with the same. Whole lower parts, including the lores and cheeks, and lining of wing, light ochraceous, very deeply ochraceous across the breast and on the sides, nearly white on the abdomen and crissum. Upper mandible deep black, lower whitish ("bright orange-yellow" in life); feet deep black. Wing-formula: second, third, and fourth quills equal and longest, 5, 6, 1. Tail very slightly emarginated, but lateral feather a little the shortest. *Male.* Length, 4.75; wing, 2.25; tail, 2.00; culmen, .54 (measured to concealed base); breadth of bill, .24; tarsus, .54; middle toe, .28. *Female.* Colors paler; deep ochraceous of breast, etc., less distinct.

Hab. Southern border of Middle Province of United States (Fort Whipple, Arizona).

The true *M. fulvifrons* of Mexico differs simply in deeper colors, the shade above being decidedly fulvous, instead of grayish, and the lower parts much more deeply ochraceous, the abdomen not approaching white; the wing-markings are also tinged with ochraceous.

Habits. This species, both new to our fauna and previously undescribed, was taken by Dr. Coues at Fort Whipple. It belongs to a newly established genus of Flycatchers, recently established by Mr. Sclater, similar to *Empidonax*. So far as known, its members are more or less tropical in their residence. It is a rare summer resident at Fort Whipple, arriving there early in May. Nothing is stated in reference to its habits, except that they correspond with those of the *Empidonaces*.

Genus **PYROCEPHALUS**, Gould.

Pyrocephalus, Gould, Zoöl. of Beagle, 1838, 44.

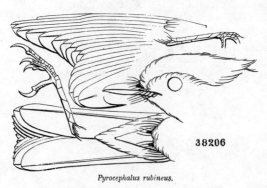

38206

Pyrocephalus rubineus.

Gen. Char. Tarsus moderate, very little longer than the middle toe; hind toe not longer than the lateral. Bill slender, very narrow at the base. Tail broad, even, considerably shorter than the wings (about four fifths), which reach beyond the middle of the tail. First quill shorter than the fifth. Head with a conspicuous rounded crest. Sexes dissimilar. Male with the crown and lower parts red (except in *E. obscurus*); tail, back, and wings dark brown.

The single North American species of this genus is readily distinguished among other Flycatchers by the bright red of the under parts. The female is quite different in color from the male, being peculiar in this respect among North American Flycatchers.

Species and Varieties.

E. obscurus.[1] Entirely uniform sepia-brown beneath, with a wine-purple tinge posteriorly and on the forehead. *Hab.* Peru.

E. rubineus. Whole crown, and entire lower parts (except lining of wing), brilliant scarlet-red; a stripe on side of the head, and entire upper parts, sepia-brownish. *Female.* Whitish anteriorly beneath, more or less reddish posteriorly; anterior portion with dusky streaks; crown dusky. *Young* without any red; feathers above bordered with lighter; streaks beneath numerous. Length, about 5.50.

The brown of a dark sepia cast, edges of wing-feathers not appreciably paler, the red with a slight carmine shade. No whitish on the edge of outer nor on tips of other tail-feathers. *Hab.* South America var. *rubineus*.[2]

Similar to last, but outer web of lateral tail-feather distinctly whitish, the rest tipped slightly with whitish. *Hab.* Northern South America (Bogota and Guayaquil) . . . . var. *nanus*.[3]

The brown of a decided grayish cast, and edges of wing-feathers very distinctly paler; red more scarlet (but equally intense). No whitish tips to tail-feathers, and no white edge to the outer. *Hab.* Middle America; north into southern border of United States . var. *mexicanus*.

Pyrocephalus rubineus, var. mexicanus, SCLATER.

RED FLYCATCHER.

Pyrocephalus rubineus, LAWRENCE, Ann. N. Y. Lyc. V, May, 1851, 115. CASSIN, Ill. I, IV, 1853, 127, pl. xvii. — BAIRD, Birds N. Am. 1858, 201. — SALVADORI, Atti. Milan. vii, 1864. — HEERM. X, *S,* 38. *Tyrannula coronata,* SWAINSON, WAGLER, Isis, 1831, 529. *Pyrocephalus nanus,* WOODHOUSE, Sitgreave's Report, 1853, 75 (not of GOULD). *Pyrocephalus mexicanus,* SCLATER, P. Z. S. 1859, 45, 56, 366; 1864, 176. — IB. Ibis, 1859, 442. — IB. Catal. 227. — SCLATER & SALVIN, Ibis, 1860, 399 (Guatemala). — CABANIS, Mus. Hein. ii, 1859, 68. — COOPER, Orn. Cal. I, 1870, 333.

SP. CHAR. Head with a full rounded or globular crest. Tail even. Crown and whole under parts bright carmine-red; rest of upper parts, including the cheeks as far as the bill, and the lining of the wing, dull grayish-brown; the upper tail-coverts darker; the tail almost black; greater and middle wing-coverts and edges of secondaries and tertials

---

[1] *Pyrocephalus obscurus,* GOULD, Zoöl. Voy. Beag. iii, 45. — SCLATER, P. Z. S. 1859, 46; Catal. Am. B. 1862, 228 (Peru).

[2] *Pyrocephalus rubineus,* (BODD.) CAB. *Muscicapa rubinea,* BODD. (ex Buff. pl. enl. cclxv, f. 1). *Pyrocephalus r.* CABANIS et HEIN. Mus. Hein. ii, p. 67. — SCLATER, Catal. Am. B. 1862, 227.

[3] *Pyrocephalus rubineus,* var. *nanus,* GOULD, Zoöl. Beag. iii, 45, pl. vii. — SCLATER, P. Z. S. 1859, 46, 144; 1860, 282, 295; Catal. Am. B. 1862, p. 228. The last is hardly separable by the characters given, as, although they are never seen in southern specimens, they are not constant in the northern ones. Specimens of *nanus* are as large as any of *rubineus,* there being in every region a great range of variation in dimensions.

dull white towards the edges. *Female* similar, without the crest; the crown brown, like the back; the under parts whitish anteriorly, streaked with brown; behind white, tinged with red or ochraceous. Length of male about 5.50; wing, 3.25; tail, 2.75. *Young* resembling the female, but lacking any trace of red, and with each feather of the upper parts bordered with whitish, producing a very variegated appearance.

HAB. Valleys of Rio Grande and Gila southward. Localities: Honduras (MOORE, P. Z. S. 1859, 55); Cordova (SCL. 1856, 296); Vera Cruz, hot to alpine regions (SUM. M. B. S. I, 557); Yucatan (LAWR. IX, 201); Arizona (COUES, P. A. N. S. 1866, 64).

Every stage between the youngest plumage described and the adult male may be found in a large series of immature specimens : the shade of the red

Pyrocephalus rubineus.

in both sexes frequently varies, it being sometimes of a slightly rosaceous tint, and again decidedly inclining to orange; its amount in the female varies almost with the individual. The two South American races (var. *nanus* and var. *rubineus;* see synopsis) differ in having the brown of upper parts, etc., very decidedly darker; no appreciable light edgings to wing-feathers, and sometimes an appreciably more intense red. One of them (*nanus*) has a distinct white outer edge to lateral tail-feather, and slight whitish tips to the other; the other has no more than a trace of these markings.

HABITS. This brilliant species is a rare summer visitant to Texas, New Mexico, Arizona, and probably Southern California. It is found throughout Middle America. It has only within a few years been known as a resident within our territory, but was first observed in Texas by Captain McCown, of the United States Army, in 1850, and its claim to a place in our fauna publicly made by Mr. G. N. Lawrence. Captain McCown, in some notes on the habits of certain Texan birds, published in the Annals of the N. Y. Lyceum, speaks of this Flycatcher as being seldom seen, and of his having noticed not more than a dozen in Western Texas. He always found them near ponds of water, in the vicinity of the Rio Grande, generally on a tree or a stake near the water. He only met with one nest, and this was inaccessible. It was built on an acacia over the water.

Lieutenant Couch, in a letter to Mr. Cassin, states that he first met with this bird at Charco Escondido, in Tamaulipas, on the 10th of March. The males had come in advance of the females, as the latter were not observed until several weeks afterwards. Early in the morning, and again about sunset, one of these birds came to the artificial lake constructed there for the supply of water to the inhabitants. It appeared to be of a very quiet and inoffensive disposition, usually sitting on the upper branches of the trees, occasionally uttering a low chirp. He subsequently met with these birds in Nueva

Leon. In their habits they appeared to be in some respects similar to the smaller northern Flycatchers.

Dr. Henry also met with these birds in the vicinity of Fort Webster, in New Mexico ; he found them exceedingly rare, and his observations were confirmatory of their partiality for the neighborhood of water. His first specimen was obtained on the Rio Mimbres, near Fort Webster, in the month of March.

Dr. Woodhouse met with an individual of this Flycatcher near the settlement of Quihi, in Texas, in the month of May. It was breeding in a thicket. He did not hear it utter any note.

According to the observations of Mr. Sumichrast, this bird is very abundant throughout the entire Department of Vera Cruz, common everywhere, at all heights, in the hot, the temperate, and the alpine regions. Mr. Dresser obtained a fine male specimen from the San Pedro River, near San Antonio, in August. Another, a young male, was obtained September 25. It was very shy, and made its way through the low bushes like the Hedge Sparrow of Europe. A third was obtained April 5, after much difficulty. It was not so shy as the others, but kept more in the open country, always perching on some elevated place. Its note resembled that of the *Milvulus forficatus.*

This bird, according to Dr. Coues, is not found as far to the north as Fort Whipple, among the mountains, though it extends up the valley of the Colorado to an equally high latitude. It is also said to be common in the valley of the Gila and in Southern Arizona generally.

Mr. E. C. Taylor (Ibis, VI, p. 86) mentions finding this Flycatcher tolerably abundant both at Ciudad Bolivar and at Barcelona, but he did not meet with a specimen on the island of Trinidad. He notes its great resemblance in habits to the *Muscicapæ* of Europe.

Dr. Kennerly reports that these birds were often observed by him at various points on the road, from Boca Grande to Los Nogales. It generally selected its perch on the topmost branch of some bush or tree, awaiting the approach of its insect food, and then sallying out to capture it. Sometimes it poised itself in a graceful manner in the air, while its bright plumage glistened in the sun like some brightly colored flower.

Dr. Heermann procured a specimen of this Flycatcher at Fort Yuma, where he was informed that it was quite common in spring. He saw other individuals of this species at Tucson in Sonora. These birds, he states, station themselves upon the topmost branches of trees, and when pursued appear quite wild, flying to a considerable distance before again alighting.

Dr. Cooper saw at Fort Mohave, May 24, a bird which he had no doubt was an individual of this species, but he was not able to procure it. It perched upon the tops of bushes, and would not suffer him to approach within shooting distance. One has since been taken by Mr. W. W. Holden in Colorado Valley, lat. 34°, April 18.

Mr. Joseph Leyland found this species common on the flats near Peten, in Guatemala, as also on the pine ridges of Belize. They have, he states, a singular habit of spinning round and round on the wing, and then dropping suddenly with wings loose and fluttering as though shot, — apparently done for amusement. They lay three or four light-colored eggs in a small nest composed of light grass and lined with cottony materials. Mr. Xantus found the nest and eggs of this species at San José, Mexico, May 16, 1861.

FAMILY **ALCEDINIDÆ.** — THE KINGFISHERS.

CHAR. Head large; bill long, strong, straight, and sub-pyramidal, usually longer than the head. Tongue very small. Wings short; legs small; the outer and middle toes united to their middle. Toes with the usual number of joints (2, 3, 4, 5).

The gape of the bill in the Kingfishers is large, reaching to beneath the eyes. The third primary is generally longest; the first decidedly shorter; the secondaries vary from twelve to fifteen in number, all nearly equal. The secondaries cover at least three quarters of the wing. The tail is short, the feathers twelve in number; they are rather narrow, the outer usually shorter. The lower part of the tibia is bare, leaving the joint and the tarsus uncovered. The tarsus is covered anteriorly with plates; behind, it is shagreen-like or granulated. The hind toe is connected with the inner, so as to form with it and the others a regular sole, which extends unbroken beneath the middle and outer as far as the latter are united. The inner toe is much shorter than the outer. The claws are sharp; the middle expanded on its inner edge, but not pectinated.

The North American species of Kingfisher belong to the subfamily *Cerylinæ,* characterized by the crested head, and the plumage varying with sex and age. The single genus *Ceryle* includes two types, *Streptoceryle* and *Chloroceryle.*

GENUS **CERYLE**, BOIE.

Ceryle, BOIE, Isis, 1828, 316, ch. (Type, *Alcedo rudis* of Africa.)
Ispida, Sw. Birds, II, 1837, 336. (Type, *A. alcyon,* in part.)

GEN. CHAR. Bill long, straight, and strong, the culmen slightly advancing on the forehead and sloping to the acute tip; the sides much compressed; the lateral margins rather dilated at the base, and straight to the tip; the gonys long and ascending. Tail rather long and broad. Tarsi short and stout.

This genus is distinguished from typical *Alcedo* (confined to the Old World) by the longer tail, an indented groove on each side the culmen, inner toe much longer than the hinder instead of equal, etc.

The two species of North American Kingfishers belong to two different subgenera of modern systematists, the one to *Streptoceryle,* Bonap., the other to *Chloroceryle,* Kaup. The characters of these subgenera are as follows:—

Streptoceryle, Bonap. (1854). Bill very stout and thick. Tarsus about equal to the hind toe; much shorter than the inner anterior. Plumage without metallic gloss; the occipital feathers much elongated, linear, and distinct. Type, *C. alcyon.*
Chloroceryle, Kaup (1849). Size smaller and shape more slender than in

the preceding. Bill long, thin. Tarsi longer than hind toe; almost or quite as long as the inner anterior. Plumage with a green metallic gloss above; the occiput with a crest of rather short, indistinct feathers. Type, *A. amazona*.

The genus *Ceryle* was established by Boie on the *Alcedo rudis*, of Linnæus, an African species. Modern systematists separate the American Kingfishers from those of the Old World, and if correct in so doing, another generic

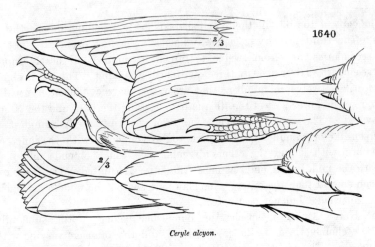

1640

Ceryle alcyon.

name must be selected for the former. If the two American sections be combined into one, *Chloroceryle* of Kaup (type, *Alcedo amazona*) must be taken as being the older, unless, indeed, *Ispida* of Swainson (1837) be admissible. This appears to have been based on *Alcedo alcyon*, although including also some Old World species.

Ceryle alcyon, Boie.

BELTED KINGFISHER.

Alcedo alcyon, Linnæus, Syst. Nat. I, 1766, 180. — Wilson, Am. Orn. III, 1811, 59. — Audubon, Orn. Biog. I, 1831, 384 ; pl. lxxvii. — Ib. Birds America. — Max. Cab. J. VI, 1858, 102. *Ceryle alcyon*, Boie, Isis, 1828, 316. — Brewer, N. Am. Oology, I, 1857, 110, pl. iv, fig. 52 (egg). — Wood, Am. Naturalist, 1868, 379 (nesting). — Baird, Birds N. Am. 1858, 158. — Cooper & Suckley, 167. — Dall & Bannister, Ch. Ac. I, i, 1869, 275 (Alaska). — Finsch, Abh. Nat. III, 1872, 29 (Alaska). — Samuels, 125. — Cooper, Orn. Cal. I, 1870, 337. — Allen, B. Fla. 300. *Megaceryle alcyon*, Reichenb. Handb. Sp. Orn. I, ii, 1851, 25, pl. ccccxii, fig. 3108 – 9. *Ispida ludoviciana*, Gmelin, Syst. Nat. I, 1788, 452. "*Alcedo jaguacate*, Dumont, Dict. Sc. Nat. I, 1816, 455" (Cassin). "*Alcedo guacu*, Vieillot, Nouv. Dict. XIX, 1818, 406," (Cassin). *Streptoceryle alcyon*, Cabanis, Mus. Hein. II, 151.

Sp. Char. Head with a long crest. Above ashy-blue, without metallic lustre. Beneath, with a concealed band across the occiput, and a spot anterior to the eye, pure white. A band across the breast, and the sides of the body under the wings, like the back.

Primaries white on the basal half, the terminal unspotted. Tail with transverse bands and spots of white. *Female* and *young* with sides of body and a band across the belly below the pectoral one light chestnut; the pectoral band more or less tinged with the same. Length of adult about 12.75 inches; wing, 6.00.

HAB. The entire continent of North America to Panama, including West Indies. Localities: Honduras (MOORE, P. Z. S. 1859, 53; SCL. Ibis, II, 116); Sta. Cruz, winter (NEWTON, Ibis, I, 67); Belize (SCL. Ibis, I, 131); York Factory, H. B. T. (MURRAY, Edinb. Phil. J. Jan 1860); Cuba (CAB. J. IV, 101; GUNDL. Rep. I. 1866, 292); Bahamas (BRYANT, Bost. Soc. VII, 1859); Jamaica (GOSSE, Birds Jam. 81; Orizaba (SCL. P. Z. S. 1860, 253); Panama (LAWR. N. Y. Lyc. 1861, 318 n.); Costa Rica (CAB. J. 1862,

Ceryle alcyon.

162; LAWR. N. Y. Lyc. IX, 118); Tobago (JARD. Ann. Mag. 19, 80); Texas (DRESSER, Ibis, 1865, 471); Arizona (COUES, P. A. N. S. 1866, 59); Sta. Bartholemy (SUND. Ofv. 1869, 585).

This species varies considerably in size with locality, as do so many others. Western specimens are appreciably larger, especially those from the northwest coast. According to Nuttall and Audubon, it is the female that has the transverse band of chestnut across the belly. In this they may be correct; but several specimens in the Smithsonian collection marked female (perhaps erroneously) show no indication of the chestnut.[1]

Two closely allied but much larger species belong to Middle and South America. They differ in having the whole body beneath of a reddish color.

HABITS. The common Belted Kingfisher of North America is a widely distributed species at all times, and in the summer is found in every portion of North America, to the Arctic Ocean on the north, and from the Atlantic to the Pacific. It is more or less resident throughout the year, and in mild and open winters a few have been known to linger throughout New England, and even in higher latitudes. In 1857 Captain Blakiston found it remaining on the lower part of the Saskatchewan River until the 7th of October; and afterwards, in 1859, at Pembina, on the 1st of May, he ob-

---

[1] This confounding of the two sexes has probably resulted from guess-work of the collector, who, noticing the marked difference between the male and female, and naturally supposing the former to be the more brightly colored, marked the rufous-breasted specimens accordingly; while the few marked correctly may have been thus labelled after careful dissection.

served them to be present, although the river was not yet open. Those that have migrated to the south make their reappearance in spring throughout the continent as soon as, and not unfrequently before, the ice has disappeared from the rivers and ponds.

It occurs in extreme northern latitudes. Mr. MacFarlane received skins from the Eskimos obtained on the Arctic coast, and Mr. Dall found them breeding at Fort Yukon, where it was quite common on all the small streams flowing into that river. It was also found by Dr. Richardson frequenting all the large streams of the fur countries, as far at least as the 67th parallel. In California a larger race than our Atlantic species is found abundantly along the coast, and about nearly every stream or lake in which the water is not turbid and muddy.

Mr. A. Newton reports this bird as a winter visitant at St. Croix, leaving the island late in April. It frequents mangrove swamps and the mouths of small streams, sometimes fishing half a mile out at sea. The stomach of one contained shells of crabs. The occurrence of two specimens of this species in Ireland is recorded by Mr. Thompson.

The Kingfisher is an eminently unsocial species. It is never found other than in solitary pairs, and these are very rarely seen together. They feed almost entirely upon fish, which they capture by plunging into the water, and which they always swallow whole on emerging from their bath. Undigested portions of their food, such as scales, bones, etc., they have the power of occasionally ejecting from their stomachs. They may usually be noticed by the side of streams, mill-ponds, and lakes, stationed on some convenient position that enables them to overlook a deep place suitable for their purpose, and they rarely make a plunge without accomplishing their object.

The cry of the Kingfisher, uttered when he is disturbed, or when moving from place to place, and occasionally just as he is about to make a plunge, is loud and harsh, and resembles the noise made by a watchman's rattle. This noise he makes repeatedly at all hours, and most especially at night, during the breeding-season, whenever he returns to the nest with food for his mate or young.

They nest in deep holes excavated by themselves in the sides of streams, ponds, or cliffs, not always in the immediate vicinity of water. These excavations are often near their accustomed fishing-grounds, in some neighboring bank, usually not many feet from the ground, always in dry gravel, and sufficiently high to be in no danger of inundation. They make their burrow with great industry and rapidity, relieving one another from time to time, and working incessantly until the result is satisfactorily accomplished. When digging through a soft fine sand-bank their progress is surprising, sometimes making a deep excavation in a single night. The pages of "The American Naturalist" contain several animated controversies as to the depth, the shape, and the equipments of these passages.

The result of the evidence thus given seems to be that the holes the Kingfishers make are not less than four nor more than fifteen feet in length ; that some are perfectly straight, while some, just before their termination, turn to the right, and others to the left ; and that all have, at or near the terminus, an enlarged space in which the eggs are deposited. Here the eggs are usually laid on the bare sand, there being very rarely, if ever, any attempt to construct a nest. The use of hay, dry grass, and feathers, spoken of by the older writers, does not appear to be confirmed by more recent testimony. Yet it is quite possible that in certain situations the use of dry materials may be resorted to to protect the eggs from a too damp soil.

The place chosen for the excavation is not always near water. In the spring of 1855 I found the nest of a Kingfisher in a bank by the side of the carriage path on Mount Washington, more than a mile from any water. It was a shallow excavation, made that season, and contained fresh eggs the latter part of May. The food of the pair was taken near the dam of a sawmill on Peabody River. In another instance a pair of Kingfishers made their abode in a sand-bank in the midst of the village of Hingham, within two rods of the main street, and within a few feet of a dwelling, and not in the near vicinity of water. Here the confidence they displayed was not misplaced. They were protected, and their singular habits carefully and curiously watched. During the day they were cautious, reticent, and rarely seen, but during the night they seemed to be passing back and forth continually, the return of each parent being announced by a loud rattling cry. Later in the season, when the young required constant attention, these nocturnal noises seemed nearly incessant, and became almost a nuisance to the family.

The Kingfisher, having once selected a situation for its nest, is very tenacious of it, and rarely forsakes it unless compelled to by too great annoyances. They will submit to be robbed time after time, and still return to the same spot and renew their attempts. They are devoted to their young, exhibit great solicitude if their safety is threatened, and will suffer themselves to be taken from their nest rather than leave it, and immediately return to it again.

Mr. Dall observed a male bird of this species digging other holes in the bank near his nest, apparently for amusement or occupation. They were never more than two feet in length and about eight inches in diameter. He seemed to abandon them as soon as made, though seen to retire into one to eat a fish he had captured.

The eggs are usually six, rarely seven, in number, and are of a beautifully clear crystal whiteness. They are very nearly spherical in shape, and measure 1.31 by 1.06 inches.

Ceryle americana, var. cabanisi, Tschudi.

TEXAS KINGFISHER; GREEN KINGFISHER.

Alcedo americana, GMELIN, Syst. Nat. I, 1788, 451 (in part). *Ceryle americana*, LAW-
RENCE, Annals N. Y. Lyceum, V, 1851, 118 (first introduction into the fauna of
United States). — CASSIN, Illustrations, I, 1855, 255. — BREWER, N. Am. Oology, I,
1857, 3, pl. iv, f. 53 (egg). — BAIRD, Birds N. Am. 1858, 159, pl. xlv. — IB. Mex.
B. II ; Birds 7, pl. vii. — COOPER, Orn. Cal. I, 1870, 339. *Alcedo viridis*, VIEILLOT,
Nouv. Dict. XIX, 1818, 413 (CASSIN). *Ceryle cabanisi*, REICHENB. Handb. sp. Orn.
I, 27. — CABAN. Mus. Hein. II, 147. *Alcedo cabanisi*, TSCHUDI.

SP. CHAR. Head slightly crested. Upper parts, together with a pectoral and abdominal
band of blotches, glossy green, as also a line on each side the throat. Under parts
generally, a collar on the back of the neck, and a double series of spots on the quills,
white. *Female* with a broad band of chestnut across the breast. *Young* of both sexes
similar to the adult, but white beneath tinged with buff, and marking on breast more
obsolete. Length about 8.00 ; wing, 3.14.

HAB. Rio Grande region of Texas and southward. Localities : Honduras (SCL. P.
Z. S. 1858, 358) ; Bogota (SCL. P. Z. S. 1853, 130) ; Cordova (SCL. P. Z. S. 1856, 286) ;
Guatemala (SCL. Ibis, I, 131) ; Honduras (Ibis, II, 117) ; S. E. Texas (DRESSER, Ibis, 1865,
472, breeds) ; Colorado River (COUES P. A. N. S. 1866, 59) ; Costa Rica (LAWR. N. Y.
Lyc. IX, 118).

This species is much smaller than the Northern or Belted Kingfisher, and
is easily distinguishable by the diagnostic marks already given. The sexes
appear to differ, like those of *C. alcyon*, namely, the female being distinguished by a rufous pectoral band, which is wanting in the male

Tschudi and Cabanis separate the northern from the more southern bird
under the name of *C. cabanisi ;* Tschudi retaining the name of *C. americana*
for specimens resident in eastern South America. The differences are
said to consist in the larger size, longer bill, greater extension of the white
of the throat, and the decided spotting on the wing-coverts and quills of
cabanisi. Though these differences are readily appreciable, they correspond
so entirely with natural laws, distinguishing northern and southern individuals of most resident species, that it is only fair to consider them as
merely modifications of a single species.

Several other species of *Chloroceryle* proper are found in Tropical America.

HABITS. So far as is certainly known, this species is only found within
our fauna as a bird of Texas, where it is occasional, rather than common, and
confined to its western limits. From information received, I am confident
that it will yet become known as at least of rare occurrence in Southern
Florida, and possibly along the whole gulf coast. It was first noticed as a
bird of the United States by Captain McCown, and added to our list by
Mr. Lawrence, in 1851. It has since then been occasionally taken near the
Rio Grande and in all the northeastern portions of Mexico. It is said to
be found nearly throughout Mexico, and to be abundant also in Central
America.

Mr. Dresser noticed several of these birds at Matamoras, in August, and afterwards found them common on the Nueces and the Leona Rivers, in which places they were breeding. In December he saw others near Eagle Pass. They were nowhere so abundant as the common belted species.

Dr. Coues states that they have been observed on several points on the Colorado River between Fort Mohave and Fort Yuma, — the only instances of their occurrence in the United States other than on the Rio Grande. We have but little information in regard to their habits, but there is no reason to suppose that they differ in this respect.

Mr. Salvin states that this species occurs abundantly everywhere upon the small streams in the Atlantic coast region, and in the interior of Central America. It was frequently observed near Dueñas, both on the Guacalate and on the outlet of Lake Dueñas. And Mr. J. F. Hamilton, in his Notes on the birds from the province of Santo Paulo, in Brazil, states that he found this species several times in the vicinity of shallow pools, most especially those of which the banks were well wooded. Several times he saw them perched on logs projecting a few feet out of the water. Dr. Burmeister speaks of this bird (var. *americana*) as the most common species of Kingfisher in Brazil. It is there met with everywhere near the small brooks, on the overhanging branches, and plunging into the water after its prey, which consists especially of small fish. It is less shy than other species, coming quite near to the settlements and being easily shot. Its nest is found in holes in the banks.

Mr. E. C. Taylor also mentions finding this species pretty common in the island of Trinidad, especially among the mangroves in the swamps and lagoons.

Eggs marked as those of Kingfishers were found in the collection of the late Dr. Berlandier, of Matamoras, and are presumed to belong to this species, though no notes in relation to their parentage, and none referring to this bird, were found among his papers. Except in size, they closely resembled eggs of the *C. alcyon*, being of a pure bright crystal-white color, and measuring 1.06 inches in length by .61 in breadth.

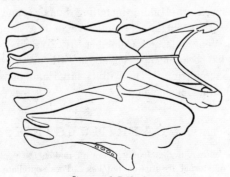

Sternum of *Ceryle alcyon.*

FAMILY **CAPRIMULGIDÆ.** — THE GOATSUCKERS.

CHAR. Bill very short; the gape enormously long and wide, opening to beneath or behind the eyes. Culmen variable. Toes connected by a movable skin; secondaries lengthened; plumage soft, sometimes very full and loose, as in the Owls.

The preceding diagnosis in connection with that of the order will suffice to separate the *Caprimulgidæ* from their allies. Their closest relatives are the *Cypselidæ*, next to which perhaps may be reckoned the *Trochilidæ*.

In defining the subdivisions of this family, we make use of an excellent monograph of the American species by Dr. Sclater, in Proceedings of the Zoölogical Society, London, 1866, 123. He establishes three subfamilies as follows : —

> I. **Podarginæ.** Claw of middle toe not pectinated; outer toe with five phalanges. Sternum with two pairs of posterior fissures.
> > Outer pair of posterior sternal fissures much deeper than inner pair; tarsus long and naked. Eggs colorless. *Podargus, Batrachostomus, Ægotheles,* Old World.
> > Outer pair of posterior fissures much deeper than inner pair; tarsus extremely short and feathered. *Nyctibius,* New World.
> II. **Steatornithinæ.** Claw of middle toe not pectinated; outer toe with five phalanges. Sternum with one pair of shallow posterior fissures. Eggs colorless. *Steatornis,* New World.
> III. **Caprimulginæ.** Claw of middle toe pectinated; outer toe with four phalanges only. Sternum with one pair of shallow posterior fissures. Eggs colored (colorless in *Antrostomus nuttalli,* Baird).
> > *a. Glabrirostres.* Rictus smooth. *Podager, Lurocalis, Chordeiles,* New World. *Lyncornis, Eurystopodus,* Old World.
> > *b. Setirostres.* Rictus armed with strong bristles. *Caprimulgus, Scotornis, Macrodipteryx,* Old World; *Antrostomus, Stenopsis, Hydropsalis, Heleothreptus, Nyctidromus, Siphonorhis,* New World.

Dr. Sclater is of the opinion that *Podargus* may ultimately have to be placed in a different family from the *Caprimulgidæ,* with or without the other genera placed under *Podarginæ;* of these *Nyctibius,* the sole New World genus has species in Middle (including Jamaica) and South America. *Steatornis caripensis,* the single representative of the second subfamily, is found in Trinidad, Venezuela, and Colombia. It lives in caverns and deep chasms of the rocks, becoming excessively fat (whence the scientific name), and is said to feed on fruits. The bill is large and powerful, more like that of a Hawk than a Goatsucker.

SUBFAMILY **CAPRIMULGINÆ.**

CHAR. Outer toes with four digits only; claw of middle toe pectinated. Sternum with one pair only of sternal fissures or notches. Toes scutellate above. Hind toe directed a little more than half forward, nostrils separated; rather nearer the commissure than the culmen.

The *Caprimulginæ* have been divided by Dr. Sclater as follows : —

A. Glabrirostres. Rictus smooth.

I. Tarsus stout, longer than middle toe, entirely naked . . . *Podager.*

II. Tarsus moderate, shorter than middle toe, more or less clothed with feathers.

    a. Tail short, almost square . . . . *Lurocalis.*

    b. Tail elongated, a little forked . . . . . . *Chordeiles.*

B. Setirostres. Rictus bristled.

III. **Aerial.** Tarsi short, more or less clothed.

    a. Wings normal, second and third quills longest.

        1. Tail moderate, rounded at tip . . . . . *Antrostomus.*

        2. Tail elongated, even at tip . . . . . . *Stenopsis.*

        3. Tail very long, forked or bifurcate . . . . *Hydropsalis.*

    b. Wings abnormal in male; outer six quills nearly equal . *Heleothreptus.*

IV. **Terrestrial.** Tarsi elongated, naked.

    a. Bill moderately broad; nasal aperture scarcely prominent . *Nyctidromus.*

    b. Bill very broad; nasal aperture much projecting (Jamaica) . *Siphonorhis.*

Of the genera enumerated above, only two certainly belong to the fauna of the United States (*Chordeiles* and *Antrostomus*), although there is some reason to suppose that *Nyctidromus* should be included, as among the manu-

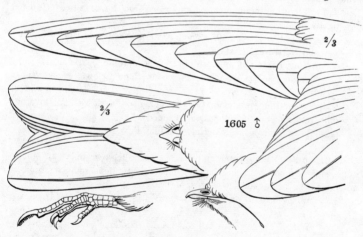

Chordeiles popetue.

script drawings of Dr. Berlandier, of birds collected at Matamoras on the Lower Rio Grande, is one that can be readily referred to no other than *N. albicollis.*[1] The briefest diagnoses of these three genera will be as follows : —

Chordeiles. Gape without bristles; tarsi moderate, partly feathered; tail narrow, slightly forked; plumage rather compact.

---

[1] *Nyctidromus albicollis. Caprimulgus albicollis* and *guianensis*, GMELIN, S. N. I, 1788, 1030. *Nyctidromus americanus*, CASSIN, Pr. A. N. S. 1851, 179. *Nyctidromus guianensis, derbyanus, grallarius, — affinis* of authors. *Nyctidromus albicollis*, SCLATER, P. Z. S. 1866, 145. *Hab.* From Northern Mexico southward to Ecuador and Brazil.

Antrostomus. Gape with bristles; tarsi moderate, partly feathered; tail broad, considerably rounded; plumage soft.

Nyctidromus. Gape with bristles; tarsi lengthened, bare; tail broad, rounded; plumage soft.

Genus **CHORDEILES**, Swainson.

Chordeiles, Swainson, Fauna Bor. Amer. II, 1831, 496. (Type, *Caprimulgus virginianus*.)

Gen. Char. Bill small, the nostrils depressed; the gape with feeble, inconspicuous bristles. Wings long, narrow, and pointed; the first quill nearly or quite equal to the second. Tail rather narrow, slightly forked; plumage quite compact. Habits diurnal or crepuscular.

Many species of this genus belong to America, although but two that are well characterized enter into the fauna of the United States. These are easily distinguished as follows : —

Species and Varieties.

C. popetue. White patch on primaries extending over the five outer quills, anterior to their middle portion. No rufous spots on quills, anterior to the white patch.

  a. Dark mottling predominating on upper parts; lower tail-coverts distinctly banded.

   Wing, 8.00; tail, 4.40. *Hab.* Eastern Province of United States and Northwest coast . . . . . . var. *popetue.*

   Wing, 6.90; tail, 4.00. More rufous mottling on scapulars and jugulum, and a decided ochraceous tinge below. *Hab.* West Indies . . . . var. *minor.*[1]

  b. Light mottling predominating on upper parts; lower tail-coverts only very indistinctly and sparsely banded.

   Size of var. *popetue. Hab.* Middle Province of United States   var. *henryi.*

C. acutipennis. White patch on primaries extending over only four outer quills, and beyond their middle portion; distinct rufous spots on quills, anterior to the white patch.

   Wing, 6.20 to 6.50; tail, 3.90 to 4.10. *Hab.* South America.
                  var. *acutipennis.*[2]

   Wing, 7.00 to 7.30; tail, 4.40 to 4.75; Colors not appreciably different. *Hab.* Middle America, north into southern border of United States . . . . var. *texensis.*

[1] *Chordeiles popetue*, var. *minor*, Cabanis. *Chordeiles minor*, Cab. Journ. f. Orn. 1856, p. 5. — Sclater, Catal. Am. B. 1862, 279. *Ch. gundlachi*, Lawr. Ann. N. Y. Lyc. VI, 165.

[2] *Chordeiles acutipennis*, (Bodd.) Cass. *Caprimulgus acutipennis*, Boddært, Tab. Pl. Enl. p. 46 (1783). *Chordeiles a.* Cassin, P. A. N. S. 1851 (Catalogue of *Caprimulgidæ*, in Mus. Philad. Acad.). *Caprimulgus acutus*, Gmel. *C. pruinosus*, Tschudi. *C. exilis*, Lesson. *Chordeiles labeculatus*, Jardine. "*Caprimulgus semitorquatus*, L., Gm., Pr. Max." Tschudi. *Chordeiles peruvianus*, Peale. *Hab.* South America.

Chordeiles popetue, var. popetue, Baird.

NIGHT-HAWK; BULL-BAT.

Caprimulgus popetue, Vieillot, Ois. Am. Sept. I, 1807, 56, pl. xxiv (♀). *Chordeiles popetue*, Baird, Birds N. Am. 1858, 151. — Lord, Pr. R. A. Inst. IV, 1864, 113 (Br. Col. nesting). — Cooper & Suckley, 166. — Samuels, 122. *Caprimulgus americanus*, Wilson, V, 1812, 65, pl. cxl. f. 1, 2. *Chordeiles americanus*, DeKay, N. Y. Zoöl. II, 1844, 34, pl. xxvii. *Caprimulgus virginianus*, Brisson, II, 1760, 477 (in part only). — Aud. Orn. Biog. II, 1834, 273, pl. cxlvii. — Max. Cab. J. VI, 1858. — Warthausen, Cab. J. 1868, 373 (nesting). *Caprimulgus (Chordeiles) virginianus*, Sw. F. Bor.-Am. II. 1831, 62. *Chordeiles virginianus*, Bon. List, 1838. — Aud. Birds Am. I, 1840, 159, pl. xliii. — Newberry, Zoöl. Cal. and Oregon Route, 79 ; Rep. P. R. R. Surv. VI, 1857. *Long-winged Goatsucker*, Pennant, Arctic Zoöl. II, 1785, 337.

Sp. Char. Male, above greenish-black, but with little mottling on the head and back. Wing-coverts varied with grayish; scapulars with yellowish-rufous. A nuchal band of fine gray mottling, behind which is another coarser one of rufous spots. A white V-shaped mark on the throat; behind this a collar of pale rufous blotches, and another on the breast of grayish mottling. Under parts banded transversely with dull yellowish or reddish-white and brown. Wing-quills quite uniformly brown. The five outer primaries with a white blotch (about half an inch long) midway between the

Chordeiles popetue.

tip and carpal joint, not extending on the outer web of the outer quill. Tail with a terminal white patch, which does not reach the outer edge of the feathers. *Female* without the caudal white patch, the white tail-bands more mottled, the white of the throat mixed with reddish. Length of male, 9.50 ; wing, 8.20.

Hab. United States and north to Hudson Bay ; in winter visits Greater Antilles, and southward to Central America (Rio Janeiro, Pelzeln) ; said to breed in Jamica. In Rocky Mountains, replaced by the variety *henryi*. Localities: Trout Lake, H. B. T. (Murray, Edinb. Phil. Journ. 1860); Bahamas (Bryant, Bost. Soc. VII, 1859); Guatemala (Scl. Ibis, II, 275) ; Cuba (Lawr.) ; Jamaica (March, P. A. N. S. 1863, 285, breeds) ; Matamoras (Dresser, Ibis, 1865, 471, breeds) ; Rio Janeiro, January (Pelz., Orn. Bras. I. 14) ; Veragua (Salvin, P. Z. S. 1870, 203).

Habits. The common Night-Hawk of North America is a very common species throughout a widely extended area, and within the United States breeds wherever found. Its range extends from Florida and Texas to the extreme northern latitudes, and from the Atlantic at least to the great Central Plains. It has been found as far to the south as Panama.

At Matamoras Mr. Dresser found this species abundant during the summer season, and towards dusk thousands of these birds and of *C. texensis* and *C. henryi* might be seen flying in towards the river from the prairies, this one being the least common of the three. In Northern Florida it is also a common species, and I have rarely received any collection of eggs from that State without the eggs of this bird being found among them. They are known there as Bull-bats.

In many of its habits, as well as in its well-marked generic distinctions, this species exhibits so many and such well-marked differences from the Whippoorwill that there seem to be no good reasons for confounding two birds so very unlike. It is especially much less nocturnal, and has, strictly speaking, no claim to its common name, as indicating it to be a bird of the night, which it is not. It is crepuscular, rather than nocturnal, and even this habit is more due to the flight of the insects upon which it feeds at morning and at evening than to any organization of the bird rendering it necessary. It may not unfrequently be seen on the wing, even in bright sunny weather, at midday, in pursuit of its winged prey. This is especially noticeable with such birds as are wont to frequent our large cities, which may be seen throughout all hours of the day sailing high in the air. Generally, however, it is most lively early in the morning and just before nightfall, when its supply of insect food is most abundant. But it is never to be found on the wing after dark. As soon as the twilight deepens into the shades of night all retire to rest as regularly, if not at quite as early an hour, as other birds in regard to the diurnal habits of which there is no question.

This species appears to be equally abundant throughout the fur countries, where, Dr. Richardson states, few birds are better known. In the higher latitudes to which these birds resort the sun does not set during their stay, and all their pursuit of insects must be made by sunlight.

In the winter this species leaves the United States, retiring to Mexico, Central America, and the northern portions of South America. Specimens from Mexico were in the Rivoli collection. They were taken by Barruel in Nicaragua, by Salvin in Guatemala, in Jamaica by Gosse, and in Cuba by both Lembeye and Gundlach.

The movements, evolutions, and general habits of this species, in the pursuit of their prey, bear little resemblance to those of the *Antrostomi*, but are much more like those of the *Falconidæ*. They fly high in the air, often so high as to be hardly visible, and traverse the air, moving backward and forward in the manner of a Hawk. At times they remain perfectly stationary for several moments, and then suddenly and rapidly dart off, their wings causing a very peculiar vibratory sound. As they fly they utter a very loud and shrill cry which it is almost impossible to describe, but often appearing to come from close at hand when the bird is high in the air. Richardson compares this sound to the vibration of a tense cord in a violent gust of wind.

In some of the peculiarities of its breeding the Mosquito-Hawk displays several very marked variations of habit from the Whippoorwill. While the latter always deposits its eggs under the cover of shady trees and in thick woods, these birds select an open rock, a barren heath, or an exposed hillside for their breeding-place. This is not unfrequently in wild spots in the vicinity of a wood, but is always open to the sun. I have even known the eggs carelessly dropped on the bare ground in a corner of a potato-field, and have found the female sitting on her eggs in all the bright glare of a noon-day sun in June, and to all appearance undisturbed by its brilliance. A more common situation for the eggs is a slight hollow of a bare rock, the dark weather-beaten shades of which, with its brown and slate-colored mosses and lichens, resembling both the parent and the egg in their color-ing, are well adapted to screen them from observation or detection.

The great abundance of insect life of certain kinds in the vicinity of our large cities has of late years attracted these birds. Each summer their number in Boston has perceptibly increased, and through June and July, at almost all hours of the day, most especially in the afternoon, they may be seen or heard sailing high in the air over its crowded streets. The modern style of house-building, with flat Mansard roofs, has also added to the inducements, affording safe and convenient shelter to the birds at night, and serving also for the deposition of their eggs. In quite a number of in-stances in the summers of 1870 and 1871 they were known to lay their eggs and to rear their young on the flat roofs of houses in the southern and western sections of the city. I have also been informed by the late Mr. Turnbull, of Philadelphia, that the flat roofs of large warehouses near the river in that city are made similar use of.

If approached when sitting on her eggs, the female will suffer herself to be almost trodden on before she will leave them, and when she does it is only to tumble at the feet of the intruder and endeavor to draw him away from her treasures by well-feigned lameness and pretended disability. Her imitation of a wounded bird is so perfect as to deceive almost any one not aware of her cunning devices.

The eggs of this bird are always two in number, elliptical in shape, and equally obtuse at either end. They exhibit marked variations in size, in ground-color, and in the shades and number of their markings. In cer-tain characteristics and in their general effect they are alike, and all resem-ble oblong-oval dark-colored pebble-stones. Their safety in the exposed positions in which they are laid is increased by this resemblance to the stones among which they lie. They vary in length from 1.30 to 1.13 inches, and in breadth from .84 to .94 of an inch. Their ground is of various shades of stone-color, in some of a dirty white, in others with a tinge of yellow or blue, and in yet others a clay-color. The markings are more or less diffused over the entire egg, and differ more or less with each specimen, the prevailing colors being varying shades of slate and of yellowish-brown.

With all these variations the eggs are readily recognizable, and bear no resemblance to any others except those of *texensis* and *henryi*. From the former they are easily distinguished by the greater size, but from the latter they can only be separated by considerations of locality.

Chordeiles popetue, var. henryi, CASSIN.

WESTERN NIGHT-HAWK.

Chordeiles henryi, CASSIN, Illust. Birds of Cal. & Tex. I, 1855, 233. — BAIRD, Birds N. Am. 1858, 153, pl. xvii. — SCLATER, P. Z. S. 1866, 133. — COOPER, Orn. Cal. I, 1870, 343.

SP. CHAR. Similar to var. *popetue*, but the male considerably lighter, with a greater predominance of the light mottlings, producing a more grayish aspect; the female more rufous. Wing-patch of the male larger (at least an inch long), and, like the tail-patch, crossing the whole breadth of the feather.

HAB. Western Province of North America, except Pacific Coast region. Matamoras to San Antonio, Texas (DRESSER, Ibis, 1865, 471); Arizona (COUES, P. A. N. S. 1866, 58).

In examining a large series of Night-Hawks, we find the differences indicated above, in specimens from the Black Hills, Rocky Mountains, and the adjacent regions, to be quite decided and constant. Skins, however, from Washington, Oregon, and California, seem darker even than the typical eastern. There is no prominent difference beyond the lighter colors of male, and greater distinctness, extent, and purity of the white or light markings, and in the white patches of wing and tail, crossing the outer webs of all the feathers; the general proportions and pattern of coloration being quite the same. It will therefore seem proper to consider *C. henryi* as a local race, characteristic of the region in which it occurs, and as such noteworthy, but not entitled to independent rank.

Another race, *C. minor*, Cab., similar to var. *popetue*, but considerably smaller (7.50, wing, 7.00), is resident in Cuba and Jamaica. *C. popetue* is also said to breed in the latter island, but *minor* is probably referred to.

HABITS. This form, whether we regard it as a good species, or only a western race of the common Night-Hawk, was first described as a new variety by Mr. Cassin, in 1855, from specimens procured at Fort Webster, New Mexico, by Dr. Henry, in honor of whom it was named. Its claim to be considered a distinct race or species rests chiefly upon its constantly different colorations.

Dr. Cooper, who regarded this form not specifically distinct from the Night-Hawk, states that it is not found near the coast border of California.

Dr. Kennerly encountered it in abundance in the vicinity of Los Nogales, in Sonora, in June. Late in the afternoon they came in great numbers around the camp. They kept circling round and round, and approached the earth nearer and nearer with the declining sun,

Mr. Dresser found them very abundant at Matamoras, and as far east as the Sal Colorado, beyond which he did not meet with any. About dusk, thousands of these birds might be seen flying in towards the river from the prairies. At San Antonio, where Mr. Dresser found both *C. popetue* and *C. texensis*, he never procured a single specimen of this bird, nor did Dr. Heermann ever meet with one there.

Dr. Coues says these birds are abundant throughout the Territory of Arizona. At Fort Whipple it is a summer resident, arriving in April and remaining until October, being particularly numerous in August and September. Mr. Drexler made a large collection of these birds at Fort Bridger, in Utah, all of which showed such constant differences from eastern specimens as to indicate in his opinion the propriety of a specific separation.

An egg of this bird taken at Fort Crook, California, by Lieutenant Fulner, measures 1.25 inches in length by .92 of an inch in breadth. While resembling in general effect an egg of *C. popetue*, it is lighter in colorings, and varies from any of that bird I have ever seen. Its ground-color is that of clay, over which are diffused curious aggregations of small spots and cloudings of yellowish-brown, mingled with lilac. These markings are quite small and separate, but are grouped in such close proximity into several collections as to give them the appearance of large blotches ; and the blending of these two shades is so general as to produce the effect of a color quite different from either, except upon a close inspection, or an examination through a magnifying glass.

This variety was met with at the Forks of the Saskatchewan, in June, 1858, by Captain Blakiston, and specimens were obtained on the Saskatchewan Plains, by M. Bourgeau, in the summer of the same year. The latter also procured its eggs. These are said to have been three in number, described as light olive, blotched with black more thickly at one end than the other. No mention of shape is made. This description, incomplete as it is, indicates a great dissimilarity with eggs of this bird, fully identified in the Smithsonian collection.

The western variety was met with by Mr. Ridgway throughout the entire extent of his route across the Great Basin. It bred everywhere, laying its eggs on the bare ground, beneath a sage-bush, usually on the foot-hills of the mountains, or on the mesas. In August and September they congregate in immense flocks, appearing in the evening. Not the slightest difference in habits, manners, or notes, was observed between this and the eastern Night-Hawk.

Chordeiles acutipennis, var. texensis, LAWRENCE.

TEXAS NIGHT-HAWK.

Chordeiles brasilianus, LAWRENCE, Ann. N. Y. Lyceum, V, May, 1851, 114 (not of
GMELIN). — CASSIN, Ill. I, 1855, 238. *Chordeiles sapiti*, BON. Conspectus Avium, I,
1849, 63. *Chordeiles texensis*, LAWRENCE, Ann. N. Y. Lyc. VI, Dec. 1856, 167. —
BAIRD, Birds N. Am. 1858, 154, pl. xliv. — IB. M. B. II, Birds, 7, pl. vi. — COOPER,
Orn. Cal. I, 1870, 345. *Caprimulgus texensis*, WARTHAUSEN, Cab. J. 1868, 376 (nest-
ing).

SP. CHAR. Much smaller than *C. virginianus*, but somewhat similar. White on the
wing extending over only four outer primaries, the bases of which, as well as the remaining ones, with other quills, have round rufous spots on both webs. Under tail-coverts
and abdomen with a strong yellowish-rufous tinge. Female more rufous and without the
white spot of the tail. Length, 8.75; wing, 7.00.

HAB. Basins of Rio Grande, Gila, and Colorado Rivers, and west to Gulf of California;
South as far, at least, as Costa Rica. Localities: Matamoras to San Antonio (DRESSER,
Ibis, 1865, 471, breeds): W. Arizona (COUES, P. A. N. S. 1866, 58); Costa Rica (LAWR.
An. N. Y. Lyc. IX, 120); Yucatan (LAWR. N. Y. Lyc. IX, 204).

The markings of this species are quite different from those of *Chordeiles
popetue*. In average specimens the prevailing color above may be described
as a mixed gray, yellowish-rusty, black, and brown, in varied but very fine
mottlings. The top of the head is rather uniformly brown, with a few
mottlings of grayish-rusty, although the concealed portion of the feathers is
much varied. On the nape is a finely mottled collar of grayish and black,
not very conspicuously defined, and rather interrupted on the median line.
A similar collar is seen on the forepart of the breast. The middle of the
back and the rump exhibit a coarser mottling of the same without any
rufous. The scapulars and wing-coverts are beautifully variegated, much as
in some of the Waders, the pattern very irregular and scarcely capable of
definition. There are, however, a good many large round spots of pale
yellowish-rusty, very conspicuous among the other markings. There is
quite a large blotch of white on the wing, situated considerably nearer the
tip than the carpal joint. It only involves four primaries, and extends
across both outer and inner webs. The four first primaries anterior to the
white blotches, and the remaining ones nearly from their tips, exhibit a
series of large round rufous spots not seen in the other North American
species. The other wing-quills have also similar markings. There is a
large V-shaped white mark on the throat, as in *C. virginianus*, though rather
larger proportionally. Posterior to this there are some rather conspicuous
blotches of rufous, behind which is the obscure finely mottled collar of gray
and brown already referred to. The breast and remaining under parts are
dull white transversely banded with brown, with a strong tinge of yellowish-
rufous on the abdomen, about the vent, and on the under tail-coverts. The
tail is dark brown with about eight transverse bars of lighter; the last are

white, and extend across both vanes; the others less continuous, and yellowish-rufous beneath as well as above, especially on the inner vane.

The females are quite similar, but lack the white patch of the tail, have more numerous rufous spots on quills, and are perhaps more fulvous in general appearance. Young birds, however, would hardly be recognized as the same, except when taken with adults, owing to the predominance of a pale cinnamon shade above, and a decided tinge of the same on all the white and gray markings. Nearly all the primaries have a border of this color.

The variety *acutipennis* of South America (see synopsis) is very similar, differing merely in smaller dimensions.

HABITS. The Texan Night-Hawk occurs in the valley of the Rio Grande from Texas on the east, through New Mexico, Arizona, Southern California, and Cape San Lucas. It is found in the northern provinces of Mexico during the summer months, and thence southward to Central America. It was found at Dueñas, in Guatemala, by Mr. Salvin, and also at Coban. Mr. Xantus found it breeding at Cape San Lucas in May.

This species was first added to our fauna by Mr. Lawrence, in 1851, as a bird of Texas, supposed to be *C. brasilianus*, and in 1856 described by the same writer as a new species.

According to Dr. Cooper, it makes its first appearance at Fort Mohave by the 17th of April, and soon after becomes quite numerous, hunting in companies after sunset, and hiding during the day on the ground under low bushes. By the 25th of May they had all paired, but continued nearly silent, making only a low croaking when approached. They flew in the manner of the common species, but seemed to sail in rather smaller circles. Dr. Cooper found them as far west as the Coast Mountains.

Dr. Coues states that this species is common in the Colorado Valley, even farther north than the latitude of Fort Whipple. It was not, however, met with by him at that port, nor indeed for some fifty miles to the south of it, and then only in the summer. He adds that it extends from the Rio Grande Valley westward to the Pacific. It was found abundant at Cape St. Lucas by Dr. Xantus.

Mr. Dresser found it very common at Matamoras during the summer season, and thence to San Antonio and to the eastward of that place. At San Antonio, in the spring, he first noticed them on the 2d of May, when he saw seven or eight flying about at noonday. A few days later they had become very numerous. They remained about San Antonio until the end of September, and soon after disappeared. He noticed none later than the first week in October.

Mr. J. H. Clark met with this species at Ringgold Barracks, Texas, in June. They were to be seen sitting about in the heat of the day, at which time they could be easily approached. During the hottest days they did not sally forth in quest of food until late in the evening. On one occasion, near

El Paso, Mr. Clark saw these birds congregated in such quantities over a mud-hole from which were issuing myriads of insects, that he felt that the discharge among them of mustard-seed shot would involve a wanton destruction.   This species is not known, according to his account, to make a swoop in the manner of the common species.   It does not utter the same hoarse sounds, nor does it ever fly so high.

Among the notes of the late Dr. Berlandier, of Matamoras, we find references to this species, to which he gives the common name of *Pauraque*, and in his collection of eggs are many that unquestionably are those of this bird, and which are, in all respects but size, in close affinity to the eggs of the common Night-Hawk.   These eggs measure 1.18 inches in length by .87 of an inch in breadth.   Their ground-color, seen through a magnifying glass, is of clear crystal whiteness, but is so closely covered by overlaying markings as not to be discernible to the eye.   They are marked over the entire surface with small irregular confluent spots and blotches, which are a blending of black, umber, and purplish-gray markings.   These combinations give to the egg the appearance of a piece of polished marble of a dark gray color. They are both smaller and of a lighter color than those of the common eastern bird.

Genus ANTROSTOMUS, Gould.

Antrostomus, Gould, Icones Avium, 1838.   (Type, *Caprimulgus carolinensis*, Gm.)

Gen. Char. Bill very small, with tubular nostrils, and the gape with long, stiff, sometimes pectinated bristles projecting beyond the end of the bill. Tarsi moderate, partly

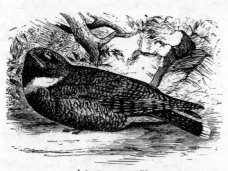

feathered above. Tail broad, rounded; wings broad and rounded; first quill shorter than third; plumage soft and lax. Habit nocturnal.

In what the genus *Antrostomus* really differs from *Caprimulgus* proper, we are quite unable to say, as in the many variations of form of both New and Old World species of these two divisions respectively, it is said to be not difficult to find species in

Antrostomus nuttalli.

each, almost identical in form.   In the want of suitable material for comparison, we shall follow Sclater in using *Antrostomus* for the New World species.

Species and Varieties.[1]

A. Bristles of gape with lateral filaments. Light tail-spaces confined to inner web of feathers.

> *Dark markings on crown longitudinal. Ochraceous or white gular collar in form of a narrow band across jugulum.*

A. carolinensis. Throat ochraceous, with sparse, narrow, transverse bars of black; jugular collar more whitish, with broader but more distant black bars. Crissum barred, and inner webs of primaries with black prevailing. Wing, 8.90; tail, 6.30. *Hab.* Louisianian region of the Eastern Province of United States (Florida and the Carolinas to Arkansas). Costa Rica.

B. Bristles of gape without lateral filaments; light tail-spaces covering both webs.

a. Throat black, with sparse, narrow, transverse bars of pale brown. Crissum barred, and inner webs of primaries with black greatly predominating.

A. macromystax. Crown pale brown and whitish very coarsely mottled with dusky; lower parts clouded with whitish, in conspicuous contrast with the ground color. Light tail patch restricted to less than terminal third, and decreasing in breadth toward the middle feathers. Bristles of gape enormously long and stout; bill compressed, nostrils large.

> White patch on end of tail confined to three outer feathers, and decreasing very rapidly in extent to the inner. Wing, 6.60; tail, 5.30; rictal bristles, 1.40. *Hab.* Mexico (Mirador, La Parada).
>
> <div align="right">var. <i>macromystax.</i>[2]</div>
>
> White patch on end of tail, on four outer feathers, and just appreciably decreasing in extent toward the inner. Wing, 7.00; tail, 5.50; rictal bristles, 2.00. *Hab.* Cuba . . var. *cubanensis.*[3]

A. vociferus. Crown ash, finely mottled or minutely sprinkled with dusky; lower parts without whitish cloudings. White tail-patch covering more than terminal half, and decreasing in breadth toward the outer feather. Bristles of gape moderate, slender; bill weaker, less compressed, and nostrils smaller. Wing, 6.40; tail, 5.10; rictal bristles, 1.50 or less. *Hab.* Eastern Province of North America, south to Guatemala.

> *Dark markings of crown transverse. Gular collar pure white, covering nearly whole throat.*

b. Throat pure white, without any markings. Crissum immaculate; inner webs of primaries with ochraceous very largely predominating.

A. nuttalli. White space of tail occupying about the terminal fourth, or less, on three feathers, and gradually decreasing inwardly. Wing, 5.75; tail, 3.90; rictal bristles less than 1.00. *Hab.* Western Province of United States, from the Plains to the Pacific.

---

[1] The females differ simply in having the light tail-space much reduced in size, and dull ochraceous, instead of whitish ; in that of *carolinensis* it is wanting altogether.

[2] *Antrostomus macromystax* (WAGL. ?) SCLATER, P. Z. S. 1866, 137 (La Parada, Mex.). ? *Caprimulgus macromystax*, WAGL. Isis, 1831, p. 533.

[3] *Antrostomus macromystax*, var. *cubanensis* (LAWR.) *Antrostomus cubanensis*, LAWR. Ann. N. Y. Lyc. VII, May, 1860, p. 260.

Antrostomus carolinensis, GOULD.

CHUCK-WILL'S WIDOW.

Caprimulgus carolinensis, GMELIN, Syst. Nat. I, 1788, 1028. — AUD. Orn. Biog. I, 1832, 273, pl. lii ; V, 1839, 401. — IB. Birds Am. I, 1840, 151, pl. xli. — WARTHAUSEN, Cab. J. 1868, 368 (nesting). *Antrostomus carolinensis,* GOULD, Icones Avium, 1838 ? — CASSIN, Illust. N. Am. Birds, I, 1855, 236. — BAIRD, Birds N. Am. 1858, 147. — ALLEN, B. Fla. 300. *Caprimulgus rufus,* VIEILLOT, Ois. Am. Sept. I, 1807, 57, pl. xxv (♀). *Caprimulgus brachypterus,* STEPHENS, Shaw's Zoöl. X, I, 1825 ? 150. *Short-winged Goatsucker,* PENNANT, Arctic Zoöl. II, 1785, 434.

SP. CHAR. Bristles of the bill with lateral filaments. Wing nearly nine inches long. Top of the head finely mottled reddish-brown, longitudinally streaked with black. The

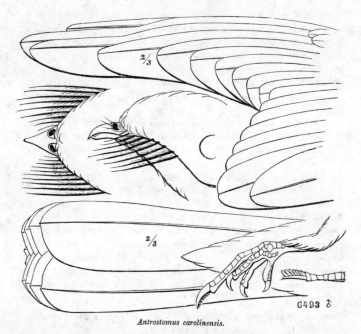

Antrostomus carolinensis.

prevailing shade above and below pale rufous. Terminal two-thirds of the tail-feathers (except the four central) rufous white ; outer webs of all mottled, however, nearly to the tips. *Female* without the white patch on the tail. Length, 12.00 ; wing, 8.50.

HAB. South Atlantic and Gulf States to Veragua ; Cuba in winter. Cuba (CABAN. J. IV, 6, winter) ; San Antonio, Texas (DRESSER, Ibis, 1865, 70, breeds) ; Costa Rica (LAWR. IX, 120) ; Veragua (SALVIN, P. Z. S. 1870, 303).

This, according to Sclater, is the largest of the *Antrostomi* and the only species with lateral filaments to the bristles of the mouth.

The extent of the white spaces on the inner webs of tail-feathers varies with the individual, but in none does it occupy less than the terminal half.

The *A. rufus (Caprimulgus rufus,* BODD. et GMEL. ex Pl. Enl. 735 (?) ;

Antrostomus r. SCLATER, P. Z. S. 1866, 136; *A. rutilus,* BURM. Syst. Ueb. II, 385) and *A. ornatus* (SCL. P. Z. S. 1866, 586, pl. xlv), of South America, appear to be the nearest relatives of this species, agreeing very closely in coloration; but both have the rictal bristles simple, without lateral filaments, and would thus seem to be distinct species. In the latter, the white spaces of the tail are found only on the second and third feathers, instead of on the outer three, while the former is said to have no such markings at all.

HABITS. The exact extent of the geographical range of this species is not very clearly defined. Rarely anywhere a very abundant species, it is more common throughout Florida than in any other State. It is also found, more or less frequently, in the States of Georgia, South Carolina, Alabama, Mississippi, Louisiana, and Texas. Dr. Woodhouse mentions finding it common in the Creek and Cherokee countries of the Indian Territory, and also extending into Texas and New Mexico. Mr. Dresser noticed several of this species on the Medina River, in Texas, April 28, and afterwards in May. On the 18th of the same month he again found it very numerous at New Braunfels, and also, on the 20th, at Bastrop. Dr. Heermann states that these birds visit the neighborhood of San Antonio in the spring, and remain there to raise their young.

James River, Virginia, has been assigned as the extreme northern limit of its migrations, but I can find no evidence of its occurring so far north, except as an accidental visitant. Wilson, indeed, claims to have met with it between Richmond and Petersburg, and also on the Cumberland River. Dr. Bachman states that it is not a common bird even in the neighborhood of Charleston. Mr. Audubon, who claimed to be a very close and careful observer of the habits of this species, states that it is seldom to be met with beyond the then southern limits of the Choctaw nation, in Mississippi, or the Carolinas on the Atlantic coast.

I have been informed by Dr. Kollock that these birds are rather common at Cheraw, in the northern part of South Carolina. Dr. Bryant found them quite abundant near Indian River, in Florida, though he makes no mention of them in his paper on the birds of that State. Mr. Cassin informed me that Colonel McCall met with this bird in New Mexico. Lembeye includes it among the birds of Cuba, but in reality refers to *cubanensis.*

These birds, according to Mr. Audubon, are not residents, but make their appearance within the United States about the middle of March. They are nocturnal in their habits, remaining silent and keeping within the shady recesses of the forests during the daytime. As soon as the sun has disappeared and the night insects are in motion, this species issues forth from its retreat, and begins to give utterance to the peculiar cries from which it receives its trivial name, and which are said to resemble the syllables *chuck-wills-wi-dow.* These sounds are said to be repeated with great rapidity, yet with clearness and power, six or seven times in as many seconds. They are are only uttered for a brief period in the early evening.

Mr. Audubon states that deep ravines, shady swamps, and extensive pine groves, are resorted to by this species for safety during the day, and for food during the night. Their notes are seldom heard in cloudy weather, and never during rain. They roost in hollow trees, standing as well as prostrate, which they never leave by day except during incubation. He adds that whenever he has surprised them in such situations they never attempt to make their escape by flying out, but draw back to the farthest corner, ruffle their feathers, open their mouths to the fullest extent, and utter a hissing sound. When taken to the light, they open and close their eyes in rapid succession, snap their bills in the manner of a Flycatcher, and attempt to shuffle off. When given their liberty, they fly straight forward until quite out of sight, readily passing between the trees in their course.

The flight of this bird is light, like that of the Whippoorwill, and even more elevated and graceful. It is performed by easy flapping of the wings, with occasional sailings and curving sweeps. It sweeps, at night, over the open fields, ascending, descending, or sailing with graceful motions in pursuit of night beetles, moths, and other insects, repeatedly passing and repassing over the same area, and occasionally alighting on the ground to capture its prey. Occasionally it pauses to alight on a stake or a tall plant, and again utters its peculiar refrain, and then resumes its search for insects. And thus it passes pleasant summer nights.

Like all the birds of this family, the Chuck-will's Widow makes no nest, but deposits her eggs on the ground, often among a collection of dry deciduous leaves, in the forest. These are two in number, and the spot chosen for them are thickets, and the darker and more solitary portions of woods. Dr. Bryant, who took several of their eggs in Florida, informed me that they were in each instance found deposited on beds of dry leaves, but with no attempt at any nest, and always in thick woods.

Sometimes, Mr. Audubon thinks, the parent bird scratches a small space on the ground, among the leaves, before she deposits her eggs. If either their eggs or their young are meddled with, these birds are sure to take the alarm and transport them to some distant part of the forest. In this both parents take part. After this removal Mr. Audubon found it impossible, even with the aid of a dog, to find them again. On one occasion he actually witnessed the act of removal of the eggs, and presumed that they also treat the young in the same manner when they are quite small. The eggs were carried off in the capacious mouths of these birds, each parent taking one and flying off, skimming closely to the ground until lost to sight among the branches and the trees. To what distance they were carried he was unable to ascertain.

During the period of incubation they are silent, and do not repeat their peculiar cries until just before they are preparing to depart on their southern migrations, in August.

The food of these birds consists chiefly, if not altogether, of the larger nocturnal insects, for swallowing which their mouths are admirably adapted, opening with a prodigious expansion, and assisted by numerous long bristles, which prevent the escape of an insect once within their enclosure. In a single instance the remains of a small bird are said to have been found within the stomach of one of this species.

The inner side of each middle claw of the *Chuck-will's Widow* is deeply pectinated. The apparent use of this appendage, as in the other species in which it is found, appears to be as an aid in adjusting the plumage, and perhaps to assist in removing vermin.

The eggs of this bird are never more than two in number. They are oval in shape, large for the size of the bird, and alike at either end. Their ground-color is a clear crystal white. They are more or less spotted, and marked over their entire surface with blotches of varying size, of a dark purplish-brown, and cloudings of a grayish-lavender color, with smaller occasional markings of a light raw-umber brown. In shape and markings they very closely resemble those of the Whippoorwill, differing chiefly in their much larger size. They measure 1.44 inches in length by 1.06 in breadth.

Antrostomus vociferus, BONAP.

WHIPPOORWILL.

Caprimulgus vociferus, WILSON, Am. Orn. V, 1812, 71, pl. xli, f. 1, 2, 3. — AUD. Orn. Biog. I, 1832, 443 ; V, 405, pl. lxxxv. — IB. Birds Am. I, 1840, 155, pl. xlii. — MAX. Cab. J. VI, 1858, 98. *Antrostomus vociferus*, BONAP. List, 1838. — CASSIN, J. A. N. Sc. II, 1852, 122. — IB. Ill. I, 1855, 236. — BAIRD, Birds N. Am. 1858, 148. — SAMUELS, 119. — ALLEN, B. Fla. 300. *Caprimulgus virginianus*, VIEILL. Ois. Am. Sept. I, 1807, 55, pl. xxv. *"Caprimulgus clamator*, VIEILLOT, Nouv. Dict. X, 1817, 234 "* (CASSIN). *Caprimulgus vociferans*, WARTHAUSEN, Cab. J. 1868, 369 (nesting).

SP. CHAR. Bristles without lateral filaments. Wing about 6.50 inches long. Top of the head ashy-brown, longitudinally streaked with black. Terminal half of the tail-feathers (except the four central) dirty white on both outer and inner webs. Length, 10.00 ; wing, 6.50. *Female* without white on the tail.

HAB. Eastern United States to the Plains ; south to Guatemala (Tehuantepec, Orizaba, Guatemala). Coban (SALV. Ibis, II, 275).

In this species the bristles at the base of the bill, though stiff and long, are without the lateral filaments of the Chuck-will's Widow. The wings are rather short ; the second quill longest ; the first intermediate between the third and fourth. The tail is rounded ; the outer feathers about half an inch shorter than the middle ones.

The colors of this species are very difficult to describe, although there is quite a similarity to those of *A. carolinensis*, from which its greatly inferior size will at once distinguish it. The top of the head is an ashy gray, finely mottled, with a broad median stripe of black ; all the feathers with a narrow stripe of the same along their centres. The back and rump are somewhat similar, though of a different shade. There is a collar of white on the under side of the neck, posterior to which the upper part of the breast is finely mottled, somewhat as on the top of the head. The belly is dirty white, with indistinct transverse bands and mottlings of brown. The wings are brown; each quill with a series of round rufous spots on both webs, quite conspicuous on the outer side of the primaries when the wings are folded. The terminal half of the outer three tail-feathers is of a dirty white.

The female is smaller; the collar on the throat is tinged with fulvous. The conspicuous white patch of the tail is wanting, the tips only of the outer three feathers being of a pale brownish-fulvous.

Mexican and Guatemalan specimens are identical with those from the United States.

HABITS. The well-known Whippoorwill has an extended range throughout the eastern portion of North America, from the Atlantic to the valley of the Missouri, and from Southern Florida to about the 50th parallel of north latitude. Dr. Richardson observed this bird on the northern shores of Lake Huron, but did not meet with it at any point farther north. It is found throughout New England and in portions of New Brunswick and Nova Scotia, but is rare in the latter places, and is not common in the vicinity of Calais. It breeds from Florida northward. It has not been found as far west as Texas. It was noticed by Mr. Say at Pembina. It is given by Dr. Hall, of Montreal, as common in that neighborhood, and by Mr. McIlwraith as an abundant summer resident around Hamilton, Canada. Dr. Lembeye names it as a resident Cuban species, and Dr. Gundlach informed me that he had taken its eggs within that island. I have also received its eggs from various portions of Florida.

The Whippoorwill is nowhere a resident species in any portion of the United States. They make their appearance in the Southern States early in March, and very gradually proceed northward, entering Pennsylvania early in April, but not being seen in New York or New England until the last of that month, and sometimes not until the 10th of May. Mr. Maynard mentions their first appearance in Massachusetts as from the 19th to the 24th of May, but I have repeatedly known them in full cry near Boston at least a fortnight earlier than this, and in the western part of the State Mr. Allen has noted their arrival by the 25th of April. They leave in the latter part of September. Mr. Allen also observed the abundant presence of these birds in Western Iowa, where he heard their notes as late as the 20th of September.

In its habits the Whippoorwill is very nearly the counterpart of the *carolinensis*. Like that bird, it is exclusively nocturnal, keeping, during the day, closely within the recesses of dark woods, and remaining perfectly silent, uttering no note even when disturbed in these retreats. In very cloudy weather, late in the day, these birds may be seen hunting for insects, but this is not usual, and they utter no sound until it is quite dark.

Like the preceding species, this bird receives its common name of Whippoorwill from its nocturnal cry, which has some slight resemblance to these three sounds; but the cry is so rapidly enunciated and so incessantly repeated that a fertile imagination may give various interpretations to the sounds. They are never uttered when the bird is in motion, but usually at short intervals, when resting on a fence, or bush, or any other object near the ground.

Their flight is noiseless to an incredible degree, and they rarely fly far at a time. They are usually very shy, and are easily startled if approached. At night, as soon as the twilight disappears, these birds issue from their retreats, and fly out into more open spaces in quest of their favorite food. As many of the nocturnal insects, moths, beetles, and others, are attracted about dwellings by lights, the Whippoorwill is frequently enticed, in pursuit, into the same vicinity. For several successive seasons these birds have appeared nearly every summer evening within my grounds, often within a few feet of the house. They never suffer a very near approach, but fly as soon as they notice any movement. Their pursuit of insects is somewhat different from that narrated of the preceding species, their flights being usually quite brief, without any perceptible sailing, and more in the manner of Flycatchers. Their song is given out at intervals throughout the night, until near the dawn.

The nocturnal habits of this bird have prevented a general or accurate knowledge of its true character. Strange as it may seem, in many parts of the country the Night-Hawk and the Whippoorwill are supposed to be one and the same bird, even by those not ill informed in other respects. This was found to be the case in Pennsylvania by Wilson, and is equally true of many portions of New England, though disputed by Mr. Audubon.

Like the Chuck-will's Widow, this species removes its eggs, and also its young, to a distant and safer locality, if they are visited and handled. Wilson once, in passing through a piece of wood, came accidentally upon a young bird of this species. The parent attempted to draw him away by well-feigned stratagems. Wilson stopped and sketched the bird, and, returning again, after a short absence, to the same place, in search of a pencil he had left behind, found that the bird had been spirited away by its vigilant parent.

When disturbed by an intrusive approach, the Whippoorwill resorts to various expedients to divert attention to herself from her offspring. She flutters about as if wounded and unable to fly, beats the ground with her wings as if not able to rise from it, and enacts these feints in a manner to deceive even the most wary, risking her own life to save her offspring.

The Whippoorwills construct no nest, but deposit their eggs in the thickest and most shady portions of the woods, among fallen leaves, in hollows slightly excavated for that purpose, or upon the leaves themselves. For this purpose elevated and dry places are always selected, often near some fallen log. There they deposit two eggs, elliptical in shape. Their young, when first hatched, are perfectly helpless, and their safety largely depends upon their great similarity to small pieces of mouldy earth. They grow rapidly, and are soon able to follow their mother and to partially care for themselves.

The egg of the Whippoorwill has a strong family resemblance to those of both species of European *Caprimulgi*, and is a complete miniature of that of *A. carolinensis*. In shape it is oblong and oval, equally obtuse at either end. Resembling the egg of the Chuck-will's Widow, it is yet more noticeable for the purity of its colors and the beauty of their contrast. The ground-color is a clear and pure shade of cream-white. The whole egg is irregularly spotted and marbled with lines and patches of purplish-lavender, mingled with reddish-brown. The former are fainter, and as if partially obscured, the brown usually much more distinct. The eggs measure 1.25 inches in length by .88 of an inch in breadth. Wilson's account of its egg is wholly inaccurate.

In the extreme Southern States these eggs are deposited in April, in Virginia and Pennsylvania about the middle of May, and farther north not until early in June. The young are hatched and able to care for themselves during July, but, with the female, rarely leave the woods. The notes of the male are once more occasionally heard in August. Mr. Allen has heard them late in September, but I have never happened to notice their cries later than August.

Mr. Nuttall states that the young of these birds, at an early age, run about with remarkable celerity, and that they utter, at short intervals a *pé-ūgh*, in a low mournful tone. Their food appears to consist of various kinds of nocturnal insects, besides ants, grasshoppers, and other kinds not nocturnal, frequenting decaying wood and shady thickets.

Left foot of *Antrostomus vociferus*.

Left foot of *Nyctibius jamaicensis*.

Antrostomus nuttalli, Cassin.

NUTTALL'S WHIPPOORWILL; POOR-WILL.

Caprimulgus nuttalli, AUD. Birds Am. VII, 1843, pl. ccccxcv, Appendix. *Antrostomus nuttalli*, CASSIN, J. A. N. Sc. Phila. 2d series, II, 1852, 123. — IB. Ill. I, 1855, 237. — NEWBERRY, Zoöl. Cal. and Oregon Route, 77 ; Rep. P. R. R. Surv. VI, IV. — BAIRD, Birds N. Am. 1858, 149. — COOPER & SUCKLEY, 166. — COOPER, Orn. Cal. I, 1870, 341.

SP. CHAR. Rictal bristles without any lateral filaments ; wing, about 5.50 ; the top of the head hoary gray, with narrow and transverse, not longitudinal bands. Tail above, except the central feathers, nearly black on the terminal half, the extreme tip only (in the outer feather of each side) being white for nearly an inch, diminishing on the second and third. Length, 8.00 ; wing, 5.50. *Female* without the white tip of tail. Audubon describes the male as follows : " Bill, black ; iris, dark hazel ; feet, reddish-purple ; scales and claws, darker ; general color of upper parts dark brownish-gray, lighter on the head and medial tail-feathers, which extend half an inch beyond the others, all which are minutely streaked and sprinkled with brownish-black and ash-gray. Quills and coverts dull cinnamon color, spotted in bars with brownish-black ; tips of former mottled with light and dark brown ; three lateral tail-feathers barred with dark brown and cinnamon, and tipped with white. Throat brown, annulated with black ; a band of white across foreneck ; beneath the latter black, mixed with bars of light yellowish-gray and black lines. Under tail-coverts dull yellow. Length, 7.25 ; wing, 5.75 ; bill, edge, .19 ; second and third quills nearly equal. Tail to end of upper feathers, 3.50 ; tarsus, .63 ; middle toe, .63 ; claw, .25 ; strongly pectinated."

HAB. High Central Plains to the Pacific coast. San Antonio, Texas (DRESSER, Ibis, 1865, 471, breeds) ; W. Arizona (COUES, P. A. N. S. 1866, 58) ; Guanajuata, Mex. (SALVIN, p. 1014).

Nuttall's Whippoorwill is readily distinguished from the other North American species by the transverse, not longitudinal, lines on the top of head, the narrow white tip of tail on both webs, and the inferior size, as well as by numerous other points of difference.

HABITS. This species was first described by Mr. Audubon from a specimen obtained near the Rocky Mountains, but with no information in regard to any peculiarities of habit. From Mr. Nuttall we learn that these birds were first observed by him on the 10th of June, amidst the naked granite hills of the sources of the Upper Platte River, called Sweet-Water. It was about twilight, and from the clefts of the rocks they were uttering at intervals a low wailing cry, in the manner of the Whippoorwill, and sounding like the cry of the young of that species, or *pē-cū*. Afterwards, on the 7th of August, when encamped on the high ravine of the insulated mountains so conspicuous from Lewis River, called the Three Buttes, this bird was again observed, as it flew from under a stone near the summit of the mountain. It flew about hawking for insects near their elevated camp, for two or three hours, but was now silent. On the 16th of June, near the banks of the Sandy River of the Colorado, Mr. Nuttall again heard its nocturnal cry, which he says sounded like *pēvai*.

Dr. Cooper did not meet with this bird in the Colorado Valley, but he heard their nocturnal call, which he says sounds like *poor-will*, on the barren mountains west of the valley, in May. He has never seen or heard any west of the Coast Range, nor in the Santa Clara Valley in the spring. They are, however, said to be common in the hot interior valleys, and remain near San Francisco as late as November, usually hiding on the ground, and flying at dusk in short, fitful courses in pursuit of insects. Dr. Cooper adds that they inhabit the almost bare and barren sage-plains east of the Sierra Nevada, where their rather sad whistle is heard all night during the spring, sounding like an echoing answer to the cry of the eastern species.

Dr. Suckley, in the Report on the Zoölogy of Washington Territory, speaks of this species as moderately abundant in the interior of that Territory, as well as of Oregon. East of the Cascade Mountains, at Fort Dalles, they can be heard on almost any fine night in spring or early summer. Their cries closely resemble those of the *vociferus*, but are more feeble, and not so incessantly kept up. Dr. Cooper, in the same report, also speaks of finding this bird common near the Yakima River, in 1853. Two specimens were killed in the daytime by a whip. Late in the evening he found them flying near the ground. Dr. Woodhouse, in passing down the Little Colorado River, in New Mexico, found this bird quite abundant, as also among the San Francisco Mountains.

Dr. Newberry met with this species in all the parts of California and Oregon visited by him. Near the shores of Rhett Lake he met with its nest containing two young nearly ready to fly. The old bird fluttered off as if disabled, and by her cries and strange movements induced one of the party to pursue her. The young resembled those of the eastern species, were of a gray-brown color, marbled with black, and had large, dark, and soft eyes. They were quite passive when caught.

This species was observed by Mr. J. H. Clark near Rio Mimbres, in New Mexico. From the manner in which it flew, it seemed so similar to the Woodcock that until a specimen was obtained it was supposed to belong to that family. He saw none east of the Rio Grande, but met with it as far west as Santa Cruz. It was nowhere abundant, and was generally solitary. It was found usually among the tall grass of the valleys, and occasionally on the plains. It was only once observed to alight upon a bush, but almost invariably, when started up, it flew down again among the grass at a short distance.

A single specimen of this bird was taken by Dr. Kennerly on the Great Colorado River. Dr. Heermann met with two specimens among the mountains bordering the Tejon Valley, and he was informed by Dr. Milhau that a small species of Whippoorwill was abundant round that fort in the spring and summer.

Dr. Heermann killed one of these birds on the Medina, in Texas; and during the summer, passing along Devil's River, he heard their notes every evening, and judged that the birds were abundant. Mr. Dresser obtained a single specimen, shot near the town of San Antonio, where it was of uncommon occurrence. He received also another specimen from Fort Stockton. During his stay at Matamoras he did not notice this bird, but was informed that a kind resembling this species was very common at a rancho about twenty-five miles distant, on the Monterey road. Dr. Coues found this species particularly abundant throughout Arizona. At Fort Whipple it was a summer resident, arriving there late in April and remaining until October. So numerous was it in some localities, that around the camp-fires of the traveller a perfect chorus of their plaintive two-syllabled notes was continued incessantly through the night, some of the performers being so near that the sharp click of their mandibles was distinctly audible.

Mr. J. A. Allen found this species abundant on the lower parts of the mountains in Colorado, and heard the notes of scores of them near the mouth of Ogden Cañon on several occasions after nightfall. Though so numerous, all efforts to procure specimens were futile, as it did not usually manifest its presence till after it became too dark for it to be clearly distinguished. He saw it last, October 7, during a severe snow-storm on the mountains north of Ogden. It had been quite common during the greater part of September. He also met with this bird at an elevation of 7,000 feet. He had previously ascertained its presence throughout Kansas from Leavenworth to Fort Hays.

From these varied observations the range of this species may be given as from the valley of the Rio Grande and the more northern States of Mexico, throughout New Mexico, Arizona, and the Great Plains nearly to the Pacific, in California, Oregon, and Washington Territory.

The egg of this species (13,587) was obtained among the East Humboldt Mountains, by Mr. Robert Ridgway, July 20, 1868. Its measurement is 1.06 inches in length by .81 of an inch in breadth. It is of a regularly elliptical form, being equally rounded at either end. Its color is a clear dead-white, entirely unspotted. The egg was found deposited on the bare ground beneath a sage-bush, on a foot-slope of the mountains. The nest was nothing more than a bare spot, apparently worn by the body of the bird. When found, the male bird was sitting on the egg, and was shot as it flew from the spot.

Mr. Salvin (Ibis, III. p. 64) mentions taking, April 20, 1860, on the mountains of Santa Barbara, Central America, a species of *Antrostomus*, a female, with two eggs. This is spoken of as nearly allied to, perhaps identical with, *A. vociferus*. Its eggs are, however, spoken of as white, measuring 1.05 inches by .80 of an inch, almost exactly the size of the eggs of this species. Mr. Salvin adds: " I do not quite understand these eggs being white, except by supposing them to be accidentally so. In other respects, i. e. in form and texture, they agree with the eggs of other species of *Caprimulgidæ*. These eggs, two in number, were on the ground at the foot of a large pine-tree. There was no nest."

In regard to the parentage of the eggs thus discovered, the coloration and size of which correspond so closely with those of the Poor-will, Mr. Salvin writes, in a letter dated March 10, 1872 : "In respect to the *Antrostomus* which lays white eggs in Guatemala, I have carefully examined the skin of the female sent to me with the eggs in question, and represented as their parent. It certainly is not *A. nuttalli,* but appears to belong to the species described by Wagler as *A. macromystax.* This species is very closely allied to *A. vociferus,* but appears to be sufficiently distinct, inasmuch as the rictal bristles are very long, the throat is almost without white feathers, and the white on the tail is more limited in extent than in *A. vociferus.* The true *A. vociferus* is frequently found in winter in Guatemala, but is probably only a migrant. The other species would certainly appear to be a resident in South Mexico and Guatemala. With respect to *A. nuttalli,* I may add that I have recently acquired a skin from Guanajuata, in Mexico. This is the first instance of the occurrence of the species in Mexico at all, that I am aware of."

Mr. Ridgway met with the Poor-will from the eastern slope of the Sierra Nevada to the Wahsatch and Uintah Mountains. He describes its notes as much like those of the eastern *A. vociferus,* except that the first syllable is left off, the call sounding like simply *poor-will,* the accent on the last syllable. It frequents chiefly the dry *mesa* and foot-hills of the mountains, and lives almost entirely on the ground, where its two white unspotted eggs are deposited beneath some small scraggy sage-bush, without any sign of a nest whatever. Both sexes incubate.

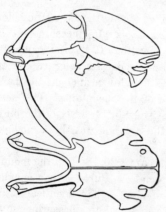

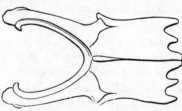

Sternum of *Nyctibius jamaicensis.*

Sternum of *Chordeiles virginianus.*

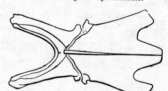

Sternum of *Caprimulgus stictomus.*

Family **CYPSELIDÆ.** — The Swifts.

CHAR. Bill very small, without notch, triangular, much broader than high; the culmen not one sixth the gape. Anterior toes cleft to the base, each with three joints, (in the typical species,) and covered with skin or feathers; the middle claw without any serrations; the lateral toes nearly equal to the middle. Bill without bristles, but with minute feathers extending along the under margin of the nostrils. Tail-feathers ten. Nostrils elongated, superior, and very close together. Plumage compact. Primaries ten, elongated, falcate.

The *Cypselidæ*, or Swifts, are Swallow-like birds, generally of rather dull plumage and medium size. They were formerly associated with the true Swallows on account of their small, deeply cleft bill, wide gape, short feet, and long wings, but are very different in all the essentials of structure, belonging, indeed, to a different order or suborder. The bill is much smaller and shorter; the edges greatly inflected; the nostrils superior, instead of lateral, and without bristles. The wing is more falcate, with ten primaries instead of nine. The tail has ten feathers instead of twelve. The feet are weaker, without distinct scutellæ; the hind toe is more or less versatile, the anterior toes frequently lack the normal number of joints, and there are other features which clearly justify the wide separation here given, especially the difference in the vocal organs. Strange as the statement may be, their nearest relatives are the *Trochilidæ*, or Humming-Birds, notwithstanding the bills of the two are as opposite in shape as can readily be conceived. The sternum of the *Cypselidæ* is also very different from that of the *Hirundinidæ*, as will be shown by the accompanying figure. There are no emargi-

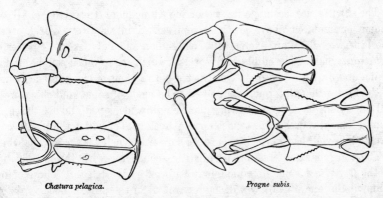

Chætura pelagica.   *Progne subis.*

nations or openings in the posterior edge, which is regularly curved. The keel rises high, for the attachment of the powerful pectoral muscles. The manubrium is almost entirely wanting.

In this family, as in the *Caprimulgidæ*, we find deviations in certain forms from the normal number of phalanges to the toes, which serve to divide it into two sections. In one, the *Chæturinæ*, these are 2, 3, 4, and 5, as usual; but in the *Cypselinœ* they are 2, 3, 3, and 3, as shown in the accompanying cut borrowed from Dr. Sclater's masterly memoir on the *Cypselidœ,* (Pr. Zoöl. Soc. London, 1865, 593), which also serves as the basis of the arrangement here presented.

Left foot of *Chœtura zonaris.*   Left foot of *Panyptila melanoleuca.*

Cypselinæ. Tarsi feathered; phalanges of the middle and outer toes three each (instead of four and five). Hind toe directed either forward or to one side, not backward.

Tarsi feathered; toes bare; hind toe directed forward . . . *Cypselus.*
Both tarsi and toes feathered; hind toe lateral . . . . *Panyptila.*

Chæturinæ. Tarsi bare; phalanges of toes normal (four in middle toe, five in outer). Hind toe directed backwards, though sometimes versatile.

Tarsi longer than middle toe.
    Tail-feathers spinous.
        Shafts of tail-feathers projecting beyond the plumage . *Chœtura.*
        Shafts not projecting, (*Nephœcetes*) . . . . *Cypseloides.*
    Tail-feathers not spinous . . . . *Collocallia.*
Tarsi shorter than middle toe . . . . . . *Dendrochelidon.*

The Swifts are cosmopolite, occurring throughout the globe. All the genera enumerated above are well represented in the New World, except the last two, which are exclusively East Indian and Polynesian. Species of *Collocallia* make the " edible bird's-nests " which are so much sought after in China and Japan. These are constructed entirely out of the hardened saliva of the bird, although formerly supposed to be made of some kind of sea-weed. All the *Cypselidœ* have the salivary glands highly developed, and use the secretion to cement together the twigs or other substances of which the nest is constructed, as well as to attach this to its support. The eggs are always white.

There are many interesting peculiarities connected with the modification of the *Cypselidœ,* some of which may be briefly adverted to. Those of our common Chimney Swallow will be referred to in the proper place. *Panyptila sancti-hieronymœ* of Guatemala attaches a tube some feet in length to the under side of an overhanging rock, constructed of the pappus or seed-down of plants, caught flying in the air. Entrance to this is from below, and the eggs are laid on a kind of shelf near the top. *Chœtura poliura* of Brazil again makes a very similar tube-nest (more contracted below) out of the seeds of *Trixis divaricata,* suspends it to a horizontal branch, and covers the outside with feathers of various colors. As there is no shelf to receive the eggs, it is believed that these are cemented against the sides of the tube, and brooded on by the bird while in an upright position. *Dendrochelidon klecho*, of Java, etc., builds a narrow flat platform on a horizontal branch, of feathers, moss, etc., cemented together, and lays in it a single egg. The nest is so small that the bird sits on the branch and covers the egg with the end of her belly.

Owing to the almost incredible rapidity in flight of the Swifts, and the great height in the air at which they usually keep themselves, the North American species are, of all our land birds, the most difficult to procure, only flying sufficiently near the surface of the ground to be reached by a gun in damp weather, and then requiring great skill to shoot them. Their nests, too, are generally situated in inaccessible places, usually high perpendicular or overhanging mountain-cliffs. Although our four species are sufficiently abundant, and are frequently seen in flocks of thousands, it is only the common Chimney Swift that is to be met with at all regularly in museums.

Subfamily CYPSELINÆ.

The essential character of this subfamily, as stated already, is to be found in the feathered tarsus; the reduction of the normal number of phalanges in the middle toe from 4 to 3, and of the outer toe from 5 to 3, as well as in the anterior or lateral position of the hind toe, not posterior. Of the two genera assigned to it by Dr. Sclater, one, *Cypselus*, is enlarged by him so as to include the small West Indian Palm Swifts, *Tachornis* of Gosse.

Genus PANYPTILA, Cabanis.

Panyptila, Cabanis, Wiegm. Archiv, 1847, i, 345. — Burmeister, Thiere Bras. Vögel, I, 1856, 368. (Type, *Hirundo cayanensis*, Gm.)
Pseudoprocne, Streubel, Isis, 1848, 357. (Same type.)

Gen. Char. Tail half as long as the wings, moderately forked; the feathers rather lanceolate, rounded at tip, the shafts stiffened, but not projecting. First primary shorter than the second. Tarsi, toes, and claws very thick and stout; the former shorter than the middle toe and claw, which is rather longer than the lateral one; middle claw longer than its digit. Hind toe very short; half versatile, or inserted on the side of the tarsus. Tarsi and toes feathered to the claws, except on the under surfaces.

Panyptila melanoleuca.

6018 ♂

Three species of this genus are described by authors, all of them black, with white throat, and a patch of the same on each side of rump, and otherwise varied with this color. The type *P. cayanensis* is much the smallest (4.70), and has the tail more deeply forked than *P. melanoleuca*.

Synopsis of Species.

P. cayanensis. Glossy intense black ; a supraloral spot of white ; white of throat transversely defined posteriorly. Tail deeply forked, the lateral feathers excessively attenuated and acute.

Wing, 4.80 ; middle tail-feather, 1.20, external, 2.30. *Hab.* Cayenne
and Brazil . . . . var. *cayanensis*.[1]
Wing, 7.30; middle tail-feather, 1.90, external, 3.60. *Hab.* Guatemala.
var. *sancti-hieronymi*.[2]

P. melanoleuca. Lustreless dull black; no supraloral white spot, but instead a hoary wash; white of throat extending back along middle of abdomen to the vent. Tail moderately forked, the lateral feathers obtuse. Wing, 5.75 ; middle tail-feather, 2.30, outer, 2.85. *Hab.* Middle Province of United States, south to Guatemala.

Panyptila melanoleuca, BAIRD.

WHITE-THROATED SWIFT.

Cypselus melanoleucus, BAIRD, Pr. A. N. Sc. Phil. VII, June, 1854, 118 (San Francisco Mountains, N. M.). — CASSIN, Illust. I, 1855, 248. *Panyptila melanoleuca,* BAIRD, Birds N. Am. 1858, 141, pl. xviii, f. 1. — SCLATER & SALVIN, Ibis, 1859, 125 (Guatemala). — SCLATER, P. Z. S. 1865, 607. — KENNERLY, P. R. R. X, b, 36, pl. xviii, f. 1. — HEERMANN, Ib. X, c, 10. — COOPER, Orn. Cal. I, 1870, 347.

SP. CHAR. Wings very long ; tail forked ; tarsi and feet covered with feathers. Black all over, except the chin, throat, middle of the belly as far as the vent, a patch on each side of the rump, the edge of the outer primary, and blotches on the inner webs of the median tail-feathers, near the base, which are white, as is also a band across the ends of the secondaries. Length, 5.50 ; wing, 5.50 ; tail, 2.70.

HAB. Nevada, Utah, Colorado, Arizona, and southern Rocky Mountains, to Guatemala. Localities : Cajon Pass (COOPER, Pr. Cal. Ac. 1861, 122) ; Arizona (COUES, P. A. N. S. 1866, 57); San Diego (COOPER).

Although there is no difference in size between Rocky Mountain and Guatemalan specimens, the only two of the latter in the collection are darker colored, showing scarcely any indication of the frontal and supraloral whitish so conspicuous in most northern skins. In the Guatemalan female (30,837, Dueñas, February 13) the dusky of the lateral, and white of the medial, portions of the breast blend gradually together, there not being that sharp

---

[1] *Panyptila cayanensis* (GMEL.), CAB. *Hirundo cay.* GMELIN, Syst. Nat. I, 1024. *Panyptila cay.* CABAN. Wiegm. Archiv, XIII, 345 (1847). — SCL. P. Z. S. 1866, 606.

[2] *Panyptila sancti-hieronymi,* SALVIN (P. Z. S. 1863, 190, pl. xxii ; SCL. P. Z. S. 1866, 607). May be the northern form of *cayanensis,* which, however, we have not seen.

line of junction seen in all the others, including the male from Guatemala (30,836, Dueñas, Nov.).

HABITS. This new species was first discovered by Dr. Kennerly on Bill Williams Fork, New Mexico, February 16, 1854. He speaks of it as a very curious and interesting bird, found by him only among the cañons of that stream, and not observed elsewhere during their journey. Large flocks could be seen at any time in the vicinity of those cañons, flying and circling around very high, and far beyond the reach of shot. Towards the close of the day, when the sun had sunk behind the hills, they occasionally descended lower. He only met with them where the walls of the cañons were very high, and consisted of almost perpendicular masses of rock. At times they

Panyptila melanoleuca.

were seen to sweep low down, and then to ascend nearly perpendicularly very near the stones, as if examining them in order to select a place for their nests. The construction of these had obviously not then commenced. Dr. Kennerly saw none engaged in the work, nor did he observe any old nests, unless they build after the manner of the common Cliff Swallow, which were also abundant in that region. Mr. Möllhausen was of the opinion that these birds build in the holes and crevices of the cliffs. In their flight and habits they appeared to closely resemble the common *Chætura pelagica*.

Dr. Heermann met with this species several times, first in San Fernando Pass, near Los Angelos, and again near Palm Spring, between the Colorado desert and Vallicita, at another time near Tucson, and once also in Texas. He always found them flying at a great height, either far beyond or on the extreme limit of gunshot range. From the extent of their wings they seemed formed to live in the air, where they pass most of their time gliding about in extensive circles, with apparently very little motion of the wings. During pleasant weather they found their insect prey in the upper air, but, when cloudy or rainy, they flew nearer the ground in their pursuit. When on the ground, they were observed to rise with difficulty, owing to the shortness of their legs and the length of their wings. When they rest, they always alight on some elevated point whence they can throw themselves into the air, and take to wing. Numbers were observed flying about the rocks near Tucson, but none were heard to utter a note. They were sociable among themselves, gathering in large flocks, but never mingled with the Swallows. He states that they construct their nests in the crevices of rocks, and that their eggs are pure white, and of an elongated form.

Dr. Coues found this species rather sparingly distributed throughout Arizona, always in the neighborhood of cliffs and precipices, which it exclusively inhabits. From Inscription Rock, about one day's march from Whipple's Pass, to the San Francisco Mountains of Arizona, he found these birds in great numbers, except along the valley of the Colorado Chiquito, where there were no suitable cliffs for their habitation. He generally found them congregated in considerable, sometimes in immense, numbers in the vicinity of huge cliffs and piles of rocks. Their note, he adds, is an often and quickly repeated twitter, loud and shrill, and quite different from that of the *C. pelagica*. He states that they build their nest upon the vertical faces of precipitous rocks.

Dr. Woodhouse met with a Swift in the same region referred to by Dr. Coues, which he called *Acanthylis saxatilis*, which may possibly be the same species, but of which no specimen was procured. They were breeding in the crevices of the rocks. The description, however, does not at all correspond.

This species has lately been met with by Mr. Salvin, in Guatemala, where it is by no means common, and so very local that its presence might readily have been overlooked. He found it near Dueñas, in a gorge with precipitous rocks on the right hand, along the course of the river Guacalate. His attention was drawn to a noise coming from the rocks, which he at first took to be bats in some of the cracks. After watching for some time, he saw two Swifts dart into a crack in the rock twenty feet from the ground, and the noise became louder than before. Resorting to several expedients, in vain, to make them fly out, he climbed up part way, and there found one of them killed by a random shot of his gun. Another discharge of his gun brought out five or six more, which were immediately pursued by the *Cotyle serripennis*. He obtained three specimens in all. The spot was evidently their common roosting-place, and by the noise they made he judged they were there in large numbers. He found them about the middle of February.

Dr. Cooper met with this species near Fort Mohave, but saw none before May. On the 7th of June, near the head of Mohave River, he found a few about some lofty granite cliffs, and succeeded in obtaining one. Their flight was exceedingly swift and changeable, and they were very difficult to shoot. He also found them about some high rocky bluffs close to the sea-shore, twelve miles north of San Diego. They were seen the last of March, but may have been there for a month previously.

Mr. Allen encountered this little-known Swift near Colorado City, where it was quite numerous about the high cliffs in the "Garden of the Gods," and of which, with great difficulty, he procured four specimens. It was nesting in inaccessible crevices and weather-beaten holes in the rocks, about midway up the high vertical cliffs, some of which were not less than three hundred feet high. It seemed to be very wary, and flew with great velocity, rarely descending within reach of the guns.

The White-throated Swift was met with in great abundance by Mr. Ridgway at the East Humboldt Mountains, and was seen by him more sparingly in the Toyabe and Wahsatch. In the former mountains it inhabited the high limestone cliffs which walled the cañons, congregating in thousands, and nesting in the chinks or crevices of the rocks, in company with the Violet-green Swallow (*Tachycincta thalassina*). It was a very noisy species, having a vigorous chatter, reminding one somewhat of the notes of young Baltimore Orioles when being fed by their parents. It was also very pugnacious, a couple now and then being seen to fasten upon one another high up in the air, and, clinging together, falling, whirling round and round in their descent, nearly to the ground, when they would let go each other, and separate. A couple would often rush by with almost inconceivable velocity, one in chase of the other. Their flight was usually very high, or, if they occasionally descended, it was so swiftly that Mr. Ridgway only succeeded in shooting three specimens, while he found it utterly impossible to reach their nests, which were in the horizontal fissures in the face of the overhanging cliff.

SUBFAMILY CHÆTURINÆ.

This subfamily is characterized by having the normal number of phalanges to the middle and outer toes (4 and 5, instead of 3 and 3), the backward position of the hind toe, and the naked tarsi, which do not even appear to be scutellate, but covered with a soft skin. Of the two North American genera, *Chætura* has spinous projections at the end of the tail-feathers, while in *Nephœcetes* the shafts of the tail-feathers, though stiffened, do not project beyond the plume.

This subfamily appears to be composed of two definable sections, with subdivisions as follows:—

A. Tail forked; spinous points of the feathers not extending far beyond the webs, or entirely wanting. Feathering of the sides of the forehead extending forward outside the nostrils nearly to their anterior end.

   a. No trace of spinous points to tail-feathers. Feathering of frontal points almost completely enclosing the nostrils between them. No light collar round the neck; sides of the forehead with a hoary suffusion . . *Nephœcetes.*

   b. Spinous points of tail-feathers distinct. A light collar round the neck.

      1. Nostril as in *Nephœcetes.* Sides of forehead with a hoary suffusion. Collar chestnut. Wing less than 5.50. (*C. rutila.*) . .

      2. Feathered frontal points narrower, not reaching anterior end of nostril. Sides of forehead without hoary suffusion. Collar white. Wing more than 8.00 . . . . *Hemiprocne.*

B. Tail rounded; spinous points of the feathers much elongated and projecting. Feathering of sides of forehead scarcely reaching beyond posterior end of nostril. Wing less than 5.50 . . . . *Chætura.*

Genus **NEPHŒCETES**, Baird.

Nephœcetes, Baird, Birds N. Am. 1858, 142. (Type, *Hirundo nigra*, Gmel.)

Gen. Char. Tail rather less than half the wings; quite deeply forked (less so in the female); the feathers obtusely acuminate; the shafts scarcely stiffened. First quill longest. Tarsi and toes completely bare, and covered with naked skin, without distinct indications of scutellæ. Tarsus rather longer than middle toe; the three anterior toes about equal, with moderately stout claws. Claw of middle toe much shorter than its

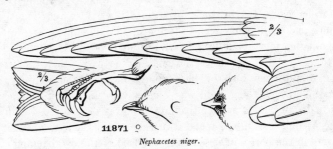

11871 ♀

Nephœcetes niger.

digit. Hind toe not versatile, but truly posterior and opposite, with its claw rather longer than the middle toe without it. Toes all slender; claws moderate. Nostrils widely ovate, the feathers margining its entire lower edge.

The comparative characters of this genus will be found in the diagnostic

Nephœcetes niger.

tables at the head of the family. According to Sclater, *Cypseloides* of Streubel (Isis, 1848, 366) with *C. fumigatus* as type, may have to be taken for this genus, as it was named by Streubel as an alternative to *Hemiprocne*, which belongs to *Chætura*. Until this question of synonymy can be decided positively, we retain *Nephœcetes*.

The single North American species, *N. niger*, has a singular distribution, being abundant near Puget Sound in summer, and again found in Jamaica and Cuba, without having been met with in any intermediate locality, except in the Province of Huatasco, Mex. The West India specimens are rather smaller, but otherwise not distinguishable.

Nephœcetes niger, BAIRD.

BLACK SWIFT.

? Hirundo niger, GMEL. S. N. I, 1788, 1025. *Cypselus niger*, GOSSE, B. Jam. 1847, 63. —
IB. Illust. B. Jam. pl. x. — GUNDL. & LAWR. Ann. N. Y. Lyc. VI, 1858, 268. — SCL.
P. Z. S. 1865, 615. *Nephocœtes niger*, BAIRD, Birds N. Am. 1858, 142. — ELLIOT,
Illust. Birds N. Am. I, xx. — COOPER, Orn. Cal. I, 1870, 349. *Cypselus borealis*,
KENNERLY, P. A. N. S. Philaḍ. IX, Nov. 1857, 202. — SCL. P. Z. S. 1865, 615.
Hirundo apus dominicensis, BRISSON, II, 1760, 514, pl. xlvi, f. 3.

SP. CHAR. Wing the length of the body. General color rather lustrous dark sooty-
brown, with a greenish gloss, becoming a very little lighter on the breast anteriorly
below, but rather more so on the neck and head above. The feathers on top of the head
edged with light gray, which forms a continuous wash on each side of the forehead
above, and anterior to the usual black crescent in front of the eye. Occasionally some
feathers of the under parts behind are narrowly edged with gray. Bill and feet black.
Length, 6.75; wing, 6.75; tail, 3.00, the depth of its fork about .45 in the male, and
scarcely .15 in the female.

HAB. Washington Territory, Oregon, Nevada, and Orizaba (var. *borealis*); Cuba and
Jamaica (var. *niger*), breeds. Vera Cruz; breeds (SUMICHRAST, Mem. Bost. Soc. I, 562).

The tail is considerably more forked in the male than in the female, in
which it is sometimes nearly even, and in the males its depth varies considerably.

Jamaican specimens (var. *niger*) are rather smaller, considerably blacker,
and seem to have narrower tail-feathers, even when the other dimensions are
about equal.

Whether the Puget Sound bird visits the West Indies is not known; but
the difference in size and colors between them and the West Indian birds
would seem to indicate that they select a more directly southern region.
The fact that the Orizaba specimen is most like the Northwest Coast birds
favors this latter supposition.

HABITS. This Swift is of irregular and local occurrence in the West
Indies and in Western North America. Specimens were obtained at Simi-
ahmoo Bay, Washington Territory, by Dr. Kennerly, in July, 1857. Dr.
Cooper saw a black Swift, which he thinks may have been this species, in
Pah-Ute Cañon, west of Fort Mohave, May 29, 1861, and again at Santa
Barbara, May, 1863.

Dr. Gundlach, in his ornithological explorations in Cuba, in 1858, met
with this species among the mountains between Cienfuegos and Trinidad, on
the southern coast of that island, and also in the eastern parts of the Sierra
Maestra. He saw these birds for the first time in the month of May, near
Bayamo, where they commonly arrived every morning about one hour after
sunrise, and flew in a circular direction over the river at a considerable
height, making their evolutions always in the same place, apparently employed in catching the insects attracted by the proximity of the river.

In the month of June they came every day towards noon, whenever it threatened to rain, and sometimes returned again after sunset. When tired of their exercise they always flew together towards the mountains, where he had no doubt their breeding-places existed. He states that when one of these birds flies in chase of another, it emits a soft continued note, not unlike a song. Having taken many young birds in the month of June, he supposes that these Swifts breed in April and May.

It is stated by Sumichrast to have been occasionally met with in the table-lands of Mexico, and that it is resident and breeds within the State of Vera Cruz, Mexico.

A single specimen of this bird was known to Gosse to have been taken near Spanishtown in Jamaica, in 1843, in company with many others. Mr. March, in his paper on the birds of this island, gives a similar account of the habits of this species to that of Dr. Gundlach. He states that it was rarely seen except at early dawn, or in dull and cloudy weather, or after rain in an afternoon. He has sometimes procured specimens from Health-shire and the St. Catharine Hills. The only place known to him as their actual resort is a cave in the lower St. Catharine Hills, near the ferry, where they harbor in the narrow deep galleries and fissures of the limestone rocks.

Mr. J. K. Lord cites this species as among the earliest of the spring visitors seen by him in British Columbia. On a foggy morning early in June, the insects being low, these birds were hovering close to the ground, and he obtained four specimens. He saw no more until the fall of the year, when they again made their appearance in large numbers, among the many other birds of that season. He again saw this Swift at Fort Colville.

Captain Prevost, R. N., obtained a single specimen of this bird on Vancouver Island, which Mr. Sclater compared with Gosse's *Cypselus niger*, from Jamaica. He, however, is not satisfied as to their identity, and is inclined to regard the two birds as distinct.

According to Captain Feilner, this species breeds in the middle of June, on high rocks on the Klamath River, about eight miles above Judah's Cave.

The Black Swift was seen by Mr. Ridgway, during his western tour, only once, when, about the middle of June, an assembly of several hundreds was observed early one morning hovering over the Carson River, below Fort Churchill, in Nevada. In the immediate vicinity was an immense rocky cliff, where he supposed they nested. In their flight they much resembled Chimney-Swallows (*Chœtura*), only they appeared much larger. They were perfectly silent. On the Truckee River, near Pyramid Lake, in May of the same year, he found the remains of one which had been killed by a hawk, but the species was not seen there alive.

Genus **CHÆTURA**, STEPHENS.

Chætura, STEPHENS, Shaw's Gen. Zoöl. Birds, XIII, II, 1825, 76.   (Type, *C. pelagica.*)
Acanthylis, BOIE, Isis, 1826, 971.   (*Cypselus spinicauda.*)

GEN. CHAR. Tail very short, scarcely more than two fifths the wings ; slightly rounded ; the shafts stiffened and extending some distance beyond
the feathers in a rigid spine.
First primary longest. Legs
covered by a naked skin,
without scutellæ or feathers.
Tarsus longer than middle
toe. Lateral toes equal,
nearly as long as the middle.
Hind toe scarcely versatile,
or quite posterior ; including

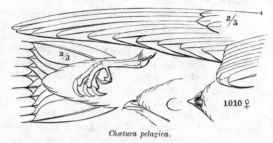

Chætura pelagica.

claw, less than the middle anterior without it. Toes slender ; claws moderate. Feathers
of the base of the bill not extending beyond the beginning of the nostrils.

By the arrangement of the genera on page 1018, the *C. rutila* and large
white-collared species are excluded from the present genus as restricted.
Chætura, as here defined, is a genus of very extensive distribution, species
occurring not only in North and South America, but also in Africa and Asia.
Among the several American members, three styles are distinguishable,
these probably representing only as many species ; the several more closely
allied forms being, in all probability, but geographical modifications of these
three types.   They may be arranged as follows : —

>   *Plumage with no marked contrast of shades.*

C. pelagica.   Nearly uniformly dusky grayish-brown, the throat, however,
very much lighter, and the rump just appreciably so.

>   Above glossy dusky-brown, hardly appreciably paler on the rump ;
>   abdomen scarcely paler than the back. Wing, 5.20. *Hab.* Eastern
>   Province North America . . . . var. *pelagica.*
>   Above glossy blackish-dusky, very decidedly paler on the rump ;
>   abdomen very much paler than the back. Wing, 4.50. *Hab.* Pacific
>   Province of North America, south to Guatemala (from whence speci-
>   mens are much darker, almost black above, and slightly smaller) var. *vauxi.*
>   Above glossy black, fading into sooty dusky on the rump ; abdomen
>   like-the rump. Wing, 4.80. *Hab.* Northern South America (Cayenne,
>   Tobago) . . . . var. *poliura.*[1]

>   *Plumage with marked contrast of shades.*

C. cinereiventris.[2]   Upper parts, except the rump, glossy, intense blue-
black ; rump and lower parts bluish-cinereous, conspicuously different.

---

[1] *Chætura poliura*, (TEMM.) SCL. Cat. Am. B. 1862, 101 ; P. Z. S. 1866, 611. (*Cypselus
polivurus*, TEMM. Tab. Méth. p. 78.)
[2] *Chætura cinerciventris*, SCL. Cat. Am. B. 1862, p. 283 ; P. Z. S. 1863, p. 101, pl. xiv, f. 1 ;
P. Z. 1866, 612. *C. sclateri*, PELZ. Orn. Braz. I, 1868, pp. 16, 56, is also referrible to it as
perhaps a race.

C. spinicauda.[1] Upper parts glossy black, with a white band across the rump. Below sooty-whitish, with indistinct black marks on the breast. wing, 3.90. *Hab.* Cayenne and Brazil.

Chætura pelagica, BAIRD.

CHIMNEY SWALLOW.

Hirundo pelagica, LINN. Syst. Nat. ed. 10, 1758, 192. *Hirundo pelasgia,* LINN. Syst. Nat. I, 1766, 345. — WILS. Am. Orn. V, 1812, 48, pl. xxxix, fig. 1. *Cypselus pelasgia,* AUD. Orn. Biog. II, 1834, 329 ; V, 419, pl. clviii. *Chætura pelasgia,* STEPHENS, in Shaw's Gen. Zoöl. Birds, XIII, II, 1825, 76. — IB. Birds America, I, 1840, 164, pl. xliv. — BAIRD, Birds N. Am. 1858, 144. — SAMUELS, 116. — ALLEN, Birds Fla. 301. *Acanthylis pelasgia,* "TEMM." — BON. Consp. 1850, 64. — CASSIN, Ill. I, 1855, 241. *Hemiprocne pelasgia,* STREUBEL, Isis, 1848, 363. *Aculeated Swallow,* PENN. Arc. Zoöl. II, 1785, 432. *Cypselus pelasgius,* MAX. Cab. Journ. 1858.

SP. CHAR. Tail slightly rounded. Sooty-brown all over, except on the throat, which becomes considerably lighter from the breast to the bill. Above with a greenish tinge ; the rump a little paler. Length, 5.25 ; wing, 5.10 ; tail, 2.15.

HAB. Eastern United States to slopes of Rocky Mountains ?

Chætura pelagica.

The etymology of the specific name of *pelasgia,* used by Linnæus, of this bird, in the twelfth edition of Systema Naturæ, has always been a question. We find that the word in the tenth edition is *pelagica,* referring probably to the supposed passage over the Caribbean Sea in its annual migrations.

Chætura vauxi, the western representative of this bird, is extremely similar, but distinguishable by considerably smaller size, much lighter, almost white, throat, paler rump, and under parts decidedly lighter than the back. *C. poliura,* which much resembles it, is blacker above, and much darker below. (See synopsis on page 1027.)

HABITS. The common Chimney Swallow of North America has an extended range throughout the eastern portions of the continent, from the Atlantic to the 50th parallel of northern latitude. It was not met with by Dr. Richardson in the fur regions, but was found by Say at Pembina, on

---

[1] *Chætura spinicauda,* SCL. *Cypselus spinicaudus,* TEM. Tabl. Méth. p. 78 (ex Buff. Pl. Enl. 726, f. 1). *Acanthylis s.* BOIE, Isis, 1826, p. 971 ; BONAP. Consp. p. 64. *Chætura s.* SCL. Catal. Am. Birds, 1862, 283. *Hirundo pelasgia,* var., LATH. Ind. Orn. II, 581. *Hab.* Cayenne and Brazil.

the Red River, in what is now the northern part of Minnesota. Its western range is not well determined, but is presumed to be terminated by the great plains. It has been found as far west as Bijoux Hill, in Nebraska.

In its habits, especially during the breeding-season, this Swift presents many remarkable differences from the European species. While the latter are shy and retiring, shunning the places frequented by man, and breeding chiefly in caves or ruined and deserted habitations, their representatives in eastern North America, like all the Swallow family here, have, immediately upon the erection of the dwellings of civilized life, manifested their appreciation of the protection they afford, by an entire change in their habits in regard to the location of their nests. When the country was first settled, these birds were known to breed only in the hollow trunks of forest trees. The chimneys of the dwellings of civilized communities presented sufficient inducements, in their greater convenience, to tempt this bird to forsake their primitive breeding-places. The change in this respect has been nearly complete. And now, in the older portions of the country, they are not known to resort to hollow trees for any other purpose than as an occasional roosting-place.

In wild portions of the country, where natural facilities are still afforded to these Swifts, they are occasionally found breeding within the hollows of decaying trees. Mr. George A. Boardman, of St. Stephen, N. B., writes that in his neighborhood this bird continues to build in the hollows of trees. He adds, that in the summer of 1863 he found them building within a hollow birch. He also met with one of their nests built against a board in an old winter logging-camp, at a distance from any chimney. Mr. Ridgway has also met with the nest of this bird inside the trunk of a large sycamore-tree, and also mentions finding another attached to the planks of an outbuilding, in the Wabash valley of Southeastern Illinois.

Mr. J. A. Allen found this species quite numerous in Kansas, where it was breeding chiefly in the hollow trees of the forests, which it always seems naturally to prefer to chimneys, to which it is compelled to resort, in most of the longer settled districts, or else wholly to abandon the country.

The Chimney Swallow is known to breed throughout the Central and Northern States, from Virginia to Canada. Dr. Woodhouse states that he found this species very abundant throughout the Indian Territory, as also in Texas, and New Mexico, even to California. It was not, however, taken at San Antonio by Mr. Dresser, nor in any portion of Texas, and was not procured by any of the naturalists in the other Western expeditions.

The Chimney Swallow is crepuscular, rather than nocturnal, in its habits, preferring to hunt for its insect prey in dull and cloudy weather, or in the early morning and the latter part of the afternoon. In this it is probably influenced by the abundance or scarcity of insects, as it is not unfrequently to be seen hawking for insects in the bright glare of noon. When they have young, they often continue to feed them until quite late at night.

They are not, however, to be regarded as nocturnal, as they are only known to do this during a brief period.

The nest of this species is a very peculiar and remarkable structure. It is composed of small twigs of nearly uniform size, wrought and interwoven into a neat semicircular basket. In selecting the twigs with which they are to construct their nests, the Swifts break from the tree the ends of living branches, which they gather with great skill and adroitness while on the wing. Sweeping upon the coveted twig somewhat as a Hawk rushes on its prey, it divides it at the desired place, and bears it off to its nest. This is a well-attested fact, familiar to all who have ever watched these birds in the early morning as they are at work constructing their nests.

Each one of these twigs is strongly fastened to its fellows by an adhesive saliva secreted by the bird, and by the same cement the whole structure is made to adhere to the side of the chimney in which it is built. This saliva, as it dries, hardens into a tough glue-like substance, as firm even as the twigs it unites. In separating nests from the sides of chimneys, I have known portions of the brick to which it was fastened part sooner than the cement. When moistened, however, by long-continued rains, the weight of their contents will sometimes cause these nests to part, and the whole is precipitated to the bottom. The young birds cling very tenaciously to the sides of the chimneys with their bills and claws. They not only are often able, in these accidents, to save themselves from falling, but even at a very early age can cling to the sides of the chimney and work their way to the top. They always leave their nest and climb to the upper part of the chimney several days before they can fly, and are there fed by their parents.

Occasionally the young birds fall to the bottom of the chimney, out of the reach or notice of their parents. I have never been able to induce them to take any food, although they keep uttering pitiful cries of hunger. In such cases the young birds placed on the roof near their native chimney soon manage to climb to its base, and there receive the aid of the old birds.

Their eggs are four in number, somewhat elliptical in form, though somewhat less obtuse at one end than the other. They are of a pure white color, and are never spotted. They vary but little in size or shape, and measure from .75 to .81 of an inch in length, and from .50 to .55 in breadth.

In New England the Chimney Swallow raises but one brood in a season. In Pennsylvania it is said to have two.

Chætura (pelagica var. ?) vauxi, (Towns.) DeKay.

OREGON CHIMNEY SWIFT.

Cypselus vauxi, Townsend, J. A. N. Sc. VIII, 1839, 148 (Columbia River). — Ib. Narrative, 1839. *Chætura vauxi*, DeKay, N. Y. Zoöl. II, 1844, 36. — Baird, Birds N. Am. 145, pl. xviii. — Sclater, Cat. 282. — Ib. P. Z. S. 1863, 100 (Guatemala). — Kennerly, P. R. R. x, b, pl. xviii, f. 2. — Cooper & Suckley, 165. — Cooper, Orn. Cal. I, 1870, 351. *Acanthylis vauxi*, Bonap. Comptes Rendus, XXVIII, 1854 ; notes Delattre, 90. — Cassin, Ill. I, 1855, 250. — Newberry, Zoöl. Cal. and Or. Route, 78 ; P. R. R. Surv. VI, 1857.

Sp. Char. Light sooty-brown ; rump and under parts paler ; lightest on the chin and throat. Length, 4.50 ; wing, 4.75 ; tail, 1.90.

Hab. Pacific coast, from Puget's Sound to California. West coast to Guatemala (Scl. P. Z. S. 1863, 100) ; Yucatan (Lawr. Ann. N. Y. Lyc. IX, 204).

This species bears a very close resemblance to the common Chimney Swallow of the Eastern States, being only readily distinguishable by its much smaller size, 4.50 inches instead of 5.25. The wing, too, is nearly an inch shorter. The tarsus and the middle toe, however, seem absolutely longer. The rump is a little paler than in *C. pelagica,* as well as the under parts, where the chin and throat are lighter, almost dirty white, and gradually becoming a little darker behind, although even the hinder part of the belly is much lighter than the back, even in strong contrast, instead of being of the same color with it. Guatemalan specimens are much darker.

Habits. This western Swift was first discovered by Mr. Townsend on the Columbia River, where he found it having the primitive habits of the eastern species, and breeding in hollow trees, forming a nest in a similar manner, and laying four pure-white eggs. It differs from the common bird in its smaller size and lighter color. It is said to occur from Puget Sound to California.

Dr. Cooper met with these birds May 4, 1864, in the Coast Range, twelve miles south of Santa Clara. He was of the opinion that they had nests in hollow trees at the summit of the mountains, but he was not able to find any. He did not observe any at Fort Vancouver in the summer of 1853, nor did he learn whether these birds are found in the central valleys of California. In 1866 they were observed to make their first appearance at Santa Cruz on the 4th of May, though as they rarely descended to the town they might have been on the hills earlier than this. On the 5th of October he observed five of them, in company with a large flock of *Hirundo bicolor,* spending the morning in hunting insects near the town. They were apparently delayed in their migration southward by a thick fog and cold south-wind. They may have been a late brood from the north.

Dr. Kennerly obtained a single specimen of this species at the Straits of Fuca, showing that these birds sometimes extend their migrations up to the 49th parallel. Neither Dr. Suckley nor Dr. Cooper was able to find this Swift anywhere in Washington Territory.

Dr. Newberry observed this species quite common in California, but could obtain no specimens, owing to the height at which they flew. He saw nothing of it in Oregon.

Two specimens of this species obtained in Mexico by M. de Saussure are in the collection of Dr. Sclater.

Mr. Ridgway saw on the Truckee River, near Pyramid Lake, in May, 1868, what he supposes to have been this species. It was not common, only a few individuals being observed every evening just before dusk, flying overhead exactly in the manner of Chimney Swallows (*C. pelagica*), which they also exactly resembled in appearance. They flew so high that specimens could not be obtained. They were entirely silent, and appeared at no other time than in the evening, in these respects differing strikingly from the eastern species.

FAMILY **TROCHILIDÆ**. — THE HUMMING-BIRDS.

CHAR. Least of all birds; sternum very deep; bill subulate, and generally longer than the head, straight, arched, or upcurved. Tongue composed of two lengthened cylindrical united tubes, capable of great protrusion, and bifid at tip; nostrils basal, linear, and covered by an operculum; wings lengthened, pointed; first quill usually longest except in *Aithurus*, where it is the second; primaries, 10; secondaries, 6; tail of ten feathers. Tarsi and feet very diminutive, claws very sharp. (GOULD.)

There is no group of birds so interesting to the ornithologist or to the casual observer as the Humming-Birds, at once the smallest in size, the most gorgeously beautiful in color, and almost the most abundant in species, of any single family of birds. They are strictly confined to the continent and islands of America, and are most abundant in the Central American and Andean States, though single species range almost to the Arctic regions on the north and to Patagonia on the south, as well as from the sea-coast to the frozen summits of the Andes. Many are very limited in their range; some confined to particular islands, even though of small dimensions, or to the summits of certain mountain-peaks.

The bill of the Humming-Bird is awl-shaped or subulate; thin, and sharp-pointed; straight or curved; sometimes as long as the head, sometimes much longer. The mandibles are excavated to the tip for the lodgement of the tongue, and form a tube by the close apposition of their cutting edges. There is no indication of stiff bristly feathers at the base of the mouth. The tongue has some resemblance to that of the Woodpecker in the elongation of the cornua backwards, so as to pass round the back of the skull, and then anteriorly to the base of the bill. The tongue itself is of very peculiar structure, consisting anteriorly of two hollow threads closed at the ends and united behind. The food of the Humming-Bird consists almost entirely of insects, which are captured by protruding the tongue in flowers of various shapes without opening the bill very wide.

The genera of Humming-Birds are very difficult to define. This is partly owing to the great number of the species, of which nearly four hundred and fifty have been recognized by authors, all of them with but few exceptions diminutive in size and almost requiring a lens for their critical examination, so that characters for generic separation, distinct enough in other families, are here overlooked or not fully appreciated. A still greater difficulty, perhaps, is the great difference in form, especially of the tail, between the male and female, the young male occupying an intermediate position. The coloration, too, is almost always very different with sex and age, and usually any generic characters derived from features other than those of bill, feet, and wing do not apply to the females at all.

In the large number of species of Humming-Birds arranged in about one hundred and thirty genera, only two subfamilies have been recognized, as follows : —

Phæthornithinæ. Anterior toes connected at the base. No metallic lustre to the dull plumage.

Trochilinæ. Anterior toes not connected at the base. Plumage brilliant, with more or less of metallic lustre, at least in the males.

The first-mentioned subfamily embraces five genera, and about fifty species, none of which are found in the United States. The *Trochilinæ* count nearly four hundred species and one hundred and twenty-five genera, and in the absence of any successful attempt to arrange them in subordinate groups, the difficulties of determination on the part of the tyro may readily be imagined.

Of the seven genera accredited to North America, with their ten species, we cannot pretend to do more than present an artificial analysis, which may serve to define them as compared with each other, but bear little reference to the family as a whole. The characters are selected partly from the shape of tail and partly from color.

COMMON CHARACTERS. All the North American *Trochilidæ* have metallic green backs, excepting *Selasphorus rufus*, this color extending over the top of head, except in *Calypte* (metallic red and violet), and *Heliopædica* (bluish-black). The latter alone has a white stripe through the eye. *Atthis heloisæ* alone has the tail tipped with white in the male. Females of all the species except *Heliopædica* have tail tipped with white; all have it rounded. All females lack the metallic throat. The males of the several genera belonging to North America may be distinguished as follows : —

I. *Bill covered with feathers between nostrils.*

A. Top of head green.
　　Feathers of throat not elongated.
　　　　Tail rounded or slightly emarginated, the feathers broad, rounded, and metallic rufous-purple, or greenish-blue. Wing more than 2.50　.　*Lampornis.*
　　　　Tail more or less forked; feathers pointed, narrow, and without rufous or blue. Wing much less than 2.00　.　.　.　.　.　*Trochilus.*
　　Throat-feathers elongated laterally into a kind of ruff. Tail-feathers edged or banded with cinnamon at base.
　　　　Tail cuneate, the outer primary attenuated at end. Innermost tail-feather green above.
　　　　　　Tail dusky at end　.　.　.　.　.　.　.　.　*Selasphorus.*
　　　　　　Tail tipped with white　.　.　.　.　.　.　.　*Atthis.*
　　　　Tail nearly even, and emarginated. Outer primary not attenuated at end. Innermost tail-feather brown above　.　.　.　.　*Stellula.*
B. Top of head metallic red or violet.
　　Metallic feathers of side of throat much elongated　.　.　.　.　*Calypte.*

II. *Bill bare of feathers between the nostrils.*

C. Top of head bluish-black ; a white line through eye.
　　Metallic feathers of side of throat not elongated.
　　　　Tail nearly even, and slightly emarginated. Lateral feathers very broad and obtuse at end　.　.　.　.　.　.　.　.　*Heliopædica.*

We have included *Lampornis* in the list of United States genera on exceedingly doubtful evidence of the occurrence of *L. mango*, which was said to have been taken at Key West, and sent to Mr. Audubon, who figured it. The species, however, proves to be one belonging to Brazil, and not the Jamaican form (*L. porphyrura*, Gould), which might possibly have straggled there.

In reference to the large number of species of *Trochilidæ*, it may be well to remark that many differ by very slight, sometimes quite inappreciable characters, and are to be looked on as only climatic or geographical varieties. All those given for the United States are, however, well marked.

Additional species of *Trochilidæ* will doubtless yet be detected within our limits, especially in Arizona, New Mexico, and Southern Texas, where almost any of the Mexican table-land species may be looked for, such as *Calypte floresi*, *Calothorax cyanopogon*, etc. South Florida will probably yet furnish to us the Bahaman *Doricha evelynæ*.

The following synopsis expresses, perhaps, a more natural arrangement of the genera : —

A. Nasal operculum entirely covered by the frontal feathers; base of the bill narrow.

    a. Tail forked, and unvariegated in the male. Outer primary strongly bowed, or curved inward at the end.

        Stellula. Tail deeply emarginated in ♂, somewhat doubly rounded in ♀, but outer feather not longest ; the feathers spatulate ; outer primary very strongly bowed, and very broad at end. ♂. Gorget feathers linear, much elongated ; only their terminal half colored ; crown green like the back. ♀. Similar in form, but the intermediate feathers of tail longer than the external, instead of shorter.

        Trochilus. Tail deeply emarginated in the male, the feathers attenuated toward tips ; doubly rounded in ♀, and broader ; outer primary strongly bowed, but narrow at end. ♂. Gorget feathers broad, short, squamate ; colored blue or crimson to their bases. Crown green like the back.

        Calypte. Tail as in *Trochilus*, but the external feather abruptly narrower than the next, with its edges nearly parallel. Outer primary as in *Trochilus*. Crown metallic (violet or crimson) like the throat. *Female* like that of *Trochilus*.

    b. Tail rounded or graduated, and variegated in the male. Outer primary only slightly bowed, and narrow at end, except in ♀ of *Atthis*.

        Selasphorus. Tail graduated in the ♂, the feathers attenuated at ends. Outer primary abruptly attenuated, the end turned outwards. Gorget feathers broad, elongated laterally, rose-purple or fire-color ; crown green like the back ; tail-feathers edged with rufous. ♀ with tail less graduated, and the feathers broader at ends. Outer primary broader, and not attenuated and turned outward at end.

        Atthis. Sexes alike in form. Tail rounded ; outer primary bowed at end, rather narrow in the ♂. Gorget feathers much elongated, posteriorly and laterally ; tail-feathers tipped with white.

    c. Tail rounded, or slightly emarginated, and usually unvariegated in either sex; the feathers very broad, and rounded at the ends; primaries normal, the outer broad to the end, and moderately bowed.

Lampornis.[1] Bill cylindrical, considerably curved. Wing very long, reaching to, or beyond, the tip of the very broad tail. Size large (wing, 2 50, or more). The male dark-colored (green or black) beneath. Sexes sometimes alike (in West Indies).

B. Nasal operculum entirely uncovered; base of bill very broad. Female with tail-feathers not tipped with white.

Heliopædica. Sexes alike in form. First primary longest, much bowed toward end. Tail more than two thirds the wing, nearly square (a little emarginated in the ♂, slightly rounded in the ♀), the feathers very broad, rounded at ends. Color, metallic green above, white or rufous glossed with green below; a conspicuous white post-ocular stripe, and an auricular one of black beneath it. ♂. Forehead and chin black or metallic blue; throat rich metallic green. ♀. Forehead dull brownish-green; chin and throat white, glossed with green, or plain ochraceous; tail plain bluish-black or purplish-rufous, the middle feathers more or less green.

Thaumatias. Sexes alike in form and color. General form of *Heliopædica*, but tail emarginated, instead of rounded. Color nearly uniform green, with or without white throat and abdomen. Tail grayish-dusky, with an obscure subterminal band of black (with basal three fourths white in *T. chionurus*).

HABITS. The habits and manners of the whole family of *Trochilidæ* are, in many striking respects, entirely peculiar to themselves, and without any known correspondence or close resemblance to those of any other kinds of birds, either in America or elsewhere. This family is found exclusively in Amer-

---

[1] Genus *Lampornis*, SWAINS. CHAR. Size large (wing, 2.50); tail large, more than half the wing, the feathers very broad; usually a little rounded, sometimes slightly emarginated (as in *L. mango, L. virginalis,* and *L. aurulentus*). Bill cylindrical, considerably curved, its vertical thickness least at about the middle. Nasal opercula nearly covered by the frontal feathers; tarsi naked. Wing very long, reaching to or beyond the tip of the tail; first primary longest, only slightly bowed, and not attenuated at tip; inner primaries normal.

The species of this genus belong chiefly to the West India Islands and to Tropical America, — principally on the Atlantic coast. They are all of more than the average size, and distinguished by broad tail-feathers, and rather dull, though handsome colors. In *L. porphyrurus* the sexes are alike in color. The following species has been accredited to North America, but probably upon erroneous data, since it belongs to northern South America, not even being an inhabitant of any of the West India Islands, except Trinidad. Still it is possible that, as alleged for *Thaumatias linnæi* (see page 1064), it may have wandered far from its usual habitat, and have reached Florida, as stated by Mr. Audubon.

Lampornis mango, (L.) SWAINS. — The Mango Hummer. *Trochilus mango,* L. S. N. I, 191. — GMEL. S. N. I. 491. — AUD. Orn. Biog. II, 1834, 486; pl. 184. — IB. Birds Am. IV, 1842, 186, pl. ccli. *Lampornis mango,* Sw. Zoöl. Journ. III, 358. — BAIRD, Birds N. Am. 1858, 130. SP. CHAR. — *Male :* Above deep golden green; beneath opaque velvety-black medially, from the bill to the anal region, separated from the lateral and superior green by a tint of metallic greenish-blue. Tail richly metallic rufous-purple, the feathers bordered terminally with blue-black; intermediæ plain dark bronzy-green. Primaries plain dull dusky. *Female.* Similar, but white beneath, except laterally, and with a medial stripe of black, from the bill to the anus. Wing, 2.60 – 2.70; tail, 1.50 – 1.70; bill, .90. *Hab.* Northern South America (Brazil, Guiana, Venezuela, New Granada, Panama, and Trinidad); accidental in Florida???

ica, either in the islands or on the continent, and number in all not far from four hundred species, distributed into various subdivisions and genera, but all possessing, to a very large degree, the same common peculiarities, of which the well-known Ruby-throat of eastern North America may be taken as eminently typical. The habits and peculiarities of this numerous family have been closely studied, and many valuable facts in relation to them have been contributed by various naturalists; by none, perhaps, with more intelligent attention than by the eminent Swiss naturalist, M. H. de Saussure, in his visit to the West India Islands and Mexico, to whose observations we are largely indebted.

On the first visit of this naturalist to a savanna in the island of Jamaica, he at once noticed what he at first took to be a brilliant green insect, of rapid flight, approaching him by successive alternations of movements and pauses, and rapidly gliding among and over the network of interlacing shrubs. He was surprised by the extraordinary dexterity with which it avoided the movements of his net, and yet more astonished to find, when he had captured it, that he had taken a bird, and not an insect.

He soon satisfied himself that this entire family not only have the form and aspect of insects, but that they have also the same movements, the same habits, and the same manner of living, with certain insects. Their flight is exactly like that of an insect, and in this respect they form a remarkably exceptional group among birds. When we notice their long wings in our cabinet specimens, we naturally suppose that they use these instruments of flight in the same manner with the Swallow or the Swift. Yet investigation shows that, so very far from this, these wings, comparatively so very long, vibrate even more rapidly than do those of birds with proportionately the smallest wings, such as the Grebe, the Loon, and the Penguin, and that, more than this, they vibrate with an intensity so vastly superior, that they become wholly invisible in the wonderful rapidity of their movements.

The altogether exceptional character of their flight is a subject for neverceasing astonishment. Until we actually witness it, we should never conceive it to be possible for a bird to vibrate its wings with so great a rapidity, and by them to support itself in the air in the same manner with the *Anthraces* and other aerial insects. This feat is rendered all the more surprising by the extreme narrowness of the wing and the comparative weight of the body, which is quite considerable, on account of the compactness of the flesh and bones, and the small size of the birds themselves, whose wings displace but a small quantity of air. The resistance of the air to the stroke of the wing of a bird should be, not in proportion to the surface of that wing, but to its square, or even to its cube, if the movement is very rapid. Hence it follows that a due proportion being required as between the weight of the body and the surface of this organ, a small bird cannot keep itself poised in the air except by means of vibrations more rapid than those of a larger kind. This is, without doubt, one explanation of the fact that Humming-Birds, in their flight, are so insect-like. They pass from bush to bush as if suspended in the air, and pause over each flower, vibrating their wings, in precisely the same manner with the Sphinxes, and with the same humming sounds.

The flight of the Humming-Bird is of two kinds. One of these is used for a horizontal movement, and is so rapid that one can hardly follow it with the eye. This is accompanied by a kind of hissing sound. The other seems to keep the body in the air immovable, in one spot. For the latter purpose the bird assumes a position nearly vertical, and beats its wings with great intensity. These organs must vibrate all the more rapidly, because the immobility of the body requires a shorter stroke, and therefore the more frequently repeated. The equilibrium of the body is preserved by the alternate up and down strokes of the wings, no inconsiderable force being required to keep its immobility, besides that requisite for neutralizing the weight of the body.

The Humming-Bird is entirely aerial. They pass with the rapidity of an arrow, stop, rest for a few seconds on some small branch, and then suddenly depart with so much rapidity that we cannot trace its flight. They disappear as if by enchantment. Their life is one of feverish excitement. They seem to live more intensely than any other being on our globe. From morning to night they traverse the air in quest of honeyed flowers. They come like a flash of light, assume a vertical position without any support, throw their tail forward, expanding it like a fan, vibrating their wings with such rapidity that they become absolutely invisible, plunging, at the same time, their thread-like tongues to the bottom of some long corolla, and then they have gone as suddenly as they came. They are never known to rest on a branch in order more at their leisure to plunge their tongue into the flower. Their life is too short for this delay; they are in too great haste; they can only stop long enough to beat their wings before each flower for a few seconds, but long enough to reach its bottom and to devour its inhabitants. When we take into consideration how entirely aerial is their life, and the prodigious relative force requisite to enable them to keep suspended in the air during the entire day, almost incessantly, either in rapid motion or accomplishing the most violent vibrations, we can but be amazed at the extraordinary powers of flight and endurance they manifest.

The Humming-Bird enjoys even the most tropical heat, avoids shade, and is easily overcome by cold. Though some travellers speak of having met with these birds in the depths of forests, Saussure discredits their statements, having never found any in such situations. They prefer open flowery fields, meadows, gardens, and shrubbery, delighting to glitter in the sun's rays, and to mingle with the swarm of resplendent insects with which tropical regions abound, and with the habits of which their own so well accord. Nearly all live in the open sun, only a very few are more or less crepuscular and never to be seen except very early in the morning or in the evening twilight.

Mr. Salvin is of the opinion that Humming-Birds do not remain long on the wing at once, but rest frequently, choosing for that purpose a small dead or leafless twig at the top, or just within the branches of the tree. While in this position they trim their feathers and clean their bill, all the time keeping up an incessant jerking of their wings and tail.

In Mexico, where these birds are very abundant, they are attracted by the blossoms of the *Agave americana*, and swarm around them like so many beetles. As they fly, they skim over the fields, rifle the flowers, mingling with the bees and the butterflies, and during the seasons of bloom, at certain hours of the day, the fields appear perfectly alive with them. The ear receives unceasingly the whistling sounds of their flight, and their shrill cries, resembling in their sharp accent the clash of weapons. Although the Humming-Bird always migrates at the approach of cold weather, yet it is often to be found at very considerable elevations. The traveller Bourcier met with them on the crater of Pichincha, and M. Saussure obtained specimens of *Calothorax lucifer* in the Sierra de Cuernavaca, at the height of more than 9,500 feet.

While we must accept as a well-established fact that the Humming-Birds feed on insects, demonstrated long since by naturalists, it is equally true that they are very fond of the nectar of flowers, and that this, to a certain extent, constitutes their nourishment. This is shown by the sustenance which captive Humming-Birds receive from honey and other sweet substances, food to which a purely insectivorous bird could hardly adapt itself.

Notwithstanding their diminutive size the Humming-Birds are notorious for their aggressive disposition. They attack with great fury anything that excites their animosity, and maintain constant warfare with whatever is obnoxious to them, expressly the Sphinxes or Hawk-Moths. Whenever one of these inoffensive moths, two or three times the size of a Humming-Bird, chances to come too early into the garden and encounters one of these birds, he must give way or meet with certain injury. At sight of the insect the bird attacks it with his pointed beak with great fury. The Sphinx, overcome in this unlooked-for attack, beats a retreat, but, soon returning to the attractive flowers, is again and again assaulted by its infuriated enemy. Certain destruction awaits these insects if they do not retire from the field before their delicate wings, lacerated in these attacks, can no longer support them, and they fall to the ground to perish from other enemies.

In other things the Humming-Bird also shows itself all the more impertinent and aggressive that it is small and weak. It takes offence at everything that moves near it. It attacks birds much larger than itself, and is rarely disturbed or molested by those it thus assails. All other birds must make way. It is possible that in some of these attacks it may be influenced by an instinctive prompting of advantages to be gained, as in the case of the spider, in whose nets they are liable to be entangled, and whose webs often seriously incommode them. When a Humming-Bird perceives a spider in the midst of its net, it rarely fails to make an attack, and with such rapidity that one cannot follow the movement, but in the twinkling of an eye the spider has disappeared. This is not only done to small spiders, which doubtless they devour, but also to others too large to be thus eaten.

Not content with thus chastising small enemies, the Humming-Bird also contends with others far more powerful, and which give them a good deal of trouble. They have been known to engage in an unequal contest with the Sparrow-Hawk, yet rarely without coming off the conquerors. In this strife they have the advantage of numbers, their diminutive size, and the rapidity and the irregularity of their own movements. Several unite in these attacks, and, in rushing upon their powerful enemy, they always aim at his eyes. The Hawk soon appreciates his inability to contend with these tormenting little furies, and beats an ignominious retreat.

Advantage is taken of this aggressive disposition of these birds, by the hunter, to capture them. In their combats with one another, or in their rash attacks upon various offensive objects, even upon the person of the snarer himself, they are made prisoners through their own rashness and reckless impetuosity.

In enumerating the prominent characteristics of this remarkable family, we should not omit to refer to the lavish profusion of colors of every tint and shade, excelling in lustre and brilliancy even the costliest gems, with which Nature has adorned their plumage. And not only are nearly all the birds of this group thus decked out with hues of the most dazzling brightness and splendor, when alive and resplendent in the tropical sun, but many also display the most wonderfully varying shades and colors, according to the position in which they are presented to the eye. The sides of the fibres of each feather are of a different color from the surface, and change as seen in a front or an oblique direction, and while living, these birds, by their movements, can cause these feathers to change very suddenly to very different hues. Thus the *Selasphorus rufus* can change in a twinkling the vivid fire-color of its expanded throat to a light green, and the species known as the Mexican Star (*Cynanthus lucifer*) changes from a bright crimson to an equally brilliant blue.

The nests and the eggs of the Humming-Birds, though in a few exceptional cases differing as to the form and position of the former, are similar, so far as known, in the whole family. The eggs are always two in number, white and unspotted, oblong in shape, and equally obtuse at either end. The only differences to be noticed are in the relative variations in size. The nests are generally saddled upon the upper side of a horizontal branch, are cup-like in shape, and are largely made up of various kinds of soft vegetable down, covered by an outward coating of lichens and mosses fastened upon them by the glue-like saliva of the bird. In *T. colubris* the soft inner portion of the nest is composed of the delicate downy covering of the leaf-buds of several kinds of oaks. In Georgia the color of this down is of a deep nankeen hue, but in New England it is nearly always white. At first the nest is made of this substance alone, and the entire complement of eggs, never more than two, is sometimes laid before the covering of lichens is put on by the male bird, who seems to amuse himself with this while his mate is sitting upon her eggs.

Genus STELLULA, GOULD.

Stellula, GOULD, Introd. Trochil. 1861, 90. (Type, *Trochilus calliope*, GOULD.)

GEN. CHAR. Bill rather longer than the head; straight. Wings much developed, reaching beyond the tail, which is short, nearly even, or slightly rounded, and with the innermost feathers abruptly short; the outer feather rather narrower and more linear than the others, which have a rather spatulate form. Metallic throat-feathers elongated and rather linear and loose, not forming a continuous metallic surface. Central tail-feather without green.

17992 ♂

This genus, established by Gould, has a slight resemblance to *Atthis*, but differs in absence of the attenuated tip of outer primary. The outer three tail-

Stellula calliope.

feathers are longest and nearly even (the second rather longest), the fourth and fifth equal and abruptly a little shorter, the latter without any green. The feathers are rather broad and wider terminally (the outermost least so), and are obtusely rounded at end. The tail of the female is quite similar. The absence of green on the tail in the male seems a good character. But one species is known of the genus.

Calothorax is a closely allied genus, in which the tail is considerably longer. One species, *C. cyanopogon*, will probably be yet detected in New Mexico.

Stellula calliope, GOULD.

THE CALLIOPE HUMMING-BIRD.

Trochilus calliope, GOULD, Pr. Z. S. 1847, 11 (Mexico). *Calothorax calliope*, GRAY, Genera, I, 100. — BON. Rev. Mag. Zoöl. 1854, 257. — GOULD, Mon. Troch. III, pl. cxlii. — XANTUS, Pr. A. N. Sc. 1859, 190. — ELLIOT, Illust. Birds N. A. I, xxiii. *Stellula calliope*, GOULD, Introd. Troch. 1861, 90. — COOPER, Orn. Cal. I, 1870, 363.

SP. CHAR. *Male* above, except on tail, golden-green, beneath white, the sides glossed with green, the flanks somewhat with rusty; crissum pure white. Throat-feathers pure white at base, terminal half violet-red, more reddish than in *Atthis heloisæ;* the sides of neck pure white. Tail-feathers brown, edged at base, especially on inner webs, but inconspicuously, with rufous; the ends paler, as if faded; central feathers like the rest; under mandible yellow. Length, 2.75; wing, 1.60; tail, 1.00; bill above to base of feathers, .55. *Female* without the metallic gorget (replaced by a few dusky specks), and the throat-feathers not elongated; no green on sides, and more tinged with rufous beneath. A white crescent under the eye. Tail more rounded and less emarginate than in the male.

The outer three feathers green at base, then black, and tipped with white; the fourth green and black; the fifth green, with a dusky shade at end; all, except central, edged internally at base with rufous. The under mandible is paler at base than elsewhere, but not yellowish-white as in the male.

HAB. Mountains of Washington Territory, Oregon, and California, to Northern Mexico. East to East Humboldt Mountains (RIDGWAY); Fort Tejon (XANTUS); Fort Crook (FEILNER).

The male bird is easily distinguished from other North American species by its very small size, the snowy-white bases of the elongated loose throat-feathers, and by the shape of the tail, as also the absence, at least in the several males before us, of decided metallic green on the central tail-feathers. The females resemble those of *A. heloisæ* most closely, but have longer bills and wings, broader tail-feathers, and their rufous confined to the edges, instead of crossing the entire basal portion. *Selasphorus platycercus* and *rufus* are much larger, and have tails marked more as in *A. heloisæ*.

HABITS. This interesting species was first met with as a Mexican Humming-Bird, on the high table-lands of that republic, by Signor Floresi. His specimens were obtained in the neighborhood of the Real del Monte mines. As it was a comparatively rare bird, and only met with in the winter months, it was rightly conjectured to be only a migrant in that locality.

This species is new to the fauna of North America, and was first brought to the attention of naturalists by Mr. J. K. Lord, one of the British commissioners on the Northwest Boundary Survey. It is presumed to be a mountain species, found in the highlands of British Columbia, Washington Territory, Oregon, California, and Northern Mexico.

Early in May Mr. Lord was stationed on the Little Spokan River, superintending the building of a bridge. The snow was still remaining in patches, and no flowers were in bloom except the brilliant pink *Ribes*, or flowering currant. Around the blossoms of this shrub he found congregated quite a number of Humming-Birds. The bushes seemed to him to literally gleam with their flashing colors. They were all male birds, and of two species; and upon obtaining several of both they proved to be, one the *Selasphorus rufus*, the other the present species, one of the smallest of Humming-Birds, and in life conspicuous for a frill of minute pinnated feathers, encircling the throat, of a delicate magenta tint, which can be raised or depressed at will. A few days after the females arrived, and the species then dispersed in pairs.

He afterwards ascertained that they prefer rocky hillsides at great altitudes, where only pine-trees, rock plants, and an alpine flora are found. He frequently shot these birds above the line of perpetual snow. Their favorite resting-place was on the extreme point of a dead pine-tree, where, if undisturbed, they would sit for hours. The site chosen for the nest was usually the branch of a young pine, where it was artfully concealed amidst the fronds at the very end, and rocked like a cradle by every passing breeze.

Dr. Cooper thinks that he met with this species in August, 1853, on the summit of the Cascade Mountains, but mistook the specimens for the young of *Selasphorus rufus.*

Early in June, 1859, Mr. John Feilner found these birds breeding near Pitt River, California, and obtained their nests.

This species was obtained by Mr. Ridgway only on the East Humboldt Mountains, in Eastern Nevada. The two or three specimens shot were females, obtained in August and September, and at the time mistaken for the young of *Selasphorus platycercus,* which was abundant at that locality.

Dr. W. J. Hoffman writes, in relation to this species, that on the 20th of July, 1871, being in camp at Big Pines, a place about twenty-seven miles north of Camp Independence, California, on a mountain stream, the banks of which are covered with an undergrowth of cottonwood and small bushes, he frequently saw and heard Humming-Birds flying around him. He at length discovered a nest, which was perched on a limb directly over the swift current, where it was sometimes subjected to the spray. The limb was but half an inch in thickness, and the nest was attached to it by means of thin fibres of vegetable material and hairs. It contained two eggs. The parents were taken, and proved to be this species. There were many birds of the same kind at this point, constantly on the tops of the small pines in search of insects.

GENUS **TROCHILUS,** LINNÆUS.

Trochilus, LINNÆUS, Systema Naturæ, 1748 (AGASSIZ).

GEN. CHAR. Metallic gorget of throat nearly even all round. Tail forked; the feathers lanceolate, acute, becoming gradually narrower from the central to the exterior. Inner six primaries abruptly and considerably smaller than the outer four, with the inner web notched at the end.

1101 ♀

Trochilus colubris ♀

1100 ♂

Trochilus colubris. ♂

The female has the outer tail-feathers lanceolate, as in the male, though much broader. The outer feathers are broad to the terminal third, where they become rapidly pointed, the tip only somewhat rounded ; the sides of this attenuated portion (one or other, or both) broadly and concavely emarginated, which distinguishes them from the females of *Selasphorus* and *Calypte,* in which the tail is broadly linear to near the end, which is much rounded without any distinct concavity.

A peculiarity is observable in the wing of the two species of *Trochilus* as restricted, especially in *T. colubris,* which we have not noticed in other North American genera. The outer four primaries are of the usual shape, and diminish gradually in size ; the remaining six, however, are abruptly much smaller, more linear, and nearly equal in width (about that of inner web of the fourth), so that the interval between the fifth and fourth is from two to five times as great as that between the fifth and sixth. The inner web of these reduced primaries is also emarginated at the end. This character is even sometimes seen in the females, but to a less extent, and may serve to distinguish both *colubris* and *alexandri* from other allied species where other marks are obscured.

The following diagnosis will serve to distinguish the species found in the United States : —

COMMON CHARACTERS. Above and on the sides metallic green. A ruff of metallic feathers from the bill to the breast, behind which is a whitish collar, confluent with a narrow abdominal stripe; a white spot behind the eye. Tail-feathers without light margins.

Tail deeply forked (.30 of an inch). Throat bright coppery-red from the chin. Tail of female rounded, emarginated . . . . . *T. colubris.*

Larger. Tail slightly forked (.10 of an inch). Throat gorget with violet, steel, green, or blue reflections behind; anteriorly opaque velvety-black. Tail of female graduated; scarcely emarginated . . . . *T. alexandri.*

Trochilus colubris, LINNÆUS.

RUBY-THROATED HUMMING-BIRD.

Trochilus colubris, LINN. Syst. Nat. I, 1766, 191. — WILSON, Am. Orn. II, 1810, 26, pl. x. — AUD. Orn. Biog. I, 1832, 248, pl. xlvii. — IB. Birds Am. IV, 1842, 190, pl. ccliii. — BAIRD, Birds N. Am. 1858, 131. — MAX. Cab. J. VI, 154. — SAMUELS, 111. — ALLEN, B. Fla. 301. *Ornisyma colubris,* DEVILLE, Rev. et Mag. Zool. May, 1852 (habits). *Trochilus aureigaster,* LAWRENCE (alcoholic specimens).

SP. CHAR. Tail in the male deeply forked; the feathers all narrow lanceolate-acute. In the female slightly rounded and emarginate; the feathers broader, though pointed. Male, uniform metallic green above; a ruby-red gorget (blackish near the bill), with no conspicuous ruff; a white collar on the jugulum; sides of body greenish; tail-feathers uniformly brownish-violet. Female, without the red on the throat; the tail rounded and emarginate, the inner feathers shorter than the outer; the tail-feathers banded with black, and the outer tipped with white; no rufous or cinnamon on the tail in either sex. Length, 3.25; wing, 1.60; tail, 1.25; bill, .65. *Young* males are like the females; the throat usually spotted, sometimes with red; the tail is, in shape, more like that of the old male.

HAB. Eastern North America to the high Central Plains; south to Brazil. Localities: Cordova (SCL. P. Z. S, 1856, 288); Guatemala (SCL. Ibis, I, 129); Cuba (CAB. J. IV, 98; Gundl. Rep. I, 1866, 291); S. E. Texas (DRESSER, Ibis, 1865, 470, breeds); Veragua (SALV. P. Z. S. 1870, 208).

The *Trochilus aureigaster* (*aureigula ?*) of Lawrence, described from an alcoholic specimen in the Smithsonian collection, differs in having a green throat, becoming golden towards the chin. It is quite probable, however, that the difference is the result of immersion in spirits.

The red of the throat appears paler in some Mexican and Guatemalan

skins ; others, however, are not distinguishable from the northern specimens.

HABITS. This species is found throughout eastern North America, as far
west as the Missouri Valley, and breeds from Florida and the valley of the
Rio Grande to high northern latitudes. Richardson states that it ranges at
least to the 57th parallel, and probably even farther north. He obtained
specimens on the plains of the Saskatchewan, and Mr. Drummond found
one of its nests near the source of the Elk River. Mr. Dresser found this
bird breeding in Southwestern Texas, and also resident there during the
winter months, and I have received their nests and eggs from Florida and
Georgia. It was found by Mr. Skinner to be abundant in Guatemala during
the winter months, on the southern slope of the great Cordillera, showing
that it chooses for its winter retreat the moderate climate afforded by a region lying between the elevations of three and four thousand feet, where
it winters in large numbers. Mr. Salvin noted their first arrival in
Guatemala as early as the 24th of August. From that date the number
rapidly increased until the first week in October, when it had become by
far the most common species about Dueñas. It seemed also to be universally distributed, being equally common at Coban, at San Geronimo, and the
plains of Salamá.

The birds of this species make their appearance on our southern border
late in March, and slowly move northward in their migrations, reaching
Upper Georgia about the 10th of April, Pennsylvania from the last of
April to about the middle of May, and farther north the last of May or the
first of June. They nest in Massachusetts about the 10th of June, and are
about thirteen days between the full number of eggs and the appearance of
the young. They resent any approach to their nest, and will even make
angry movements around the head of the intruder, uttering a sharp outcry.
Other than this I have never heard them utter any note.

Attempts to keep in confinement the Humming-Bird have been only partially successful. They have been known to live, at the best, only a few
months, and soon perish, partly from imperfect nourishment and unsuita-
ble food, and probably also from insufficient warmth.

Numerous examinations of stomachs of these birds, taken in a natural
state, demonstrate that minute insects constitute a very large proportion of
their necessary food. These are swallowed whole. The young birds feed
by putting their own bills down the throats of their parents, sucking probably a prepared sustenance of nectar and fragments of insects. They raise,
I think, but one brood in a season. The young soon learn to take care of
themselves, and appear to remain some time after their parents have left.
They leave New England in September, and have all passed southward beyond our limits by November.

A nest of this bird, from Dr. Gerhardt, of Georgia, measures 1.75 inches
in its external diameter and 1.50 in height. Its cavity measures 1.00

in depth and 1.25 inches in breadth. It is of very homogeneous construction, the material of which it is made being almost exclusively a substance of vegetable origin, resembling wool, coarse in fibre, but soft, warm, and yielding, of a deep buff color. This is strengthened, on the outside, by various small woody fibres; the whole, on the outer surface, entirely and compactly covered by a thatching of small lichens, a species of *Parmelia*.

A nest obtained in Lynn, Mass., by Mr. George O. Welch, in June, 1860, was built on a horizontal branch of an apple-tree. In measures 1.50 inches in height, and 2.25 in its external diameter. The cavity is more shallow, measuring .70 of an inch in depth and 1.00 in diameter. It is equally homogeneous in its composition, being made of very similar materials. In this case, however, the soft woolly material of which it is woven is finer in fibre, softer and more silky, and of the purest white color. It is strengthened on the base with pieces of bark, and on the sides with fine vegetable fibres. The whole nest is beautifully covered with a compact coating of lichens, a species of *Parmelia*, but different from those of the Georgian nest.

The fine silk-like substance of which the nest from Lynn is chiefly composed is supposed to be the soft down which appears on the young and unexpanded leaves of the red-oak, immediately before their full development. The buds of several of the oaks are fitted for a climate liable to severe winters, by being protected by separate downy scales surrounding each leaf. In Massachusetts the red-oak is an abundant tree, expands its leaves at a convenient season for the Humming-Bird, and these soft silky scales which have fulfilled their mission of protection to the embryo leaves are turned to a good account by our tiny and watchful architect. The species in Georgia evidently make use of similar materials from one of the southern oaks.

The eggs measure .50 by .35 of an inch, and are of a pure dull white.

Trochilus alexandri, Bourc. & Mulsant.

BLACK-CHINNED HUMMING-BIRD.

Trochilus alexandri, Bourcier & Mulsant, Ann. de la Soc. d'Agric. de Lyons, IX, 1846, 330. — Heermann, Jour. A. N. Sc. Phila. 2d ser. II, 1853, 269. — Cassin, Ill. N. Am. Birds, I, v, 1854, 141, pl. xxii. — Gould, Mon. Trochilidæ, xiv, Sept. 1857, plate. — Baird, Birds N. Am. 1858, 133, pl. xliv, f. 3. — Ib. M. B. II, Birds, 6, pl. v, f. 3. — Heerm. X, *S*, 56. — Cooper, Orn. Cal. I, 1870, 353.

Sp. Char. Very similar to *Trochilus colubris*. Tail slightly forked; the chin and upper part of the throat opaque velvety-black, without metallic reflections, which are confined to the posterior border of the gorget, and are violet, sometimes changing to steel blue or green, instead of coppery-red. *Female* without the metallic scales; the tail-feathers tipped with white; the tail graduated, not emarginated; the innermost feather among the longest. Length of male, 3.30; wing, 1.70; tail, 126; bill, .75.

Hab. Coast of California, southward, and east to the Wahsatch and Uintah Mountains, Utah.

The chief characters of this species are to be found in the violet, steel-blue, or steel-green reflections of the hinder part of the gorget, varying with the situation of the feathers and the specimen, as distinguished from the bright fiery or coppery red of the other. The chin and upper part of the throat extending beneath the eyes are opaque velvety or greenish black, without metallic lustre, while in *T. colubris* it is only the extreme chin which is thus dull in appearance. The bill is about .10 of an inch longer, the tail less deeply forked, and tinged with green at the end.

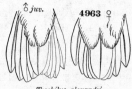

Trochilus alexandri.

It is exceedingly difficult to distinguish the female of this species from

Trochilus alexandri.

that of *T. colubris.* The size is rather larger, and the tail rounded, without any distinct emargination ; the middle feathers being .15 of an inch longer than the lateral ones, instead of actually shorter. The color is much the same. The primaries are also much broader in the present species.

In both species the outer tail-feathers, though broader than in the male, are quite acutely pointed on the terminal third, one side or the other of which is slightly concave, instead of being linear to near the end, and rounded without any concavity, as in *Selasphorus* and *Calypte.*

HABITS. This Humming-Bird, originally described as a Mexican species, is found from the highlands of that republic northward, not only to the southern borders of the western United States, but as far north as the 58th parallel. It was first discovered on the table-lands of Mexico, east of the city, by Signor Floresi, a distinguished naturalist, who devoted himself to the study of the *Trochilidæ* of Mexico, but was first added to the fauna of North America by Dr. Heermann, who detected it, and obtained several specimens, within the burying-ground of Sacramento City, Cal. There several pairs remained during the period of incubation, and reared their young, finding both food and shelter among the flowering plants of that cemetery. He found several of their nests which were essentially similar to the *T. colubris.*

Dr. Cooper met with this species along the Mohave River. He saw the first on the 3d of June. He also found one of their nests built in a dark willow-thicket in the fork of a tree, eight feet from the ground. Those afterwards found near Santa Barbara were all built near the end of hanging branches of the sycamore, constructed of white down from willow catkins, agglutinated by the bird's saliva, and thus fastened to the branch on which it rested. These were built in the latter part of April, and early in May contained two eggs, exactly resembling those of the *T. colubris*, and measuring .51 by .32 of an inch.

Afterwards Mr. W. W. Holden obtained a specimen in the Colorado Valley, March 20.

Mr. J. K. Lord, one of the English commissioners of the Northwestern Boundary Survey, met with this species near his camping-place on the western slope of the Rocky Mountains. This was near a lake, by the margin of which, with other trees, grew a number of the black birch. On these trees he found a sweet gummy sap exuding plentifully from splits in the bark, and on this sap hosts of insects, large and small, were regaling themselves. As the sap was very sticky, numbers of the smaller winged insects were trapped in it. Busily employed in picking off and devouring these captive insects were several very sombre-looking Humming-Birds, poising themselves over the flowers, and nipping off, as with delicate forceps, the imprisoned insects. Upon securing one of these birds, he ascertained that it belonged to this species. This was pretty satisfactory proof that they are insect-eaters. Not only on this occasion, but many times afterwards, Mr. Lord saw this bird pick the insects from the tree; and the stomachs of those he killed, on being opened, were filled with various kinds of winged insects. He found this bird lingering around lakes, pools, and swamps, where these birches grow. They generally build in the birch or alder, selecting the fork of a branch high up.

This species bears a very close resemblance in size, appearance, and markings, to the common eastern species, but is readily distinguishable by the difference in the color of the chin and the shape of the tail.

In the spring of 1851, on a trip to Sonora, Mexico, Dr. Heermann found these birds abundant in the arid country around Guaymas, where amid the scanty vegetation they had constructed their nests in the month of April. He also afterwards found them on Dry Creek and the Cosumnes River.

According to the observations of Mr. Ridgway, this species has quite an extended distribution in the West. He found it in varying abundance from the Sacramento Valley, in California, to the Wahsatch and Uintah Mountains in Utah.

At Sacramento it was more abundant than the *C. anna*, nesting in the door-yards and in gardens, but particularly in the thick copses of small oaks in the outskirts of the city. In the Great Basin it associated with the *Selasphorus rufus* in the western portion, and with *S. platycercus* to the eastward, nesting everywhere, from the lowest valleys to a height of eight or nine thousand feet in the mountains.

Genus **CALYPTE**, Gould.

Calypte, Gould, Introd. Trochilidæ, 1861, 87.   (Type, *Ornysmya costæ*.)

Gen. Char. Bill longer than the head, straight or slightly curved; tail rather short. Outer primary not attenuated at end. Top of head, as well as throat, with metallic scale-like feathers, a decided and elongated ruff on each side the neck.

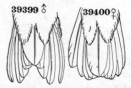

Calypte costæ.

The metallic feathers on top of head, the attenuated outer tail-feathers (except in *C. helenæ*), and the elongated ruff, distinguish the males of this genus very readily from any other in North America.

Calypte costæ.

Species.

A. No rufous on tail-feathers; tail forked or emarginated.

    a. Lateral tail-feather as broad as the others; tail emarginated. Rump and middle tail-feathers blue.

        C. helenæ.[1] Very small (wing, 1.15); metallic hood and ruff of the male purplish-red. *Hab.* Cuba.

    b. Lateral tail-feather abruptly narrower than the others, tail forked. Rump and middle tail-feathers green.

        C. anna.   Large (wing, 2.00); outer tail-feather with a double curve, the end inclining outward. Metallic hood and ruff of the male purplish-red. *Hab.* California.

        C. costæ.   Small (wing, 1.75); outer tail-feather with a simple curve, the end inclining inward. Metallic hood and ruff of the male violet-blue. *Hab.* Southern California, Arizona, and Mexico.

B. Inner webs of tail-feathers mostly rufous, and outer webs edged with the same. Tail rounded. Lateral tail-feather abruptly narrower than the others.

        C. floresi.[2] Size of *C. anna.* Hood and ruff of the male crimson. *Hab.* Table-lands of Mexico (Bolanos).

---

[1] *Calypte helenæ*, (Lemb.) Gould, Monog. Troch. III, pl. cxxxvi. *Orthorhynchus helenæ*, Lemb. Aves de l'Isle de Cuba, p. 70, pl. x, fig. 2.   *O. boothi*, Gundl. MSS. (Gould, Monog.).

[2] *Calypte floresi*, (Lodd.) *Trochilus floresi*, Lodd. MSS. *Selasphorus floresi*, Gould, Monog. Troch. III, pl. cxxxix. There are certainly few reasons for considering this bird as a *Selasphorus*, while there are many for referring it to *Calypte*. The only feature that it shares with the former is the peculiar coloration, and to some extent the shape, of the tail. However, in *Selasphorus* the outer primary is always (in the male) attenuated and acute at the tip, and the crown is never metallic, while in *Calypte* the outer primary is never attenuated nor acute, and the crown of the male is always metallic. The form and coloration of the tail are nothing more than a specific character, since no two species, of either genus, agree in this respect. In view, then, of these considerations, we find *floresi* to be strictly congeneric with the other species of *Calypte*.

Calypte anna, GOULD.

ANNA HUMMING-BIRD.

Ornismya anna, LESSON, Oiseaux Mouches, 1830, (?) pl. cxxiv. *Trochilus anna*, JARDINE, Nat. Lib. Humming-Birds, I, 93, pl. vi. — AUD. Orn. Biog. V, 1839, 428, pl. ccccxxviii. — IB. Birds America, IV, 1842, 188, pl. cclii. — HEERM. X, *S*, 56 (nest). *Calliphlox anna*, GAMBEL, Pr. A. N. Sc. Phil. III, 1846, 3. — IB. Journ. 2d ser. I, 1847, 32. *Trochilus (Atthis) anna*, REICHENBACH, Cab. Jour. Extraheft for 1853, 1854, App. 12. *Trochilus icterocephalus*, NUTTALL, Man. I, (2d ed.,) 1840, 712 (male with forehead covered with yellow pollen). *Atthis anna*, BAIRD, Birds N. Am. 1858, 137. *Calypte annæ*, GOULD, Introd. Trochilidæ. — COOPER, Orn. Cal. I, 1870, 358.

SP. CHAR. Largest of North American species of Humming-Bird. Tail deeply forked; external feather narrow, linear. Top of the head, throat, and a moderate ruff, metallic crimson-red, with purple reflections. Rest of upper parts and a band across the breast green. Tail-feathers purplish-brown, darkest centrally. In the female the tail is slightly rounded, not emarginate; the scales of the head and throat are wanting. Tail barred with black, and tipped with white. Length, about 3.60; wing, 2.00; tail, 1.45.

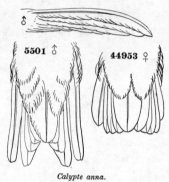

5501 ♂   44953 ♀

Calypte anna.

HAB. Mexico and coast region of California.

The *C. floresi* of the table-lands of Mexico resembles this species in every respect except the tail, which is somewhat like that of *Selasphorus rufus*. The only North American species to which the male of this bird bears any resemblance is the *A. costæ*, which has the same metallic crown and other generic features. The latter, however, is much smaller; has the metallic reflections varied, chiefly violet, instead of nearly uniform purplish-red. The tail is much less deeply forked, the depth being only about .10 of an inch, instead of .32; the outer feather is much narrower. The females of the two, however, appear to be distinguishable only by their relative size. The absence of rufous, and the

Calypte anna.

rounded, not graduated, tail always separates the female of *anna* from that of *Selasphorus rufus*. The larger size is the chief distinction from the female *Calypte costæ*, while the size and less acutely pointed outer tail-feathers distinguish it from the female *Trochilus colubris*.

We have never seen any specimens of this bird taken out of California, nor quoted of late years as occurring in Mexico, although stated by Gould to belong to the table-lands.

HABITS. This beautiful Humming-Bird is found from the high table-lands of Mexico throughout the western portions of that region, and through all the coast country of California, from the slopes of the Sierra to the ocean. It was first taken in Mexico, and named in honor of Anna, Duchess of Rivoli. Mr. Nuttall was the first of our own naturalists to take it within our territory. He captured a female on its nest near Santa Barbara. This was described and figured by Audubon. The nest was attached to a small burnt twig of *Photinia*, and was small for the bird, being only 1.25 inches in breadth. It was somewhat conic in shape, made of the down of willow catkins, intermixed with their scales, and a few feathers, the latter forming the lining. It had none of the neatness of the nests of our common species, and was so rough on the outside that Mr. Nuttall waited several days in expectation of its being completed, and found the female sitting on two eggs when he caught her. Dr. Cooper, however, thinks this description applies much better to the nest of *T. alexandri*, as all that he has seen of this species are twice as large, and covered externally with lichens, even when on branches not covered with these parasites.

Dr. Gambell, in his paper published in 1846 on the birds of California, describes this as a very abundant species, numbers of which pass the entire winter in California. At such times he found them inhabiting sheltered hillsides and plains, where, at all seasons, a few bushy plants were in flower and furnished them with a scanty subsistence. In the latter part of February and during March they appeared in greater numbers. About the Pueblo the vineyards and the gardens were their favorite resort, where they build a delicate downy nest in small flowering bushes, or in a concealed spot about a fence. In April and May they may be seen in almost every garden.

In the wilder portions of the country Dr. Gambel found them attaching their nest almost exclusively to low horizontal branches of the *Quercus agrifolia*, or evergreen oak, so common in that region. The nest he describes as small, only about an inch in depth, and 1.25 inches in diameter, formed in the most delicate manner of pappus and down of various plants matted into a soft felt, with spider's-webs, which he frequently observed them collecting for the purpose, in the spring, along hedges and fence-rows. The base of the nest is formed of a few dried male aments of the oak, which, with the adjoining felt-like matting of pappus, are agglutinated and bound around the twig with a thick layer of spider's-webs. The note of this bird, he states, is a slender *chep*, frequently repeated. During the breeding-season they are very pugnacious, darting like meteors among the trees, uttering a loud and repeated twittering scold. They also have the habit of ascending to a considerable height, and then of descending with great rapidity, uttering at the same time a peculiar cry. The glutinous pollen of a tubular flower upon which these birds feed often adheres to the rigid feathers of the crown, and causes the bird to seem to have a bright yellow head. Nuttall, who never obtained the male of this species, but saw them in this condition, supposed this to be a yellow spot in the crown, and hence his supposed species of *icterocephalus*.

In California, south of San Francisco, this species was also observed, by Dr. Cooper, to be a constant resident in mild winters, remaining among the foot-hills of the Sierra Nevada, at least fifteen hundred feet above the sea. There he has found them quite common in February. At that season flowers, and consequently insects, are more abundant than in the dry summers. The males are in fine plumage early in January.

Dr. Cooper states that the nests of this species are built at various heights and positions, often in gardens, and sometimes on dead branches, without any attempt at concealment except the outside covering of lichens. He has found them made almost wholly of mosses, with only a lining of feathers and down of plants. In the neighborhood of San Francisco the young are sometimes hatched as early as the middle of March. This species appears to be more hardy than the others, being common along the coast border, though Dr. Cooper saw none near the summits of the Sierra Nevada.

The notes of the male bird, he states, are like the sound produced by the filing of a saw or the whetting of a scythe. They enter familiarly into the city of San Francisco, and even venture into rooms, attracted by the flowers. They are bold and confident, approach to within a few feet of man, but at the least motion disappear like a flash.

Dr. Heermann found this species quite common at San Diego in March, and in its full spring plumage. In September he procured a number of specimens on a small island in the Cosumnes River. While on the wing in pursuit of insects, or after alighting on a small branch, he heard them utter a very weak twitter, continued for a minute or more.

A nest of this species from Petaluma is about 1.50 inches in diameter, and 1.00 in height, and bears no resemblance to the one described by Nuttall. It is made of a commingling of mosses and vegetable down, covered externally with a fine yellow lichen. The eggs measure .60 by .40 of an inch, and are about ten per cent larger than those of any other North American Humming-Bird.

Another nest of this Humming-Bird, obtained in Petaluma, Cal., by Mr. Emanuel Samuels, measures 1.75 inches in diameter, and about 1.00 in height. Its cavity is one inch in diameter at the rim, and half an inch in depth. Its lining is composed of such soft materials that its limits are not well defined. The base of the nest is made of feathers, mosses, and lichens of several varieties of the smaller kinds. The periphery and rim of the nest are of nearly the same materials. The inner fabric consists of a mass of a dirty-white vegetable wool, with a lining of the very finest and softest of feathers, intermingled with down from the seeds of some species of silkweed. The predominant lichen in the base and sides of the nest is the *Ramalina menziesii*, which is peculiar to California. The nest contained a single egg.

Calypte costæ, GOULD.

COSTA'S HUMMING-BIRD; RUFFED HUMMER.

Ornismya costæ, BOURCIER, Rev. Zoöl. Oct. 1839, 294 (Lower California). — IB. Ann. Sc. Phys. et d'Hist. Nat. de Lyon, 1840, 225, tab. ii. — PREVOST & DES MURS, Voyage de la Venus, Zool. I, 1855, 194, Atlas, tab. ii, f. 1, 2. *Selasphorus costæ*, BON. Conspectus Avium, I, 1850, 82. *Atthis costæ*, REICHENBACH, Cab. Jour. für Orn. Extraheft, 1853, 1854. — BAIRD, Birds N. Am. 1858, 138, pl. xix. — KENNERLY, P. R. R. x, b, 36, pl. xix. *Calypte costæ*, GOULD, Mon. Humming-Birds. — COOPER, Orn. Cal. I, 1870, 360.

SP. CHAR. Tail very slightly emarginated and rounded; exterior feather very narrow, and linear. A very long ruff on each side of the throat. Head above and below, with the ruff, covered with metallic red, purple and violet (sometimes steel green). Remaining upper parts and sides of the body green. Throat under and between the ruffs, side of head behind the eye, anal region, and under tail-coverts whitish. Female with the tail rounded, scarcely emarginate; barred with black, and tipped with white. The metallic colors of the head wanting. Length, 3.20; wing, 1.75; tail, 1.10; bill, .68.

HAB. Mexico, Southern California, and the Colorado Basin, Monterey (NEBOUX). Arizona (COUES, P. A. N. S, 1866, 57).

Specimens vary considerably in the color of the ruff, which, however, is only occasionally green; violet being the prevailing shade. The length of this appendage varies considerably.

The female of this species differs much from the male in the absence of the metallic scales on the head and throat. It has a close resemblance to the female *T. colubris,* although the bill is smaller and narrower. The tail-feathers are narrower, more linear, and less acutely pointed at the tip. The black on the outer tail-feathers, instead of extending very nearly to the base, is confined to the terminal half, the basal portion being green. All the tail-feathers are terminated by white, although that on the fourth and fifth is very narrow. In *T. colubris* this color is confined to the three outer ones. The much smaller size will alone distinguish it from the female of *C. anna.*

HABITS. This species is a Mexican bird, first discovered by Signor Floresi among the valleys of the Sierra Madre, in that country, throughout the western portions of which it is said to be an abundant species, as well as along our southern borders, whence it extends into New Mexico, the Colorado Valley, Southern California, and Arizona. It was first described by Bourcier in 1839, and named in honor of the Marquis de Costa, of Chambery.

Mr. Xantus found this species exceedingly abundant at Cape St. Lucas. It has also been found on the eastern coast of the Gulf of California, at Guaymas, and Mazatlan, and also on the table-lands of Mexico.

It was first added to our fauna by Dr. Kennerly, who obtained specimens near Bill Williams Fork, in New Mexico, February 9, 1854. At that early season a few flowers had already expanded beneath the genial rays of the sun, and around them the party rarely failed to find these beautiful birds.

They had already paired, and were constantly to be seen hovering over the flowers. Their notes consisted of a rapid chirping sound. As Dr. Kennerly's party approached the coast of California, where the valleys abounded with flowers of every hue, these birds continued flitting before them in great numbers. Dr. Coues states that this species was not taken at Fort Whipple, though abundantly distributed throughout the Territory, particularly in its southern and southwestern portions, and found about fifty miles south of Prescott. It is presumed to winter within the Territory, and also within the valley of the Colorado. Dr. Cooper did not observe any at Fort Mohave until March 5, and they were not numerous afterwards. At San Diego, in 1862, when the spring was unusually backward, he saw none before April 22, and he has since met with them as far north as San Francisco, where, however, they are rare. The notes uttered by the male he compares to the highest and sharpest note that can be drawn from a violin. Nothing more is known as to their distinctive specific peculiarities.

Genus SELASPHORUS, Swainson.

Selasphorus, Swainson, F. B. A. II, 1831, 324. (Type, *Trochilus rufus*.)

As already stated, the characters of *Selasphorus*, as distinguished from *Calypte* (to which it is most nearly related, through the *C. floresi*), consist in

2896 ♂

Selasphorus rufus.

the lack of metallic feathers on the crown, and in the attenuation of the outer primary, and the pointed and acuminate cuneate (instead of forked) tail.

As distinguished from *Trochilus*, the quills diminish gradually, instead of showing an abrupt transition between the fourth and fifth, so characteristic of the two species of *Trochilus*, as restricted. The very attenuated tip of the outer primary is a character entirely peculiar to *Selasphorus*.

The two North American species, though strictly congeneric, differ from each other considerably in details of form, as well as in color. They may be distinguished from each other and from their two Central American allies as follows : —

Species and Varieties.

A. Feathers of the metallic gorget not elongated laterally.

    S. platycercus. Above continuous metallic green; tail-feathers merely edged with rufous. Gorget purplish-red.

        Wing, 1.90; tail, 1.40; bill (from forehead), .66. Gorget rich solferino-purple, the feathers grayish-white beneath the surface. Outer primary with its attenuated tip turned outward. *Hab.* Rocky Mountains and Middle Province of United States, south to Guatemala . var. *platycercus*.

Wing, 1.65; tail, 1.20; bill, .41. Gorget dull velvety-crimson, the feathers ochraceous beneath the surface. Outer primary apparently with its attenuated tip curved inward. *Hab.* Costa Rica . var. *flammula*.[1]

B. Feathers of the metallic gorget much elongated laterally.

S. rufus. Above chiefly rufous, overlaid by green (except in *S. scintilla*, which is almost wholly green above); tail-feathers rufous with a shaft-streak of dusky. Gorget fiery red. Attenuated tip of outer primary curved inwards.

Wing, 1.60; tail, 1.30; bill, .65. Rufous prevailing above; gorget very brilliant. *Hab.* Western Province of North America, from East Humboldt Mountains to the Pacific. North to Sitka, south to Mirador . . . . var. *rufus*.

Wing, 1.35; tail, 1.00 to 1.10; bill, .42. Continuous green above; gorget not brilliant, but with a dusty appearance. Tail less graduated. *Hab.* Costa Rica and Chiriqui . . . . . . var. *scintilla*.[2]

Selasphorus rufus, SWAINSON.

RUFOUS-BACKED HUMMING-BIRD.

Trochilus rufus, GMELIN, Syst. Nat. I, 1788, 497. — AUD. Orn. Biog. IV, 1838, 555, pl. ccclxxii. *Selasphorus rufus,* SWAINSON, F.-Bor. Am. II, 1831, 324. — AUD. Birds Am. IV, 1842, 200, pl. ccliv. — BAIRD, Birds N. Am. 1858, 134. — COOPER & SUCKLEY, 164. — DALL & BANNISTER, Tr. Chic. Ac. I, 1869, 275 (Alaska). — FINSCH, Abh. Nat. III, 1872, 29 (Alaska). — COOPER, Orn. Cal. I, 1870, 355. *Trochilus collaris,* LATH. (Bonaparte). *Trochilus sitkensis,* RATHKE (Bonaparte). *Ornysmia sasin,* LESSON (Bonaparte).

SP. CHAR. Tail strongly cuneate and wedge-shaped. Upper parts, lower tail-coverts, and breast cinnamon. A trace of metallic green on the crown, which sometimes extends over the back, never on the belly. Throat coppery red, with a well-developed ruff of the same; below this a white collar. Tail-feathers cinnamon, edged or streaked at the end with purplish-brown. *Female* with the rufous of the back covered or replaced with green; less cinnamon on the breast. Traces only of metallic feathers on the throat. Tail rufous, banded with black and tipped with white; middle feathers glossed with green at the end. Tail still cuneate. Length of male, 3.50; wing, 1.55; tail, 1.30.

HAB. West coast of North America, and across from Gulf of California to the Upper Rio Grande Valley, and along the table-lands of Mexico, south; in Middle Province east to East Humboldt Mountains.

[1] *Selasphorus (platycercus,* var. ?) *flammula* (SALV.). *Selasphorus flammula,* SALVIN, P. Z. S. 1864 (Costa Rica). (Described above from specimen in Mr. Lawrence's collection.)

[2] *Selasphorus (rufus* var. ?) *scintilla* (GOULD). *Selasphorus scintilla,* GOULD, P. Z. S. 1850, 162, Monog. Troch. III, pl. cxxxviii. The foregoing species are so similar in all essential respects to the northern *S. platycercus* and *S. rufus,* that it is exceedingly probable that they are merely the southern forms of those species. Both differ in exactly the same respects from their northern representatives, namely, in smaller size and less burnished throat, and to a very slight degree only in form. The only specimen of the *S. flammula* that we have examined is a badly shot male in Mr. Lawrence's collection; what appears to be the outer primary in this specimen is not attenuated at the tip, which is curved inward, instead of acutely attenuated and turned outward as in *platycercus;* the wings are badly cut with shot, however, and the first primary may be wanting.

Specimens from the table-lands of Mexico are smaller than those from Oregon, and have yellower, less ruby throats.

HABITS. This brilliant species has an extended distribution throughout the western part of North America, being found from the valley of the Rio

Grande to the Pacific, and from Mexico to Sitka. It was first discovered near Nootka Sound, by that distinguished navigator, Captain Cook, and described by Latham, and has been met with as far to the south as Real del Monte, on the table-lands of Mexico, by Mr. Taylor, whose specimens were described by Mr. Swainson.

Selasphorus rufus.

Dr. Coues found it very abundant at Arizona, near Fort Whipple, as it is also along the whole slope of the Rocky Mountains. It is a summer resident in that Territory, and breeds there abundantly, arriving at Fort Whipple April 10, and remaining until the middle of September, being found in all situations, particularly meadows, open copses, ravines, etc., where flowers are most abundant.

Mr. Dall gives them as common summer residents at Sitka. Bischoff obtained sixteen specimens. Dr. Suckley says they are very abundant in the western provinces of both Oregon and Washington Territory, and in Vancouver Island. They appear to be very hardy, and are one of the earliest of the migratory birds to arrive in spring. At Fort Steilacoom, latitude 47°, they appeared April 10. They are supposed to commence their southern migrations from that region in September, — a move induced by the scarcity of flowers and lack of means of captivating insects, rather than by cold. In Washington Territory their incubation commences about the 10th of May, and is made evident by the fierce and angry battles continually occurring between the male birds, in which they tilt at each other at full speed, at the same time keeping up a loud and vociferous squeaking and buzzing.

A nest with eggs, of this species, obtained by Dr. Cooper near Fort Slaughter, May 23, was found in the forked branch of a snowberry-bush. It was composed principally of fine green moss, lined internally with the delicate floss of the cottonwood, and externally bordered most artistically with rock lichens. The female was on the nest, and allowed so near an approach as almost to admit of being grasped by the hand. The nest was 2.00 inches in diameter and 1.50 in height. The eggs measured .45 by .33 of an inch, and were white, as in all the species.

Dr. Cooper states that the appearance of this species at the Straits of Fuca is coincident with the blossoming of the red-flowering currant, which begins to bloom on the Columbia March 10. The male of this species has a remarkable habit, when a stranger or a wild animal approaches its nest, of rising to a great height in the air, and of then darting down perpendicularly upon the intruder, producing a hollow rushing sound, like that of the Night-Hawk, but of a much sharper tone.   These sounds are produced by the wings.   In July, when flowers are more abundant among the mountain summits, they leave the lower country.   Dr. Cooper found them abundant in August at an elevation of nearly six thousand feet, and where ice was formed at night in their camp.

In California, Dr. Cooper has not found any of this species remaining in winter, even at San Diego, where, however, he has known them to arrive as early as the 5th of February.   He also saw several on the 22d of the same month feeding among the flowers of the evergreen gooseberry.   By the first of April they were swarming about San Diego.   Their young are hatched before the middle of June.   When perching, this species is said to utter a shrill wiry call, like the highest note of a violin.   They also produce a curious kind of bleating sound.   They are among the most noisy and lively of their race, are very quarrelsome, chase each other away from favorite flowers, rising into the air until out of sight, chirping as they go in the most excited manner.

Mr. Lord noticed the arrival of this species at Little Spokan River, in latitude 49°, early in May.   He found their nests usually in low shrubs and close to rippling streams.   The females of this and other species are said to arrive about a week later than the males.

Dr. Heermann for several successive seasons found many pairs of these birds breeding in the vicinity of San Francisco.

Mr. Nuttall compares the appearance of the male birds of this species, when he approached too near their nests, to an angry coal of brilliant fire, as they darted upon him, passing within a few inches of his face as they returned again and again to the attack, making a sound as of a breaking twig.

Dr. Woodhouse, who found this bird abundant in New Mexico, particularly in the vicinity of Santa Fé, speaks of the great noise they make for so small a bird, and of their quarrelsome and pugnacious disposition.

Mr. R. Brown, in his synopsis of the birds of Vancouver Island, notes the appearance of this species, from the end of March to the beginning of May, according to the state of the season.   Its nest was built on the tips of low bushes, or the under branches of trees.   This was the only species of Humming-Bird seen west of the Cascade Mountains.

The Rufous Hummer was first noticed by Mr. Ridgway in the valley of the Truckee River, in August, where it was the only species shot, and was extremely abundant among the sunflowers which ornament the meadows.   In May of the succeeding year, when the same locality was again visited, not one of this species was to be found, its place being apparently supplied by the *T. alexandri*, which was quite common, and breeding.   Eastward it was met with as far as the East Humboldt Mountains, where, however, only a single pair was seen, and one of them shot, in September.

Selasphorus platycercus, Gould.

BROAD-TAILED HUMMING-BIRD.

Trochilus platycercus, Sw. Philos. Mag. I, 1827, 441 (Mexico). *Selasphorus platycercus*,
Gould, Mon. Trochilid. or Humming-Birds, iii, May, 1852. — Baird, Birds N. Am.
1858, 135, pl. xliii, figs. 1 and 2. — Cooper, Pr. Cal. Ac. 1868 (Lake Tahoe). — Ib.
Orn. Cal. I, 1870, 357. *Ornismia tricolor*, Lesson, Colibris, 125 (no date), pl. xiv
(Brazil). — Ib. Trochilide. 1831, 156, pl. lx (Mexico). — Jardine, Nat. Lib. II, 77,
pl. xiii. *Ornismya montana*, Lesson, Trochilid. 1831, 161, pl. lxiii, adult, and 163 ;
pl. lxiv, young (Mexico).

Sp. Char. Outer primaries greatly attenuated at the end and turned outward. Outer
tail-feathers nearly linear, but widening a little from the base ; its width .20 of an inch.

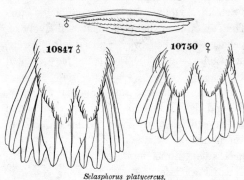

Tail slightly graduated and emarginate. *Male* above and on the
sides metallic green ; chin and
throat light reddish-purple, behind which, and along the belly
to the tail, is a good deal of white.
Wings and tail dusky purplish ;
the tail-feathers, excepting the
internal and external ones, edged
towards the base with light
cinnamon. *Female* without the
metallic gorget ; the throat-feathers with dusky centres. The tail
somewhat cuneate, as in the male,

Selasphorus platycercus.

the feathers less pointed ; the outer three cinnamon-rufous at base (this extending somewhat along the outer edges), then black, and broadly tipped with white (much as in the
male *Atthis heloisa*), the inner two feathers green, the fourth with black spot at end, and
only edged at base with rufous. The sides and crissum also tinged with cinnamon.
Length, 3.50 ; wing, 1.92 ; tail, 1.40. Bill, gape, .80.

Hab. Table-lands of Mexico and Rocky Mountains, and Middle Province of United
States, north to Wyoming Territory ; Uintah, Wahsatch, and East Humboldt Mountains
(Ridgway) ; Sierra Nevada (Cooper) ; Cordova (Scl. P. Z. S, 1856, 288) ; Guatemala
(Scl. Ibis, I, 129) ; Arizona (Coues, P. A. N. S, 1866, 57).

A decided character of this species among its North American relatives is
the rufous outer border of the exterior tail-feathers. This rufous in *S. rufus*
pervades most of the feathers, instead of being restricted as above. Females
of the two species are not dissimilar : those of *S. platycercus* are larger, less
rufous beneath ; the tail-feathers broader and less pointed, and with the
inner two (on each side) entirely green to base (the fourth edged with
rufous), instead of being principally rufous, except at tip.

Specimens from Mirador, Mexico, are undistinguishable from those of
Fort Bridger ; those from Guatemala are smaller than the Mexican.

Habits. Until recently this Humming-Bird has been presumed to be an
exclusively Mexican and Central American species. Until taken within our
limits, it had been supposed to be confined on the north to the Mexican plateau,

westward to the city, and thence southward to Guatemala, while throughout this region it is said to be very generally and very plentifully distributed. It was first taken, in 1851, by Mr. J. H. Clark, near El Paso, Texas. Subsequently numerous specimens were seen by Dr. Coues on the summit of Whipple's Pass of the Rocky Mountains, in July, feeding among clumps of wild roses. It was not noticed near Fort Whipple, though the range of this species is now well known to include New Mexico and Arizona, as far north, at least, as Fort Bridger in Wyoming. It was found breeding abundantly in the vicinity of Fort Grant, Arizona, by Dr. Palmer.

This Humming-Bird was found by Mr. Allen more or less common among the foot-hills, as well as among the mountains, of Colorado, and extending several miles out on the plains. On Mount Lincoln, in Colorado, he found it exceedingly numerous, and though larger and otherwise different from the eastern Ruby-throat, it might easily be mistaken for it. The shrill whistling of its wings, he adds, is a peculiarity one is sure to notice. This Humming-Bird continued to be common on the sides of Mount Lincoln to far above the timber line, being apparently as much at home among the bright flowers growing on the highest parts of the mountain as in the valleys.

At Lake Tahoe, at an elevation of six thousand feet, Dr. Cooper found the young of this species quite common near the middle of September. Supposing them to be the more common *S. rufus*, he only obtained a single specimen. He thinks that these birds extend their northern migrations as far as the Blue Mountains, near Snake River, Oregon, and that they are the ones referred to by Nuttall as seen by him in autumn, and supposed to be the *rufus*.

The nests of this species procured by Dr. Palmer were large for the size of the bird, unusually broad and shallow, composed of soft downy pappus from seeds of plants, and vegetable down, with the outer walls covered with mosses and lichens. The eggs are not distinguishable from those of the other species.

The Rocky Mountain or Broad-tailed Hummer, according to Mr. Ridgway's observations, is the most abundant species in the Great Basin, though he did not see it to recognize it west of the East Humboldt Mountains. It is essentially a bird of the mountains, since in that region there are few flowers elsewhere; yet in the gardens of Salt Lake City, an altitude far below its usual habitat, it was abundant. Its favorite resorts are the flowery slopes of the higher and well-watered mountain-ranges of the Great Basin and Rocky Mountain system, at an average elevation of about eight or nine thousand feet, yet it will be found wherever flowers are abundant. Mr. Ridgway saw one at an altitude of about twelve thousand feet, in July, on the East Humboldt Mountains, but it merely passed rapidly by him. In the Wahsatch Mountains, particularly in the neighborhood of Salt Lake City, this species was most plentiful. It there nested abundantly in the scrub-oaks on the hills or slopes of the cañons.

The male bird is very pugnacious, and was observed to attack and drive away an *Accipiter fuscus,* the Hawk retreating as rapidly as possible. When the nest is approached, the male often rises high into the air and then sweeps down almost to the head of the intruder, its swift descent being accompanied by a very peculiar shrill, screeching buzz, of an extraordinary degree of loudness to be produced by so small a creature. The same sound Mr. Ridgway noticed when the bird was passing overhead, in a manner not observed in any other species, its horizontal flight being by a peculiar undulating course. The shrill noise made by the male of this species he suggests may be caused by the curious attenuated and stiffened outer primary. He noticed a curious piece of ingenuity in nest-making on the part of this species. The nest in question was fastened upon a dead twig of a small cottonwood-tree ; the loosening bark, which probably had separated after the nest was finished, had allowed the nest to turn around so as to hang beneath the branch, thus spilling the eggs upon the ground. The owners, however, built another nest upon the top of the branch, fastening its sides to that of the old one, and making the new nest lighter and less bulky, so that the weight of the older nest kept the other in a permanently upright position.

Genus **ATTHIS**, Reichenbach.

Atthis, Reich. Cab. Jour. f. Orn. extraheft für 1853, 1854. Appendix B. (Type, *Ornys-mya heloisa,* Lesson, Del.)

Gen. Char. Size very diminutive ; bill short, scarcely longer than the head. Outer primary attenuated nearly as in *Selasphorus ;* the tail graduated, the feathers, however, not lanceolate-acute, but rounded at end, and tipped with white in the male.

Atthis heloisa.

This genus seems closely related to *Selasphorus,* agreeing in character of throat, the curious attenuation of outer primary, and the general shape of the tail, with its rufous base and edging. The feathers, however, are not lanceolate and pointed, either sharply as in *S. rufus,* or obtusely as in *platycercus,* but are more equal to near the end, where they round off. The white tip of the tail in the male seems to be the principal reason why Mr. Gould removes the single species from *Selasphorus,* where it was previously placed by him, and where perhaps it might have not inappropriately remained.

Atthis heloisa, LESS. & DEL.

HELOISA'S HUMMING-BIRD.

Ornysmya heloisa, LESSON & DELATTRE, Rev. Zoöl. 1838, 15 (Xalapa). *Mellisuga heloisa*, GRAY & MITCHELL, Gen. Birds, I, 113. *Tryphœna heloisa*, BONAP. Consp. Troch. Rev. Mag. Zoöl. 1854, 257. *Selasphorus heloisæ*, GOULD, Mon. Trochil. III, pl. cxli. *Atthis heloisæ*, REICH. Cab. Jour. extraheft, 1853, App. 12. — GOULD, Introd. Trochil. 1861, 89. — ELLIOT, Illust. Birds N. Am. I, xxi, xii, plate. — COOPER, Orn. Cal. I, 1870, 361.

SP. CHAR. *Male.* Above metallic green with golden reflections; beneath white; the sides of breast glossed with green; the flanks with rufous, which tinges the crissum very faintly; gorget brilliant violet or light purplish-red, bordered behind by clear white. All the tail-feathers rufous-cinnamon for basal half; the three outer black centrally and tipped with white (mixed with reddish on the third); the fourth green, centrally tipped with black; the central entirely green for the exposed portion, perhaps glossed with blackish at the end. Length, 2.70; wing, 1.35; tail, 1.00; exposed part of bill above, .45. *Female.* Outer primary not attenuated. Colors similar to male, wanting the metallic gorget; the feathers spotted with dusky; crissum and flanks more rufous; innermost tail-feathers entirely green; other feathers as in male, but with the central black encroaching on the basal rufous; third and fourth feathers tipped with reddish-white.

HAB. Southern New Mexico and Texas, to Guatemala.

The introduction of this species into the fauna of the United States is based on a female specimen collected by Mr. J. H. Clark at El Paso, Texas, and for a time supposed to be *Selasphorus rufus*, but after a careful examination by Mr. Lawrence, pronounced to belong to this species. Its range is southward along the highlands to Guatemala.

The species is very much like *Selasphorus* in shape, and hardly differs more than *S. rufus* and *platycercus* do from each other. The male is easily distinguished from its allies; the females are closely related to those of *rufus*, differing in much shorter bill (.55 to .65), much less rufous on the more nearly even tail, with broader feathers, etc.

HABITS. This species claims a place within the fauna of North America, probably only as an accidental visitor, on the ground of a single specimen, — a female, taken by Mr. J. H. Clark at El Paso, Texas. It was at first mistaken for *Selasphorus rufus*. It is a Mexican and Central American species, ranging throughout the highlands at least as far to the south as Guatemala, where it was taken by Mr. Salvin.

It was first discovered on the highlands of Mexico by Mr. Delattre, who procured his specimens between Jalapa and Quatepu. It is crepuscular in its habits, collecting its food only in the morning or in the evening. Mr. Delattre states that the male bird is known to rise very early in the morning, and is never seen in quest of food later than nine in the forenoon. It very seldom goes to any distance from its mate or young, seeming to prefer to frequent the flowers in the edge of forests, but does not disdain those of the open fields. Mr. Salvin received specimens of this species taken in a place called Chimachoyo near Calderas, in the Volcan de Fuego, and other specimens taken in the *tierra caliente,* near Coban, showing that, like many other species, it is found in very different climates.

Genus **HELIOPÆDICA**, Gould.

Heliopædica, Gould, Mon. Trochilidæ, II, Introd. Trochil. 1861, 60. (Type, *Trochilus melanotus,* Swainson.)

Gen. Char. Bill longer than head, depressed, broad at its exposed base; the frontal feathers not advancing forward beyond the beginning of the nostrils, nor so far as those of the chin. Hind toe shorter than the lateral, tarsi feathered; outer primary not attenuated. Tail nearly even, slightly rounded and emarginate, the feathers broad, the webs nearly even. Metallic feathers of throat not elongated. Female quite similar in form.

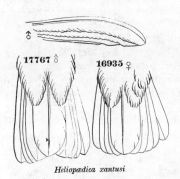

17767 ♂   16935 ♀

Heliopædica xantusi.

This genus is quite peculiar among those of North America in the exposure of the base of bill, which is entirely bare between the lengthened nostrils, instead of covered by the frontal feathers. This makes the bill appear very broad, although it really is more so than in the other genera. The feathers on the chin extend considerably beyond those of the forehead, instead of to about the same line. The tail and its feathers are much broader than in the other genera.

The two known species of this genus may be distinguished by the following characters: —

Common Characters. Above metallic green; tail plain black or chestnut, glossed with green, and without white in either sex. A conspicuous white postocular stripe, and a blackish auricular one beneath it; beneath with more or less green. ♂. Forehead, chin, and side of head deep black or metallic dark blue; throat and jugulum brilliant green. ♀. Front dull brownish-green; chin, throat, and jugulum white or ochraceous, with or without a green gloss.

H. melanotis.[1] *Male.* Belly white, glossed with green; tail black beneath; base of bill, all round, brilliant blue; white cheek-stripe beginning back of the eye. *Female.* Beneath white glossed with green; tail bluish-black. *Hab.* Guatemala and table-lands of Mexico.

H. xantusi. *Male.* Belly cinnamon; tail beneath purplish-cinnamon; chin black; white cheek-stripe beginning at the bill. *Female.* Beneath plain pale rufous; tail deep rufous. *Hab.* Cape St. Lucas.

[1] *Heliopædica melanotis,* (Swains.) Gould, Monog. Troch. II, pl. lxiv. *Trochilus melanotus,* Swains. Phil. Mag. 1827, 441. *Trochilus leucotis,* Vieill. *Ornismyia arsenni,* Less. *Hab.* Mexico and Guatemala.

Heliopædica xantusi, LAWRENCE.

XANTUS'S HUMMING-BIRD.

Amazilia xantusi, LAWRENCE, Ann. N. Y. Lyc. VII, April, 1860, 109. *Heliopædica xantusi,* GOULD, Mon. Troch. II, pl. lxv. — IB. Introd. Troch. 61. — ELLIOT, Ill. Birds N. Am. XI, plate. — COOPER, Orn. Cal. I, 1870, 365. *Heliopædica castaneocauda,* LAWRENCE, Ann. N. Y. Lyc. 1860, 145 (female). — ELLIOT, Illust. Birds N. Am. I, xxii.

SP. CHAR. *Male.* Above metallic green; the forehead, cheeks, and chin velvety black (the former with a deep blue gloss). A distinct white stripe from bill, through and behind the eye. Throat and forepart of breast brilliant metallic green; rest of under parts cinnamon-rufous; all the tail-feathers purplish-rufous, — the central glossed with green above, near the edges, the others obscurely edged with blackish along ends. Bill red at base, black at end. Length, 3.50; wing, 2.10; tail, 1.40; exposed portion of bill above, .65. *Female.* Forehead and all under parts light cinnamon beneath, without any green, or any dusky specks on throat; white cheek-stripe appreciable, but tinged with rufous. Tail as in male, but the central feathers entirely green above, the other, except the outer, with a dusky greenish or purplish spot on each web near the end. Whole upper mandible apparently dusky; base of lower, red.

Heliopædica xantusi.

HAB. Cape St. Lucas.

This well-marked and interesting species we owe to Mr. Xantus, together with many other birds of the west coast. It is sufficiently distinct to require no comparison other than that given under the general head; it can be separated from *H. melanotis* in all stages of plumage by the rufous tail.

Specimens vary sometimes in the intensity of the rufous shade, and, as stated, it is probable that the forehead, instead of being black, in full plumage is deep blue, as in *melanotis.*

HABITS. This is a new and well-marked species, and although belonging to the North American fauna cannot be claimed for the United States, having thus far been only taken at Cape St. Lucas by Mr. Xantus, and described by Mr. Lawrence in 1860. Nothing is known as to its specific habits.

GENUS **THAUMATIAS**, BONAP.

GEN. CHAR. Very similar in general form to *Heliopœdica*, but the tail emarginated, instead of rounded, the feathers narrower and less rounded at the ends. The coloration quite different. Sexes alike, in all the species. Color nearly uniform green, with the anal region white, the wings and tail dusky. Many species with the whole lower parts, except laterally, pure white. One species (*T. chionurus*) with the tail white, except the ends of the feathers and the intermediæ.

The species are all of rather small size and rather plain appearance, from the uniformity of their green, or green and white, coloring. They belong to northern South America, and to Central America north to Guatemala.

The genus is included in the North American fauna solely upon the accidental occurrence of one species (*T. linnœi*) in Eastern Massachusetts.

Thaumatias linnæi, BONAP.

LINNÆUS'S EMERALD.

Thaumatias linnœi, BONAP. Rev. et Mag. de Zool. 1854, 255. *Thaumatias l.* GOULD, Monog. Trochilid. pl. ? *Trochilus tobaci*, GMEL. Syst. Nat. I, 498. ? *Trochilus toba-gensis*, LATH. Ind. Orn. I, 316. ? *Trochilus tobago*, SHAW, Gen. Zoöl. viii, 350. *Or-nismya viridissima*, LESS. Hist. Nat. 257, pl. lxxv. ? *L'Oiseau-mouche à poitrine verte* (*Trochilus maculatus*), AUD. et VIEILL. Ois. Dor. tom. I, 87, pl. xliv. *Argyrtria maculata*, MAYNARD, Birds E. Mass. 1870, 128 (Cambridge, Mass.!).

SP. CHAR. Continuous green, darker above, more brilliant, and of an emerald tint on the throat and jugulum ; crissum, anal region, and middle of the abdomen, white. Primaries plain dusky. Tail blackish, with a faint reflection of dark blue subterminally, and of dull green basally, the lateral feathers obscurely tipped with dull dark ashy. Sexes alike. Wing, about 2.00 ; bill, .70.

HAB. Northern Brazil, Guiana, Tobago, and Bogota (GOULD) ? ? Accidental in the eastern United States (Cambridge, Mass., MAYNARD).

This race much resembles the *T. albiventris*, (REICHENB.) BONAP. (GOULD, Monog. Troch., Vol. V, p. ccci), of Brazil, but is said to be smaller and with less white on the abdomen and the under tail-coverts tinged with gray.

HABITS. The single specimen of this Humming-Bird, referred to by both Mr. Maynard and Mr. Allen[1] as having been taken in Massachusetts, is said to have been shot by Mr. William Brewster in the summer of 1868, in Cambridge, near Mount Auburn. It was secured by accident, and was presumed to be, when taken, a female specimen of *Trochilus colubris*. It was sent to Mr. Vickary, of Lynn, to be mounted, and the question has been raised if by chance a South American bird may not have been substituted for the original. This, however, Mr. Vickary is positive could not have happened. Nothing distinctive was observed as to its habits. In view, however, of the possibility of an error, the propriety of including it in our fauna is very questionable.

[1] Am. Naturalist, 1869 – 70.

The three families next in order are those generally known as the *Zygodactyli*, in their more restricted sense, that is, having the toes arranged in pairs, two before and two behind. In the present case the anterior toes are the inner and the middle (the second and third), the posterior being the hinder and outer (the first and fourth); where, as is sometimes the case, a hind toe is wanting, it is the first, or the hind toe proper.

By this definition we exclude the *Trogonidæ*, the *Bucconidæ*, and the *Galbuilidæ*, which likewise have the toes in pairs, but in which they are differently combined.

The North American families, the *Cuculidæ*, the *Picidæ*, and the *Psittacidæ*, are defined as follows : —

A. Upper mandible not movable nor hinged. Tarsus with transverse scutellæ. Bill without a naked skin, or cere, at the base; lower mandible much longer than deep, the end not truncated.

    a. Tongue short, and not extensible; not barbed at the point.

        Bill hooked or curved at tip; not constructed for hammering. No nasal tufts . . . . *Cuculidæ.*

    b. Tongue long and cylindrical, and generally capable of great extension; barbed at the point.

        Bill not hooked, but nearly straight; strong, and constructed for hammering. Thick nasal tufts at base of the bill (except in the *Nudinares*).

                                              Picidæ.

B. Upper mandible movable or hinged. Tarsus without transverse scutellæ. Bill with a naked skin, or cere, at the base; lower mandible not longer than deep, its end truncated.

    c. Tongue short and thick, fleshy.

        Bill enormously large, much curved, the upper mandible hooked, both much arched . . . . *Psittacidæ.*

FAMILY CUCULIDÆ. — THE CUCKOOS.

CHAR. Bill compressed, usually more or less lengthened and with decurved culmen. Rictal bristles few or none. Nostrils exposed, no nasal tufts. Tail long and soft, of eight to twelve feathers. Toes in pairs, deeply cleft or not united, the outer anterior toe usually versatile, but directed rather laterally than backward.

The *Cuculidœ* form a strongly marked group of birds, easily distinguished among the *Zygodactyli* by the characters given above. The outer toe is versatile, but in the American form is more lateral than posterior in the skin, standing sideways, or even anterior, more frequently than behind.

Modern systematists divide the family into six or more subfamilies, of which two only are American, none of these having more than ten tail-feathers. These may be characterized as follows: —

Coccyginæ. Face covered with feathers; bill elongated, more or less cylindrical, straight or curved. Tail of ten feathers.
    Bill about the length of the head, or not longer; curved. Loral feathers soft. Legs weak, tarsus shorter than the toes. Arboreal . *Coccygus.*
    Bill longer than the head; straight. Loral feathers stiff, bristly. Tarsi much longer than the toes. Terrestrial . . . . . *Geococcyx.*
Crotophaginæ. Face naked. Bill much compressed, with a sharp crest. Tail of eight feathers. Bill shorter than and nearly as high as the head.
    Crotophaga.

SUBFAMILY COCCYGINÆ.

GENUS GEOCOCCYX, WAGLER.

Geococcyx, WAGLER, Isis, 1831, 524.
Leptostoma, SWAINSON, Classification Birds, II, 1837, 325.

GEN. CHAR. Bill long and strong, slightly compressed, and at least as long as the head; head crested; loral feathers, and those at base of bill, stiffened and bristly. Nostrils elongated, linear. A naked colored skin around and behind the eye; the eyelids ciliated. Tarsi longer than the toes; very stout. Wings very short and concave; the tertials as long as the primaries. Tail longer than the head and body; composed of ten narrow, much graduated feathers.

This remarkable genus is represented in the United States by a single species, known as the Paisano, Chaparral Cock, or sometimes Road-Runner, on account of its frequenting public highways. Its very long legs enable it to run with great rapidity, faster even than a fleet horse. A second species occurs in Mexico, the *Geococcyx affinis* of Hartlaub. This is smaller, and differently proportioned. In both the feathers above are bronzed brown and green; nearly all with opaque white edges; beneath white, with black

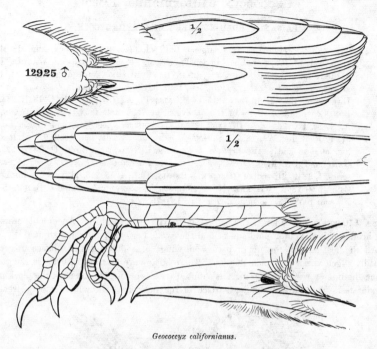

Geococcyx californianus.

streaks on the sides of neck and breast; the feathers with broad white tips; the principal differences are as follows:—

G. californianus. Bill above, about 2.00; gape nearly straight to near tip; nostril behind middle of gape. Feathers of throat and upper part of breast light brownish, with shaft-streaks of black. *Hab.* Southwestern United States, from Cape St. Lucas and Southern California to Texas.

G. affinis.[1] Bill above about 1.60; gape gently curved throughout. Nostril opposite middle of gape. Feathers of throat and breast fulvous-white, without shaft-streaks, except on the sides, where they are broad and abruptly defined. *Hab.* Mexico, from Mazatlan to Xalapa.

This last species is common at Mazatlan, as well as elsewhere in Mexico, and may yet be found in Arizona.

[1] *Geococcyx affinis*, HARTLAUB, Rev. Zoöl. 1844, 215. — BONAP. 97. — SCL. P. Z. S. 1858, 305. — SCLATER & SALVIN, Ibis, 1859, 134. — SCLATER, Catal. 1862, 325. *Geococcyx velox*, KARW. BONAP. 97.

Geococcyx californianus, BAIRD.

PAISANO; ROAD-RUNNER; CHAPARRAL COCK.

Saurothera californiana, LESSON, Complem. Buff. VI, 1829, 420. — BOTTA, Ann. du Mus. 1835, 121, pl. (Cape St. Lucas to San Francisco). *Geococcyx variegata*, WAGLER, Isis, V, 1831, 524. *Saurothera bottæ* (BLAINVILLE), LESSON, Traité d'Orn. I, 1831, 145. *Diplopterus viaticus* (LICHT.) BOIE, Isis, 1831, 541 (no description). *Geococcyx viaticus*, HARTLAUB, Rev. Zoöl. 1844, 215. — M'CALL, Pr. A. N. Sc. III, July, 1847, 234. — BON. Consp. 1850, 97. — IB. Consp. Zygod. in Aten. Ital. 1854, 5. — HEERMANN, J. A. N. Sc. Ph. 2d series, II, 1853, 270. — NEWBERRY, Zoöl. Cal. and Oregon Route, 91, P. R. R. Rep. VI, 1857. *Saurothera marginata*, KAUP, Isis, 1832, 991 ; tab. xxvi (fig. of head and foot). *Leptostoma longicauda*, SWAINSON, Birds, II, 1837, 325. — GAMBEL, Pr. A. N. S. I, 1843, 263. *Geococcyx mexicanus*, GAMBEL, J. A. N. Sc. 2d series, I, 1849, 215 (not of GMELIN). — CASSIN, Ill. I, 1855, 213, pl. xxxvi. — SCLATER, Catal. 324, 1862. — HEERM. X, *S*, 59 (nest). *Geococcyx californianus*, BAIRD, Birds N. Am. 1858, 73. — COOPER, Orn. Cal. I, 1870, 368.

SP. CHAR. Tail very long; the lateral feathers much shortest. An erectile crest on the head. A bare skin around and behind the eye. Legs very long and stout.

All the feathers of the upper parts and wings of a dull metallic olivaceous-green, broadly edged with white near the end. There is, however, a tinge of black in the green along the line of white, which itself is suffused with brown. On the neck the black preponderates. The sides and under surface of the neck have the white feathers streaked

Geococcyx californianus.

centrally with black, next to which is a brownish suffusion. The remaining under parts are whitish, immaculate. Primary quills tipped with white, and with a median band across the outer webs. Central tail-feathers olive-brown; the others clear dark green, all edged, and (except the central two) broadly tipped with white. Top of the head dark blackish-blue. Length, 20 to 23 inches; wing, about 6.50; tail, 12 to 13. Size generally very variable.

HAB. Middle Texas, New Mexico, and California to Central Mexico. Seen as far north as Fort Reading, California, and Fort Chadbourne, Texas. Localities: Southeast Texas (DRESSER, Ibis, 1865, 466, resident); W. Arizona (COUES, P. A. N. S. 1866, 57); Cape St. Lucas (XANTUS); Kioway Agency (DR. PALMER).

There are seemingly no differences of plumage depending on sex, age, or season.

In calling this species *Geococcyx californianus* we do not feel entirely sure that we have selected the earliest name. Hartlaub and other authors give 1829 as the date of Lesson's Vol. VI, of complement to Buffon (VI, 420). A copy of this volume in the Library of Congress bears date of 1834 upon the titlepage. It is, however, quoted at the date of 1829 by Engelmann, so that the copy referred to above may possibly be a second edition, or with a new post-dated titlepage. In this uncertainty, however, we prefer to retain the name of *californianus*.

Botta, in his description of the bird (the original of Lesson's species), speaks of it as occurring from Cape St. Lucas to San Francisco. Specimens from Cape St. Lucas, brought by Mr. Xantus, are smaller than those of Upper California, but otherwise apparently identical.

Habits. This very remarkable bird, variously named, in Mexico, Texas, and California, the Paisano, the Road-Runner, the Chaparral Cock, the Ground Cuckoo, the Prairie Cock, and the Corre-camino, is one of the most curious and interesting of the recent additions to our ornithological lists. It is found throughout Northern Mexico, Texas as far north as Fort Chadbourne, and in California as far as Fort Reading. It is also abundant in portions of Arizona and New Mexico, and is supposed to be resident in all these districts. It is described as very remarkable for great swiftness of foot, in which it appears to be equalled by no other North American bird. In Mexico, and in some parts of the United States, it is not unusual to hunt these birds, as a matter of amusement, on horseback, and to pursue them with hounds, — a test of their fleetness in which they are said to often make a longer race than their pursuers anticipated.

This bird habitually frequents the ground. When walking or running, its long tail is borne in an erect position, and often assumes a variety of grotesque positions. While thus more or less terrestrial in its habits, and sharing with gallinaceous birds many of their peculiarities, it has no other affinities with them, but ranks in a very different ornithological division, being classed with the Cuckoos.

This bird was first brought to the attention of American naturalists by Dr. William Gambel, who published a description of it in 1845. Two years afterwards Colonel McCall published the first satisfactory account that has been given of its habits and manners of life. He states that though this bird is zygodactyle, with toes disposed in opposite pairs, yet that the reversibility of the outer toe favors its use for climbing or perching, as well as for movements on the ground.

The food of the Ground Cuckoo consists of coleopterous and almost every other description of insects, and where snails abound they also are greedily eaten. These are usually taken either from the ground or a branch, and carried to a particular spot, where the shell is broken and its contents eaten.

Piles of these shells are often found thus collected in places frequented by them. They are also said to be ready and expert in catching their prey in the air, sometimes springing up to the height of eight or ten feet In these performances the wings and tail are expanded for but a moment, the bill is heard to snap as the insect is seized, and the bird drops again suddenly to the ground.

Colonel McCall adds that the general impression that its powers of flight are very limited is not correct. When suddenly alarmed in open ground, it rises with a light quick motion, and flies some hundreds of yards continuously with an ease that attests its ability to maintain even a longer flight. He has often seen it climb to the top of a straight leafless branch, and there sit, apparently to enjoy the first rays of the morning sun.

They are shy and retiring in disposition, wary, vigilant, and cautious, so that it is generally difficult to approach them on the open ground. When suddenly surprised and driven to fly a considerable distance for cover, though they fly with evident ease, they rarely rise higher than six or eight feet from the ground. In evidence of its wonderful swiftness of foot, Colonel McCall states that when on one occasion, approaching Limpia Creek, in Texas, with a small party, he discovered a Chaparral Cock in the open road, about a hundred yards in advance, for his amusement he put spurs to his horse, and dashed after the bird with one of the men. It was thus pursued for full four hundred yards along a smooth and level road, over which with straightened neck and slightly expanded wings it swiftly glided without seeming to touch the ground. When at last it sought shelter in the thicket, they had not gained upon it more than fifty yards.

Captain McCown kept a young half-grown bird in confinement, but it refused to eat, and soon died; others, however, have been more fortunate, and have succeeded in taming them.

Dr. Heermann states that the stomachs of all these birds examined by him were filled with the grasshoppers and the large black beetles found on the plains. A nest of this bird was found by him, built on the branches of the cactus, and constructed of loose sticks put negligently together in a manner similar to the nests of the Yellow-billed Cuckoos. It contained two large white and nearly spherical eggs.

Dr. Gambel states that these birds devour reptiles as well as other insects, which is also confirmed by the observations of Mr. Arthur Schott.

Lieutenant Couch mentions that this bird, called Paisano by the Mexicans, is also held in high estimation by them on account of its enmity to the rattle-snake, which it usually succeeds in killing in fair combat. Though by no means deficient in courage, it is represented as remarkably quiet and harmless in its habits. The only note he heard from it was a weak scream, which is seldom uttered. It is unsocial, is never seen in flocks, and rarely wanders from its restricted locality.

In regard to their note, Dr. Cooper mentions hearing one at Fort Mohave making a low cooing noise like that of a dove, for which it was at first mistaken. He afterwards heard it cooing harshly and chattering its mandibles together, at the same time jerking up its tail and erecting its crest.

Where not molested, Dr. Cooper states that they become quite tame, and seem to have a preference for towns and houses. At Santa Barbara he observed one young bird nearly fledged as early as May.

Mr. A. J. Grayson had one of these birds in confinement, which became quite tame, and readily fed upon any kind of raw meat, but preferred lizards and small birds, the latter of which it swallowed, feathers and all. If given to him alive, he would play with them awhile before swallowing them, as a cat does with a mouse. They are sometimes tamed, and kept about gardens to kill mice and insects. Dr. Kennerly also states that when taken alive they soon become quite tame, and willingly remain about a house, soon destroying all the mice in the vicinity, which they catch with as much dexterity as a cat.

Mr. Dresser found this bird abundant throughout the mesquite regions, and more particularly so near the Rio Grande. He found its eggs near San Antonio in April and May, and received them even as late as the 23d of September. They build a clumsy nest of mesquite twigs, placed at some height on a bough or in a hollow tree, and lay from two to four pure white eggs. The stomachs examined by Mr. Dresser were found to contain small snakes, lizards, and ticks. He had one in a semi-domesticated state at Matamoras, which became very tame, and was so mischievous that he could not let it remain in the house. It would steal and hide everything that it could carry off, and was particularly fond of tearing up letters and upsetting the inkstand. It was never caged or tied up, and would frequently pay the neighbors a visit, always returning before evening. He fed it on raw meat and lizards. It flew with great ease, and was very fond of perching on the house-top. This bird had a singular antipathy to a tame parrot, and whenever the latter was let out of the cage, it would get into a rage, and either go to the house-top or decamp to some of the neighbors.

The eggs are white, of a rounded oval, equal at either end, and measure 1.60 by 1.22 inches.

Genus COCCYGUS, Vieillot.

Coccyzus, Vieillot, Analyse, 1816. (Type, *Cuculus americanus*, Linn.)
Erythrophrys, Swainson, Class. Birds, II, 1837, 322.

Gen. Char. Head without crest; feathers about base of bill soft; bill nearly as long as the head, decurved, slender, and attenuated towards the end. Nostrils linear. Wings lengthened, reaching the middle of the tail; the tertials short. Tail of ten graduated feathers. Feet weak; tarsi shorter than the middle toe.

The species of *Coccygus* are readily distinguished from those of *Geococcyx* by their arboreal habits, confining themselves mainly to trees, instead of living habitually on the ground. The plumage is soft, fine, and compact.

The American Cuckoos differ from the European (*Cuculus*) by having lengthened naked tarsi, instead of very short feathered ones. The nostrils, too, are elongated instead of rounded. The habits of the two are entirely

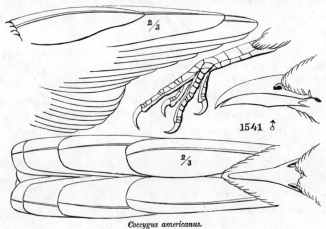

Coccygus americanus.

different, the American species rearing their own young, instead of laying the eggs in the nests of other birds, like the European Cuckoo and the American Cowbird (*Molothrus pecoris*).

The following synopsis will serve to distinguish the North American species of *Coccygus*, with their more nearly related southern allies, all of them being of a light greenish color above, tinged with ashy towards the head : —

Species and Varieties.

A. Tail-feathers except two middle ones black, with broad, sharply defined terminal spaces of white.

    a. Lower mandible yellow.

        C. americanus. Beneath pure white, with an ashy shade across the jugulum. Inner webs of primaries mostly rufous. Auriculars nearly concolor with the nape. Length, 12.00 ; wing, 5.45 ; tail, 5.64 ; culmen, 1.00 ; tarsus, .90. *Hab.* United States (very rare in the Western Province), Jamaica, Porto Rico.

        2. **C. minor.** Beneath ochraceous, generally paler anteriorly. Inner webs of primaries without any rufous. Auriculars blackish, conspicuously different from the nape. Length, 12.00 ; wing, 5.30 ; tail, 7.50 ; graduation of tail, 2.75. Tail-spots about 1.00 long. *Hab.* West Indies, and Northern and Eastern South America, Southern Florida.

    b. Lower mandible blackish like the upper (pale blue in life).

        3. **C. melanocoryphus.**[1] Colors similar to those of *C. minor*, but upper parts more brown. Wing, 4.50 ; tail, 5.85 ; graduation of the tail, 2.00. Tail-spots about .50 long. *Hab.* South America (Buenos Ayres, Peru, La Plata, Cayenne, etc.).

[1] *Coccygus melanocoryphus*, VIEILLOT, Nouv. Dict. VIII, 271. — SCLATER, Catal. 1862, 323. — IB. P. Z. S. 1864, 122.

B. Tail-feathers all grayish-brown, with narrow terminal, obscure spots of white.

  c. Lower mandible blackish like the upper (pale blue in life ?).

  C. erythrophthalmus. No rufous on primaries, except in young (which have black bill, brown tail-feathers, etc.). Beneath continuous white, with a faint ashy-buff shade across the jugulum; above grayish-brown. Bare eyelids bright red in the adult. Length, 11.30; wing, 5.12; tail, 6.24; tarsus, .90; culmen, 1.00. *Hab.* Eastern Province of the United States, south through eastern Middle America to Bogota.

Coccygus americanus, Bonap.

YELLOW-BILLED CUCKOO.

Cuculus americanus, Linn. Syst. Nat. I, 1766, 170, 10. *Coccyzus americanus,* Bon. Obs. Wilson, 1825, No. 47. — Ib. Conspectus, 1850, IV. — Aud. Orn. Biog. I, 1832, 18, V; 520, pl. ii. — Ib. Birds Am. IV, 1842, 293, pl. cclxxv. — Baird, Birds N. Am. 1858, 76. — Scl. Cat. 1862, 322. — Cooper, Pr. Cal. Ac. 1868 (Sacramento, Cal.) — Samuels, 83. — Cooper, Orn. Cal. I, 1870, 371. *Erythrophrys americanus,* Sw. Birds II, 1837. — Bon. List, 1838. *Cureus americanus,* Bon. List, Eur. Birds, 1842. *? Cuculus dominicensis,* Linn. Syst. Nat. I, 1766, 170, 13. *? Cuculus dominicus,* Latham, Syst. I, 1790, 221 (considered distinct by Bonaparte). *Coccygus dominicus,* Baird, pl. *Cuculus carolinensis* (Brisson), Wilson, Am. Orn. IV, 1811, 13, pl. xxviii. *Cuculus cinerosus,* Temminck, Man. IV, 1835, 277. *Coccyzus pyrrhopterus,* Vieill. Dict. *Coccygus bairdi,* Sclater, P. Z. S. March, 1864, 120 (Jamaica; no rufous externally on wing). *? Coccygus julieni,* Lawr. Ann. N. Y. Lyc. VIII, June, 1864, 42, 99 (Sombrero Island; no rufous on wing).

Sp. Char. Upper mandible and tip of lower, black; rest of lower mandible and cutting edges of the upper, yellow. Upper parts of a metallic greenish-olive, slightly tinged with ash towards the bill; beneath white. Tail-feathers (except the median, which are like the back) black, tipped with white for about an inch on the outer feathers, the external one with the outer edge almost entirely white. Quills orange-cinnamon; the terminal portion and a gloss on the outer webs olive; iris brown. Length, 12.00; wing, 5.95; tail, 6.35.

Coccygus americanus.

Hab. Eastern United States to the Missouri plains. California and Nevada (Ridgway); Mazatlan; Jamaica; Porto Rico. Localities: ? Sta. Cruz (Newton, Ibis, I, 149, eggs!); Cuba (Cab. J. IV, 154; Gundl. Rep. I, 1866, 295); Jamaica (Gosse, B. Jam. 279 ?) Costa Rica (Cab. J. 1862, 167); Lower Rio Grande (Dresser, Ibis, 1865, 466, breeds).

There is considerable variation in the amount of rufous in the quills; sometimes this shows very distinctly externally, sometimes it is entirely replaced by the bronzed olive of the back. A greater amount of the rufous seems to characterize the more southern and Jamaica specimens, which also are smaller; northern specimens, however, show similar variations. In the immature birds the under surface of the tail-feathers is gray, not black, so that the contrast with the white tips is very indistinct, as in *erythrophthalmus*, in which, however, these light tips are much narrower, while the bill is entirely black.

Specimens of this bird from regions west of the Missouri, and especially one from Cantonment Burgwyn, New Mexico, are appreciably larger than eastern, with decidedly longer bill. One brought from Mazatlan by Mr. Xantus is undistinguishable from the long-billed western variety.

HABITS. The Yellow-billed Cuckoo is distributed throughout North America from Canada to Florida, and from the Atlantic coast to California. It has been met with in all the principal West India Islands. I have received specimens of its eggs and nest from Southwestern Texas. Audubon mentions finding this bird high up on the Mississippi River, on the upper branches of the Arkansas, and in Upper Canada, as well as in every State between these limits. Mr. Newton found it breeding in the island of St. Croix, Mr. Gosse mentions it as a bird of Jamaica, and Lembeye gives it among those of Cuba, and Mr. Salvin found it in Central America. It is known to breed from the West Indies and Florida to Minnesota, and from New Brunswick to Texas. It does not appear to have been met with in any of the government expeditions, except by Dr. Woodhouse, who speaks of it as very common in the Indian Territory, Texas, and New Mexico.

This species was seen on one occasion, and heard at other times, near Sacramento City, Cal., by Mr. Ridgway, in June, 1867. It was there rare, or at least not common, and found principally in the willow-thickets. It was again met with in July, of the same year, along the Truckee River, in Nevada, where, also, it appeared to be very rare.

Wilson traced it as far north as Lake Ontario, and speaks of finding it numerous in the Chickasaw and Choctaw nations, and as breeding in the upper part of Georgia. He seems to have observed very carefully its habits, and to have enjoyed favorable opportunities for his observations. His account of their nesting is interesting. He states that, in marked contrast to the singularly unparental conduct of their European relatives, the American Cuckoos build their own nest, hatch their own eggs, and rear their own young, and that in conjugal and parental affection they seem to be surpassed by no other birds. He adds that they begin to pair early in May, and commence building about the 10th of that month. He describes their nest as usually fixed among the horizontal branches of an apple-tree ; sometimes in a solitary thorn, crab, or cedar, in some retired part of the woods. It is constructed with little art, and scarcely any concavity, of small sticks and twigs, intermixed with green weeds and blossoms of the maple. On this almost flat bed the eggs, usually three or four in number, are placed ; these are of a uniform greenish-blue color, and of a size proportionate to that of the bird. While the female is sitting, the male is usually not far distant, and gives the alarm by his notes when any person is approaching. The female sits so close that you may almost reach her with your hand, and then precipitates herself to the ground, feigning lameness to draw you away from the spot, fluttering, trailing her wings, and tumbling over in the manner of the Woodcock and other birds. Both parents unite in providing food for the young. This consists chiefly of caterpillars, particularly such as infest apple-trees.

Mr. Audubon speaks of this species as not abundant anywhere, therein differing from Wilson's statements, but more in accordance with my own observations. They are, as a species, pretty generally distributed, but at the same time their numbers are materially affected by the character of the locality, as they are chiefly to be met with on low grounds and in damp places. Mr. Audubon also describes their nest as simple and flat, composed of a few dry sticks and grass, formed much like that of the Carolina Dove, and like it fastened to a horizontal branch, often within reach. He subsequently states that when in Charleston, S. C., in the early part of June, 1837, he was invited by Mr. Rhett to visit his grounds in the vicinity of that city, for the purpose of viewing a nest of this bird. The following is his account of it : " A nest, which was placed near the centre of a tree of moderate size, was reached by a son of the gentleman on whose grounds we were. One of the old birds, which was sitting upon it, left its situation only when within a few inches of the climber's hand, and silently glided off to another tree close by. Two young Cuckoos, nearly able to fly, scrambled off from their tenement among the branches of the tree, and were caught. The nest was taken, and carefully handed to me. It still contained three young Cuckoos, all of different sizes, the smallest apparently just hatched, the next in size probably several days old, while the largest, covered with pin-feathers, would have been able to leave the nest in about a week. There were also in the nest two eggs, one containing a chick, the other fresh or lately laid. The two young birds which escaped from the nest clung so firmly to the branches by their feet, that our attempts to dislodge them were of no avail, and we were obliged to reach them with the hand. On looking at all these birds, our surprise was great, as no two of them were of the same size, which clearly showed that they had been hatched at different periods, and I should suppose the largest to have been fully three weeks older than any of the rest. Mr. Rhett assured us that he had observed the same in another nest, placed in a tree within a few paces of his house. He stated that eleven young Cuckoos had been successively hatched and reared in it by the same pair of old birds in one season, and that young birds and eggs were to be seen in it at the same time for many weeks in succession."

Mr. Nuttall states that the nest of this bird is usually forsaken by the owner if the eggs are handled before the commencement of incubation. They are very tenacious and affectionate towards their young, and sit so close as almost to allow of being taken off by the hand. They then frequently precipitate themselves to the ground, fluttering, tumbling, and feigning lameness, in the manner of many other affectionate and artful birds, to draw the intruder away from the vicinity of the brood. At such times, the mother also utters the most uncouth guttural sounds as she runs along the ground. While the female is engaged in sitting on her charge, the male takes his station at no great distance, and gives alarm by his notes, on the approach of an intruder. When the young are hatched, both unite in the labor of providing them with food. He subsequently states that these birds hatch several broods in a season, which he inferred from the fact of his meeting with a nest containing eggs as late as the 28th of August. He also speaks of finding in one instance an egg of the Cuckoo laid in the nest of a Catbird, and in another instance (June 15) an egg in the nest of a Robin. Such instances must, however, be very rare. No other writer mentions any similar instance, and none have ever fallen under my observations.

Mr. Gosse, in his Birds of Jamaica, describes the Yellow-bill as among the birds of that island, speaks of it as among the regular visitants in spring, but makes no mention of its breeding there.

Mr. Edward Newton, in his paper on the birds of St. Croix (Ibis, 1859, p. 149), gives an interesting account of its breeding in that locality. He adds his testimony to the general credit given to this species for the conjugal affection they evince. On one occasion, he says, a male having been shot, and shrieking as it fell, the female instantly flew to the spot, and fluttered along the ground in the manner that an old hen Partridge or other bird would do, to lead astray the pursuer of her young. On June 2, 1858, he shot a female of this species, having an egg in her ovary nearly ready for exclusion; it was quite soft, but had its proper color. On the 29th of the same month, while riding, he saw the white terminal spots of a Cuckoo's tail projecting from a small nest on a manchineel that overhung the path. It was built in a very open situation, and the bird, as he rode underneath, was not more than a yard above his head. She sat with nearly all her neck and breast outside the nest, which was only just large enough to contain the eggs. She did not fly off until after he had tied up the pony hard by, and had almost touched her with his whip. There were three eggs, laid side by side in a row, *along* which the bird had been sitting. The nest was at some distance from the stem of the tree, and placed loosely on the bough. It was a mere platform of small sticks laid one across another, with a few finer twigs and a little grass as a lining; so slightly was it put together, that, on attempting to take it from the tree, it fell to pieces.

No writer besides Mr. Audubon makes any mention of, or appears to have been aware of, the peculiar habits of these birds in hatching out their successive depositions of eggs, one by one. In this respect they are eccentric, and do not always exhibit this trait. While I have repeatedly observed facts exactly corresponding with those noticed by Mr. Audubon in the garden of Mr. Rhett, at other times I have found in the opening of the season three or four eggs laid before incubation commenced, and all hatched before others were deposited. Then the parents seemed to depend, in no small degree, upon the warmth of the bodies of the older offspring to compensate to the younger for their own neglect, as well as for the exposed and insufficient warmth of the nest. I have repeatedly found in a nest three young and two eggs, one of the latter nearly fresh, one with the embryo half developed, while of the young birds one would be just out of the shell, one half fledged, and one just ready to fly. My attention was first called to these peculiarities of hatching as early as 1834, by finding, in Cambridge, in a nest with three young birds, an egg which, instead of proving to be addled, as I anticipated, was perfectly fresh, and evidently just laid. Subsequent observations in successive seasons led to the conviction that both this species and the Black-billed Cuckoo share in these' peculiarities, and that it is a general, but not a universal practice. These facts were communicated to Mr. Audubon, but not before his attention had been called to the same thing.

In referring to these peculiarities of the American Cuckoo, Mr. Audubon finds in them a closely connecting link with the European bird, and Mr. Darwin, carrying still farther the same idea, finds in them also data for regarding our birds as only one remove from the vagaries of the European Cuckoo. At the first glance there may seem to be some plausibility in these deductions. The mere apology for a nest of our Cuckoos and their alternations of laying and hatching may, to some extent, be regarded as but one remove from the total neglect of the European to build any nest, making, instead, successive depositions in the nests of other birds. But there are other peculiarities of our Cuckoos to be taken into consideration, totally variant from the polygamous, unconjugal, and unparental European. Their devotion to their mates and to their offspring, in which both sexes vie with each other ; their extended breeding-season, varying from one to nearly four months, — all these characteristics separate them by a long interval from their namesakes of the Old World.

If the nests of the Cuckoos are incomplete and insufficient, so are also those of the most exemplary of parents, the whole tribe of Pigeons, and, like the latter, our Cuckoos more than atone for such deficiencies by the devoted fidelity with which they adhere to their post of duty even in the face of imminent dangers ; while, after the first offspring of the season have been hatched, the warmth of their bodies becomes an additional protection from the exposure of the bare platform on which they are deposited.

The eggs of this species are of an oblong-oval shape, equally obtuse at either end, and measure 1.30 inches in length by 1.00 in breadth. They vary considerably in size, their minimum breadth being .90 of an inch, and the length 1.20 inches. Their color is a uniform light bluish-green, extremely fugitive, and fading even in the closed drawer of a cabinet.

Coccygus minor, CABANIS.

MANGROVE CUCKOO.

? *Cuculus minor*, GMELIN, Syst. Nat. I, 1788, 411. *? Coccyzus minor*, CABANIS, Cab.
Journal für Orn. 1856, 104 (Cuba). — BAIRD, Birds N. Am. 1858, 78. — *Cuculus
seniculus*, LATH. Ind. I, 1790, 219. *Coccyzus seniculus*, NUTTALL, Man. I, 1832, 558.
— AUD. Orn. Biog. II, 1834, 390, pl. clxix. — IB. Birds America, IV, 1842, 303, pl.
cclxxvii. — GOSSE, Birds Jamaica, 281. — BON. Conspectus, 1850, III. *Erythrophrys
seniculus*, BON. List, 1838. *Coccygus dominicus*, SCL. Cat. 1862, 323.

SP. CHAR. Lower mandible yellow, except at the tip. Body above olivaceous, strongly
tinged with ashy towards and on the head. Beneath pale yellowish-brown, darkest on
the legs and abdomen, becoming lighter to the bill. An elongated spot of dark plumbeous
behind the eye. Inner edges of the quills and under wing-coverts like the belly. Tail-
feathers, except the central, black, with a sharply defined tip of white for about an inch,
this color not extending along the outer web of the quill. Length about 12.00; wing
about 5.25.

HAB. Florida Keys to West Indies. Localities: ? Sta. Cruz (NEWTON, Ibis, I, 150);
Cuba (CAB. J. IV, 154; GUNDL. Repert. I, 1866, 295); Jamaica (GOSSE, B. Jam. 281).

This species is readily distinguishable by its fulvous under parts, dark ear-
coverts, and lack of rufous on inner webs of quills. It has the yellow bill
and dark tail, with broad white tips, of *C. americanus*, although the white
does not extend along the outer web of the feathers.

According to Mr. Audubon, this species is a regular summer visitor to
Key West and the other Florida keys.

This species is more especially West Indian, occurring in nearly all the
islands. There are some local variations in color (Porto-Rican being much
redder, Bahaman paler), as well as in size, but in a large series from the same
island there will be found such differences as to warrant us in considering
all as one species. In a very large series before us, we cannot see any
tangible difference, although Cabanis and Sclater recognize a *C. nesiotes* from
the Antillean West Indies, as distinguished from *C. seniculus* from South
American and the windward West Indies; the former, smaller and paler,
and, according to Cabanis, with the white of tip of tail confined to the inner
web; the latter darker beneath, and larger. These characters I do not find
substantiated, nor have I seen one specimen without white in both webs at
the ends of the tail-feathers.

As the name of *C. minor* is the earliest one for at least the South American race, we retain it in preference to *seniculus*, as although scarcely *minor*
in this genus, it is so compared with *Piaya, Geococcyx*, and *Saurothera*.

HABITS. This species claims a place in the fauna of North America as a
resident of the Florida keys. This is the only locality positively known as
its habitat within the limits of the territory of the United States. The
only specimen referred to in the ninth volume of the Pacific Railroad Surveys was supposed to have been obtained in Florida. Mr. Nuttall, who

was the first to include the Mangrove Cuckoo among North American birds, speaks of it as an inhabitant chiefly of Cayenne, and as occasionally visiting the extreme Southern States. Mr. Audubon, who was the first to meet with the species within the limits of the United States, only obtained specimens of it in Florida, near Key West. I have seen a specimen which was given to Mr. John G. Bell as having been procured in Southern Mississippi. Mr. Gosse obtained specimens of this bird in Jamaica, though he had no opportunity of observing its domestic economy. In the month of January the specimens he dissected had eggs in their ovaries as large as duckshot. Dr. Gundlach gives it as a Cuban bird, but does not mention it as one that breeds on that island. The Newtons met with this species in St. Croix, but appear to have regarded it as not a summer resident, but only in the light of a visitant in the winter.

Mr. March, referring without doubt to this species, mentions it as a constant resident in the island of Jamaica, where it is common in the lowlands during summer. It is said to breed from March to July, building in the low branches of trees or in shrubs. The nest is described as a structure composed of a few dry sticks, so loosely put together that it falls to pieces on any attempt to remove it. Three, rarely four, eggs are laid, which are of a glaucous-green color, oval, generally round at both ends, and varying in size from 1.25 inches by .90 to 1.38 inches by 1 inch.

Of late years no specimens seem to have been obtained in Florida, either by Maynard or by the many other explorers of the Peninsula; and even if the earlier notices are correct, we may have to consider it as merely a straggler from the Bahamas, like *Certhiola bahamensis, Crotophaga ani, Phonipara zena, Vireosylvia barbatula*, etc.

Mr. Audubon, who was the only one of our naturalists who met with the nest and eggs, discovered them near Key West. He describes the nest as slightly constructed of dry twigs, and as almost flat, nearly resembling that of the Yellow-billed Cuckoo. The eggs are the same in number and form as those of that species, but are somewhat larger. It is said to raise two broods in one season, and to feed its young on insects until they are able to provide for themselves. An old bird, caught on its nest, which Mr. Audubon saw confined in a cage, refused all food and soon pined itself to death, — thus evincing, in his opinion, the great affection these birds have for their own eggs. An egg in the Smithsonian Institution collection, given me by Mr. John G. Bell of New York, is said to have been obtained in Mississippi with the parent bird. Its color has slightly faded, and, except in its greater comparative breadth, it is not distinguishable from the eggs of the Yellow-bill.

Coccygus erythrophthalmus, Bon.

BLACK-BILLED CUCKOO.

Cuculus erythrophthalmus, WILSON, Am. Orn. IV, 1811, 16, pl. xxviii. *Coccyzus erythrophthalmus*, BON. Obs. Wils. 1825, 48. — IB. Consp. 1850, IV. — AUD. Orn. Biog.
I, 1832, 170 ; V, 523, pl. xxxii. — IB. Birds America, IV, 1842, 300, pl. cclxxvi. —
BAIRD, Birds N. Am. 1858, 77. — SCL. Cat. 1862, 323. — SAMUELS, 85. *Erythrophrys erythrophthalmus*, BON. List, 1838. *Coccyzus dominicus*, (LATH.) NUTT.
Man. I, 1832, 556 (not of LATHAM, which belongs rather to *C. americanus*, on account
of the red quills and white edge of outer tail-feather).

SP. CHAR. Bill entirely black. Upper parts generally of a metallic greenish-olive, ashy
towards the base of the bill ; beneath pure white, with a brownish-yellow tinge on the
throat. Inner webs of the quills tinged with cinnamon. Under surface of all the tail-
feathers hoary ash-gray. All, except the central on either side, suffused with darker to
the short, bluish-white, and not well-defined tip. A naked red skin round the eye.
Length, about 12.00 ; wing, 5.00 ; tail, 6.50.

HAB. United States to the Missouri plains, south to Bogota. Localities : Cuba (CAB. J.
IV, 154, nests ; GUNDL. Repert. I, 1866, 295)) ; Guatemala (SALVIN, Ibis, II, 276) ;
Mexico and Bogota (SCL. Cat. 323) ; Isth. Panama (LAWR. Ann. N. Y. Lyc. VII, 62) ;
Costa Rica (LAWR. N. Y. Lyc. IX, 128).

This species differs from the *C. americanus* in the black bill, and the
absence of black on the tail-feathers, the white tips of which are much
shorter and less abruptly defined. One specimen (5,253) from the Upper
Missouri has a much stronger tinge of yellowish-cinnamon on the inner
webs of the quills than the others. The sexes are quite similar.

HABITS. The Black-billed Cuckoo, so closely allied with the common
species in respect to size, appearance, habits, and all its general characteristics, is also distributed throughout very nearly the same localities, where,
however, it is usually regarded as a much less abundant bird. It is found
throughout the United States as far west as the Missouri plains. Dr.
Woodhouse met with this bird in his expedition down the Zuni and Colorado Rivers, but states that he saw but very few, either in Texas or in the
Indian Territory. Lembeye, De la Sagra, and Dr. Gundlach include it as a
visitant, in the winter months, to Cuba. Mr. Audubon met with this
Cuckoo in Louisiana only a few times in the course of his various researches, and never in any Western State except Ohio. He does not seem
to have been aware that it ever breeds south of North Carolina. From
thence to Maine, and even as far north as the Canadas, Nova Scotia, and
Southern Labrador, he gives as its distribution during the breeding-season. He also regarded it as much more common in low and wooded ground
on the borders of the sea, where it frequents the edges of woods rather than
their interior, and chiefly on the edges of creeks, and in damp places. Mr.
Nuttall appeared to have regarded it as very nearly as common as the Yellow-bill throughout the United States, and as extending its migrations as far
north as Nova Scotia and Newfoundland. He states that it is found in St.

Domingo and Guiana, and also, on the authority of Mr. Abbott, that it breeds in Georgia as early as the 1st of April. Mr. Audubon says it was never met with by Dr. Bachman in South Carolina. It certainly breeds, however, as far south, at least, as Georgia, as the nest and eggs of this species were taken at Varnell Station, in the northwestern part of that State, by the late Dr. Alexander Gerhardt.

It is not mentioned by either Dr. Gambel or Dr. Heermann as among the birds of the Pacific Coast, and it does not appear to have been actually obtained by any of the expeditions to the Pacific beyond the Indian Territory. Its distribution, therefore, during the breeding-season, would seem to be from Georgia to Canada, and from Texas to Minnesota, inclusive of all the intermediate territory. Dr. Newberry frequently saw and heard what he supposed to have been this species, in the trees bordering Cow Creek, near Fort Reading, but as he did not secure a specimen, he may have been mistaken. It has been taken at Devil's Lake, in Minnesota, and in the Red River Settlement.

Wilson describes the nest of this bird as generally built in a cedar, much in the same manner, and of nearly the same materials, as that of the Yellow-bill; the eggs are smaller than those of that bird, usually four or five in number, and of a deeper greenish-blue.

Mr. Audubon speaks of the nest as built in places similar to those chosen by the other species, as formed of the same materials, and arranged with quite as little art. He gives the number of eggs as from four to six, of a greenish-blue, nearly equal at both ends, but rather smaller than those of the Yellow-bill, rounder, and of a much deeper tint of green. He gives their measurement as 1.50 inches in length and .87 of an inch in breadth.

Mr. Nuttall, whose description more nearly corresponds with my own observations, speaks of this species as usually retiring into the woods to breed, being less familiar than the former species, and choosing an evergreen bush or sapling for the site of the nest, which is made of twigs pretty well put together, but still little more than a concave flooring, and lined with moss occasionally, and withered catkins of the hickory. The eggs are described as smaller, and three to five in number, of a bluish-green. The female sits very close on the nest, admitting a near approach before flying. He also speaks of this species as being less timorous than the Yellow-billed, and states that near the nest, with young, he has observed the parent composedly sit and plume itself for a considerable time without showing any alarm at his presence.

In all the instances in which I have observed the nest of this species, I have invariably found it in retired damp places, usually near the edges of woods, and built, not in trees, after the manner of the Yellow-billed Cuckoo, but in bushes and in low shrubbery, often not more than two or three feet from the ground. The nest, without being at all remarkable for its finish, or the nicety of its arrangement, is much more artistic and elaborate than that of the Yellow-bill. It is composed of twigs, roots, fine strips of bark, and moss, and is sometimes interwoven and partially lined with the soft catkins of trees and blossoms of plants. The eggs vary from three to six in number, and are often found to have been deposited, and incubation commenced on them, at irregular intervals, and to be in various stages of development in the same nest. I have hardly been able to observe a sufficient number of their nests to be able to state whether this species carries this irregularity so far as the Yellow-bill, nor am I aware that it has ever been known to extend its incubations into so late a period of the season. It is, if anything, more devoted to its offspring than the Yellow-bill. Both parents are assiduous in the duties of incubation, and in supplying food to each other and to their offspring. In one instance, where the female had been shot by a thoughtless boy, as she flew from the nest, the male bird successfully devoted himself to the solitary duty of rearing the brood of five. At the time of the death of the female the nest contained two eggs and three young birds. The writer was present when the bird was shot, and was unable to interpose in season to prevent it. Returning to the spot not long afterwards, he found the widowed male sitting upon the nest, and so unwilling to leave it as almost to permit himself to be captured by the hand. His fidelity and his entreaties were not disregarded. His nest, eggs, and young, were left undisturbed; and, as they were visited from time to time, the young nestlings were found to thrive under his vigilant care. The eggs were hatched out, and in time the whole five were reared in safety. This single incident shows how wide is the interval between these Cuckoos and their European namesakes.

The egg resembles that of the other, but is more spherical and of a much darker shade of green. The color is equally fugitive, and even in a close cabinet fades so that the eggs of the two species are undistinguishable, except in size and shape. This egg averages 1.10 inches in length by .90 of an inch in breadth.

Genus CROTOPHAGA, Linnæus.

Crotophaga, Linnæus, Systema Naturæ, 1756. (Type, *C. ani*, Linn).

Gen. Char. Bill as long as the head, very much compressed; the culmen elevated into a high crest, extending above the level of the forehead. Nostrils exposed, elongated. Point of bill much decurved. Wings lengthened, extending beyond the base of the tail, the fourth or fifth quill longest. Tail lengthened, of eight graduated feathers. Toes long, with well-developed claws.

The feathers in this genus are entirely black; those on the head and neck with a peculiar stiffened metallic or scale-like border. The species are not numerous, and are entirely confined to America.

Of *Crotophaga*, two species have heretofore been recognized in the United

States, *C. ani* and *C. rugirostris.* We are, however, satisfied that there is but one here and in the West Indies, *C. ani* (extending to South America). *C.*

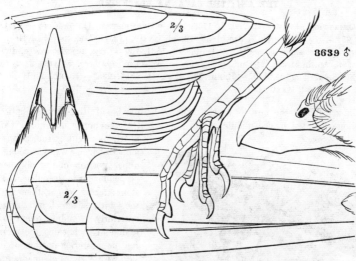

2/3

3639 ♂

2/3

Crotophaga ani.

major of South America, and *C. sulcirostris,* found from Mexico southward, are the other species, and are easily distinguishable by the following characters among others : —

C. major.[1] Length, 17.00; wing, 7.50; outline of culmen abruptly angulated in the middle. *Hab.* Brazil and Trinidad.
C. ani. Length, 13.00 to 15.00; wing, 6.00; culmen gently curved from base. Bill smooth or with a few tranverse wrinkles. *Hab.* North-eastern South America, West Indies, and South Florida.
C. sulcirostris.[2] Length, 12.00; wing, 5.00; culmen gently curved. Bill with several groves parallel to culmen. *Hab.* Middle America, from Yucatan, south to Ecuador.

[1] *Crotophaga major,* LINN. Syst. Nat. I, 363. — MAX. Beitr. IV, 319. — SCL. Cat. 1862, 320. *C. ani,* VIEILL. Gal. Ois. II, 35, pl. xliii.
[2] *Crotophaga sulcirostris,* SWAINSON, Phil. Mag. 1827, I, 440. — BONAP. Consp. 89. — SCL. P. Z. S. 1856, 309, 1859, pp. 59, 368, 388, et 1860, pp. 285, 297. — IB. Catal. 1862, 320. *C. casasi,* LESS. Voy. Coq. Zoöl. I, pl. ii, 619, et Cent. Zoöl. pl. ix.

Crotophaga ani, LINN.

THE ANI; THE SAVANNA BLACKBIRD.

Crotophaga ani, LINN. Syst. Nat. I, 1766, 154. — BURMEISTER, Th. Bras. (Vögel.) 1856, 254. — BAIRD, Birds N. Am. 1858, 72, pl. lxxxiv, f. 2. — CABANIS, Mus. Hein. IV, 100. *Crotophaga minor*, LESS. Traite Orn. 1831, 130. *Crotophaga lævirostra*, SWAINSON, An. in Menag. 2¼ Cent. 1838, 321. *Crotophaga rugirostra*, SWAINSON, 2¼ Cent. 1838, 321, fig. 65, bill. — BURM. Th. Bras. II, 1856, 235. — BAIRD, Birds N. Am. 1858, 71, pl. lxxxiv, f. 1.

SP. CHAR. Bill at the nostrils nearly twice as high as broad; the nostrils elliptical, a little oblique, situated in the middle of the lower half of the upper mandible. Gonys nearly straight. Indications of faint transverse wrinkles along the upper portion of the bill, nearly perpendicular to the culmen. Legs stout; tarsus longer than middle toe, with seven broad scutellæ anteriorly extending round to the middle of each side; the remaining or posterior portion of each side with a series of quadrangular plates, corresponding nearly to the anterior ones, the series meeting behind in a sharp ridge. The wings reach over the basal third of the tail. The primary quills are broad and acute, the fourth longest; the first about equal to the tertials. The tail is graduated, the outer about an inch and a half shorter than the middle ones.

Crotophaga ani.

The color generally is black, with steel-blue reflections above, changing sometimes into violet; duller beneath. The pointed feathers of the head, neck, and breast, with a bronzy metallic border, appearing also to some extent on the wing-coverts and upper part of back. Iris brown. Length, 13.20; wing, 6.00; tail, 8.30; tarsus, 1.48.

HAB. West Indies; South Florida. Accidental near Philadelphia. Localities: Sta. Cruz (NEWTON, Ibis, I, 148).

As already remarked, we do not find reason to admit more than one species of *Crotophaga* in the United States and the West Indies, as in the great variation in size, and to some extent in shape of bill, there is nothing constant. The species can hardly be considered more than a straggler in the United States, although a considerable number of specimens have been seen or taken within its limits. That in the Smithsonian collection was killed on the Tortugas; but there is one in the collection of the Philadelphia Academy, killed near Philadelphia by Mr. John Krider, and presented by him. Mr. Audubon also possessed a pair said to have been killed near New Orleans.

HABITS. This species, the common Savanna Blackbird of the West India Islands, is probably only an accidental visitant of the United States, and may not strictly belong to the avi-fauna of North America.

It is common throughout the West Indies, and in South America as far south as Brazil. Gosse states it to be one of the most abundant birds of Jamaica· In speaking of its breeding habits he mentions that it was universally maintained by the inhabitants that these birds unite and build in company an immense nest of basket-work, made by the united labors of the flock. This is said to be placed on a high tree, where many parents bring forth and educate a common family. This statement is reiterated by Mr. Hill, who says that a small flock of about six individuals build but one large and capacious nest, to which they resort in common, and rear their young together.

In July Mr. Gosse found the nest of one of these birds in a *guczuma* tree. It was a large mass of interwoven twigs, and was lined with leaves. There were eight eggs in the nest, and the shells of many others were scattered beneath the tree.

Mr. Newton found these birds very common in St. Croix. He mentions meeting with a nest of this species June 17. It was about five feet from the ground, on a large tamarind-tree. He speaks of it as a rude collection of sticks and twigs, large and deep, partly filled with dry leaves, among which were fourteen eggs, and around the margin were stuck upright a few dead twigs of tamarind. Five days afterwards he went to the nest, where he found but nine eggs, two of which he took. Three days later he found but four eggs in the nest, it having been robbed in the interim; but six days afterwards the number had again been increased to eight. He never found the eggs covered up as if intentionally done. The nest was evidently common property. There were generally two or three birds sitting close to or on it, and up in the tree perhaps four or five more, who would continue screeching all the time he was there. Mr. Newton adds that when the egg is fresh the cretaceous deposit on the shell is very soft and easily scored, but it soon hardens. It is mentioned in De Sagra's list as one of the common birds of Cuba.

Mr. J. F. Hamilton, in his interesting paper (Ibis, July, 1871) on the birds of Brazil, mentions finding this species very common at Santo Paulo. There was scarcely an open piece of ground where there were but few bushes that had not its flock of these birds. They were especially fond of marshy ground. They were also often to be seen running about among·a herd of cattle, picking up the insects disturbed by the animals. They seemed utterly regardless of danger, and would scarcely do more than flit from one bush to another, even when the numbers of their flock were being greatly thinned. When concealed in the long grass, they would allow themselves to be almost trodden on before rising. The Brazilians seldom molest them, as their flesh is not good to eat.

This bird is known as the Black Witch in St. Croix,— a name Mr. Newton supposes to be due to its peculiar call-note, which sounds like *que-yuch*. Its familiar habits and its grotesque appearance make it universally known. It is a favorite object of attack to the Chickaree Flycatcher, in which encounters it is apt to lose its presence of mind, and to be forced to make an ignominious retreat.

These birds are said to be attracted by collections of cattle and horses, upon the bodies of which they are often seen to alight, feeding upon the ticks with which they are infested. They are at once familiar and wary, permitting a limited acquaintance, but a too near approach sets the whole flock in motion. It moves in a very peculiar gliding flight. In feeding it is omnivorous; besides insects of all kinds, such as ticks, grasshoppers, beetles, etc., it eats berries of various kinds, lizards, and other kinds of food. It catches insects on the ground by very active jumps, pursues them on the wing, and with its sharp thin bill digs them out in the earth. They hop about and over the bodies of cattle, especially when they are lying down, and when grazing they have been observed clinging to a cow's tail, picking insects from it as far down even as its extremity.

Mr. Hill states that these birds are downward, not upward, climbers. They enter a tree by alighting on the extremity of some main branch, and reach its centre by creeping along the stem, and seldom penetrate far among the leaves.

The eggs of this species are of a regularly oval shape, equally obtuse at either end. In color they are of a uniform light-blue, with a very slight tinge of green. This is usually covered, but not entirely concealed, by a white cretaceous coating. When fresh, this may readily be rubbed off, but becomes hard and not easily removed. The eggs vary in size from 1.40 to 1.50 inches in length, and in breadth from 1.10 to 1.15 inches.

FAMILY **PICIDÆ.** — THE WOODPECKERS.

CHAR. Outer toe turned backwards permanently, not versatile laterally, the basal portion of the tongue capable of great protrusion.

The preceding characters combined appear to express the essential characters of the *Picidæ.* In addition, it may be stated that the tongue itself is quite small, flat, and short, acute and horny, usually armed along the edges with recurved hooks. The horns of the hyoid apparatus are generally very long, and curve round the back of the skull, frequently to the base of the bill, playing in a sheath, when the tongue is thrown forward out of the mouth to transfix an insect.

There are twelve tail-feathers, of which the outer is, however, very small and rudimentary (lying concealed between the outer and adjacent feathers), so that only ten are usually counted. The tail is nearly even, or cuneate, never forked, the shafts very rigid in the true Woodpeckers ; soft in *Picumninæ* and *Yunginæ.* The outer primary is generally very short, or spurious, but not wanting. The bill is chisel or wedge shaped, with sharp angles and ridges and straight culmen ; sometimes the culmen is a little curved, in which case it is smoother, and without the ridges. The tarsi in the North American forms are covered with large plates anteriorly, posteriorly with small ones, usually more or less polygonal. The claws are compressed, much curved, very strong and acute.

The *Picidæ* are found all over the world with the exception of Madagascar, Australia, the Moluccas, and Polynesia. America is well provided with them, more than half of the described species belonging to the New World.

The subfamilies of the *Picidæ* may be most easily distinguished as follows, although other characters could readily be given : —

Picinæ. Tail-feathers pointed, and lanceolate at end; the shafts very rigid, thickened and elastic.

Picumninæ. Tail soft and short, about half the length of wing; the feathers without stiffened shafts, rather narrow, linear, and rounded at end.

Yunginæ. Tail soft and rather long, about three fourths the length of wing; the feathers broad, and obtusely rounded at end.

Of these subfamilies the *Picinæ* alone occur north of Mexico. The *Yunginæ,* to which the well-known Wryneck of England (*Jynx torquilla*) belongs, are exclusively Old World ; the *Picumninæ* belong principally to the tropical regions of America, although a few species occur in Africa and India. One species, *Picumnus micromegas,* Sundevall, belongs to St. Domingo, although erroneously assigned to Brazil. This is the giant of the group, being about the size of the White-bellied Nuthatch (*Sitta carolinensis*) the other species being mostly very diminutive, varying from three to four inches in length.

Subfamily PICINÆ.

The diagnosis on the preceding page will serve to distinguish this group from its allies, without the necessity of going into greater detail. It includes by far the largest percentage of the *Picidæ*, and in the great variations of form has been variously subdivided by authors into sections. Professor Sundevall, in his able monograph,[1] establishes the following four series, referring all to the single genus *Picus*: —

> I. **Angusticolles.** Neck slender, elongated. Nostrils concealed by bristles. Tail-feathers black or brownish, immaculate.
> II. **Securirostres.** Neck not slender, and shorter. Nostrils concealed by bristles. Bill stout, cuneate, with the nasal ridges widely distant from each other.
> III. **Ligonirostres.** Neck not slender. Nostrils covered, nasal ridges of bill placed near the culmen (or at least nearer it than the lower edge of the upper mandible), for the most part obsolete anteriorly.
> IV. **Nudinares.** Nostrils open, uncovered by bristly hairs. Neck and bill various.

Of these series, the first and second correspond with *Piceæ*, as given below, while *Centureæ* and *Colapteæ* both belong to *Ligonirostres*. The *Nudinares* are not represented in North America, and by only one group, *Celeus*, in any portion of the continent.

In the following account of the *Picinæ*, we shall not pretend to discuss the relationship of the North American species to the *Picinæ* in general, referring to Sundevall's work, and the monographs of Malherbe and Cassin, for information on the subject. For our present purposes they may be conveniently, even if artificially, arranged in the following sections: —

> **Piceæ.** Bill variable in length; the outlines above and below nearly straight; the ends truncated; a prominent ridge on the side of the mandible springing from the middle of the base, or a little below, and running out either on the commissure, or extending parallel to and a little above it, to the end, sometimes obliterated or confluent with the lateral bevel of the bill. Nostrils considerably overhung by the lateral ridge, more or less linear, and concealed by thick bushy tufts of feathers at the base of the bill. Outer posterior toe generally longer than the anterior.
> **Centureæ.** Bill rather long; the outlines, that of the culmen especially, decidedly curved. The lateral ridge much nearest the culmen, and, though quite distinct at the base, disappearing before coming to the lower edge of the mandible; not overhanging the nostrils, which are broadly oval, rounded anteriorly, and not concealed by the bristly feathers at the base. Outer pair of toes nearly equal; the anterior rather longer.
> **Colapteæ.** Bill rather long, much depressed, and the upper outline

---

[1] *Conspectus avium picinarum.* Stockholm, 1866.

much curved to the acutely pointed (not truncate) tip. The commissure considerably curved. Bill without any ridges. The nostrils broadly oval, and much exposed. Anterior outer toe longest.

The preceding diagnoses will serve to distinguish the three groups sufficiently for our present purposes ; the bill being strongest in the *Picinæ* and best fitted for cutting into trees by its more perfect wedge-shape, with strengthening ridges, as well as by the lateral bevelling of both mandibles, which are nearly equal in thickness at the base, and with their outlines nearly straight. The lateral ridge is prominent, extending to the edge or end of the bill, and overhangs the nostrils, which are narrow and hidden. The *Centureæ* and the *Colapteæ* have the upper mandible more curved (the commissure likewise), the lower mandible smaller and weaker, the bill with little or no lateral bevelling. The nostrils are broadly oval and exposed. In the former, however, there is a distinct lateral ridge visible for a short distance from the base of the bill ; while in the other there is no ridge at all, and the mandible is greatly curved.

In all the species of North American Woodpeckers, there is more or less red on the head in the male, and frequently in the female. The eggs of all are lustrous polished white, without any markings, and laid in hollow trees, upon a bed of chips, no material being carried in for the construction of the nest.

Section PICEÆ.

With the common characters, as already given, there are several well-marked generic groups in this section of Woodpeckers which may be arranged for the United States species as follows : —

A. Posterior outer toe longer than the anterior outer one. (Fourth toe longer than third.)

   a. Lateral ridge starting above the middle of the base of the bill, and extending to the tip.

      1. **Campephilus.** Lateral ridge above the middle of the lateral profile of the bill when opposite the end of the nostrils, which are ovate, and rounded anteriorly. Bill much depressed, very long; gonys very long. Posterior outer toe considerably longer than the anterior. Primaries long, attenuated towards the tip. Spurious quill nearly half the second. Shafts of four middle tail-feathers remarkably stout, of equal size, and abruptly very much larger than the others; two middle tail-feathers narrower towards bases than towards end.[1] A pointed occipital crest.

      2. **Picus.** Lateral ridge in the middle of the lateral profile opposite the end of the nostrils, which are ovate and sharp-pointed anteriorly. Bill moderate, nearly as broad as high.

---

[1] A character common to all the members of the genus, and distinguishing them from the species of every other ; this peculiar form of the middle tail-feathers is caused principally by a folding of the webs downward, almost against each other. The under surfaces of the shafts have a very deep groove their whole length, which is seen in no other genus.

Outer hind toe moderately longer than the outer fore toe. Primaries broad to the tip, and rounded. Spurious primary not one third the second quill.

3. **Picoides.** Lateral ridge below the middle of the profile, opposite the end of the ovate acute nostrils, which it greatly overhangs. Bill greatly depressed ; lower mandible deeper than the upper. Inner hind toe wanting, leaving only three toes. Tufts of nasal bristles very full and long.

b. Lateral ridge starting below the middle of the base of the bill, and running as a distinct ridge into the edge of the commissure at about its middle; the terminal half of the mandible rounded on the sides, although the truncate tip is distinctly bevelled laterally.

4. **Sphyropicus.** Nostrils considerably overhung by the lateral ridge, very small, linear. Gonys as long as the culmen, from the nostrils. Tips of tail-feathers elongated and linear, not cuneate. Wings very long; exposed portion of spurious primary about one fourth that of second quill.

B. Posterior outer toe considerably shorter than the anterior outer one. (Fourth toe shorter than third).

5. **Hylotomus.** Bill depressed. Lateral ridge above the middle of the lateral profile near the base. Nostrils elliptical, wide, and rounded anteriorly. Tail almost as in *Sphyropicus*. A pointed occipital crest, as in *Campephilus*, and not found in the other genera.

The arrangement in the preceding diagnosis is perhaps not perfectly natural, although sufficiently so for our present purpose. Thus, *Hylotomus*, in having the lateral ridge extending to the end of the bill, is like *Picus*, but the nostrils are broader, more open, and not acute anteriorly. The tail-feathers of *Sphyropicus* differ greatly from those of the others in being abruptly acuminate, the points elongated, narrow, and nearly linear, instead of being gently cuneate at the ends. *Campephilus* and *Hylotomus* belong to Sundevall's *Angusticolles*, with their long slender neck, and elongated occipital crest (*Dryocopinæ*, Cab.) ; the other genera to *Securirostres*, with shorter, thicker neck, and no crest (*Dendrocopinæ*, Cab.). But no two genera in the subfamily are more distinct than *Campephilus* and *Hylotomus*.

GENUS **CAMPEPHILUS**, GRAY.

Campephilus, GRAY, List of Genera ? 1840. (Type, *C. principalis.*)
Megapicus, MALHERBE, Mém. Ac. de Metz, 1849, 317.

GEN. CHAR. Bill considerably longer than the head, much depressed, or broader than high at the base, becoming somewhat compressed near the middle and gradually bevelled off at the tip. Culmen very slightly curved, gonys as concave, the curve scarcely appreciable ; commissure straight. Culmen with a parallel ridge on each side, starting a little above the centre of the basal outline of the bill, the ridge projecting outwards and downwards, and a slight concavity between it and the acute ridge of the culmen. Gonys considerably more than half the commissure. Nostrils oval below the lateral ridge near the base of the bill ; concealed by the bristly feathers directed forward. Similar feathers are seen at the sides of the lower jaw and on the chin.

Feet large; outer hind toe much longest; claw of inner fore toe reaching to middle of outer fore claw; inner hind toe scarcely more than half the outer one; its claw reaching as far as the base of the inner anterior claw, considerably more than half the outer anterior toe. Tarsus rather shorter than the inner fore toe. Tail long, cuneate; shafts of the four middle feathers abruptly much larger than the others, and with a deep groove

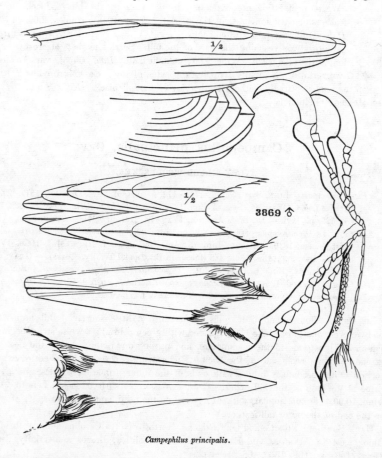

Campephilus principalis.

running continuously along their under surface; webs of the two middle feathers deflected, almost against each other, so that the feathers appear narrower at the base than terminally. Wings long and pointed, the third, fourth, and fifth quills longest; sixth secondary longest, leaving six "tertials," instead of three or four as usual; primaries long, attenuated. Color continuous black, relieved by white patches. Head with a pointed occipital crest.

This genus embraces the largest known kind of Woodpecker, and is confined to America. Of the two species usually assigned to it, only one occurs within the limits of the United States, *C. imperialis,* given by Audubon, and by subsequent authors on his credit, really belonging to Southern Mexico and Central America. The diagnoses of the species are as follows : —

COMMON CHARACTERS. Bill ivory-white. Body entirely glossy blue-black. A scapular stripe, secondaries, ends of inner primaries, and under wing-coverts, white. Crest scarlet in the male, black in the female.

1. **C. principalis.** A white stripe on each side of the neck. Bristly feathers at the base of the bill white.

  White neck-stripe not extending to the base of the bill. Black feathers of crest longer than the scarlet. Wing, 10.00; culmen, 2.60. *Hab.* Gulf region of United States . . . . var. *principalis.*

  White stripe reaching the base of the bill. Scarlet feathers of crest longer than the black. Wing, 9.50; culmen, 2.40. *Hab.* Cuba . var. *bairdi.*[1]

2. **C. imperialis.** No white stripe on the sides of the neck. More white on the wings. Bristly feathers at the base of the bill black. *Hab.* South Mexico; Guatemala.

Campephilus principalis, GRAY.

IVORY-BILLED WOODPECKER.

Picus principalis, LINN. Syst. Nat. I, 1766, 173. — WILSON, Am. Orn. IV, 1811, 20, pl. xxxix, f. 6. — WAGLER, Syst. Avium, 1827, No. 1. — AUD. Orn. Biog. I, 1832, 341 ; V, 525, pl. lxvi. — IB. Birds America, IV, 1842, 214, pl. cclvi. — SUNDEVALL, Consp. Pic. 4. *Dendrocopus principalis,* BON. List, 1838. *Campephilus principalis,* GRAY, List Genera, 1840. — BAIRD, Birds N. Am. 83. — CAB. & HEIN. Mus. Hein. IV, II, 100. — DRESSER, Ibis, 1865, 468 (breeds in Brazos and Trinity, Texas). — GRAY, Cat. 53. — ALLEN, Birds E. Florida, 301. *Dryotomus (Megapicus) principalis,* BON. Con. Zyg. Aten. Ital. 1854, 7. *Dryocopus principalis,* BON. Consp. 1850, 132. *White-billed Woodpecker,* CATESBY, Car. I, 16. — PENNANT, LATHAM.

SP. CHAR. Fourth and fifth quills equal; third a little shorter. Bill horn-white. Body entirely of a glossy blue-black (glossed with green below) ; a white stripe beginning half an inch posterior to the commissure, and passing down the sides of the neck, and extending down each side of the back. Under wing-coverts, and the entire exposed portion of the secondary quills, with ends of the inner primaries, bristles, and a short stripe at the base of the bill, white. Crest scarlet, upper surface black. Length, 21.00; wing, 10.00. *Female* similar, without any red on the head, and with two spots of white on the end of the outer tail-feather.

HAB. Southern Atlantic and Gulf States. North to North Carolina and mouth of the Ohio ; west to Arkansas and Eastern Texas. Localities : Brazos and Trinity Rivers, Texas (DRESSER, Ibis, 1865, 468, breeds).

In the male the entire crown (with its elongated feathers) is black. The scarlet commences just above the middle of the eye, and, passing backwards a short distance, widens behind and bends down as far as the level of the under edge of the lower jaw. The feathers which spring from the back of the head are much elongated above ; considerably longer than those of the crown. In the specimen before us the black feathers of the crest do not reach as far back as the scarlet.

Reference has already been made to the Cuban variety of the Ivory-billed

---

[1] *Campephilus bairdi,* CASSIN, Pr. A. N. Sc. 1863, 322 (Cuba). — GUNDLACH, Repertorium, I, 1866, 293. — IB. Cab. Jour. 1866, 352. *Hab.* Cuba.

Woodpecker named *C. bairdi* by Mr. Cassin, and differing in smaller size; extension of the white cheek-stripe to the very base of the bill, and the excess in length of the upper black feathers of the crest over the scarlet. These features appear to be constant, and characteristic of a local race.

For the reasons already adduced, we drop *C. imperialis* from the list of North American birds, although given as such by Audubon.

HABITS. So far as we have information in regard to the geographical distribution of the Ivory-billed Woodpecker, it is chiefly restricted in its range to the extreme Southern States, and especially to those bordering on the Gulf of Mexico. Wilson states that very few, if any, are ever found north of Virginia, and not many even in that State. His first specimen was obtained near Wilmington, N. C. It is not migratory, but is a resident where found.

Mr. Audubon, who is more full than any other writer in his account of this bird, assigns to it a more extended distribution. He states that in descending the Ohio River he met with it near the confluence of that river with the Mississippi, and adds that it is frequently met with in following the windings of the latter river either downwards towards the sea, or upwards in the direction of the Missouri. On the At-

Campephilus principalis.

lantic he was inclined to make North Carolina the limit of its northern distribution, though now and then individuals of the species have been accidentally met with as far north as Maryland. To the westward of the Mississippi he states that it is found in all the dense forests bordering the streams which empty into it, from the very declivities of the Rocky Mountains. The lower parts of the Carolinas, Georgia, North Florida, Alabama, Louisiana, and Mississippi, are, however, its favorite resorts, and in those States it constantly resides.

It was observed by Dr. Woodhouse in the timber on the Arkansas River, and in Eastern Texas, but quite rarely in both places. It was not, however, met with in any other of the government expeditions, either to the Pacific, in the survey of the railroad routes, or in that for the survey of the Mexican boundary line. It is given as a bird of Cuba by De la Sagra, in his catalogue of the birds of that island, as observed by him, October, 1850, and by Dr. John Gundlach, in his list of the birds that breed in Cuba. It is not mentioned by Gosse among the birds of Jamaica, nor by the Newtons as found in St. Croix. As it is not a migratory bird, it may be regarded as breeding in all its localities, except where it is obviously an accidental visitant.

Wilson, who never met with the nest of this Woodpecker, states, on the authority of reliable informants, that it breeds in the large-timbered cypress swamps of the Carolinas. In the trunks of these trees at a considerable height from the ground, both parents working alternately, these birds dig out a large and capacious cavity for their eggs and young. Trees thus dug out have frequently been cut down with both the eggs and the young in them. The hole was described to Wilson as generally a little winding, to keep out the rain, and sometimes five feet deep. The eggs were said to be generally four, sometimes five in number, as large as pullets', pure white, and equally thick at both ends. The young make their appearance about the middle or end of June.

Mr. Audubon, whose account of the breeding-habits of the Ivory-bill is given from his own immediate observations, supplies a more minute and detailed history of its nesting. He states that it breeds earlier in spring than any other species of its tribe, and that he has observed it boring a hole for that purpose as early as the beginning of March. This hole he believed to be always made in the trunk of a live tree, generally an ash or a hackberry, and at a great height. It pays great regard to the particular situation of the tree and the inclination of the trunk, both with a view to retirement and to secure the aperture against rains. To prevent the latter injury, the hole is generally dug immediately under the protection of a large branch. It is first bored horizontally a few inches, then directly downward, and not in a spiral direction, as Wilson was informed. This cavity is sometimes not more than ten inches in depth, while at other times it reaches nearly three feet downward into the heart of the tree. The older the bird, the deeper its hole, in the opinion of Mr. Audubon. The average diameter of the different nests which Mr. Audubon examined was about seven inches in the inner parts, although the entrance is only just large enough to admit the bird. Both birds work most assiduously in making these excavations. Mr. Audubon states that in two instances where the Woodpeckers saw him watching them at their labors, while they were digging their nests, they abandoned them. For the first brood, he states, there are generally six eggs. These are deposited on a few chips at the bottom of the hole, and are of a pure white color. The young may be seen creeping out of their holes about a fortnight before they venture to fly to any other tree. The second brood makes its appearance about the 15th of August. In Kentucky and Indiana the Ivory-bill seldom raises more than one brood in a season. Its flight is described by Audubon as graceful in the extreme, though seldom prolonged to more than a few hundred yards at a time, except when it has occasion to cross a large river. It then flies in deep undulations, opening its wings at first to their full extent, and nearly closing them to renew their impulse. The transit from tree to tree is performed by a single sweep, as if the bird had been swung in a curved line from the one to the other.

Except during the love-season it never utters a sound when on the wing. On alighting, or when, in ascending a tree, it leaps against the upper parts of the trunk, its remarkable voice may be constantly heard in a clear, loud, and rather plaintive tone, sometimes to the distance of half a mile, and resembling the false high note of a clarionet. This may be represented by the monosyllable *pait* thrice repeated.

The food of this Woodpecker consists principally of beetles, larvæ, and large grubs. They are also especially fond of ripe wild grapes, which they eat with great avidity, hanging by their claws to the vines, often in the position of a Titmouse. They also eat ripe persimmons, hackberries, and other fruit, but are not known to disturb standing corn nor the fruits of the orchard.

These birds attack decaying trees so energetically as often to cause them to fall. So great is their strength, that Audubon has known one of them to detach, at a single blow, a strip of bark eight inches long, and, by beginning at the top branch of a dead tree, tear off the bark to the extent of thirty feet in the course of a few hours, all the while sounding its loud notes.

Mr. Audubon further states that this species generally moves in pairs, that the female is the least shy and the most clamorous, and that, except when digging a hole for the reception of their eggs, they are not known to excavate living trees, but only those attacked by worms. When wounded, they seek the nearest tree, and ascend with great rapidity by successive hops. When taken by the hand, they strike with great violence, and inflict severe wounds with their bills and claws.

Mr. Dresser states that these birds were found on the Brazos River, and also on the Trinity, where they were by no means rare.

Wilson dwells at some length and with great force upon the great value of these birds to our forests. They never injure sound trees, only those diseased and infested with insects. The pine timber of the Southern States is often destroyed, thousands of acres in a season, by the larvæ of certain insects. In Wilson's day this was noticeable in the vicinity of Georgetown, S. C., and was attributed by him to the blind destruction of this and other insect-eating birds.

An egg of this species (Smith. Coll., No. 16,196) taken near Wilmington, N. C., by Mr. N. Giles, measures 1.35 inches in length by .95 of an inch in breadth. It is of a highly polished porcelain whiteness, and is much more oblong in shape and more pointed than are the eggs of *Hylotomus pileatus.*

GENUS PICUS, LINNÆUS.

Picus, LINN. Syst. Nat. 1748.   (Type, *Picus martius*, L.)

GEN. CHAR. Bill equal to the head, or a little longer; the lateral ridges conspicuous,

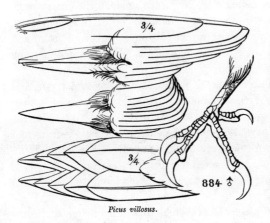

starting about the middle of the base of the bill; the basal elongated oval nostrils nearest the commissure; the ridges of the culmen and gonys acute, and very nearly straight, or slightly convex towards the tip; the bill but little broader than high at the base, becoming compressed considerably before the middle. Feet much as in *Campephilus;* the outer posterior toe longest; the outer anterior about intermediate between it and the inner anterior; the inner posterior reaching to the base of the claw

Picus villosus.

of the inner anterior. Tarsus about equal to the inner anterior toe; shorter than the two other long toes. Wings rather long, reaching to the middle of the tail, rather rounded; the fourth and fifth quills longest; the quills rather broad and rounded.

In the genus *Picus*, as characterized above, are contained several subdivisions more or less entitled to distinct rank, and corresponding with peculiar patterns of coloration. Thus, taking the *P. villosus* as the type, *P. borealis* has proportionally much longer primaries; the spurious primary smaller; the bill is considerably more attenuated, and even concave in its lateral outlines. The wings are still longer in *P. albolarvatus*. The species may be arranged as follows : —

A. Black above, and white beneath. Wings spotted with white; a black maxillary stripe.

    a. Two white stripes on the side of the head, one above, and the other below, the ear-coverts, which are mostly black. First quill shorter than sixth. Tail-feathers broad and obtuse at ends, the narrowed tips of middle feathers very short.

        DRYOBATES, BOIE. Middle of back streaked longitudinally and continuously with white. Maxillary and auricular black stripes not confluent; the latter running into the black of the nape. Beneath white without spots. Red of head confined to a narrow nuchal band.

            1. **P. villosus.** Outer tail-feathers immaculate white, great variation in size with latitude. Length, 7.00 to 10.00.

                All the quills, with middle and greater wing-coverts, with large white spots. *Hab.* Eastern North America . var. *villosus*. Innermost quills and some of the coverts entirely black, or unspotted with white. Remaining spots reduced in size.

(Var. *jardini* similar, but much smaller, 7.00, and lower parts smoky-brown.) *Hab.* Middle and western North America, and south to Costa Rica . . . . var. *harrisi*.

2. **P. pubescens.** Outer tail-feather white, with transverse black bands; length about 6.25.

All the quills, with middle and greater wing-coverts, with large white spots. *Hab.* Eastern North America . var. *pubescens*.

Innermost quills and some of the coverts entirely black; remaining white spots reduced in size. *Hab.* Western North America . . . . var. *gairdneri*.

DYCTIOPICUS, Bon. Whole back banded transversely with black and white. Beneath white, with black spots on sides. Maxillary and auricular black stripes confluent at their posterior ends, the latter not running into the nape. In the males at least half of top of head red. Length, about 6.50.

3. **P. scalaris.** Anterior portion of the back banded with white; lores and nasal tufts smoky brown. Black stripes on sides of the head very much narrower than the white ones, and not connected with the black of the shoulders. *Male* with the whole crown red.

Outer web of lateral tail-feathers barred with black to the base. White bands on back exceeding the black ones in width; red of the crown very continuous, on the forehead predominating over the black and white. (Sometimes the black at base of inner web of lateral tail-feather divided by white bars.) *Hab.* Southern and Eastern Mexico, and Rio Grande region of United States . . . . . var. *scalaris*.

Outer web of lateral tail-feather barred with black only toward end. Red of crown much broken anteriorly, and in less amount than the black and white mixed with it. White bands of the back not wider, generally much narrower than the black ones.

Bill, .90; tarsus, .70. Red of crown extending almost to the bill. *Hab.* Western Mexico, up to Western Arizona.

var. *graysoni*.

Bill, 1.10; tarsus, .75. Red of crown disappearing about on a line above the eye. *Hab.* Cape St. Lucas.

var. *lucasanus*.

4. **P. nuttalli.** Anterior portion of back not banded with white; lores and nasal tufts white. Black stripes on side of the head very much broader than the white ones, and connected by a narrow strip with the black of the shoulders. *Male* with only the nape and occiput red. *Hab.* California (only).

b. One white stripe, only, on side of head, and this occupying whole auricular region. Tail-feathers narrowed at ends, the points of the middle ones much elongated. First quill longer than sixth. Bill very small, much shorter than head.

PHRENOPICUS, Bonap. Back and wings transversely banded with black and white, and sides spotted with black, as in *Dyctiopicus*.

5. **P. borealis.** Red of male restricted to a concealed narrow line on each side of the occiput, at the junction of the white and black. Maxillary black stripe very broad and conspicuous, running back to the series of black spots on sides of breast. Three outer

tail-feathers more or less white, with a few bars of black near their ends, principally on inner webs. *Hab.* South Atlantic States.

B. Body entirely continuous black; head all round immaculate white. First quill shorter than sixth.

XENOPICUS, BAIRD. Tail and primaries as in "A," but much more lengthened. Bill as in *Dryobates,* but more slender.

6. **P. albolarvatus.** Red of male a narrow transverse occipital crescent, between the white and the black. Basal half, or more, of primaries variegated with white, this continuous nearly to the end of outer webs; inner webs of secondaries with large white spots toward their base. *Hab.* Sierra Nevada and Coast Ranges, Pacific Province, United States.

SUBGENUS DRYOBATES, BOIE.

Dryobates, BOIE, 1826. (Type, *Picus pubescens, fide* CABANIS, Mus. Hein.)
Trichopicus, BONAP. 1854.
Trichopipo, CAB. & HEIN. Mus. Hein. 1863, 62.

According to Cabanis, as above cited, *Dryobates,* as established by Boie in 1826, had the *Picus pubescens* as type, although extended in 1828 to cover a much wider ground. As a subgeneric name, therefore, it must take preference of *Trichopicus* of Bonaparte, which, like all the allied names of this author, Cabanis rejects at any rate as hybrid and inadmissible.

The synopsis under the head of *Picus* will serve to distinguish the species in brief.

The small black and white Woodpeckers of North America exhibit great variations in size and markings, and it is extremely difficult to say what is a distinct species and what a mere geographical race. In none of our birds is the difference in size between specimens from a high and a low latitude so great, and numerous nominal species have been established on this ground alone. There is also much variation with locality in the amount of white spotting on the wings, as well as the comparative width of the white and black bars in the banded species. The under parts, too, vary from pure white to smoky-brown. To these variations in what may be considered as good species is to be added the further perplexities caused by hybridism, which seems to prevail to an unusual extent among some Woodpeckers, where the area of distribution of one species is overlapped by a close ally. This, which can be most satisfactorily demonstrated in the *Colaptes,* is also

Picus harrisi.

probably the case in the black and white species, and renders the final settlement of the questions involved very difficult.

After a careful consideration of the subject, we are not inclined to admit any species or permanent varieties of the group of four-toed small white and black Woodpeckers as North or Middle American, other than those mentioned in the preceding synopsis.

Picus villosus, LINNÆUS.

HAIRY WOODPECKER; LARGER SAPSUCKER.

Var. canadensis. — Northern and Western regions.

? *Picus leucomelas,* BODDÆRT, Tabl. Pl. Enl. 1783 (No. 345, f. 1, GRAY). — CASS. P. A. N. S. 1863, 199. *Dryobates leucomelas,* CAB. & HEIN. Mus. Hein. IV, 67. ? *Picus canadensis,* GMELIN, Syst. Nat. I, 1788, 437. — ? LATHAM, Ind. Orn. I, 1790, 231. — AUD. Orn. Biog. V, 1839, 188, pl. cccxvii. — IB. Syn. 1839, 177. — IB. Birds America, IV, 1842, 235, pl. cclviii. — BONAP. Consp. 1850, 137. — IB. Aten. Ital. 1854, 8. *Picus villosus,* FORSTER, Philos. Trans. LXII, 1772, 383. — BAIRD, Birds N. Am. 1858, 84. — CASSIN, P. A. N. S. 1863, 199. — GRAY, Catal. 1868, 45. — DALL & BANNISTER, Tr. Chicago Ac. Sc. I, 1869, 274 (Alaska). — FINSCH, Abh. Nat. III, 1872, 60 (Alaska). — SAMUELS, 87. *Picus (Dendrocopus) villosus,* SW. F.-Bor. Am. II, 1831, 305. *Picus phillipsi,* AUD. Orn. Biog. V, 1839, 186, pl. cccxvii. — IB. Syn. 1839, 177. — IB. Birds Amer. IV, 1842, 238, pl. cclix (immature, with yellow crown). — NUTTALL, Man. I, (2d ed.,) 1840, 686. — CASS. P. A. N. S. 1863, 199. *Picus martinæ,* AUD. Orn. Biog. V, 1839, 181, pl. cccxvii. — IB. Syn. 1839, 178. — IB. Birds Amer. IV, 1842, 240, pl. cclx (young male, with red feathers on crown). — CASS. P. A. N. S. 1863, 199. *Picus rubricapillus,* NUTTALL, Man. I, (2d ed.,) 1840, 685 (same as preceding). *Picus septentrionalis,* NUTTALL, Man. I, (2d ed.,) 1840, 684.

Var. villosus. — Middle States.

Picus villosus, LINNÆUS, Syst. Nat. I, 1758, 175. — VIEILLOT, Ois. Am. Sept. II, 1807, 64, pl. cxx. — WILSON, Am. Orn. I, 1808, 150, pl. ix. — WAGLER, Syst. Av. 1827, No. 22. — AUD. Orn. Biog. V, 1839, 164, pl. cccxvi. — IB. Birds Amer. IV, 1842, 244, pl. cclxii. — BONAP. Conspectus, 1850, 137. — SUNDEVALL, Mon. Pic. 17. — BAIRD, Birds N. Am. 1858, 84. *Picus leucomelanus,* WAGLER, Syst. Av. 1827, No. 18 (young male in summer). *Hairy Woodpecker,* PENNANT, LATHAM. *Dryobates villosus,* CAB. & HEIN. Mus. Hein. IV, 2, 66.

Var. auduboni. — Southern States.

Picus auduboni, SWAINSON, F. B. A. 1831, 306. — TRUDEAU, J. A. N. Sc. Ph. VII, 1837, 404 (very young male, with crown spotted with yellow). — AUD. Orn. Biog. V, 1839, 194, pl. cccxvii. — IB. Birds Amer. IV, 1842, 259, pl. cclxv. — NUTT. Man. I, (2d ed.,) 1840, 684. — CASS. P. A. N. S. 1863, 199. *Picus villosus,* BRYANT, Pr. Bost. Soc. 1859 (Bahamas, winter). — ALLEN, B. E. Fla. 302.

SP. CHAR. Above black, with a white band down the middle of the back. All the middle and larger wing-coverts and all the quills with conspicuous spots of white. Two white stripes on each side of the head; the upper scarcely confluent behind, the lower not at all so; two black stripes confluent with the black of the nape. Beneath white. Three outer tail-feathers with the exposed portions white. Length, 8.00 to 11.00; wing, 4.00 to 5.00; bill, 1.00 to 1.25. *Male,* with a nuchal scarlet crescent (wanting in the female) covering the white, generally continuous, but often interrupted in the middle.

Immature bird of either sex with more or less of the whole crown spotted with red or yellow, or both, sometimes the red almost continuous.

HAB. North America, to the eastern base of the Rocky Mountains, and (var. *canadensis*) along the 49th parallel to British Columbia; Sitka; accidental in England.

In the infinite variation shown by a large number of specimens in the markings of the wings, so relied on by authors to distinguish the species of the black and white spotted North American Woodpeckers having a longitudinal band of white down the back, it will be perhaps our best plan to cut them rigorously down to two, the old-fashioned and time-honored *P. villosus* and *pubescens ;* since the larger and more perfect the series, the more difficult it is to draw the line between them and their more western representatives. The size varies very greatly, and no two are alike in regard to the extent and number of the white spots. Beginning at one end of the chain, we find the white to predominate in the more eastern specimens. Thus in one (20,601) from Canada, and generally from the north, every wing-covert (except the smallest) and every quill shows externally conspicuous spots or bands of white ; the middle coverts a terminal band and central spot ; the greater coverts two bands on the outer web, and one more basal on the inner ; and every quill is marked with a succession of spots in pairs throughout its length, — the outer web as bands reaching nearly to the shaft ; the inner as more circular, larger spots. The alula alone is unspotted. This is the typical marking of the *P. leucomelas* or *canadensis* of authors. The white markings are all larger respectively than in other forms.

The next stage is seen in typical or average *P. villosus* for the Middle States. Here the markings are much the same, but the white is more restricted, and on the outer webs of the feathers forms rounded spots rather than bands. Some Carlisle specimens have two spots on the middle coverts as described, others lack the basal one. Another stage is exhibited by a specimen from Illinois, in which with two spots on the middle coverts there is but one terminal on the outer web of the greater, and a reduction in number of spots on the inner webs of innermost secondaries, terminal outer spots not having the corresponding inner. This form is quite prevalent westward and on the Upper Missouri, but cannot be considered as strictly geographical, since a Massachusetts and a Georgia skin agree in the same characters.

In all this variation there is little diminution in the number of spots visible externally, nor so far have we seen any from the region east of the Missouri plains that lack white spots on every covert (except the smallest ones) and every quill, and with few exceptions on both webs of the latter. It is therefore this style that we propose to consider as pure *P. villosus*, irrespective of variations in the size or shape of the spots, of the amount of white on tail and back, or of the bird itself. Any deviation from this may be called a variety. It has the distribution already mentioned, and extends along the Upper Missouri to British Columbia and Sitka, straggling into Washington Territory, where, however, it is found with the more typical western form, var. *harrisi.* A specimen collected by Mr. Hepburn at Caribou, on the Upper Fraser, is absolutely undistinguishable from typical *P. canadensis* in size and markings.

We now come to the western race or variety, hardly to be called species, the *P. harrisi* of Audubon. Here the extreme of condition most opposed to typical *villosus* is shown by the entire absence of white on the exposed surface of the wing, except on the outer webs of the four or five longest primaries, where the spots are very small. (We have never seen them entirely wanting.) The white of the back, too, may be normal in amount, or else much restricted. Concealed white spots on some of the feathers will be seen on raising them. The white of tail-feathers sometimes shows black spots or blotches, especially on the inner web of the second. These features belong more especially to specimens from the coast region of Oregon and Washington.

Proceeding eastward from the Northern Pacific Coast we next find specimens showing a few white streaks on the greater coverts and next on the middle coverts. The spots on the secondaries, too, begin to show themselves; but as a general rule they do not occur on the innermost of the greater coverts and of the secondaries. This, therefore, may be considered as the limit of a variety, characterized by the absence at least of spots in these members of the wing.

With the variation in spots in the western variety we have, as already remarked, differences in amount of white on the tail and the back, as well as in the color of the belly, which is sometimes pure white, sometimes of a smoky gray; this latter variation not at all parallel with other differences or with geographical distribution, and equally observable in eastern *villosus.* The size, too, varies somewhat, but not to the same extent as on the Atlantic side. Here, however, we have *Picus jardini* of Mexico and Central America, as the small southern race, absolutely undistinguishable from dark-breasted Oregon specimens, except in size (length, 7.00; wing, 3.90; bill above, .85), and perhaps a more fulvous tinge on the under parts. The specimens before me have one or two black spots on the inner web of the next to the outer tail-feather, as in darker varieties of *harrisi,* but these are not symmetrical or constant in either, and are to be looked on as mere indications of the general tendency to melanism.

HABITS. This common and familiar species of Woodpecker has an extended range throughout eastern North America. Specimens in the Smithsonian Institution have been collected from almost every portion of North America east of the Rocky Mountains. Wilson speaks of it as common throughout the continent from Hudson's Bay to Carolina and Georgia. Mr. Audubon, who regarded *Picus martinæ, P. phillipsi,* and *P. canadensis* as distinct species, instead of varieties of this Woodpecker, states, in regard to its distribution, that the *P. villosus* is a constant resident both in the maritime and inland districts from Texas to New Hampshire, as well as in all the wooded tracts intervening between the junction of the Missouri and Mississippi, and the northern borders of the great lake. He adds that not an individual was found by him or by his sons in Maine, where he did, however, obtain in great abundance the variety he called *P. canadensis*. According to Sir John Richardson it is found as far to the north as the 63d parallel. It remains all the year round in the fur countries, and is the most common species up to the fifty-sixth degree of latitude, north of which it yields in frequency to the three-toed species. Dr. Woodhouse speaks of it as common in Texas and in the Indian Territory. Although not crossing the Rocky Mountains in the United States, it reaches the Pacific Coast of British Columbia, and is found north as far as Sitka, and perhaps still farther, thus replacing the var. *harrisi*. It is a resident, and not a migratory, species, and wherever found it also breeds. Several specimens have been killed in England.

According to the observations of Wilson, this Woodpecker frequents the orchards and cultivated grounds, and is less wild and more domestic than most of the species. In May, with its mate, it seeks the retirement of the woods to breed, selecting a branch already hollowed, or excavating one for itself. In the former case the nest has been known to be four or five feet from the opening. When it excavates its own opening, it digs horizontally six or eight inches into the body of the tree, and then downward to about twice that distance, carrying up the chips in the bill or scraping them out with the feet. They not unfrequently breed in orchards, and have been even known to excavate their holes in the rails of old fences. The female lays five white eggs, which are usually hatched out early in June.

Mr. Audubon observed these birds, at all seasons, in almost every possible locality, from the isolated trees of large towns and cities, even to the very midst of the salt marshes about the mouth of the Mississippi. He found the excavation for the nest more frequently running obliquely than perpendicularly. In the Southern States they rear two broods in a season, the first appearing the last of May, the second usually about the first of August. In the middle and northern districts they rarely raise more than one. Those which Mr. Audubon observed to raise more than one brood in a season made use of the same excavation for both, and not unfrequently within a few yards of a house. The eggs of the first brood he found usually six in number, and of the second four. Where they have but one brood, the number varies from four to six, and in two instances he has found seven. The measure given by him is one inch in length by .69 of an inch in breadth. They are elliptical or almost equally rounded at both ends, smooth, pure white, and translucent. The young remain in the nest until well able to fly.

Mr. Audubon states that the Hairy Woodpecker becomes, during the winter months, a very common bird in all parts of the Southern States, coming to the farm-yards with the downy species to glean the grains of corn left by the cattle. At this season their visits to the corn-cribs are extremely frequent. They may also be seen clinging to the stalks of the sugar-cane, boring them, and evidently enjoying the sweet juices of that plant.

Their flight is short and rapid, resembling that of other allied species. They are not social, never more than the members of one family being seen together. They feed chiefly on insects and their larvæ, often seizing the former on the wing. In the autumn they occasionally eat berries, seeds, and small fruit. Their notes are sharp and loud, uttered in monosyllables, at times with great frequency.

An egg of this species, taken in Roxbury, Mass., is of a pure crystal whiteness, oblong in shape, and equally rounded at either end, measuring 1.01 inches in length by .72 of an inch in breadth. Another, from Georgia, is more rounded at one end, and measures 1.02 inches in length and .75 of an inch in breadth.

Picus villosus, var. harrisi, AUD.

HARRIS'S WOODPECKER.

Picus harrisi, AUD. Orn. Biog. V, 1839, 191, pl. ccccxvii. — IB. Syn. 1839, 178. — IB. Birds America, IV, 1842, 242, pl. cclxi (dark-bellied variety). — NUTTALL, Man. I, (2d. ed.,) 1840, 627. — BAIRD, Birds N. Am. 1858, 87. — SUNDEVALL, Mon. 17. — LORD, Pr. R. Art. Ass. IV, 111 (nesting). — COUES, Pr. A. N. S. 1866, 52 (Oregon). SUMICHRAST, Mem. Bost. Soc. I, 1869, 562 (Alpine regions of Vera Cruz). — GRAY, Catal. 1868, 47. — CABAN. J. 1862, 175. — CASSIN, P. A. N. S. 1863, 200. — COOPER & SUCKLEY, 159. — COOPER, Orn. Cal. I, 1870, 375. *? Picus inornatus*, LICHT. (Bon. Consp.). *Picus (Trichopicus) harrisi*, BP. Consp. Zyg. Aten. Ital. 1854, 8. *Dryobates harrisi*, CAB. & HEIN. Mus. Hein. IV, 2, 68 (*jardini*, 69.) *Picus jardini*, MALH. Rev. Zoöl. Oct. 1845, 374 (Mexico). — CAB. Jour. 1862, 175. *Picus hyloscopus*, CAB. & HEIN. Mus. Hein. IV, 2, 1863, 69 (white-bellied form).

SP. CHAR. Similar to typical *villosus ;* the innermost of the greater wing-coverts and of the secondary quills without any white spots externally ; varying from this to the entire absence of exposed white on wing except on the outer web of longest primaries. Belly varying from pure white to smoky or fulvous gray, white of tail-feathers very rarely blotched with black. Average length, in north, 9.00 ; wing, 5.00 ; exposed part of culmen, 1.15.

Var. *jardini* much smaller. Length, 7.00 ; wing, 3.90 ; culmen, .85.

HAB. Whole of Western United States, west of the Missouri plains, extending into Mexico and Central America, where it passes into the smallest and darkest southern extreme, known as *P. jardini*. Localities : West Arizona (COUES, P. A. N. S. 1866, 52) ; Vera Cruz, Alpine regions (SUMICHRAST, M. Bost. Soc. I, 1869, 562).

In the preceding article we have given some general remarks on Harris's Woodpecker, and shown why we cannot consider it a well-defined species. If the specimens from the extreme west were constant in themselves, and the variations, as with *Colaptes hybridus*, occurred along the line of contact with *villosus*, we might refer to hybrids many of the intermediate forms ; but as scarcely any two are alike, even on the Pacific coast, such a view is inadmissible. As, however, in the extreme limits of variation, there is yet a difference from eastern specimens, and this is characteristic of a large area of country, it may be proper to recognize the form by the name *harrisi*.

The *P. jardini* appears to be nothing more than the most southern race of this dark western form of *P. villosus*, and shows the smallest, as well as the darkest, extreme to which the species attains. In Southern Mexico typical *P. harrisi* and this form grade insensibly together. The minimum of size and maximum darkness of colors are reached in Costa Rica.

HABITS. This variety was first described by Mr. Audubon from specimens obtained by Mr. Townsend on the Columbia River. No information was obtained in regard to its habits, which, it may be presumed, do not vary very essentially from those of the more familiar *pubescens* and *villosus*. In regard to its geographical distribution, it has been found in more or less abundance from Nebraska to the Pacific, and from Mexico to British America. It is known to occur in Texas on the Rio Grande, in New Mexico, in Arizona, Nebraska, California, Oregon, and Washington Territory.

This indicates a very general distribution throughout Western North America from the eastern slope of the Rocky Mountains to the Pacific, and from New Mexico and Texas probably to the limits of the forests in the northwest. It seems to take the place of the *P. villosus* in the far west. Dr. Heermann, in his notes on the birds of California (Journal of Philadelphia Academy, II, 270), says it is not a common bird, although it is occasionally met with in that State. Dr. Gambel, however, states that it occupies, on the western coast, the same place that the *P. villosus* does on the Atlantic, but seems to have a greater partiality for the pine woods. Dr. Woodhouse did not meet with it in the expedition to the Zuñi and Colorado. Dr. Newberry speaks of it (U. S. P. R. R. Survey, VI, — Zoölogy, p. 89) as not uncommon in the wooded districts of Northern California and Oregon. Dr. Kennerly, in his report on the birds obtained by Lieutenant Whipple's party, states that Harris's Woodpecker was found along the Little Colorado River in the month of December, wherever the cottonwood trees grew (U. S. P. R. R. Survey, X, Pt. VI, 21). It is not mentioned by Dr. Heermann in his Report on the birds of Lieutenant Parke's explorations near the 32d parallel. The same writer, in his Report on the birds of Lieutenant Williamson's party, speaks of this bird as having been occasionally observed during the survey, but as a somewhat rare species, though procured in Northern California and at Tejon Pass. Dr. Suckley speaks of it as quite abundant at Fort Dalles, where he found it among the true pines, and at Fort Steilacoom, among the firs (*D. douglasi*), and as a winter resident in both localities (Natural History of Washington Territory, Zoölogy, p. 159). Dr. Cooper states that Harris's Woodpecker is the most abundant species in Washington Territory, being found on both sides of the Cascade Mountains, frequenting the lower parts of the great coniferous trees. He found it a constant resident in May, burrowing out a nest in a dead tree, sometimes only four feet from the ground. He describes its cries and habits as so exactly like those of the larger Sapsucker (*P. villosus*) of the Atlantic States, that, were there not constant and unchangeable differences in plumage, it would be taken for the same species. He furnishes no description of the eggs, but it is quite probable that there is no appreciable difference between them and those of the *Picus villosus*.

Dr. Coues mentions this species as one of the most common and characteristic birds in the vicinity of Fort Whipple. Dr. Heermann speaks of its having clear trumpet-like notes that betray its locality and render it an easy bird to shoot.

In California Dr. Cooper found this chiefly a northern bird, frequenting the forests of all kinds up to the summits of the Sierra Nevada, and also resident as far south as Santa Barbara, descending, in winter, to the eastern branches of the Colorado and to Tejon Pass. He found it more common in the higher Coast Range near Santa Cruz, and still more so toward the Columbia River. Its cry, he adds, is louder than that of most of the small Woodpeckers, and it is rather shy, especially when it imagines itself pursued. It feeds at times on fruits and berries, and sometimes it visits gardens. It is known as one of the "Sapsuckers," but does more good than harm in the orchard, destroying both insects and their larvæ.

Mr. John K. Lord states that this Woodpecker is by far the most abundant species in the district through which his party passed. He found it on Vancouver's Island, and along the entire course of the boundary-line, south through Oregon and California, and north to Fort Simpson. A few remained at Colville during the winter, but the greater number retired to the coast and returned in April and May. In the latter month they mate, and bore out a hole in a dead tree. They use no lining for the nest, but lay the eggs on the bare wood. Their favorite haunts are the stumps of trees growing round swamps or prairie-land.

This Woodpecker was met with by Mr. Ridgway in all wooded portions of the Great Basin, but was most abundant among the pines on the mountains. In all respects, it is a perfect counterpart of the *P. villosus* of the east.

Picus pubescens, LINN.

DOWNY WOODPECKER; LESSER SAPSUCKER.

Picus pubescens, LINN. Syst. Nat. I, 1766, 15. — VIEILLOT, Ois. Am. Sept. II, 1807, 65, pl. cxxi. — WILSON, Am. Orn. I, 1808, 153, pl. ix. — WAGLER, Syst. Avium, 1827, No. 23. — AUD. Orn. Biog. II, 1834, 81 ; V, 539, pl. cxii. — IB. Birds Am. IV, 1842, 249, pl. cclxiii. — BAIRD, Birds N. Am. 1858, 89. — SUNDEVALL, Mon. Pic. 17. — MALB. Mon. Pic. I, 119, pl. xxix. — CASSIN, Pr. 1863, 20. — SCL. Cat. 1862, 334. — GRAY, Cat. 1868, 44. — DALL & BANNISTER, Tr. Chicago Ac. I, 1869, 274 (Alaska). — FINSCH, Abh. Nat. III, 1872, 60 (Alaska). — SAMUELS, 89. — ALLEN, B. E. Fla. 304. *Picus* (*Dendrocopus*) *pubescens*, SW. F. B. A. II, 1831, 307. *Picus* (*Trichopicus*) *pubescens*, BONAP. Consp. Zyg. Ateneo Italiano, 1854, 8. *? Picus medianus*, SW. F. B. A. II, 1831, 308. *Picus meridionalis*, SW. F. B. A. II, 1831, 308 (small southern race). *Picus leconti*, JONES, Ann. N. Y. Lyc. IV, 1848, 489, pl. xviii (Georgia ; three-toed specimen, first toe wanting. Type of *Tridactylia*, BP.) *Dryobates pubescens*, CAB. & HEIN. Mus. Hein. 1863, 63.

Sp. Char. A miniature of *P. villosus*. Above black, with a white band down the back. Two white stripes on the side of the head; the lower of opposite sides always separated behind, the upper sometimes confluent on the nape. Two stripes of black on the side of the head, the lower not running into the forehead. Beneath white; all the middle and greater coverts and all the quills with white spots, the larger coverts with two series each; tertiaries or inner secondaries all banded with white. Two outer tail-feathers white, with two bands of black at end; third white at tip and externally, crissum sometimes spotted with black. Length, about 6.25; wing, 3.75. *Male* with red, terminating the white feathers on the nape. *Young* with whole top of head red.

HAB. Eastern United States, towards the eastern slope of the Rocky Mountains, into British Columbia and the Humboldt Mountains, and north to the limits of the woods; along whole Yukon River; perhaps to the Pacific, north of the 49th parallel; Kodiak. Localities: San Antonio, Texas (DRESSER, Ibis, 1865, 468). Accidental in England.

The remarks already made on the variation of *Picus villosus* apply equally well here; all the differences in size and markings with locality being almost exactly reproduced. The western variety, *P. gairdneri*, is equally uncertain in characters as *P. harrisi*, and as little entitled to specific distinction. As in the previous instance, we shall call typical *pubescens* those specimens in which all the middle and greater coverts and all the quills including the innermost secondaries are spotted with white, while those in which any of these feathers, whether all the coverts, as in Oregon birds, or only a few of them, are unspotted, may be called var. *gairdneri*.

Of typical *pubescens* in the Eastern States there are minor variations, but not of much account. Thus the forehead itself, apart from the white nasal tufts, is sometimes white, connecting with the white superciliary stripe; more frequently, however, the whole forehead is black. Northern specimens are larger and have larger white spots, and not unfrequently the black cheek-stripe is invaded anteriorly by white, which, however, is appreciable at the base of the feathers. The black bars on the tail are much restricted in specimens from the Yukon. Southern specimens are smaller and darker, with smaller spots on the wings.

In all the changes of the two species, there is no difficulty in distinguishing *P. pubescens* from *P. villosus* by the black bars on outer tail-feathers of the former, and their absence in the latter. The crissum of *pubescens* is sometimes somewhat spotted with blackish. The white markings on the coverts are larger in proportion, and there are almost always two series of white spots on the greater coverts, as in northern varieties of *villosus*, not one, as in most of those from the Middle States.

HABITS. This species, like the Hairy Woodpecker, is a resident rather than a migratory species, and breeds wherever it is met with. It also seems to have very nearly the same geographical distribution with that species. Dr. Woodhouse found it common throughout the Indian Territory, Texas, and New Mexico. It does not, however, appear to have been collected by any of the parties engaged in the Pacific Railroad surveys, nor by that upon the survey of the Mexican boundary. Of seventeen specimens given by

Professor Baird in 1858 as in the collections of the Smithsonian Institution, six are from Pennsylvania, two from Massachusetts, two from Missouri, one from Bonhomme Island in Nebraska, and the rest from Fort Leavenworth, Salt Creek, Fort Riley, and Platte River in Kansas. It is quite common throughout the coast region of Alaska, exclusive of the Aleutians, and throughout the entire valley of the Yukon. Wilson makes no mention of its geographical distribution, probably because he found it everywhere common, to the extent of his own investigations. Audubon speaks of it as very generally distributed from the lower parts of Louisiana to Labrador, and as far westward as he travelled.

Sir John Richardson states that this species is a constant inhabitant of the fur countries up to the 58th parallel. It seeks its food principally on the maple, elm, and ash, and, north of latitude 54°, where these trees are not found, on the aspen and birch.

According to Wilson, these birds select a suitable place for the excavation of their nest, about the middle of May. An apple, pear, or cherry tree, often in the near neighborhood of a farm-house, is generally fixed upon for this purpose. The work of excavation is begun by the male, who cuts a hole in the solid wood as circular as if described with a pair of compasses. He is occasionally relieved by the female, both parties working with the most indefatigable diligence. The direction of the hole, when made in the body of the tree, is downward by an angle of forty degrees for the distance of six or eight inches, and then directly downward for ten or twelve more. Within, the excavation is roomy, capacious, and as smooth as if polished by the hand of the most finished workman. The entrance is, however, left only just large enough to admit the bodies of the birds. During their labor they even take the pains to carry their chips to a distance, to prevent suspicion. This operation sometimes occupies the chief part of a week. The eggs are generally six in number, pure white, and laid on the smooth bottom of the cavity. The male supplies the female with food while she is sitting. The young generally leave the nest about the last of June.

The same writer also gives an interesting account of the impudent coolness of the House Wren, who, coveting the well-built home of this Woodpecker, and unable to excavate such an apartment for itself, waits until the poor Woodpeckers have completed their work, and then attacks them with violence and drives them off from the nest they have been at so much pains to prepare. He states that he saw a striking example of this, where the Woodpeckers, after commencing in a cherry-tree, within a few yards of the house, and having made considerable progress, were turned out by the Wren. They began again on a pear-tree in the garden, a few yards off, when, after digging out a most complete apartment, and laying one egg, they were once more assaulted by the same impertinent intruder, and finally forced to abandon the place.

Mr. Audubon gives substantially the same account of their nesting, only he assigns an earlier period, the middle of April, for its commencement, and describes the entrance to the excavation as often being at right angles to the trunk for a few inches before it descends. He states that in the Southern and Middle States two broods are raised in a season, farther north seldom more than one.

Mr. C. S. Paine, of Randolph, Vt., speaks of this Woodpecker as being one of the most common and familiar, in Vermont, of the family. They are to be met with in his neighborhood at all seasons of the year, though he is of the opinion that many of them go south to spend the winter. They deposit their eggs about the first of June in the very snug little excavations they prepare. The male bird will sometimes prepare a separate apartment for himself, apart from his mate. Mr. Paine has taken the male in such a hole by himself, and without any nest or eggs, evidently only prepared for shelter.

This Woodpecker has a single note or cry, sounding like *chink*, which it frequently repeats. When it flies, and often when it alights, this cry is more shrill and prolonged. They are very industrious, and are constantly employed in search of insects, chiefly in orchards and the more open groves. The orchard is its favorite resort, and it is particularly fond of boring the bark of apple-trees for insects. This fact, and the erroneous impression that it taps the trees for the sap, has given to these birds the common name of Sapsuckers, and has caused an unjust prejudice against them. So far from doing any injury to the trees, they are of great and unmixed benefit. Wilson, who was at great pains to investigate the matter, declares that he invariably found that those trees that were thus marked by the Woodpecker were uniformly the most thriving and the most productive. " Here, then," adds Wilson, " is a whole species — I may say genus — of birds, which Providence seems to have formed for the protection of our fruit and forest trees from the ravages of vermin, which every day destroy millions of those noxious insects that would otherwise blast the hopes of the husbandman, and even promote the fertility of the tree, and in return are proscribed by those who ought to have been their protectors."

The egg of this species is nearly spherical, pure white, and measures .83 by .72 of an inch.

Picus pubescens, var. gairdneri, Aud.

GAIRDNER'S WOODPECKER.

Picus gairdneri, Aud. Orn. Biog. V, 1839, 317. — Ib. Syn. 1839, 180. — Ib. Birds Amer. IV, 1842, 252 (not figured). — Baird, Birds N. Am. 1858, 91, pl. lxxxv, f. 2, 3. — Sundevall, Consp. 1866, 17. — Gray, Cat. 1868, 44. — Cooper & Suckley, 159. — Sclater, Catal. 1862, 334. — Malh. Monog. Picidæ, I, 123. — Cass. P. A. N. S, 1863, 201. — Cooper, Orn. Cal. I, 1870, 377. — Lord, Pr. R. Art. Inst. IV, 1864, 111. *Picus meridionalis*, Nutt. Man. I, (2d ed.,) 1840, 690 (not of Swainson). — Gambel, J. A. N. Sc. I, 1847, 55, 105. *Picus turati*, Malherbe, Mon. Pic. I, 125, tab. 29 (small race, 5.50, from Monterey, Cal., nearest *pubescens*). *Dryobates turati*, Cab. & Hein. Mus. Hein. IV, 2, 1863, 65. *Dryobates homorus*, Cab. & Hein. Mus. Hein. IV, 2, 1863, 65 (larger, more spotted style).

Sp. Char. Similar to *pubescens* in size and markings, but with less white on the wings.
Varies from entire absence of exposed white spots on the middle and greater wing-coverts
and innermost secondaries, with small spots on the quills, to spots on most of their
feathers, but absent on some, and the spots generally larger.

Hab. Pacific coast of United States to Rocky Mountains. Darkest and with least
white in Western Oregon and Washington.

In the preceding article we have given the comparative characters of this
form, which we can only consider as a variety, and not very permanent or
strongly marked at that.

As in *pubescens*, this race varies much in the color of the under parts,
which are sometimes pure white, sometimes smoky-brown. It is suggested
that this is partly due to a soiling derived from inhabiting charred trees.
It is, at any rate, of no specific value.

Habits. Gairdner's Woodpecker is the western representative and counterpart of the Downy Woodpecker of the east, resembling it in size and
general habits, and only differing from it in certain exceptional characteristics already mentioned. It is found throughout western North America,
probably from Mexico to the British Possessions, and from the eastern base
of the Rocky Mountains to the Pacific.

Dr. Cooper met with it in California, chiefly in the northern parts of the
State, but did not observe any south of the Santa Clara Valley. Dr. Coues
saw none in Arizona, or possibly a single specimen not positively ascertained.

Dr. Cooper found one of its nests near Santa Clara, on the 24th of May,
containing young. It had been burrowed in a small and partly rotten tree,
and was about five feet from the ground. From the fact that they were
found breeding so far south he infers that among the mountains they probably occur much farther to the south, as do most other northern birds. He
found them frequenting chiefly the smaller trees in the vicinity of the evergreen woods, where they were to be seen at all seasons industriously tapping
the bark to obtain insects.

Dr. Newberry mentions finding them very common in Oregon, and also
in Northern California. In Washington Territory, Dr. Suckley found them
extremely common on the Lower Columbia, especially among the willow-
trees lining its banks. They were resident throughout the winter, and in these
situations were very abundant. In January, 1856, he found them so abundant among the willows growing on the islands in the delta of the Willa-
mette, that he readily obtained eight specimens in the space of an hour. At
that season they were very unwary, giving little heed to the presence of man,
not even allowing the near discharge of a gun to interfere with their busy
search for food.

Dr. Heermann speaks of it as neither common nor especially rare. He
obtained several specimens among the mountains of Northern California.

Mr. Lord met with these Woodpeckers abundantly in the Northwestern

Boundary Survey. They differed slightly in their habits from the *P. harrisi*, generally hunting for insects on the maples, alders, and stunted oaks, rather than on the pine-trees. Specimens were taken on Vancouver Island, Sumass Prairie, Colville, and the west slope of the Rocky Mountains at an altitude of seven thousand feet above the sea-level.

Mr. Ridgway found this Woodpecker to be unaccountably rare in the Sierra Nevada and all portions of the Great Basin, as well as in the Wahsatch and Uintah Mountains, even in places where the *P. harrisi* was at all times abundant. Indeed, he only met with it on two or three occasions, in the fall : first in the Upper Humboldt Valley, in September, where it was rare in the thickets along the streams ; and again in the Wahsatch Mountains, where but a single brood of young was met with in August.

An egg of this species from Oregon, obtained by Mr. Ricksecker, is larger than that of the *pubescens*, but similar in shape, being very nearly spherical. It measures .96 of an inch in length by .85 in breadth.

SUBGENUS **DYCTIOPICUS**, BONAP.

Dyctiopicus, BONAP. Ateneo Ital. 1854, 8. (Type, *Picus scalaris*, WAGLER.)
Dyctiopipo, CABANIS & HEIN. Mus. Hein. IV, 2, 1863, 74. (Same type.)

CHAR. Small species, banded above transversely with black or brown and white.

Of this group there are two sections, — one with the central tail-feathers entirely black, from Mexico and the United States (three species) ; the other with their feathers like the lateral black, banded or spotted with white (three species from southern South America). The northern section is characterized as follows : —

COMMON CHARACTERS. All the larger coverts and quills with white spots becoming transverse bands on innermost secondaries. Cheeks black with a supra-orbital and a malar stripe of white. Back banded alternately with black and white, but not on upper tail-coverts, nor four central tail-feathers. Beneath whitish, sides with elongated black spots ; flanks and crissum transversely barred. Tail-feathers, except as mentioned, with spots or tranverse bars of black. Head of male with red patch above (restricted in *nuttalli*), each feather with a white spot below the red. *Female* without red.

The characters of the species *scalaris*, with its varieties, and *nuttalli*, will be found under *Picus*.

Picus scalaris, WAGLER.

LADDER-BACKED WOODPECKER.

Picus scalaris, WAGLER, Isis, 1829, V, 511 (Mexico). — BONAP. Consp. 1850, 138. — SCL.
P. Z. S. 1856, 307. — SUND. Consp. 18. — BAIRD, Birds N. Am. 1858, 94, pl. xli, f. 1.
— IB. Rep. Mex. Bound. II, 4, pl. iii. — SCL. Cat. 1862, 333. — CASS. P. A. N. S.
1863, 195. — GRAY, Cat. 1868, 48. — HEERM. X, c, p. 18. — COOPER, Orn. Cal. I,
1870, 379. *Picus (Dyctiopicus) scalaris*, BON. Consp. Zygod. Aten. Ital. 1854, 8. *Dyc-
tiopipo scalaris*, CAB. & HEIN. Mus. 74. *Picus gracilis*, LESS. Rev. Zoöl. 1839, 90
(Mexico). *Picus parvus*, CABOT, Boston Jour. N. H. V, 1845, 90 (Sisal, Yucatan).
Picus orizabœ, CASSIN, Pr. A. N. S. 1863, 196 (Orizaba). *Picus bogotus*, CASSIN, Pr.
A. N. S. 1863, 196 ; Jour. A. N. S. V, 1863, 460, pl. lii, f. 1 (Mex.). *Picus bairdi*
(SCL. MSS.), MALHERBE, Mon. Pic. I, 118, t. xxvii, f. 7, 8. — SCL. Cat. 333, (?) P. Z. S.
64, 177 (city of Mex.). — CAB. & HEIN. Mus. Hein. IV, 2, 76. — CASSIN, Pr. A. N. S.
1863, 196. — COUES, Pr. A. N. S. 1866, 52 (perhaps var. *graysoni*). — DRESSER, Ibis,
1865, 468. *Hab.* Texas and New Mexico, to Arizona ; south through Eastern Mexico
to Yucatan. *Picus scalaris*, var. *graysoni*, BAIRD, MSS. *Hab.* Western Arizona ;
Western Mexico and Tres Marias.

SP. CHAR. Back banded transversely with black and white from nape to rump (not
upper tail-coverts). Quills and coverts with spots of white; forming bands on the
secondaries. Two white stripes on sides of head. Top of head red, spotted with white.
Nasal tufts brown. Beneath brownish-white, with black spots on sides, becoming bands
behind. Outer tail-feathers more or less banded. Length, about 6.50; wing, 3.50 to
4.50; tail, about 2.50.

HAB. Guatemala, Mexico, and adjacent southern parts of United States. Localities:
Xalapa (SCL. P. Z. S. 1859, 367) ; Cordova (SCL. 1856, 357) ; Guatemala (SCL. Ibis, I,
136) ; Orizaba (SCL. Cat. 333) ; S. E. Texas (DRESSER, Ibis, 1865, 468, breeds) ; W.
Arizona (COUES, P. A. N. S. 1866, 52) ; Yucatan (LAWR. Ann. N. Y. Lyc. IX, 205).

In the above diagnosis we have endeavored to express the average of
characters belonging to a Woodpecker to which many names, based on
trifling geographical variations, have been assigned, but which legitimately
can be only considered as one species. This is among the smallest of the
North American Woodpeckers, and in all its variations the wings are long,
reaching as far as the short feathers of the tail. The upper parts generally
are black, on the back, rump, and exposed feathers of the wings banded
transversely with white, the black bands rather the narrower ; the quills and
larger coverts spotted with the same on both webs, becoming bands on the
innermost secondaries. The upper tail-coverts and two inner tail-feathers
on either side are black. The white bands of the back extend all the way
up to the neck, without any interscapular interruption. The under parts
are of a pale smoky brownish-white, almost with a lilac tinge ; on the sides
of the breast and belly are a few scattered small but elongated spots. The
posterior parts of the sides under the wing and the under tail-coverts are
obscurely banded transversely with black. The top of the head, extending
from a narrow sooty frontlet at the base of the bill to a short, broad nuchal
crest, is crimson in the male, each feather with a white spot between the

crimson and the dark brown base of the feathers.   The brown nasal tuft is
scarcely different from the feathers of the forehead.

In a large series of specimens of this species, from a wide area of distribution,
considerable differences are appreciable in size, but fewer in coloration than
might be expected.   Yucatan birds are the least (*Picus parvus*, Cabot; *vaga-
tus*, Cassin), the wing measuring 3.30 inches.   Those from Southern Mexico
are but little larger (wing, 3.60).   In Northern Mexico the wing is nearly
4 inches; in New Mexico it is 4.30.   The markings vary but little.   The black
and white bands on the back are about of equal width, but sometimes one,
sometimes the other, appears the larger ; the more eastern have, perhaps, the
most white.   The pattern on the tail is quite constant.   Thus, assuming the
three outer feathers to be white, banded with black, the outermost may be
said to have seven transverse bars of black, of which the terminal four
(sometimes five) are distinct and perfect, the basal three (or two) confluent
into one on the inner web (the extreme base of the feather white).   The
next feather has, perhaps, the same number of dark bands, but here only
two (sometimes three) are continuous and complete ; the innermost united
together, the outer showing as scallops.   The third feather has no continuous
bands (or only one), all the inner portions being fused ; the outer mere scallops, sometimes an oblique edging ; generally, however, the interspaces of
the dark bands are more or less distinctly traceable through their dusky suffusion, especially on the inner web of the outer feather.   The number of free
bands thus varies slightly, but the general pattern is the same.   This condition prevails in nearly all the specimens before us from Yucatan and Mexico
(in only one specimen from Arizona, and one or two from Texas), and is
probably the typical *scalaris* of Wagler.

In specimens from the Rio Grande and across to Arizona the seven bands
of the outer feather are frequently continuous and complete on both webs
to the base, a slight suffusion only indicating the tendency to union in the
inner web.   The other feathers are much as described, except that the white
interspaces of the black scallops penetrate deeper towards the shaft.   This
is perhaps the race to which the name of *P. bairdi* has been applied.   We do
not find, however, any decided reduction in the amount of red on the anterior portion of the head, as stated for this species (perhaps it is less continuous towards the front), except in immature birds ; young females possibly
losing the immature red of the crown, as with typical *scalaris*.

A third type of tail-marking is seen in specimens from the Pacific coast,
and from the Tres Marias especially ; also in some skins from Southwestern
Arizona.   Here the extreme forehead is black, with white spots ; the red of
the crown not so continuous anteriorly even as in the last-mentioned race.
The general pattern of tail is as described, and the bars on the inner webs
are also confluent towards the base, but we have only two or three transverse bars at the end of the outer feathers ; the rest of outer web entirely
white, this color also invading the inner.   The second feather is similarly

marked, sometimes with only one spot on outer web; the third has the black scallops restricted. This may be called var. *graysoni*, as most specimens in the Smithsonian collection were furnished by Colonel Grayson. The size is equal to the largest typical *scalaris*.

We next come to the Cape St. Lucas bird, described by Mr. Xantus as *P. lucasanus*. Here the bill and feet become disproportionally larger and more robust than in any described; the black bands of the back larger than the white, perhaps fewer in number. The continuous red of the head also appears restricted to a stripe above and behind the eye and on the occiput, although there are some scattered feathers as far forward as above the eyes. The specimens are, however, not in very good plumage, and this marking cannot be very well defined; the red may really be as continuous forward as in the last variety. The nasal tufts are brown, as in the typical *scalaris*. The outer three tail-feathers in most specimens show still more white, with one or two indistinct terminal bands only on the outer two; one or two additional spots, especially on inner web, and the sub-basal patch of inner web greatly reduced. Specimens vary here in this respect, as in other races of *scalaris*, but the average is as described.

Notwithstanding the decided difference between typical *scalaris* and *lucasanus*, the discovery of the variety *graysoni* makes it possible to consider both as extremes of one species. To *nuttalli*, however, it is but one step farther; a restriction of the red to the posterior half of the top of head, the white instead of brown nasal feathers, and the whiter under parts being the only positive characters. The markings of the tail are almost identical with those of *lucasanus*. The anterior portion of the back is, however, not banded, as in the several varieties described. For this reason it may therefore be questioned whether, if *lucasanus* and *scalaris* are one, *nuttalli* should not belong to the same series.

We thus find that the amount of black on the tail is greatest in Southern and Southeastern Mexican specimens, and farther north it begins to diminish; in Western Mexico it is still more reduced, while at Cape St. Lucas the white is as great in amount as in the Upper Californian *P. nuttalli*.

The characters given above for the different varieties or races of *Picus scalaris*, as far as they relate to the tail, may be expressed in the following table, illustrated by the accompanying diagram, showing the markings of outer tail-feather in *scalaris* and *nuttalli*.

Outer tail-feathers with seven distinct transverse black bands.
    These bands confluent on inner web near the base . . var. *scalaris*.
    Bands distinct on inner web . . . . var. *bairdi*.
Bands on outer tail-feather distinct on outer webs at end only, obsolete or wanting towards base (as in *nuttalli*).
    Tarsus, .68. Bill and legs as in average . . . . var. *graysoni*.
    Tarsus, .78. Bill and legs very stout . . . . var. *lucasanus*.

HABITS. This species belongs to our southern and southwestern fauna, entering our borders from Mexico, occurring from the valley of the Rio Grande to Southeastern California, and the slopes of the Rocky Mountains south of the 35th parallel. It is found throughout Mexico to Yucatan and Guatemala.

6105

4482

Outermost tail-feather of *Picus scalaris*.

Outermost tail-feather of *Picus nuttalli*.

Dr. Samuel Cabot obtained a single specimen of this bird at Yucatan, which he described under the name of *P. parvus*, in the Boston Journal of Natural History, V, p. 92. It was procured early in December, 1841, in the neighborhood of Ticul, Yucatan. Dr. Kennerly considered it a not uncommon species in the vicinity of Boca Grande; especially wherever there were large trees. The same naturalist, in his Report on the birds of Lieutenant Whipple's expedition, states that he very often saw this bird near San Antonio, Texas, as well as during the march several hundred miles west of that place, but that, after leaving the Rio Grande, he did not meet with it until he reached the head-waters of Bill Williams Fork. From thence to the Great Colorado River he saw it frequently, wherever there was any timber; but it was very shy, alighting on the tops of the leafless cotton-wood trees, and keeping a vigilant lookout.

Dr. Heermann, in his Report on the birds of Lieutenant J. G. Parke's expedition, states that he observed this Woodpecker in the southernmost portion of California, and found it more and more abundant as he advanced towards Texas, where it was quite common. The same naturalist, in his Report on the birds of Lieutenant Williamson's expedition, remarks that he procured this bird first at Vallicita, but found it abounding in the woods about Fort Yuma. He considered the species as new to the California fauna, though frequently seen in Texas, several of the expeditions having collected it.

Dr. Woodhouse, in his Report on the birds of Sitgreaves's expedition to the Zuñi and the Colorado speaks of finding this beautiful little Woodpecker abundant in Texas, east of the Pecos River. During his stay in San Antonio and its vicinity, he became quite familiar with it. It was to be seen, at all times, flying from tree to tree, and lighting on the trunk of the mesquites (*Algarobia*), closely searching for its insect-food. In its habits and notes, he states, it much resembles the common Hairy Woodpecker. Dr. Woodhouse elsewhere remarks that he did not meet with this bird west of the Rio San Pedro, in Texas. In regard to its breeding-habits, so far as I am aware, they are inferred rather than known. It is quite probable they are not unlike those of the *Picus pubescens*, which it so closely resembles. The eggs in the collection of the Smithsonian were obtained with the collections of the late Dr. Berlandier of Matamoras, in the province of Tamaulipas, Mexico.

Dr. Cooper states that this Woodpecker is abundant in the Colorado Valley, and that they are sometimes seen on the bushes covering the neighboring mountains. In habits he regards them the exact counterpart of *P. nuttalli*, to which they are allied.

Mr. Dresser found them resident and very common throughout all Texas and Northeastern Mexico. It breeds abundantly about San Antonio, boring into any tree it finds most suitable for its purposes.

Dr. Coues regards Fort Whipple as about the northern limit of this species in Arizona. It is not very common, is only a summer resident, and breeds sparingly there. Farther south, throughout the Territory, and in the Colorado Valley, he found it abundant. It does not cross the Colorado Desert into California, and is there replaced by *P. nuttalli*. It extends south into Central America. A bird shot by Dr. Coues, June 5, appeared to be incubating; young birds were taken just fledged July 10. The nest was in the top of a live-oak tree. Malherbe, who speaks of this Woodpecker as exclusively Mexican, states that he has been informed that it is abundant in that country, where it may be seen at all times, climbing over the trunks and branches of trees. It is said to be very familiar and unwary, living commonly in gardens and orchards through the greater part of the year, and many of them nesting there, though in regard to their manner of nesting he has no information.

The egg of this Woodpecker in shape is most similar to the *P. villosus*, being of an oblong-oval. It is larger than the *pubescens*, and not of so clear a white color. It measures exactly one inch in length by .75 of an inch in breadth.

Picus scalaris, var. lucasanus, Xantus.

THE CAPE WOODPECKER.

Picus lucasanus, Xantus, Pr. A. N. S. 1859, 298, 302. — Malherbe, Mon. Picidæ, I, 166. — Cassin, Pr. A. N. S. 1863, 195. — Cooper, Orn. Cal. I, 1870, 381.

Sp. Char. General appearance that of *Picus nuttalli* and *scalaris*. Bill stout, as long as or longer than the head. Above black, banded transversely with white on the back and scapulars to the nape, the white narrower band, the rump and inner tail-feathers entirely black; quills with a row of white spots on each web; the outer square, the inner rounded, these spots on the tertials becoming transversely quadrangular. Beneath brownish-white, with rounded black spots on the sides of the breast, passing behind on the flanks and under tail-coverts into transverse bars. Greater inner wing-coverts transversely barred. Outer two tail-feathers white, with one, sometimes two terminal bars, next to which are one or two bars on the inner web only; third feather black, the outer web mostly white, with traces of a terminal black bar; sometimes there is a greater predominance of black on the inner web. Two white stripes on side of head, one starting above, the other below the eye, with a tendency to meet behind and form a whitish collar on the nape. Male with the entire top of the head streaked with red, becoming more conspicuous behind; each red streak with a white spot at base. Feathers covering the nostrils smoky-brown. Length, 7.15; extent, 12.15; wing, 4.00; bill above, 1.00; middle toe and claw, .80; tarsus, .76.

HAB. Cape St. Lucas.

Of the distinctness of this bird as a species from *P. nuttalli* and *scalaris* I had at one time no doubt; but the discovery that the otherwise typical *scalaris* from Mazatlan and Western Mexico generally have the same markings on the tail has induced me to consider it as a kind of connecting link. I have, however, thought it best to give a detailed description for comparison. Of about the same size with *nuttalli*, the bill and feet are much larger. The legs, indeed, are nearly, if not quite, as large as those of male *P. villosus* from Pennsylvania; the bill, however, is somewhat less. The relations to *P. scalaris* are seen in the dorsal bands extending to the nape, the smoky-brown feathers of the nostrils, the red on the whole top of head (scattering anteriorly), the brownish shade beneath, the width of the white cheek-bands, etc. On the other hand, it has the black bands of the back rather wider than the white, as in *nuttalli,* and the white outer tail-feathers even less banded with black. The two outer are entirely white, with one terminal black bar; one or two spots on the outer web; and two or three bands on the inner, with a sub-basal patch on the inner web, even smaller than in *nuttalli*. It is rarely that even two continuous transverse bands can be seen to cross both webs of the tail. The bill and feet are much larger.

The following measurements taken from the largest specimens before us of *Dyctiopicus*, and one of *P. villosus*, will illustrate what has been said of the size of bill and feet of *P. lucasanus*.

	P. villosus.	P. lucasanus.	P. nuttalli.	P. scalaris.
	884 ♂	♂ 12939	♂ 4482	♂ 6105
Bill from forehead, . .	1.26	1.10	.90	.99
Tarsus, ...	.76	.76	.70	.68
Middle toe and claw, . .	.87	.84	.75	.65
Claw alone, . . .	.39	.34	.32	.31
Outer hind toe and claw, .	.95	.84	.79	.80
Claw alone, . . .	.40	.32	.31	.31

HABITS. Nothing distinctive is known of the habits of this race.

Picus nuttalli, GAMBEL.

NUTTALL'S WOODPECKER.

Picus nuttalli, GAMBEL, Pr. A. N. Sc. I, April, 1843, 259 (Los Angeles, Cal.). — BAIRD, Birds N. Am. 1858, 93. — SUNDEVALL, Consp. Pic. 19. — MALH. Mon. Pic. I, 100. — CASSIN, P. A. N. S. 1863, 195. — GRAY, Cat. 1868, 50. — COOPER, Orn. Cal. I, 1870, 378. *Picus scalaris*, (WAGLER) GAMBEL, J. A. N. Sc. Ph. 2d ser. I, Dec. 1847, 55, pl. ix, f. 2, 3 (not of WAGLER). *Picus wilsoni*, MALHERBE, Rev. Zoöl. 1849, 529. — BONAP. Consp. 1850, 138. *Picus* (*Trichopicus*) *wilsoni*, BONAP. Consp. Zyg. Aten. Ital. 1854, 8.

SP. CHAR. Back black, banded transversely with white, but not on upper tail-coverts, nor as far forward as the neck. Greater and middle coverts and quills with spots or bands of white. Crown black, with white spots, sometimes wanting. On the nape a patch of white, behind this unbanded black. Occiput and nape crimson in the male. Tufts of feathers at the base of the bill white. Sides of the head black, with two white stripes, one above the eye and passing down on the side of the neck, the other below and cut off behind by black. Under parts smoky yellowish-white, spotted on the sides of the breast, and banded on flank and crissum with black. Predominant character of the outer tail-feather white, with two or three interrupted bands towards end; none at base. Length, about 7.00; wing, 4.50. *Female* with the top of the head uniform black, or sometimes spotted with white.

HAB. Coast region of California.

Third, fourth, and fifth quills nearly equal and longest; second intermediate between the seventh and eighth. General color above black, barred transversely with white on the back, rump, and flanks; the upper surface of tail and tail-coverts, and a broad patch on the upper part of the back about half an inch long, pure black. The white bands measure about .12 of an inch, the black about twice as much. The top of the head is black, each feather with a short streak of white; on the extreme occiput and the nape is a transverse patch of crimson, each feather having a white spot just below the crimson. The crimson patch is usually as far from the base of the bill above as this is from its point. The sides of the head may be described as black; a white stripe commences on the upper edge of the eye, and, passing backwards, margins the crimson, and extends on down the side of the neck to a patch of white, apparently connected with its fellow on the opposite side by white spots. Another narrow white stripe commences at the nostrils, (the bristles of which are whitish,) and passes as far as the occiput, where it ceases in the middle of the black of the cheeks. There are thus two white streaks on the side of the head bordering a black one passing through the eye. The under parts generally are white, with a dirty yellow tinge. The sides of the breast and body are faintly streaked with black; the flanks barred with the same. The under coverts are barred with black.

The three outer tail-feathers are yellowish-white, with two or three interrupted bars of black on the posterior or terminal fourth, and a concealed patch of black on the inner web near the end. Only the terminal band is continuous across, sometimes the others ; always interrupted along the shaft, and even reduced to rounded spots of black on one or both webs. No distinct bands are visible on raising the crissum. The black patch on inner web of outer tail-feather near the base increases on the second and third, on the latter leaving the end only with an oblique white patch. The bands on the under surface have a tendency to a transversely cordate and interrupted, rather than a continuous, linear arrangement.

Young birds have the whole top of head red, as in *P. scalaris*, with or without white at the base of the red. The white nasal tufts and other characters will, however, distinguish them.

This bird, though widely different in appearance from *scalaris*, may nevertheless, without any violence, be regarded as but one extreme of a species of which the lighter examples of *scalaris* (*bairdi*) are the other, the transition towards *nuttalli* being through var. *scalaris*, var. *graysoni*, and var. *lucasanus*, each in that succession showing a nearer approach to the distinctive features of *nuttalli*. We have not seen any intermediate specimens, however. The pure white instead of smoky-brown nasal tufts, and their greater development, are the only characters which show a marked difference from the varieties of *scalaris ;* but the other differences are nothing more than an extension of the black markings and restriction of the red in the male, the result of a melanistic tendency in the Pacific region.

HABITS. This species was first discovered by Dr. Gambel near Los Angeles, Cal., and described by him in the Proceedings of the Philadelphia Academy. Afterwards, in his paper on the birds of California, published in the Academy's Journal, mistaking it for the *P. scalaris* of Wagler, he furnished a fuller description of the bird and its habits, and gave with it illustrations of both sexes. So far as now known, it appears to be confined to the regions in California and Oregon west of the Coast Range, extending as far south as San Diego, representing, in its distribution on the Pacific, the *P. borealis* of the Atlantic States. One specimen in the Smithsonian collections was obtained on Umpqua River, in Oregon Territory ; the others at Santa Clara, San Francisco, Petaluma, Bodega, and Yreka, in California. Dr. Woodhouse says, in his Report on the birds of the Zuñi and Colorado expedition, that he has only seen this bird in California, from which region he has examined numerous specimens. Dr. Heermann, in his Report on the birds of Lieutenant Williamson's expedition, states that this Woodpecker is occasionally found in the mountains of Northern California, but that it is much more abundant in the valleys. Dr. Gambel found it abundant in California at all seasons. He describes it as having the usual habits of Woodpeckers, familiarly examining the fence-rails and orchard-trees for its insect-fare. He found it breeding at Santa Barbara, and on the 1st of May discovered a nest containing young in the dead stump of an oak, about fifteen feet from the ground. The hole for entrance was remarkably small, but inside appeared large and deep. The parents were constantly bringing insects and larvæ.

Dr. Cooper states that this Woodpecker is quite abundant towards the coast of California, and among the foothills west of the Sierra Nevada. It frequents the oaks and the smaller trees almost exclusively, avoiding the coniferous forests. It is very industrious, and not easily frightened, when engaged in hammering on the bark of trees allowing a very near approach. At other times, when pursued, it becomes more wary and suspicious. April 20, 1862, Dr. Cooper discovered a nest of this bird near San Diego. It was in a rotten stump, and was only about four feet from the ground. He captured the female on her nest, which contained five eggs of a pure pearly whiteness.

These birds are said to remain throughout the year in the valleys, and to migrate very little, if at all. Dr. Cooper has not observed it west of the Coast Range, except near Santa Barbara, nor has he seen any around gardens or orchards. None have been observed north or east of the State. East of the mountains it is replaced by the *scalaris*.

Mr. Xantus mentions finding a nest containing two eggs in a hole in the *Cereus giganteus*, about fifteen feet from the ground. The excavation made by the bird was about a foot and a half deep and six inches wide.

This Woodpecker Mr. Ridgway saw only in the Sacramento Valley, where, in June, it appeared to be a common species among the oaks of the plains. He did not learn anything of its habits, but describes its notes as very peculiar, the usual one being a prolonged querulous rattling call, unlike that of any other bird known to him.

Subgenus **PHRENOPICUS**, Bonap.

Phrenopicus, Bonap. Consp. Vol. Zygod. Ateneo Ital. 1854. (Type, *Picus borealis*, Vieill.)
Phrenopipo, Cab. & Hein. Mus. Hein. 1863, 70. Same type.

This subgenus is closely related in external form to the preceding, differing in rather longer and more pointed wings and tail, the latter especially, and a very small, short bill. The first quill (excluding the spurious one) is considerably longer than the sixth, not shorter. The tail-feathers are much attenuated at end. The most marked differences in coloration of the type species, *P. borealis*, consists in the absence of the post-ocular black patch, leaving the whole auricular region white, and in the restriction of the red to a very narrow line on each side, usually concealed.

Some authors place *Picus stricklandi* of Mexico (*Phrenopipo* or *Xylocopus stricklandi*, Cab. and Hein.) in this section, to which it may indeed belong as far as the wing is concerned, but the markings are entirely different.

Picus borealis, VIEILL.

RED-COCKADED WOODPECKER.

Picus borealis, VIEILLOT, Ois. Am. Sept. II, 1807, 66, pl. cxxii. — STEPHENS, in Shaw's
Gen. Zoöl. IX, 1817, 174. — BAIRD, Birds N. Am. 1858, 96. — CASSIN, Pr. A. N. S.
1863, 201. — GRAY, Catal. 1868, 50. — ALLEN, B. E. Fla. 305. — SUNDEVALL, Consp.
1866, 21. *Threnopipo borealis*, CAB. & HEIN. Mus. Hein. IV, 2, 70. *Picus querulus*,
WILSON, Am. Orn. II, 1810, 103, pl. xv, f. 1. — WAGLER, Syst. Av. 1827, No. 21. —
IB. Isis, 1829, 510. — AUD. Orn. Biog. V, 1839, 12, pl. ccclxxxix. — IB. Birds Am. IV,
1842, 254, pl. cclxiv. — BP. Consp. 1850, 137. — CASSIN, Pr. A. N. S. 1863 (southernmost
race). *Picus (Phrenopicus) querulus*, BP. Consp. Zyg. Aten. Ital. 1854, 8. *Picus leucotis*,
ILLIGER (fide Lichtenstein in letter to Wagler ; perhaps only a catalogue name). —
LICHT. Verzeich. 1823, 12, No. 81. *Picus vieilloti*, WAGLER, Syst. Av. 1827, No. 20.

SP. CHAR. Fourth quill (not counting the spurious) longest. First nearer tip of fifth
than of sixth, intermediate between the two. Upper parts, with top and sides of the
head, black. Back, rump, and scapulars banded transversely with white; quills spotted
with white on both webs; middle and greater coverts spotted. Bristles of bill, under
parts generally, and a silky patch on the side of the head, white. Sides of breast and
body streaked with black. First and second outer tail-feathers white, barred with black
on inner web. Outer web of the third mostly white. A short, very inconspicuous
narrow streak of silky scarlet on the side of the head a short distance behind the eye,
along the junction of the white and black (this is wanting in the female) ; a narrow short
line of white just above the eye. Length, about 7.25 ; wing, 4.50 ; tail, 3.25.

HAB. Southern States, becoming very rare north to Pennsylvania.

This species differs from the other banded Woodpeckers, as stated in the
diagnosis, in having a large patch of white behind the eye, including the
ears and sides of head, and not traversed by a black post-ocular stripe. The
bands of the back, as in *P. nuttalli*, do not reach the nape, nor extend over
the upper tail-covert. The white patch occupies almost exactly the same
area as the black one in *nuttalli;* the white space covered by the supra-
orbital and malar stripes, and the white patch on side of nape, of the latter
species being here black.

According to Mr. Cassin, southern specimens which he distinguishes as
P. querulus from *P. borealis* of Pennsylvania, differ in smaller number of
transverse bars on the back, and shorter quills, and in fewer white spots on
the wing-coverts and outer primaries. The black band on the back of neck
is wider. This therefore exhibits the same tendency to melanism, in more
southern specimens, that has been already indicated for *P. villosus, scalaris,*
etc.

HABITS. The Red-cockaded Woodpecker has a restricted distribution to the
Southeastern Atlantic States, being rarely met with so far north as Pennsylvania. Georgia and Florida are the only localities represented in the Smithsonian collection, though other Southern States not named have furnished
specimens. It has been met with as far to the west as Eastern Texas and the
Indian Territory, where Dr. Woodhouse speaks of having found them com-

mon. (Report of an Expedition down the Zuñi and Colorado Rivers, Zoölogy, p. 89.) Wilson only met with it in the pine woods of North Carolina, Georgia, and South Carolina, and does not appear to have been acquainted with its habits. Audubon speaks of it as being found abundantly from Texas to New Jersey, and as far inland as Tennessee, and as nowhere more numerous than in the pine barrens of Florida, Georgia, and the Carolinas. He found these birds mated in Florida as early as January, and engaged in preparing a breeding-place in February. The nest, he states, is not unfrequently bored in a decayed stump about thirty feet high. The eggs he describes as smooth and pure white, and as usually four in number, though he has found as many as six in a nest. The young crawl out of their holes before they are able to fly, and wait on the branches to receive the food brought by their parents until they are able to shift for themselves. During the breeding-season the call of these birds is more than usually lively and petulant, and is reiterated through the pine woods where it is chiefly found.

Wilson compares the common call-notes of these birds to the querulous cries of young birds. His attention was first directed to them by this peculiarity. He characterizes the species as restless, active, and clamorous.

Though almost exclusively a Southern species, and principally found south of North Carolina, individuals have been known to wander much farther north. Mr. G. N. Lawrence obtained a specimen of this bird in Hoboken, N. J., opposite New York City.

In quickness of motion this Woodpecker is said to be equalled by very few of the family. Mr. Audubon states that it glides upwards and sideways, along the trunks and branches, on the lower as well as the upper sides of the latter, moving with great celerity, and occasionally uttering a short, shrill, clear cry, that can be heard at a considerable distance. Mr. Audubon kept a wounded one several days. It soon cut its way out of a cage, and ascended the wall of the room as it would a tree, seizing such spiders and insects as it was able to find. Other than this it would take no food, and was set at liberty.

In the stomach of one dissected were found small ants and a few minute coleopterous insects. In Florida it mates in January and nests in February. In the winter it seeks shelter in holes, as also in stormy weather. Mr. Audubon states that it occasionally feeds on grain and on small fruits. Some go to the ground to search for those that have fallen from trees. They are always found in pairs, and during the breeding-season are very pugnacious.

An egg of this species obtained near Wilmington, N. C., by Mr. N. Giles, measures .95 by .70 of an inch. It is pure white, appeared less glossy than the eggs of most Woodpeckers, and was of a more elliptical shape. Another egg of this bird sent to me by Mr. Samuel Pasco of Monticello, Fla., measures .98 by .70 of an inch, being even more oblong in shape, and corresponds also in the absence of that brilliant polish so common in most Woodpeckers.

SUBGENUS **XENOPICUS**, BAIRD.

Xenopicus, BAIRD, Birds N. Am. 1858, 83. (Type, *Leuconerpes albolarvatus*, CASS.) *Xenocraugus*, CAB. & HEIN. Mus. Hein. IV, 2, 1863, 74. (Same type.)

This section of *Picus* is not appreciably different in form from *Picus villosus*, which may be taken as the American type of the genus *Picus*. The plumage appears softer, however, and the uniformly black body with white head and white patch at base of primaries will readily distinguish it from any allied group.

Picus albolarvatus, BAIRD.

WHITE-HEADED WOODPECKER.

Leuconerpes albolarvatus, CASSIN, Pr. A. N. Sc. V, Oct. 1850, 106 (California). BONAP. Consp. Zyg. At. Ital. 1854, 10. *Melanerpes albolarvatus*, CASSIN, Jour. A. N. Sc. 2d series, II, Jan. 1853, 257, pl. xxii. — NEWBERRY, Zoöl. Cal. and Oreg. Route, 9, Rep. P. R. R. VI, 1857. *Picus (Xenopicus) albolarvatus*, BAIRD, Birds N. Am. 1858, 96. — CASSIN, Pr. A. N. Sc. 1863, 202. — LORD, Pr. R. Art. Ins. IV, 1864, 112 (Ft. Colville ; nesting). — COOPER & SUCKLEY, 160. — ELLIOT, Birds N. Am. IX, plate. *Picus albolarvatus*, SUNDEVALL, Consp. Pic. 29. — COOPER, Orn. Cal. I, 1870, 382. *Xenocraugus albolarvatus*, CAB. & HEIN. Mus. Hein. IV, 2, 1863, 74. *Xenopicus albolarvatus*, ELLIOT, Illust. Birds Am. I, pl. xxix.

SP. CHAR. Fourth and fifth quills equal and longest ; tip of first equidistant between sixth and seventh. Entirely bluish-black, excepting the head and neck, and the outer edges of the primaries (except outermost), and the concealed bases of all the quills, which are white. Length, about 9.00 ; wing, 5.25. Male with a narrow crescent of red on the occiput.

HAB. Cascade Mountains of Oregon and southward into California. Sierra Nevada.

Picus albolarvatus.

HABITS. This very plainly marked Woodpecker, formerly considered very rare, is now known to be abundant in the mountains of Northern California and Nevada, as also in the mountain-ranges of Washington Territory and Oregon. Dr. Cooper found it quite common near the summits of the Sierra Nevada, latitude 39°, in September, 1863, and procured three specimens. Three years previously he had met with it at Fort Dalles, Columbia River. He thinks that its chief range of distribution will be found to be between those two points. He also found it as far north as Fort Colville, in the northern part of Washington Territory, latitude 49°. He characterizes it as a rather silent bird.

Dr. Newberry only met with this bird among the Cascade Mountains, in Oregon, where he did not find it common.

Mr. J. G. Bell, who first discovered this species, in the vicinity of Sutter's Mills, in California, on the American River, represents it as frequenting the higher branches of the pines, keeping almost out of gunshot range. Active and restless in its movements, it uttered at rare intervals a sharp and clear note, while busily pursuing its search for food.

Mr. John K. Lord states that the only place in which he saw this very rare bird was in the open timbered country about the Colville Valley and Spokan River. He has observed that this Woodpecker almost invariably haunts woods of the *Pinus ponderosa*, and never retires into the thick damp forest. It arrives in small numbers at Colville, in April, and disappears again in October and November, or as soon as the snow begins to fall. Although he did not succeed in obtaining its eggs, he saw a pair nesting in the month of May in a hole bored in the branch of a very tall pine-tree. It seldom flies far, but darts from tree to tree with a short jerking flight, and always, while flying, utters a sharp, clear, chirping cry. Mr. Ridgway found it to be common in the pine forests of the Sierra Nevada, in the region of the Donner Lake Pass. It was first observed in July, at an altitude of about five thousand feet, on the western slope of that range, where it was seen playing about the tops of the tallest dead pines. On various occasions, at all seasons, it was afterwards found to be quite plentiful on the eastern slope, in the neighborhood of Carson City, Nevada. Its habits and manners are described as much like those of the *P. harrisi*, but it is of a livelier and more restless disposition. Its notes have some resemblance to those of that species, but are of a more rattling character. It is easily recognized, when seen, by its strikingly peculiar plumage.

Genus **PICOIDES**, Lacep.

Picoides, Lacep. Mem. Inst. 1799.   (Type, *Picus tridactylus.*)
Tridactylia, Steph. Shaw, Gen. Zoöl. 1815.
Apternus, Sw. F. B. A. II, 1831, 311.

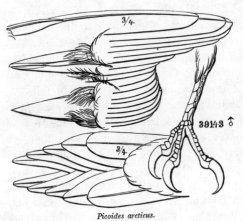

Gen. Char. Bill about as long as the head, very much depressed at the base; the outlines nearly straight; the lateral ridge at its base much nearer the commissure than the culmen, so as to bring the large, rather linear nostrils close to the edge of the commissure. The gonys very long, equal to the distance from the nostrils to the tip of the bill. Feet with only three toes, the first or inner hinder one being wanting; the outer lateral a little longer than the inner, but slightly exceeded by the hind toe, which is about equal to the tarsus. Wings very long, reaching beyond the middle of the tail, the tip of the first quill between those of sixth and seventh.

Picoides arcticus.

Color black above, with a broad patch of yellow on the crown; white beneath, transversely banded on the sides. Quills, but not wing-coverts, with round spots. Lateral tail-feathers white, without bands on exposed portion, except in European specimens.

The peculiarities of this genus consist in the absence of the inner hind toe and the great depression of the bill. The figure above fails to represent the median ridge of the bill as viewed from above.

Common Characters. The American species of *Picoides* agree in being black above and white beneath; the crown with a square yellow patch in the male; a white stripe behind the eye, and another from the loral region beneath the eye; the quills (but not the coverts) spotted with white; the sides banded transversely with black. The diagnostic characters (including the European species) are as follows: —

Species and Varieties.

P. arcticus. Dorsal region without white markings; no supraloral white stripe or streak, nor nuchal band of white. Four middle tail-feathers wholly black; the next pair with the basal half black; the outer two pairs almost wholly white, without any dark bars. Entire sides heavily banded with black; crissum immaculate; sides of the breast continuously black. ♂. Crown with a patch of yellow, varying from lemon, through gamboge, to orange, and not surrounded by any whitish markings or suffusion. ♀. Crown lustrous black, without any yellow, and destitute of white streaks or other markings. Wing, 4.85 to 5.25; tail, 3.60; culmen, 1.40 to 1.55. *Hab.* Northern parts of North America. In winter just within the northern border of the United States, but farther south on high mountain-ranges.

P. tridactylus. Dorsal region with white markings, of various amount and direction ; a more or less distinct supraloral white streak or stripe, and a more or less apparent nuchal band of the same. Four to six middle tail-feathers entirely black ; when six, the remainder are white, with distinct black bars to their ends ; when four, they are white without any black bars, except occasionally a few toward the base. Sides always with black streaks or markings, but they are sometimes very sparse ; crissum banded with black, or immaculate ; sides of the breast not continuously black.   ♂. Crown with a patch of gamboge, amber, or sulphur-yellow, surrounded by a whitish suffusion or markings.   ♀. Crown without any yellow, but distinctly streaked, speckled, or suffused with whitish (very seldom plain black).

    a. Six middle tail-feathers wholly black.   Europe and Asia.

        Sides and crissum heavily barred with black (black bars about as wide as the white ones).

           Back usually transversely spotted with white ; occasionally longitudinally striped with the same in Scandinavian examples. Wing, 4.80 to 5.10 ; tail, 3.80 to 4.00 ; culmen, 1.20 to 1.35. *Hab.* Europe . . . . . . var. *tridactylus.*[1]

        Sides and crissum almost free from black bars ; black bars on the outer tail-feathers very much narrower than the white.

           Back always (?) striped longitudinally with white. Wing, 4.70 to 4.75 ; tail, 3.65 to 3.90 ; culmen, 1.20 to 1.35. *Hab.* Siberia and Northern Russia . . . var. *crissoleucus.*[2]

    b. Four middle tail-feathers, only, wholly black.   North America.

        Sides heavily barred with black, but crissum without bars, except beneath the surface. Three outer tail-feathers without black bars, except sometimes on the basal portion of the inner webs. Wing, 4.40 to 5.10 ; tail, 3.40 to 3.70 ; culmen, 1.10 to 1.25.

           Back transversely spotted or barred with white. *Hab.* Hudson's Bay region ; south in winter to northern border of Eastern United States . . . . . var. *americanus.*

           Back longitudinally striped with white at all seasons. *Hab.* Rocky Mountains ; north to Alaska . . . . var. *dorsalis.*

---

[1] *Picoides tridactylus*, var. *tridactylus.   Picus tridactylus*, LINN. S. N. 12th ed. I, 177 (1766). — DEGLAND, Orn. Eur. I, 161 (1849). *Apternus tridactylus*, BONAP. Birds (1838), p. 9. — GOULD, Birds of Europe, pl. ccxxxii. *Picoides tridactylus*, GRAY. *Picoides europæus*, LESS. Orn. p. 217 (1831).

[2] *Picoides tridactylus*, var. *crissoleucus.   Picus crissoleucus*, BRANDT, Mus. Petrop. *Apternus crissoleucus*, BONAP. Consp. — REICH. Syn. p. 362, No. 836 ; pl. dcxxxi, f. 4197, 4198. *Picoides crissoleucus*, MALH. Monog. Pic. I, 180. *"Apternus kamtchatkensis,* BONAP." — MALH. Monog. Pic. I, 180 (in synonymy). *Apternus tridactylus*, Mus. de Mayence. — PALLAS, Zoogr. Ros. As. I, 415.

Picoides arcticus, GRAY.

THE BLACK-BACKED THREE-TOED WOODPECKER.

Picus (Apternus) arcticus, Sw. F. Bor. Am. II, 1831, 313. *Apternus arcticus*, Bp. List, 1838. — IB. Consp. 1850, 139. — NEWBERRY, Zoöl. Cal. and Oreg. Route, 91, Rep. P. R. R. Surv. VI, 1857. *Picus arcticus*, AUD. Syn. 1839, 182. — IB. Birds Amer. VI, 1842, 266, pl. cclxviii. — NUTTALL, Man. I, (2d ed.,) 1840, 691. — SUNDEVALL, Consp. I, 1866, 15. *Picus tridactylus*, BON. Am. Orn. II, 1828, 14, pl. xiv, f. 2. — AUD. Orn. Biog. II, 1834, 198, pl. cxxxii. *Tridactylia arctica*, CAB. & HEIN. *Picoides arcticus*, GRAY, Gen. — BAIRD, Birds N. Am. 1858, 98. — LORD, Pr. R. Art. Inst. Woolwich, IV, 1864, 112 (Cascade Mountains). — COOPER, Pr. Cal. Ac. Sc. 1868 (Lake Tahoe and Sierra Nevada). — SAMUELS, 94. — COOPER, Orn. Cal. I, 1870, 384.

SP. CHAR. Above entirely uniform glossy bluish-black; a square patch on the middle of the crown saffron-yellow, and a few white spots on the outer edges of both webs of the primary and secondary quills. Beneath white, on the sides of whole body, axillars, and inner wing-coverts banded transversely with black. Crissum white, with a few spots anteriorly. A narrow concealed white line from the eye a short distance backwards, and a white stripe from the extreme forehead (meeting anteriorly) under the eye, and down the sides of the neck, bordered below by a narrow stripe of black. Bristly feathers of the base of the bill brown; sometimes a few gray intermixed. Exposed portion of two outer tail-feathers (first and second) white; the third obliquely white at end, tipped with black. Sometimes these feathers with a narrow black tip.

Picoides arcticus.

HAB. Northern North America; south to northern borders of United States in winter. Massachusetts (MAYNARD, B. E. Mass., 1870, 129). Sierra Nevada, south to 39°. Lake Tahoe (COOPER); Carson City (RIDGWAY).

This species differs from the other American three-toed Woodpeckers chiefly in having the back entirely black. The white line from the eye is usually almost imperceptible, if not wanting entirely. Specimens vary very little; one from Slave Lake has a longer bill than usual, and the top of head more orange. The size of the vertex patch varies; sometimes the frontal whitish is inappreciable. None of the females before me have any white spots in the black of head, as in that of *americanus*.

The variations in this species are very slight, being chiefly in the shade of the yellow patch on the crown, which varies from a sulphur tint to a rich orange. Sometimes there is the faintest trace of a whitish post-ocular streak, but usually this is wholly absent. Western and Eastern examples appear to be identical.

HABITS. This species has a well-defined and extended distribution, from the Pacific to the Atlantic, and from the northern portions of the United States to the extreme Arctic regions. In the United States it has been found as far south as Massachusetts, New York, and Ohio, but rarely; and, so far as I am aware, it is a winter visitant only to any but the extreme northern portions of the Union, except along the line of the Rocky Mountains and the Sierra Nevada. Audubon says it occurs in Northern Massachusetts, and in all portions of Maine that are covered by forests of tall trees, where it constantly resides. He saw a few in the Great Pine Forest of Pennsylvania, and Dr. Bachman noticed several in the neighborhood of Niagara Falls, and was of the opinion that it breeds in the northern part of New York. The same writer describes the nesting-place of the Arctic Woodpecker as generally bored in the body of a sound tree, near its first large branches. He observed no particular choice as to the timber, having seen it in oaks, pines, etc. The nest, like that of most of this family, is worked out by both sexes, and requires fully a week for its completion. Its usual depth is from twenty to twenty-four inches. It is smooth and broad at the bottom, although so narrow at its entrance as to appear scarcely sufficient to enable one of the birds to enter it. The eggs are from four to six, rather rounded and pure white. Only one brood is raised in the season. The young follow their parents until the autumn. In the southern districts where these Woodpeckers are found, their numbers are greatly increased in the winter by accessions from the North.

Dr. Cooper found this species quite numerous, in September, in the vicinity of Lake Tahoe and the summits of the Sierra Nevada, above an altitude of six thousand feet. From thence this bird has a northern range chiefly on the east side of these mountains and of the Cascade Range. None were seen near the Lower Columbia. At the lake they were quite fearless, coming close to the hotel, and industriously rapping the trees in the evening and in the early morning. Farther north Dr. Cooper found them very wild, owing probably to their having been hunted by the Indians for their skins, which they consider very valuable. He noticed their burrows in low pine-trees near the lake, where he had no doubt they also raise their young. Dr. Cooper has always found them very silent birds, though in the spring they probably have more variety of calls. The only note he heard was a shrill, harsh, rattling cry, quite distinct from that of any other Woodpecker.

The flight of this Woodpecker is described as rapid, gliding, and greatly undulated. Occasionally it will fly to quite a distance before it alights, uttering, from time to time, a loud shrill note.

Professor Verrill says this bird is very common in Western Maine, in the spring, fall, and winter, or from the middle of October to the middle or end of March. It is not known to occur there in the summer. Near Calais a few are seen, and it is supposed to breed, but is not common. In Massachusetts it is only a rare and accidental visitant, occurring usually late in winter or in March. Two were taken near Salem in November. It is also a rare winter visitant near Hamilton in Canada.

Mr. Ridgway met with but a single individual of this species during his Western explorations. This was shot in February, near Carson City, Nevada; it was busily engaged in pecking upon the trunk of a large pine, and was perfectly silent.

Mr. John K. Lord obtained a single specimen of this bird on the summit of the Cascade Mountains. It was late in September, and getting cold; the bird was flying restlessly from tree to tree, but not searching for insects. Both when on the wing and when clinging to a tree, it was continually uttering a shrill, plaintive cry. Its favorite tree is the *Pinus contorta*, which grows at great altitudes. It is found chiefly on hill-tops, while in the valleys and lower plains it is replaced by the *Picoides hirsutus*.

Eggs of this species were obtained by Professor Agassiz on the northern shore of Lake Superior. They were slightly ovate, nearly spherical, rounded at one end and abruptly pointed at the other, of a crystal whiteness, and measured .91 of an inch in length by .70 in breadth.

An egg received from Mr. Krieghoff is small in proportion to the size of the bird, nearly spherical in form, and of a uniform dull-white color. It measures .92 of an inch in length by .76 in breadth.

Picoides tridactylus, var. americanus, BREHM.

THE WHITE-BACKED THREE-TOED WOODPECKER.

Picus hirsutus, VIEILLOT, Ois. Am. Sept. II, 1807, 68, pl. cxxiv (European specimen). — WAGLER, Syst. Av. 1827, No. 27 (mixed with *undulatus*). — AUD. Orn. Biog. V, 1839, 184, pl. ccccxvii. — IB. Birds Amer. IV, 1842, pl. cclxix. — NUTTALL, Man. I, (2d ed.,) 1840, 622. *Apternus hirsutus*, BON. List. *Picoides hirsutus*, BAIRD, Birds N. Am. 1858, 98. — SAMUELS, 95. ? *Picus undulatus*, VIEILLOT, Ois. Am. Sept. II, 1807, 69 (based on Pl. enl. 553, fictitious species?) *Picus undatus*, TEMM. *Picus undosus*, CUV. R. A. 1829, 451 (all based on same figure). *Tridactylia undulata*, CAB. & HEIN. Mus. Hein. IV, 2, 1863, 28. *Picus tridactylus*, SW. F. Bor. Am. 1831, 311, pl. lvi. *Picoides americanus*, BREHM Vögel Deutschlands, 1831, 195. — MALHERBE, Mon. Picidæ, I, 176, pl. xvii, 36. — SCLATER, Catal. — GRAY, Cat. Br. Mus. III, 3, 4, 1868, 30. *Apternus americanus*, SWAINSON, Class. II, 1837, 306. *Picus americanus*, SUNDEVALL, Consp. Av. Picin. 1866, 15. *Picoides dorsalis*, BAIRD, Birds N. Am. 1858, 100, pl. lxxxv, f. 1. — COOPER, Orn. Cal. I, 1870 (under *P. americanus*). *Tridactylia dorsalis*, CAB. & HEIN. *Picus dorsalis*, SUNDEVALL, Consp. 1866, 14.

SP. CHAR. Black above. The back markings of white, transverse in summer, and longitudinal in winter; these extend to the rump, which is sometimes almost wholly white. A white line from behind the eye, widening on the nape, and a broader one under the eye from the loral region, but not extending on the forehead; occiput and sides of head uniform black. Quills, but not coverts, spotted on both webs with white, seen on inner webs of inner secondaries. Under parts, including crissum, white; the sides, including axillars and lining of wing, banded transversely with black. Exposed portion of outer three tail-feathers white; that of third much less, and sometimes with a narrow tip of black. Upper tail-coverts sometimes tipped with white, and occasionally, but very rarely, banded with the same. Top of the head spotted, streaked, or suffused with white; the crown of the male with a yellow patch. Nasal bristles black, mixed with gray. Female with the whole top of head usually spotted with white, very rarely entirely black.

HAB. Arctic regions of North America ; southward in the Rocky Mountains to Fort Buchanan; northern border of the Eastern United States, in winter (Massachusetts, MAYNARD).

This species varies considerably in its markings, especially in the amount of white above. The head is sometimes more coarsely spotted with white than in the average ; very rarely are the white spots wanting, leaving merely the broad malar and interrupted post-ocular stripe. The rictal black stripe is sometimes much obscured by white. In typical specimens from the Hudson Bay and Labrador Provinces, which seem to be darkest, the feathers of the centre of the back have three transverse bars of white (one of them terminal), rather narrower than the intermediate black bars ; the basal white ones disappearing both anteriorly and posteriorly, leaving but two. In specimens from the Mackenzie River district there is a greater development of white ; the white bands being broader than the black, and sometimes extending along the shafts so as to reduce the black bars to pairs of spots. The next step is the disappearance of these spots on one side or the other, or on both, leaving the end of the feathers entirely white, especially anteriorly, where the back may have a longitudinal stripe of white, as in *Picus villosus*. Usually, however, in this extreme, the upper tail-coverts remain banded transversely. In all the specimens from the Rocky Mountains of the United States, especially Laramie Peak, this white back, unbarred except on the rump, is a constant character, and added to it we have a broad nuchal patch of white running into that of the back and connected with the white post-ocular stripe. The bands, too, on the sides of the body, are less distinct. It was to this state of plumage that the name of *P. dorsalis* was applied, in 1858, and although in view of the connecting links it may not be entitled to consideration as a distinct race, this tendency to a permanence of the longitudinal direction of the white markings above seems to be especially characteristic of the Rocky Mountain region, appearing only in winter birds from elsewhere. This same character prevails in all the Rocky Mountain specimens from more northern regions, including those from Fort Liard, and in only one not found in that region, namely, No. 49,905, collected at Nulato by Mr. Dall. Here the middle of the back is very white, although the nuchal band is less distinct. Other specimens from that locality and the Yukon River generally, as also from Kodiak, distinctly show the transverse bars.

In one specimen (29,126) from the Mackenzie River, all the upper tail-coverts are banded decidedly with white, and the wing-coverts spotted with the same. Even the central tail-feathers show white scallops. The back is, however, banded transversely very distinctly, not longitudinally.

P. americanus in all stages of color is distinguished from *arcticus* by the white along the middle of the back, the absence of distinct frontal white and black bands, more numerous spots of white on the head, etc. The inner webs of inner secondaries are banded with white, not uniform black. The maxillary black stripe is rather larger than the rictal white one, not smaller. The size is decidedly smaller. Females almost always have the top of head spotted with white instead of uniform black, which is the rule in *arcticus*.

It is probable that the difference in the amount of white on the upper parts of this species is to some extent due to age and season, the winter specimens and the young showing it to the greatest degree. Still, however, there is a decided geographical relationship, as already indicated.

This race of *P. tridactylus* can be easily distinguished from the European form of Northern and Alpine Europe by the tail-feathers; of these, the outer three are white (the rest black) as far as exposed, without any bands; the tip of the third being white only at the end. The supra-ocular white stripe is very narrow and scarcely appreciable; the crissum white and unbanded. The back is banded transversely in one variety, striped longitudinally in the other. In *P. tridactylus* the outer two feathers on each side are white, banded with black; the outer with the bands regular and equal from base; the second black, except one or two terminal bands. The crissum is well banded with black; the back striped longitudinally with white; the supra-ocular white stripe almost as broad as the infra-ocular. *P. crisoleucus*, of Siberia, is similar to the last, but differs in white crissum, and from both species in the almost entire absence of dark bands on the sides, showing the Arctic maximum of white.

We follow Sundevall in using the specific name *americanus*, Brehm, for this species, as being the first legitimately belonging to it. *P. hirsutus* of Vieillot, usually adopted, is based on a European bird, and agrees with it, though referred by the author to the American. The name of *undulatus*, Vieillot, selected by Cabanis, is based on Buffon's figure (Pl. enl. 553) of a bird said to be from Cayenne, with four toes; the whole top of the head red from base of bill to end of occiput, with the edges of the dorsal feathers narrowly white, and with the three lateral tail-feathers regularly banded with black, tipped with red; the fourth, banded white and black on outer web, tipped with black. None of those features belong to the bird of Arctic America, and the markings answer, if to either, better to the European.

HABITS. This rare and interesting species, so far as has been ascertained, is nowhere a common or well-known bird. It is probably exclusively of Arctic residence, and only occasionally or very rarely is found so far south as Massachusetts. In the winter of 1836 I found a specimen exposed for sale in the Boston market, which was sent in alcohol to Mr. Audubon. Two specimens have been taken in Lynn, by Mr. Welch, in 1868. They occur, also, in Southern Wisconsin in the winter, where Mr. Kumlien has several times, in successive winters, obtained single individuals.

Sir John Richardson states that this bird is to be met with in all the forests of spruce and fir lying between Lake Superior and the Arctic Sea, and that it is the most common Woodpecker north of Great Slave Lake, whence it has frequently been sent to the Smithsonian Institution. It is said to greatly resemble *P. villosus* in habits, except that it seeks its food principally upon decaying trees of the pine tribe, in which it frequently makes holes large enough to bury itself. It is not migratory.

Genus **SPHYROPICUS**, BAIRD.

Pilumnus, BON. Consp. Zygod. Ateneo Italiano, May, 1854. (Type *P. thyroideus*) preoccupied in crustaceans.

Sphyropicus, BAIRD, Birds N. Am. 1858, 101. (Type, *Picus varius*, LINN., COUES, Pr. A. N. S. 1866, 52 (anatomy).

Cladoscopus, CAB. & HEIN. Mus. Hein. IV, 2, 1863, 80. (Type, *P. varius*.)

GEN. CHAR. Bill as in *Picus*, but the lateral ridge, which is very prominent, running out distinctly to the commissure at about its middle, beyond which the bill is rounded without any angles at all. The culmen and gonys are very nearly straight, but slightly convex, the bill tapering rapidly to a point; the lateral outline concave to very near the slightly bevelled tip. Outer pair of toes longest; the hinder exterior rather longest; the inner posterior toe very short, less than the inner anterior without its claw.

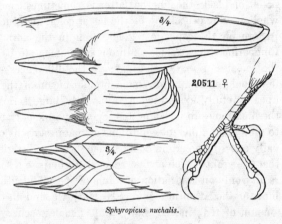

Sphyropicus nuchalis.

Wings long and pointed; the third, excluding the spurious, longest. Tail-feathers very broad, abruptly acuminate, with a very long linear tip. Tongue scarcely extensible.

The genus *Sphyropicus*, instituted in 1858, proves to be so strongly marked in its characters that Dr. Coues proposes to make it the type of a distinct subfamily, *Sphyropicinæ* (Pr. Phil. Acad. 1866, 52). In addition to the peculiarities already indicated, there is a remarkable feature in the tongue, which, according to Dr. Coues, Dr. Hoy, Dr. Bryant, and others, is incapable of protrusion much beyond the tip of the bill, or not more than the third of an inch. Dr. Coues states that the apo-hyal and cerato-hyal elements of the hyoid bone do not reach back much beyond the tympano-maxillary articulation, instead of extending round, as in *Picus*, over the occiput to the top of the cranium, or even curving into an osseous groove around the orbit. The basihyals supporting the tongue are shorter and differently shaped. The tongue itself is short and flattened, with a superior longitudinal median groove and a corresponding inferior ridge; the tip is broad and flattened and obtusely rounded, and with numerous long and soft bristly hairs. This is, of course, very different from the long, extensile, acutely pointed tongue of other Woodpeckers, with its tip armed with a few strong, sharp, short, recurved barbs.

Dr. Hoy and Dr. Coues maintain that the food of these Woodpeckers consists mainly of the cambium or soft inner bark of trees, which is cut out in patches sometimes of several inches in extent, and usually producing square holes in the bark, not rounded ones. As may be supposed, such proceedings are very injurious to the trees, and justly call down the vengeance of their proprietors. This diet is varied with insects and fruits, when they can be had, but it is believed that cambium is their principal sustenance.

This strongly marked genus appears to be composed of two sections and three well-defined species; the first being characterized by having the back variegated with whitish, and the jugulum with a sharply defined crescentic patch of black, though the latter is sometimes concealed by red, when the whole head and neck are of the latter color, and the sharply defined striped pattern of the cephalic regions, seen in the normal plumage, obliterated. Comparing the extreme conditions of plumage to be seen in this type, as in the females of *varius* and of *ruber*, the differences appear wide indeed, and few would entertain for a moment a suspicion of their specific identity; yet upon carefully examining a sufficiently large series of specimens, we find these extremes to be connected by an unbroken transition, and are thus led to view these different conditions as manifestations of a peculiar law principally affecting a certain color, which leads us irresistibly to the conclusion that the group which at first seemed to compose a section of the genus is in reality only an association of forms of specific identity. Beginning with the birds of the Atlantic region (*S. varius*), we find in this series the minimum amount of red; indeed, many adult females occur which lack this color entirely, having not only the whole throat white, but the entire pileum glossy-black; usually, however, the latter is crimson. In adult males from this region the front and crown are always crimson, sharply defined, and bordered laterally and posteriorly with glossy-black; and below the black occipital band is another of dirty white; the crimson of the throat is wholly confined between the continuous broad, black malar stripes, and there is no tinge of red on the auriculars; there is a broad, sharply defined stripe of white beginning with the nasal tufts, passing beneath the black loral and auricular stripe, and continuing downward into the yellowish of the abdomen, giving the large, glossy-black pectoral area a sharply defined outline; the dirty whitish nuchal band is continued forward beneath the black occipital crescent to above the middle of the eye. The pattern just described will be found in ninety-nine out of a hundred specimens from the Eastern Province of North America (also the West Indies and whole of Mexico); but a single adult male, from Carlisle, Penn. (No. 12,071, W. M. Baird), has the whitish nuchal band distinctly tinged with red, though differing in this respect only, while an adult female, from Washington, D. C. (No. 12,260, C. Drexler), has the lower part of the throat much mixed with red.

Taking next the specimens from the Rocky Mountains and Middle Province of the United States (*S. nuchalis*), we find that *all* the specimens possess *both* these additional amounts of the red, there being always a red, instead of dirty-white, nuchal crescent, while in the female the lower part of the throat is always more or less red ; in addition, the male has the red of the throat reaching laterally to the white stripe, thus interrupting the black malar one, which is always unbroken in the eastern form ; and in addition, the auriculars are frequently mixed with red. Proceeding towards the Columbia River, we find the red increasing, or escaping the limits to which it is confined in the normal pattern, staining the white and black areas in different places, and tingeing the whitish which borders the black pectoral area.

Lastly, in the series from the Pacific coast (*S. ruber*), we find the whole normal pattern rendered scarcely definable — sometimes entirely obliterated — by the extension of the red, which covers continuously the whole head, neck, and breast ; but nearly always the normal pattern may be traced, the feathers of the normally black areas being dusky beneath the surface, and those of the usual white stripes very white for the concealed portion. Usually, in this form, the red of the breast covers only the black pectoral area ; but in extreme specimens it reaches back to the middle of the body beneath, and stains the white spots of the back.

With the increase of the red as we proceed westward, there is also a decrease in the amount of white above ; thus, in *varius* the whole back is irregularly spotted with dirty white and black, — the former predominating, the latter most conspicuous as a medial, broken broad stripe, — and the lateral tail-feathers are much variegated by white spots. In *nuchalis* the back is mostly unbroken glossy-black, with two parallel *narrow* stripes of white converging at their lower ends ; and the lateral tail-feather is almost wholly black, having merely a narrow white border toward the end. *S. ruber* is most like *nuchalis*, but has the white still more restricted.

In *varius* the bill is dark brown, in *nuchalis* it is deep black, and in *ruber* wax-brown. In *varius* the yellow of the lower parts is deepest, in *nuchalis* just appreciable.

Species and Varieties.

A. Wing with a white patch on the middle and greater coverts. Markings along the sides with a longitudinal tendency.

    1. **S. varius.** Back variegated medially with brownish-white ; secondaries with transverse rows of white spots.

        White and black stripes on side of head sharply defined, as is also the black pectoral crescent. Red confined to isolated patches, — two large ones, one on the crown and one on the throat ; when there is more, only a tinge on the auriculars, and a crescent on nape.

      Crown sometimes glossy black without a trace of red on the female ; no tinge of scarlet on the nape. Red of the throat entirely confined within the broad, continuous black maxillary stripe. *Female* with the throat wholly white. *Hab.* Eastern Province North America, south in winter into West Indies, and over whole of Mexico, to Guatemala . . . . var. *varius.*

Crown always red in adult. A nuchal crescent of scarlet in both sexes. Red of the throat not confined by the black maxillary stripe, which is interrupted by it in the middle, allowing the red to touch the white stripe; a tinge of red on the auriculars. *Female* always with more or less red on lower part of the throat. *Hab.* Rocky Mountains and Middle Province of United States . . . . var. *nuchalis.*

White and black stripes on side of head obsolete, as is also the black pectoral crescent, caused by being overspread by a continuous red wash extending over whole head, neck, and breast.

Whole head, neck, and breast red, with the light and dark stripes of the normal pattern only faintly traceable. Sexes similar. *Hab.* Pacific Province of United States, north to British Columbia . . var. *ruber.*

2. **S. williamsoni.** Back unvariegated; secondaries without bands of white spots.

Whole crown and upper parts (except lower part of rump and upper tail-coverts, and wing-patch), a stripe on side of head, a broader one on side of the throat, and the whole jugulum and sides of the breast, unbroken glossy-black; abdomen bright lemon-yellow. *Male* with a narrow stripe of scarlet on middle of the throat. *Female* with it white. *Young* like the adult. *Hab.* Western Province of United States.

B. Wing without a white patch. Markings on sides regularly transverse.

3. **S. thyroideus.** Head all round light brown; abdomen bright lemon-yellow; rump and upper tail-coverts white. Entire upper surface, with sides, regularly and continuously barred with black and white, in nearly equal amount; the black bars usually coalesced on the jugulum into a more or less extensive patch. *Male* with the throat tinged medially with scarlet. *Female* without any red. *Hab.* Western Province of United States.

Sphyropicus varius, var. varius, BAIRD.

THE YELLOW-BELLIED WOODPECKER.

Picus varius, L. Syst. Nat. I, 1766, 176. — VIEILLOT, Ois. Am. II, 1807, 63, pl. cxviii, cxix. — WILSON, Am. Orn. I, 1808, 147, pl. ix, f. 2. — WAGLER, Syst. Av. 1827, No. 16. — AUD. Orn. Biog. II, 1834, 519 ; V, 537, pl. 190. — IB. Birds Amer. IV, 1842, 263, pl. cclxvii. — BON. List, 1838. — IB. Consp. 1850, 138. — MAXIM. Cab. Jour. VI, 1858, 416 (refers to peculiar tongue). — GOSSE, Birds Jam. 270 (Jamaica). — NEW-TON, Ibis, 1860, 308 (St. Croix). — TAYLOR, Ibis, 1860, 119 (Honduras). — SUNDE-VALL, Consp. 33. — GRAY, Cat. 51. *Picus (Dendrocopus) varius.* SW. F. B. A. II, 1831, 309. *Pilumnus varius,* BON. Consp. Zygod. Aten. Ital. 1854, 8. *Cladoscopus varius,* CAB. & HEIN. Mus. 80. ? *Picus atrothorax,* LESSON, Traité d'Ornithologie, I, 1831, 229. — PUCHERAN, Rev. Zoöl. VII, 1835, 21. (Refers it to *Picus varius.*) *Yellow-bellied Woodpecker,* PENNANT, LATHAM. *Sphyropicus varius,* BAIRD, Birds N. Am. 1858, 103. — SCLATER, P. Z. S. 1859, 367 (Xalapa). — IB. Catal. 335 (Orizaba). — IB. Ibis, 1859, 136 (Guatemala). — IB. 1860, 119 (Honduras). — CAB. Journal, IV, 1856, 102. — GUNDLACH, Repertorium, I, 1866, 294 (Cuba). — BRYANT, Pr. Bost. Soc. 1859 (Bahamas). — IB. 1865, 91 (Anatomy of tongue.) — DRESSER, Ibis, 1865, 468 (breeds in Texas). — SAMUELS, 96. — ALLEN, B. E. Fla. 306.

SP. CHAR. Third quill longest; second a little shorter; first between fourth and fifth considerably shorter. General color above black, much variegated with white. Feathers of the back and rump brownish-white, spotted with black. Crown crimson, bordered by black on the sides of the head and nape. A streak from above the eye, and a broad stripe from the bristles of the bill, passing below the eye, and into the yellowish of the belly, enclosing a black post-ocular one, and a stripe along the edges of the wing-coverts, white. A triangular broad patch of scarlet on the chin, bordered on each side by black stripes from the lower mandible which meet behind, and extend into a large quadrate spot on the breast. Rest of under parts yellowish-white, or yellow, streaked and banded on the sides with black. Inner web of inner tail-feather white, spotted with black. Outer feathers black, edged and spotted with white.

Sphyropicus varius.

Quills spotted with white. Length, 8.25 ; wing, about 4.75 ; tail, 3.30. *Female* with the red of the throat replaced by white. Immature bird without black on the breast, or red on top of the head, as in every intermediate stage to the perfect plumage.

HAB. Atlantic coast to the eastern slopes of the Rocky Mountains ; Greenland ; West Indies ; whole of Mexico, to Guatemala. Localities : ? Oaxaca (SCL. P. Z. S. 1858, 305) ; Orizaba (SCL. Cat. 335) ; Xalapa (SCL. 1859, 367) ; Yucatan (LAWR. Ann. N. Y. Lyc. IX, 205) ; Guatemala (SCL. Ibis, I, 136) ; Honduras (SCL. Ibis, II, 119) ; Cuba (CAB. J. IV, 102) ; (GUNDL. Repert. I, 1866, 294) ; Bahamas (BRYANT, Pr. Bost. Soc. VII, 1859 ; IB. 1867, 65) ; Jamaica (GOSSE, B. Jam. 270) ; St. Croix (SCL. Ibis, II, 308) ; E. Texas (DRESSER, Ibis, 1865, 468 ; breeds).

There is an occasional variation in the markings of the tail-feathers. Thus, in No. 782, from Carlisle, the innermost one is entirely black, while in 4,631, from the Upper Missouri, the outer web of the same feather has nearly, and in 2,107, from Carlisle, it has quite, as much white as the inner web. The outer webs do not appear to vary so much.

Specimens from the whole of Mexico, including even the west coast, are referrible to *varius;* they are probably winter migrants from the eastern United States.

A female, from Washington, D. C. (No. 12,260, C. Drexler), has the lower half of the throat much mixed with red, as in var. *nuchalis;* but there is no trace of this color on the nape. A male from Carlisle (No. 12,071, W. M. Baird) has the nape distinctly tinged with red, as in *nuchalis,* but the black malar stripe is uninterrupted. Similar specimens have been taken in New England, by Messrs. Brewster and Henshaw.

Many females occur with the entire pileum glossy-black, there being no trace of red, though there are sometimes specks of white.

HABITS. The Yellow-bellied Woodpecker is found throughout the United States, from the Gulf of Mexico on the south and the Atlantic on the east to the Rocky Mountains, and is met with as far to the north as the 61st parallel of latitude. Sir John Richardson found it common in the fur countries, being the only Woodpecker that visits those regions in flocks. He observed the Yellow-bellied Woodpecker on the north shore of Lake Huron on the 14th of April, in 1825, and in 1827 it made its first appearance for the season, on the plains of the Saskatchewan, on the 14th of May. Swainson received specimens of this Woodpecker from Mexico. De la Sagra and Dr. Gundlach both give it in their list of Cuban birds, though not as breeding on that island. Gosse obtained several specimens in the months of December, January, and February, in Jamaica, where he regarded it as only a winter migrant from the northern continent. It is not given by the Newtons among the birds of St. Croix, but appears in Sclater's list of the birds of Central America, on the authority of Mr. George M. Skinner. Two specimens have been taken in Greenland.

Wilson, in his account of its breeding habits, speaks of it as a resident bird from Cayenne to Hudson's Bay, as being common in the States of Kentucky and Ohio, and as having been found in the neighborhood of St. Louis. He describes the habits of this species as similar to those of the Hairy and Downy Woodpeckers, with which it generally associates. The only nest of this bird which Wilson ever met with was in the body of an old pear-tree, about ten or eleven feet from the ground. The hole was almost exactly circular, small for the size of the bird, so that it crept in and out with difficulty; but the excavation suddenly widened, descending by a small angle, and then running downward about fifteen inches. On the smooth solid wood lay four white eggs. This was about the 25th of May.

Mr. Audubon, on the other hand, speaks of this species as returning to Louisiana and the other Southern States only about the beginning of October, remaining there during the winter, and again taking its departure before the beginning of April, after which period he never observed it in those districts. A few only, according to the same authority, breed in Kentucky, but the greater number migrate to the more northern parts of the Union. He describes it, in its habits, as preferring the interior of the forest during the spring and summer, seldom showing itself near the habitation of man at those seasons. It generally, he adds, bores its nest at a considerable height, and usually in the trunk of an undecayed tree, immediately beneath a large branch, and on its southern side. The hole is worked out by the male as well as the female, in the manner followed by the other species, and to the depth of from fifteen to twenty-four inches. The aperture is just large enough to admit the birds, but the whole widens gradually towards the bottom, where it is large and roomy. The eggs, which are from four to six, and pure white, with a slight blush, are deposited on the chips without any nest. The young seldom leave the hole until they are fully fledged.

Mr. Audubon elsewhere speaks of having found this species extremely abundant in the upper parts of the State of Maine and in the Provinces of Nova Scotia and New Brunswick; but he saw none in Newfoundland or Labrador.

For my specimens of the eggs of this species and valuable information as to its habits, I am indebted to Mr. Charles S. Paine, of East Bethel, Vt., in which State it seems to be quite abundant. In a letter written in the summer of 1860, he furnishes the results of his observations relative to their habits, so far as they have fallen under his notice.

The Yellow-bellied Woodpeckers reach the central and northern parts of that State about the 10th of April. They soon make their presence known there by their loud and continued drumming, rather than tapping, on the trunks and larger branches of decaying trees. Of this drumming they seem to be peculiarly fond, especially where they can produce a loud ringing sound. Sometimes, when Mr. Paine had been engaged in the process of preparing maple sugar, he had left a few empty wooden buckets hanging on the branches of trees, until needed for use. Upon these the bird will drum, apparently with the greatest delight. At times they would experiment upon the tin pails, but, being unable to obtain good standing-ground, they did not follow it up. On such occasions their drumming did not appear to be done in the pursuit of worms or food, but was very evidently for their own entertainment, or in a spirit of rivalry one with another, as if seeking to please their mates. When two male birds meet, they pursue each other through the woods with great clamor. They have a loud, distinct, and lively note, but their favorite music appears to be this drumming. They mate and commence the excavation of their nests the last week in April. Their eggs are usually deposited, in this section, somewhere between the 20th of May and the first of June. The excavations for their nests are usually made in the tops of large decaying trees. He adds that he found four or five of these nests that year. The eggs of one of these he was able to obtain without much trouble, the others had hatched. When the young leave their nests they usually keep together, and often four or five may be seen playing about the bark of the same tree while waiting for their parents to bring them their food.

This species is far more abundant at the West than it is in the New England States. In the States of Rhode Island, Connecticut, and Massachusetts it is very rarely met with. It is commonly known as the Sap-Sucker, and much better deserves that name than do other species to which this term is also applied. Owing to the peculiar formation of its tongue and the muscles connected with it, it feeds less readily upon insects, and they form a smaller proportion of its food. In the spring of the year these birds prey largely upon the inner bark of trees, and where they exist in great numbers often do a great deal of mischief. In April, 1868, I visited gardens in Racine, in company with Dr. Hoy, where these Woodpeckers had every successive spring committed their ravages, and was eyewitness to their performance. Their punctures were unlike those of the *pubescens*, being much deeper, penetrating the inner bark, and, being repeated in close proximity, becomes entirely stripped off after a while, often resulting in the girdling and complete destruction of the tree. In one garden of some considerable size, all the mountain-ash and white-pine trees had thus been killed. In prairie countries, where trees are a deficiency and their cultivation both important and attended with difficulty, these birds prove a great pest, and in a few hours may destroy the labor of many years. These habits, so well known to most of our Western farmers, appear to have entirely escaped the notice of our older ornithologists.

Mr. Dresser found these birds near San Antonio at all seasons of the year, but rather rare. He shot a couple near the Medina River, and Dr. Heermann also procured the eggs in that neighborhood.

Mr. Ridgway says that in Southern Illinois this Woodpecker is only a winter resident, coming from the north in September or October, and departing in April. It is the only one of the eight species of Woodpeckers of that section which does not breed there, and also the only one which is not resident.

Specimens of its eggs from Vermont measure .95 by .70 of an inch. They are of an oval shape, a little less rounded at one end than at the other.

Sphyropicus varius, var. nuchalis, BAIRD.

THE RED-NAPED WOODPECKER.

Sphyropicus varius, var. *nuchalis*, BAIRD, Birds N. Am. 1858, 103, pl. xxxv, figs. 1, 2. *Sphyropicus nuchalis*, BAIRD, Ib. 921. — COUES, Pr. A. N. Sc. 1866, 53. — COOPER, Pr. Cal. Ac. 1861, 122. — CASS. P. A. N. S. 1863, 204. — COOPER, Orn. Cal. I, 1870, 390. *Picus varius occidentalis*, SUNDEVALL, Consp. Pic. 1866, 34. *Cladoscopus nuchalis*, CAB. & HEIN. 82.

Sp. Char. Markings, generally, as in *S. varius*. A red nuchal crescent. Belly yellowish-white. The red of the throat extending over and obliterating the black stripe from the lower mandible, except on the side of the jaw. Post-ocular black patch tinged with red. Secondaries with little or no white on outer webs. Tail-feathers black, scarcely varied; the innermost with inner web, as in *varius*. Female similar, but with the chin white; the throat red, bordered, as in male, by a black stripe from the bill to the black pectoral patch. Length, 8.00; wing, 5.00; tail, 3.50.

Hab. Middle Province of United States. Localities: Fort Mohave (Cooper, Pr. Cal. Ac. 1861, 122); W. Arizona (Coues, P. A. N. S. 1866, 53).

This bird, first indicated as a simple variety of *S. varius*, is yet as decidedly distinct and constant in its markings as a large number of what are considered to be valid species. The principal differences from *varius* have been mentioned above: they consist mainly in the greater development of red, as seen in wider throat-patch; nuchal crescent; tinge on cheek; a greater amount of black, shown in unspotted outer webs of secondaries and blacker tail, and in the paler colors below. The most striking peculiarity is in the half-red throat of the female, which is entirely white in *varius*. The light markings of the back are more distinctly arranged in two lines enclosing a median of black, which show no concealed white spots as in *varius*. The breast is much paler, only slightly tinged with yellow, instead of the rich color to which *S. varius* owes its trivial name.

Young birds vary in color to the same excessive degree as in *varius*.

Habits. This form, closely allied to the *varius*, was at first known only from the southern Rocky Mountains. Afterwards a large number of specimens were obtained by Mr. C. Drexler at Fort Bridger, in Utah.

Dr. Cooper procured a female specimen of this species at Fort Mohave, on the 20th of February, 1861, which had probably wandered in a storm from the mountains, and which was the only one he met with. Dr. Heermann states, also, that they were not rare at Fort Yuma. Dr. Cooper's bird was silent and inactive, as if exhausted by a long flight. He also saw these birds rather common as he crossed the mountains near latitude 48° in September, 1860, and noticed a great similarity in their habits to those of the *S. varius*. They chiefly frequented small deciduous trees, fed in the usual manner of other Woodpeckers, and had also a shrill, unvaried call or note of alarm.

Dr. Coues found this Woodpecker an abundant and a permanent resident in Arizona. Its distinctness as a species he did not question. Everywhere common, it seemed to prefer live cottonwood-trees and willows. Two specimens of this race have been taken in New England, — one in New Hampshire by Mr. William Brewster, the other in Cambridge by Mr. Henshaw.

The Red-naped Woodpecker was found by Mr. Ridgway to be one of the most abundant and characteristic species of the Wahsatch and Uintah Mountains. It was also found, in greater or less numbers, throughout the Great Basin, in the region of his route, and was even obtained on the eastern Sierra Nevada, where, however, only one specimen was seen. Its favorite resort, during summer, was the aspen groves in the mountains, at an altitude averaging about seven thousand feet; and even when pine woods were near the aspens were invariably chosen as nesting-places. Its excavations were always in living trees, and the abandoned ones were taken possession of by Purple Martins and White-bellied Swallows (*Progne subis* and *Tachycineta bicolor*) as nesting-places. In winter it was found among the cottonwoods and willows of the river valleys. Its habits, manners, and notes are described as almost perfectly similar to those of *S. varius.*

Sphyropicus varius, var. ruber, Baird.

THE RED-BREASTED WOODPECKER.

Picus ruber, Gm. Syst. Nat. I, 1788, 429. — Wagler, Syst. Av. 1827, No. 151. — Aud. Orn. Biog. V, 1839, 179, pl. ccccxvi. — Ib. Birds Amer. IV, 1842, 261, pl. cclxvi. — Sundevall, Consp. Pic. 32. *Melanerpes ruber*, Rich. List, Pr. Br. Assoc. for 1835. — Bonap. List, 1838. — Ib. Consp. 1850, 115. *Pilumnus ruber*, Bon. Consp. Zyg. Aten. Ital. 1854, 8. *Picus flaviventris*, Vieillot, Ois. Am. Sept. II, 1807, 67. *Sphyropicus ruber*, Baird, Birds N. Am. 1858, 104. — Cooper & Suckley, 160. — Gray, Cat. 51. — Cooper, Orn. Cal. I, 1870, 392. *Cladoscopus ruber*, Cab. & Hein. Mus. Hein. IV, 1863, 82.

Sp. Char. Fourth quill longest; third intermediate between fourth and fifth. Bill brown wax-color. Head and neck all round, and breast, carmine-red. Above black, central line of back from nape to rump spotted with whitish; rump, wing-coverts, and inner web of the inner tail-feathers white, the latter with a series of round black spots. Belly sulphur-yellow, streaked with brown on the sides. Narrow space around and a little in front of the eye black. A yellowish stripe from the nostrils, a short distance below and behind the eye. Length, about 8.50; wing, 5.00; tail, 3.40. Sexes similar.

Hab. Pacific slopes of the United States.

As stated in the remarks before the synopsis on page 1133, there is every reason for considering this as merely a geographical race of a species, of which *nuchalis* and *varius* are the other forms. The differences from *varius* consist merely in an excessive amount of red, this obliterating the normal pattern of the cephalic portions; and in an increased amount of black, or a manifestation of the melanistic tendency so often distinguishing birds of the Pacific coast region from their eastern co-specific representatives.

S. nuchalis is exactly intermediate in all respects between *S. ruber* and *S. varius*, — the extremes, — while each of the latter is connected with the intermediate race by specimens combining the characters of both races.

Habits. The geographical distribution of this form seems to be restricted to the Pacific coast region.

Dr. Cooper only met with these birds three times in Washington Territory. This was in spring and fall. He speaks of them as being very shy, silent, and retiring, remaining among the dense tops of the dark forest trees. Whether it resides and breeds in the Territory he had no means of determining. Dr. Suckley saw but one specimen, and regarded it as confined, for the most part, to the close vicinity of the coast.

Mr. Audubon assigns to it the same distribution, but is only able to give the information in regard to its habits which he derived from the observations of Mr. Nuttall, which, however, do not correspond with those of Dr. Cooper. Mr. Nuttall states that this species, seen in the forests of the Columbia and the Blue Mountains, has most of the habits of the common Red-headed species. He concedes that it is less familiar, and that it keeps generally among the tall fir-trees, in the dead trunks of which it burrows out a hole for a nest, sometimes at a great elevation. On approaching one that was feeding its young in one of these situations, it uttered a loud reverberating *t'rr*, and seemed angry and solicitous at his approach. He adds that this species also inhabits California, as well as the northwest coast up to Nootka, and that it is found eastward as far as the central chain of the Rocky Mountains. An egg taken from a nest which contained four was 1.25 iu length and .75 of an inch in breadth. It was smooth, equally rounded at both ends, though somewhat elongated, and pure white.

We are confident that there must be some mistake in this statement. The disproportion between the length and the breadth is unprecedented. Even in the most oblong egg there is rarely so much as twenty-five per cent difference.

Dr. Cooper, in his Birds of California, speaks of it as rather a northern bird, having seen none south of Santa Clara, and there only in the mountains of the Coast Range in early spring.

Dr. Heermann found this form not at all rare in the Sierra Nevada Mountains, and occasionally met a stray one among the valleys. Their call-note was similar to the cry of a child in distress, and was very disagreeable. In their quick, restless motions, and their untiring diligence in quest of food, they resemble the rest of the Woodpecker family.

It was noticed by Mr. Ridgway only on the Sierra Nevada, and he is not certain that he saw it on the eastern slope of that range.

Sphyropicus williamsoni, BAIRD.

WILLIAMSON'S WOODPECKER.

Picus williamsoni, NEWBERRY, Zoöl. California and Oregon Route, 89, P. R. R. Repts. VI, 1857, pl. xxxiv, fig. 1. — SUNDEVALL, Consp. 32. *Melanerpes rubrigularis*, SCL. Annals and Mag. N. H. 3d series, I, Feb. 1858, 127. — Pr. Zoöl. Soc. 1858, 2, pl. cxxxi. *Sphyropicus williamsoni*, BAIRD, Birds N. Am. 1858, 105, pl. xxxiv, f. 1. — COUES, Pr. 1866, 54. — CASS. P. A. N. S. 1863, 204. — COOPER, Orn. Cal. I, 1870, 393. *Cladoscopus williamsoni*, CAB. & HEIN. Mus. Hein. IV, 1863, 82. *Melanerpes williamsoni*, GRAY, Catal. Br. Mus. 1868, 116.

SP. CHAR. Rich black ; middle line of belly yellow ; central line of chin and throat above red. A large patch on the wing, rump, and upper tail-coverts, a line from the forehead beneath the eye, and another from its upper border, white. Tail entirely black. Exposed surface of quills without any white, except on the outer primaries. Female with the chin white instead of red. Length, 9.00; wing, 5.00; tail, 4.70.

HAB. Rocky Mountains to the Cascade Mountains, Sierra Nevada. Localities: West Arizona (COUES, P. A. N. S. 1866, 54).

Head and neck all round, sides of breast and body, upper parts generally, wings, and tail, glossy greenish-black. A well-defined white stripe from the nostrils (including the bristly nasal feathers) passing backwards under the eye; another, nearly parallel, starting at the upper part of the eye, and nearly meeting its fellow on the occiput. Chin and throat red along their central line. A large patch on the wing, including the exposed portions of the middle and greater coverts, white, although the anterior lesser coverts are black. The inner face of the wings, excepting the smaller coverts, is black, banded transversely on the inner primaries with white; the sides of body behind and under tail-coverts white, with broadly V-shaped bands of black, which color on the latter occupies the whole central portion of the feathers. Rump and upper tail-coverts pure white; back with a few indistinct and concealed spots of the same. Quills black; the margins of exterior primaries spotted with white, the inner margins only of the remaining quills with similar but larger and more transverse blotches. Middle of the body, from the breast to the vent, sulphur-yellow, with the exception of the type which had been preserved in alcohol (which sometimes extracts the red of feathers). We have seen no specimen (except young birds, marked female), in a considerable number, without red on the chin, and are inclined to think that both sexes exhibit this character. Young birds from the Rocky Mountains are very similar to the adult, but have the throat marked white, and the inner web of innermost tail-feather banded with the same color. No. 16,090, ♂ ad. (Fort Crook, California), has a single crimson feather in the middle of the forehead.

HABITS. This comparatively new species of Woodpecker was first discovered by Dr. Newberry in the pine forest on the eastern border of the upper Klamath Lake. Its habits appeared to him to be very similar to those of *P. harrisi* and *P. gairdneri*, which inhabit the same region. The individual he procured was creeping up the trunk of a large yellow pine (*P. brachyptera*), searching for insects in the bark. Its cry was very like that of *P. harrisi*. Although killed by the first fire, a second discharge was required to detach it from the limb to which it clung fast.

According to Dr. Coues, it is resident and not uncommon in the Territory of Arizona, occurring exclusively among the pine-trees. It is said to range from both slopes of the Rocky Mountains to the Pacific, from as far north at least as Oregon. Fort Whipple is supposed to be about its southern limit. Dr. Coues states that this species possesses the anatomical peculiarities of the *S. varius*, and that its habits entirely correspond. Mr. Allen found it abundant on the sides of Mount Lincoln, in Colorado Territory.

Dr. Cooper met with a straggler of this species in the valley of the Colorado, shot on the 12th of March, 1861. In September, 1863, he found them rather common near the summit of the Sierra Nevada, latitude 39°, where he shot two. It has since been met with at Laramie Peak, and near the mouth of the Klamath River.

It was found by Mr. Ridgway on the eastern slope of the Sierra Nevada, and again on the Wahsatch Mountains; in both regions inhabiting the pine forests exclusively, and in neither place at all common. It occurred so seldom that Mr. Ridgway could learn but little concerning the peculiarities of its habits, etc. Its common note is a plaintive wailing squeal, much like that of *S. varius* (common to all the members of the genus), but other notes were heard which were quite peculiar.

Sphyropicus thyroideus, BAIRD.

BROWN-HEADED WOODPECKER.

Picus thyroideus, CASSIN, Pr. A. N. Sc. V, Dec. 1851, 349 (California). — HEERMANN, J. A. N. Sc. Ph. 2d ser. II, 1853, 270. — SUNDEVALL, Consp. 32. *Melanerpes thyroideus*, CASSIN, Ill. I, 1854, 201, pl. xxxii. *Pilumnus thyroideus*, BON. Consp. Zygod. Aten. Ital. 1854, 8. *Sphyropicus thyroideus*, BAIRD, Birds N. Am. 1858, 106. — ELLIOT, Ill. Birds N. Am. II, pl. — COUES, P. A. N. S. 1866, 54. — CASS. P. A. N. S. 1863, 204. — GRAY, Cat. 52. — ELLIOT, B. Am. I, pl. xxxv. — COOPER, Orn. Cal. I, 1870, 394. ? ? *Picus nataliæ*, MALHERBE, Cab. Journ. f. Ornith. 1854, 171.

SP. CHAR. About the size of *P. varius*. Head dark ashy-brown; general color ashy-brown; head and neck scarcely marked; middle line of belly sulphur-yellow; rump and upper coverts pure white; rest of body apparently encircled by narrow transverse and continuous bands (crossing the wings and tail) of black, the outer spaces becoming whiter behind; a large round black patch on the breast. No red on top of the head. Male with reddish chin. Length, about 9.00; wing, 5.00; tail, 4.10.

HAB. Cascade and Coast Ranges of California and Oregon; Sierra Nevada, Wahsatch, and Rocky Mountains. Localities: West Arizona (COUES, P. A. N. S. 1866, 54).

In addition to the characters already assigned, the crown of the head is indistinctly streaked or spotted with black. The under coverts are barred with black. The tail-feathers are black, the inner and outer barred transversely with white on both webs; the shafts, however, entirely black. The quills are all spotted with white on both webs.

The jugular black patch shows more or less indication of the transverse bands, and is sometimes wanting, leaving the bands distinct. In one specimen (38,285 ♀, Laramie Peak) it is remarkably large and almost unbroken, while the black malar stripe is decidedly indicated; on the back the black bars much exceed in width the light ones, which are nearly white. The generic rictal white stripe is usually inappreciable, as also the black maxillary one, although both can be detected in some specimens.

A young bird is not appreciably different from the adult.

HABITS. Dr. Cooper regards this bird as quite a rare species. He has never met with it, and doubts if it is ever found so far south as San Francisco. Mr. J. G. Bell, of New York, was the first to meet with this bird in the Lower Sierra Nevada.

Dr. Heermann procured specimens among the southern mines, near the Colorado River, where they were especially frequenting the pine-trees in search of their food. He saw none of them alight on an oak, though those trees were abundant in that locality. It has since been met with near Fort Crook, and Dr. Cooper thinks it probable they may be more common in the mountains of Eastern Oregon and in those of Central Utah.

Dr. Coues says that it is resident, but very rare, in Arizona. It frequents pine-trees by preference. Its range is said to include both slopes of the Rocky Mountains, from Oregon to the Rio Grande, and probably to Sonora.

Mr. Ridgway met with this rare Woodpecker on the Sierra Nevada and Wahsatch Mountains, where it inhabited the same woods with the *S. williamsoni*; it appeared to have the same manners and notes as that species, but it was so seldom met with that nothing satisfactory could be learned concerning its habits. Its conspicuously barred coloration gives it much the appearance of a *Centurus*, when flying.

GENUS **HYLOTOMUS**, BAIRD.

Dryotomus, MALHERBE, Mém. Ac. Metz, 1849, 322. (Not of SWAINSON, 1831.)
Dryopicus, BONAP. Consp. Zygod. in Aten. Ital. May, 1854. (Not of MALHERBE.)
Hylatomus, BAIRD, Birds N. Am. 1858, 107. (Type, *Picus pileatus*.)
Phlœotomus, CAB. & HEIN. 1863. (Same type.)

GEN. CHAR. Bill a little longer than the head; considerably depressed, or broader than high at the base; shaped much as in *Campephilus*, except shorter, and without the bristly feathers directed forwards at the base of the lower jaw. Gonys about half the length of the commissure. Tarsus shorter than any toe, except the inner posterior. Outer posterior toe shorter than the outer anterior, and a little longer than the inner anterior. Inner posterior very short, not half the outer anterior; about half the inner anterior one. Tail long, graduated; the longer feathers much incurved at the tip. Wing longer than the tail, reaching to the middle of the exposed surface of tail; considerably graduated, though pointed; the fourth and fifth quills longest. Color uniform black. Head with pointed occipital crest. A stripe from nasal tufts beneath the eye and down side of neck, throat, lining of wing, and basal portion of under surface of quills, white; some species with the abdomen and sides barred black and brownish-white; others with a white scapular stripe in addition. Male with whole crown and crest and maxillary patch red; female with only the crest red.

This genus is similar in general appearance and size to *Campephilus*, but differs essentially in many respects; the differences being, however, mostly those which distinguish all other Woodpeckers from the species of *Campephilus*, which is unique in the peculiar structure of the tail-feathers, the great graduation of the tertials (sixth, instead of third or fourth, longest), and very long gonys with the flat tuft of hair like feathers at its base. The less development of the outer hind toe in *Hylotomus*, which is about exactly intermediate between the outer and inner anterior, the outer largest, instead of being longest, and having the outer anterior intermediate between it and the inner, the shorter bill, the gonys fully half the length of the commissure, are additional distinctive features.

Of *Hylotomus* there are several species in tropical America, all differing, however, in transversely banded lower parts, while some have a broad white

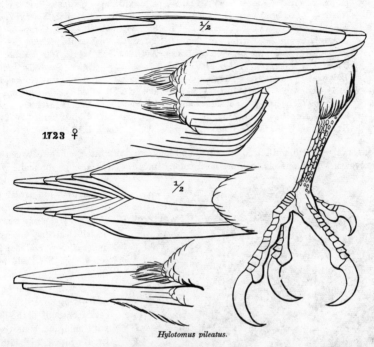

Hylotomus pileatus.

scapular stripe ; in these features of coloration (but in these only, for the head pattern is always much as in the *H. pileatus*) they resemble closely species of *Campephilus* (*C. guatemalensis, C. albirostris, C. malherbei,* etc.,) found in the same region ; one (*H. scapularis*, of Mexico) even has a whitish ivory-like bill. They may all be distinguished from the species of *Campephilus*, however, by the generic differences.

Hylotomus pileatus, BAIRD.

BLACK WOODCOCK; LOG-COCK.

Picus pileatus, LINN. Syst. Nat. I. 1766, 173. — VIEILLOT, Ois. Am. Sept. II, 1807, 58, pl. cx. — WILSON, Am. Orn. IV, 1811, 27, pl. xxix, f. 2. — WAGLER, Syst. Av. 1827, No. 2. — AUD. Orn. Biog. II, 1834, 74 ; V, 533, pl. cxi. — IB. Birds Amer. IV, 1842, 266, pl. cclvii. — MAXIM. Cab. Jour. VI. 1858, 352. — SUNDEVALL, Consp. 8. *Picus (Dryotomus) pileatus,* Sw. F. Bor. Am. II, 1831, 304. *Dryotomus pileatus,* BP. List, 1838. *Dryocopus pileatus,* BONAP. Consp. Av. 1850, 132. *Dryopicus pileatus,* BON. Consp. Zyg. Aten. Ital. I. — SCLATER, Catal. 1862, 332. — GRAY, Catal. 59. *Pileated Woodpecker,* PENNANT. — LATHAM. *Hylotomus pileatus,* BAIRD, Birds N. Am. 1858, 107. — LORD, Pr. R. Art. Inst. IV, 212. — COOPER & SUCKLEY, 161. — DRESSER, Ibis, 1865, 469 (E. Texas, but not Rio Grande). — COOPER, Orn. Cal. I, 1870, 396. *Ceophloeus pileatus,* CAB. Jour. 1862, 176. (*Hylotoma,* preoccupied by Latreille ! !) CAB. & HEIN. Mus. Hein. IV, II, 1863. — SAMUELS, 99. — ALLEN, B. E. Fla. 302.

SP. CHAR. Fourth and fifth quills equal and longest; third intermediate between sixth and seventh. Bill blue-black; more horn-color beneath. General color of body, wings, and tail dull greenish-black. A narrow white streak from just above the eye to the occiput; a wider one from the nostril feathers (inclusive), under the eye and along the side of the head and neck; sides of the breast (concealed by the wing), axillaries, and under wing-coverts, and concealed bases of all the quills, with chin and beneath the head, white, tinged with sulphur-yellow. Entire crown from the base of the bill to a well-developed occipital crest, as also a patch on the ramus of the lower jaw, scarlet-red. A few faint white crescents on the sides of the body and on the abdomen. Longer primaries generally tipped with white. Length, about 18.00; wing, 9.50. *Female* without the red on the cheek, and the anterior half of that on the top of the head replaced by black.

Hylotomus pileatus.

HAB. Wooded parts of North America from Atlantic to Pacific. Localities : E. Texas (not Rio Grande !), (DRESSER, Ibis, 1865, 469, breeds).

Specimens of this species from Fort Liard in the Northern Rocky Mountains, and from Puget Sound region, are nearly four inches longer than those from the Southern Atlantic States, and are scarcely exceeded in size by the Ivory-billed Woodpecker.

Specimens from the northwest coast region (Columbia River, British

Columbia, etc.) have no trace of the white spots on ends of outer primaries, always found in eastern specimens.

HABITS. No member of this large family has a wider distribution than the Pileated Woodpecker, extending from the Gulf of Mexico to the extremest limits of the northern forests, and from the Atlantic to the Pacific. It seems to be a resident everywhere but in its extreme northern localities, rather than a migratory species. There are specimens in the Smithsonian collection from Nelson River, on the north, to St. Johns River, Florida, on the south, and from Pennsylvania on the east to the Rio Grande and the Columbia on the west. Sir John Richardson (*Fauna Boreali-Americana*, II, p. 304) speaks of it as resident all the year in the interior of the fur countries, up to the 62d or 63d parallels, rarely appearing near Hudson's Bay, but frequenting the gloomiest recesses of the forests that skirt the Rocky Mountains. Dr. Woodhouse, in his Report on the natural history of the expedition down the Zuñi and the Colorado Rivers, speaks of this Woodpecker as having been found abundant in the Indian Territory, Texas, and New Mexico. Neither Dr. Gambel nor Dr. Heermann give it in their lists of the birds of California, nor does Dr. Newberry mention meeting with it in his Report of the zoölogy of his route. Dr. Suckley, however, speaks of the Log-Cock as abundant in the vicinity of Fort Steilacoom, Washington Territory, during summer, and Dr. Cooper also mentions it as an abundant and constant resident in the forests of the Territory. I have occasionally met with it in the wilder portions of New Hampshire and Maine, but have nowhere been so fortunate as to observe its nest or its breeding-habits. It has always seemed a very shy bird, difficult of approach, always keeping at a safe distance, and ever greeting your attempts for a nearer view with a loud, cackling cry, not unlike a derisive laugh.

According to the observations of Wilson, their eggs are deposited in the hole of a tree dug out by themselves, no other materials being used but the soft chips of rotten wood. The female lays six eggs, of a snowy whiteness, and they are said to raise two broods in a season.

Mr. Audubon states that it almost always breeds in the interior of the forest, and frequently on trees placed in deep swamps over the water, appearing to give a preference to the southern side of the tree, on which side the hole is usually found to which they retreat in the winter and during stormy weather. The hole is sometimes bored perpendicularly, but occasionally in the form of that of the Ivory-billed Woodpecker. The usual depth is from twelve to eighteen inches, the breadth from two and a half to three, and at the bottom five or six. He believed they raise but a single brood in a season. The young follow their parents a long while, sometimes until the return of spring.

Rev. Dr. Bachman gives an interesting account of a pair of Pileated Woodpeckers building a nest in an old elm-tree in a swamp, and occupying it the first year. Early the next spring two Bluebirds took possession of it, and there had young. Before they were half grown the Woodpeckers returned to the place, and, despite the cries and reiterated attacks of the Bluebirds, took out the young and carried them away to some distance. Next, the nest itself was disposed of, the hole cleaned and enlarged, and there they raised their brood. The tree was large, but so situated that Dr. Bachman could reach the nest from the branches of another. The hole was eighteen inches deep, and he could touch the bottom with his hand. The eggs, six in number, were laid on fragments of chips expressly left by the birds, and were large, white, and translucent. Before the Woodpeckers began to sit, he robbed them of their eggs to see if they would lay a second time. They waited a few days as if undecided, and then he heard the female at work again, deepening the hole and making it broader at the bottom. She soon recommenced laying, this time depositing five eggs. He suffered her to bring out her young, both birds alternately incubating, and each visiting the other at intervals, looking in at the hole to see if all were right and well there, and flying off afterwards in search of food. When the young were old enough, he took them home and endeavored to raise them. Three died, refusing all food. With two he was more successful. But even these he found untamable and destructive and troublesome pets, which he was at last glad to release.

Dr. Cooper, who observed this species in Washington Territory, discovered a pair early in April on Whitby's Island, burrowing out a hole for their nest in a dead trunk, about thirty feet from the ground. They worked alternately, and were very watchful, keeping perfectly silent while they heard any noise near by. He found the place by noticing chips on the bushes below, and after watching silently for some time, one of them began to work, now and then protruding its bill full of chips, and, after cautiously looking round, dropping them.

According to Mr. C. S. Paine, of Randolph, Vt., the Pileated Woodpecker is very rare in Vermont, and extremely shy. It is difficult to approach one nearer than from fifteen to twenty rods, except by surprise. He adds that in only a single instance has he been able to shoot one. This fell with a broken wing. Before he could reach it, the bird commenced climbing a tree, and nearly escaped. When overtaken, it fought furiously, and wounded Mr. Paine severely in the hand, setting up at the same time a loud outcry, not unlike that of a domestic hen. He has never met with its nest, although he has several times seen the young when just able to leave it. The elder Mr. Paine states that, some fifty years previous, this species was abundant in Vermont, and not at all timid, and is of the opinion that their present shyness is all that exempts them from extermination.

Mr. Dresser found this Woodpecker resident and quite numerous in Texas near all the large rivers, where the timber is heavy. A few were seen on the Medina, and their eggs obtained there, but they were not abundant in that district. On the Colorado and Brazos Rivers these birds were very common, and Mr. Dresser found several nests in huge cottonwood-trees, but had no means of getting to them.

Mr. J. K. Lord assigns to this species a wide western range, being common both east and west of the Cascades, and on the west slope of the Rocky Mountains. He met with it north as far as Fort Rupert in Vancouver Island, and south through Oregon and California. He found them at Colville during the winter. He states that they nest in May, generally in a tall dead pine-tree, at a great height.

For my first specimens of the eggs of this species I am under obligations to Dr. Cornelius Kollock, of Cheraw, S. C. They were obtained by him from excavations made in large trees at the height of about twenty-five feet from the ground, and in localities at no great distance from the inhabited parts of the country.

The eggs of this species from South Carolina and Florida are of a very brilliant crystalline whiteness, of a rounded-oval shape, and measure 1.25 inches in length by 1.02 in breadth. Northern specimens are probably larger.

Section CENTUREÆ.

The United States genera of this section are very similar to each other, and may be most easily distinguished by color, as follows : —

Centurus. Back and wings banded transversely with black and white. Crown more or less red; rest of head with under parts grayish, and with red or yellow tinge on the middle of the abdomen. Rump white.

Melanerpes. Upper parts uniform black, without bands, with or without a white rump; variable beneath, but without transverse bands.

Genus CENTURUS, Swainson.

Centurus, Sw. Class. Birds, II, 1837, 310. (Type, *C. carolinus*.)
Zebrapicus, Malh. Mém. Acad. Metz, 1849, 360. (Type, *C. carolinus*.)

Gen. Char. Bill about the length of the head, or a little longer; decidedly compressed, except at the extreme base. A lateral ridge starting a little below the culmen at the base of the bill, and angular for half the length of the bill, then becoming obsolete, though traceable nearly to the tip. Culmen considerably curved from the base; gonys nearly straight. Nostrils very broad, elliptical; situated about midway on the side of the mandible, near the base; partly concealed. Outer pairs of toes unequal, the anterior toe longest. Wings long, broad; third to fifth primaries equal and longest. Tail-feathers rather narrow, stiffened.

The species are all banded above transversely with black and white; the rump white. The head and under parts are brown, or grayish, the latter sometimes much the lighter. The belly with a red or yellow tinge. The under tail-coverts with V-shaped dark marks. The North American species of *Centurus* may be arranged as follows : —

C. carolinus. Middle of belly reddish; whole crown and nape red in male. Nape, only, red in female.

Forehead reddish; beneath soiled ashy-white; abdomen pinkish-red; crissum with sagittate marks of dusky. Wing, 5.25; tail, 3.80; bill, 1.30. *Hab.* Eastern Province United States . . . var. *c a r o l i n u s.*

Forehead smoky-white; beneath smoky-olive, middle of abdomen carmine-red; crissum with broad transverse bars of dusky. Wing, 4.50; tail, 2.60; bill, 1.08. *Hab.* Central America; Venezuela . var. *t r i c o l o r.*[1]

C. aurifrons. Middle of belly yellowish; red of crown, in male, confined to an ovoid vertical patch. Nape and forehead gamboge-yellow; white of rump and upper tail-coverts immaculate. *Female* without any red on the crown.

Inner webs of middle tail-feathers unvariegated black. Lower parts dirty ashy-whitish, abdomen dilute gamboge-yellow. Wing, 5.20; tail, 3.60; bill, 1.50. *Hab.* Eastern Mexico, north to the Rio Grande.

var. *a u r i f r o n s.*

Inner webs of middle tail-feathers spotted with white. Lower parts smoky-olive, belly bright orange-yellow. Wing, 4.70; tail, 2.80; bill, 1.16. *Hab.* Costa Rica . . . . var. *h o f f m a n n i.*[2]

C. uropygialis. Middle of the belly yellowish. Nape and forehead soft smoky grayish-brown. *Female* without red or yellow on head. White of rump and upper tail-coverts with transverse dusky bars. Inner webs of middle tail-feathers spotted with white. Wing, 5.30; tail, 3.70; bill, 1.35. *Hab.* Western Mexico, north into Colorado, region of Middle Province of United States.

Centurus carolinus, BONAP.

RED-BELLIED WOODPECKER.

Picus carolinus, LINN. Syst. Nat. I, 1766, 174. — WILSON, Am. Orn. I, 1808, 113, pl. vii, f. 2. — AUD. Orn. Biog. V, 1839, 169, pl. ccccxv. — IB. Birds Amer. IV, 1842, 270, pl. cclxx. — MAX. Cab. Jour. 1858, 418. — SUNDEVALL, Consp. 53. *Centurus carolinus,* Sw. BP. List, 1838. — IB. Conspectus, Av. 1850, 119. — BAIRD, Birds N. Am. 109. — CAB. Jour. 1862, 324. — DRESSER, Ibis, 1865, 469 (resident in Texas). — SCL. Cat. 1862, 342. — GRAY, Cat. 99. — ALLEN, B. E. Fla. 306. *Centurus carolinensis,* Sw. Birds, II, 1837, 310 (error). *Picus griseus,* VIEILL. Ois. Am. Sept. II, 1807, 52, pl. cxvi. *? Picus erythrauchen,* WAGLER, Syst. Avium, 1827. *Picus zebra,* BODDÆRT, Tabl. pl. enl. (Gray, genera).

SP. CHAR. Third, fourth, and fifth quills nearly equal, and longest; second, or outermost, and seventh about equal. Top of the head and nape crimson-red. Forehead whitish, strongly tinged with light red, a shade of which is also seen on the cheek, still stronger on the middle of the belly. Under parts brownish-white, with a faint wash of yellowish on the belly. Back, rump, and wing-coverts banded black and white; upper tail-covert white, with occasional blotches. Tail-feathers black; first transversely banded with white; second less so; all the rest with whitish tips. Inner feathers banded with white on the

---

[1] *Centurus carolinus,* var. *tricolor. Picus tricolor,* WAGL. Isis, 1829, 512. *Centurus tri.* SCL. Catal. Am. B. 1862, 343. *C. subelegans,* SCL. P. Z. S. 1855, 162; 1856, 143.

[2] *Centurus aurifrons,* var. *hoffmanni. Centurus hoffmanni,* CABANIS, Journ. Sept. 1862, 322 (Costa Rica).

inner web; the outer web with a stripe of white along the middle. Length, 9.75; wing, about 5.00. Female with the crown ashy; forehead pale red; nape bright red.

HAB. North America, from Atlantic coast to the eastern slope of the Rocky Mountains. Localities : Texas (DRESSER, Ibis, 1865, 469, resident).

Specimens vary considerably in size (with latitude), and in the tinge of reddish on chin, breast, etc. The width of the dorsal bands differs in different specimens. The rump is banded; up-

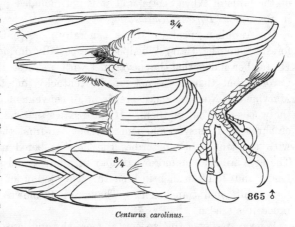

Centurus carolinus.

per tail-coverts are generally immaculate, but are sometimes dashed with black. Specimens from the Mississippi Valley are generally more brightly colored than those from the Atlantic States, the lower parts more strongly tinged with red. Florida examples are smaller than northern ones, the black bars broader, the lower parts deeper ashy and strongly tinged with red, but of a more purplish shade than in western ones.

Centurus carolinus.

HABITS. The Red-bellied Woodpecker is distributed throughout North America, from the Atlantic Coast to the eastern slope of the Rocky Mountains. It is, however, much more abundant in the more southern and western portions. In the collections of the Smithsonian Institution none are recorded from farther north than Pennsylvania on the east and Nebraska Territory on the west, while others were obtained as far south as Florida. Nor am I aware that it is found, except very rarely, north of Pennsylvania on the Atlantic coast. I have never met with it in Eastern Massachusetts, although Mr. Audubon speaks of it as breeding from Maryland to Nova Scotia. Dr. Woodhouse found it common in the Indian Territory and in Texas. Wilson speaks of having found it abundant in Upper Canada, and in the northern parts of the State of New York. He also refers to its inhabiting the whole Atlantic States as far as Georgia and the southern extremity of Florida. Its absence in Eastern Massachusetts was noticed by Mr. Nuttall. It is not given by Thompson or Paine as one of the birds of Vermont, nor does Lieutenant Bland mention it as one of the birds of Nova Scotia, and it is not included by Sir John Richardson in the *Fauna Boreali-Americana.*

Mr. Audubon speaks of it as generally more confined to the interior of forests than the Hairy Woodpecker, especially during the breeding-season. He further states that he never met with its nest in Louisiana or South Carolina, but that it was not rare in Kentucky, and that, from the State of Maryland to Nova Scotia, it breeds in all convenient places, usually more in the woods than out of them. He also states that he has found the nests in orchards in Pennsylvania, generally not far from the junction of a branch with the trunk. He describes the hole as bored in the ordinary manner. The eggs are seldom more than four in number, and measure 1.06 inches in length and .75 of an inch in breadth. They are of an elliptical form, smooth, pure white, and translucent. They are not known to raise more than one brood in a season.

Wilson speaks of this species as more shy and less domestic than the Red-headed or any of the other spotted Woodpeckers, and also as more solitary. He adds that it prefers the largest high-timbered woods and the tallest decayed trees of the forest, seldom appearing near the ground, on the fences, or in orchards or open fields. In regard to their nesting, he says that the pair, in conjunction, dig out a circular cavity for the nest in the lower side of some lofty branch that makes a considerable angle with the horizon. Sometimes they excavate this in the solid wood, but more generally in a hollow limb, some fifteen inches above where it becomes solid. This is usually done early in April. The female lays five eggs, of a pure white, or almost semi-transparent. The young generally make their appearance towards the latter part of May. Wilson was of the opinion that they produced two broods in a season.

Mr. Dresser found this bird resident and abundant in Texas. It is also equally abundant in Louisiana and in Florida, and Mr. Ridgway considers it very common in Southern Illinois. Neither Mr. Boardman nor Mr. Verrill have found it in Maine. Mr. McIlwraith has, however, taken three specimens at Hamilton, Canada West, May 3, near Chatham. Mr. Allen gives it as a summer visitant in Western Massachusetts, having seen one on the 13th of May, 1863. It has also been taken several times in Connecticut, by Professor Emmons, who met with it, during the breeding-season, in the extreme western part of the State. Mr. Lawrence has found it near New York City, and Mr. Turnbull in Eastern Pennsylvania.

The eggs vary from an oblong to a somewhat rounded oval shape, are of a bright crystalline whiteness, and their measurements average 1.02 inches in length by .88 of an inch in breadth.

Centurus aurifrons, GRAY.

YELLOW-BELLIED WOODPECKER.

Picus aurifrons, WAGLER, Isis, 1829, 512. — SUNDEVALL, Consp. Pic. 53. *Centurus auri-frons*, GRAY, Genera. — CABANIS, Jour. 1862, 323. — COOPER, Orn. Cal. I, 1870, 399. *Centurus flaviventris*, SWAINSON, Anim. in Menag. 1838 (2½ centenaries), 354. — BAIRD, Birds N. Am. 1858, 110, pl. xlii. — HEERMANN, P. R. Rep. X, c, 18. — DRESSER, Ibis, 1865, 469 (resident in Texas). — IB. Rep. Mex. Bound. II, 5, pl. iv. *Centurus elegans*, LAWRENCE, Ann. N. Y. Lyc. V, May, 1851, 116. *Centurus santacruzi*, LAWRENCE, Ann. N. Y. Lyc. V, 1851, 123 (not of Bonap.). *Picus ornatus*, LESS. Rev. Zoöl. 1839, 102.

SP. CHAR. Fourth and fifth quills nearly equal; third a little shorter; longer than the fourth. Back banded transversely with black and white; rump and upper tail-coverts pure white. Crown with a subquadrate spot of crimson, about half an inch wide and long; and separated from the gamboge-yellow at the base of the bill by dirty white, from the orbit and occiput by brownish-ash. Nape half-way round the neck orange-yellow. Under part generally, and sides of head, dirty white. Middle of belly gamboge-yellow. Tail-feathers all entirely black, except the outer, which has some obscure bars of white. Length about 9.50; wing, 5.00. Female without the red of the crown.

HAB. Rio Grande region of the United States, south into Mexico. Probably Arizona. Localities: Orizaba (SCL. P. Z. S. 1860, 252); Texas, south of San Antonio (DRESSER, Ibis, 1865, 469, resident).

Young birds are not different from adults, except in showing indication of dark shaft-lines beneath, becoming broader behind on the sides. The yellow of the nape extends over the whole side of the head.

HABITS. This beautiful Woodpecker is abundant throughout the valley of the Rio Grande, from Eagle Pass to its mouth; how far to the west within our boundaries it occurs, I am not able to state. It is common throughout Mexico, and was found in the Guatemalan collection of Van Patten, though not mentioned by Sclater and Salvin. Dr. Woodhouse, in his Report on the zoölogy of Captain Sitgreaves's expedition, speaks of finding it quite abundant in the neighborhood of San Antonio, Texas. He adds that west of the Rio San Pedro he did not meet with it. He speaks of it as having a loud, sharp cry, which it utters as it flies from tree to tree. He observed it mostly on the trunks of the mesquite (*Algarobia*), diligently searching in the usual manner of Woodpeckers. In the Report upon the birds of the Mexican Boundary Survey, it is mentioned by Mr. Clark as abundant on the Lower Rio Grande, as very shy, and as keeping chiefly about the mesquite. Lieutenant Couch speaks of it as very common throughout Tamaulipas.

Mr. Dresser found the Yellow-bellied Woodpecker plentiful from the Rio Grande to San Antonio, and as far north and east as the Guadaloupe, after which he lost sight of it. Wherever the mesquite-trees were large, there it was sure to be found, and very sparingly elsewhere. Near San Antonio it is quite common, but not so much so as the *C. carolinus*. At Eagle Pass, however, it was the more abundant of the two. He found it breeding near San Antonio, boring for its nest-hole into a mesquite-tree. Mr. Dresser was informed by Dr. Heermann, who has seen many of their nests, that he never found them in any other tree.

These birds were found breeding by Dr. Berlandier, and his collection contained quite a number of their eggs. Nothing was found among his papers in relation to their habits or their manner of breeding. Their eggs, procured by him, are of an oblong-oval shape, and measure 1.05 inches in length by .85 of an inch in breadth.

Centurus uropygialis, Baird.

GILA WOODPECKER.

Centurus uropygialis, Baird, Pr. A. N. Sc. Ph. VII, June, 1854, 120 (Bill Williams River, N. M. — Ib. Birds N. Am. 1858, 111, pl. xxxvi. — Cab. Jour. 1862, 330. — Sundevall, Consp. 54. — Kennerly, P. R. R. X, b, pl. xxxvi. — Heermann, X, c, 17. Coues, Pr. Avi. 1866, 54 (S. Arizona). — Cooper, Orn. Cal. I, 1870, 399. *Centurus hypopolius*, (Bp.) Pucheran, Rev. et Mag. 1853, 163 (not *Picus (Centurus) hypopolius*, Wagler). *Zebrapicus kaupii*, Malherbe, 1855. — Gray, Catal. Br. Mex. *Centurus sulfureiventer*, Reichenbach, Handbuch, Picinæ, Oct. 1854, 410, figs. 4411, 4412.

Sp. Char. Third, fourth, and fifth quills longest, and about equal. Back, rump, and upper tail-coverts transversely barred with black and white, purest on the two latter. Head and neck all round pale dirty-brown, or brownish-ash, darkest above. A small subquadrate patch of red on the middle of the crown, separated from the bill by dirty white. Middle of the abdomen gamboge-yellow; under tail-coverts and anal region strongly barred with black. First and second outer tail-feathers banded black and white, as is also the inner web of the inner tail-feather; the outer web of the latter with a white stripe. Length, about 9.00; wing, 5.00. Female with the head uniform brownish-ash, without any red or yellow.

Hab. Lower Colorado River of the West, to Cape St. Lucas. South to Mazatlan. Localities: W. Arizona (Coues, P. A. N. S, 1866, 54).

Habits. This species was first discovered by Dr. Kennerly in his route along the 35th parallel, and described by Professor Baird, in 1854. The Doctor encountered it almost continually during the entire march along the Big Sandy, Bill Williams Fork, and the Great Colorado; but it was so very shy that he had great difficulty in procuring specimens. Seated in the top of the tree, it was ever on guard; and, upon the approach of danger, flew away, accompanying its flight with the utterance of very peculiar notes. Its flight was in an undulating line, like that of other birds of this class.

Dr. Heermann found this Woodpecker abundant on the banks of the Gila River among the mesquite-trees. The giant cactus, often forty feet high, which grows abundantly on the arid hillsides throughout that whole section of country, was frequently found filled with holes bored out by this bird. The pith of the plant is extracted until a chamber of suitable size is obtained, when the juice exuding from the wounded surface hardens, and forms a smooth dry coating to the cavity, thus making a convenient place for the purposes of incubation. At Tucson, in Arizona, he found it frequenting the cornfields, where it might be seen alighting on the old hedge-posts in search of insects. Its note, he adds, resembles very much that of the Red-headed Woodpecker. He afterwards met with this bird in California, in considerable numbers, on the Colorado. Besides its ordinary notes, resembling those of the *Melanerpes erythrocephalus*, it varies them with a soft plaintive cry, as if hurt or wounded. He found their stomachs filled with the white gelatinous berry of a parasitic plant which grows abundantly on the mesquite-trees, and the fruit of which forms the principal food of many species of birds during the fall.

Dr. Coues gives this bird as rare and probably accidental in the immediate vicinity of Fort Whipple, but as a common bird in the valleys of the Gila and of the Lower Colorado, where it has the local name of *Suwarrow*, or *Saguaro*, on account of its partiality for the large cactuses, with the juice of which plant its plumage is often found stained.

Dr. Cooper found this Woodpecker abundant in winter at Fort Mohave, when they feed chiefly on the berries of the mistletoe, and are very shy. He rarely saw them pecking at the trees, but they seemed to depend for a living on insects, which were numerous on the foliage during the spring. They have a loud note of alarm, strikingly similar to that of the *Phœnopepla nitens*, which associated with them in the mistletoe-boughs.

About the 25th of March he found them preparing their nests in burrows near the dead tops of trees, none of them, so far as he saw, being accessible. By the last of May they had entirely deserted the mistletoe, and were probably feeding their young on insects.

Genus MELANERPES, Swainson.

Melanerpes, Swainson, F. B. A. II, 1831. (Type, *Picus erythrocephalus*.)
Melampicus (Section 3), Malherbe, Mém. Ac. Metz, 1849, 365.
Asyndesmus, Coues, Pr. A. N. S. 1866, 55. (Type, *Picus torquatus*.)

Gen. Char. Bill about equal to the head ; broader than high at the base, but becoming compressed immediately anterior to the commencement of the gonys. Culmen and gonys with a moderately decided angular ridge ; both decidedly curved from the very base. A rather prominent acute ridge commences at the base of the mandible, a little below the ridge of the culmen, and proceeds but a short distance anterior to the nostrils (about one third of the way), when it sinks down, and the bill is then smooth. The lateral outlines are gently concave from the basal two thirds ; then gently convex to the tip, which does not exhibit any abrupt bevelling. Nostrils open, broadly oval ; not concealed by the feathers, nor entirely basal. Fork of chin less than half lower jaw. The outer pair of toes equal. Wings long, broad ; lengthened. Tail-feathers broad, with lengthened points.

The species all have the back black, without any spots or streaks anywhere.

Dr. Coues places *M. torquatus* in a new genus, *Asyndesmus*, characterized by a peculiar texture of the under part and nuchal collar, in which the fibres are disconnected on their terminal portion, enlarged and stiffened, almost bristle-like; otherwise the characters are much as in *Melanerpes*. It

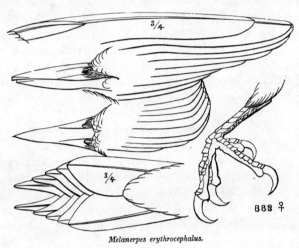

Melanerpes erythrocephalus.

should, however, be noted, that the feathers of the red portion of the head in the other species have the same texture.

Species and Varieties.

A. Sexes similar. *Young* very different from the adult.

M. torquatus. Feathers of the lower parts, as well as of frontal, lateral, and under portions of the head, with the fibres bristle-like. (*Asyndesmus*, Coues.) Upper parts wholly uniform, continuous, very metallic blackish-green. *Adult.* Forehead, lores, cheeks, and chin deep crimson, of a burnt-carmine tint; jugulum, breast, and a ring entirely around the nape, grayish-white; abdomen light carmine. Back glossed with purplish-bronze. *Young* without the red of the head, and lacking the grayish nuchal collar; abdomen only tinged with red, no purple or bronze tints above. Wing, 6.70; tail, 4.50. *Hab.* Western Province of the United States, from the Black Hills to the Pacific.

M. erythrocephalus. Feathers generally soft, blended; those of the whole head and neck with stiffened and bristle-like fibres in the adult. Secondaries, rump, and upper tail-coverts, with whole lower parts from the neck, continuous pure white. Two lateral tail-feathers tipped with white. *Adult.* Whole head and neck bright venous-crimson or blood-red, with a black convex posterior border across the jugulum; back, wings, and tail glossy blue-black. *Young.* Head and neck grayish, streaked with dusky; back and scapulars grayish, spotted with black; secondaries with two or three black bands; breast tinged with grayish, and with sparse dusky streaks. Wing, 5.90; tail, 3.90. *Hab.* Eastern Province of the United States, west to the Rocky Mountains.

B. Sexes dissimilar; young like the adult.

M. formicivorus. Forehead and a broad crescent across the middle of the throat (the two areas connected by a narrow strip across the lore), white, more or less tinged with sulphur-yellow. Rump, upper tail-coverts, abdomen, sides, and crissum, with patch on base of primaries, pure white, the sides and breast with black streaks. Other portions glossy blue-black.

♂. Whole crown and nape carmine. ♀ with the occiput and nape alone red.

> *More than the anterior half of the pectoral band immaculate.*

♀ with the white frontal, black coronal, and red occipital bands of about equal width. Forehead and throat only slightly tinged with sulphur-yellow. Wing, 5.80; tail, 3.90; bill, 1.27. *Hab.* Pacific Province of United States, and Northern and Western Mexico . . . . var. *formicivorus.*

♀ with the white frontal band only about half as wide as the black coronal, which is only about half as wide as the red occipital, band or patch. Forehead and throat bright sulphur-yellow. Wing, 5.40; tail, 3.65; bill, 1.23. *Hab.* Lower California.

var. *angustifrons.*

> *Nearly the whole of the black pectoral band variegated with white streaks.*

Relative width of the white, black, and red areas on the crown as in *formicivorus.* Wing, 5.50; tail, 3.75; bill, 1.22. *Hab.* Middle America, south of Orizaba and Mirador . . . . var. *striatipectus.*[1]

♂. Nape, only, red (as in females of preceding races); ♀ without any red.

Whole breast streaked, the black and white being in about equal amount. Wing, 5.70; tail, 3.90; bill, 1.20. *Hab.* New Granada.

var. *flavigula.*[2]

Melanerpes torquatus, BONAP.

LEWIS'S WOODPECKER.

Picus torquatus, WILSON, Am. Orn. III, 1811, 31, pl. xx. — WAGLER, Syst. Av. 1827, No. 82. — AUD. Orn. Biog. V, 1839, 176, pl. ccccxvi. — IB. Birds Amer. IV, 1842, 280, pl. cclxxii. — SUNDEVALL, Consp. 51. *Melanerpes torquatus,* BP. Consp. 1850, 115. — HEERMANN, J. A. N. Sc. Phil. 2d ser. II, 1853, 270. — NEWBERRY, Zoöl. Cal. & Or. Route, 90, in P. R. R. Surv. VI, 1857. — BAIRD, Birds N. Am. 115. — COOPER & SUCKLEY, 161. — CASSIN. Pr. A. N. S. 1863, 327. — LORD, Pr. R. A. Inst. IV, 1864, 112 (nesting). — COOPER, Orn. Cal. I, 1870, 406. *Picus montanus,* ORD. in Guthrie's Geog. 2d Am. ed. II, 1815, 316. *Picus lewisii,* DRAPIEZ. (Gray.) *Asyndesmus torquatus,* COUES, Pr. A. N. S. 1866, 55.

SP. CHAR. Feathers on the under parts bristle-like. Fourth quill longest; then third and fifth. Above dark glossy-green. Breast, lower part of the neck, and a narrow collar all round, hoary grayish-white. Around the base of the bill and sides of the head to

---

[1] *Melanerpes formicivorus,* var. *striatipectus,* RIDGWAY. In view of the very appreciable difference from the other races named, it appears necessary to name this one, in order that it may rank equally with the rest. The almost entirely streaked breast is only an approach to what we see, in its extreme phase, in the var. *flavigula.* The black vertex of the female appears broader than in specimens of var. *formicivorus.*

[2] *Melanerpes formicivorus,* var. *flavigula,* NATT. *Melampicus flavigula* (NATT.), MALH. Rev. Zool. 1849, 542, Monog. Pic. II, 202, pl. xcix, f. 5, 6. *Melanerpes flavigularis,* SCL. P. Z. S. 1856, 161. This can only be considered the melanistic extreme of a species of which the var. *formicivorus* is the rubescent one, the transition being gradual through the var. *striatipectus* of the intermediate region.

behind the eyes, dark crimson. Belly blood-red, streaked finely with hoary whitish. Wings and tail entirely uniform dark glossy-green. Female similar. Length about 10.50; wing, 6.50. Young without the nuchal collar, and the red of head replaced by black.

HAB. Western America from Black Hills to Pacific.

The peculiarities in the feathers of the under parts have already been adverted to. This structure appears to be essentially connected with the red feathers, since these have the same texture in the other species of the genus, wherever the color occurs. The remark may perhaps apply generally to the red feathers of most, if not all, Woodpeckers, and may be connected with some chemical or physical condition yet to be determined.

HABITS. Lewis's Woodpecker would seem to have a distribution throughout the Pacific Coast, from the sea-shore to the mountains, and from Puget Sound to the Gulf of California, and extending to the eastern border of the Great Plains, within the limits of the United States. They were first observed by Messrs. Lewis and Clarke, in their memorable journey to the Pacific. Subsequently Mr. Nuttall met with them in his westward journey, in the central chain of the Rocky Mountains. This was in the month of July. Among the cedar and pine woods of Bear River, on the edge of Upper California, he found them inhabiting the decayed trunks of the pine-trees, and already feeding their young. Afterwards, at the close of August, he met them in flocks on the plains, sixty miles up the Wahlamet. He describes them as very unlike Woodpeckers in their habits, perching in dense flocks, like Starlings, neither climbing branches nor tapping in the manner of their tribe, but darting after insects and devouring berries, like Thrushes. He saw them but seldom, either in the dense forests of the Columbia or in any settled part of California.

Townsend speaks of their arriving about the first of May on Bear River and the Columbia. Both sexes incubate, according to his observations.

Dr. Gambel first observed this Woodpecker in a belt of oak timber near the Mission of St. Gabriel, in California, and states that it was abundant. He also describes its habits as peculiar, and unlike the generality of Woodpeckers. Dr. Heermann, too, speaks of finding it in all the parts of California which he visited. Dr. Newberry, in his Notes on the zoölogy of Lieutenant Williamson's expedition, refers to it as most unlike the California Woodpecker in the region it occupies and in its retiring habits. He describes it as seeming to choose, for its favorite haunts, the evergreen forests upon the rocky declivities of the Cascade and Rocky Mountains. He first observed it in Northern California, but subsequently noticed it in the mountains all the way to the Columbia. Though often seen in low elevations, it was evidently alpine in its preferences, and was found most frequently near the line of perpetual snow; and when crossing the snow lines, in the mountain-passes, it was often observed flying far above the party. He describes it as being always shy, and difficult to shoot.

Dr. S. W. Woodhouse describes this species as being common in the Indian

Territory and in New Mexico; while Dr. Cooper, in his Report on the zoölogy of Washington Territory, speaks of it as being common, during summer, in all the interior districts, but seldom or never approaching the coast. It arrives at Puget Sound early in May, and some even remain, during mild winters, in the Territory. According to his account, it burrows holes for its nests at all heights from the ground, but commonly in dead trees. The eggs are described as pure white, and, when fresh, translucent, like those of all the Woodpecker tribe, and hardly distinguishable in size and general appearance from those of the Golden-winged Woodpecker (*Colaptes auratus*). Its harsh call is rarely uttered in summer, when it seems to seek concealment for itself and nest. The flocks of young, which in fall associate together to the number of eight or ten, are more noisy. Dr. Suckley, in the same Report (page 162), speaks of this Woodpecker as being very abundant throughout the more open portions of the timbered region of the northwest coast, preferring oak openings and groves. At Fort Dalles, on the Columbia, they are extremely numerous, not only breeding there during summer, but also found as winter residents. Their breeding-places are generally holes in oak and other trees, which, from the appearance of all he examined, seemed to have been excavated for the purpose. At Puget Sound this species was found less frequently than at Fort Dalles, on the Columbia. At the latter place they were constant winter residents. Dr. Suckley also speaks of them as being semi-gregarious in their habits.

Mr. Lord thinks that this Woodpecker is not to be met with west of the Cascade Mountains, but says it is very often found between the Cascades and the Rocky Mountains, where it frequents the open timber. The habits and modes of flight of this bird, he states, are not the least like a Woodpecker's. It flies with a heavy flapping motion, much like a Jay, feeds a good deal on the ground, and chases insects on the wing like a Shrike or a Kingbird. Whilst mating they assemble in large numbers, and keep up a continual, loud, chattering noise. They arrive at Colville in April, begin nesting in May, and leave again in October. The nest is in a hole in a dead pine-tree, usually at a considerable height from the ground.

Dr. Coues says this bird is very common at Fort Whipple, in Arizona, where it remained in moult until November.

Mr. J. A. Allen found this the most numerous of the *Picidæ* in Colorado Territory. He also states that it differs considerably in its habits from all the other Woodpeckers. He frequently noticed it rising high into the air almost vertically, and to a great height, apparently in pursuit of insects, and descending again as abruptly, to repeat the same manœuvre. It was met with by Mr. Ridgway in the Sacramento Valley, along the eastern base of the Sierra Nevada, and in the East Humboldt Mountains. In the first-mentioned locality it was the most abundant Woodpecker, and inhabited the scattered oaks of the plains. In the second region it was very abundant — perhaps more so than any other species — among the scattered pines along the very base of the eastern slope ; and in the last-mentioned place was observed on a few occasions among the tall aspens bordering the streams in the lower portions of the cañons. In its habits it is described as approaching most closely to our common Red-headed Woodpecker (*M. erythrocephalus*), but possessing many very distinctive peculiarities. In the character of its notes it quite closely approximates to our common Redhead, but they are weaker and of a more twittering character ; and in its lively playful disposition it even exceeds it. It has a very peculiar and characteristic habit of ascending high into the air, and taking a strange, floating flight, seemingly laborious, as if struggling against the wind, and then descending in broad circles to the trees.

The eggs are more spherical than are usually those of the *Colaptes auratus*, are of a beautiful crystalline whiteness, and measure 1.10 inches in length and .92 of an inch in breadth.

Melanerpes erythrocephalus, SWAINSON.

RED-HEADED WOODPECKER.

Picus erythrocephalus, LINN. Syst. Nat. I, 1766, 174. — VIEILLOT, Ois. Am. Sept. II, 1807, 60, pl. cxii, cxiii. — WILSON, Am. Orn. I, 1810, 142, pl. ix, fig. 1. — WAGLER, Syst. Av. 1827, No. 14. — IB. Isis, 1829, 518 (young). — AUD. Orn. Biog. I, 1832, 141 ; V, 536, pl. xxvii. — IB. Birds America, IV, 1842, 274, pl. cclxxi. — MAX. Cab. J. VI, 1858, 419. *Melanerpes erythrocephalus*, SW. F. B. A. II, 1831, 316. — BON. List, 1838. — IB. Conspectus, 1850, 115. — GAMBEL, J. Ac. Nat. Sc. Ph. 2d ser. I, 1847, 55. — BAIRD, Birds N. Am. 1858, 113. — SCL. Cat. 1862, 340. — SAMUELS, 102. — COOPER, Orn. Cal. I, 1870, 402. — ALLEN, B. E. Fla. 307. *Picus obscurus*, GM. I, 1788, 429 (young). — *Red-headed Woodpecker*, PENNANT, KALM, LATHAM. *White-rumped Woodpecker*, LATHAM.

SP. CHAR. Head and neck all round crimson-red, margined by a narrow crescent of black on the upper part of the breast. Back, primary quills, and tail bluish-black. Under parts generally, a broad band across the middle of the wing, and the rump, white. The female is not different. Length, about 9.75 ; wing, 5.50. Bill bluish-white, darker terminally ; iris chestnut; feet olive-gray. Young without any red, the head and neck being grayish streaked with dusky ; breast with an ashy tinge, and streaked sparsely with dusky ; secondaries with two or three bands of black ; dorsal region clouded with grayish.

HAB. Eastern Province of United States to base of Rocky Mountains, sometimes straggling westward to coast of California (GAMBEL). Salt Lake City, Utah (RIDGWAY). Other localties : Nueces to Brazos, Texas (DRESSER, Ibis, 1865, 469, breeds).

Western specimens frequently have the abdomen strongly tinged with salmon-red, or orange-red, and are generally more deeply colored than eastern.

HABITS. The Red-headed Woodpecker is one of the most familiar birds of this family, and ranges over a wide extent of territory. Excepting where it has been exterminated by the persecutions of indiscriminate destroyers, it is everywhere a very abundant species. Once common, it is now rarely met with in the neighborhood of Boston, though in the western part of Massachusetts it is still to be found. In the collections of the Smithsonian Institution are specimens from Pennsylvania, Wyoming, Nebraska, Kansas, Missouri, Louisiana, the Indian Territory, etc. Sir John Richardson speaks of it as ranging in summer as far north as the northern shores of Lake Huron. He also remarks that in the Hudson Bay Museum there is a specimen from the banks of the Columbia River. Dr. Gambel, in his paper on the birds of California, states that he saw many of them in a belt of oak timber near the Mission of St. Gabriel. As, however, Dr. Heermann did not meet with it in California, and as no other collector has obtained specimens in that State, this is probably a mistake. With the exception of Dr. Woodhouse, who speaks of having found this species in the Indian Territory and in Texas, it is not mentioned by any of the government exploring parties. It may therefore be assigned a range extending, in summer, as far north as Labrador, and westward to the eastern slopes of the Rocky Mountains. Throughout the year it is a permanent resident only of the more southern States, where it is, however, much less abundant in summer than it is in Pennsylvania.

Wilson, at the time of his writing (1808), speaks of finding several of the nests of this Woodpecker within the boundaries of the then city of Philadelphia, two of them being in buttonwood-trees and one in the decayed limb of an elm. The parent birds made regular excursions to the woods beyond the Schuylkill, and preserved a silence and circumspection in visiting their nest entirely unlike their habits in their wilder places of residence. The species is altogether migratory, visiting the Middle and Northern States early in May and leaving in October. It begins the construction of its nest almost immediately after its first appearance, as with other members of its family, by excavations made in the trunk or larger limbs of trees, depositing six white eggs on the bare wood. The cavities for their nests are made almost exclusively in dead wood, rarely, if ever, in the living portion of the tree. In Texas, Louisiana, Kentucky, and the Carolinas, they have two broods in a season, but farther north than this they rarely raise more than one. Their eggs are usually six in number, and, like all the eggs of this family, are pure white and translucent when fresh. They vary a little in their shape, but are usually slightly more oval and less spherical than those of several other species. Mr. Nuttall speaks of the eggs of this bird as being said to be marked at the larger end with reddish spots. I have never met with any thus marked, and as Mr. Nuttall does not give it as from his own observations I have no doubt that it is a mistake. Mr. Paine, of Randolph, Vt., writes that he has only seen a single specimen of this Woodpecker in that part of Vermont, while on the western side of the Green Mountains they are said to be very common. He adds that it is a tradition among his older neighbors that these Woodpeckers were formerly everywhere known throughout all portions of the State.

Mr. Ridgway saw a single individual of this species in the outskirts of Salt Lake City, in July, 1869.

Their eggs vary both in size and in shape, from a spherical to an oblong-oval, the latter being the more usual. Their length varies from 1.10 to 1.15 inches, and their breadth from .80 to .90 of an inch.

Melanerpes formicivorus, var. formicivorus, BONAP.

CALIFORNIA WOODPECKER.

Picus formicivorus, SWAINSON, Birds Mex. in Philos. Mag. I, 1827, 439 (Mexico). — VIGORS, Zool. Blossom, 1839, 23 (Monterey). — NUTTALL, Man. I, 2d ed. 1840. *Melanerpes formicivorus,* BP. Conspectus, 1850, 115. — HEERMANN, J. A. N. Sc. Phil. 2d series, II, 1853, 270. — CASSIN, Illust. II, 1853, 11, pl. ii. — NEWBERRY, Zool. Cal. & Oregon Route, 90, P. R. R. Surv. VI, 1857. — BAIRD, Birds N. Am. 1868, 114. — SUMICHRAST, Mem. Bost. Soc. I, 1865, 562 (correcting an error of Saussure). — CASSIN, Pr. A. N. S. 63, 328. — HEERMANN, P. R. R. X, 58 (nesting). — BAIRD, Rep. M. Bound. II, Birds, 6. — SCLATER, Pr. Z. S. 1858, 305 (Oaxaca). — IB. Ibis, 137 (Honduras). — CAB. Jour. 1862, 322 (Costa Rica). — COUES, Pr. A. N. S. 1866, 55. — COOPER, Orn. Cal. I, 1870, 403. *Picus melanopogon,* TEMMINCK, Pl. Color. IV, (1829 ?) pl. ccccli. — WAGLER, Isis, 1829, v, 515. — SUNDEVALL, Consp. 51.

SP. CHAR. Fourth quill longest, third a little shorter. Above and on the anterior half of the body, glossy bluish or greenish black; the top of the head and a short occipital crest red. A white patch on the fore-head, connecting with a broad crescentic collar on the upper part of the neck by a narrow isthmus, white tinged with sulphur-yellow. Belly, rump, bases of primaries, and inner edges of the outer quills, white. Tail-feathers uniform black. Female with the red confined to the occipital crest, the rest replaced by greenish-black; the three patches white, black, and red, very sharply defined, and about equal. Length about 9.50; wing, 6.00; tail, 3.75.

Melanerpes formicivorus.

HAB. Pacific Coast region of the United States and south; in Northern Mexico, eastward almost to the Gulf of Mexico; also on the Upper Rio Grande; south to Costa Rica. Localities: Oaxaca (SCL. P. Z. S. 1858, 305); Cordova (SCL. 1856, 307); Guatemala (SCL. Ibis, I, 137); Honduras (SCL. Cat. 341); Costa Rica (CAB. J. 1862, 322); W. Arizona (COUES, P. A. N. S. 1866, 55).

In most specimens one or two red feathers may be detected in the black of the breast just behind the sulphur-yellow crescent. The white of the breast is streaked with black; the posterior portion of the black of the breast and anterior belly streaked with white. The white of the wing only shows externally as a patch at the base of the primaries.

Dr. Coues calls attention to extraordinary differences in the color of the iris, which varies from white to red, blue, yellow, ochraceous, or brown. A mixture of blue, he thinks, indicates immaturity, and a reddish tinge the full spring coloration.

The male of this species has a white forehead extending a little backwards of the anterior edge of the eye, the rest of the top of head to the nape being red. The female has the white forehead, and a quadrate occipito-nuchal red patch, a black band about as broad as the white one separating the latter from the occipital red. The length of the two anterior bands together is decidedly greater than that of the posterior red. In both sexes the jugulum is entirely and continuously black. Anteriorly (generally with a red spot in its anterior edge) and on the feathers of its posterior border only are these elongated white spots, on each side the shaft, the feathers of the breast being streaked centrally with black. The inner webs of the secondaries have an elongated continuous patch of white along their internal edge, with a very slight, almost inappreciable, border of black; this white only very rarely converted partly or entirely into quadrate spots, and that never on the innermost quills marked with white. Specimens from California are very similar to those from the Rocky Mountains and the Rio Grande Valley, except, perhaps, in being larger, with longer and straighter bill.

In *M. flavigula* from Bogota, the male has the head marked with the red, black, and white (the red much less in extent, however) of the female *M. formicivorus*, while the female has no red whatever. All, or nearly all, the feathers of the jugulum have the two white spots, and (as pointed out by Reichenbach) the white of the inner webs of the inner quills is entirely converted into a series of non-confluent quadrate spots. The black streaks on the sides and behind appear to be of greater magnitude, and more uniformly distributed. In both species all the tail-feathers are perfectly black.

A Guatemalan bird, received from Mr. Salvin as *M. formicivorus*, — and indeed all specimens from Orizaba and Mirador to Costa Rica, — agrees in the main with the northern bird, except that all the black feathers of the jugulum have white spots, as in *M. flavigula*. The outermost tail-feather of Mr. Salvin's specimen has two narrow transverse whitish bands, and a spot indicating a third, as well as a light tip. The white markings on the inner quills are more like the northern bird, though on the outermost ones there is the same tendency to form spots as in a few northern specimens (as 6,149 from Los Nogales, &c.). The bill is very different from either in being shorter, broader, much stouter, and the culmen more decurved.

These peculiarities, which are constant, appear to indicate a decided or strongly marked variety, as a series of almost a hundred specimens of the northern bird from many localities exhibit none of the characters mentioned, while all of an equally large series from Central America agree in possessing them.

A series of Jalapan specimens from the cabinet of Mr. Lawrence show a close relationship to skins from the Rio Grande, and do not approach the Guatemalan bird in the peculiar characters just referred to, except in the shortness and curvature of the bill. In one specimen there is an approach to the Bogotan in a moderate degree of barring on the white inner edgings of the tertials ; in the rest, however, they are continuously white.

HABITS. This handsome Woodpecker, distinguished both by the remarkable beauty of its plumage and the peculiarity of its provident habits, has a widely extended area of distribution, covering the Pacific Coast, from Oregon throughout Mexico. In Central America it is replaced by the variety *striatipectus*, and in New Grenada by the var. *flavigula*, while at Cape St. Lucas we find another local form, *M. angustifrons*. So far as we have the means of ascertaining their habits, we find no mention of any essential differences in this respect among these races.

Suckley and Cooper did not meet with this bird in Washington Territory, and Mr. Lord met with it in abundance on his journey from Yreka to the boundary line of British Columbia. Mr. Dresser did not observe it at San Antonio. Mr. Clark met with it at the Coppermines, in New Mexico, in great numbers, and feeding principally among the oaks. Lieutenant Couch found it in the recesses of the Sierra Madre quite common and very tame, resorting to high trees in search of its food. He did not meet with it east of the Sierra Madre. Dr. Kennerly first observed it in the vicinity of Santa Cruz, where it was very frequent on the mountain-slopes, always preferring the tallest trees, but very shy, and it was with difficulty that a specimen could be procured. Mr. Nuttall, who first added this bird to our fauna, speaks of it as very plentiful in the forests around Santa Barbara. Between that region and the Pueblo de los Angeles, Dr. Gambel met with it in great abundance, although neither writer makes mention of any peculiarities of habit. Mr. Emanuel Samuels met with it in and around Petaluma, where he obtained the eggs.

Dr. Newberry, in his Report on the zoölogy of Lieutenant Williamson's route (P. R. R. Reports, VI), states that the range of this species extends to the Columbia, and perhaps above, to the westward of the Cascade Range, though more common in California than in Oregon. It was not found in the Des Chutes Basin, nor in the Cascade Mountains.

In the list of the birds of Guatemala given by Mr. Salvin in the Ibis, this Woodpecker is mentioned (I, p. 137) as being found in the Central Region, at Calderas, on the Volcan de Fuego, in forests of evergreen oaks, where it feeds on acorns.

Dr. Heermann describes it as among the noisiest as well as the most abundant of the Woodpeckers of California. He speaks of it as catching insects on the wing, after the manner of a Flycatcher, and mentions its very extraordinary habit of digging small holes in the bark of the pine and the oak, in which it stores acorns for its food in winter. He adds that one of these acorns is placed in each hole, and is so tightly fitted or driven in that it is with difficulty extracted. Thus, the bark of a large pine forty or fifty feet high will present the appearance of being closely studded with brass nails, the heads only being visible. These acorns are thus stored in large quantities, and serve not only the Woodpecker, but trespassers as well. Dr. Heermann speaks of the nest as being excavated in the body of the tree to a depth varying from six inches to two feet, the eggs being four or five in number, and pure white.

These very remarkable and, for a Woodpecker, somewhat anomalous habits, first mentioned among American writers by Dr. Heermann, have given rise to various conflicting statements and theories in regard to the design of these collections of acorns. Some have even ventured to discredit the facts, but these are too well authenticated to be questioned. Too many naturalists whose accuracy cannot be doubted have been eyewitnesses to these performances. Among these is Mr. J. K. Lord, who, however, was constrained to confess his utter inability to explain why the birds did so. He was never able to find an acorn that seemed to have been eaten, nor a trace of vegetable matter in their stomachs, and at the close of his investigations he frankly admitted this storing of acorns to be a mystery for which he could offer no satisfactory explanation.

M. H. de Saussure, the Swiss naturalist, in an interesting paper published in 1858 in the *Bibliothèque Universelle* of Geneva, furnishes some very interesting observations on the habits of a Woodpecker, which he supposed to be the *Colaptes mexicanoides* of Mexico, of storing collections of acorns in the hollow stems of the maguay plants. Sumichrast, who accompanied Saussure in his excursion, while recognizing the entire truth of the interesting facts he narrates, is confident that the credit of all this instinctive forethought belongs not to the *Colaptes*, but to the Mexican race of this species. Saussure's article being too long to quote in full, we give an abstract.

The slopes of a volcanic mountain, Pizarro, near Perote, in Mexico, are covered with immense beds of the maguay (*Agave americana*), with larger growths of yuccas, but without any other large shrubs or trees. Saussure was surprised to find this silent and dismal wilderness swarming with Woodpeckers. A circumstance so unusual as this large congregation of birds, by nature so solitary, in a spot so unattractive, prompted him to investigate the mystery. The birds were seen to fly first to the stalks of the maguay, to attack them with their beaks, and then to pass to the yuccas, and there repeat their labors. These stalks, upon examination, were all found to be riddled with holes, placed irregularly one above another, and communicating with the hollow cavity within. On cutting open one of these stalks, he found it filled with acorns.

As is well known, this plant, after flowering, dies, its stalk remains, its outer covering hardens into a flinty texture, and its centre becomes hollow. This convenient cavity is used by the Woodpecker as a storehouse for provisions that are unusual food for the tribe. The central cavity of the stalk is only large enough to receive one acorn at a time. They are packed in, one above the other, until the cavity is full. How did these Woodpeckers first learn to thus use these storehouses, by nature closed against them ? The intelligent instinct that enabled this bird to solve this problem Saussure regarded as not the least surprising feature. With its beak it pierces a small round hole through the lower portion into the central cavity, and thrusts in acorns until the hollow is filled to the level of the hole. It then makes a second opening higher up, and fills the space below in a like manner, and so proceeds until the entire stalk is full. Sometimes the space is too small to receive the acorns, and they have to be forced in by blows from its beak. In other stalks there are no cavities, and then the Woodpecker creates one for each acorn, forcing it into the centre of the pith.

The labor necessary to enable the bird to accomplish all this is very considerable, and great industry is required to collect its stores ; but, once collected, the storehouse is a very safe and convenient one. Mount Pizarro is in the midst of a barren desert of sand and volcanic *débris*. There are no oak-trees nearer than the Cordilleras, thirty miles distant, and therefore the collecting and storing of each acorn required a flight of sixty miles.

This, reasons Saussure, is obviously an instinctive preparation, on the part of these birds, to provide the means of supporting life during the arid winter months, when no rain falls and everything is parched. His observations were made in April, the last of the winter months ; and he found the Woodpeckers withdrawing food from their depositories, and satisfied himself that the birds were eating the acorn itself, and not the diminutive maggots a few of them contained.

The ingenuity with which the bird managed to get at the contents of each acorn was also quite striking. Its feet being unfit for grasping the acorn, it digs a hole into the dry bark of the yuccas, just large enough to receive the small end of the acorn, which it inserts, making use of its bill to split it open, as with a wedge. The trunks of the yuccas were all found riddled with these holes.

There are several remarkable features to be noticed in the facts observed by Saussure, — the provident instinct which prompts this bird to lay by stores of provisions for the winter ; the great distance traversed to collect a kind of food so unusual for its race ; and its seeking, in a spot so remote from its natural abode, a storehouse so remarkable. Can instinct alone teach, or have experience and reason taught, these birds, that, better far than the bark of trees, or cracks in rocks, or cavities dug in the earth, or any other known hiding-place, are these hidden cavities within the hollow stems of distant plants ? What first taught them how to break through the flinty coverings of these retreats ? By what revelation could these birds have been informed that within these dry and closed stalks they could, by searching, find suitable places, protected from moisture, for preserving their stores in a state most favorable for their long preservation, safe from gnawing rats, and from those acorn-eating birds whose bills are not strong or sharp enough to cut through their tough enclosures?

M. Sumichrast, who afterwards enjoyed unusual opportunities for observing the habits of these Woodpeckers in the State of Vera Cruz, states that they dwell exclusively in oak woods, and that near Potrero, as well as in the alpine regions, trunks of oak-trees are found pierced with small holes in circular lines around their circumference. Into each of these holes these birds drive the acorns by repeated blows of their beaks, so as to fix them firmly. At other times they make their collection of acorns in openings between the raised bark of dry trees and the trunks. This writer states that he has sought in vain to explain such performances satisfactorily. The localities in which these birds reside, in Mexico, teem at all seasons with insects; and it seems absurd, therefore, to suppose that they can be in quest of the small, almost microscopic, larvæ contained in the acorns.

Dr. C. T. Jackson sought to account for these interesting performances on the ingenious hypothesis that the acorns thus stored are always infested with larvæ, and never sound ones; that they are driven into the tree cup-end foremost, so as to securely imprison the maggot and prevent its escape, and thus enable the Woodpecker to devour it at its leisure. This would argue a wonderful degree of intelligence and forethought, on the part of the Woodpecker, and more than it is entitled to; for the facts do not sustain this hypothesis. The acorns are not put into the tree with the cup-end in, but invariably the reverse, so far as we have noticed; and the acorns, so far from being wormy, are, in nine cases out of ten, sound ones. Besides, this theory affords no explanation of the large collections of loose acorns made by these birds in hollow trees, or in the stalks of the maguay plants. Nor can we understand why, if so intelligent, they make so little use of these acorns, as seems to be the almost universal testimony of California naturalists. And, as still further demonstrating the incorrectness of this hypothesis, we have recently been informed by Dr. Canfield of Monterey, Cal., that occasionally these Woodpeckers, following an instinct so blind that they do not distinguish between an acorn and a pebble, are known to fill up the holes they have drilled with so much labor, not only with acorns, but occasionally with stones. In time the bark and the wood grow over these, and after a few years they are left a long way from the surface. These trees are usually the sugar-pine of California, a wood much used for lumber. Occasionally one of these trees is cut, the log taken to mill without its being known that it is thus charged with rounded pieces of flint or agate, and the saws that come in contact with them are broken.

Without venturing to present an explanation of facts that have appeared so contradictory and unsatisfactory to other naturalists, such as we can claim to be either comprehensive or entirely satisfactory, we cannot discredit the positive averments of such observers as Saussure and Salvin. We believe that these Woodpeckers do eat the acorns, when they can do no better.

And when we are confronted with the fact, which we do not feel at liberty to altogether disregard, that in very large regions this bird seems to labor in vain, and makes no use of the treasures it has thus heaped together, we can only attempt an explanation. This Woodpecker is found over an immense area. It everywhere has the same instinctive promptings to provide, not "for a rainy day," but for the exact opposite, — for a long interval during which no rain falls, for nearly two hundred days at a time, in all the low and hot lands of Mexico and Central America. There these accumulations become a necessity, there we are informed they do eat the acorns, and, more than this, many other birds and beasts derive the means of self-preservation in times of famine from the provident labors of this bird. That in Oregon, in California, and in the mountains of Mexico and elsewhere, where better and more natural food offers throughout the year, it is rarely known to eat the acorns it has thus labored to save, only seems to prove that it acts under the influences of an undiscriminating instinct that prompts it to gather in its stores whether it needs them or not.

It may be, too, that writers have too hastily inferred that these birds never eat the acorns, because they have been unable to obtain complete evidence of the fact. We have recently received from C. W. Plass, Esq., some interesting facts, which, if they do not prove that these birds in the winter visit their stores and eat their acorns, render it highly probable. Mr. Plass resides near Napa City, Cal., near which city, and on the edge of the pine forests, he has recently constructed a house. The gable-ends of this dwelling the California Woodpeckers have found a very convenient storehouse for their acorns, and Mr. Plass has very considerately permitted them to do so unmolested. The window in the gable slides up upon pullies its whole length, to admit of a passage to the upper verandah, and the open space in the wall admits of the nuts falling down into the upper hall, and this frequently happens when the birds attempt to extricate them from the outside. Nearly all these nuts are found to be sound, and contain no worm, while those that fall outside are empty shells. Empty shells have also been noticed by Mr. Plass under the trees, indicating that the acorns have been eaten.

The Smithsonian Institution has received specimens of the American race of this Woodpecker, collected at Belize by Dr. Berendt, and accompanied by illustrations of their work in the way of implantation of acorns in the bark of trees.

The eggs of this Woodpecker, obtained by Mr. Emanuel Samuels near Petaluma, Cal., and now in the collection of the Boston Society of Natural History, are undistinguishable from the eggs of other Woodpeckers in form or color, except that they are somewhat oblong, and measure 1.12 inches in length by .90 of an inch in breadth.

Melanerpes formicivorus, var. angustifrons, BAIRD.

THE NARROW-FRONTED WOODPECKER.

Melanerpes formicivorus, var. *angustifrons*, BAIRD, COOPER, Orn. Cal. I, 1870, 405.

SP. CHAR. Compared with *M. formicivorus*, the size is smaller. The light frontal bar is much narrower; in the female scarcely more than half the black one behind it, and not reaching anything like as far back as the anterior border of the eye, instead of exceeding this limit. The light frontal and the black bars together are only about two thirds the length of the occipital red, instead of exceeding it in length; the red patch reaches forward nearly or quite to the posterior border of the eye, instead of falling a considerable distance behind it, and being much broader posteriorly. The frontal band too is gamboge-yellow, much like the throat, and not white; the connection with the yellow throat-patch much broader. The white upper tail-coverts show a tendency to a black edge. Length, 8.00; wing, 5.20; tail, 3.20.

HAB. Cape St. Lucas.

As the differences mentioned are constant, we consider the Cape St. Lucas bird as forming at least a permanent variety, and indicate it as above. A single specimen from the Sierra Madre, of Colima, is very similar.

HABITS. We have no information as to the habits of this singular race of the *M. formicivorus*, found at Cape St. Lucas by Mr. John Xantus. It will be an interesting matter for investigation to ascertain to what extent the totally different character of the region in which this bird is met with from those in which the *M. formicivorus* is found, may have modified its habits and its manner of life.

SECTION COLAPTEÆ.

This section, formerly embracing but one genus additional to *Colaptes*, has recently had three more added to it by Bonaparte. The only United States representative, however, is *Colaptes*.

GENUS COLAPTES, SWAINSON.

Colaptes, SWAINSON, Zool. Jour. III, Dec. 1827, 353. (Type, *Cuculus auratus*, LINN.)
Geopicos, MALHERBE, Mém. Acad. Metz, 1849, 358. (*G. campestris*.)

GEN. CHAR. Bill slender, depressed at the base, then compressed. Culmen much curved, gonys straight; both with acute ridges, and coming to quite a sharp point with the commissure at the end; the bill, consequently, not truncate at the end. No ridges on the bill. Nostrils basal, median, oval, and exposed. Gonys very short; about half the culmen. Feet large; the anterior outer toe considerably longer than the posterior. Tail long, exceeding the secondaries; the feathers suddenly acuminate, with elongated points.

There are four well-marked representatives of the typical genus *Colaptes* belonging to Middle and North America, three of them found within the

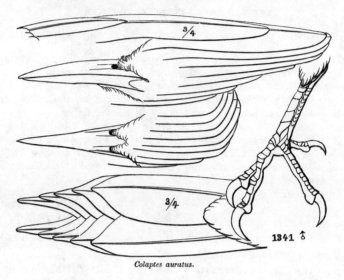

Colaptes auratus.

limits of the United States, in addition to what has been called a hybrid between two of them. The common and distinctive characters of these four are as follows : —

Species and Varieties.

COMMON CHARACTERS. Head and neck ashy or brown, unvaried except by a black or red malar patch in the male. Back and wings brown, banded transversely with black; rump and upper tail-coverts white. Beneath whitish, with circular black spots, and bands on crissum; a black pectoral crescent. Shafts and under surfaces of quills and tail-feathers either yellow or red.

A. Mustache red; throat ash; no red nuchal crescent.

   a. Under surface and shafts of wings and tail red.

      1. **C. mexicanoides.**[1] Hood bright cinnamon-rufous; feathers of mustache black below surface. Upper parts barred with black and whitish-brown, the two colors of about equal width. Shafts, etc., dull brick-red. Rump spotted with black; black terminal zone of under surface of tail narrow, badly defined. Wing, 6.15; tail, 4.90; bill, 1.77. *Hab.* Southern Mexico and Guatemala.

      2. **C. mexicanus.**[2] Hood ashy-olivaceous, more rufescent anteriorly, light cinnamon on lores and around eyes; feathers of mustache light ash below surface. Upper parts umber-brown, barred with black, the black only about one fourth as wide as the brown. Shafts, etc., fine salmon-red, or pinkish orange-red. Rump unspotted; black terminal

[1] *Colaptes mexicanoides*, LAFR. Rev. Zool. 1844, 42. — SCL. & SALV. Ibis, 1859, 137. — SCL. Catal. Am. B. 1862, 344. *Colaptes rubricatus*, GRAY, Gen. B. pl. cxi. *Geopicus rub.* MALH. Monog. Pic. II, 265, pl. cx, figs. 1, 2. *Picus submexicanus*, SUND. Consp. Pic. 1866, 72.

[2] A series of hybrids between *mexicanus* and *auratus* is in the Smithsonian collection, these specimens exhibiting every possible combination of the characters of the two.

zone of tail broad, sharply defined. Wing, 6.70; tail, 5.00; bill, 1.60. *Hab.* Middle and Western Province of United States, south into Eastern Mexico to Mirador and Orizaba, and Jalapa.

b. Under surface and shafts of wings and tail gamboge-yellow.

3. **C. chrysoides.** Hood uniform light cinnamon; upper parts raw umber with sparse, very narrow and distant, bars of black. Rump immaculate; black terminal zone of tail occupying nearly the terminal half, and very sharply defined. Wing, 5.90; tail, 5.70; bill, 1.80. *Hab.* Colorado and Cape St. Lucas region of Southern Middle Province of United States.

B. Mustache black; a red nuchal crescent. Throat pinkish, hood ashy.

4. **C. auratus.** Shafts, etc., gamboge-yellow; upper parts olivaceous-brown, with narrow bars of black, about half as wide as the brown.

Rump immaculate; black terminal zone of under surface of tail broad, more than half an inch wide on outer feather. Edges of tail-feathers narrowly edged, but not indented, with whitish. Outer web of lateral feathers without spots of dusky. Wing, 6.10; tail, 4.80; bill, 1.58. *Hab.* Eastern Province of North America . . . . var. *auratus.*

Rump spotted with black; black terminal zone of tail narrow, consisting on outer feather of an irregular spot less than a quarter of an inch wide. Edges of all the tail-feathers indented with whitish bars; outer web of lateral feathers with quadrate spots of dusky along the edge. Wing, 5.75; tail, 4.75; bill, 1.60. *Hab.* Cuba . . . . var. *chrysocaulosus.*[1]

Colaptes auratus, SWAINSON.

FLICKER; YELLOW-SHAFTED WOODPECKER; HIGH-HOLDER.

Cuculus auratus, LINN. Syst. Nat., I, (ed. 10,) 1758, 112. *Picus auratus,* LINN. Syst. Nat. I, (ed. 12,) 1766, 174. — FORSTER, Phil. Trans. LXII, 1772, 383. — VIEILLOT, Ois. Am. Sept. II, 1807, 66, pl. cxxiii. — WILSON, Am. Orn. I, 1810, 45, pl. iii, f. 1. — WAGLER, Syst. Av. 1827, No. 84. — AUD. Orn. Biog. I, 1832, 191; V, 540, pl. xxxvii. — IB. Birds Amer. IV, 1842, 282, pl. cclxxiii. — SUNDEVALL, Consp. 71. *Colaptes auratus,* Sw. Zoöl. Jour. III, 1827, 353. — IB. F. Bor. Am. II, 1831, 314. — BON. List, 1838. — IB. Conspectus, 1850, 113. — BAIRD, Birds N. Am. 1858, 118. — MAX. Cab. Jour. 1858, 420. — DRESSER, Ibis, 1865, 470 (San Antonio, one specimen only seen). — SCL. Cat. 1862, 344. — GRAY, Cat. 1868, 120. — FOWLER, Am. Nat. III, 1869, 422. — DALL & BANNISTER, Tr. Chicago Ac. I, 1869, 275 (Alaska). — SAMUELS, 105. — ALLEN, B. E. Fla. 307.

SP. CHAR. Shafts and under surfaces of wing and tail feathers gamboge-yellow. Male with a black patch on each side of the cheek. A red crescent on the nape. Throat and stripe beneath the eye pale lilac-brown. Back glossed with olivaceous-green. Female without the black cheek-patch.

ADDITIONAL CHARACTERS. A crescentic patch on the breast and rounded spots on the belly black. Back and wing-coverts with interrupted transverse bands of black. Neck above and on the sides ashy. Beneath pale pinkish-brown, tinged with yellow on the

---

[1] *Colaptes auratus,* var. *chrysocaulosus.* *Colaptes chrysocaulosus,* GUNDLACH, Boston Journal. — IB. Repert. I, 1866, 294.

abdomen, each feather with a heart-shaped spot of black near the end. Rump white. Length, 12.50 ; wing, 6.00.

HAB. All of eastern North America to the eastern slopes of Rocky Mountains ; farther north, extending across along the Yukon as far at least as Nulato, perhaps to the Pacific. Greenland (REINHARDT). Localities : San Antonio, Texas, only one specimen (DRESSER, Ibis, 1865, 470).

Specimens vary considerably in size and proportions ; the more northern ones are much the larger. The spots vary in number and in size ; they may be circular, or transversely or longitudinally oval. Western specimens appear paler. In a Selkirk Settlement specimen the belly is tinged with pale sulphur-yellow, the back with olivaceous-green.

This species, in general pattern of coloration, resembles the *C. mexicanus*, although the colors are very different. Thus the shafts of the quills, with their under surfaces, are gamboge-yellow, instead of orange-red. There is a conspicuous nuchal crescent of crimson wanting, or but slightly indicated, in *mexicanus*. The cheek-patch is pure black, widening and abruptly truncate behind, instead of bright crimson, pointed or rounded behind. The shade of the upper parts is olivaceous-green, instead of purplish-brown. The top of the head and the nape are more ashy. The chin, throat, neck, and sides of the head, are pale purplish or lilac brown, instead of bluish-ash ; the space above, below, and around the eye of the same color, instead of having reddish-brown above and ashy below.

The young of this species is sufficiently like the adult to be readily recognizable. Sometimes the entire crown is faintly tipped with red, as characteristic of young Woodpeckers.

HABITS. The Golden-winged Woodpecker is altogether the most common and the most widely distributed of the North American representatives of the genus. According to Sir John Richardson, it visits the fur countries in the summer, extending its migrations as far to the north as the Great Slave Lake, and resorting in great numbers to the plains of the Saskatchewan. It was found by Dr. Woodhouse very abundant in Texas and the Indian Territory, and it is given by Reinhardt as occurring in Greenland. Mr. McFarlane found it breeding at Fort Anderson ; Mr. Ross at Fort Rae, Fort Resolution, and Fort Simpson ; and Mr. Kennicott at Fort Yukon. All this testimony demonstrates a distribution throughout the entire eastern portion of North America, from the Gulf of Mexico almost to the Arctic Ocean, and from the Atlantic to the Rocky Mountains.

In the more northern portions of the continent this bird is only a summer visitant, but in the Southern and Middle, and to some extent in the New England States, it is a permanent resident. Wilson speaks of seeing them exposed for sale in the markets of Philadelphia during each month of a very rigorous winter. Wilson's observations of their habits during breeding, made in Pennsylvania, were that early in April they begin to prepare their nest. This is built in the hollow body or branch of a tree, sometimes, though not always, at a considerable height from the ground. He adds that he has frequently known them to fix on the trunk of an old apple-tree, at a height not more than six feet from the root. He also mentions as quite surprising the sagacity of this bird in discovering, under a sound bark, a hollow limb or trunk of a tree, and its perseverance in perforating it for purposes of incubation. The male and female alternately relieve and encourage each other by mutual caresses, renewing their labors for several days, till the object is attained, and the place rendered sufficiently capacious, convenient, and secure. They are often so extremely intent upon their work as to be heard at their labor till a very late hour in the night. Wilson mentions one instance where he knew a pair to dig first five inches straight forward, and then downward more than twice that distance, into a solid black-oak. They carry in no materials for their nest, the soft chips and dust of the wood serving for this purpose. The female lays six white eggs, almost transparent, very thick at the greater end, and tapering suddenly to the other. The young soon leave the nest, climbing to the higher branches, where they are fed by their parents.

According to Mr. Audubon this Woodpecker rears two broods in a season, the usual number of eggs being six. In one instance, however, Mr. MacCulloch, quoted by Audubon, speaks of having found a nest in a rotten stump, which contained no less than eighteen young birds, of various ages, and at least two eggs not quite hatched. It is not improbable that, in cases where the number of eggs exceeds seven or eight, more females than one have contributed to the number. In one instance, upon sawing off the decayed top of an old tree, in which these birds had a nest, twelve eggs were found. These were not molested, but, on visiting the place a few days after, I found the excavation to have been deepened from eighteen to twenty-four inches.

Mr. C. S. Paine, of Randolph, Vt., writing in October, 1860, furnishes some interesting observations made in regard to these birds in the central part of that State. He says, " This Woodpecker is very common, and makes its appearance about the 20th of April. Between the 1st and the 15th of May it usually commences boring a hole for the nest, and deposits its eggs the last of May or the first of June." He found three nests that year, all of which were in old stumps on the banks of a small stream. Each nest contained *seven* eggs. The boy who took them out was able to do so without any cutting, and found them at the depth of his elbow. In another nest there were but three eggs when first discovered. The limb was cut down nearly to a level with the eggs, which were taken. The next day the nest had been deepened a whole foot and another egg deposited. Mr. Paine has never known them go into thick woods to breed, but they seem rather to prefer the edges of woods. He has never known one to breed in an old cavity, but in one instance a pair selected a partially decayed stump for their operations. When they are disturbed, they sometimes fly around their nests, uttering shrill, squeaking notes, occasionally intermixing with them guttural or gurgling tones.

It is probably true that they usually excavate their own burrow, but this is not an invariable rule. In the fall of 1870 a pair of these Woodpeckers took shelter in my barn, remaining there during the winter. Although there were abundant means of entrance and of egress, they wrought for themselves other passages out and in through the most solid part of the sides of the building. Early in the spring they toók possession of a large cavity in an old apple-tree, directly on the path between the barn and the house, where they reared their family. They were very shy, and rarely permitted themselves to be seen. The nest contained six young, each of which had been hatched at successive intervals, leaving the nest one after the other. The youngest was nearly a fortnight later to depart than the first. Just before leaving the nest, the oldest bird climbed to the opening of the cavity, filling the whole space, and uttering a loud hissing sound whenever the nest was approached. As soon as they could use their wings, even partially, they were removed, one by one, to a more retired part of the grounds, where they were fed by their parents.

Throughout Massachusetts, this bird, generally known as the Pigeon Woodpecker, is one of the most common and familiar birds. They abound in old orchards and groves, and manifest more apparent confidence in man than the treatment they receive at his hands seems to justify. Their nests are usually constructed at the distance of only a few feet from the ground, and though Wilson, Audubon, and Nuttall agree upon six as the average of their eggs, they frequently exceed this number. Mr. Audubon gives as the measurement of the eggs of this species 1.08 inches in length and .88 of an inch in breadth. Their length varies from 1.05 to 1.15 inches, and their breadth from .91 to .85 of an inch. Their average measurement is 1.09 by .88 of an inch.

Colaptes mexicanus, SWAINSON.

RED-SHAFTED FLICKER.

Colaptes mexicanus, Sw. Syn. Mex. Birds, in Philos. Mag. I, 1827, 440. — IB. F. Bor. Am. II, 1831, 315. — NEWBERRY, Zoöl. Cal. & Or. Route, 91 ; P. R. R. Rep. VI, 1857. — BAIRD, Birds N. Am. 1858, 120. — MAX. Cab. Jour. 1858, 420, mixed with *hybridus*. — LORD, Proc. R. Art. Inst. I, IV, 112. — COOPER & SUCKLEY, 163. — SCLATER, P. Z. S. 1858, 309 (Oaxaca). — IB. Cat. 1862, 344. — DRESSER, Ibis, 1865, 470 (San Antonio, rare). — COUES, Pr. A. N. S. 1866, 56. — SUMICHRAST, Mem. Bost. Soc. I, 1869, 562 (alpine district, Vera Cruz). — GRAY, Cat. 1868, 121. — DALL & BANNISTER, Pr. Chicago Ac. I, 1869, 275 (Alaska). — COOPER, Orn. Cal. I, 1870, 408. *Picus mexicanus*, AUD. Orn. Biog. V, 1839, 174, pl. ccccxvi. — IB. Birds America, IV, 1842, 295, pl. cclxxiv. — SUNDEVALL, Consp. 72. *Colaptes collaris*, VIGORS, Zoöl. Jour. IV, Jan. 1829, 353. — IB. Zoöl. Beechey's Voy. 1839, 24, pl. ix. *Picus rubricatus*, WAGLER, Isis, 1829, V, May, 516. ("Lichtenstein Mus. Berol.") *Colaptes rubricatus*, BON. Pr. Zoöl. Soc. V, 1837, 108. — IB. List, 1838. — IB. Conspectus, 1850, 114. *? Picus cafer*, GMELIN, Syst. Nat. I, 1788, 431. — LATH. Index Ornith. II, 1790, 242. *? Picus lathami*, WAGLER, Syst. 1827, No. 85 (Cape of Good Hope ?).

Sp. Char. Shafts and under surfaces of wing and tail feathers orange-red. Male with a red patch on each side the cheek; nape without red crescent; sometimes very faint indications laterally. Throat and stripe beneath the eye bluish-ash. Back glossed with purplish-brown. Female without the red cheek-patch. Length, about 13.00; wing, over 6.50.

Additional Characters. Spots on the belly, a crescent on the breast, and interrupted transverse bands on the back, black.

Hab. Western North America from Pacific to the Black Hills; north to Sitka on the coast. Localities: Oaxaca (Scl. P. Z. S. 1858, 305); Vera Cruz, alpine regions (Sumichrast, Mem. Bost. Soc. I, 1869, 562); San Antonio, Texas (Dresser, Ibis, 1865, 470); W. Arizona (Coues, P. A. N. S. 1866, 56).

Colaptes mexicanus.

The female is similar in every way, perhaps a little smaller, but lacks the red mustache. This is, however, indicated by a brown tinge over an area corresponding with that of the red of the male.

In the present specimen (1,886) there is a slight indication of an interrupted nuchal red band, as in the common Flicker, in some crimson fibres to some of the feathers about as far behind the eye as this is from the bill. A large proportion of males before us exhibit the same characteristic, some more, some less, although it generally requires careful examination for its detection. It may possibly be a characteristic of the not fully mature bird, although it occurs in two out of three male specimens.

There is a little variation in the size of the pectoral crescent and spots; the latter are sometimes rounded or oblong cordate, instead of circular. The bill varies as much as three or four tenths of an inch. The rump, usually immaculate, sometimes has a few black streaks. The extent of the red whisker varies a little. In skins from Oregon and Washington the color of the back is as described; in those from California and New Mexico it is of a grayer cast. There is little, if any, variation in the shade of red in the whiskers and quill-feathers. The head is washed on the forehead with rufous, passing into ashy on the nape.

There is not only some difference in the size of this species, in the same locality, but, as a general rule, the more southern specimens are smaller.

This species is distinct from the *C. mexicanoides* of Lafresnaye, though somewhat resembling it. It is, however, a smaller bird; the red of the cheeks is deeper; the whole upper part of the head and neck uniform reddish-cinnamon without any ash, in marked contrast to that on the sides of the head. The back is strongly glossed with reddish-brown, and the black transverse bars are much more distinct, closer and broader, three or four on each feather, instead of two only. The rump and upper tail-coverts are closely barred, the centre of the former only clearer white, but even here each feather has a cordate spot of white. The spots on the flanks posteriorly exhibit a tendency to become transverse bars.

Specimens from Mount Orizaba, Mexico, are very similar to those from Oregon in color, presenting no appreciable difference. The size is, however, much less, a male measuring 10.50, wing 6.00, tail 4.60 inches, instead of 12.75, 6.75, and 5.25 respectively. While, however, the feet are smaller (tarsus 1.00 instead of 1.15), the bill is fully as large, or even larger.

Most young birds of this species have a tinge of red on top of the head, and frequently a decided nuchal crescent of red; but these are only embryonic features, and disappear with maturity.

HABITS. This species, the counterpart in so many respects of the Golden-winged Woodpecker, appears to take the place of that species from the slopes of the Rocky Mountains to the Pacific, throughout western North America. Dr. Woodhouse speaks of finding it abundant along the banks of the Rio Grande. And in the fine collection belonging to the Smithsonian Institution are specimens from the Straits of Fuca, Fort Steilacoom, and Fort Vancouver, in Washington Territory, from the Columbia River, from various points in California, New Mexico, Arizona, Utah, Kansas, Nebraska, Texas, Mexico, etc. Dr. Gambel, in his Paper on the birds of California, first met with the Red-shafted Woodpecker soon after leaving New Mexico, and it continued to California, where he found it very abundant. He describes it as a remarkably shy bird, and adds that he always saw it on the margins of small creeks, where nothing grew larger than a willow-bush. Dr. Heermann also found it abundant in California. Dr. Newberry, in his Report on the zoölogy of Lieutenant Williamson's expedition, speaks of the Red-shafted Flicker as rather a common bird in all parts of California and Oregon which his party visited. He describes many of its habits as identical with those of the Golden Flicker (*C. auratus*), but regards it as much the shyer bird. Dr. Cooper also mentions the fact of the great abundance of this bird along the western coast, equalling that of its closely allied cousin on the eastern side of the Mississippi. It also resembles, he adds, that bird so exactly in habits and notes that the description of one will apply with exactness to the other. It is a constant resident in Washington Territory, or at least west of the Cascade Mountains. He observed it already burrowing out holes for its nests in April, at the Straits of Fuca. About June 1 he found a nest containing seven young, nearly fledged, which already showed in the male the distinguishing red mustache. Dr. Suckley, in the same report, also says that it is extremely common in the timbered districts of Washington Territory, and adds that its habits, voice, calls, etc., are precisely similar to those of the Yellow-Hammer of the Eastern States. Mr. Nuttall, as quoted by Mr. Audubon, states that he first came upon this bird in the narrow belt of forest which borders Laramie's Fork of the Platte, and adds that he scarcely lost sight of it from that time until he reached the shores of the Pacific. Its manners, in all respects, are so entirely similar to those of the common species that the same description applies to both. He also regards it as the shyer bird of the two, and less frequently seen on the ground. They burrow in the oak and pine trees, and lay white eggs, after the manner of the whole family, and these eggs are in no wise distinguishable from those of the Golden-wing.

Dr. Cooper, in his Report upon the birds of California, refers to this as a common species, and found in every part of the State except the bare plains. It even frequents the low bushes, where no trees are to be seen for miles. In the middle wooded districts, and towards the north, it is much more abundant than elsewhere.

Their nesting-holes are at all heights from the ground, and are usually about one foot in depth. In the southern part of the State their eggs are laid in April, but farther north, at the Columbia, in May.

Dr. Cooper attributes their shyness in certain localities to their being hunted so much by the Indians for their bright feathers. Generally he found them quite tame, so that their interesting habits may be watched without difficulty. He regards them as an exact counterpart of the eastern *auratus*, living largely on insects and ants, which they collect without much trouble, and do not depend upon hard work, like other Woodpeckers, for their food. During the season they also feed largely on berries. Their curved bill is not well adapted for hammering sound wood for insects, and they only dig into decayed trees in search of their food. Like the eastern species, the young of these birds, when their nest is approached, make a curious hissing noise. They may be seen chasing each other round the trunk of trees, as if in sport, uttering, at the same time, loud cries like *whittoo, whittoo, whittoo*. Dr. Kennerly found these birds from the Big Sandy to the Great Colorado, but they were so shy that he could not obtain a specimen. They were seen on the barren hills among the large cacti, in which they nest. Their extreme shyness was fully explained afterwards by finding how closely they are hunted by the Indians for the sake of their feathers, of which head-dresses are made.

Mr. Dresser states that this bird is found as far east as San Antonio, where, however, it is of uncommon occurrence. In December he noticed several near the Nueces River, and in February and March obtained others near Piedras Negras.

Dr. Coues gives it as abundant and resident in Arizona, where it is found in all situations. Its tongue, he states, is capable of protrusion to an extent far beyond that of any other North American Woodpecker.

This bird, in some parts of California, is known as the Yellow-Hammer, a name given in some parts of New England to the *Colaptes auratus*. Mr.

C. W. Plass, of Napa City, writes me that this Woodpecker "makes himself too much at home with us to be agreeable. He drills large holes though the weather-boards of the house, and shelters himself at night between them and the inner wall. He does not nest there, but simply makes of such situations his winter home. We have had to shoot them, for we find it is of no use to shut up one hole, as they will at once make another by its side."

Mr. J. A. Allen mentions finding this species, in the absence of suitable trees on the Plains, making excavations in sand-banks.

According to Mr. Ridgway, the Red-shafted Flicker does not differ from the Yellow-shafted species of the east in the slightest particular, as regards habits, manners, and notes. It is, however, more shy than the eastern species, probably from the fact that it is pursued by the Indians, who prize its quill and tail-feathers as ornaments with which to adorn their dress.

Their eggs are hardly distinguishable from those of the *auratus*, but range of a very slightly superior size. They average 1.12 inches in length by .89 of an inch in breadth. Their greatest length is 1.15 inches, their least 1.10, and their breadth ranges from .87 to .90.

Colaptes hybridus, BAIRD.

HYBRID FLICKER.

Colaptes ayresii, AUD. Birds Am. VII, 1843, 348, pl. ccccxciv. *Colaptes hybridus*, BAIRD, Birds N. Am. 1858, 122. *Colaptes mexicanus*, MAX. Cab. Jour. 1858, 422 (mixed with *mexicanus*). *Picus hybridus aurato-mexicanus*, SUNDEVALL, Consp. Pic. 1866, 721.

SP. CHAR. Yellow shafts or feathers on wing and tail combined with red, or red spotted cheek-patches. Orange-red shafts combined with a well-defined nuchal red crescent, and pinkish throat. Ash-colored throat combined with black cheek-patch or yellow shafts. Shafts and feathers intermediate between gamboge-yellow and dark orange-red.

HAB. Upper Missouri and Yellowstone; Black Hills.

The general distribution of *Colaptes mexicanus*, as already indicated, is from the Pacific coast of the United States, eastward to the Black Hills and the Upper Missouri and Yellowstone; that of the *C. auratus* from the Atlantic Coast to about the eastern limits of *mexicanus*. But little variation is seen in the two species up to the region mentioned; slight differences in shade of color, size, and frequency of spots, etc., being all. Where they come together, however, or overlap, a most remarkable race is seen, in which no two specimens, nay, scarcely the two sides of the same bird, are alike, the characters of the two species becoming mixed up in the most extraordinary manner. Thus, the shafts show every shade from orange-red to pure yellow; yellow shafts combine with red cheek-patch (as in *C. ayresii* of Audubon); a red nape, with orange-red shafts; cheek-patches red with black feathers intermixed, or *vice versa*; perhaps the feathers red at base and black at tip, or black at base and red at tip, etc. As the subject has been presented in sufficient detail in the Birds of North America, as quoted above, it need not be repeated here, except to say that collections received since 1858 only substantiate what has there been stated.

To the race thus noted, the name *hybridus* was given, not as of a variety, since it is not entitled to this rank, but as of a heterogeneous mixture, caused by the breeding together of two different species, and requiring some appellation. Whether the presumed hybrids are fertile, and breed with each other or with full-blooded parents, has not yet been ascertained; perhaps not, since the area in which they occur is limited, and it is only occasionally that individuals of the kind referred to have been found beyond the bounds mentioned. It is very rarely, however, that pure breeds occur in the district of *hybridus*, a taint being generally appreciable in all.

The conditions in the present instance appear different from those adverted to under the head of *Picus villosus*, where the question is not one of hybridism between two strongly marked and distinct species, but of the gradual change, between the Atlantic and the Pacific, from one pattern of coloration to another.

Colaptes chrysoides, MALH.

THE CAPE FLICKER.

Geopicus chrysoides, MALH. Rev. et Mag. Zool. IV, 1852, 553. — IB. Mon. Pic. II, 261, tab. 109. *Colaptes chrysoides*, BAIRD, Birds N. Am. 1858, 125. — ELLIOT, Ill. Birds N. Am. VI, plate. — COOPER, Pr. Cal. Ac. 1861, 122 (Fort Mohave). — COUES, Pr. A. N. Sc. 1866, 56 (Arizona). — SCL. Cat. 1862, 344. — ELLIOT, Illust. Am. B. I, pl. xxvi. — COOPER, Orn. Cal. I, 1870, 410. *Picus chrysoides*, SUNDEVALL, Consp. 72.

SP. CHAR. Markings generally as in other species. Top of head rufous-brown; chin, throat, and sides of head ash-gray. Shafts of quills and tail-feathers, with their under surfaces in great part, gamboge-yellow; no nuchal red. Malar patch of male red; wanting in the female. Length, 11.50; wing, 5.75; tail, 4.50.

HAB. Colorado and Gila River, north to Fort Mohave, south to Cape St. Lucas. Localities: Fort Mohave (COOPER, Pr. Cal. Ac. 1861, 122); W. Arizona (COUES, P. A. N. S. 1866, 56).

This interesting species is intermediate between *auratus* and *mexicanus* in having the yellow shafts and quills of the former; a red malar patch, an ashy throat, and no nuchal crescent, as in the latter. To *mexicanoides* the relationship is still closer, since both have the rufous-brown head above. A hybrid between this last species and *auratus* would in some varieties come very near *chrysoides*, but as it does not belong to the region of *chrysoides*, and there is no transition from one species to the other in any specimens, as in *hybridus*, there is no occasion to take this view of the species.

Cape St. Lucas specimens, where the species is exceedingly abundant, are considerably smaller than those from Arizona, and appear to be more strongly marked with black above and below; otherwise there seems to be no difference of special importance.

As neither *C. auratus* nor *mexicanus* has the top of the head rufous-brown, (though slightly indicated anteriorly in the latter), this character has not been noted in the hybrids between the two (*hybridus*), and its presence in *chrysoides* will serve to distinguish it from *hybridus*.

HABITS. This comparatively new form of Woodpecker was first described in 1852 by Malherbe, from a California specimen in the Paris Museum, which had been at first supposed to be a female or immature *ayresii*. What Dr. Cooper thinks may have been this species was met with by Dr. Heermann among the mountains bordering upon the Cosumnes River, in California, where it was rare, and only two specimens were taken. In February, 1861, other specimens of this bird were taken at Fort Mohave by Dr. Cooper. They were feeding on larvæ and insects among the poplar-trees, and were very shy and wary. The bird is supposed to winter in the Colorado Valley, and wherever found has been met with in valleys, and not on mountains. It is an abundant and characteristic member of the Cape St. Lucas fauna.

According to Dr. Cooper these birds were already mated at Fort Mohave after February 20. They had the same habits, flight, and cries as the *C. mexicanus*. They appeared to be migratory, having come from the south.

Mr. Xantus, in his brief notes on the birds of Cape St. Lucas, makes mention of finding this bird breeding, May 19, in a dead *Cereus giganteus*. The nest was a large cavity about fifteen feet from the ground, and contained only one egg. The parent bird was also secured. In another instance two eggs were found in a *Cereus giganteus*, at the distance of forty feet from the ground. The eggs were not noticeably different from those of the common *Colaptes mexicanus*.

Family **PSITTACIDÆ**. — The Parrots.

Char. Bill greatly hooked ; the maxilla movable and with a cere at the base. Nostrils in the base of the bill. Feet scansorial, covered with granulated scales.

The above diagnosis characterizes briefly a family of the *Zygodactyli* having representatives throughout the greater part of the world, except Europe, and embracing about three hundred and fifty species, according to the late enumeration of Finsch,[1] of which one hundred and forty-two, or nearly one half, are American (seventy Brazilian alone). The subfamilies are as follows : —

    I. **Stringopinæ**. Appearance owl-like; face somewhat veiled or with a facial disk, as in the Owls.
    II. **Plyctolophinæ**. Head with an erectile crest, of variable shape.
    III. **Sittacinæ**. Head plain. Tail long, or lengthened, wedge-shaped or graduated.
    IV. **Psittacinæ**. Head plain. Tail short or moderate, straight or rounded.
    V. **Trichoglossinæ**. Tip of tongue papillose. Bill compressed ; tip of maxilla internally smooth, not crenate ; gonys obliquely ascending.

Of these, Nos. III and IV alone are represented in the New World, and only the *Sittacinæ* occur in the United States, with one species.

Subfamily **SITTACINÆ**.

The lengthened cuneate tail, as already stated, distinguishes this group from the American *Psittacinæ* with short, square, or rounded tail. The genera are distinguished as follows : —

    Sittace. Culmen flattened. Face naked, except in *S. pachyrhyncha*. Tail as long as or longer than wings.
    Conurus. Culmen rounded. Face entirely feathered, except a curve around the eye. Tail shorter than wings.

Of the genus *Sittace*, which embraces eighteen species, two come sufficiently near to the southern borders of the United States to render it not impossible that they may yet be found to cross the border. Of one of these, indeed, (*S. pachyrhyncha*,) there is a specimen in the Museum of the Philadelphia Academy of Natural Sciences, presented by J. W. Audubon as shot on the Rio Grande of Texas ; and another (*S. militaris*) is common at Mazatlan, and perhaps even at Guaymas. There is considerable reason for doubt as to the authenticity of the alleged locality of the *S. pachyrhyncha*, but for the

---

[1] Die Papageien. Monographisch bearbeitet von Otto Finsch. 2 vols. Leiden, 1867, 1868.

purpose of identification, should either species present itself, we give diagnoses in the accompanying foot-note.[1]

Genus **CONURUS**, Kuhl.

Conurus, Kuhl, Consp. Psittac. 4, 1830. — Ib. Nova Acta K. L. C. Acad. X, 1830.

Gen. Char. Tail long, conical, and pointed; bill stout; cheeks feathered, but in some species leaving a naked ring round the eye; cere feathered to the base of the bill.

The preceding diagnosis, though not very full, will serve to indicate the essential characteristics of the genus among the Middle American forms

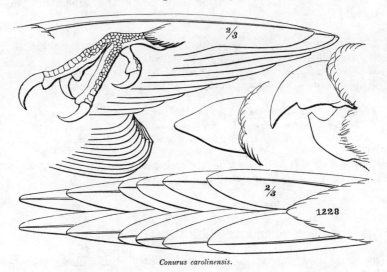

Conurus carolinensis.

with long pointed tails, the most prominent feature consisting in the densely feathered, not naked, cheeks. But one species belongs to the United States,

[1] **A.** Tail longer than the wings; lores and cheeks naked; the latter with narrow lines of small feathers.

    S. militaris. Green; forehead red; posterior portion of back, upper and under tail-coverts with quills and tip of tail, sky-blue; under side of tail dirty orange-yellow. Wing, 14.00; middle tail-feathers, 15.00; tarsus, 1.08. *Hab.* North-western Mexico to Bolivia.

        Synonymy : *Psittacus militaris*, Linn. S. N. 1767, 139. *Sittace militaris*, Finsch, Die Papageien, I, 1867, 396.

B. Tail about equal to the wings; lores and cheeks feathered.

    S. pachyrhyncha. Green; the forehead, edge of wings, and the tibiæ red; greater under wing-coverts yellow. Wing, 8.00 to 10.00; middle tail-feather, 6.50. *Hab.* Southern Mexico (Jalapa and Anguangueo), given probably erroneously from the Rio Grande of Texas. Synonymy : *Macrocercus pachyrhynchus*, Sw. Syn. Birds Mex. in Philos. Mag. I, 1827, 439, No. 79. *Rhynchopsitta pachyrhyncha*, Bon. Tableau des Perroquets, Rev. et Mag. de Zool. 1854, 149. *Sittace pachyrhyncha*, Finsch, Die Papageien, I, 1867, 428. *Psittacus pascha*, Wagler, Isis, 1831, 524. *Psittacus strenuus*, Licht. Preis-Verzeichiss, 1830.

though three others are found in Mexico, and many more in South and Central America. A few species occur in the West Indies.

Conurus carolinensis, KUHL.

PARAKEET; CAROLINA PARROT; ILLINOIS PARROT.

Psittaca carolinensis, BRISSON, Ornith. II, 1762, 138. *Psittacus carolinensis,* LINN. Syst. Nat. I, 1758, 97 ; 1766, 141 (nec SCOPOLI). — WILSON, Am. Orn. III, 1811, 89, pl. xxvi, fig. 1. — AUD. Orn. Biog. I, 1832, 135, pl. xxvi. *Conurus carolinensis,* KUHL, Nova Acta K. L. C. 1830. — BON. List, 1838. — PR. MAX. Cabanis Journ. für Orn. V, March, 1857, 97. — BAIRD, Birds N. Am. 1858, 57. — FINSCH, Papagei. I, 1857, 478. — SCL. Cat. 1862, 347. — ALLEN, B. E. Fla. 308. *Centurus carolinensis,* AUD. Syn. 1839, 189. — IB. Birds Am. IV, 1842, 306, pl. cclxxviii. *Psittacus ludovicianus,* GM. Syst. I, 1788, 347. *Psittacus thalassinus,* VIEILL. Ency. Meth. 1377. *Conurus ludovicianus,* GRAY. Catal. Br. Mus. Psittac. 1859, 36 (makes distinct species from *carolinensis*). *Carolina parrot,* CATESBY, Car. I, tab. xi. — LATHAM, Syn. I, 227. — PENNANT, II, 242. *Orange-headed parrot,* LATHAM, Syn. I, 304.

SP. CHAR. Head and neck all round gamboge-yellow ; the forehead, from above the eyes, with the sides of the head, pale brick-red. Body generally with tail green, with a yellowish tinge beneath. Outer webs of primaries bluish-green, yellow at the base; secondary coverts edged with yellowish. Edge of wing yellow, tinged with red; tibiæ yellow. Bill white. Legs flesh-color. Length, about 13.00 ; wing, 7.50 ; tail, 7.10. Young with head and neck green. Female with head and neck green ; the forehead, lores, and suffusion round the eyes, dark red, and without the yellow of tibiæ and edge of wing. Size considerably less.

HAB. Southern and Southwestern States and Mississippi Valley ; north to the Great Lakes and Wisconsin.

Conurus carolinensis.

This species was once very abundant in the United States east of the Rocky Mountains, being known throughout the Southern States, and the entire valley of the Mississippi, north to the Great Lakes. Stragglers even penetrated to Pennsylvania, and one case of their reaching Albany, N. Y., is on record. Now, however, they are greatly restricted. In Florida they are yet abundant, but, according to Dr. Coues, they are scarcely entitled to a place in the fauna of South Carolina. In Western Louisiana, Arkansas, and the Indian Territory, they are still found in considerable numbers, straggling over the adjacent States, but now seldom go north of the mouth of the Ohio. We have seen no note of their occurrence south of the United States, and in view of their very limited area and rapid diminution in numbers, there is little doubt but that their total extinction is only a matter of years, perhaps to be consummated within the lifetime of persons now living. It is a question whether both sexes are similarly colored, as in most American Parrots, or whether the female, as just stated, lacks the yellow of the head. Several female birds killed in Florida in March agree in the characters indicated above for that sex; but the material at our command is not sufficient to decide whether all females are similarly marked, or whether the plumage described is that of the bird of the second year generally. There is no trace whatever of yellow on the head.

HABITS. In determining the geographical distribution of the Carolina Parrot, a distinction should be made between its accidental occurrence and its usual and habitual residence. Strictly speaking, this species, though of roving habits, is not migratory. Its movements are irregular, and dependent upon the abundance or the scarcity of its food. Where it breeds, it is usually a permanent resident. An exceptional visit to a place cannot be taken as certain evidence that it will reappear in that locality.

When Wilson wrote, it inhabited the interior of Louisiana and the country lying upon the banks of the Mississippi and Ohio Rivers, and their tributary waters, even beyond the Illinois River, to the neighborhood of Lake Michigan, in latitude 42° north. The same writer insisted that, contrary to the generally received opinion, it was at that time resident in all those places. Eastward of the great range of the Alleghanies it has been very seldom seen north of the State of Maryland, though straggling parties have been occasionally observed among the valleys of the Juniata. Barton states that a very large flock of these birds was observed in January, 1780, about twenty-five miles northwest of Albany.

The occurrence of this species in midwinter so far to the north, and its constant residence west of the Alleghanies throughout the year in colder regions, justify the conclusion of its being a very hardy bird. In evidence of this, Wilson mentions the fact of his having seen a number of them, in the month of February, on the banks of the Ohio, in a snow-storm, flying about like Pigeons, and in full cry.

The very evident preference which the Carolina Parakeet evinces for western localities, though in the same parallel of latitude with those east of the Alleghanies, which it rarely or never visits, is attributed by the same attentive observer to certain peculiar features of the country to which it is particularly and strongly attached. These are the low, rich alluvial bottoms along the borders of creeks, covered with a gigantic growth of buttonwood, deep and impenetrable swamps of the cypress, and those peculiar salines — or, as they are called, salt-licks — so frequent throughout that region, all of which are regularly visited by the Parakeets. The great abundance of the seeds of the cockle-bur (*Xanthium strumarium*) is also given as a still greater inducement for their frequenting the banks of the Ohio and the Mississippi, where these plants are found in the greatest abundance. The seeds of the cypress-trees are another powerful attraction, while the abundance of the mast of the beech, on which it feeds freely, may explain their occasional visits to more northern regions, and even to places where they were before unknown.

In descending the Ohio in the month of February, Wilson met the first flock of Parakeets at the mouth of the Little Scioto. He was informed by an old inhabitant of Marietta that they were sometimes, though rarely, seen there. He afterwards observed flocks of them at the mouth of the Great and Little Miami, and in the neighborhood of the numerous creeks which discharge themselves into the Ohio. At Big Bone Lick, near the mouth of the Kentucky River, he met them in great numbers. They came screaming through the woods, about an hour after sunrise, to drink the salt water, of which, he says, they are remarkably fond.

Audubon, writing in 1842, speaks of the Parakeets as then very rapidly diminishing in number. In some regions where twenty-five years before they had been very plentiful, at that time scarcely any were to be seen. At one period, he adds, they could be procured as far up the tributary water of the Ohio as the Great Kanawha, the Scioto, the head of the Miami, the mouth of the Maumee at its junction with Lake Erie, and sometimes as far northeast as Lake Ontario. At the time of his writing very few were to be found higher than Cincinnati, and he estimated that along the Mississippi there was not half the number that had existed there fifteen years before.

According to Nuttall, this species constantly inhabits and breeds in the Southern States, and is so hardy as to make its appearance commonly, in the depth of winter, along the wooded banks of the Ohio, the interior of Alabama, and the banks of the Mississippi and Missouri, around St. Louis, and other places, when nearly all the other birds have migrated.

Its present habitat seems to be the Southern and Southwestern States, as far west as the Missouri. They occur high up that river, although none were seen or collected much farther west than its banks. In the enumeration of the localities from which the specimens in the Smithsonian collection were derived, Florida, Cairo, Ill., Fort Smith, Arkansas, Fort Riley, Kansas, Nebraska, and Bald Island, Missouri River, and Michigan are given.

In regard to the manner of nesting, breeding-habits, number of eggs in a nest, and the localities in which it breeds, I know nothing from my own personal observations, nor are writers generally better informed, with the single exception of Mr. Audubon. Wilson states that all his informants agreed that these birds breed in hollow trees. Several affirmed to him that they had seen their nests. Some described these as made with the use of no additional materials, others spoke of their employing certain substances to line the hollows they occupied. Some represented the eggs as white, others as speckled. One man assured him that in the hollow of a large beech-tree, which he had cut down, he found the broken fragments of upwards of twenty Parakeet's eggs, which he described as of a greenish-yellow color. He described the nest as formed of small twigs glued to each other and to the side of the tree in the manner of the Chimney-Swallow! From all these contradictory accounts Wilson was only able to gather, with certainty, that they build in companies and in hollow trees. The numerous dissections which he made in the months of March, April, May, and June led him to infer that they commence incubation late in spring or very early in summer.

Mr. Audubon, who speaks from his own observations, describes their nests, or the places in which they deposit their eggs, as simply the bottom of such cavities in trees as those to which they usually retire at night. Many females, he thinks, deposit their eggs together; and he expresses the opinion that the number of eggs which each individual lays is two, although he was not able absolutely to assure himself of this. He describes them as nearly round, and of a light greenish-white. An egg of this species from Louisiana is of a rounded oval shape, equally obtuse at either end, and of a uniform dull-white color. It measures 1.40 by 1.10 inches.

INDEX TO PLATES OF LAND BIRDS.

PLATE XXVII.

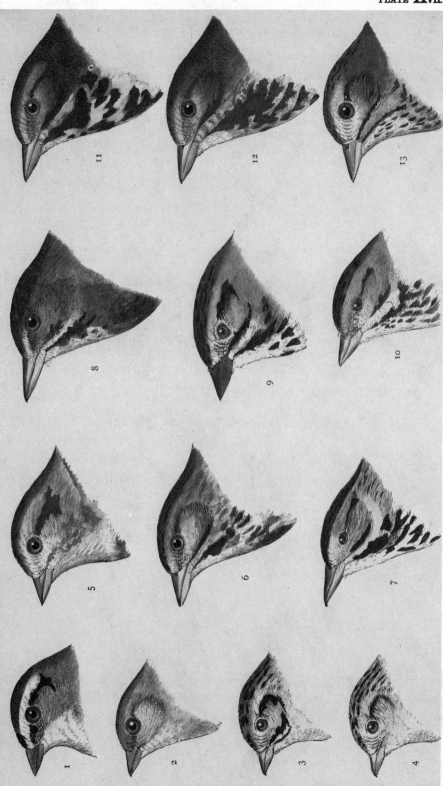

1. Spizella socialis. *Ad.* Pa., 10150.
2. " pusilla. ♀ Pa., 1378.
3. " pallida. *Ad.*
4. " breweri. *Ad.* Rocky Mts., 2890.

5. Spizella monticola. Pa., 2637.
6. Melospiza melodia. Pa., 2637.
7. " samuelis. Cal., 7008.

8. Melospiza insignis. Kodiak, 5247.
9. " heermanni. ♂ Sierra Nevada, 53509.
10. " fallax. ♀ Nevada, 53537.

11. Melospiza rufina. Sitka, 46007.
12. " guttata. Washington Ter.
13. " lincolni. Pa., 937.

PLATE XXVIII.

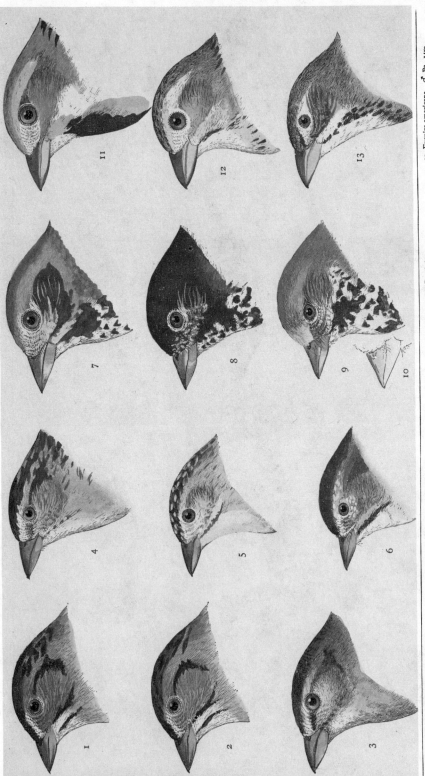

1. Melospiza palustris. ♂ D. C., 3846.
2.   "   "   ♀ Pa.
3. Embernagra rufivirgata. Orizaba, 29229.

4. Peucæa æstivalis. Ga., 10245.
5.   "   cassini. Texas, 6329.
6.   "   ruficeps. Cal., 6241.

7. Passerella iliaca. Ad, Pa., 846.
8.   "   townsendi. ♀ Columbia R., 2874.
9.   "   schistacea. Utah, 11234.
10.   "   var. megarhyncha. ♂ Utah.

11. Euspiza americana. ♂ Pa., 1459.
12.   "   townsendi. ♀ D. C., 1033.
13.   "   townsendi. Pa., 10082. (Type.)

PLATE XXIX.

1. Poocætes gramineus.   D. C., 10147.
2. Calamospiza bicolor.   ♂ Neb., 5720.
3.   "   "   ♀ N. Mex., 6306.
4. Guiraca cærulea.   ♂ Philad., 6480.
5.   "   "   ♀ Cal.

6. Cyanospiza parellina.   ♂ N. Leon, Mex., 4074.
7.   "   ciris.   ♂ Texas, 6271.
8.   "   "   ♀.
9.   "   versicolor.   ♂ N. Leon, Mex., 4075.
10.   "   "   ♀ C. St. Lucas, 12984.
11.   "   amœna.   ♂ Ft. Union, Dak., 1898.

12. Cyanospiza amœna.   ♀ Nevada, 5355l.
13.   "   cyanea.   ♂ Pa., 2645.
14.   "   "   ♀ Ga., 32426.
15. Phonipara zena.   ♂ Bahamas.
16.   "   "   ♀
17. Spermophila moreleti.   ♂ Costa Rica, 30524.

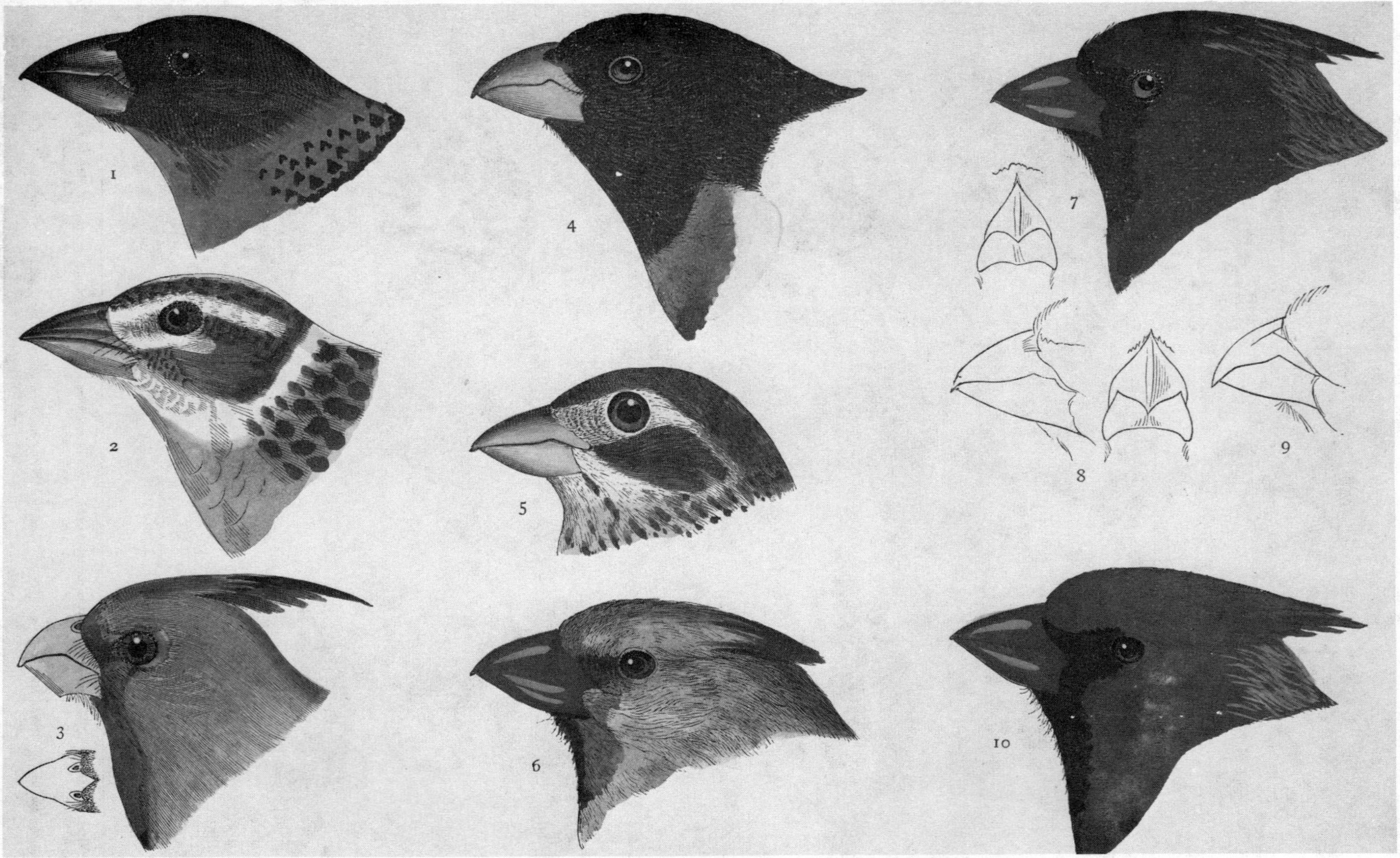

1. Hedymeles melanocephalus. ♂ Ft. Bridger, 11241.
2. " " ♀ Dakota, 1868.

4. Hedymeles ludovicianus. ♂ Iowa, 34206.
5. " " ♀ Pa., 2425.

7. Cardinalis virginianus. ♂ S. Ill., 58586.
8. " coccineus. ♂ 29702.

PLATE XXXI.

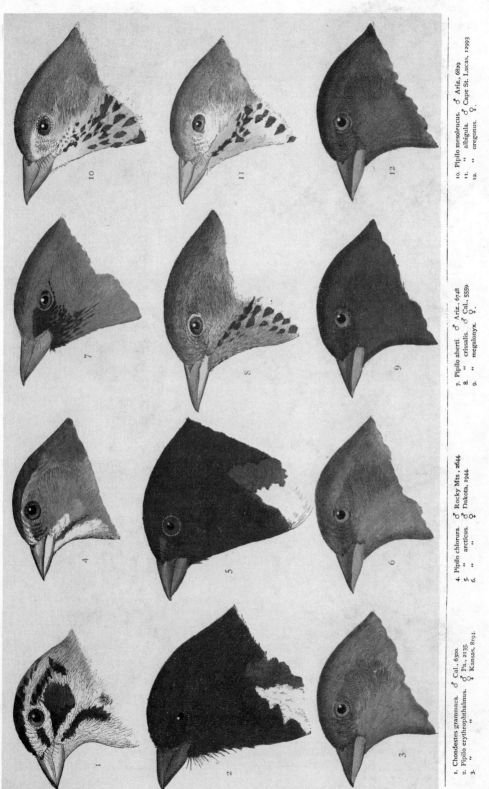

1. Chondestes grammaca. ♂ Cal. 6300.
2. Pipilo erythrophthalmus. ♂ Pa., 2135.
3. " " ♀ Kansas, 8191.

4. Pipilo chlorura. ♂ Rocky Mts. 2644
5. " arcticus. ♂ Dakota, 1944.
6. " " ♀

7. Pipilo aberti. ♂ Ariz. 648
8. " crissalis. ♂ Cal. 5559.
9. " megalonyx. ♀.

10. Pipilo mesoleucus. ♂ Ariz. 6829
11. " albigula. ♂ Cape St. Lucas, 12993
12. " oregonus. ♀.

PLATE XXXII.

PLATE XXXIII.

1. Agelaius phœniceus. ♂ Pa., 1386.
2.   "   "   ♀ Pa., 2174.
3.   "   "   ♂ shoulder.
4.   "   gubernator. ♂ "
5.   "   tricolor. ♂   "

6. Agelaius tricolor. ♂ Cal., 2836.
7.   "   "   ♀ Cal., 5532.
8.   "   gubernator. ♀ Cal., 5530.
9. Xanthocephalus icterocephalus. ♀ Kansas, 6557.

PLATE XXXIV

1. Sturnella neglecta. ♂ Nevada, 53592.
2.   "   magna. ♂ Pa., 1303.
3. Icterus bullocki. ♂ Ft. Bridger, 11282.

4. Icterus spurius. ♂ La., 4286.
5.   "   "   ♂ juv., Pa., 1437.
6.   "   "   ♀ Pa., 150.
7.   "   bullockii. ♀ Cal., 3900.

PLATE XXXV.

1. Icterus auduboni. ♂ Tamaulipas. Mex., 4063.
2. " wagleri. ♂ Guat., 8089.
3 Scolecophagus cyanocephalus. ♀ Nevada, 53596.
4. " ferrugineus. ♂ Pa., 1322.

5. Icterus baltimore. ♂ Ft. Garry, 27046.
6 " cucullatus. ♂ Tamaulipas, Mex., 4066.
7 " parisorum. ♂ N. Leon, Mex., 4056.
8. Sturnus vulgaris. ♂ France, 19020.

PLATE XXXVI.

1. Quiscalus macrourus. ♂ Texas, 3948.
2. " " ♀ Texas, 3949.

3. Quiscalus major. ♀ S. Car., 39005.
4. " " ♂ S. Car., 39003.

PLATE XXXVII.

1. Quiscalus purpureus. ♂ Pa., 1363.
2. "   aglæus. ♂ Fla., 10342.
3. Corvus caurinus. ♂ Sitka, 46662.

4. Corvus mexicanus. ♂ Mazatlan, 52802.
5. "   americanus. ♂ D. C.
6. "   carnivorus. ♀ Neb., 4546.

7. Corvus ossifragus. D. C., 4515.
8. "   cryptoleucus. Tex., 46798.
9. "   floridanus. Fla., 10374.

PLATE XXXVIII

PLATE XXXIX.

1. Cyanura stelleri. ♂ Oregon, 16040.
2. " " var. frontalis. ♂ Sierra Nevada, 53699.
3. Cyanura macrolopha. ♂ Ariz., 11015.
4. " coronata. ♂ Xalapa, 16313.

PLATE XI.

2. Cyanocitta woodhousii ♂ Nev., 1867.

PLATE XLI.

1. Cyanocitta sordida. Orizaba, 38209.
2.   "   "   var. arizonae. ♂ Ariz., 18279.

3. Perisoreus canadensis. ♂ Nova Scotia, 26540.
4.   "   "   var. capitalis. ♂ Colorado, 51642.

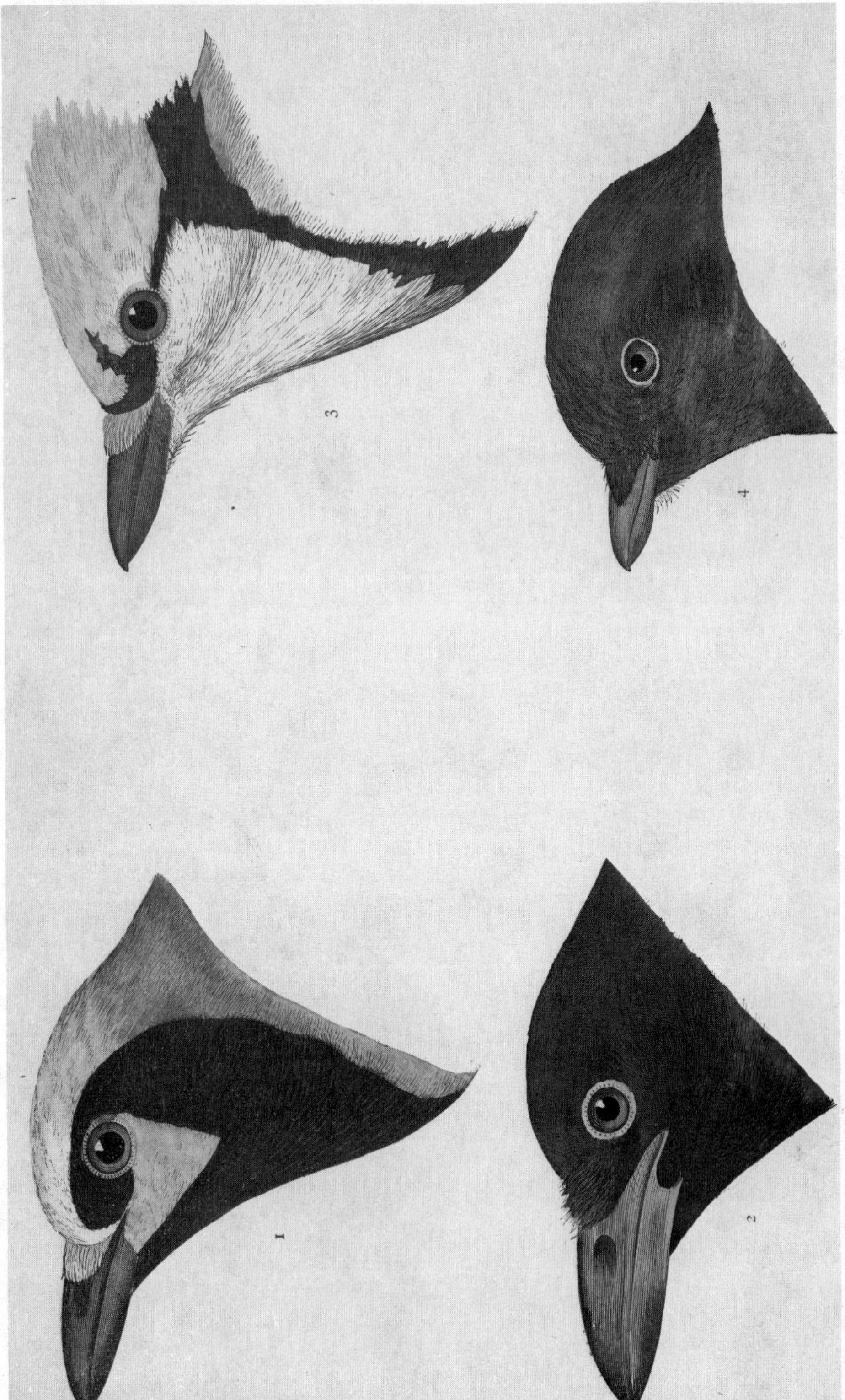

1. Xanthoura luxuosa. New Leon, New Mex., 4052.
2. Psilorhinus morio. ♀ New Leon, Mex., 4114.
3. Cyanura cristata. ♂ D. C., 12408.
4. Perisoreus canadensis. *Juv.*, Maine, 1920.

PLATE XLIII.

1. Milvulus forficatus. ♂ Texas, 7375.
2. Tyrannus verticalis. ♂ Cal., 16137.
3. Myiarchus crinitus. ♂ Pa., 1489.

4. Tyrannus carolinensis. ♂ E. U. S., 6482.
5. " vociferans. ♂ Cal., 31887.
6. Myiarchus cinerascens. ♂ Cal., 13719.

7. Tyrannus couchi. ♂ Tamaulipas, 4001.
8. " dominicensis. ♂ Fla., 13737.
9. Myiarchus lawrencii. ♂ N. Mex., 29344.

PLATE XLIV.

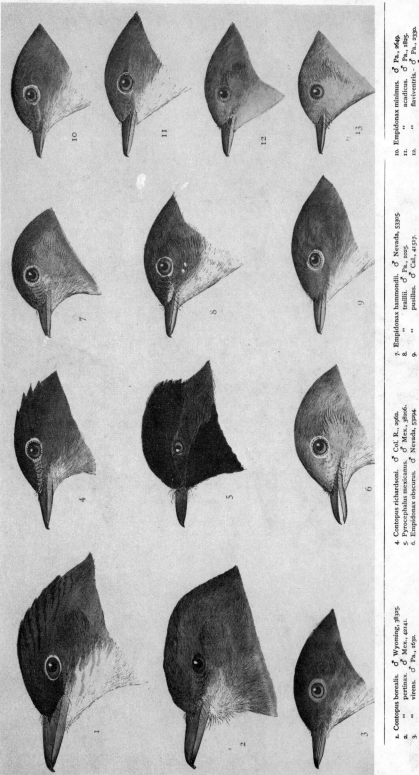

PLATE XLV.

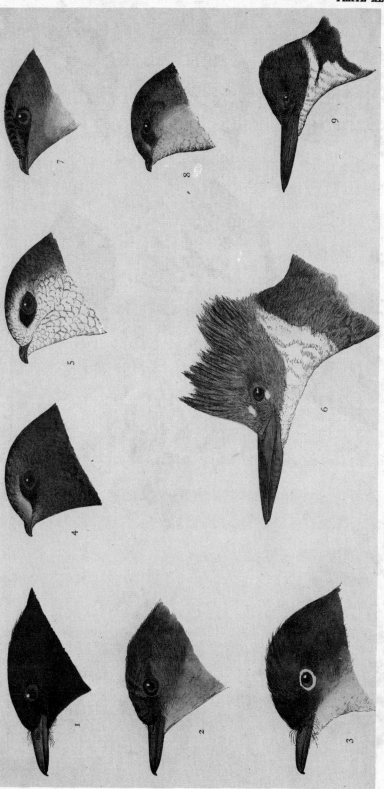

7. Chætura pelagica. ♂ Pa., 1010.
8. " vauxi. ♀ Puget Sound, 13955.
9. Ceryle americana, *var.* cabanisi. ♂ Texas, 6194. ½ nat. size.

4. Nephœcetes niger. ♀ Puget Sound, 1187I.
5. Panyptila melanoleuca. ♂ Nevada, 5327?.
6. Ceryle alcyon. ♂ D. C., 2520?. ½ nat. size.

1. Sayornis nigricans. ♂ Cal., 3906.
2. " fuscus. ♂ Pa., 957.
3. " sayus. ♂ Nevada, 5286.

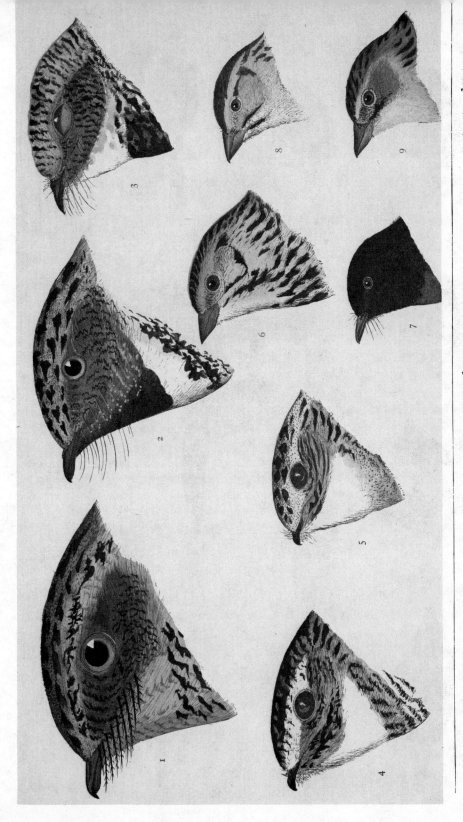

1. Antrostomus carolinensis. ♂ Florida, 1716.
2.   "   vociferus. ♂ D. C., 1208;
3.   "   nuttalli. ♂ Wyoming, 3824.

4. Chordeiles henryi. ♂ Wyoming, 3823.
5.   "   texensis. ♂ Texas, 4218;
6. Centronyx ochrocephalus. Colorado.

7. Setophaga picta. ♂ Mexico, 3970s.
8. Peucæa carpalis. Arizona, 6372.
9. Passerculus caboti. Nahant, 6373.

PLATE XLVII.

1. Trochilus alexandri.   ♂ Cal, 44959.
2.   "   colubris.   ♂ Pa, 2713.
3. Heliopædica xantusi.   ♂ Cape St. Lucas.

4. Selasphorus rufus.   ♂ Oregon, 2896.
5.   "   platycercus.   ♂ Rocky Mts, 10847.
6. Atthis heloise.   ♂ Mex., 2874.

7. Calypte anna.   ♂ Cal, 5501.
8.   "   costæ.   ♂ Cal, 39397.
9. Stellula calliope.   ♂ Cal, 17992.

PLATE XLVIII.

1. Geococcyx californianus.   ♂ Cal, 12925.
2. Crotophaga ani.   ♀ Fla., 8639.

3. Coccygus americanus.   ♂ Penn., 1541.
4.   "   "   minor.
5.   "   "   erythrophthalmus.   27028.

PLATE XLIX.

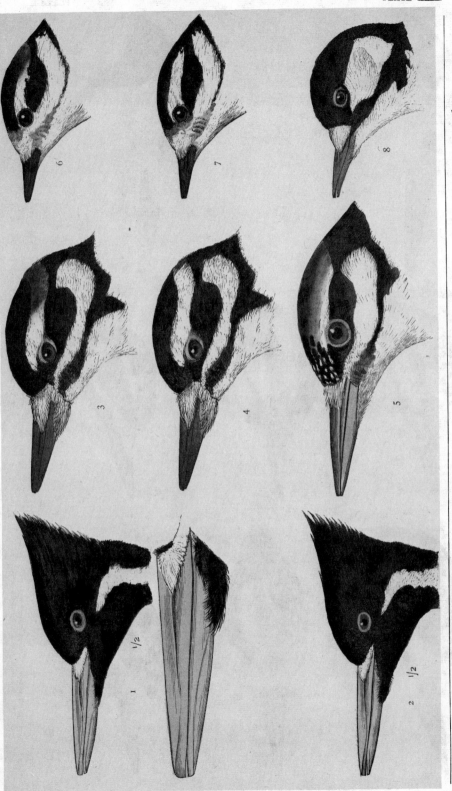

1. Campephilus principalis. ♂ Fla., 3869.
2.   "   "   ♀ Arkansas. ?

3. Picus villosus. ♂ Pa., 884.
4.   "   "   ♀ Pa.
5.   "   "   ♂ juv. Iowa, 1372.

6. Picus pubescens. ♂ Pa, 1291.
7.   "   "   ♀ Pa.
8.   "   borealis.   ♂ Georgia, 1378.

PLATE L.

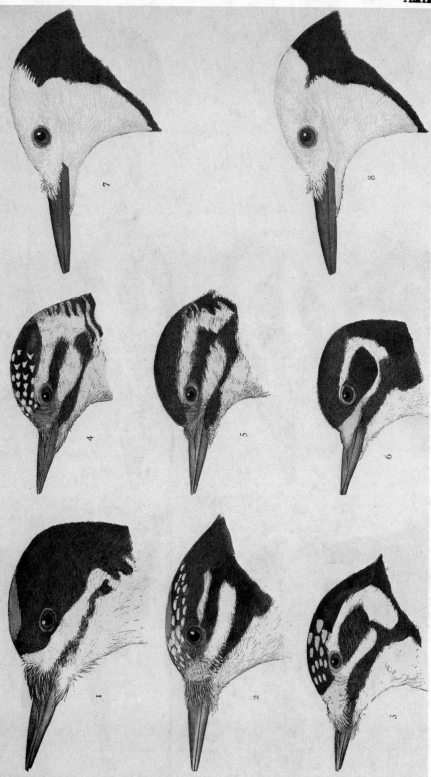

1. Picoides arcticus. ♂ Nova Scotia, 26923.
2. " americanus. ♂ New Brunswick, 39143.
3. Picus nuttalli. ♂ Cal., 482.

4. Picus scalaris. ♂ Texas, 46804.
5. " " ♀ Texas, 9933.
6. " " nuttalli. ♀ Cal, 5400.

7. Picus albolarvatus. ♂ Cal., 16666.
8. " " ♀ Cal.

PLATE LI.

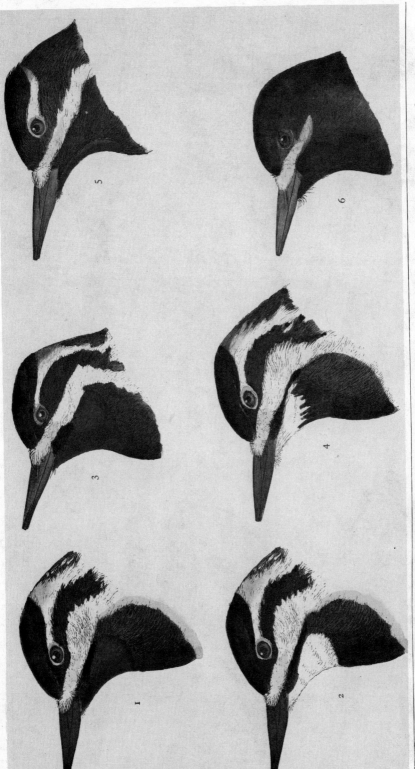

PLATE LII.

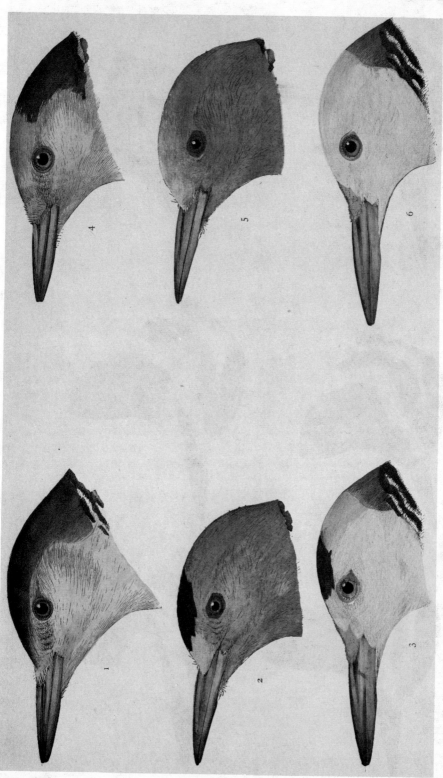

1. Centurus carolinus. ♂ Pa., 868.
2.   "   uropygialis. ♂ Ariz., 6128.
3.   "   aurifrons. ♂ Texas, 6121.

4. Centurus carolinus. ♀ 6118.
5.   "   uropygialis. ♀ Ariz.
6.   "   aurifrons. ♀ Texas.

PLATE LIII.

1. Melanerpes formicivorus.   ♂ Cal, 5495.
2.   "   "   "   " 25035.

3. Melanerpes angustifrons.   ♂ Cape St. Lucas, 25947.
4.   "   "   ♀   "   "   "   25949.

PLATE LIV.

1. Colaptes chrysoides.   ♂ Arizona, 107.
2.   "   "   ♀ Cape St. Lucas.
3.   "   hybridus.   ♂ Neb., 5214.
4. Melanerpes erythrocephalus.   ♂ Neb., 38393.
5.   "   torquatus.   ♀ Cal., 6138.

PLATE LV.

1. Colaptes auratus. ♂ 2122.
2. " " " ♀.

3. Colaptes mexicanus. ♂.
4. " " " ♀.

PLATE LVI.

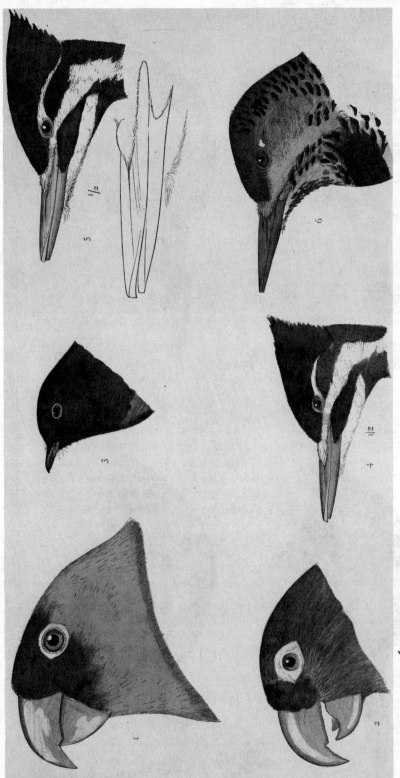

1. Conurus carolinensis. *Ad.*, Mich., 1228.
2.   "   "   *Juv.*, Fla., 54812.

3. Setophaga picta. ♂ Guat., 39705.
4. Hylotomus pileatus. ♀ Pa., 1723.

5. Hylotomus pileatus. ♂ Selkirk Settlement, 51863.
6. Sphyropicus thyroideus. ♂ Cal., 16098.

NATURAL SCIENCES IN AMERICA

An Arno Press Collection

Allen, J[oel] A[saph]. **The American Bisons,** Living and Extinct. 1876

Allen, Joel Asaph. **History of the North American Pinnipeds:** A Monograph of the Walruses, Sea-Lions, Sea-Bears and Seals of North America. 1880

American Natural History Studies: The Bairdian Period. 1974

American Ornithological Bibliography. 1974

Anker, Jean. **Bird Books and Bird Art.** 1938

Audubon, John James and John Bachman. **The Quadrupeds of North America.** Three vols. 1854

Baird, Spencer F[ullerton]. **Mammals of North America.** 1859

Baird, S[pencer] F[ullerton], T[homas] M. Brewer and R[obert] Ridgway. **A History of North American Birds:** Land Birds. Three vols., 1874

Baird, Spencer F[ullerton], John Cassin and George N. Lawrence. **The Birds of North America.** 1860. Two vols. in one.

Baird, S[pencer] F[ullerton], T[homas] M. Brewer, and R[obert] Ridgway. **The Water Birds of North America.** 1884. Two vols. in one.

Barton, Benjamin Smith. **Notes on the Animals of North America.** Edited, with an Introduction by Keir B. Sterling. 1792

Bendire, Charles [Emil]. **Life Histories of North American Birds** With Special Reference to Their Breeding Habits and Eggs. 1892/1895. Two vols. in one.

Bonaparte, Charles Lucian [Jules Laurent]. **American Ornithology:** Or The Natural History of Birds Inhabiting the United States, Not Given by Wilson. 1825/1828/1833. Four vols. in one.

Cameron, Jenks. **The Bureau of Biological Survey:** Its History, Activities, and Organization. 1929

Caton, John Dean. **The Antelope and Deer of America:** A Comprehensive Scientific Treatise Upon the Natural History, Including the Characteristics, Habits, Affinities, and Capacity for Domestication of the Antilocapra and Cervidae of North America. 1877

Contributions to American Systematics. 1974

Contributions to the Bibliographical Literature of American Mammals. 1974

Contributions to the History of American Natural History. 1974

Contributions to the History of American Ornithology. 1974

Cooper, J[ames] G[raham]. **Ornithology.** Volume I, Land Birds. 1870

Cope, E[dward] D[rinker]. **The Origin of the Fittest:** Essays on Evolution and **The Primary Factors of Organic Evolution.** 1887/1896. Two vols. in one.

Coues, Elliott. **Birds of the Colorado Valley.** 1878

Coues, Elliott. **Birds of the Northwest.** 1874

Coues, Elliott. **Key To North American Birds.** Two vols. 1903

Early Nineteenth-Century Studies and Surveys. 1974

Emmons, Ebenezer. **American Geology:** Containing a Statement of the Principles of the Science. 1855. Two vols. in one.

Fauna Americana. 1825-1826

Fisher, A[lbert] K[enrick]. **The Hawks and Owls of the United States in Their Relation to Agriculture.** 1893

Godman, John D. **American Natural History:** Part I — Mastology and **Rambles of a Naturalist.** 1826-28/1833. Three vols. in one.

Gregory, William King. **Evolution Emerging:** A Survey of Changing Patterns from Primeval Life to Man. Two vols. 1951

Hay, Oliver Perry. **Bibliography and Catalogue of the Fossil Vertebrata of North America.** 1902

Heilprin, Angelo. **The Geographical and Geological Distribution of Animals.** 1887

Hitchcock, Edward. **A Report on the Sandstone of the Connecticut Valley,** Especially Its Fossil Footmarks. 1858

Hubbs, Carl L., editor. **Zoogeography.** 1958

[Kessel, Edward L., editor]. **A Century of Progress in the Natural Sciences: 1853-1953.** 1955

Leidy, Joseph. **The Extinct Mammalian Fauna of Dakota and Nebraska,** Including an Account of Some Allied Forms from Other Localities, Together with a Synopsis of the Mammalian Remains of North America. 1869

Lyon, Marcus Ward, Jr. **Mammals of Indiana.** 1936

Matthew, W[illiam] D[iller]. **Climate and Evolution.** 1915

Mayr, Ernst, editor. **The Species Problem.** 1957

Mearns, Edgar Alexander. **Mammals of the Mexican Boundary of the United States.** Part I: Families Didelphiidae to Muridae. 1907

Merriam, Clinton Hart. **The Mammals of the Adirondack Region,** Northeastern New York. 1884

Nuttall, Thomas. **A Manual of the Ornithology of the United States and of Canada.** Two vols. 1832-1834

Nuttall Ornithological Club. **Bulletin of the Nuttall Ornithological Club:** A Quarterly Journal of Ornithology. 1876-1883. Eight vols. in three.

[Pennant, Thomas]. **Arctic Zoology.** 1784-1787. Two vols. in one.

Richardson, John. **Fauna Boreali-Americana;** Or the Zoology of the Northern Parts of British America, Containing Descriptions of the Objects of Natural History Collected on the Late Northern Land Expeditions Under Command of Captain Sir John Franklin, R. N. Part I: Quadrupeds. 1829

Richardson, John and William Swainson. **Fauna Boreali-Americana:** Or the Zoology of the Northern Parts of British America, Containing Descriptions of the Objects of Natural History Collected by the Late Northern Land Expeditions Under Command of Captain Sir John Franklin, R. N. Part II: The Birds. 1831

Ridgway, Robert. **Ornithology.** 1877

Selected Works By Eighteenth-Century Naturalists and Travellers. 1974

Selected Works in Nineteenth-Century North American Paleontology. 1974

Selected Works of Clinton Hart Merriam. 1974

Selected Works of Joel Asaph Allen. 1974

Selections From the Literature of American Biogeography. 1974

Seton, Ernest Thompson. **Life-Histories of Northern Animals: An Account of the Mammals of Manitoba.** Two vols. 1909

Sterling, Keir Brooks. **Last of the Naturalists:** The Career of C. Hart Merriam. 1974

Vieillot, L. P. **Histoire Naturelle Des Oiseaux de L'Amerique Septentrionale,** Contenant Un Grand Nombre D'Especes Decrites ou Figurees Pour La Premiere Fois. 1807. Two vols. in one.

Wilson, Scott B., assisted by A. H. Evans. **Aves Hawaiienses:** The Birds of the Sandwich Islands. 1890-99

Wood, Casey A., editor. **An Introduction to the Literature of Vertebrate Zoology.** 1931

Zimmer, John Todd. **Catalogue of the Edward E. Ayer Ornithological Library.** 1926